METHODOLOGY AND TACIT KNOWLEDGE
Two Experiments in Econometrics

Jan R. Magnus and **Mary S. Morgan**

The two experiments reported in this book are designed to help understand and assess the competing methodologies of econometrics and the tacit knowledge content of the discipline. They provide an unrivalled insight into the practice of econometrics.

Previous accounts of methodology in econometrics have been at the abstract level. This new research is at the applied level, and the design, reporting and assessment of the two experiments illustrate how the different methodologies used in modern econometrics work in practice.

The first experiment is a field trial experiment: participating teams, with different methodological positions, answer specific economic questions using a given data set. The second experiment is a tacit knowledge experiment: an "apprentice" tries to emulate the approaches of three "master" econometricians on the same applied problem.

The book contains a number of applied econometrics papers, all written by professional econometricians, each of which uses the same data set and tries to answer the same questions, but each uses different techniques and provides different answers. In addition, the book contains analyses and comparative assessments of these papers. The data are described in detail, and are freely available on the Internet.

This book will be of considerable interest to economists and to econometricians interested in the methodology of their own discipline, and will provide valuable material for researchers in science studies and for teachers of econometrics.

Methodology and Tacit Knowledge:
Two Experiments in Econometrics

JAN R. MAGNUS

CentER, Tilburg University, the Netherlands

AND

MARY S. MORGAN

University of Amsterdam, the Netherlands,
and London School of Economics, UK

JOHN WILEY & SONS

Chichester • New York • Weinheim • Brisbane • Singapore • Toronto

Other Wiley Editorial Offices

John Wiley & Sons, Inc., 605 Third Avenue,
New York, NY 10158-0012, USA

WILEY-VCH Verlag GmbH, Pappelallee 3,
D-69469 Weinheim, Germany

Jacaranda Wiley Ltd, 33 Park Road, Milton,
Queensland 4064, Australia

John Wiley & Sons (Canada) Ltd, 22 Worcester Road,
Rexdale, Ontario M9W 1L1, Canada

John Wiley & Sons (Asia) Pte Ltd, 2 Clementi Loop #02-01,
Jin Xing Distripark, Singapore 129809

Library of Congress Cataloging-in-Publication Data

Methodology and tacit knowledge Jan R. Magnus, Mary S.
  Morgan.
       p.   cm.
    Includes bibliographical references and index.
    ISBN 0-471-98297-0 (hardcover : alk. paper)
    1. Econometrics — Methodology. 2. Econometrics — Field work.
  3. Tacit knowledge — Econometric models. 4. Food consumption — United
  States — Econometric models. 5. Food consumption — Netherlands —
  Econometric models.   I. Magnus, Jan R. II. Morgan, Mary S.
  HB139.M477   1999
  330'.01'5195 — dc21   98–47539
                                                            CIP

British Library Cataloguing in Publication Data

A catalogue record for this book is available from the British Library

ISBN 0 471 98297 0

Typeset in 10/12pt Times by Laser Words, Madras, India
Printed and bound in Great Britain by Bookcraft (Bath) Ltd
This book is printed on acid-free paper responsibly manufactured from sustainable forestry,
for which at least two trees are planted for each one used for paper production.

CONTENTS

ACKNOWLEDGEMENTS

In this book we report on two experiments in applied econometrics: a field trial experiment and a tacit knowledge experiment. The success of these experiments has depended to a large extent on the trust and respect between participants and organizers. We feel exceptionally fortunate that we were able to work with an outstanding group of scholars who put time, thought and effort into this project. Without them there would have been no experiment, no special issue of the *Journal of Applied Econometrics* and no book.

About half of the material in this book has appeared in the September/October 1997 special issue of the *Journal of Applied Econometrics*. In addition to the material in the special issue, the book contains all eight contributions to the field trial experiment (rather than six in the special issue), comparative assessments by five of the assessors and analysis of the results. The book also contains a description, report and assessments of the tacit knowledge experiment, and an attempt to link our experiments with the literature on applied science.

The participants: Eight teams, comprising 23 scholars, completed the field trial experiment and submitted reports; of these, 16 attended the December 1996 workshop in Tilburg. The participants were:

Heather Anderson, Peter Bearse, Hamparsum Bozdogan, Denis de Crombrugghe, Hans van Driel, Rune Höglund, Markus Jäntti, Johan Knif, Edward Leamer, Xiaming Liu, G. S. Maddala, Venuta Nadall, Leif Nordberg, Franz Palm, Peter Romilly, Gunnar Rosenqvist, Alan Schlottmann, Haiyan Song, Jean-Pierre Urbain, Farshid Vahid, Shaowen Wu, Yong Yin, and Kees Zeelenberg.

We thank the participants to the field trial experiment for their enthusiasm, their willingness to put time and effort into an uncertain project, and their positive collaboration throughout the year.

The assessors: We asked eight assessors to comment on the submitted papers, to act as referees for the special issue, and to write comparative assessments. They were:

Anton Barten, J. S. Cramer, Arie Kapteyn, Michael McAleer, Hashem Pesaran, Peter Schmidt, Ken Wallis, and Michael Wickens.

The assessors played a crucial role in the project, before, during and after the Tilburg workshop. They put more time into the experiment than we could have reasonably expected and we are most grateful to them.

Our star guest: James Tobin, whose inspired work served as our base study, was willing to come to Tilburg and share his thoughts and insights with us.

The 'master craftsmen': In the tacit knowledge experiment, Edward Leamer and David Hendry were strongly supportive, as was Adrian Pagan in his overall assessments.

The 'apprentice': The apprentice in the tacit knowledge experiment, Wiebe Siegert, performed his task with great determination and little guidance. We thank him for taking on this difficult task, and also for his general support and help with the analysis.

The advisors: Many advised us in different stages of the experiment. Clive Granger, David Hendry and Peter Phillips served as nominated referees in various grant applications. Harry Collins and Rob Evans provided helpful advice on tacit knowledge and experimental design. Richard Blundell and Kevin Hoover shared their thoughts with us during the Tilburg workshop.

The data: Adriaan Kalwij, Adam Sutton, and Paolo Zaffaroni helped us collect the US and Dutch data. This proved very much more difficult than we had anticipated. We are grateful for their persistence and precision. The Dutch data are provided courtesy of Statistics Netherlands, and some (the budget data) were not orginally in the public domain.

Secretarial help: We gratefully acknowledge the secretarial support at CentER for Economic Research at Tilburg University, the Department of Macroeconomics at the University of Amsterdam, and the Department of Economic History at the London School of Economics.

Financial support: CentER for Economic Research provided the money for organizing the workshop in Tilburg without which there would have been no experiment.

The publishers: Finally, we thank Hashem Pesaran and the editors of the *Journal of Applied Econometrics* and Gill Smith for their generous support, and the editor and staff at John Wiley for keeping their promises and helping us keep ours.

Tilburg/Amsterdam/London   Jan R. Magnus
July 1998   Mary S. Morgan

LIST OF CONTRIBUTORS

HEATHER M. ANDERSON
Department of Economics, Texas A&M University, USA

ANTON P. BARTEN
Department of Economics, Catholic University of Leuven, Belgium

PETER M. BEARSE
Department of Economics, Centre for Business and Economic Research, University of Tennessee, USA

HAMPARSUM BOZDOGAN
Department of Statistics, University of Tennessee, USA

J. S. CRAMER
Department of Economics, University of Amsterdam, the Netherlands

DENIS DE CROMBRUGGHE
Faculty of Economics and Business Administration, Maastricht University, the Netherlands

HANS VAN DRIEL
Statistics Netherlands, the Netherlands

DAVID F. HENDRY
Nuffield College, Oxford, UK

RUNE HÖGLUND
Department of Statistics, Abo Akademi University, Finland

MARKUS JÄNTTI
Department of Statistics, Abo Akademi University, Finland

ARIE KAPTEYN
CentER, Tilburg University, the Netherlands

JOHAN KNIF
Swedish School of Economics and Business Administration, Vasa, Finland

EDWARD E. LEAMER
Anderson Graduate School of Management, UCLA, USA

XIAMING LIU
Division of Economics, School of Social Sciences, University of Abertay Dundee, UK

G. S. MADDALA
Department of Economics, Ohio State University, USA

JAN R. MAGNUS
CentER, Tilburg University, the Netherlands

MICHAEL McALEER
Department of Economics, University of Western Australia, Perth, Australia

MARY S. MORGAN
University of Amsterdam, the Netherlands and London School of Economics, UK

VENUTA NADALL
Statistics Netherlands, the Netherlands

LEIF NORDBERG
Department of Statistics, Abo Akademi University, Finland

ADRIAN R. PAGAN
Australian National University, Canberra, Australia

FRANZ C. PALM
Faculty of Economics and Business Administration, Maastricht University,
the Netherlands

M. HASHEM PESARAN
Trinity College, Cambridge, UK

PETER ROMILLY
Division of Economics, School of Social Sciences, University of Abertay Dundee, UK

GUNNAR ROSENQVIST
Swedish School of Economics and Business Administration, Helsingfors, Finland

ALAN M. SCHLOTTMANN
Department of Economics, University of Tennessee, USA

PETER SCHMIDT
Michigan State University, USA

WIEBE K. SIEGERT
Department of Economics, Tilburg University, the Netherlands

HAIYAN SONG
Department of Management Studies, University of Surrey, UK

JAMES TOBIN
Cowles Foundation for Research in Economics, Yale University, USA

JEAN-PIERRE URBAIN
Faculty of Economics and Business Administration, Maastricht University,
the Netherlands

FARSHID VAHID
Department of Economics, Texas A&M University, USA

KENNETH F. WALLIS
Department of Economics, University of Warwick, UK

MICHAEL R. WICKENS
Department of Economics, University of York, UK

SHAOWEN WU
Department of Economics, The Ohio State University, USA

YONG YIN
Department of Economics, SUNY at Buffalo, USA

KEES ZEELENBERG
Statistics Netherlands, the Netherlands

INTRODUCTION: APPLIED ECONOMETRICS AND DESIGN OF TWO EXPERIMENTS

JAN R. MAGNUS AND MARY S. MORGAN

1. THE PROBLEM BEHIND THE EXPERIMENTS

For the last 10 to 15 years, econometricians have been debating amongst themselves the right way to do econometrics. The discussions have ranged widely over questions about the concept of probability appropriate for economics, associated statistical inference procedures, criteria of economic versus statistical significance, the kinds of models appropriate for econometrics, the process of modelling, and so forth. The debate has been joined at many levels, from abstract methodological discussions to arguments over the rival merits of software packages. The classic critical survey of three main approaches is Pagan (1987, updated 1995).

These discussions have been informative and innovative. In marked contrast to other areas of methodological debate inside economics, they have often managed to combine both philosophical sophistication and practicality (see, for example, the papers on econometrics contained in Hamminga and De Marchi, 1994). They are a sign of a healthy and active econometrics profession. Apart from the critiques, the arguments have connected to some thoroughly innovative developments in econometrics: for example, methods to compare models, to compare forecasts, to assess the usefulness of calibration versus estimation, and so forth.

The problem is not a new one. Indeed, there have been periodic debates within economics about how to do econometrics, going back to the Tinbergen-Keynes debate of 1939–40 and the 'measurement without theory' debate of 1946–47 (see Hendry and Morgan, 1995). But the current debate has gone on longer and been more fruitful than earlier ones in generating a greater number of clearly established methodological positions and practical methods associated with them. We see in these new developments real attempts to produce tools and establish practices in line with methodological pronouncements. To some degree, these have been conveniently enshrined in software packages which enable econometricians to combine their preferred choice of econometric theory, methodology and data treatment in one approach.

Despite the activity of the debate, it has been somewhat disquieting that few matters have been resolved. Nevertheless, econometrics remains a very important part of applied economics and plays a vital role in economics. Because of this, the establishment of a credible applied econometrics is possibly the most important task of econometrics today.

Discussions about how to do econometrics have been dominated by the view that there are 'right' and 'wrong' ways to do things, that the matter is one of agreeing on one correct methodology. So far, despite the years of discussion, no meta-principle has

Methodology and Tacit Knowledge: Two Experiments in Econometrics
Jan R. Magnus and Mary S. Morgan © 1997 John Wiley & Sons Ltd

been seen by participants as strong enough to settle the differences between them. Given this situation, we are concerned to clarify and perhaps assess the practical usefulness of different approaches in applied circumstances by conducting two experiments in applied econometrics. These experiments aim to move the debate over econometric methodology to the practical domain in harmony with recent research into the role and importance of 'practice' in applied science.

2. APPLIED SCIENCE: METHODOLOGIES AND THEIR 'PRACTICE'

A conventional position in methodology of science is that good applied science consists of applying scientific theories to the world in accordance with certain principles of scientific procedure. Recent detailed studies of the practice of science place the focus the other way around: successful applied science relies on knowing exactly when specific principles matter (and when they don't) and exactly how far (or not) theories will take you in solving a particular problem and achieving a particular goal. The lessons from such studies are that applied science involves making many choices and using experienced judgement at a resolutely practical level. Stephen Turner's (1994) study suggests the conclusion that: 'our practices are the sole means by which we have access to the world' (p. 86). This is a strong conclusion, but we do not have to go so far; we need only to recognise that though we may need theories and principles to guide us, they are not sufficient knowledge upon which to do applied econometrics.

Accounts of the kind of practical knowledge involved in successful applied science often draw on Michael Polanyi's (1958) notion 'personal knowledge'. This term denotes expert knowledge in any field, with a range extending from the cognitive domain of our abilities to assess chances or recognize order and patterns, to the kinds of practical expertise involved in manual or bodily skills, when it is more often described by the term 'tacit knowledge'. Tacit knowledge enters many of our daily actions, one of the standard examples being the ability to ride a bicycle, a skill which can not easily be either imitated by a learner or articulated into a set of maxims or rules. Perhaps because of the reverence with which scientific knowledge and the 'scientific method' has been held, it is only comparatively recently that students of science have followed Polanyi in recognizing how critical such personal knowledge is to the successful practice of science.

How can we characterize personal knowledge in terms useful for understanding applied econometrics? One way to understand Polanyi's notion is to characterize personal knowledge as the knowledge base of the master craftsman. In the economic historian's mind, the master craftsman's skill-set is epitomized as involving both breadth and depth of skills. The master has the abilities to assess and take into account the qualities and characteristics of different materials, to use many different types of tools in sequence according to need, and to fashion a range of objects using different processes. This ability to deal skilfully with, and create, variety is what distinguishes the master craftsman of the medieval or guild era from the limited industrial skills needed for the highly divided task performed by a worker of the Fordist era skilled at one task, using one material and one tool to make one part of one thing (epitomized by Charlie Chaplin in *Modern Times*).

Polanyi's account is not limited to technology, but there are two points of difference with applied science which we might want to note. First, whereas the personal knowledge base of master-craft production is acquired and practised in an acknowledged technological realm and while the personal knowledge base involved in scientific work may be just as instrumental, the situations in which it is applied are often more open-ended in terms of new domains or combinations and the requirement for innovation. Second, in science, as opposed to technology, 'hammers and probes can be replaced by intellectual tools' (Polanyi, 1958, p. 59) ranging from things which look like tools (such as computers, equations and theorems) to cognitive elements, often hidden from view (such as interpretative frameworks and unspecified assumptions, scientific theories and methodological commitments). Of course, we can write down theorems or equations, we can see the computer on the desk; the point to emphasize is that the process by which the applied scientist uses the intellectual (non-physical) tools, whether they are hidden or obvious, is also riven with tacit knowledge.

Recent work in the field of science studies has considered questions about personal knowledge and its transmission in terms of the 'practice' of science. Attempts to develop a theoretical account of practices, defining exactly what personal or tacit knowledge is and providing a theory of how it is transmitted, have not been especially successful. Turner (1994), reviewing the attempts by philosophers and social theorists in this respect, comes to rather dismal conclusions. As far as definitions of practice are concerned, these have ranged from the broad social concepts of 'tradition' and 'inherited background' to ones more obviously associated with science, such as Kuhn's 'paradigm'. (Kuhn's paradigm is associated with his 'normal science' and is rather well-known to econometricians from Kuhn (1962).) Turner suggests that these ideas of practices can be divided into two rough categories: 'shared presuppositions' (which amount to the 'hidden premises of deductive theories') and 'embodied knowledge' (which includes skill along with other competencies or dispositions). But, as he notes for us,

> 'the appeal of many of these concepts [of practice] rests on the fact that they neglect this distinction or trespass against it. Kuhn's notion of paradigm, like Polanyi's notion of tacit knowledge, trades on the interdependence of skill and presupposition that is part of the scientist's way.'   (Turner, 1994, p. 3)

Applied science requires a combination of intellectual, cognitive and manual knowledge and skills which, it seems, cannot be disentangled: methodological principles are embedded in practices.

This recent concentration of study on the practical processes of modern science, and the diversity of practices revealed, have to some extent reversed the notions of how we might understand the role of practice in claims to scientific knowledge. This is most neatly put, once again, by Turner:

> 'Truth, validity and correctness are held to be *practice-relative* rather than *practice-justifying* notions. Where we used to say that our practices, for example in science, were justified by the fact that they led us to truth, now we can see that truth is only that which our practices of representation enable us to construct as true.'
> (Turner, 1994, p. 9)

Whereas some might see this statement as dangerous and radical, Turner's claim is relevant for applied econometrics and for our experiments.

Turner's claim does not seem so problematic when the context is the comparison of different ways of doing science, for each mode of doing science works by different principles. The principles and practices used in experimental science are different from those used in statistical analysis, and the criteria for judging the integrity of practices within each mode are therefore different. Within each mode, we use practices to construct what we conceive to be the true answer to some question within the context and limits of those principles and within the range of our theoretical preconceptions. Within a mode, the internal methodological principles are normally shared, and provide the criteria for judging the success of the applied science practice. But, as we know, within econometrics, different approaches involve different versions of the principles. These principles are to some extent incompatible: the notions of probability and associated inference procedures are different between Bayesian econometricians and those following classical statistics; the modelling procedures, loosely tied to notions of falsification and confirmation, differ between groups. As we noted in Section 1, within the econometrics profession, different principles hold, they are attached to different associated practices, ask different questions, and provide different answers. Each econometric approach, carried out in accordance with its principles, and with care and integrity in practice, constructs an answer which we can consider to be true in terms of those principles.

This is exactly the point of Kuhnian paradigms: a set of shared and interdependent principles and practices within which the scientific community aims to arrive at the 'truth' relative to those principles and practices. Though we can criticize the performance of applied scientists within each approach, and may be able to explain the differences in outcomes observed between them, each set of practices can potentially provide its own 'true' answer to the questions. Nevertheless, as Fish (1989) has pointed out, this still leaves room for persuasion, provided that a common goal or purpose is involved. In the December 1996 Tilburg workshop for our first experiment, it was open to all participants to persuade each other that their way was best, for they shared the same questions set in the experimental tasks, and there were some shared criteria (not all) in terms of statistical and economic judgements.

Given the state of the debate in econometrics, that no one set of abstract methodological principles has proven sufficiently superior to the others that it has displaced them, our aim was to adopt an alternative way of investigating econometric methodologies via their practices. In accordance with the arguments in this section, we take it for granted in setting up both our experiments that there may be many ways of doing good applied science and of gaining an understanding of the economy: no methodology is pre-judged. But the discussion of this section also points to the difficulties involved, for in applied science, methodology cannot be separated clearly from practice and practice depends on personal knowledge. Such personal knowledge involves both the cognitive level of beliefs that contain theoretical presuppositions and scientific principles along with practical skills involving knowledge of materials, tools and how to make things work.

3.   THE FIELD TRIAL EXPERIMENT

The first experiment reported in this book was designed to assess different ways of doing econometrics by a controlled field trial experiment in applied econometrics. The basic idea of the experiment is very simple, namely to take a specified data set and let several researchers carry out the same set of applied econometrics tasks, but with their own (different) methods, approaches and beliefs. Our overall aim was to assess, within the environment of our experiment, the differences between the several ways of doing econometrics in a practical application.

As far as we know, this is the first time such an applied econometrics field trial experiment has been undertaken. Ed Leamer planned an experiment in applied macro econometrics (to take place in 1990–91), but this never took place. Jan Magnus first proposed a field trial experiment for econometric methodology in 1991. But despite being highly rated as innovative, appropriate and important by the Netherlands Organization for the Advancement of Research (NWO), the project was not funded. A similar fate met further attempts by the two organizers (Magnus and Morgan) to obtain funds from the Economic and Social Research Council (ESRC) in the UK in 1992–3 and 1993–4. Assessors agreed it was a good idea and that the experiment was sufficiently well thought out to be worth supporting, but we failed to get the funds necessary. We were delighted when the opportunity to do part of the planned experiment was made possible by the support of the editorial board of the *Journal of Applied Econometrics*, and are grateful for the opportunity this gave us to conduct the experiment. We are equally grateful to CentER for Economic Research at Tilburg University for their funding of the workshop where the experimental results were discussed.

The aim of the experiment was to assess competing methodologies of econometrics in an applied field trial. This sounds simple enough, but the design of such an experiment is not simple; indeed, our experience suggests that it is fraught with difficulties (on which, see also Chapter 14). We have learnt much from conducting this experiment, which is to say that there are many aspects of our design that could be improved. No doubt we made many beginners' mistakes, the most important one of which was that we were too ambitious: we tried to do too much in one experiment. This was partly due to our lack of experience, but also because of the history of our attempts to get this experiment off the ground. This had proved so difficult that when we finally succeeded we were tempted to do as much as possible with our opportunity.

Our field trial experiment posed a number of design problems. The main problem of field trials is to establish sufficient control in the design that one can, in principle, expect to learn from the results. In the classic cases where experimental design techniques have been worked out (see Fisher, 1960, originally 1935) there is always an untreated group which acts as the control against which the difference in outcome can be measured. In our case, there appeared to be no possible 'control group' or 'untreated group' against which to measure the differences between one econometric methodology and another. In order to establish a neutral base line against which to judge the different approaches we picked a 'classic paper' in applied econometrics, one which everyone could agree had been, at its time, the best that applied econometrics could offer. The chosen paper was James Tobin's 'A statistical demand function for food in the USA', published in 1950 in the *Journal of the Royal Statistical Society*, Series A (and reproduced here as Chapter 2). This solution, and our associated choice of classic paper, had the immediate implication that we widened our aims. Our aims, as we expressed it in our experimental information pack, were to assess not only 'the differences between the several ways of doing econometrics in a practical application' but also, since Tobin's paper was not a contemporary one, 'the advantage (if any) of 45 years of econometric theory since Tobin's paper' and 'the impact of new economic theories' (Magnus and Morgan, 1995, p. 3).

Another level of design control required us to hold constant as many as possible of the other circumstances which might vary, or at least hold them equal between participants, so that one could see more clearly the differences due to different methodologies. There are three main areas of control we tried to instil in the design here.

First, we constrained participants to use only the data we provided. We aimed to control for particular local knowledge by supplying data from two economies: the USA and the Netherlands believing that no participant would have expert local knowledge of both.

Second, we had to choose the qualities or criteria on which the methodologies were to be assessed; that is: what should a practical econometrician be able to do in working on this data set? We believed that these criteria should involve at least four elements: measurement (estimation), testing of an economic hypothesis, policy implications, and forecasting. This required that we set well-specified tasks so that each methodology could be assessed as far as possible on the same tasks.

Third, we feared 'contamination' between our participating 'subjects', and so asked them not to communicate with each other, or publicly report the results, until after a specific date by which all experimental reports were due.

Our experimental design was complicated by the fact that, although we wanted comparability in order to be able to assess the methodologies on the same tasks, we were quite aware that the existing methodological approaches were, in part, designed for different kinds of problems and different types of data sets. We thus had to satisfy two objectives in our design: comparability and diversity, and these were relevant both for our choice of tasks and of data sets.

On the one hand, we wanted the data to be sufficiently simple so that we could isolate the impact of the changes in technology and theory since 1950. On the other hand, we wanted sufficient richness in the data sets so that the study was interesting for its own sake (to motivate participation) and would allow the participants to shine in their own specialities. We therefore chose, in addition to Tobin's data set, two further sets of data. The data used in the experiment consisted of:

1. the set used by Tobin,
2. further data (after 1950) for the USA,
3. data of same type, but from the Dutch economy.

The US data consisted of both time-series and cross-section data in the same spirit as Tobin's data. This data set was somewhat narrow, but it fulfilled our requirement to enhance comparability of the various approaches. The Dutch data set, on the other hand, was much richer. This set combined time-series (1948–1988) data with three budget studies, two of which are quite detailed. (A full description of the data is included in Chapters 21 and 22 and was included in Magnus and Morgan, 1995.) Taken together, the US and Dutch data sets involved time-series, cross-section and household-level data and thus satisfied our requirement for diversity in type of data.

The tasks were set to allow both for the full range of what one might expect practical econometrics to achieve, and to allow different methodologies, even specialized ones, to show their best efforts. The tasks are fully described in Chapter 1. Suffice it to say here that they involved a measurement task using the US data directly comparable to the one that Tobin had undertaken; a 'measurement with related information' task involving the Dutch and US data; a forecasting task involving the Dutch data; a policy question task, and a self-chosen task. Since we were interested in assessing the advantages and disadvantages of the different methodologies, there was, of course, freedom on how the tasks were performed. And because of the specialisms associated with different methodologies and with participants' own skills and interests, we did not expect all participants to undertake all tasks.

In summary, we selected Tobin's 1950 paper as an example of 'good applied econometrics' to provide the baseline for the participants' own analysis. The experiment was designed to show first what difference modern approaches and technologies make to Tobin's results. Beyond that base level, we wanted to generate information which would enable comparative assessment of the different approaches. By constraining the participants to the same data set and asking all participants to carry out a well-specified set of 'tasks' (how they performed the tasks was up to them), the experiment aimed to provide the raw material for explicit and constructive assessment.

From the beginning of the experiment we planned to ask the help of a panel of independent experts for commentary on the experiment and to help us assess the results reported by our participants in the field trial. This aspect of the experiment also included several issues of design. In order to avoid the problem of having assessors who were all in one 'camp', and to make sure all participants had the chance of nominating assessors who were sympathetic to their approach, we asked each participant to nominate two assessors. (In fact, few participants nominated assessors, and not all assessors nominated by participants, or selected by ourselves, were willing to participate.) The role of these assessors was to act as commentators on the submitted reports. As a further procedure to minimize bias, we asked each assessor to comment on several papers, not only on the one for which they had been nominated. These commentaries follow the relevant experimental reports in Chapters 3–10. By asking a panel of independent assessors to comment on the reports, we hoped this would maintain our own position as neutral between participants in the field trial. We believed it would be invidious for us to be assessing the individual reports as well as running the experiment. We were also aware that the *Journal of Applied Econometrics* provided an important, professionally neutral, place to report the results, but again, only if we ensured its neutrality with respect to the different approaches of the participants in carrying out our editorial responsibilities. We therefore announced that, as guest editors of the special issue, we would be assuming complete editorial responsibility. Our aim for the special issue was that it would contain the most interesting reports, as judged by the independent assessors (who also acted as referees on quality for the journal submissions). In the event we found that our assessors were most responsive and, in their comparative comments, helped us and the participants understand more clearly why results from the different teams differed; see Ken Wallis' comments following Chapter 8 and Chapter 12. Our own comparative analysis of the results and assessment of the experiment are given in Chapters 13 and 14.

4. THE TACIT KNOWLEDGE EXPERIMENT

While the first experiment was a field trial, primarily designed to assess different ways of doing econometrics, it also included a small tacit knowledge component. We asked all participants of the field trial to keep logbooks, recording the process of how they did their work, in what order, what mistakes they made, and so forth. We hoped that these logbooks would make our participants conscious of the process of their thinking, and might provide a resource for future study of tacit knowledge. The current volume contains brief versions of these logbooks as part of each report on the field trial experiment.

Our second experiment was designed to find out more directly how important 'tacit knowledge' is in applied econometrics. As in our field trial experiment, there were knotty problems of design and we also experienced difficulty in funding the experiment. Consequently, our tacit knowledge experiment was modest in aims and design. Just how modest is revealed by a brief discussion of the design principles in tacit knowledge elicitation. The most experienced researcher in the field, Harry Collins, has adopted several different methods to explore the content and role of tacit knowledge in different physical sciences. For example, in Collins (1985), he studied the attempts to make a new type of laser by working as an apprentice alongside the scientist and questioning each move made. He made use of a two-person team in his 1990 examination of tacit knowledge in crystal growing. This experiment was designed to elicit the difference between apprenticeship learning and the knowledge-elicitation procedures of an 'expert systems' approach (which became embodied in a computerized advice programme). In practice, the comparison became three way involving also a comparison with textbook knowledge. In this case, the apprentice ended up as a go-between between the expert chemist and the expert-systems person. Both cases point to the difficulties of such experiments, the importance of practical experience in attempts to elicit tacit rules, and the minimum requirement of an inexperienced apprentice along with an experienced master.

In discussing our own attempts to design a tacit knowledge experiment in 1992, Collins suggested an alternative design he called 'the proxy stranger'. This seemed appropriate, since both of us were ruled out from playing the role of the ignorant apprentice in eliciting tacit knowledge. This design involves a two-person team, one who is a stranger to the field and is apprenticed to the relevant field expert and the other the tacit knowledge researcher who observes, asks questions about why things are done in a certain way and records the information flow as the apprentice learns the craft (see Collins, 1992). The luxury of such an experimental design was beyond us (we tried but failed to get funding for such a design); we did have an apprentice willing to learn the art of the master (in fact, three masters) though we had to be content with an arms-length connection with the masters.

Our tacit knowledge experiment involved Wiebe Siegert, a Master's student at Tilburg University, as the apprentice willing to learn the art of three masters: David Hendry, Ed Leamer and Chris Sims. We asked ourselves to what extent the apprentice could learn the tacit knowledge of the master econometricians solely by reading their published works. More precisely, our design asked: could an apprentice working from the texts do a reasonably good job, on a specified task, of using three different approaches to applied econometrics as judged by the three relevant masters involved. Siegert was set the same project, data and one of the tasks as used in the field trial experiment (see Chapter 15), and asked to imitate the three master econometricians. Minimal guidance was provided by one of us (Jan Magnus). We expected that both the logbook comments of our apprentice, and the comments from our master econometricians (each of whom was asked to comment on the apprenticeship work) would reveal large gaps attributable to tacit knowledge. The interest lay in trying to access the nature of these gaps and at what points they occurred to reveal something of the comparable tacit knowledge involved in the different approaches. Since there was only one apprentice, we can assume his personal knowledge remained rather constant (of course there was some learning about the data during the course of the experiment), making comparison rather easier than in the first experiment.

In the event, only two of the three master econometricians commented (see Chapters 17 and 18) on the apprenticeship piece (Chapter 16), but we were delighted that Adrian Pagan (whose own assessments of the master-methodologies are well known — see Pagan, 1987 and 1995) took on the task of making an assessment of the tacit knowledge gap revealed by this second experiment (see Chapter 19). We comment on tacit knowledge, from the experience of both experiments, in Chapter 20.

5. CONCLUSION

We began this introduction by discussing the debate over how to do econometrics. In an early version of the debate, the Tinbergen-Keynes debate, Tinbergen asked that econometrics be assessed on its success in application, rather than by philosophy and general arguments. Keynes responded by asking Tinbergen to undertake an experiment modelled on the case of the translation of the Septuagint wherein seventy-two translators (rather than the seventy as Keynes said) were shut up in separate rooms and came up with identical translations. Keynes asked in 1940: 'Would the same miracle be vouchsafed if seventy multiple correlators were shut up with the same statistical material?' The answer of course is 'No', for as Keynes himself recognized, theoretical beliefs would make a difference:

> 'I suppose, if each had a different economist perched on his *a priori*, that would make a difference to the outcome.'   (Keynes, 1940, p. 156–7)

But perhaps, Keynes missed another point: the question of what we can infer from the results of the original experiment. Bible scholars suggest that the quality of the Septuagint translation varies dramatically from section to section. Was there a miracle? Or was there perhaps collusion and division of labour between the translators, each taking responsibility for a different section and each bringing their own personal knowledge and experience to their allotted section? The aim of our two experiments was not to seek consensus, but to learn what we could about the differences in applied econometric methodologies and the personal knowledge base involved. Like Tinbergen, we want to assess econometrics as an applied science.

The two experiments: the field trial and the tacit knowledge experiments, are described and reported in Parts I and II of this book, including in each case, assessments of the experiments. The full data description is provided in Part III.

REFERENCES

Collins, H. M. (1985), *Changing Order. Replication and Induction in Scientific Practice*, Sage, London.
Collins, H. M. (1990), *Artificial Experts. Social Knowledge and Intelligent Machines*, MIT Press, Cambridge, USA.
Collins, H. M. (1992), 'Reproducing historical experiments: Three ways of assembling a cultural inventory', Paper presented to the International Workshop on Reproduction of Historic Experiments, Carl von Ossietzky University of Oldenburg, August 24–28, 1992.
Fish, S. (1989), *Doing What Comes Naturally*, Duke University Press, Durham, USA.
Fisher, R. A. (1960), *Design of Experiments*, 8th edition, Oliver and Boyd, Edinburgh and London.
Hamminga, B. and N. De Marchi (1994), *Idealization in Economics*, Rodopi, Amsterdam.
Hendry, D. F. and M. S. Morgan (1995), *The Foundations of Econometric Analysis*, Cambridge University Press, Cambridge, UK.
Keynes, J. M. (1940) 'Comment', *Economic Journal*, **49**, 154–156.
Kuhn, T. S. (1962), *The Structure of Scientific Revolutions*, University of Chicago Press, Chicago.

Magnus, J. R. and M. S. Morgan (1995), *The Experiment in Applied Econometrics: Information Pack* (54 pages), CentER for Economic Research, Tilburg University.

Pagan, A. (1987), 'Three econometric methodologies: a critical appraisal', *Journal of Economic Surveys*, **1**, 3–24.

Pagan, A. (1995), 'Three econometric methodologies: an update', in L. Oxley, D. A. R. George, C. J. Roberts and S. Sayer (eds), *Surveys in Econometrics*, Basil Blackwell, Oxford, 30–41.

Polanyi, M. (1958), *Personal Knowledge: Towards a Post-Critical Philosophy*, Routledge, London.

Tobin, J. (1950), 'A statistical demand function for food in the USA', *Journal of the Royal Statistical Society*, Series A, **113**, Part II, 113–141 [reprinted in Chapter 2, this volume].

Turner, S. (1994), *The Social Theory of Practices, Tradition, Tacit Knowledge and Presuppositions*, Polity Press, Cambridge.

Part I

The Field Trial Experiment

CHAPTER 1

ORGANIZATION OF THE FIELD TRIAL EXPERIMENT*

JAN R. MAGNUS AND MARY S. MORGAN

1. INTRODUCTION

For many years we had been thinking about an experiment in applied econometrics and discussed it with many people. The experiment in its current form was first announced in the May 1995 issue of the *Journal of Applied Econometrics* (Magnus and Morgan, 1995a). We told prospective participants that we had selected one classic paper — Tobin (1950) — and we briefly summarized the purpose, the data, the tasks, and the assessments of the experiment. Then we invited participants to come forward and perform the described tasks within one year. In total, 39 individuals or teams wrote to us. (Four teams who wanted to participate after the deadline were allowed to do so.) The teams were geographically distributed as follows:

	Participants	Completed
USA	14	4
UK	7	1
Netherlands	4	2
Rest of Europe	8	1
Rest of World	6	0

On 1 July 1995 we sent to each participant:

- the *Experiment Information Pack*, see Magnus and Morgan (1995b)
- a reprint of the Tobin (1950) article
- one diskette containing the data.

We anticipated that there would be questions from the participants during the year. In order to sustain complete equality of information, we promised that, if at all appropriate, we would send the question and our answer to all participants. We also promised that, if we discovered relevant papers, we would inform participants about these. Papers mentioned at the start as possibly useful were Chetty (1968), Maddala (1971) and, in particular, Izan (1980).

In Section 2 we describe the rules of the experiment. Section 3 contains the tasks that we set to the participating teams. Section 4 covers our request to participants to keep a logbook and provides our instructions on reporting. A summary of our correspondence with the participants by e-mail during the year is given in Section 5. The assessors

---

* Reprinted, with minor changes, from the *Journal of Applied Econometrics*, **12**, 467–476 (1997).

Methodology and Tacit Knowledge: Two Experiments in Econometrics
Jan R. Magnus and Mary S. Morgan © 1997 John Wiley & Sons Ltd

and their role in the experiment is described in Section 6, while Section 7 explains the organization of the workshop in Tilburg. Finally, Section 8 summarizes our activities between the workshop and the publication of the Special Issue of the *Journal of Applied Econometrics*.

2.   THE RULES

We believed that strict rules were necessary for the success of the experiment. Comparability of the results (difficult in the best of worlds) would depend on strict controls of certain aspects of the experiment. We attempted, however, to keep the rules as simple as possible. These were our rules.

Use of the Data

(a)   Only data supplied by Magnus and Morgan (hereafter MM) can be used. However, there is no restriction on the use of economic theory and econometrics.
(b)   The US data is drawn from official published reports and is in the public domain. Please credit the relevant US government department and cite the relevant publications (all references are given in Chapters 7 and 8 of the *Experiment Information Pack*[1]) when you make use of these data. Some of the Dutch data can only be used courtesy of Statistics Netherlands. Each report should contain a note of thanks to Statistics Netherlands.
(c)   Participants are not permitted to provide the data supplied by MM to anybody other than members of their research team.

Time Schedule

A strict time schedule is a necessary condition for the success of this experiment. The date and location of the workshop are fixed and the date that copy will have to be with the *Journal of Applied Econometrics* is fixed as well.

1 July 1995	Information packs have been sent out
1 July 1996	All experiment reports with MM
1 September 1996	Selected reports to assessors
14–17 December 1996	Workshop at CentER, Tilburg University, the Netherlands
1 March 1997	Assessors comments to MM
1 October 1997	Publication of Special Issue of the *Journal of Applied Econometrics* (Volume 12, Supplement)

The time schedule is holy.

Exchange of Information

No information concerning the ongoing experiment should be exchanged between participating experimenters before 1 July 1996.

---

[1] This information is reprinted in Chapters 21 and 22.

Reporting[2]

(a) The focus of each report must be the tasks set by MM.
(b) All results must be reproducible.
(c) A logbook of the process by which the results have been obtained must be kept and a summary logbook must be submitted as one section of the final report.

Publication of the Results

Participants are obliged to submit their reports to MM on or before 1 July 1996. The report shall be considered as a submission to the Special Issue of the *Journal of Applied Econometrics* and will be refereed according to the highest academic standards. The report (or parts of it) should not be published elsewhere until after publication of the Special Issue.

Role of MM

(a) MM will act as organizers and administrators of the project.
(b) MM will serve as guest editors of the Special Issue of the *Journal of Applied Econometrics* and have been given complete editorial responsibility.
(c) MM will not participate as one of the research teams producing a report and aim to be neutral between approaches.
(d) In cases where the above rules do not apply or where a change of the rules is deemed necessary, the decision by MM is final.

3. THE TASKS

There were five tasks. We hoped participants would attempt to undertake all five tasks, but we made it clear that this was not necessary if a particular task could not be performed within the framework of the participant's methodology. The tasks were described as follows.

3.1. Measurement

(a) Using the original Tobin data set for the USA:
   (i) Estimate the income elasticity of food demand;
   (ii) Test the 'homogeneity postulate' of the family food demand function;
   (iii) Comment on the differences between your results and Tobin's.

   Note: You may use the data set as used by Tobin (with or without our corrections) and, if you wish, the additional data that Tobin could have used but didn't.
(b) Using the full set of US data provided, perform the tasks specified under (a).

---

[2] See also Section 4–The logbook and report.

3.2. Measurement with Related Information

(a) Assume now that you have no access to the US data set, only to the Dutch set. However, a colleague of yours (whose work you moderately admire) has recently published a study on the US demand for food in the *Journal of Applied Econometrics* using the US data set. The *results* of this study (estimates, standard errors, tests, predictions) are available to you, but *not* the underlying data. In particular, your American colleague has performed Task 1(b).

　　You are asked to undertake the tasks specified under 1(a) for the Netherlands using the Dutch data set. In doing so, you wish to take account of the American article. You also wish to take advantage of the experience of your American colleague. Upon your request you are given the logbook underlying the American study. How do you take account of the American article and/or the logbook in your Dutch study? If you had completely ignored the American article, would your results have been any different?

(b) Assume next that both data sets are available to you. Thus you have more information than in Task 1(b) (because you may use the Dutch set) and Task 2(a) (because you can now use the US data set, not just the resulting US estimates). Answer the questions in Task 1(a) again for both the USA and the Netherlands and comment on the difference (if any) between the results of Task 1(b) and Task 2(b) for the USA and between the results of Task 2(a) and Task 2(b) for the Netherlands.

3.3. Forecasting

In 1988 (the last year of the Dutch time series available to you) the research department of an important food manufacturer, operating mainly in the Dutch market, wishes to make economic forecasts until the year 2000. You are hired as a consultant. Produce forecasts for the demand for food in the Netherlands as it will develop in the twelve years from 1989 to 2000.

3.4. Policy

Governments and policy makers are now worried about the differential impact of changes in the economy on different population groups. One aspect of this problem is the relationship between income distribution and aggregate economic performance (or real income performance). Is a flat income distribution good or bad for the economic performance of an economy? Does an improved economic performance change the income distribution? If so, how? The relationship between income distribution and economic performance thus has a causality aspect as well as a quantitative aspect.

(a) Construct an index of aggregate real income performance for each of the two economies.

(b) Investigate the relation between income distribution and aggregate real income performance.

(c) What would be the effects (if any) of tax policies designed to redistribute incomes?

Note: Some references relating to this question are: Blank and Blinder (1986), Blinder and Esaki (1978), Carroll and Summers (1991), Cutler and Katz (1991), and Quah (1994).

3.5. Own Task

Define your own task (within the context of the data sets provided). Describe the problem, your procedures and results.

4. THE LOGBOOK AND REPORT

The Logbook

Most scientific research relies on a large amount of 'tacit knowledge' — knowledge which is not part of formal theoretical ideas (either statistical or economic), but which is an essential element in conducting applied scientific research. It is this knowledge, gained from experience, which guides the scientist in deciding what to do next and how to do it. It seems reasonable to assume that this is the case in econometrics as well.

In an attempt to learn more about the process of applied econometrics, and to access the sort of tacit knowledge involved, we asked all participants to join us in an attempt to throw light on this important aspect of econometric research. As a mechanism for keeping track of the process we suggested the 'logbook'. It is commonplace in other scientific fields to keep lab notebooks. These record the procedures used, the various steps taken as the research progresses, false avenues, interim results, and other details the scientist wishes to keep track of. These records, directly or indirectly, can reveal much about the research process. We asked all our participants to keep such 'logbooks'; these form an important element of the experiment.

There are no hard and fast rules about what should be in a logbook. Different participating groups might keep note of different aspects. But at a minimum we think it should include notes on data preparation work, the order of work on each task, failed steps as well as successful ones, and so forth. The logbook record ought to be sufficient for the author to reconstruct the path of the author's work and the reasoning behind it.

We asked that a summary of the logbook be included in the final report in a shortened form (2–3 pages). In this way, other participants (and later the readers of the reports), would be able to learn about the process of applied econometrics.

The Report

We told participating teams that the Special Issue of the *Journal of Applied Econometrics* would include a full description of the experiment including the tasks, data description and sources. These should therefore *not* be repeated in each author's report. Instead, participants' reports should focus on how the tasks were undertaken, the outcomes interpreted, and the results assessed according to self-set criteria.

We asked the authors to bear in mind the following guidelines and requests:

(a) Please keep to a maximum of 25 pages.
(b) Please include a short summary of your overall approach/methodology (include references to longer explanations where necessary).
(c) Please outline your own criteria of success.

(d) Please include a brief, honest summary account (including false moves) of your progress on each task based on your logbook record.

(e) Please do not change the variable names unnecessarily.

(f) Please include your interpretation/assessment of your results, including those things you are disappointed with as well as those you are pleased with.

(g) Please describe the self-set task and its results.

(h) Please remember that all results should be reproducible.

5. E-MAIL MESSAGES SENT TO PARTICIPANTS

During the year we kept in touch with all participants through e-mail. We encouraged them to ask for clarification if necessary, informed them about new participants, asked their advice about possible assessors, reminded them of the deadlines and the rules of the experiment, and corrected some errors. Of these messages, one (19 August 1995) contained some additional data for the 1941 US budgets survey. On 1 May 1996 we provided a corrected data set for Dutch population figures — with our apologies. Because of this error on our part, and because of requests from participants, we postponed the deadline for completion of the experimental reports until 1 August 1996. These two e-mail messages and associated data are provided in Part III of this book, and are also available as additional information to the data archived with the *Journal of Applied Econometrics*.

Only one e-mail message related to clarification of the experimental design: On 29 August 1995 we e-mailed participants as follows in reply to one participant's comment on Task 2 (measurement with related information; see Section 3.2):

Comment:

(a) This question could be interpreted as asking for a hypothetical response to hypothetical stimuli, which (as the participant pointed out) contrasts greatly to the implicit philosophy of everything else, namely real responses to real stimuli.

(b) The first sentence: 'Assume next that both sets are available to you' might suggest a hypothetical circumstance which was not intended.

Our reply:

(a) The idea here is to use your own estimation results on the USA. Thus the 'colleague whose work you moderately admire' is yourself. This is slightly schizophrenic but it is the only way this task can be realistically performed.

(b) The sentence should read: 'Next use both data sets available to you.'

6. THE ASSESSORS

During the summer of 1996 we were able to find eight assessors to read and comment on the reports presented at the workshop. They were (in alphabetical order):

Short name	Assessor	Affiliation
AB	Anton Barten	Catholic University of Leuven, Belgium
JSC	J. S. Cramer	University of Amsterdam, the Netherlands
AK	Arie Kapteyn	CentER, Tilburg University, the Netherlands
MMc	Michael McAleer	University of Western Australia, Australia
HP	Hashem Pesaran	Trinity College, Cambridge, UK
PS	Peter Schmidt	Michigan State University, USA
KWa	Kenneth Wallis	University of Warwick, UK
MWi	Michael Wickens	University of York, UK

We received reports from eight teams who completed the experiment. They are (in the order of presentation at the December workshop):

Short name	Authors	Assessed by
CBS	van Driel/Nadall/Zeelenberg	AK, HP, MWi
Texas	Anderson/Vahid	JSC, PS, HP
Leamer	Leamer	AB, MMc, PS
Maddala	Maddala/Wu/Yin	JSC, AK, MWi
Maastricht	de Crombrugghe/Palm/Urbain	AB, MMc, KWa
Finland	Höglund/Jäntti/Knif/Nordberg/Rosenqvist	AB, PS, KWa
Dundee	Song/Liu/Romilly	JSC, KWa, MWi
Tennessee	Bearse/Bozdogan/Schlottmann	AK, MMc, HP

There are thus eight reports and eight assessors. Each report was sent to three assessors and each assessor was asked to assess/referee three reports.

In our letter of 26 August 1996 to the assessors we sent each of them:

- The information pack (54 pages)
- Data diskette (9 original files +5 ASCII files concerning the US data)
- The Tobin article
- E-mail messages sent to participants (4 pages of clarifications/corrections)
- Three reports to assess.

We asked each assessor to undertake the following assessments:

(1) To act as a referee to us as guest editors of the special issue of the *Journal of Applied Econometrics* (JAE) and tell us whether each report is of sufficient quality to be published in the JAE. We have a severe space constraint in the Special Issue, which means that we are aiming at an average of 13 journal pages per report. Therefore we would be particularly grateful for your advice as to which parts of each report are particularly interesting and worth publishing.

(2) To provide detailed comments for each report on how to improve the presentation, etc. The idea here is *not* to impose your ideas on the author on how the problem should be approached. Rather do we hope you will help the authors to clarify their own ideas, to improve the presentation, to suggest possible cuts (given space constraints), etc.

(3)   To act as comparative assessor for the three reports. That is, to analyse how the three reports differ and possibly why. We emphasize that the experiment is not a competition with a winner or a prize. Rather, it is a field trial in applied econometrics, designed to assess both the degree to which econometrics has 'progressed' since Tobin's article, and also the performance of different approaches to the applied problems we set as tasks. In this respect, we would all like to understand why report A gets different results from report B. The assessors will get sufficient time during the workshop to present their assessments and we would like to publish a 2- or 3-page edited version of your comments in the Special Issue.

7.   THE WORKSHOP

The workshop took place in Tilburg from Sunday 15 until Tuesday 17 December 1996. Each of the eight teams was represented by at least one author, except Professor G. S. Maddala who could not participate due to health problems and his co-author due to visa problems. All eight assessors were present, as was, by special invitation, Professor James Tobin. The eight papers and the written assessments were distributed to all participants at the beginning of the workshop. Thirty-three people attended the workshop:

Teams:

CBS	Hans van Driel/Venuta Nadall/Kees Zeelenberg
Texas	Heather Anderson/Farshid Vahid
Leamer	Edward Leamer
Maddala	—
Maastricht	Denis de Crombrugghe/Franz Palm/Jean-Pierre Urbain
Finland	Leif Nordberg/Gunnar Rosenqvist
Dundee	Xiaming Liu/Peter Romilly
Tennessee	Peter Bearse/Hamparsum Bozdogan/Alan Schlottmann
Assessors:	See Section 6

Others:

Richard Blundell	University College London
Bert Hamminga	Tilburg University
Marco Hoeberichts	Tilburg University
Kevin Hoover	University of California, Davis, USA
Franc Klaassen	Tilburg University
Jan Magnus	Tilburg University
Mary Morgan	University of Amsterdam and London School of Economics
Wiebe Siegert	Tilburg University
James Tobin	Yale University

We started on Sunday after lunch. After a brief welcome by Jan Magnus, three reports were presented (CBS, Texas, and Leamer). Each report was given 70 minutes: 30 minutes for the author(s) to present the report, 20 minutes for the three assessors to give their comments, and 20 minutes for a reply and general discussion. Each presentation was followed by a 20-minute interval. On Monday, following the same format, Maddala and Maastricht presented their results. Since nobody from the Maddala team could be present, Michael Wickens kindly agreed to present the report in their place. Then followed a one-hour general discussion on the experiment as a whole, where the participants gave their views on the strong and (more often) weak points of the set-up. After lunch, the three final reports were presented: Finland, Dundee, and Tennessee. On Tuesday, Kevin Hoover gave his general views about the experiment. This was followed by James Tobin's address, and a 90-minute general discussion chaired by Richard Blundell. Mary Morgan closed the workshop before lunch.

8.   AFTER THE WORKSHOP

In December 1996, immediately after the workshop, we set the parameters for reporting the results of the experiment as a whole. This involved the collaboration of us, as organizers of the experiment and guest editors for the Special Issue of the *Journal of Applied Econometrics* (and editors of the current enlarged book version), the assessors who assessed the reports for us, and the participating teams.

Our main constraint was space, and our main publication considerations were accurate reporting of the experiment in conjunction with interest, variety and quality of the experimental reports. On the basis of the assessors' comments and general discussion at the workshop, we first decided to drop our policy question task (item 3.4 above). It was generally agreed that the policy task had been poorly conceived by us. We also emphasized (again) that all reports should have a short logbook. On the basis of the assessors' comments on the intrinsic interest of the various approaches to the other experimental tasks and the quality of the reported work, we set individual page/word lengths for the revised reports, and indicated, for some reports, those sections we thought appropriate to cut. We decided to publish six reports in the special issue, and all eight of them in the enlarged volume.

We wrote to the participating teams: 'The most important point, which we have stressed before, is that this is not a normal academic paper, but a report on an experiment. We ask you therefore to stick to the spirit of our enquiry by keeping to your original reporting both in content of the choices you made and results obtained as well as to the style of reporting. Of course you should correct typos and obvious errors in your reporting. You will need to make some cuts due to the restrictions of length imposed by the Journal. You will also want to take account of the assessors' comments where they suggested clarification of your procedures were needed. But please do not redo the work or rewrite your paper as if the assessors' comments were referees' reports. Recalculated results or changed procedures can be reported in your published 'reply' to the assessors. For example, if in your first report you used expenditure rather than income data, or you used nominal income rather than real income—these were your choices and you should leave them intact. You can come back to this point in your 'reply' and provide your response.'

The revised reports were received by 1 March 1997. Although most teams adhered to the spirit of the experiment in making revisions, one participant (Leamer) did substantial reworking on his time-series results as these were queried at the workshop. Another team (Dundee), at our suggestion, corrected some calculation mistakes suspected by one of the assessors. Both these changes, and other minor ones, are clearly reported by authors in their final reports. Because of our requests to cut the size of some reports, several teams were obliged to present fewer results and in more succinct form, necessitating a number of new tables.

After a final check of the team reports, we summarized the changes made for every report, and sent all reports back to the assessors on 19 March 1997. We asked them to revise their assessment comments on each report in the style of the discussion published after papers in the *Journal of the Royal Statistical Society* (an ideal role model, since this was the place of publication for Tobin's original article). We also asked our assessors for any comparative comments and remarks on the experiment itself for publication in the enlarged book report of the experiment.

The final round in May 1997 was to invite the participating teams to write brief responses to the assessors' comments again taking the *Journal of the Royal Statistical Society* as the model.

REFERENCES

Blank, R. M. and A. S. Blinder (1986), 'Macroeconomics, income distribution, and poverty', in S. H. Danziger and D. H. Weinberg (eds), *Fighting Poverty: What Works and What Doesn't*, Harvard University Press, Cambridge USA.

Blinder, A. S. and H. Y. Esaki (1978), 'Macroeconomic activity and income distribution in the postwar United States', *Review of Economics and Statistics*, **60**, 604–9.

Carroll, C. D. and L. H. Summers (1991), 'Consumption growth parallels income growth: some new evidence', in B. D. Bernheim and J. B. Shoven (eds), *National Saving and Economic Performance*, NBER Research Project Report, University of Chicago Press, Chicago.

Chetty, V. K. (1968), 'Pooling of time series and cross section data', *Econometrica*, **36**, 279–90.

Cutler, D. M. and L. F. Katz (1991), 'Macroeconomic performance and the disadvantaged', *Brookings Papers on Economic Activity*, **2**, 1–73.

Izan, H. Y. (1980), 'To pool or not to pool: a reexamination of Tobin's food demand problem', *Journal of Econometrics*, **13**, 391–402.

Maddala, G. S. (1971) 'The likelihood approach to pooling cross-section and time-series data', *Econometrica*, **39**, 939–53.

Magnus, J. R. and M. S. Morgan (1995a), 'An experiment in applied econometrics: call for participants', *Journal of Applied Econometrics*, **10**, 213–16.

Magnus, J. R. and M. S. Morgan (1995b), *The Experiment in Applied Econometrics: Information Pack* (54 pages), CentER for Economic Research, Tilburg University.

Quah, D. (1994), 'One business cycle and one trend from (many) many disaggregates', *European Economic Review*, **38**, 605–13.

Tobin, J. (1950), 'A statistical demand function for food in the USA', *Journal of the Royal Statistical Society*, Series A, **113**, Part II, 113–41 [reprinted in Chapter 2, this volume].

A STATISTICAL DEMAND FUNCTION FOR FOOD IN THE USA*

JAMES TOBIN[1]

Quantitative data relating to the demand for consumers' goods and services are, for the most part, of two very different kinds, time series and family budget surveys. Time series are generally aggregate data: observations in successive periods of the total national consumption of a commodity and of possible explanatory variables, priniipally national income and prices. A family budget survey is a set of observations, for a single time period, of the expenditures on the goods by families who differ in income, size and other characteristics. The premise of this paper is that a statistical demand function should be consistent with both kinds of observations.

Most statistical analysis of consumer behaviour has relied exclusively on one or the other of the two types of data.[2] The relationship of national consumption to other national aggregates has been found from time series, without investigation of the consistency of this aggregate demand function with the evidence concerning family behaviour. Or budget data have been analyzed to determine the effects of family income and other variables on family expenditures, without considering the consistency of the estimates of these effects with time series of aggregate variables.

There are both economic and statistical reasons for basing quantitative demand analysis on a combination of time series and budget data. The economic reason is the obvious fact that aggregate consumption and income are the sums of the consumptions and incomes of families.[3] Any relationship among these and other aggregates is the reflection of a multitude of family consumption decisions. A hypothesis concerning the determination of aggregate demand should be derived from a hypothesis about family expenditure. The connection between the family demand function and its aggregate counterpart will, in general, involve the joint distribution of families by income and by the other variables in the family demand function.[4]

Statistically, widening the scope of the observations on which statistical demand analysis is based increases the possibility of rejecting hypotheses and improves the estimates

---

* Reprinted from the *Journal of the Royal Statistical Society*, Series A, Volume 113, Part II, 1950, 113–149 (including discussion and reply).

[1] The author wishes to express his gratitude for the hospitality of the Department of Applied Economics of the University of Cambridge in making their facilities available to him for the completion of this work.

[2] Two exceptions, to which the approach of the present paper owes much, should be noted: Marschak (1943) and Staehle (1945).

[3] For convenience, a single individual will be considered a 'family' of one person.

[4] The theoretical connection between the family demand function and the aggregate demand function, via the distribution of families by income, has been considered by Marschak (1939a), Staehle (1937) and de Wolff (1941). A more general treatment is given by Haavelmo (1947).

Methodology and Tacit Knowledge: Two Experiments in Econometrics
Jan R. Magnus and Mary S. Morgan © 1950 Royal Statistical Society

of the parameters of demand functions (Marschak, 1939b, p. 487, and 1943, p. 42). The increase in statistical power is due not merely to the addition of new information, but to the addition of information of a different nature. Economic time series are notoriously poor material for choosing among hypotheses; and simply extending the length of their span does not eliminate the difficulty. The estimation of parameters from time series encounters many statistical pitfalls, which need not be rehearsed here (Stone, 1948). These difficulties are mitigated if it is possible on the basis of other information to restrict the field of acceptable hypotheses and the range of possible parameter values.

Budget studies provide observations in which the persistent correlations of some explanatory variables over time are broken; indeed, they constitute an experiment in which certain relevant variables, such as prices, are constant while others, chiefly income, vary. Moreover, microeconomic data escape some of the difficulties of identification to which aggregate time series are subject. For example, an observation of aggregate demand is also an observation of total supply, and the observed relationship of total consumption to other macro-economic variables may reflect the operation of a supply function as well as a demand function. But the observed consumption of a family is unambiguously a point on its demand function, since a single family could have bought more or less of the commodity without affecting its price. For these reasons, the use of budget data may help to rescue statistical demand analysis from the traps encountered in relying exclusively on time series. But for the same reasons, budget statistics are by themselves insufficient to test a complete hypothesis concerning demand or to estimate all the parameters of a demand function, at least until surveys made at different times are much more numerous than at present. Some of the relevant variables change only with time, and their effects cannot be evaluated without appeal to time series of aggregates.

This paper is an attempt to derive two related statistical demand functions for food for the United States, one the family demand function and the other the aggregate demand function, by combining information from budget surveys and from time series. 'Food' is treated as a single commodity, and variations over time in the quantity and price of this commodity are measured by index numbers. The variables determining family food demand are assumed to be disposable family income in the current and preceding years, family size, the food price index and the index of prices of other consumers' goods. The form of the function assumed implies that the elasticity of demand with respect to each of these variables is constant. In Section 1 the elasticities of family food expenditure with respect to family income and size, with prices constant, are estimated from budget data. The estimate of income-elasticity is interpreted as the sum of the elasticity with respect to current income and the elasticity with respect to income of the previous year. This interpretation is justified by the evidence for a lag in adjustment of food expenditure to changes in income and by the high correlation of family incomes in two successive years. In Section 2 the aggregate demand function is derived from the family function. Under certain realistic assumptions concerning the distribution of families by income and size, it is shown that the aggregate function has the same form and the same elasticities as the family function. Given the estimate of the sum of the two income-elasticities obtained in Section 1, the parameters of the two demand functions are estimated in Section 3 by multiple correlation of time series of aggregates. Section 4 examines the relationships between food expenditure and family income in budget surveys made at different times to see if the differences among these relationships can, with the parameter estimates obtained in Section 3, be attributed to differences in prices and lagged income.

1. THE FAMILY FOOD DEMAND FUNCTION

1.1. The Form of the Function

The family food demand function is assumed to be:

$$c_t = k y_t^{\alpha_1} y_{t-1}^{\alpha_2} P_t^{\beta} Q_t^{\gamma} n_t^{\delta} \qquad\qquad 1$$

where

c_t = quantity of food consumed by a family in year t, whether purchased, received in kind, or home-produced.

y_t = disposable family income for year t: money income plus income in kind, including gifts in money or in kind from other families, less direct taxes and gifts to other families.

P_t = index of food prices, average for year t.

Q_t = index of prices of other consumers' goods, average for year t.

n_t = number of persons in the family in year t, counting a person in the family for a fraction of the year as the same fraction of a full person.

α_1 = elasticity of food demand with respect to current income.

α_2 = elasticity of food demand with respect to previous year's income.

β = elasticity of food demand with respect to food price index.

γ = elasticity of food demand with respect to non-food price index.

δ = elasticity of food demand with respect to family size.

k is a constant which depends on the units in which the variables are measured. (In general, lower-case letters indicate micro-economic variables, and capital letters macro-economic variables. Greek letters are used for the elasticities.)

Function (1) is chosen in preference to a linear relationship for a combination of reasons: (a) The relationship between family income and food expenditure in budget data is obviously not linear; as would be expected on *a priori* grounds, the marginal propensity to consume food decreases with income. A linear relationship between the logarithms gives a good fit to the data without requiring additional parameters. (b) This form of the family demand function implies, under certain simple and plausible aggregation assumptions, an aggregate relationship of the same functional form with the same elasticities. (See Section 2.) (c) Consistency of consumer behaviour requires that the sum of the elasticities of demand with respect to variables of a monetary dimension be identically zero. This theoretical proposition is, of course, not a licence to impose the zero-sum restriction on statistical estimates of elasticities. But it is a reason for adopting a form for statistical demand functions which permits but does not enforce results conforming with the 'homogeneity postulate.' Function (1) has this property: if y_t, y_{t-1}, P_t and Q_t exhaust the variables of monetary dimension relevant to food demand, then the 'homogeneity postulate' implies:

$$\alpha_1 + \alpha_2 + \beta + \gamma = 0. \qquad\qquad 2$$

A linear function in the same variables does not have this property unless it goes through the origin. It is true that the use of functions of the form of (1) for more than one commodity is inconsistent with another requirement of the theory of consumer choice, namely the Slutsky condition on cross-elasticities. Moreover, such a function could not be used for every consumer's good, including saving, without violating the identity of the sum of expenditures and income. But the present investigation concerns only one commodity (Stone, 1945, pp. 293–294.)

1.2. The Effect of Previous Year's Income

Information from budget surveys can provide only two of the five equations required to evaluate all the exponents in (1). The remaining equations must be determined by time series correlation of aggregate data. Budget data can yield, under certain assumptions to be set forth in this section, an estimate of the sum $\alpha_1 + \alpha_2$, which will be called α, and of δ.

Since the observations reported in a budget study refer to a common time period, P_t and Q_t are constant over all families. Consequently (1) becomes

$$c_t = k_t' y_t^{\alpha_1} y_{t-1}^{\alpha_2} n^{\delta} \qquad 3$$

where $k_t' = kP_t^{\beta} Q_t^{\gamma}$ is constant over all families in year t.

If a budget study classified families according to their previous year's income, current income and size, the three elasticities α_1, α_2 and δ could be estimated directly from budget data. In the absence of data concerning lagged income, none of the three exponents can be estimated without assuming either an equation involving the parameters or a relationship between y_t and y_{t-1}.

The usual procedure is to assume $\alpha_2 = 0$, i.e. that there is no lag in the adjustment of consumption to income. Then α_1 can be evaluated from budget data by regression of consumption on current income, taking account of family size.

However, the adjustment of consumption, even food consumption, to family income is in fact not instantaneous. The hypothesis of a lag in the relationship of food demand to income is supported not only by common sense but by the evidence of budget data. The 1941–42 survey for the United States shows food expenditures in the first quarter of 1942 separately for two classes of urban families, those whose annual rates of income were lower than in 1941 by 5% or more, and those whose incomes were higher than in 1941

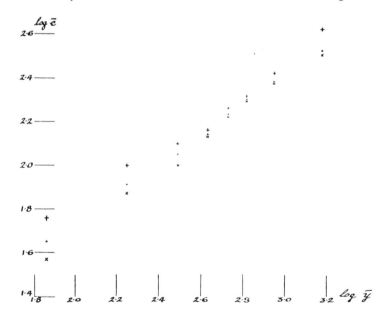

Figure 1. Money expenditure for food and disposable income, all urban families, first quarter 1942
• All families. × Families with incomes 5% or more higher than 1941. + Families with incomes 5% or more lower than 1941.

Table I. Percentage distribution of 1942 money incomes for city families of six 1941 income classes

1941 Money Income (Dollars)	1942 Money Income (Dollars, Annual Rate Based on First Quarter)					
	0–500	500–1000	1000–1500	1500–2000	2000–3000	Over 3000
0–500	78	16	5	—	1	—
500–1000	9	66	18	5	2	—
1000–1500	2	10	52	27	8	1
1500–2000	1	1	11	50	35	2
2000–3000	—	1	2	7	63	27
Over 3000	—	—	—	—	13	85

Source: B.L.S. (1942), Table 4, p. 423, and Table 6, p. 424.

by 5% or more. Figure 1 shows the average food expenditure at eight 1942 income levels for these two groups of families, and for the sample as a whole (including families who experienced less than 5% change in income).[5] The comparison is strong evidence of a lag in adjustment of food expenditure to income level. For each of the eight current income-classes of families, average expenditure is higher for those who suffered a fall in income than for those who experienced a rise. These data do not permit the evaluation of α_2, but they indicate that it is significantly bigger than zero.[6] Moreover, current family income is certainly highly correlated with previous year's income. Table I shows the distribution of families of six 1941 income classes by 1942 income. Average income in the first quarter of 1941 was at an annual rate 7% higher than 1941 average income, and Table I therefore shows that more families moved to higher brackets than to lower.

The correlation between the two years' incomes means that the regression coefficient of family consumption on current income reflects the effect of past income as well. Neglect of the lag results in an over-estimate of α_1 as well as an under-estimate of α_2. The customary assumption that $\alpha_2 = 0$ must be replaced by an alternative assumption which recognizes the importance of past income and its correlation with current income.

Assume, therefore, that the geometric average previous year's income $\bar{y}_{t-1}$ of an income class of families of given size with current income $\bar{y}_t$ is given by

$$\bar{y}_{t-1} = \frac{Y_{t-1}}{Y_t} \bar{y}_t \qquad 4$$

where Y_t is average disposable income per family in year t.[7] Every group of families, classified by current income, is assumed to have undergone the same relative change in

---

[5] US Bureau of Labor Statistics (hereafter referred to as BLS), 1945. The sources of the data on which Figure 1 is based are as follows: Table 11, p. 38, gives food consumption by 1942 income classes for families with changed incomes. Table 20, p. 107, gives this information for the whole sample. Only money income and money expense for food are considered. Families of all sizes are included; the data of Table 11 do not permit elimination of the effects of family size. Since Table 11 does not give average incomes for the various income classes, the average disposable incomes for the whole sample have been used in plotting all three sets of observations in Figure 1. These are computed from Table 19, p. 103, by subtracting 'Personal tax payments' from 'Money income.'

[6] Convincing evidence that income change is an important variable not only for food but for other consumption categories and for saving is given by Mack (1948). This evidence is based not only on the 1941–42 budget survey, but on continuing samples of farm families, whose behaviour under rising incomes is summarized in Cochrane (1947).

[7] Since $\bar{y}_{t-1}$, $\bar{y}_t$ are geometric means and Y_{t-1}, Y_t are arithmetic means the question arises whether $\bar{y}_{t-1} = K\bar{y}_t$, summed over all groups of families, implies $Y_{t-1} = KY_t$. This is not in general true, but it

income; it is not required that each individual family experience the same change. From (3) it follows that the geometric average consumption $\bar{c}_t$ of a group of families of size n with geometric average incomes $\bar{y}_t$ and $\bar{y}_{t-1}$ is given by

$$\bar{c}_t = k_t' \bar{y}_t^{\alpha_1} \bar{y}_{t-1}^{\alpha_2} n^{\delta}. \qquad\qquad 5$$

Substituting (4) in (5),

$$\bar{c}_t = k_t'' \bar{y}_t^{\alpha} n^{\delta} \qquad\qquad 6$$

where $\alpha = \alpha_1 + \alpha_2$

$$k_t'' = \left(\frac{Y_{t-1}}{Y_t}\right)^{\alpha_2} \quad k_t' = k \left(\frac{Y_{t-1}}{Y_t}\right)^{\alpha_2} P_t^{\beta} Q_t^{\gamma}$$

is constant over all income-size groups of families.

This method of allowing for the influence of lagged income is compelled by the inadequacy of data concerning the quantitative effect of past income on food consumption and concerning the joint distribution of families by incomes in two successive years. Table I indicates that assumption (4) is not far wide of the mark. There is some evidence (Mack, 1948) that assumption (4) errs by attributing too low a lagged income to families of low current income and too high a lagged income to families of high current income.[8] If this is true, the use of assumption (4) will give too low an estimate of α; more of the observed consumption of low-income families and less of that of high-income families will be due to past income than assumed in (6). In Figure 1 this bias should be revealed in a flatter slope for the whole sample than for the two groups classified by direction of income change. Figure 1 does not show serious bias of this kind.

is true under the assumption (13) concerning the joint distribution of families by income and size which will be introduced in Section 2 below.

Let $\bar{Y}_{t-1}$ and $\bar{Y}_t$ be the geometric means in the two years. Clearly $\bar{y}_{t-1} = K\bar{y}_t$ implies $\bar{Y}_{t-1} = K\bar{Y}_t$. Assumption (13) is that for all $\lambda > 0$, $\lambda f(\lambda y, n; \lambda Y) = f(y, n; Y)$ where $f(y, n; Y)$ is the density function of the joint distribution when mean income is Y.

$$\log \bar{Y}_{t-1} = \int_0^{\infty} \log y f(y, n; Y_{t-1}) \, dy = \log K + \int_0^{\infty} \log y f(y, n; Y_t) \, dy = \log K \bar{Y}_t.$$

Let $Y_{t-1} = K' Y_t$. Then, using assumption (13),

$$\log \bar{Y}_{t-1} = \int_0^{\infty} \log K' y f(K' y, n; K'Y) K' \, dy = \int_0^{\infty} \log K' y f(y, n; Y_t) \, dy$$

$$= \log K' \int_0^{\infty} f(y, n; Y_t) \, dy + \int_0^{\infty} \log y f(y, n; Y_t) \, dy$$

$$= \log K' Y_t.$$

Therefore $K = K'$.

[8] Mrs. Mack's contention is based on the distributions of income-change by income level in the 1941–42 budget survey and in the Wisconsin sample of identical taxpayers, 1929–35. However, her 1941–42 data give only direction of income change, not magnitude. The Wisconsin figures cited by Mrs. Mack detect a change in income only when a taxpayer moves from one $500-wide bracket to another, and are confined to incomes below $3000. No quantitative relationship between income and income change can be formulated from these sources. Moreover, Mrs. Mack also cites a study of Delaware taxpayers for two years, 1937 and 1938, which evidently conforms more closely to assumption (4) than to the pattern of the other two samples.

1.3. The Family Demand Function Estimated from 1941 Budget Data

The parameters of function (6) can now be estimated from budget data. In terms of the logarithms of the variables (6) becomes

$$\log \bar{c}_t = \log k_t'' + \alpha \log \bar{y}_t + \delta \log n. \qquad 7$$

In fitting (7) to budget data, a difficulty arises because of the manner in which the basic observations are summarized for publication. Observations of $(\bar{c}, \bar{y}, n)$ are not presented. The reported observations are arithmetic rather than geometric means for consumption and income. The arithmetic means will not be far from function (6) except for income-classes within which the function diverges markedly from a straight line. Clearly the reported averages for the open-ended upper income-classes in budget studies should not be used in fitting non-linear demand functions. In the present case inclusion of these observations would seriously over-estimate income-elasticity. For other income-classes, the reported arithmetic means have been treated as observations of $(\bar{c}, \bar{y}, n)$.

With this qualification, the 1941 urban budget study (BLS, 1945) provides observations of $(\bar{c}, \bar{y}, n)$ for $n = 1, 2, 3, 4$. Observations for $n \geq 5$ are also reported, and it is possible to compute for each income-class the average size of families of five or more. It is assumed that the variances of n about these averages are so small that no significant error is introduced by assuming that all the large $(n \geq 5)$ families in each income-class are of the average size of large families in that class. With this assumption, there are 37 observations $(\bar{c}, \bar{y}, n)$. These are shown in Table II.

These data yield the following regression of $\log \bar{c}$ on $\log \bar{y}$ and $\log n$:

$$\log \bar{c} = 0.82 + 0.56(\pm 0.03) \log \bar{y} + 0.25(\pm 0.07) \log n \qquad 8$$
$$R^2 = 0.93.$$

In Figure 2 function (6) with constants based on regression (8) is plotted on income and consumption axes, separately for $n = 1, 2, 3, 4, 6$. The observations on which the regression is based are also shown, each tagged with the value of n for the observation. (The points labelled '6' refer to families of five or more persons.)

The values computed for α and δ confirm a fact noted in previous analyses of budget data and known to every housewife, the economies of large family food consumption. Since the sum of α and δ is less than one, a doubling of both income and family size would not double food consumption. At the same *per capita* income, *per capita* food expenditure is smaller the larger the size of the family. This is, of course, partly due to lower consumption by children. But it may also be explained partly by indivisibilities in kitchen inputs and partly by external economies. Recipes which require one egg and serve four persons are not available to the woman who is cooking for two. The bargains obtained by purchasing large quantities do not help the small family which cannot use up a large can before it either spoils or crowds the refrigerator.

1.4. The Evidence of Other Budget Studies

The 1941 urban budget study has been used, in preference to other surveys of national scope, to derive the income-elasticity of family food demand for two reasons. The concepts of income and food consumption used in the 1941 urban sample are the most

Table II. Observations of average food consumption, $\bar{c}$, average disposable income, $\bar{y}$, and family size, n, for 37 groups of urban families classified by income and size, 1941.

$\bar{y}$ (dollars)	$\bar{c}$ (dollars)	n (number)	$\bar{y}$ (dollars)	$\bar{c}$ (dollars)	n (number)
421	210	1	2872	770	3
824	301	1	3864	934	3
1287	369	1	6925	1198	3
1703	433	1	799	419	4
2150	506	1	1401	531	4
2655	621	1	1939	658	4
520	239	2	2414	725	4
869	319	2	2878	935	4
1379	454	2	3895	907	4
1846	517	2	5983	1349	4
2262	600	2	484	279	6.4
2855	723	2	873	409	6.4
3611	849	2	1364	569	6.2
5593	673	2	1849	732	6.1
456	417	3	2345	866	5.8
936	368	3	2891	1020	5.8
1357	499	3	3936	1197	6.3
1837	562	3	6056	1708	6.3
2408	629	3			

Source: (BLS, 1945):-

Disposable income, $\bar{y}$: for each size category.
    'Average amount of income: Total' (Table 18, pp. 96–100).
    — 'Personal tax payments' (Table 19, pp. 102–105).
    $-\frac{1}{2}$ 'Gifts and contributions' (Table 19, pp. 102–105).

The last item is subtracted in order to avoid counting twice those transfers in money or in kind which are included in the income of the recipient. Not all of the amount reported under the heading 'gifts and contributions' is of this nature. Support of religious and educational institutions and community enterprises are properly consumption expenditures which create income rather than transfers. Not all gifts in kind from other families were reported in the income and consumption of the recipient; only gifts in the major categories of consumption were so treated (p. 17). Accordingly not all gifts in kind should be excluded from the income and consumption of the donors. Averages for seven kinds of 'gifts and contributions' are presented only for large groups of families, not for the income-size-classes considered here. The fraction 1/2 is a guess of the proper amount to subtract, based on a rough division of the average amount of 'gifts and contributions' for all urban families (Table 12, p. 87) between transfers and consumption.

Food consumption $\bar{c}$: for each size category.
    'Food: Total' (Table 20, pp. 111–119).

Family size n:
The last eight entries in this column are estimates of the average size of families of 5 or more. Table 1a, p. 69, gives for each of six income-classes the number of families of each size from 1 to 6, and the number of size 7 or larger. Table 1, p. 68, gives the total number of urban families of all sizes in each income-class, and Table 2, p. 70, gives the average size of families in each income-class. The total number of persons in families of five or more and the total number of such families can therefore be computed for each income-class.

inclusive, and this study permits the most satisfactory allowance for family size, which on *a priori* grounds would be expected to be the most important variable other than income.

The estimate of income-elasticity derived from 1941 urban data will be applied in Section 3 to time series observations for the whole economy. Is the estimate applicable to the rural part of the population? Is the estimate applicable to years other than 1941? The present section endeavours both to check the estimate against the evidence of urban

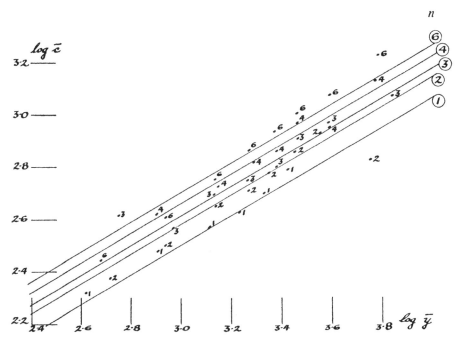

Figure 2. Family income and food expenditure for various sizes of family, 1941
Budget study observations •n. Regression $\log \bar{c} = 0.82 + 0.56 \log \bar{y} + 0.25 \log n$.

budget surveys made in other years and to see whether rural families have the same income-elasticity of demand as urban families.

Unfortunately, for the same reasons that the 1941 urban study is superior to others, it is impossible to duplicate the calculation of income-elasticity in (8) for other years. Comparisons can usually be made only by limiting the 1941 data to the concepts of income and food consumption used in the other studies. Also, a less precise adjustment for the effects of family size must be made. It is then possible to examine the consistency of the income-consumption relationships in various budget studies, but not to check the exact magnitude of the income-elasticity obtained in (8).

1.4.1..

The other urban budget studies of national scope with which the 1941 results should be compared are the 1918 survey of urban workers with families of 4 or more (BLS, 1924) and the all-inclusive survey of 1935–36 (US National Resources Committee, 1939 and 1941). Two less extensive studies made in 1927–28 provide material for another inter-temporal comparison of income-food consumption relationships.[9] One of these concerns federal employees in five cities; the other covers railroad maintenance-of-way employees

---

[9] The data for the 1927–28 studies are given in Leven et al. (1934), Appendix B, Table 1, pp. 246–249, designations D and E. The original sources and the coverage and concepts of the two studies are described on p. 241.

in ten states. The samples are considerably smaller than those of the three national surveys, and they are samples of two special groups. Moreover, it is necessary to splice the two studies together in order to cover a wide income range. For these reasons, the relationship between income and food consumption obtained from 1927–28 data is less reliable than those derived from the other studies. Finally, the only post-war budget data available refer to families in three cities, Richmond, Va., Washington, DC, and Manchester, NH, for the year 1947 (BLS, 1949). Since prediction is the ultimate objective of quantitative economics, comparison of pre-war and post-war budget data has a special interest which justifies using these limited data. In addition, samples of two kinds of rural families, farm and non-farm, are available for 1941 (US Department of Agriculture, 1943) and for 1935–36 (US National Resources Committee, 1941). These studies permit an examination of the difference between rural and urban consumption behaviour as well as additional checks of the consistency of income-elasticity over time.

1.4.1.1.

These other studies do not present data classified according to family size. Instead of observations of $(\bar{c}, \bar{y}, n)$, like those of the 1941 urban study, they report only observations of $(\bar{c}, \bar{y}, \bar{n}(\bar{y}))$ where $\bar{n}(\bar{y})$ is the average size of families in a given income class, with mean income $\bar{y}$.[10] To eliminate the effects of differences in family size on the comparison of one budget sample with another, observations of this kind must be adjusted to a common value of $\bar{n}$. The adjustment must not require information on the distribution of family sizes about the means $\bar{n}(\bar{y})$.

The approximate adjustment here employed assumes that the 1941 urban relationship between family size and food consumption applies to the other samples. The term n^{δ} in (6) is replaced by a linear expression in n:

$$\bar{c} = k_t'' \bar{y}^{\alpha}(a + bn).   \qquad 9$$

Therefore the average consumption of families of all sizes in a given income class is given by

$$\bar{c} = k_t'' \bar{y}^{\alpha}(a + b\bar{n}(\bar{y})).   \qquad 10$$

An actual observation $(\bar{c}, \bar{y}, \bar{n}\,(\bar{y}))$ is adjusted to a hypothetical observation $(\bar{c}', \bar{y}, \bar{n}')$ for the same income but for a standard size $\bar{n}'$ by

$$\bar{c}' = \bar{c}\left(\frac{a + b\bar{n}'}{a + b\bar{n}}\right).   \qquad 11$$

This adjustment assumes nothing concerning the value of α.

In practice the comparisons between budget studies concern only families of two or more persons. For $2 \leq n \leq 7$, $n^{0.25}$ can be approximated linearly by $1.032 + 0.092n$.

---

[10] The 1935–36 study does classify data by family size, but not in a manner useful for the purposes of this paper. Families are classified by seven 'types', which depend on age composition as well as size. Only in the cases of one- and two-person families is there one-to-one correspondence between 'type' and size. Moreover, detailed breakdown of the observations by 'type' appears only in publications dealing with specific localities or regions. On the treatment of family size in the 1935–36 survey, see Staehle (1945), pp. 249–251.

Table III. Definitions of disposable income and food consumption in various budget data

Type	Definition of disposable income	Definition of food consumption	Budget data available for comparison
I	Disposable money income + Rent imputed to owner-occupiers + Other income in kind, including food	Money expenditure + Value received in kind (compensation, gifts, relief, home-grown)	Rural non-farm families, 1935–36 and 1941 Farm families, 1935–36 and 1941
II	Disposable money income + Imputed rent	Money expenditure	Urban families, 1927–28, 1935–36 and 1941
III	Disposable money income	Money expenditure	Urban families, 1918, 1941 and 1947

1.4.1.2.

The differences among the budget studies with respect to definitions of income and food consumption are set forth in Table III. Three types of information are distinguished; to each type correspond two definitions, one of income and the other of food expenditure. The table lists budget surveys which can be compared on the basis of information of each type.

1.4.1.3.

The observations reported in all the studies were adjusted to an average family size of 3.5 by the method outlined in Section 1.4.1.1. For each sample a line was then fitted by least squares to the logarithms of the observations of disposable income and food consumption. The slope of this line is an estimate of the income-elasticity of food demand. The estimates from those samples which use the same type of information can then be compared to check the consistency of the family income-elasticity over time. Only for information of Type I is there any reason to expect the estimates of income-elasticity to agree with the estimate of 0.56 obtained in regression (8). The other types of information exclude food received in kind; since this is most important, relative to money expenditures, for low-income families, its omission should result in a higher estimate of income-elasticity.

Table IV reports the regressions between the logarithms of food consumption and family income for each of the samples listed in Table III. The regressions, together with the adjusted observations on which they are based, are shown in Figures 3–6.

The significance of the difference between two estimates of the coefficient of log $\overline{y}$ can be tested for each pair of regressions based on the same type of information (Fisher, 1946, pp. 140–2.) With only one exception, a difference as large as observed would occur in over 10% of samples from a population in which the coefficients were equal. The exception is the pair of regressions 8 and 9; in this case the difference is not significant at the 1% level.

All the regressions reported in Table IV are based on grouped data. None of these studies report budgets of individual families, nor do they estimate the variance of the basic observations about the means for the income-classes. Consequently a better statistical test of the significance of the differences among various sample estimates of the coefficient of log $\overline{y}$ is not possible. These differences must be judged chiefly by the grosser criterion of the degree of accuracy to which the econometrician can aspire.

Table IV. Relationships of food consumption, adjusted to family size 3.5, to disposable income in various budget data for families of two or more persons

Type of information		Budget sample	Regression $\log \bar{c} =$
1.	I	Rural non-farm, 1935–36	$0.92 + 0.55 \log \bar{y}$
2.	I	Rural non-farm, 1941	$1.02 + 0.53 \log \bar{y}$
3.	I	Farm, 1935–36	$1.16 + 0.37 \log \bar{y}$
4.	I	Farm, 1941	$1.15 + 0.35 \log \bar{y}$
5.	II	Urban, 1927–28	$0.57 + 0.68 \log \bar{y}$
6.	II	Urban, 1935–36	$0.76 + 0.61 \log \bar{y}$
7.	II	Urban, 1941	$0.64 + 0.65 \log \bar{y}$
8.	III	Urban, 1918	$0.89 + 0.57 \log \bar{y}$
9.	III	Urban, 1941	$0.68 + 0.64 \log \bar{y}$
10.	III	Richmond, Va., 1947	$0.81 + 0.64 \log \bar{y}$
11.	III	Washington, D.C., 1947	$0.96 + 0.59 \log \bar{y}$
12.	III	Manchester, N.H., 1947	$1.00 + 0.59 \log \bar{y}$

Sources of data on which the regressions were calculated:
1. US National Resources Committee (hereafter, NRC) (1941), Table 161, p. 56.
2. and 4. US Department of Agriculture (hereafter, USDA) (1943), Table 49, pp. 156–7, and Table 50, pp. 159–160.
3. NRC (1941), Table 144, p. 51.
5. Leven et al. (1934), Appendix B, Table 1, pp. 246–249, lines D and E.
6. NRC (1941), Table 178, p. 61.
7. and 9. BLS (1945), Table 19, p. 102, and Table 20, p. 109.
8. BLS (1924), Table 1, p. 4. This study does not report tax payments. However, in 1918, families of the large size to which the sample was confined had such small direct tax liabilities that it is safe to take money income before taxes as a measure of disposable money income.
10, 11, and 12. BLS (1949).
In regressions 6 and 7, the observations for the lowest-income class of each sample were omitted. If they are included the slopes are, respectively, 0.57 and 0.69; the erratic nature of the lowest-income observations in the two years can be seen in Figure 5. The explanation, and the justification for their omission, is that the exclusion of food received in kind affects the 1935–36 and 1941 samples unequally. The 1935–36 sample does not include recipients of relief; the 1941 sample does. Relief recipients rely much more on food received in kind than non-relief families of the same income. Consequently the 1935–36 low-income group shows higher money expenditures for food than the 1941 sample, and in both years the low-income point is out of line with the other observations.

By this standard the agreement in income-elasticity over time is remarkable. The table contains no evidence to prevent the application of the 1941 estimate to previous or, indeed, postwar years. The error in attributing to rural non-farm families the urban estimate of income-elasticity appears to be negligible. But the behaviour of farm families is significantly different from that of non-farm families. The lower income-elasticity characteristic of farm families, and their higher mean level of food consumption relative to income, are probably associated with the greater importance of home-produced food in farm diets. The increase in urban expenditure for food as income rises represents a shift to higher-quality foods more than an increase in total intake. This shift is perhaps neither as easy nor as necessary for farmers who produce a large part of their own food.

1.5. The Omission of Variables Other than Income and Family Size

Family size is the only variable other than family income appearing in (6), the food demand function applicable to budget data. Failure to include family size as a variable would result in a biased estimate of income elasticity, because family size is correlated with income.

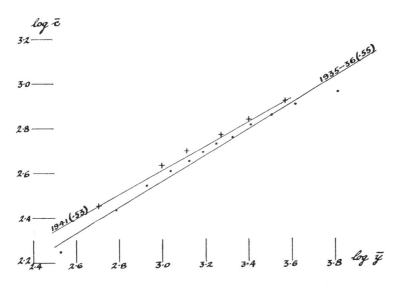

Figure 3. Rural non-farm families' income and food consumption
• 1935–36. + 1941.

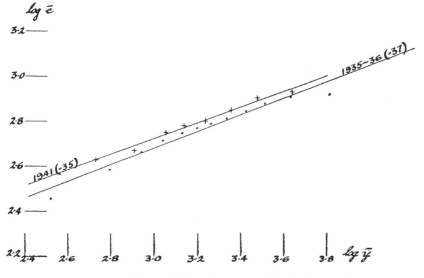

Figure 4. Rural farm families' income and food consumption
• 1935–36. + 1941.

The omission of other variables may be a source of similar bias. Sub-groups of the population may not be homogeneous in food consumption behaviour; there may be significant geographical or occupational differences. These differences may be of two kinds:

(1) Sub-groups may have significantly different income elasticities. In this case the relationship of food consumption to family income could not properly be described by a single coefficient for the whole population.

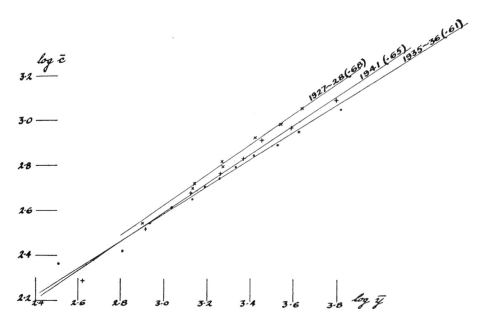

Figure 5. Urban families' income and food consumption
× 1927–28. • 1935–36. + 1941.

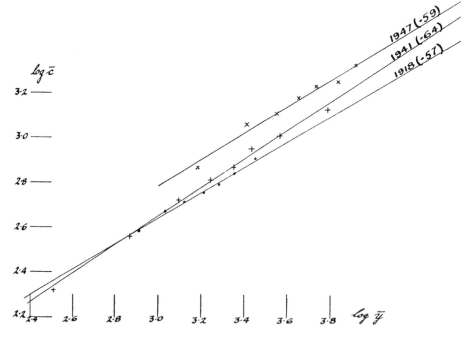

Figure 6. Urban families' income and food consumption
• 1918. + 1941. × 1947 (Washington, D.C.).

(2) Sub-groups may show differences in income-elasticity no larger than can be attributed to sampling errors, but may differ significantly in their levels of food consumption. If, in addition, the subgroups are represented in systematically differing proportions at various income levels, the estimate of income-elasticity based on the whole population will not correspond to the true income-elasticity common to the subgroups. For example, suppose, as some evidence in the 1935–36 study (NRC, 1941) suggests, that food expenditures are highest for given incomes and sizes of family in Eastern metropolises. The high-income portion of the population contains relatively more families from these communities than the low-income groups. This will be reflected in a budget study whose sampling method gives every family in the population an equal chance to be selected. Income-elasticity computed from the whole sample will be an over-estimate, since it will reflect variation in food consumption due not solely to income but also to geography.

The 1941 budget study permits consideration of only one possible determinant of food consumption other than income and family size, namely type of community: urban, rural non-farm, or farm. The discrepancy between farm and non-farm behaviour presents a difficulty in passing from the family demand function to the national demand function. In Section 2 the family function is to be summed over all families in the nation. For purposes of aggregation the simplicity of function (6) is of course a convenience. If the function involved characteristics of families other than income and family size the process of aggregation would be more complicated. If a separate function, with a different income-elasticity, were attributed to the farm population, it would be necessary also to estimate two separate aggregate functions with differing price-elasticities. The required times series are not available. The error of attributing urban behaviour to farm families must be accepted. It is desirable, therefore, to have some indication of its size. In 1941 use of the urban function to estimate farm consumption at all levels of family income yields an estimated average 5% below the actual average consumption of farm families. Since farm consumption was less than one-sixth of national food consumption the error from this source in estimating the average for all families is less than 1%.

Within the urban population there may be divergences of behaviour which are concealed in the 1941 budget data and bias the estimate of income-elasticity. Occupation, size of city, and region may be determinants of food consumption, and the impossibility of allowing for them in the 1941 study may lead to errors.[11] These errors are the price paid for the advantages of the 1941 study, pointed out above, and for a family demand function which can be aggregated without involving in the national function a collection of variables which would place an impossible burden on available time series.

---

[11] Some evidence of the influence of region and size of city may be found in NRC (1941), where urban families are classified, first, by four sizes of cities and, second, by five regions. Unfortunately they are not cross classified. Regressions for each of the four sizes of city will yield slopes of 0.51, 0.51, 0.53 and 0.46. Regressions for each of the five regions yield slopes of 0.48, 0.50, 0.60, 0.49 and 0.46. Only in the case of the region with slope 0.60 is it necessary to reject the hypothesis that these subgroups are samples from a population with a common slope. Once again the absence of individual family observations or of estimates of the variances of these observations about the income-class means makes a more satisfactory statistical test of the significance of these differences impossible. Since the slope for the whole sample (0.57) is greater than for all but one of the subgroups, it is probable that it reflects differences in level of food consumption, due not solely to income but also to size of city or to region. But the errors due to ignoring these determinants of food demand do not appear to be large.

An interesting analysis of the heterogeneity of the family food demand function over various occupational and geographical groups, based on Dutch data for individual families, has been made by G. Stuvel and S. F. James at the Department of Applied Economics, Cambridge, *J. R. Statist. Soc.*, **113**, 59.

2.   AGGREGATION OF THE FAMILY FOOD DEMAND FUNCTION

The problem of aggregation is to derive from the relationship between family income and family consumption a relationship between aggregate income and aggregate consumption. In general aggregate consumption, given the family demand function, depends on the distribution of income, and not simply on the mean of the distribution. Moreover, if family consumption depends on variables other than income–such as family size, in the case of food–aggregate consumption depends on the joint distribution of families by income and these other variables. Whenever this joint distribution is known, an estimate of aggregate consumption can be made by weighting the family demand function according to the joint distribution. The problem of aggregation arises because estimates are required when mean income is the only available information concerning the distribution. Consequently any aggregate relationship requires some assumption concerning the manner in which the joint distribution changes when aggregate income changes. In the nature of the case the assumption cannot be checked every time it is used; otherwise it would not be needed.

2.1.   Aggregation under the Assumption of a 'Constant' Income Distribution

In the particular case of food demand, summing (6) over all families gives mean consumption:

$$C(Y) = k_t'' \sum_{n=1}^{m} \int_0^\infty y^\alpha n^\delta f(y, n; Y) \, dy. \qquad 12$$

where m is the largest size of family and $f(y, n; Y)$ is the density function of the distribution of families by y and n when mean income is Y. The following assumption is made concerning this density function:

$$\lambda f(\lambda y, n, \lambda Y) = f(y, n, Y) \qquad \lambda > 0. \qquad 13$$

A sufficient but not necessary condition for (13) to be satisfied is that every family share a change in aggregate income in proportion to its income and remain of the same size.[12]

From assumption (13) it follows that aggregate food consumption (12) becomes:

$$C(Y) = M k_t'' Y^\alpha \qquad 14$$

where M is a constant depending on the distribution of families by income and size.[13]

---

[12] This is the condition assumed by Marschak (1939a, p. 164, and 1943). It is stronger than necessary.

[13] The proof of (14) is as follows.

$$\text{Let } M(Y) = \sum_{n=1}^{m} \int_0^\infty \left(\frac{y}{Y}\right)^\alpha n^\delta f(y, n; Y) \, dy.$$

$$\text{Then } M(\lambda Y) = \sum_{n=1}^{m} \int_0^\infty \left(\frac{y}{\lambda Y}\right)^\alpha n^\delta f(y, n; \lambda Y) \, dy \quad \lambda > 0$$

$$= \sum_{n=1}^{m} \int_0^\infty \left(\frac{\lambda y}{\lambda Y}\right)^\alpha n^\delta f(\lambda y, n; \lambda Y) \lambda \, dy$$

$$= \sum_{n=1}^{m} \int_0^\infty \left(\frac{y}{Y}\right)^\alpha n^\delta f(y, n; Y) \, dy \quad \text{by (13)}$$

$$= M(Y) \text{ for all } \lambda > 0.$$

The same result can be reached from an assumption somewhat weaker than (13) if approximation (9) is used for the family demand function. In this case, knowledge of the entire joint distribution of y and n is not required; since the demand function is linear in n, it is sufficient to know the average family size corresponding to each income level. Let

$$g(y; Y) = \sum_{n=1}^{m} f(y, n; Y)$$

$$\overline{n}(y; Y) = \frac{\sum_{n=1}^{m} n f(y, n; Y)}{g(y; Y)}.$$

Then (13) can be replaced by the weaker conditions:

$$\lambda g(\lambda y; \lambda Y) = g(y; Y) \quad \lambda > 0^{14}$$ 15

$$\overline{n}(\lambda y; \lambda Y) = \overline{n}(y; Y) \quad \lambda > 0$$ 16

Summing (9) over all families,

$$C(Y) = \int_0^\infty k_t'' y^\alpha (a + b\overline{n}(y; Y)) g(y; Y)\, \mathrm{d}y.$$ 17

From assumptions (15) and (16) it follows that (17) becomes:

$$C(Y) = M' k_t'' Y^\alpha$$ 18

where M' is a constant.[15]

Under the assumptions made in this section, then, the demand function of Section 1 is preserved under aggregation. That is, the relationship between aggregate consumption and aggregate income is of the same form as the relationship between family consumption and family income, and the aggregate income-elasticity is equal to the family income-elasticity α.

---

[14] It can be shown that (15) is a necessary and sufficient condition for the invariance of the Lorenz curve under changes in mean income.

[15] (17) can be written:

$$C(Y) = (aM_1(Y) + bM_2(Y)) k_t'' Y^\alpha$$

$$\text{where } M_1(Y) = \int_0^\infty \left(\frac{y}{Y}\right)^\alpha g(y; Y)\, \mathrm{d}y$$

$$\text{and } M_2(Y) = \int_0^\infty \left(\frac{y}{Y}\right)^\alpha \overline{n}(y; Y) g(y; Y)\, \mathrm{d}y.$$

The proof that $M_1(Y)$ and $M_2(Y)$ are constants is analogous to the proof in the preceding footnote that $M(Y)$ is a constant. Strictly, (9) is an approximation of the family demand function for families of two or more persons. Assumptions (17) and (18) should apply only to $n > 2$ and (13) should be retained for $n = (1)$. Then if the proportion of single individuals to larger families is constant, the aggregate function $C(Y)$ will be of the form (14) or (18).

2.2. Evidence Concerning the 'Constancy' of the Income Distribution

The reason for introducing the weaker assumptions concerning the income-family size distribution is that some data bearing on (15) are available. Figure 7 presents the cumulative distributions of families of two or more persons by income for 1935–36 and 1941, based on the budget surveys for those years (NRC, 1939, Table 24A, p. 86, and BLS, 1945, Table 1, p. 68). In Figure 7 the horizontal axis measures y/Y, the ratio of family income to mean income. The ordinate of each point gives the percentage of families whose incomes, relative to mean income, were lower than the abscissa. If assumption (15) is correct, plotting the distributions in this way should make the 1935–36 and 1941 points fall along the same curve. Figure 8 is a similar comparison of the 1941 and 1947 cumulative distributions of families of all sizes by income after federal income tax (*Economic Report*, 1949; Table B–3, p. 93, and Table 2, p. 14).

The coincidence of the income distribution observations in different years, when plotted as in Figures 7 and 8, is of course not conclusive confirmation of the invariance of the distribution either over time or with respect to changes in aggregate income.[16] It does indicate that, in the absence of time series of measures of income inequality,[17] the assumption of a constant degree of inequality will not lead to serious errors in statistical demand analysis.

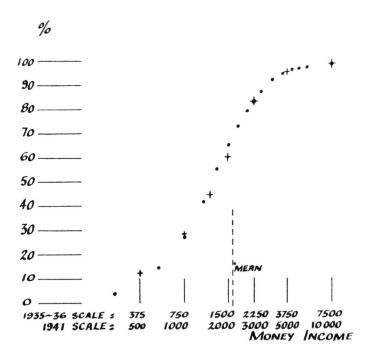

Figure 7. Cumulative income distribution of families of two or more persons, 1935–36 and 1941
● 1935–36. + 1941.

---

[16] Mendershausen (1946) has shown that inequality was greater in the depression year of 1933 than in the boom year of 1929, and has presented a convincing explanation of this phenomenon.

[17] The only time series on this subject are based on income tax statistics, and concern only the top of the income distribution. Consequently they are useless for the purposes of this paper.

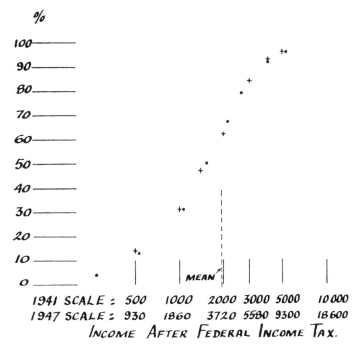

Figure 8. Cumulative income distribution of families, including single individuals, 1941 and 1947
+ 1941. ● 1947.

Assumption (15) does not, of course, imply either (13) or (17). But if (15) — constancy of the Lorenz curve – is correct, errors of aggregation will be due to failure of the assumptions regarding the distribution of families by size. These errors are not likely to be large. For one thing, overall average family size is nearly constant over the period 1913–41, varying in the narrow range 3.20–3.36.[18] With a constant average family size, it would be difficult to have a reshuffling of the joint distribution of families by income and size which would change aggregate food consumption appreciably. Suppose, to take an extreme and unlikely example, that in the 1941 distribution the average size of families below the median income of $1500 were cut in half and the average size of families with higher incomes increased by 35%. This would leave average family size unchanged. It would increase aggregate food consumption, computed by (12) only 1%.

2.3. The Aggregate *per capita* Demand Function

The aggregate demand function (14) or (18) expresses food consumption per family in terms of disposable income per family. For the purposes of Section 3 it is more convenient to measure consumption and income *per capita*. In accordance with assumption (13) or (16), the average size of family N is taken to be constant; in fact, as pointed out above, it varied only slightly over the period under consideration.

---

[18] Computed by dividing annual US population estimates (US Department of Commerce, 1945, p. 8) by annual estimates of the number of consumer units in the US (National Industrial Conference Board, 1948, p. 334).

Consequently (14) implies:

$$C' = \frac{Mk_t''}{N^{1-\alpha}} Y'^\alpha \qquad\qquad 19$$

where $C' = C/N$, *per capita* food consumption

and $Y' = Y/N$, *per capita* disposable income.

Substituting the value of k_t'' from (6) gives the complete aggregate demand function:

$$C_t' = K Y_t'^{\alpha_1} Y_{t-1}'^{\alpha_2} P_t^\beta Q_t^\gamma \qquad\qquad 20$$

where $K = \dfrac{Mk}{N^{1-\alpha}}$ is a constant.

3. ESTIMATION OF PARAMETERS FROM TIME SERIES

In accordance with Sections 1 and 2, the sum of the two income-elasticities of food demand is taken to be 0.56, both for the family demand function and for the aggregate demand function. This sum must be split into an estimate of current-income-elasticity α_1, and an estimate of past-income-elasticity α_2. The two price elasticities β and γ must also be evaluated. The purpose of the present section is to obtain these estimates by multiple correlation of time series of aggregate data. The parameters, however, apply to the family demand function (1) as well as to the aggregate demand function (20). In Section 4, therefore, the estimates obtained in this section are tested by applying them to family budget observations made in different years.

3.1. A Simple Model of the Retail Food Market

The procedure used in the time series correlation assumes the following simple model of the retail food market:

$$S_t = C_t' = K Y_t'^{\alpha_1} Y_{t-1}'^{\alpha_2} P_t^\beta Q_t^\gamma \qquad\qquad 21$$

where S_t is *per capita* food supply for domestic consumption. Y_t', Q_t and S_t are assumed to be exogenous in the sense that none of them depends on the simultaneous values of the other variables in the system. Thus the supply of food, for example, may depend on the price of food in the preceding year, and still be a datum in the year in which it comes on the market.

Over the time period under consideration, 1913–41, both the *per capita* production of food and the *per capita* supply for domestic consumption were nearly constant. Total food production was insensitive in the short run to current economic conditions and was determined instead by weather, government policy, and the state of agricultural technique. The possibility remains that, even though food production may be considered exogenous to our model, the supply for domestic consumption may be influenced by the current price level of food. Changes in stocks of foodstuffs and sales abroad may depend on current prices. A significant relationship of this kind between supply and price would mean that use of the simple model would yield biased estimates of the parameters in the demand equation (Stone, 1948, p. 4, and Leontief, 1948). The possibility of bias from this source will be considered in Section 3.4 below.

The assumptions that income and non-food prices are exogenous to the food market have less theoretical justification. But a model which would explain these variables would cover the whole economy, and the statistical estimation of the parameters in an all-inclusive model is much beyond the scope of this paper.

3.2. The Multiple Regression

The 'reduced form' of the simple system (21) is an equation expressing P as a function of the three exogenous variables. In terms of the logarithms of the variables, the equation is:

$$\log P_t = -(1/\beta) \log K + (1/\beta) \log S_t - \left(\frac{\alpha_1}{\beta}\right) \log Y'_t - \left(\frac{\alpha_2}{\beta}\right) \log Y'_{t-1} - (\gamma/\beta) \log Q_t.$$

22

This equation can be written:

$$\log P_t = b_0 + b_1(\log S_t - \alpha \log Y'_t) + b_2(\log Y'_t - \log Y'_{t-1}) + b_3 \log Q_t.$$ 23

Since the value of α is taken as known, the constants b_0, b_1, b_2, b_3 can be estimated by multiple correlation of $\log P_t$ against three variables $(\log S_t - \alpha \log Y'_t)$, $(\log Y'_t - \log Y'_{t-1})$ and $\log Q_t$. The parameters of the demand function (20) can then be found as follows:

$$\beta = \frac{1}{b_1}, -\gamma = \frac{b_3}{b_1}, \alpha_2 = \frac{b_2}{b_1}, \alpha_1 = \alpha - \frac{b_2}{b_1}.$$ 24

This multiple correlation has been computed from annual data for the 29 years 1913–41. The statistical series used to represent the variables are shown in Table V and described in the notes to that table.

The results of the regression are as follows:

Regression coefficients:	Demand function parameters:
$b_1 = -1.97(\pm 0.27)$	$\alpha_1 = 0.44$
$b_2 = -0.24(\pm 0.16)$	$\alpha_2 = 0.12$
$b_3 = -0.06(\pm 0.14)$	$\beta = -0.51$
	$\gamma = -0.03$
$(R^2 = 0.87)$	$\alpha + \beta + \gamma = 0.02$

25

In this regression, the coefficient of $\log Q_t$ differs insignificantly from zero, and the significance of the correlation is increased by omitting this variable. The results are then as follows:

Regression coefficients:	Demand function parameters:
$b_0 = 2.95$	$\log K = 1.57$
$b_1 = -1.88(\pm 0.14)$	$\alpha_1 = 0.45$
$b_2 = -0.2 \ (\pm 0.12)$	$\alpha_2 = 0.11$
$(b_3 = 0)$	$\beta = -0.53$
	$(\gamma = 0)$
$(R^2 = 0.87)$	$\alpha + \beta + \gamma = 0.03$

26

Table V. Time series of food consumption *per capita*, disposable income *per capita*, food price-index, non-food price index, and food production *per capita*

Year t	Food consumption S_t (Index 1935–39 = 100)	Disposable income Y'_t (Dollars)	Food price P_t (Index 1935–39 = 100)	Non-food price Q_t (Index 1935–39 = 100)	Food production Z_t (Index)
1912	—	332	—	—	—
1913	96	343	79.9	65.9	80
1914	97	335	81.8	66.7	82
1915	96	352	80.9	68.3	83
1916	96	408	90.8	71.2	79
1917	96	483	116.9	78.6	79
1918	95	534	134.4	93.7	86
1919	98	603	149.8	105.3	86
1920	97	627	168.8	130.5	82
1921	94	486	128.3	127	78
1922	99	517	119.9	119.5	83
1923	101	589	124	120.9	85
1924	102	584	122.8	121.9	85
1925	101	610	132.9	121.5	80
1926	102	623	137.4	120.7	83
1927	101	618	132.3	119.8	81
1928	102	625	130.8	118.4	83
1929	102	653	132.5	117.4	80
1930	100	574	126	116.1	80
1931	100	480	103.9	111	81
1932	98	365	86.5	103.4	77
1933	97	354	84.1	96.6	77
1934	99	403	93.7	96.7	79
1935	96	442	100.4	97	73
1936	99	509	101.3	97.8	76
1937	100	537	105.3	101.1	78
1938	100	485	97.8	102.3	79
1939	104	517	95.2	101.7	81
1940	105	552	96.6	102.3	84
1941	108	666	105.5	105.1	86
1945	114	1070	139.1	122.9	—
1946	118	1127	159.6	129	—
1947	117	1205	193.8	141	—
1948	113	1299	210.7	—	—

Sources and explanation of the series:

S_t: Cohen (1948), Table 1, p. 13. The 1948 figure is from *Economic Report* (1949), p. 54. The series is a price-weighted index of quantities computed by the US Bureau of Agricultural Economics. It measures the disappearance of physical quantities of food to domestic civilian consumption. It does not measure changes in the amount of servicing of food in restaurants or retail outlets, nor does it measure in all cases changes in the amount of processing. For these reasons the series is not strictly comparable to the measure of food consumption in budget data, and it probably understates the amount of variation over time in the supply of 'finished' foodstuffs.

Y'_t: Computed by dividing figures for national disposable income (Dewhurst *et al.*, 1947, Appendix 4, p. 696) by annual estimates of population (US Department of Commerce, 1945, p. 8). The figures for 1945–48 are from *Economic Report* (1949), Table C–6, p. 104.

P_t and Q_t: US Department of Commerce (1945), p. 423. The figures for 1945–48 are from *Economic Report* (1949), Table C–20, p. 1949. Both series are based on the Bureau of Labor Statistics Consumers' Price Index for moderate-income families in large cities. The series P_t is the Bureau's food price index. The series Q_t is computed from the equation $wP_t + (1 - w)Q_t = I_t$, where I_t is the index for all items and w is the weight given food in the computation of I_t. (BLS, 1943, p. 13a.)

Z_t: Bureau of Agricultural Economics weighted index of physical production of foodstuffs (US Department of Agriculture, 1948), adjusted for changes in population.

Figure 9 shows the actual time series of the food price index (P_t, not $\log P_t$) and the values of P_t estimated from regression (26). The correlation between the original and calculated series is 0.93.

Confidence limits, with 95% probability, have been computed for β and α_2.[19] They are:

$$-0.63 < \beta < -0.46$$

$$-0.03 < \alpha_2 < 0.24.$$

Taking α as known from budget data, confidence limits for α_1 can be derived from those for α_2:

$$0.32 < \alpha_1 < 0.59.$$

The sum of the estimates of elasticities in either (25) or (26) does not differ significantly from zero.[20] The results do not contradict the 'homogeneity postulate' of economic theory.

3.3. Estimates Obtained with No Restriction on the Parameters

In the correlation just described, the sum of the two income-elasticities is taken as known from budget data. How do the estimates of the parameters obtained subject to that restriction compare with estimates based on time series alone? A multiple correlation, using the same variables, has been computed to estimate the constants in the following equation:

$$\log P_t = b_0 + b_1 \log S_t - b_2 \log Y'_{t-1} + b_3 \log Q_t + b_4 \log Y'_t. \qquad 27$$

---

[19] The following method for computing these confidence limits was kindly pointed out to me by Mr. J. Durbin and Mr. G. Watson, Department of Applied Economics, University of Cambridge. In the case of α_2, consider $(b_2 - \alpha_2 b_1)/S(\alpha_2)$. Here b_2 and b_1 are the regression coefficients in (26) and $[S(\alpha_2)]^2 = \operatorname{var} b_2 + \alpha_2^2 \operatorname{var} b_1 - 2\alpha_2 \operatorname{covar} b_2 b_1 = s^2[(\Sigma x_1^2 + \alpha_2^2 \Sigma x_2^2 + 2\alpha \Sigma x_1 x_2)/(\Sigma x_1^2 \Sigma x_2^2 - (\Sigma x_1 x_2)^2)]$, where $s^2 = (N(1 - R^2) \operatorname{var} \log P)/(N - 3)$, $x_1 = \log S_t - \alpha \log Y'_t$, and $x_2 = \log Y'_t - \log Y'_{t-1}$. Given any α_2, $(b_2 - \alpha_2 b_1)/S(\alpha_2)$ is distributed according to Student's t distribution with $N - 3$ degrees of freedom. Consequently, the probability that $[(b_2 - \alpha_2 b_1)/S(\alpha_2)]^2 < t^2_{0.025} = 0.95$, where $t_{0.025}$ is the value of t exceeded with probability 0.025, or exceeded in absolute value with probability 0.05. Therefore $P[(b_2 - \alpha_2 b_1)^2 < t^2_{0.025}[S(\alpha_2)]^2] = 0.95$

$$P[b_2^2 + \alpha_2^2 b_1^2 - 2\alpha_2 b_1 b_2 - t^2_{0.025}[S(\alpha_2)]^2 < 0] = 0.95$$

$(b_2^2 + \alpha_2^2 b_1^2 - 2\alpha_2 b_1 b_2 - t^2_{0.025}[S(\alpha_2)]^2)$ is quadratic in α_2 and can be represented by $(\alpha_2 - c_1)(\alpha_2 - c_2)$. Take $c_1 < c_2$. Then

$$P[(\alpha_2 - c_1)(\alpha_2 - c_2) < 0] = 0.95.$$

But $(\alpha - c_1)(\alpha - c_2) < 0$ implies, since $c_1 < c_2$, $\alpha_2 - c_1 > 0$ and $\alpha_2 - c_2 < 0$, and therefore $c_1 < \alpha_2 < c_2$.

$$P[(c_1 < \alpha_2 < c_2)] = 0.95.$$

A similar procedure applies to the case of β. Here $(1 - \beta b_1)/(\beta \sigma_{b_1})$ is distributed by the t distribution with $N - 3$ degrees of freedom. Compare Fisher (1946), pp. 142–145.

[20] This conclusion follows for (26) from testing the significance of the deviation of the estimate of $\beta(= (1/b_1) = -0.53)$ from the assumed true value of $\beta(\bar{\beta} = -\alpha = -0.56)$ according to the 'homogeneity postulate.' $(1 - \bar{\beta} b_1)/(\bar{\beta} \sigma_{b_1})$ is distributed by Student's t-distribution with $N - 3 = 26$ degrees of freedom (see preceding footnote). With the estimates of (26) $t = -0.66$. A deviation of β from $\bar{\beta}$ as large as or larger than that observed in (26) and in the same direction would be obtained in over 25% of samples. A deviation at least as large in absolute value would occur in over 50% of samples. A similar test, with similar results, can be made for the sum of the elasticities estimated in (25).

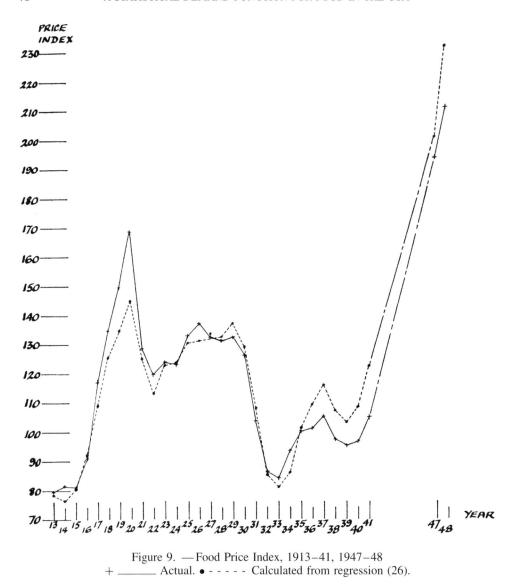

Figure 9. —Food Price Index, 1913–41, 1947–48
+ ———— Actual. • - - - - - Calculated from regression (26).

The coefficient b_2 is not significant. With $\log Y'_{t-1}$ omitted from the regression, the results are as follows:

Regression coefficients:

$$b_1 = -3.56(\pm 0.42)$$

$$(b_2 = 0)$$

$$b_3 = 0.22(\pm 0.09)$$

$$b_4 = 0.97(\pm 0.09)$$

$$(R^2 = 0.93)$$

Demand function parameters:

$$\alpha_1 = -b_4/b_1 = 0.27$$

$$(\alpha_2 = b_2/b_1 = 0)$$

$$\beta = 1/b_1 = -0.28$$

$$\gamma = -b_3/b_1 = 0.06$$

28

The 95% probability confidence limits for the parameters of the demand function, computed in the same manner as those for regression (26), are as follows:

$$0.22 < \alpha_1 < 0.35$$

$$-0.38 < \beta < -0.23$$

$$0.01 < \gamma < 0.12.$$

The unrestricted correlation thus gives significantly lower numerical values for the income- and price-elasticities than the regression restricted by the budget-study estimate. But the regression in which the budget-study estimate is assumed fits the time series almost as well as the unrestricted regression. The reverse is not true. The estimate of income-elasticity in (28) is not consistent with budget data. Moreover, the rejection in (28) of previous year's income as a significant variable is contradicted by the evidence of a lag in the 1941–42 budget study.

The unrestricted correlation is more likely than the restricted regression to give unreliable estimates because of collinearity (Stone, 1948, p. 3). The vulnerability of Equation (27) to this danger is due to high correlations among the explanatory variables. A bunch map analysis (Stone, 1945, pp. 306–310) is given in Figure 10.[21] It shows that

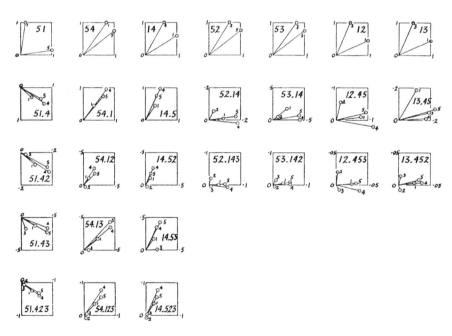

Figure 10.

[21] In Figure 10 the numbers 1, 2, 3, 4, 5 refer, respectively, to $\log S_t$, $\log Y'_{t-1}$, $\log Q_t$, $\log Y'_t$, $\log P_t$. The label on each diagram indicates both the partial regression to which it refers and the set of variables in the complete regression. Thus diagram 51.42 shows the regression coefficients of 5 on 1 in the four regressions involving 5, 1, 4 and 2. The slope of a beam indicates the value of the normalized regression coefficient, and the number at the end of beam indicates the direction of minimization of the regression. Figure 10 is not a complete bunch map analysis for the five variables, because it is clear on economic as well as statistical grounds that 1, 4, 5 must be included in the regression.

$\log Y'_{t-1}$ and $\log Q_t$ are not useful variables. Their addition to the multiple regression does not improve the bunch maps of the three regressions involving $\log P_t$, $\log Y'_t$, and $\log S_t$. (See the first three columns of diagrams in Figure 10.) Moreover, the bunch maps for the regressions of $\log P_t$ on $\log Y'_{t-1}$ and of $\log P_t$ on $\log Q_t$ are exploded by the introduction of $\log Y'_t$ and $\log S_t$. (See the fourth and fifth columns of diagrams.) Similarly, the bunch maps for the regressions of $\log S_t$ on $\log Y'_{t-1}$ and $\log S_t$ on $\log Q_t$ are exploded by adding the other variables. (See the last two columns of diagrams.) The correlations of $\log Y'_{t-1}$ and $\log Q_t$ with $\log Y'_t$ and $\log S_t$ are too high to enable α_2 and γ to be estimated from time series alone. But if these other variables influence food consumption — and budget data indicate that lagged income, at least, does — the estimates of α_1 and β will reflect their influence.

The restricted correlation is less vulnerable to this kind of error. The independent variables in regression (23) are not the highly correlated variables which appear in (27). The introduction of an outside estimate of α permits a transformation of the variables which eliminates most of the correlation. Between the two explanatory variables used in (26) the correlation is -0.20.

3.4.   The Possibility of Bias due to a Relationship between Supply and Prices

The danger that a relationship between food supply and price might bias the estimates of the parameters in the demand equation has already been mentioned. The present section fulfills the promise to investigate the possibility by fitting supply and demand equations simultaneously.

The two equations of the model are:

$$S_t = KY'^{\alpha}_t P^{\beta}_t Q^{\gamma}_t \quad \text{Demand}$$

$$S_t/Z_t = AP^{\beta'}_t Q^{\gamma'}_t \quad \text{Supply} \qquad\qquad 29$$

In this model *per capita* domestic food supply is no longer assumed to be exogenous. Instead, *per capita* food production, Z_t, is taken as a predetermined variable. The supply equation states that the share of production going into the domestic retail market depends on food prices and on other prices. A serious study of the determinants of food supply would involve other variables and a more complicated scheme (Girschick and Haavelmo, 1947). The purpose of model (29) is only to discover whether the influence of current prices on supply is strong enough to bias the single-equation estimates of the demand parameters. In the demand equation of (29), α is assumed to be known. For the sake of simplicity, past income Y'_{t-1} is omitted from the demand function and α is entirely assigned to current income.

Expressed in terms of logarithms measured from their means, the system is:

$$\log S_t - \alpha \log Y'_t - \beta \log P_t - \gamma \log Q_t = u_{1t} \qquad \text{Demand}$$

$$\log S_t \qquad\quad - \beta' \log P_t - \gamma' \log Q_t - \log Z_t = u_{2t} \quad \text{Supply.} \qquad 30$$

Here u_{1t} and u_{2t} are stochastic variables assumed to be distributed normally with zero means. System (30) can be reduced to two equations, one expressing $\log P_t$ and the other

$\log S_t$ in terms of the independent variables:

$$\log P_t - \frac{\alpha}{\beta' - \beta} \log Y'_t - \frac{\gamma - \gamma'}{\beta' - \beta} \log Q_t + \frac{1}{\beta' - \beta} \log Z_t = v_{1t}$$

$$\log S_t - \frac{\beta'\alpha}{\beta' - \beta} \log Y'_t - \frac{\beta'\gamma - \beta\gamma'}{\beta' - \beta} \log Q_t + \frac{\beta}{\beta' - \beta} \log Z_t = v_{2t} \qquad 31$$

where:

$$v_{1t} = \frac{u_{1t} - u_{2t}}{\beta' - \beta} \quad \text{and} \quad v_2 = \frac{\beta' u_{1t} - \beta u_{2t}}{\beta' - \beta}$$

are distributed normally with means zero.

Since α is known, and since $(\beta/(\beta' - \beta)) = (\beta'/(\beta' - \beta)) - 1$, these two equations may be rewritten:

$$\log P_t - b_{11}(\log Z_t - \alpha \log Y'_t) - b_{12} \log Q_t = v_{1t}$$

$$(\log S_t - \log Z_t) - b_{21}(\log Z_t - \alpha \log Y'_t) - b_{22} \log Q_t = v_{2t}. \qquad 32$$

Maximum likelihood estimates of b_{11} and b_{12} can be obtained by least squares regression of $\log S_t$ on $(\log Z_t - \alpha \log Y_t)$ and $\log Q_t$, and maximum likelihood estimates of b_{21} and b_{22} can be obtained by regression of $(\log S_t - \log Z_t)$ on the same two variables. From these four coefficients maximum likelihood estimates of the four unknown structural parameters can be derived:

$$\beta = \frac{b_{21} + 1}{b_{11}} \qquad \gamma = b_{22} - \beta b_{12}$$

$$\beta' = \frac{b_{21}}{b_{11}} \qquad \gamma' = b_{22} - \beta' b_{12}. \qquad 33$$

The estimates of the regression coefficients are as follows:

$$b_{11} = \begin{array}{c} -1.06 \\ (\pm 0.35) \end{array} \qquad b_{12} = \begin{array}{c} 0.29 \\ (\pm 0.19) \end{array} \qquad (R^2 = 0.65)$$

$$b_{21} = \begin{array}{c} -0.15 \\ (\pm 0.11) \end{array} \qquad b_{22} = \begin{array}{c} -0.02 \\ (\pm 0.06) \end{array} \qquad (R^2 = 0.1). \qquad 34$$

These estimates give the following values for the structural parameters:

$$\beta = -0.80 \quad \gamma = 0.21$$

$$\beta' = 0.14 \qquad \gamma' = -0.06. \qquad 35$$

However, the fit of the second reduced form equation is extremely poor. The multiple correlation coefficient is not significant at the 5% level (Snedecor, 1946, Table 13.6, p. 351). The hypothesis that both b_{21} and b_{22} are zero cannot be rejected. Even if $\log Q_t$ is omitted, the regression is not significant; a correlation between $\log S_t/Z_t$ and $(\log Z_t - \alpha \log Y'_t)$ numerically as large as observed could occur in over 10% of samples from a population in which the correlation is zero. If b_{21} and b_{22} are zero, so are the supply equation parameters β' and γ'. Consequently, the hypothesis that β' and γ' are zero cannot be rejected. But if β' and γ' are zero, the supply relation is reduced to

$$\log S_t = \log Z_t + u_{2t}. \qquad 36$$

Provided that u_{2t} is not correlated with u_{1t}, the error term in the demand equation, the maximum likelihood estimates of the demand parameters are the single-equation estimates. The fact that $\log S_t$ appears in both the demand and supply equations is now irrelevant. The only danger in ignoring (36) is that u_{1t} and u_{2t} are correlated. The error terms u_{2t} are a known observed series ($\log S_t - \log Z_t$). Fitting the demand equation so as to maximize the probability that its errors and the known errors u_{2t} come from a joint normal distribution makes no more sense than considering the possibility that the errors u_{1t} are correlated with any other observed series. (Compare Leontief, 1948, p. 400.) In any case (36) is not a convincing hypothesis; the correlation (0.38) between $\log S_t$ and $\log Z_t$ is barely significant.

The investigation of this section gives no reason for rejecting the hypothesis of the initial single-equation model that food supply is an exogenous variable. There is no evidence of a significant relationship between supply and prices. Whatever bias may be introduced by ignoring a possible supply relation is surely preferable to the wide bands of error attached to estimates based on the two-equation model.

3.5. The Problem of Serial Correlation

One more statistical difficulty must be considered (Stone, 1948, p. 12). The parameter estimates of (26) were obtained under the assumption that Equation (23) is satisfied every year subject to an error which is distributed independently of the errors in previous years. This assumption is contradicted by the time series of the estimated residuals. The differences between actual food price and food price calculated from the regression show a cyclical pattern (see Figure 9). They also show an over-all downward trend: actual price tends to fall relative to calculated price. The ratio (δ^2/s^2) of the mean square successive difference of the residuals to the variance of the residuals is 0.68. So low a value would occur in less than 0.1% of samples of this size from a population in which the errors in different years are independently distributed (Hart, 1942).

The addition of a time trend to the multiple regression does not eliminate serial correlation. The cyclical pattern of the residuals remains. The ratio δ^2/s^2 is increased to 1.08, but this is still significant at the 1% probability level.

A correlation has been computed using the first differences of the variables involved in regression (26). The results are as follows:

Regression coefficients:	Demand parameters:	
$b_1 = -1.74 \ (\pm 0.18)$	$\beta = -0.57$	
$b_2 = -0.08 \ (\pm 0.08)$	$\alpha_2 = 0.05$	37
$(R^2 = 0.82)$		

These estimates of the demand parameters are well within the confidence limits for the estimates based on regression (26). Correlation of first differences does not yield significantly different estimates from correlation of the original variables. But the residuals of the regression of first differences do not show the auto-correlation evident in the residuals of the other regression. The ratio δ^2/s^2 is 1.99 — not significant; indeed, the expected value of this ratio for samples of 28 from a population where the errors are not auto-correlated is 2.07.

3.6. Application to Post-war Experience

Post-war data offer a considerable challenge to any formula for food demand based on prewar experience. The war-time expansion of agricultural production has raised the *per capita* supply of food some 15% above the level which persisted with only slight variation over the period 1913–41. Consumer income, in real or money terms, has far exceeded any previous peace-time levels. The price variables too have been carried by inflation beyond the range of experience from which a statistical formula must be derived. The war may have distorted the operation of any time trend detected in peacetime. Abnormal influences on consumer demand — the backlog of demand for durable goods, the extraordinary accumulation of savings during the war, the continuation of rent control — may have indirect repercussions on food expenditure. Finally, years within which prices and other variables change markedly are not a promising period for application of a function in which each variable covers an entire year.

In extrapolating a demand function to new ranges of aggregate income, the use of budget data to estimate income-elasticity has, in theory at least, an advantage over exclusive reliance on time series. Aggregate income may be unprecedentedly high without taking the bulk of families beyond the range of family incomes observed in budget data. An estimate of income-elasticity derived from budget data, applied to a record level of aggregate income, is not necessarily being employed beyond the range of the observations on which it is based.

Judged by food demand functions based solely on pre-war time series, the inflation of food prices after the expiration of price control and the increasing share of consumer income devoted to food expenditure were a mystery. The Department of Commerce found food expenditure in 1948 eight billion dollars more than expected from its pre-war regression of aggregate income and food expenditure (Gilbert, 1948, and Cohen, 1948). The food demand function of Girschick and Haavelmo (1947), obtained by estimating the parameters of this function simultaneously with those of other equations embracing the entire economy, fails to indicate an inflationary gap in food at the end of price control in 1946, or during the inflation of 1947.[22]

Thanks to the use of budget data, the statistical food demand function obtained in this study contains a higher estimate of income elasticity than functions based on time series alone (0.56 compared to 0.3 in the Girschick-Haavelmo study).[23] The function estimated in (26) correctly shows excess demand in 1946. Table VI compares the actual averages

Table VI. Average of food price index

Year	Actual	'Predicted'
1946	160	185
1947	194	201
1948	211	232

---

[22] For the year 1946 their food demand function yields *a per capita* demand 114% of average consumption for 1935–39, and for 1947, 110% Actual food supply for domestic consumption was 118% in 1946 and 117% in 1947.

[23] Stone (1945), pp. 325–26, obtains from time series 1929–41 estimates of α and β which agree closely with the estimates of this paper. However, his estimate of γ (approximately 0.55) is radically different.

of the food price index for three post-war years with values of the index 'predicted' by (26); the comparison is also shown in Figure 9.

4. THE FAMILY FOOD DEMAND FUNCTION OVER TIME

The estimates of elasticities obtained in Section 3 are intended to apply to the family demand function as well as to the aggregate demand function. In Section 1.4 it was shown that budget observations for different years agree fairly well in regard to the slope of the line relating the logarithms of food expenditure and income. They differ, as inspection of Figures 3–6 readily reveals, in the level of this line. These differences in level should, according to the family demand function assumed in Section 1, be explained by differences in variables other than current income. The purpose of this section is to see to what extent this explanation is possible.

The family food demand function (1) gives food consumption in physical units or in constant food dollars. For expenditure x_t in current dollars the function becomes

$$x_t = c_t P_t = k y_t^{\alpha_1} y_{t-1}^{\alpha_2} P_t^{\beta+1} Q_t^{\gamma} n^{\delta}. \tag{38}$$

By assumption (4) concerning the relation of current to past income, the expenditure function is:

$$x_t = k y_t^{\alpha} \left(\frac{Y_{t-1}}{Y_t} \right)^{\alpha_2} P_t^{\beta+1} Q_t^{\gamma} n^{\delta}. \tag{39}$$

For a given year t, P_t, Q_t, and Y_{t-1}/Y_t are constant over all families. If the observations in a budget study for that year are adjusted to a standard family size $\hat{n}$, the relationship between current income and food consumption which the budget data should obey is

$$x_t = m_t y_t^{\alpha}$$

where

$$m_t = k \left(\frac{Y_{t-1}}{Y_t} \right)^{\alpha_2} P_t^{\beta+1} Q_t^{\gamma} \hat{n}^{\delta}. \tag{40}$$

For two years i and j:

$$\frac{m_i}{m_j} = \left(\frac{P_i}{P_j} \right)^{\beta+1} \left(\frac{Q_i}{Q_j} \right)^{\gamma} \left(\frac{Y_{i-1}}{Y_i} \right)^{\alpha_2} \left(\frac{Y_{j-1}}{Y_j} \right)^{-\alpha_2}. \tag{41}$$

If this ratio exceeds one, the logarithmic income-expenditure line should be higher for year i than for year j. Given the estimates of β, γ and α_2 obtained in (26) and the values of P_t, Q_t, Y_{t-1} and Y_t in the two years, the ratio can be computed. Table VII shows its value for five years, with $j = 1941$ in each case.

Table VII. Calculated
values of m_i/m_j

$i =$	$(j = 1941)$
1918	1.13
1927–28	1.16
1935–36	0.99
1941	1.00
1947	1.35

Table VIII. Shifts in urban income — food consumption relationship

Budget studies compared		Observed shift (antilog $(a_i - a_j)$)	Calculated shift (m_i/m_j)
i	j		
1935–36	1941	0.95	0.99
1918	1941	0.94	1.13
1927–28	1941	1.09	1.16
1927–28	1935–36	1.14	1.15
1947 Washington	1941	1.30	1.35
1947 Manchester	1941	1.39	1.35
1947 Richmond	1941	1.24	1.35

The levels of the logarithmic income-food expenditure lines based on budget observations in those five years should correspond in rank to the numbers in Table VII. Except for 1918, the ranks of the budget study lines with respect to level are consistent with the hypothesis (Figures 3–6).

The amount as well as the direction of the shift in the income-consumption lines can be measured and compared with the calculated shift ratios. Lines were fitted by least squares to the observations shown on Figures 3–6. Comparison of the levels of these lines is unambiguous only if they are of the same slope. Actually the slopes computed by regression differ slightly (Table IV). Therefore, in each comparison of two budget studies the mean of the two least squares slopes is taken as the slope for both lines. The level constant is then chosen so as to obtain the line of best fit with the given slope. For two years i and j we have two lines:

$$\log x_i = a_i + b \log y_i$$
$$\log x_j = a_j + b \log y_j.$$

This pair of lines provides the material for an independent estimate of the shift ratios already calculated, namely antilog $(a_i - a_j)$. If families behaved over time exactly according to the statistical demand function, this would be equal to m_i/m_j. The two estimates of shift ratios are compared in Table VIII.

5. SUMMARY AND CONCLUSION

This investigation of food demand in the US has been an experiment in the combination of time series and budget data in statistical demand analysis. The aggregate food demand function has been derived from a family food demand function, and the parameters of both functions have been estimated. Some estimates, applicable to both functions, have been obtained from budget data, and the remaining parameters have been evaluated from time series. Finally, the estimates have been checked by reference to budget observations made in different years.

Refinement of the method is certainly necessary. In particular, estimates from budget data should not be introduced into time series correlation as known with certainty. A maximum likelihood estimate of income-elasticity, for example, would utilize the two kinds of data simultaneously. The practical obstacle to this improvement is the absence of individual family observations in most published budget surveys; the use of grouped data, with no knowledge of the variation of families about the group means, gives a deceptive appearance of precision to budget study estimates. The discrepancy between budget study and unrestricted time series estimates of the same parameter should be eliminated by the use of additional variables to a greater extent than was possible in this study. But this experiment indicates, it is hoped, that further use and development of the method will be fruitful in statistical demand analysis.

REFERENCES

Cochrane, W. W. (1947), 'Farm family budgets — a moving picture,' *Review of Economic Statistics*, **29**, 189.

Cohen, M. (1948), 'Food consumption, expenditures, and prices,' *Survey of Current Business*, January, p. 12.

Dewhurst, F., and Associates (1947), *America's Needs and Resources*. Twentieth Century Fund, New York.

de Wolff, P. (1941), 'Income-elasticity of demand; a micro-economic and a macro-economic interpretation,' *Economic Journal*, **51**, 140.

Fisher, R. A. (1946), *Statistical Methods for Research Workers*, 10th ed. Oliver & Boyd, Edinburgh.

Gilbert, M. (1948), Speech to American Marketing Association, quoted in *New York Times*, June 15.

Girschick, M. A., and T. Haavelmo (1947), 'Statistical analysis of the demand for food,' *Econometrica*, **15**, 79.

Haavelmo, T. (1947), 'Family expenditures and the marginal propensity to consume,' *Econometrica*, **15**, 335.

Hart, B. I. (1942), 'Significance levels for the ratio of the mean square successive difference to the variance,' *Annals of Mathematical Statistics*, **13**, 446.

Leontief, W. (1948), 'Econometrics,' in H. Ellis (Ed.), *Survey of Contemporary Economics*. Blakiston, Philadelphia, p. 388.

Leven, M., H. G. Moulton and C. Warburton (1934), *America's Capacity to Consume*, Brookings Institution, Washington.

Mack, R. P. (1948), 'The direction of change in income and the consumption function,' *Review of Economics and Statistics*, **30**, 239.

Marschak, J. (1939a), 'Personal and collective budget functions,' *Review of Economic Statistics*, **21**, 161.

Marschak, J. (1939b), 'Review of Schultz, *Theory and Measurement of Demand*,' *Economic Journal*, **49**, 486.

Marschak, J. (1943), 'Money illusion and demand analysis,' *Review of Economic Statistics*, **25**, 40.

Mendershausen, H. (1946), *Changes in Income Distribution during the Great Depression*. National Bureau of Economic Research, New York.

National Industrial Conference Board (1948), *Economic Almanac*, New York.

Snedecor, G. W. (1946), *Statistical Methods*, 4th ed. Iowa State College Press, Ames, Iowa.

Staehle, H. (1937), 'Short period variations in the distribution of incomes,' *Review of Economic Statistics*, **19**, 133.

Staehle, H. (1945), 'Relative prices and post-war markets for animal food products,' *Quarterly Journal of Economics*, **59**, 237.

Stone, R. (1945), 'The analysis of market demand,' *Journal of the Royal Statistical Society*, **108**, 286.

Stone, R. (1948), 'The analysis of market demand: an outline of methods and results,' *Review of the International Statistical Institute*, **16**, 1.

US Bureau of Labor Statistics (1924), *Bulletin no. 357: Cost of Living in the United States*. Government Printing Office, Washington.

US Bureau of Labor Statistics (1942), 'Income and spending and saving of city families in wartime,' *Monthly Labor Review*, **55**, 419.

US Bureau of Labor Statistics (1943), *Description of the Cost-of-Living Index of the Bureau of Labor Statistics*. Government Printing Office, Washington.

US Bureau of Labor Statistics (1945), *Bulletin no. 822: Family Spending and Saving in Wartime*. Government Printing Office, Washington.

US Bureau of Labor Statistics (1949), 'Family income and expenditures in 1947,' *Monthly Labor Review*, **68**, 389.

US Department of Agriculture (1943), *Miscellaneous Publication no. 520: Rural Family Spending and Saving in Wartime*. Government Printing Office, Washington.

US Department of Agriculture (1948), *Agricultural Statistics*, Government Printing Office, Washington.

US Department of Commerce (1945), *Statistical Abstract of the United States*, 1944–45. Government Printing Office, Washington.

US National Resources Committee (1939), *Consumer Expenditures in the United States*. Government Printing Office, Washington.

US National Resources Committee (1941), *Family Expenditures in the United States*. Government Printing Office, Washington.

DISCUSSION ON DR. TOBIN'S PAPER

Mr. J. R. N. STONE: It gives me great pleasure to move a vote of thanks to Dr. Tobin on his excellent Paper. In recent years the Society has had presented to it Papers on demand analysis based on time series (such as my Paper in 1945) and on budget studies (such as J. L. Nicholson's Paper in 1949), but it has not before received one which made systematic use of both these sources. By his ingenious and skillful combination of these two kinds of information Dr. Tobin has produced a demand function which fits in with each. The superiority of his methods is demonstrated by the fact first that they do not simply reproduce earlier results but lead to different values for some of the parameters, and second that, unlike these earlier studies, they give good results when used to predict the level of the demand for food after the war. The Paper is one of which the author and the Society may justly be proud.

An interesting feature of the Paper is the use of the 1941 budget enquiry to demonstrate the need for including past incomes, a need not apparent from a study of time series alone. By assuming that the distribution of income is unchanged in a certain sense between last year and this, Dr. Tobin demonstrates that the income elasticity derived from budget studies will approximate to the sum of the elasticities with respect to this year's and last year's income. By an extension of his argument it can be seen that, on the same assumption about the constancy of the distribution of income, the income elasticity derived from budget studies will approximate to the sum of the elasticities with respect to current and past incomes, and so will approximate to the ultimate response of consumption to a given change in income not all of which, unless $\alpha = \alpha_1$, will be felt in the first year of this change. Furthermore, since the levels of income in the recent past (which is the important period) are highly but by no means perfectly correlated with present income, analyses based on time series which make use of present income only will tend to under-estimate the importance of income in determining consumption. If past incomes are introduced without restriction on the income parameters the effect, usually small, of past incomes is likely to be masked and hard to determine.

Examples such as this justify, if justification is needed, the detailed econometric methods which Dr. Tobin has employed. The remaining matters I wish to discuss relate to some of the data he has used and to a comparison of his results with earlier investigations.

In the budget data used, total food expenditure is measured, and so a full allowance is made for the cost of processing food and for the various services connected with food whether in retailing or in the catering trade. The time series for food consumption on the other hand is a retail price-weighted index of the quantity of foodstuffs, prepared by the Bureau of Agricultural Economics (for a brief description see 'Food Consumption, Expenditures and Prices,' by Morris Cohen, in the *Survey of Current Business*, January, 1948). As Dr. Tobin points out, it does not measure changes in the amount of services rendered by caterers or in retail outlets nor in all cases does it measure the amount of processing involved. As can be seen from Table V, it is remarkably stable over the period 1913–41, and the main justifications for using it are that it is the only uniform series available over the whole period and that it is the series used in an elaborate study by Girschick and Haavelmo (see 'Statistical Analysis of the Demand for Food: Examples of Simultaneous Estimation of Structural Equations,' in *Econometrica*, April, 1947). From 1929 onwards the Department of Commerce has prepared (National Income Supplement to *SCB*, July, 1947) as part of its study of aggregate consumers' expenditure a series of total food expenditure which conceptually is more nearly related to the budget data than the series used by Dr. Tobin. This series can be deflated by means of the food component of the cost of living index but the trouble with it is that it cannot easily be taken back to 1913. Some information for the earlier years is given in the pioneer study of W. H. Lough. (*High-Level Consumption*, 1935) and a very rough attempt may be made to interpolate this series for non-census years by means of a series given by W. H. Shaw (*Value of Commodity Output since 1869*, 1947). This pieced-together series shows, even when alcoholic drinks are removed from it following the repeal of prohibition, a movement different from and much more variable than that shown by the Bureau of Agricultural Economics index. In as much as this series, while statistically lacking in uniformity, is conceptually more appropriate, I have included analyses based on it in the comparative table given below. For want of a better label I have referred to these analyses as Tobin-Stone without in any way wishing to implicate Dr. Tobin in the use of such a dubious statistical series.

Comparison of Demand Analyses for Food in the United States of America

	Period	α_1	α_2	β	γ	Σ
Tobin:						
(1)	1913–41	0.44	0.12	−0.51	−0.03	0.02
(2)	1913–41	0.45	0.11	−0.53	—	0.03
(3)	1913–41	0.27	—	−0.28	0.06	0.05
Girschick and Haavelmo:						
(4)	1922–41	0.25	0.05	−0.25	0	0.05
Stone:						
(5)	1929–41	0.59	—	−0.58	−0.01	0
(6)	1929–41	0.53	—	−0.62	0.55	0.46
(7)	1929–41	0.83	—	−0.90	0.07	—
Tobin-Stone:						
(8)	1913–41	0.61	−0.05	−0.43	−0.11	0.02
(9)	1913–41	0.62	0.12	−0.39	−0.31	0.04
(10)	1913–41	0.69	0.12	−0.51	−0.29	0.01

Analyses (1) to (4) are based on the Bureau of Agricultural Economics series of food consumption, while analyses (5) to (10) are based on the Department of Commerce series continued backwards in the case of the last three by the method outlined above. In analyses (4), (6) and (7) allowance was made for a residual trend but this was not done in any of the others. Analysis (4) used a linear equation while in all the others the expression used was linear in the logarithms of the variables. In analyses (1), (2) and (8) but not in the others a restriction was placed on the sum $\alpha_1 + \alpha_2$. A zero indicates the estimated value of a parameter whereas a '—' indicates that the parameter in question was assumed to be zero or, in the final column (analysis (7)), that the sum $\alpha_1 + \beta + \gamma$ was restricted *a priori* to zero.

The first point to notice is that apart from (6) (and (7), which does not count in this connection) the sums of the elasticities shown in the final column are close to zero. This indicates that the proportionality condition is approximately satisfied in each case, which is in accordance with theoretical expectations. Second, the mean values of the parameters in (4) are similar to those in (3) so that the objection to (3) that they do not square with what is known from budget studies can equally be raised against the results of Girschick and Haavelmo as it can against Dr. Tobin's unrestricted equation. Third, (5), apart from the fact that no allowance is made for last year's income, gives results very close to (1). It was not, however, given in my original article ('The Analysis of Market Demand,' this *Journal*, pts. III–IV, 1945) because, while it showed a closed bunch map and a high coefficient of multiple correlation, it also showed a highly systematic residual which could be removed by the introduction of a residual trend with the effect on the parameters here listed shown in (6). Thus, of the two equations which I did give, (6) was unsatisfactory since the proportionality condition was so far from being satisfied, while (7) was unsatisfactory since it involved such a large negative residual trend.

Finally, the last analyses make use of the extended Department of Commerce series. In all cases the value of α_1 is substantially higher than in (1) and (2). In (8), where a restriction is placed on the sum $\alpha_1 + \alpha_2$, a negative (though not significant) value is found for α_2 which is not consistent with budget data. In (9) and (10) the income elasticities are determined without restriction. In (9) food consumption is treated as the dependent variable as in (5) to (7), whereas in (10) the food price index is treated as the dependent variable as in (1) to (3). These two analyses do not revert to the values of α_1 given by (3); on the contrary the values obtained are consistently above, not below, those derived from (1) and (2). In addition the value of α_2 is in each case the same as in (1) so that the unrestricted income effect exceeds the value obtained from budget data. This increased effect of income is largely offset by substantial negative values of γ. Thus the use of this alternative series which, for all its shortcomings, seems more appropriate than the one used by Dr. Tobin for combination with the budget data he has used, leads to results which still stand in need of reconciliation. There is clearly a need for a more satisfactory time series of food expenditure at constant prices for the years before 1929 than anything available at present.

Mr. NICHOLSON (seconding the vote of thanks): I am very glad of this opportunity of expressing my admiration for Dr. Tobin's extremely interesting paper. Having worked on part of the same field, I am the better able to appreciate Dr. Tobin's skill and finesse in handling a subject which bristles with difficulties on all sides. I am only sorry not to have been able to give the paper the careful study it so obviously deserves, and must apologize if some of my remarks appear to be based on hasty reflections. I am sure that the paper will provide food for thought for some time to come, and that future workers in this field will be very much in his debt.

I will begin by commenting on some of the assumptions implicit in Dr. Tobin's basic demand function (1). At first sight one feels rather startled at the author's boldness; for it is assumed that all the demand elasticities are constant with respect to *all* the variables included in the model. The income elasticity of demand, for instance, is assumed to be the same not only at all levels of income but also for all sizes of family. This assumption is not borne out, at any rate by my own study of pre-war budgets of British working-class families (*JRSS*, Vol. CXII, 1949, Part IV), where the income elasticity of demand for food was found to vary, for different levels of income and different sizes of family, between 0.3 and 0.9.

Another and probably more vulnerable assumption is that variations in expenditure with respect to the composition and size of the family can be accounted for simply by introducing *n* (the number of persons in the family) as one of the variables. In the past the numbers have sometimes been adjusted for differences in age and sex by means of equivalence scales and expressed in terms of the equivalent number of adult males. This method has been criticized for not conforming to family expenditure habits. But Dr. Tobin goes even further in using the simple numbers, regardless of age, sex, or of how many members of the family are at work. Further, the assumption that elasticity with respect to size does not depend either on size — that expenditure would show the same change whether the number of persons increased from 2 to 3 or from 4 to 6 — or on the level of income is hard to accept. The pre-war working-class budgets for this country reveal the following discrete values of δ (elasticity of demand for food with respect to family size) for different levels of income and size of family:

Number of children increased from —	Values of δ at total weekly expenditure of —		
	50s. 0d	72s. 8d	100s. 0d
0 to 1	0.04	0.19	0.19
1 to 2	0.18	0.10	0.10

These figures show only moderate variability, but it must be remembered that they relate to a homogeneous group of families, all of them working-class families with two adults (one of either sex), of whom only one is at work, varying numbers of children and no other person. Since expenditure on food is likely to increase, but not by much, as the size of family increases, income being constant, the values of δ for these families are likely to be small and positive, and the range of possible values is limited. But higher up the income scale families will have savings to draw on and we are likely to find a systematic connection between δ and the level of income.

There are also some interesting problems connected with the form of function (1). Dr. Tobin admits that the use of this function for all consumer goods and savings would be inconsistent with the identity between disposable family income and total expenditure plus savings. I would suggest that the conditions implicit in this identity should form an important part of any generalized description of family expenditure. It is very useful to have an anchor of this kind when working with sets of figures which, at best, are only estimates, and not always of the relevant categories. In any work which covers the whole field of expenditure it provides, as Mr. Marris has found, a valuable check on the consistency of the estimated elasticities. It is, however, easier to ensure consistency if the functions for different commodities all have the same general form. Dr. Tobin's demand function for food implies a different type of function for, at least, some of the remaining items of expenditure. The complications thus introduced would detract from the simplicity which seems to be the great merit of his model.

Dr. Tobin also refers to what he calls the 'homogeneity postulate.' This appears to be the same as what might be termed the assumption of rational consumer's behaviour, namely, that the consumer does not suffer from 'money illusion,' and that his demand is unaffected if his income and all prices simultaneously rise (or fall) in the same proportion. This hypothesis relates to income and prices at a single date, and seems to imply, using Dr. Tobin's notation, that:

$$\alpha_1 + \beta_1 + \gamma_1 = 0. \tag{i}$$

Dr. Tobin interprets his 'homogeneity postulate' as implying that:

$$\alpha_1 + \alpha_2 + \beta_1 + \gamma_1 = 0$$

(subscripts 1 and 2 referring to the current year and the previous year respectively). But, if they were discussing the same hypothesis, the inclusion in this expression of α_2 (elasticity of demand with respect to previous year's income) would appear to be incorrect.

If the assumption of rational consumer's behaviour applied to income and prices in the previous year, the inclusion in the demand function of previous year's income would have to be accompanied by previous year's prices (P_{t-1} and Q_{t-1}) with corresponding elasticities (β_2 and γ_2) and a second condition would be obtained, viz.:

$$\alpha_2 + \beta_2 + \gamma_2 = 0. \tag{ii}$$

If people behave in accordance with the hypothesis, the inclusion of previous year's income without previous year's prices implies that Y_{t-1} is used as a measure of 'real,' not merely of money, income. If this reasoning were correct, it affected the test given at the end of Section 3.2 of the paper.

The most interesting part of Dr. Tobin's paper is his attempt to combine two sets of evidence: family budgets and time series. The translation of the family demand function into an aggregate demand function depends on the various assumptions discussed above, and on the further assumption of a constant distribution of incomes, as defined by the Lorenz curve. It may be reasonable to assume constancy of the Lorenz curve in the United States for the period included in the analysis. But the assumption will not hold good for the United Kingdom, certainly not for a period which includes the last war.

Although several of Dr. Tobin's assumptions can be criticized for being unrealistic, it is useful and, indeed, even necessary, in pioneering work of this kind, to start by using a good many simplifying assumptions. The possibilities of modifying some of these assumptions can quite properly be considered at a later stage. Moreover, the data that are at present available are hardly adequate to support a more elaborate model. One of the most important lessons, in fact, of the paper is the need to extend and improve the basic statistical data; and, in particular, to have more frequent family budget inquiries.

I should like to comment briefly on a few other points. Dr. Tobin attempts to test the significance between two regression coefficients in Section 1.4.1.3, although, as he points out, no valid error can be obtained, since only grouped data are available. In the circumstances I think that very little weight can be attached to the result of this 'test.'

As Dr. Tobin would probably also agree, the method applied in Section 3.5 does not give a conclusive answer to the problem of serial correlation. The fact that two methods produce consistent results does not prove that his conclusions are unaffected by this particular difficulty.

Section 3.2 gives the results of fitting a regression equation to 4 variables, on the assumption that errors are concentrated in one of them ($\log P_t$). Different results would have been obtained if it had been assumed that errors were concentrated in any of the other variables. Calculations which I have made on different assumptions produce the following approximate values for the demand function parameters (ignoring the case where errors are concentrated in $\log Q_t$).

Errors concentrated in:

	$\log S_t$	$\log Y'_t$	$\log P_t$
α_2	0.20	0.64	0.12
β	−0.36	−0.2	−0.52
γ	−0.15	−0.33	−0.02

The last column of figures does not quite agree with Dr. Tobin's figures, because I have assumed $\alpha = 0.56$ exactly, whereas Dr. Tobin worked with a value to five places of decimals. It is obvious that very different results can be obtained, according to the assumption made; and, even though the middle column of figures is clearly absurd, one is hardly justified in pinning one's faith to one set of results alone.

Having worked on family budgets, I am glad to find, in Section 3.3, that they provide more reliable estimates of income elasticities than the time series.

Mr. R. L. MARRIS spoke as one whose job it was to try to make practical use of the work of men like Dr. Tobin, and he welcomed the paper from that point of view. This meant, however, that not only was he not qualified to make strictly technical comments but that he possessed a vested interest in trying to push research workers farther and faster than they thought it safe at this stage to go. He apologized for this.

He was particularly interested in the prospects of obtaining a similar equation for the United Kingdom. The significance of the paper from this point of view was that it developed an equation for food as a whole whereas in this country in the past, work had to be concentrated on individual items. An equation for all food was of vital importance in the UK, since with imports largely consisting of food and raw materials (and raw material requirements for a given national income being partly determined by technical factors), the demand equation for food was fundamental in deciding what was necessary to reconcile balance of payments of equilibrium with full employment. The great difficulty in this country — if an equation valid for the post-war period was to be produced — was that pre-war time series would have to be used since it would be some years before any post-war series would be long enough. It would be necessary, therefore, to allow for the known discontinuous change in the distribution of incomes which had taken place during the war. This apparently could only be done if budget data were used which gave a distribution of families by this year's income and expenditure and last year's, providing the assumption of a lag in expenditure were to be maintained. This information was not available in the United States budget data and as a result Dr. Tobin had been forced to make awkward approximations. The implication was that information of this type should be considered an essential requirement of any budgets that were to be taken in the future. In any case the existing budgets — those taken by the Ministry of Labour for the working classes and the Massey budgets for the middle classes just before the war — were not very satisfactory since the working class budgets excluded the unemployed and the middle class budgets were based only on a sample of civil servants and others whose expenditure habits might not be very representative. If, however, an attempt were made to superimpose post-war budgets on pre-war time series (and this would involve the difficult assumption that the elasticities had not changed) there would still be the difficulty of obtaining a pre-war time series for food consumption as a whole. He thought some attempt might be made by taking an index of the volume of food imports from the Trade and Navigation Accounts and adding this, with appropriate weights, to some index which it should be possible to construct of the home output of U.K. agriculture.

He supported Mr. Nicholson in what he had said about consistency. This was particularly important in practical use since applications nearly always had to be made in conjunction with estimates of other types of expenditure. An estimate or forecast was usually part of an aggregate of estimates of some kind, and nearly always had to be reconcilable with a figure of total income. He knew there was the difficulty that a good fit could only be obtained if all the relevant social variables were taken into account. For instance, Dr. Tobin would no doubt say that the existing stock of consumers' durables should be treated as a variable. But to say this was not to avoid the problem. Dr. Tobin had already implicitly assumed that family size was a factor affecting non-food consumption and, similarly, the stock of durables would on this basis become a factor affecting food consumption. He wondered if it would be possible to delimit a number of 'general' economic and social variables which could be taken as a standard list to apply to all commodities and to avoid using special variables for particular commodities. This might reduce the quality of the fit in individual cases but might increase the value of the results by increasing their generality. There would be no objection of course to finding modified forms with a larger number of variables in individual cases for use when consistency was not required, i.e. where the application was concerned only with that commodity.

The problem of consistency arose in acute form where a lag was assumed. Dr. Tobin seemed to be saying that when family income went down people cut down first on non-food expenditure and later increased this and adjusted downwards their food expenditure. This did not seem *a priori* either particularly likely or unlikely, but he suspected the truth was that there was a lag in all consumption expenditure and the whole brunt of the initial adjustment fell on savings. This result would, of course, be obtained if a large number of families reacted to a reduction of income by dissaving which could not be continued. This seemed *a priori* likely and could be tested by examination of the US data.

He wondered whether some of these questions could be looked into in the following manner. From the data that Dr. Tobin had used it must be possible to derive a time series of all non-food expenditure plus savings. A distribution of families by income and non-food expenditure could also be obtained. From these data an equation of similar type for non-food expenditure could be obtained by exactly the same methods as Dr. Tobin had used for food — if for the moment one were content with the same set of variables. There also existed a residual equation for non-food expenditure, not derived from any data, implied in Dr. Tobin's equation for food. This latter would be bound to be different from that derived by the method he had just suggested because, as had already been discussed, the mathematical form was such as to make consistency impossible. But it would be interesting to see how different they were, how much loss of accuracy appeared to have occurred as a result of using this mathematical form and how this loss would compare with the loss which might be experienced by using a limited 'general' list of variables. For instance, how did it compare with the loss if the family size variable were dropped?

Mr. L. G. K. STARKE said that, although on matters of economic analysis he could speak only as a layman, it seemed to him difficult to justify the assumption that the income-elasticity of food consumption was constant throughout the very wide range of incomes covered by the family budget data. One's physical capacity for food must have a limit, and there must be some limit also to the extent to which food expenditure could be increased by purchase of the most luxurious and expensive types of food. He would therefore expect the formula connecting food expenditure with income to be asymptotic.

If some such formula were adopted it might well be that the relationship would not lend itself to analysis by the standard methods of multiple regression; but it seemed to him that one ought not to ignore *a priori* considerations merely for the sake of expediency, i.e. in order to bring the problem within the range of normal technique.

The position in regard to the time series was different. The national *per capita* income was not likely to vary sufficiently — even over a considerable span of years — to vitiate the assumption of a constant income-elasticity for *per capita* food expenditure. But in view of what he (the speaker) had just said, he did wonder whether, despite the reasons given in the paper, the author was right in discarding the income-elasticity parameter derived from the time-series themselves in favour of the parameter derived from the budget study.

He hoped Dr. Tobin would accept these tentative remarks primarily as evidence of the interest and enjoyment with which a layman had read his paper. Finally, he wondered whether the time had now come when the Ministry of Food could introduce a little variety into the statistical diet by providing some data on food expenditure in relation to income as well as over-all consumption levels in terms of the eternal calorie.

Mr. K. S. LOMAX said he was sure that any points he might raise would clarify themselves on a closer reading of Dr. Tobin's most interesting and valuable paper on an absorbing subject — a subject of great importance both to the economist, who must attempt to measure the concepts he deals with in his economic theory, and to the statistician who would be keenly interested in the problems of fitting models to data — particularly the simultaneous fitting of demand and supply functions.

The first point he would raise concerned the scope of the paper. Was there not some danger in treating food as a single commodity? The demand functions for different types of food surely must vary quite a lot. Indeed, at one point, Section 1.4.1.3, Dr. Tobin stated that 'the increase in urban expenditure for food as income rises represents a shift to higher-quality foods more than an increase in total intake,' which surely implies that some of the lower quality foods are probably inferior goods. Yet Dr. Tobin's income elasticities of demand are all positive.

On the purely statistical or methodological side he (the speaker) must confess a certain amount of confusion.

The agreement between single equation least squares values and maximum likelihood estimates in the case of the pair of demand and supply equations in the reduced form and not in the original form seemed logically dissatisfying.

The supply equation introduced in Section 3.4 was a very simple one. Had Dr. Tobin tried the effect of introducing other variables, say agricultural costs of production, into the supply equation? And then again, would it not be more realistic, in the case of food or of agricultural products, to introduce time lags into the supply equation. That is, relate supply in period t to price in period $(t - 1)$?

Thirdly, in view of the dangers of collinearity, particularly, mentioned by Dr. Tobin in Section 3.3, but for general reasons as well, would it not have been desirable to test, by one of the tests of significance which had been suggested, how many structural relationships the data did, in fact, contain?

Finally, might it not be that the increasing share of consumer income devoted to food expenditure, referred to as a mystery by Dr. Tobin in Section 3.6, could be explained on the basis of a shift in the distribution of income?

Mr. C. F. CARTER said that Dr. Tobin's paper was very valuable and he hoped this type of work would increase in volume as time went on. He was still a little worried about n, the number of persons in the family. This number was a curious variable to have in the regression equation, giving rise to many problems including its discontinuity, and the decision to count children as equal to adults. It was presumably reflected in an obscure way by Y_t, the disposable family income for the year, which depended on the number of wage-earners in the family. On the other hand, the number of children might be related to the income of the family. He suggested that some correction for family size might be made to the data before the main regression analysis was undertaken. He was, incidentally, surprised to learn that it was possible to assume average family size as constant over so long a period.

There were one or two other points which might perhaps be made clearer in the paper, not for themselves but for future generations who would consult the *Journal* of the Society in order to use these results in practical work. For instance, 'quantity' of food presumably meant value at constant prices, and not caloric content: food appeared in this case to exclude drink: and it would be useful to have a record of how the families in the US budget studies were chosen. It might be possible to get more data on the whole subject of the paper by studies of the same group of families over a period of time, and he hoped that this, and other work on the lines laid out by Dr. Tobin, would be undertaken.

Professor J. H. RICHARDSON joined in expressing appreciation to Dr. Tobin for devising the ingenious method used in the Paper, and for obtaining such interesting results. This was another illustration of an investigation in which the delicate mathematical technique was far ahead of the quality of the data available. It would be valuable if studies of this kind could be made in a number of countries, but in Great Britain it would be a long time before the method could be used with any hope of reliable results. They had had in Great Britain a period of rationing, which precluded use of the time series. There had also been the effects of changes in habits of consumption, price control, subsidies, and of changes in the distribution of income.

With regard to the variables, although the data were at present inadequate in relation to the mathematical techniques used, he would like to suggest that in future investigations variations in the size and composition of the family should be adjusted by the method devised by Quetelet and developed by others to reduce the food consumption of children of different ages to terms of a common adult unit. Consideration might also be given, especially in countries with population trends similar to those in Britain, to the relative food consumption of adults in the prime of life and of elderly retired people. Few data were available about the food consumption of aged people, and if investigations showed their food consumption to be considerably less than that of younger adults an appropriate allowance could be made. This refinement would probably be unnecessary for the data for the United States used by Dr. Tobin.

He, too, was doubtful about the desirability of treating food as a single commodity, especially as there were considerable differences in the food consumption habits of different sections of the community. Better qualities of food were consumed by the higher than by the lower income groups. Different components of the food group were in effect different commodities from the point of view of demand functions.

He had been specially interested in the differences in food consumption between the rural and urban populations of the United States, and it seemed to him that if international comparisons were made it was likely that food consumption in agricultural countries would, other things being equal, be higher than in industrial countries. One would expect to find many conclusions of that kind as this pioneer work was extended to more and more countries.

Dr. TOBIN (in reply):

1. THE TIME SERIES FOR FOOD CONSUMPTION

Mr. Stone has quite correctly emphasized the conceptual difference between food consumption measured in dollars in budget data and food consumption measured over time by the BAE price-weighted index of physical quantities. This difference has much more serious effects on estimates of income elasticity than I had anticipated. The discrepancy between analyses (3) and (10) in Mr. Stone's table shows the effects on estimates derived without restriction from time series. Evidently a similar discrepancy arises in estimates from budget data. I have recently received, unfortunately only after the preparation and reading of my paper, Miscellaneous Publication 691 of the US Department of Agriculture, *Consumption of Food in the United States*, 1909–48 (Washington, 1949). (This publication provides for the first time a complete explanation of the BAE index.) Table 50 (p. 143) of this report is an attempt to measure food consumption of families at various income levels not in dollars but by the same weighted index of physical quantities used to measure national *per capita* food consumption over time. These estimates are extremely rough (see p. 141 of the report), and they leave out of account the most elastic component of food demand, consumption away from home. But they indicate a much lower income-elasticity — in the neighbourhood of 0.2 — than is obtained from budget data when consumption is measured in dollars. In the light of this information I have, of course, to withdraw my objections to the results of analyses (3) and (4) of Mr. Stone's compilation. The values of α in those regressions are not inconsistent with budget data when the same measure of food consumption is used. The time series used in the 'Tobin-Stone' analyses, however imperfect, is conceptually the appropriate one to use in conjunction with my analysis of budget data.

2. LAGS AND THE 'HOMOGENEITY POSTULATE'

Concerning my use of lagged income as a variable in the demand function, Mr. Nicholson has, it seems to me, raised two logically distinct questions. The first is: how is the 'homogeneity postulate' to be interpreted in the case of a dynamic demand function? The second is: does it make sense to include the lagged value of one variable, here money income, and not the lagged values of others, here prices?

The theory of consumer choice, on which the homogeneity condition is based, is a static theory. To apply it, we must convert our demand function from a dynamic to a static function. In the present case, this means simply that $y_{t=1}$ is set equal to y_t. Then my Equation (1) becomes

$$c = ky_1^\alpha + \alpha_2 P^\beta Q^t.$$

Imagine two situations in both of which previous income is equal to current income. In the second situation, income and prices are double their values in the first situation. 'Rational' behaviour requires demand to be unchanged. This requirement is simply my Equation (2), which Mr. Nicholson has criticized. According to his version of the theory (Equation (i)) demand would not be the same in the two situations.

Since the theory of rational consumer behaviour assumes static conditions, it places no restrictions on the manner of introducing lags. It provides no justification for Mr. Nicholson's Equations (i) and (ii). If lagged prices as well as lagged income are introduced into the demand function, the only requirement which the theory places on their elasticities is the one found by assuming equality of the lagged and current values of all variables, namely:

$$\alpha_1 + \alpha_2 + \beta_1 + \beta_2 + \gamma_1 + \gamma_2 = 0.$$

The second question is, therefore, empirical rather than theoretical. It may be implausible to say, as my demand function does, that consumers will adjust expenditure more rapidly to a rise (or fall) of prices than to an equivalent fall (or rise) in money income. But it involves no contradiction of the 'homogeneity postulate,' which says only that the eventual amounts of adjustment in the two cases must be the same and is silent concerning the relative speeds of adjustment. I agree with Mr. Nicholson's preference for a symmetrical treatment of lags. The variable we want, in order to embody the hypothesis that consumption habits are 'sticky' is not y_{t-1}, or any combination of y_{t-1} and lagged prices. It is c_{t-1} and perhaps, in addition, $c_{t-2}, c_{t-3}; \ldots$. That is, the evidence cited in my Section 1.2 can be interpreted as showing that, other things being equal, the current consumption of families is larger the greater was their past *consumption*. Since in a budget study sample past income and past consumption are doubtless highly correlated, this interpretation squares with the observations (Figure 1) as well as the interpretation I gave in Section 1.2. However, an autoregressive family demand function presents formidable difficulties both in aggregation and in estimation of parameters from aggregate time series.

Mr. Marris's conjecture that, given current income, consumption expenditure as a whole is related positively, and saving negatively, to past income is confirmed by United States budget data (Mack, 1948).

3.   THE FORM OF THE FUNCTION

Tractable formulae seldom do justice to the full complexity of human behaviour; I can only agree with Mr. Nicholson and Mr. Starke that, in fact, the various elasticities probably are not constant but depend on the values of the variables — and on many other things, too. (However, Mr. Nicholson's figures for δ scarcely support his complaint.)

Mr. Marris and Mr. Nicholson also criticize the form of the function because it cannot be used exhaustively without violating the identity of income and consumption plus saving.

The particular function adopted to display an economic relationship is an approximation dictated by statistical convenience. Economic theory does not tell us what functional form its relationships take. It certainly does not tell us that all consumer demand functions are of the same form. I doubt that my critics would be better satisfied by a simple linear function; the marginal propensity to consume food falls with income (whether or not, as Mr. Starke suggests, it approaches zero at a finite level of food consumption). If not, they are asking for more parameters, whose estimation would increase the statistical burden on a limited number of budget and time series observations. Additional parameters would also complicate the problem of aggregation and the comparison of parameter estimates from budget studies of varying detail. In view of these practical requirements of the inquiry, I believe the function I used was the most suitable. Unfortunately we lack any objective means of judging whether simplifications imposed by such practical requirements are over-simplifications or not.

I consider it an advantage of the method I advocated and attempted to illustrate that it calls attention to simplifying assumptions which are rarely apparent but no less necessary in demand analysis employing only aggregate time series.

4. THE TREATMENT OF FAMILY SIZE

I agree that some scale of equivalent adults would provide a better measure of family size than number of heads. Unfortunately the budget data which I used did not permit the application of such a scale. I do not believe, however, that the estimate of income-elasticity, which was my main objective in using budget data, would be greatly changed. For the 1935–36 survey it is possible to relate average food consumption per equivalent adult to average income per equivalent adult. This relationship gives very much the same income elasticity as I have obtained.

I do not understand Mr. Carter's concern over the discontinuity of the family size variable and I should have thought that difficulties due to the possible relationships Mr. Carter mentions between family income and size were dodged by the use of observations classified by both variables.

5. OTHER POINTS

I am sorry to have left doubt concerning the other points which Mr. Carter has raised. 'Quantity' of food, in budget data, does mean value at constant prices, and it *in*cludes drink. The methods of selection of families for the various budget studies are described in the sources I have cited, and I do not see any gain in repeating those descriptions.

I agree with Mr. Lomax that individual foods have widely varying income-elasticities, some of which are probably negative. But I fail to see why this is a reason for surprise that my 'income elasticities of demand [which refer to food as a whole and not to individual foods] are all positive.'

The supply equation in Section 3.4 is, as Mr. Lomax says, extremely simple. But Mr. Lomax appears to have overlooked the fact that I am taking production as a prede-termined variable and considering whether the share of production going to the home market is sensitive to current prices.

In view of Figure 8, I doubt that the high post-war expenditure on food can, as Mr. Lomax suggests, be attributed to a change in income distribution.

CHAPTER 3

ON THE CORRESPONDENCE BETWEEN INDIVIDUAL AND AGGREGATE FOOD CONSUMPTION FUNCTIONS: EVIDENCE FROM THE USA AND THE NETHERLANDS*

HEATHER M. ANDERSON AND FARSHID VAHID

1. INTRODUCTION

Many theories of microeconomic behaviour assume that an individual's behaviour is determined by both individual specific characteristics as well as variables which characterize the economy as a whole. Such theories predict that aggregate behaviour over time is determined by the evolution of those variables which affect all individuals in the economy, and also by the (possibly changing) distributions of individual-specific variables. Ideally, one uses panel data to simultaneously study all the empirical implications of such theories, but cross-sectional regressions are routinely used to assess the impact that individual specific variables have on individual behaviour, and time-series regressions are routinely used to relate aggregates of individual-specific variables to variables affecting the economy as a whole. One problem related to empirical cross-sectional and time-series studies is that they rarely lead to mutually consistent parameter estimates. Deaton (1992) points out many instances of this inconsistency in his survey of consumption studies, and suggests that more research on issues relating to aggregation might help to reconcile these two sets of results.

One of the earliest attempts to carefully integrate economic theory with both cross-sectional micro-data and time-series macro-aggregates was made by Tobin (1950) in the context of studying a log-linear model of food consumption. Tobin gave a set of sufficient conditions under which a log-linear micro model would lead to a log-linear macro model, and a sufficient condition under which long-run relationships could be estimated from cross-sectional data sets. He assumed that these conditions were satisfied, and then pooled information from both cross-sectional and time-series data to develop his 'statistical demand function for food'. Use of the log-linear specification avoided non-linearities which might have complicated the dynamics and specification of the aggregated consumption function, and the conditions which Tobin assumed,[1] ensured that the parameters relating to the aggregate macro-equations were theoretically the same as the underlying parameters associated with the micro-equations, even though the distributions of income and family size might have changed over time.

---

* Reprinted from the *Journal of Applied Econometrics*, **12**, 477–507 (1997).

[1] These conditions were later called 'mean-scaling' by Lewbel (1992). A definition of 'mean-scaling' is provided in Section 2.

Methodology and Tacit Knowledge: Two Experiments in Econometrics
Jan R. Magnus and Mary S. Morgan © 1997 John Wiley & Sons Ltd

Tobin was unable to test his log-linear specification or to formally assess his 'poolability' assumptions in 1950, but since then, the literature has made considerable advances on specification testing, dynamics, aggregation, and more recently on non-linear econometrics. This report re-analyzes and extends Tobin's work, so as to learn more about developing appropriate cross-sectional specifications for food consumption, and how aggregate time-series studies can be related to the underlying microeconomic relationships which characterize the cross-sections. Past research has suggested that the apparent disparity between cross-section estimates of income elasticity with time-series aggregates can be attributed to any combination of the following:

1. There are measurement errors in the budget surveys (including recording errors), and also in the aggregate data prepared by government agencies.
2. The available macroeconomic data is not compatible with the microeconomic data because it measures different entities.
3. The standard specification of a log-linear consumption function is incorrect.
4. The distributions of income and family size do not satisfy 'mean scaling'.
5. The estimated aggregate relationships model equilibrium food consumption, rather than the demand for food and/or
6. The dynamics in the estimated aggregate models are misspecified.

Tobin (1950) paid special attention to (2), (4), (5) and (6), and Izan (1980) considered (1) and (6). Our research concentrates on (3) and (4), but also considers (5) and (6). Theory developed by Stoker (1986) shows that if cross-sectional functional relationships are not log-linear (or linear), then the assumption of a log-linear (or linear) aggregate relationship leads to an omitted variables bias. Additional theory developed by Lewbel (1992) emphasizes that the aggregation of a log-linear microeconomic specification leads to biased parameter estimates of a corresponding aggregate function, unless the income distribution satisfies a 'mean-scaling' condition. We explore the consequences of income related heteroscedasticity in a situation in which the true microeconomic specification is log-linear and income is 'mean-scaled'. In such a situation, the income-dependent heteroscedasticity implies that the parameters of the aggregated log-linear specification differ from the corresponding microeconomic parameters. This last point has not been previously stressed in the aggregation literature, so we pay considerable attention to it here.

Our approach is to develop cross-sectional models very carefully, making sure that they pass specification tests, and then to examine their implications for the aggregate time-series models. We find evidence of non-linearities and income-related heteroscedasticity in the cross-sectional specifications, and argue that both of these characteristics imply a complicated aggregate function which differs from the underlying microeconomic function. Evidence from the cross-sections suggest that elasticities change with both an individual's income and the passage of time. This leads us to conclude that it is inappropriate to interpret the aggregate equation parameters as microeconomic parameters. Due to the unavailability of panel data, we are unable to properly model the changing cross-sectional distributions and hence link our micro model to our macro model. We therefore treat our time-series equations as largely atheoretical constructs, which simply relate aggregate series, and which are potentially useful for forecasting aggregates.

Our report is structured as follows. Section 2 briefly outlines some econometric aspects of aggregation which are relevant for our empirical work. Here, we state the results of Stoker (1986) and Lewbel (1992) which we use, and also sketch our relevant theory on how heteroscedasticity affects aggregation. Section 3 re-analyzes Tobin's data set, and finds evidence of non-linearity in the microeconomic and macroeconomic equations. Section 4 then looks at the more extensive US data set, and shows that non-linearities in the mean and heteroscedasticity in the residual errors which can potentially affect aggregation, are indeed present. Despite these problems, we are able to find a stable log-linear specification for the aggregate, but we do not attempt to interpret the parameters of this aggregate model. Section 5 finds similar patterns in the data for the Netherlands. This section also presents our forecasts for the Netherlands. Section 6 presents some derivations of the form of an aggregate relationship based on a specific assumption about income distribution, and then Section 7 summarizes and concludes.

2.   AGGREGATION OF LOG-LINEAR MODELS

Cross-sectional consumption studies are frequently based on the log-linear specification given by $\ln(c_i) = \alpha + \beta \ln(y_i) + \varepsilon_i$, where i indexes a household, c_i and y_i measure household i's consumption and income, respectively, and one assumes that $\varepsilon_i \sim N(0, \sigma_\varepsilon^2)$. It is well known that in this context the parameter β provides a direct measure of a household's income elasticity, and it is common to assume that the same conclusion about β is true if one has aggregated time series and runs the regression given by $\ln(C_t) = \alpha + \beta \ln(Y_t) + u_t$, where t now indexes time and one now assumes that $u_t \sim N(0, \sigma_u^2)$. Lewbel (1992) emphasizes that unless the distribution of income is mean scaled, i.e.

$$f(y_{it}; Y_t, \theta_t) = \frac{1}{Y_t} g(y_{it}/Y_t; \theta_t)$$ 1

where f is the probability distribution of y_{it} (with parameters θ_t), and g is the probability distribution of y_{it}/Y_t, then the $\hat{\beta}$ estimated from the time-series regression provides a biased estimate of the β in the underlying microeconomic specification. The mean-scaling condition requires that changes in the parameters θ_t are independent of Y_t.

Another requirement for the above type of log-linear aggregation to lead to an interpretable $\hat{\beta}$ from the time-series regression is that errors of the micro relationship be independent of the explanatory variables (see Lewbel, 1992). We believe that the relevance of this requirement for studying consumption has not been fully explored in the literature, so we outline a simplified example to highlight the importance of this independence assumption. Suppose that the income distribution satisfies 'mean scaling', and that the log-linear micro equation at time t is

$$\ln(c_{it}) = \alpha + \beta \ln(y_{it}) + \varepsilon_{it}.$$ 2

If there is income-dependent heteroscedasticity such that $(\varepsilon_{i\tau}|y_{i\tau}) \sim N(0, \omega_0 + \omega_1 \ln(y_{i\tau}))$, then it is easy to show that under these conditions the macro relationship will be log-linear with

$$\ln(C_t) = \left(\alpha + \frac{\omega_0}{2}\right) + \left(\beta + \frac{\omega_1}{2}\right) \ln(Y_t) + u(\theta_t).$$ 3

The parameters in this macro equation are different from the micro parameters, even though functional form is preserved. This result seems particularly relevant in this context, because it is frequently thought that the variance of food consumption changes with income.

Stoker (1986) considers a different but related aggregation problem, showing that if the micro-economic specification is not linear or log-linear, then the aggregate specification has a functional form quite different from the micro specification, containing different explanatory variables (which account for underlying changes in the moments of the cross-sectional distributions), as well as additional dynamics. In Section 6, we derive the implied functional form for the aggregate function in the special case in which the micro relationship takes a log-quadratic form, and the income has a Gamma distribution.

We have insufficient data to test the mean scaling assumption, so simply assume, as did Tobin (1950), that it is satisfied.[2] We are, however, able to examine estimated cross-sectional log-linear regressions for evidence of income-related heteroscedasticity and non-linearity, and we pursue this in the empirical sections which follow. Given that some of our data sets are small, our non-linearity tests are limited to LM tests based on Volterra expansions, (see e.g. Granger and Teräsvirta, 1993). These tests simply see if the squares and cross-product of the logarithms of household income and size provide additional explanatory ability to the log-linear regressions. Our heteroscedasticity tests are standard LM tests.

We find evidence of conditional income-related heteroscedasticity in the errors of the cross-section models based on the US budget surveys in 1950, 1960, and 1972, and in the 1980 and 1988 Dutch budget surveys (this is in addition to heteroscedasticity due to difference in cell sizes).[3] However, the functional form of the conditional variance is not a simple log-linear form, and even after controlling for heteroscedasticity, we find evidence of non-linearity in conditional mean. These results lead us to the conclusion that non-linearity of the micro relationship is more complex than log-linear form, and hence the functional form of the aggregate model will not be the same as the micro model, even if the mean-scaling assumption is correct.

3. PRELIMINARY MEASUREMENT EXERCISES (FOR THE USA 1913–41)

We first ran Tobin's original cross-sectional regression using his (uncorrected) data for 1941, and obtained[4]

$$\log FOODCON_i = \underset{(0.10)}{0.82} + \underset{(0.03)}{0.56} \log HINC_i + \underset{(0.04)}{0.25} \log AHSIZE_i + \hat{\varepsilon}_i \qquad 4$$

which agreed with Tobin's original specification, and with Izan (1980). Diagnostic specification tests showed strong evidence of heteroscedasticity and non-normality in the residuals,[5] and although these problems might have been due to the outliers noted by Izan (1980), we felt that they could also be due to the fact that the regression had been

---

[2] We approximated the joint pdf's of income and family size for the various US budget surveys, and used these to examine the mean-scaling assumption. This provided weak *ad-hoc* evidence against the validity of the mean scaling assumption for the USA. However, as discussed in Section 6, we found that the income distribution in the Netherlands is consistent with the mean scaling assumption.

[3] The LM test of additional heteroscedasticity, under the maintained assumption that error variance is inversely proportional to cell size, is derived along the lines of Breusch and Pagan (1979) or Engle (1984).

[4] Throughout this paper, the computations were done with ECSLIB, EVIEWS, GAUSS, MICROFIT, PC-GIVE and SAS. The graphs were generated by EVIEWS.

[5] *P*-values for a White (1980) heteroscedasticity test and a Jarque-Bera (1987) normality test were 0.012 and 0.000, respectively.

run on grouped data. An LM test which looked for whether heteroscedasticity was a function of the reciprocal of the group size, strongly rejected the null of homoscedasticity, indicating that a weighted regression was appropriate. Running the appropriate weighted regression, we obtained

$$\log FOODCON_i = \underset{(0.07)}{0.73} + \underset{(0.02)}{0.59} \log HINC_i + \underset{(0.03)}{0.23} \log AHSIZE_i + \hat{\varepsilon}_i. \qquad 5$$

Tests for heteroscedasticity and non-normality in the residuals now failed to find evidence of misspecification, leading us to conclude that Izan's outliers were not really outliers after all.

Next, we considered the appropriateness of Tobin's specification of the consumption function. Tobin had chosen the log-linear specification because he believed that consumption was non-linear in income and household size, but he wanted to account for this non-linearity in a way that would not jeopardize his subsequent aggregation arguments. Our LM tests for omitted non-linearity indicated that the log-linear specification was inappropriate, and that the following (weighted) regression better approximated consumption:

$$\log FOODCON_i = \underset{(0.11)}{0.91} + \underset{(0.04)}{0.54} \log HINC_i - \underset{(0.22)}{0.43} \log AHSIZE_i$$
$$+ \underset{(0.08)}{0.17} (\log AHSIZE_i)(\log HINC_i) \qquad 6$$
$$+ \underset{(0.09)}{0.14} (\log AHSIZE_i)^2 + \hat{\varepsilon}_i.$$

Diagnostic tests based on this specification failed to find any evidence of misspecification, and the implied elasticities (calculated at the means of the regression variables) were 0.62 (for income) and 0.26 (for family size).

Given the evidence of non-linearities in the family consumption function, it seemed unlikely that an aggregate consumption function would have the simple log-linear form assumed by Tobin. Instead, the aggregate (family) function could be expected to contain quadratic and higher-order terms in the logarithms of both income and family size, and the (per capita) aggregate function could be expected to contain higher order terms in the logarithm of income (assuming family size remained constant).[6] From Stoker's (1986) observation that changes in microeconomic distributions introduce dynamics into the aggregate equation, it is also reasonable to expect extra dynamics in the aggregate equations, and not just the first lag of the logarithm of income, as Tobin assumed.

An analysis of the residuals of Tobin's estimated aggregate function (his Equation (25) which relates to 1913–41) shows that they trend downwards, and, with a Dickey–Fuller (τ) test statistic of -2.73, it appears that they are not stochastically stationary. This indicates severe dynamic misspecification, and suggests that this equation cannot be viewed as a long-run (cointegrating) relationship. Relaxing Tobin's 'poolability restriction' that the elasticity of income is 0.56 leads to a regression with stochastically stationary residuals (the relevant Dickey–Fuller (μ) test statistic is -3.65). Hence it appears that the dynamic misspecification in Tobin's aggregate equation is largely due to the pooling restriction. However, the unrestricted equation still shows evidence of misspecification. A Chow test

---

[6] Tobin claimed that family size was constant, but this is not apparent from the data we had at hand. Our calculations suggest that average family size was 4.55 in 1913, and had dropped to 3.35 by 1941.

with a break between 1927 and 1928 shows evidence of structural change (the p-value for the test is 0.0131), and a Reset test strongly rejects the null of correct specification. Further, omitted variable tests find strong evidence for the presence of a (log of) family size variable, as well as for quadratic terms in the (log of) family size and the (log of) income variables. The first of these results is consistent with a failure of Tobin's assumption that family size did not change, while the second supplies evidence of a non-linearity in food consumption.

Tobin used price as the dependent variable in his aggregate equation because of endogeneity considerations, but Stone, in his comments on Tobin and in his previous work, used consumption. We followed Stone, since normalization on consumption led to a clearer rejection of non-stationary residuals (with a Dickey–Fuller test statistic of -4.10), and also since endogeneity is not a problem for consistently estimating cointegrating regressions. Our preferred long-run per capita equation for 1913–41 was

$$
\begin{aligned}
\log TOBPCFC_t = \; & 4.76 \; - \; 2.05 \; \log TOBPCY_t \; - \; 0.22 \; \log TOBFP_t \\
& (0.83) \quad (0.62) \qquad\qquad\qquad (0.02) \\[4pt]
& + \; 0.05 \; \log TOBNF_t \; + \; 0.43 \; (\log TOBPCY_t)^2 + \hat{\varepsilon}_t. \\
& \;\; (0.02) \qquad\qquad\quad (0.14)
\end{aligned}
\tag{7}
$$

The R^2 for this specification was 0.91, and the implied elasticities (calculated at the means of the regression variables) were 0.25 (for income) and 0.22 (for price). The residuals of this equation appeared to be stochastically stationary, and specification tests for serial correlation, heteroscedasticity, and omitted variables failed to find any evidence of misspecification. A per family consumption function was also estimated for comparison. This long-run equation was

$$
\begin{aligned}
\log TOBPHFC_t = \; & 7.12 \; - \; 3.03 \; \log TOBPHY_t \; - \; 0.26 \; \log TOBFP_t \\
& (1.55) \quad (0.93) \qquad\qquad\qquad (0.04) \\[4pt]
& + \; 0.05 \; \log TOBNF_t + \; 0.78 \; \log(POP/NOH_t) \\
& \;\; (0.02) \qquad\qquad\quad (0.06) \\[4pt]
& + \; 0.50 \; (\log TOBPHY_t)^2 + \hat{\varepsilon}_t \\
& \;\; (0.14)
\end{aligned}
\tag{8}
$$

where the $TOBPH$ ... variables are their $TOBPC$ ... analogues, multiplied by POP_t/NOH_t, so that they provide per-household rather than per capita measures. The per-household equation had an R^2 of 0.94, and implied elasticities (calculated at the means of the regression variables) of 0.29 (for income) and 0.26 (for price). Specification tests based on this regression failed to find any problems with the model.

Our family cross-sectional equation and our family aggregate time-series equation suggested quite different income (and family size) elasticities. Both equations were non-linear in (log) income, which shows first, that the log-linear specification is inappropriate, and second, that changes in the mean of (log) income provided insufficient information about how the distribution of (log) income affects (the log of) food consumption. Our estimate of income elasticity comes from the cross-sectional equation (and is 0.62), because we have found sufficient evidence to suggest that the parameters in the aggregate time-series equation cannot be interpreted as microeconomic coefficients.

4.　MEASUREMENT FOR THE EXTENDED US DATA SET

4.1.　Estimates from the Budget Surveys for 1941, 1950, 1960, and 1972

Table I shows a summary of the estimation and specification test results of our analysis of the four available US budget surveys. All observations are weighted by the cell size or estimated population of households in that category, whichever is available. Observation

Table I. Elasticity estimates from US budget surveys

	$\partial \ln(FOODCON)/$ $\partial \ln(y)$	$\partial \ln(FOODCON)/$ $\partial \ln(N)$	$H_0 : \sigma_i^2 = (\sigma^2/n_i)$vs $H_1 : \sigma_i^2 = f(\ln Y_i)/n_i$	H_0 : log-linear
BS41	0.59 (0.02)[b]	0.23 (0.02)	Not rejected	Rejected[c]
BS41	0.54 + 0.08 $\ln N$[d] (0.02)　(0.03)	−0.43 + 0.08 $\ln Y$ (0.16)　(0.03) + 0.12 $\ln N$[e] (0.05)	Not rejected	—
BS50	0.52 (0.02)	0.29 (0.01)	Rejected	Not rejected
BS50[a]	0.42 (0.05)	0.33 (0.03)	Rejected	Rejected
BS60	0.54 (0.01)	0.33 (0.01)	Rejected	Not rejected
BS60[a]	0.42 (0.05)	0.38 (0.02)	Rejected	Not rejected
BS72	0.35 (0.02)	0.45 (0.01)	Rejected	Rejected
BS72[a]	0.38 (0.02)	0.37 (0.05)	Rejected	Rejected
BS72	−0.62 + 0.11 $\ln Y$ (0.16)　(0.02) − 0.03 $\ln N$[f] (0.01)	0.70 − 0.03 $\ln Y$[g] (0.14)　(0.01)	Rejected	—
Pooled[h]	0.48 (0.02)	0.34 (0.01)	Rejected	Rejected

In this table Y and N denote household income ($HINC$) and average household size ($AHSIZE$), respectively.

[a]Socio-demographic variables were included in the regression. These variables are age and education of the household head, percentage of homeowners and average number of full-time earners for 1950 and 1960 budget surveys. For the analysis of 1972 budget survey, these are age of the household head, percentage of homeowners and percentage of nonwhites.

[b]All standard errors reported in parentheses underneath the parameter estimates are White's heteroscedasticity-consistent standard errors. All estimations are weighted by the cell size or estimated population of households within the cell, whichever was available. Tests for log-linearity are also performed using heteroscedasticity-consistent covariance matrices.

[c]The level of significance of the reported tests is 5%, although in almost all cases where the null hypotheses were rejected, the p-values were less than 0.01.

[d]The value at sample mean is 0.61. The 10th, 50th, and 90th percentiles within the sample are (0.54, 0.62, 0.68).

[e]The value at sample mean is 0.25. The 10th, 50th, and 90th percentiles within the sample are (0.13, 0.27, 0.38).

[f]The value at sample mean is 0.35. The 10th, 50th, and 90th percentiles within the sample are (0.25, 0.34, 0.45).

[g]The value at sample mean is 0.46. The 10th, 50th, and 90th percentiles within the sample are (0.44, 0.46, 0.48).

[h]The pooled regression includes year dummies to account for year-specific price and other effects. Socio-demographic variables were not included, since 1941 budget survey does not include any such information.

weights are normalized prior to pooling of the budget surveys. All logically inconsistent observations (such as the larger than five-person households with income between 0 and 1000 in 1960, for whom an average income of 2079 is recorded!) are deleted prior to the analysis.

The main conclusions from this table can be summarized as follows:

1. Even after controlling for the effects of cell size, there is significant heteroscedasticity in the errors of the cross-section regressions for the 1950, 1960, and 1972 budget surveys. Breusch–Pagan tests of the null of no heteroscedasticity other than the cell size effect, versus the alternative that the variance depends on logarithm of income and the square of the logarithm of income, reject the null. As we discussed in Section 2, even if the log-linearity and mean-scaling assumptions were satisfied, the exact correspondence between micro and macro parameters is broken by this type of heteroscedasticity.

2. The data reject the hypothesis that the parameters across the four cross-sections are equal. We find significant evidence that the income elasticity of food has declined over the four decades, whereas the family size elasticity of demand has increased. The data only support pooling of the 1950 and 1960 budget surveys, and provide strong evidence that the family food demand schedules for 1941 and 1972 are different from each other, and different from the 1950–60 schedule. If we control for other relevant characteristics such as the age of the head of household, then this lowers the income elasticity estimated from the 1950 and 1960 budget surveys, but this does not alter the qualitative conclusion that the demand schedule is different in different decades.

3. Our analysis of the budget surveys for 1941 and 1972 finds significant evidence that the functional form of the consumption function is non-log-linear, and this implies that the elasticities are themselves, functions of the logarithm of household income and size.[7] Also, it seems that in addition to the decline in the average household's income elasticity of food consumption over 1941–72, the variation of this elasticity over the population of households has increased (compare the (0.54, 0.68) income elasticity range for 1941 to the (0.25, 0.45) range for 1972 in Table I). The opposite is true for the family size elasticity. Here, the value of the size elasticity for the average household has increased over the decades, but its range over the population of households is tighter in 1972 than it was in 1941.

Our overall conclusion from the analysis of this section is that the log-linear homoscedastic specification is inadequate for modelling household food consumption. Furthermore, the food consumption schedule has not been constant over decades. Because of the complex trends in the food demand elasticities one has to use available data from the most recent years if one wants to analyze the short- to medium-run effect of income redistribution policies on the demand for food. The implication of our results for the pooling of cross-section and time-series data is that the micro relationship is too complex to have any straightforward implication for the aggregate model without knowledge of income distribution. In a later section we discuss the implication of non-linearity in the

---

[7] This accords with the result of Benus, Kmenta, and Shapiro (1976) who use data from Panel Study of Income Dynamics for the years 1968 to 1972.

micro relation for the macro equation, assuming a simple parametric form for the income distribution.

4.2. An Aggregate Food Expenditure Schedule for the USA

Does our analysis of budget survey data imply that we cannot find, or should not even attempt to find, a constant parameter, log-linear relationship between aggregate food consumption and aggregate income? Our answer is no. While it is true that the cross-section analysis implies that exact log-linear aggregation does not hold, this does not necessarily preclude the possibility of a constant-parameter log-linear relationship among the macro variables. It does, however, warn us that the macro parameters should not be interpreted as micro elasticities, and that we should carefully analyze the dynamics of the aggregate equation to ensure that the effects of changes in the income/family distributions have been appropriately captured. It also warns us to be 'on the look-out' for non-linearities; if they are present in the micro equations then they may also be present in the macro equation.

For the longer US time series, we used the aggregate expenditure on food and aggregate income series and divided them by the number of households to construct per-household, rather than per capita variables. The per-household variables then corresponded more closely to the available budget survey variables, and this also avoided the need to assume that the average household size had remained constant. Per-household expenditure on food was then deflated by the food price to yield real per-household consumption of food. The logarithm of this variable was our dependent variable, and the logarithms of nominal income per-household, food price, non-food price and average household size constituted our independent variables.

Detailed analysis of the time-series data revealed that finding a constant-parameter model for the entire sample period was difficult. A glance at the graphs of the variables (see Figure 1) indicates that the post-war period is quite different from the earlier period. This is especially apparent in the consumption variable. Splitting the sample into two parts, fitting separate models for the two subsamples, and looking at the total of the error sum of squares of the two subsamples, we found that the year 1948 was chosen by the data as the most likely break point. Incidentally, this year corresponds to the date that the Dutch time-series data starts. Hence we have focused attention on building an aggregate model for the post-war period.[8] Our analysis covers the years from 1948 to 1989.

Preliminary analysis suggested that all five variables had unit roots, and the residuals of a static regression of the dependent on the independent variables were stationary, suggesting that the variables were cointegrated. The Johansen test of cointegration indicated that there was only one cointegrating relationship among the variables. Since the food consumption equation was the only object of interest, we chose a single equation rather than a system method for estimation. An efficient estimate of the cointegrating vector was derived from a dynamic OLS regression (Stock and Watson, 1993) which included one lag and one lead of the income and price variables, and this was used

---

[8] Attempts to include the earlier observations by interacting a dummy variable with all independent variables were unsuccessful, because the dynamics of the earlier part of the data, especially the cointegration properties of the variables, were quite different from the latter part.

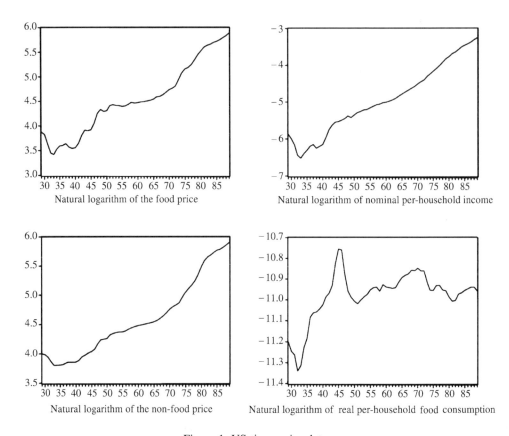

Figure 1. US time-series data

to build an error correction model. Household size and the non-food price variables contributed little and were dropped from the specification to obtain the model:

$$\Delta \ln(AGGEXPF /FP * NOH)_t = - \underset{(0.79)}{4.13} + \underset{(0.10)}{0.32} \; \Delta \ln(AGGY /NOH)_t$$

$$- \underset{(0.06)}{0.53} \; \Delta \ln(FP)_t - \underset{(0.12)}{0.62} \; ECT_{t-1} + \hat{\varepsilon}_t \qquad 9$$

$$ECT_t = \ln \left(\frac{AGGEXPF}{FP * NOH} \right)_t - 0.40 \ln \left(\frac{AGGY}{NOH} \right)_t - 0.51 \ln(FP)_t \quad ESS = 0.0040.$$

This model passed a battery of specification tests assessing its dynamic adequacy and parameter stability. The common factor restriction of equality of the short- and long-run elasticities was tested by comparing the error sum of squares of the above model with the sum of squares of the errors of the regression of *ECT* on a constant and its own lag (*ESS* = 0.0042). The common factor restrictions could not be rejected in the above model, so they were imposed. The level variables were quasi-differenced using the first autocorrelation of *ECT* and the dynamic OLS regression was re-estimated with the quasi-differenced data, which led to new estimates of the parameters of the cointegrating relationship. This procedure was iterated until it converged to the following estimated model:

$$\ln \left(\frac{AGGEXPF}{FP * NOH} \right)_t = -6.57 + 0.41 \ln \left(\frac{AGGY}{NOH} \right)_t - 0.52 \ln(FP)_t + \hat{u}_t$$

$$\hat{u}_t = 0.49\hat{u}_{t-1} + \hat{\varepsilon}_t$$

10

which implies that the elasticity of per-household real expenditure on food with respect to per-household income is 0.41 and the elasticity with respect to food price is 0.52. We do not attach any micro-structural interpretation to the estimated entities.

We feel that the homogeneity assumption for the aggregate data can be tested, but that the result of this test does not have implications about rationality or money illusion for any specific household. Additional tests indicate that the logarithm of per-household real expenditure on food is not cointegrated with *real* per-household income. This indicates a failure of homogeneity in the long run. Further, if we ignore the common factor restrictions and test for short-run homogeneity in the context of an unrestricted error correction model, then short-run homogeneity is also clearly rejected for the aggregate schedule.

In summary, we find a simple, stable, log-linear relationship between the logarithms of real per-household expenditure on food and nominal per-household income and food price, despite the fact that our cross-section analysis of the previous section indicates that the individual household demand schedule for food in 1972 was quite different from 1950 to 1960. The dynamics of this schedule satisfy two common factor restrictions which allow us to express the relationship as a regression in levels with autoregressive errors.[9] The hypothesis of the homogeneity of the aggregate schedule is clearly rejected.

5. MEASUREMENT WITH RELATED INFORMATION

The Dutch budget-survey data leads to the same conclusion as the US budget-survey data; i.e. that the log-linear homoscedastic specification is inadequate for modelling household food consumption. We conclude that even if the assumption of mean scaling of the income distribution is correct, attempts to relate the time-series estimate of the coefficient of the logarithm of income to the representative individual's income elasticity of food consumption would be incorrect. We direct our modelling search in two separate directions: (a) finding cross-section models that allow the elasticity of income to depend on household income, size, and other characteristics (this might be useful for policy analysis), and (b) developing a fixed-parameter dynamic specification of the aggregate data for the purpose of forecasting aggregates. We make no attempt to pool the cross-section and time-series information. Later, in the own task section, we derive the specification implied for the aggregate model by a cross-section log-quadratic specification, assuming that the distribution of income is Gamma.

---

[9] Recall that the aggregation over households leads to a residual term that is a function of all other parameters (other than mean income) of the income distribution. In theory, these parameters can be time varying as long as their variation is independent of the mean income. Hence, one can justifiably expect to find a regression model with autoregressive residuals for the aggregate variables.

5.1. Data Anomalies and the Question of Group Averaging

The Dutch budget-survey data descriptions warned us that the income data were top-coded, but did not tell us that all the consumption items were also top-coded.[10] We stumbled on this discovery by looking at the empirical density of food consumption. We decided to eliminate all households which were top-coded in either the income or food categories, and since there was little correlation between the income top-coded households and the food top-coded households, this involved deleting more than 200 observations from each of the budget surveys.

The budget surveys do not report average household size for households with five or more members. We derived the average size of these households by combining information about the total population and number of households from the 1980 and 1988 time-series data, with the cross-section information. Our estimates of average size of the households of five or more members are 5.6 for 1980 and 5.7 for 1988, and we use these estimates in our subsequent cross-sectional analysis.

We considered organizing the data into income groups, similar to the US data, and working with group averages. On the surface, this looked like a way to attenuate the errors in measurement of income and food consumption, and to obtain high measures of R^2. However, for obvious reasons R^2 for the group-averaged models and individual household models are not comparable, and as shown by Pakes (1982),[11] grouping based on a variable which is suspected to be measured with errors will make the OLS estimates of the group-averaged data biased and inconsistent. We therefore conducted our analysis on the individual household data. This opened up the possibility of investigating the effects of household characteristics on food consumption, leading us to a better analysis of the effects of changes in income distribution and demographics on food consumption. The complex non-linearity that we find in the individual household regressions points to the fact that group averaging would have been inappropriate and might have led to a substantial loss of information.

5.2. Estimates from Dutch Budget Survey

Table II provides a summary of our estimation results based on the 1980 and 1988 budget surveys.[12] We have also included the results of the misspecified log-linear models for comparison purposes. All estimations are weighted with the reported observation weights, but tests indicate additional heteroscedasticity related to income. We created dummy variables for all but one class for each of the categorical variables which were included in the Dutch budget survey. These included age, education, and labour force participation status of the head of the household (for a full list of these variables, refer to the organizers' data section). Our 'fully interacted' model includes these dummy variables and their interaction (i.e. product) with household income and household size.

The hypothesis that the 1980 and 1988 data can be pooled is rejected when the household characteristics are not fully interacted with income and size. When these interactions

---

[10] We reported this to the experiment organizers.

[11] We thank Peter Schmidt for this reference.

[12] We did not use the 1965 budget survey because of its coarse cell aggregation.

Table II. Elasticity estimates from the Dutch budget surveys[a]

	$\partial \ln(FOODCON)/\partial \ln Y$	$\partial \ln(FOODCON)/\partial \ln N$
BS80	0.34 (0.03)[c]	0.47 (0.02)
BS80[b]	0.30 (0.03)	0.46 (0.03)
BS80	$-1.8 + 0.2\ \ln Y - 0.2\ \ln N$[d] (0.43) (0.04) (0.03)	$2.7 - 0.2\ \ln Y - 0.2\ \ln N$[e] (0.33) (0.03) (0.05)
BS88	0.42 (0.06)	0.49 (0.04)
BS88[b]	0.37 (0.06)	0.49 (0.04)
BS88	$-2.1 + 0.3\ \ln Y - 0.2\ \ln N$[f] (1.0) (0.04) (0.03)	$2.6 - 0.2\ \ln Y - 0.2\ \ln N$[g] (0.52) (0.03) (0.06)
Pooled[h]	0.39 (0.04)	0.47 (0.03)

In this table *FOODCON* denotes household's expenditure on food (variable *V*11), and *Y* and *N* denote household's income (*HINC*) and size (*HSIZE*), respectively.
[a] The results of heteroscedasticity and non-linearity tests are not reported. The null of homoscedasticity is always rejected, and the null of linearity is rejected in all relevant cases.
[b] Socio-demographic variables are included in the regression. These variables are dummy variables characterizing age group, education level, and the labour force participation status of the household head. In the results reported in this table, these categorical variables are not interacted with income and size. The results of the fully interacted model are reported in the text.
[c] All standard errors reported in parentheses underneath the parameter estimates are White's heteroscedasticity consistent standard errors. All estimations are weighted by the reported weights. The estimates of the non-linear models are feasible GLS estimates which account for heteroscedasticity.
[d] The value at sample mean is 0.35. The 10th, 50th, and 90th percentiles within the sample are (0.21, 0.32, 0.47).
[e] The value at sample mean is 0.46. The 10th, 50th, and 90th percentiles within the sample are (0.25, 0.41, 0.69).
[f] The value at sample mean is 0.44. The 10th, 50th, and 90th percentiles within the sample are (0.32, 0.45, 0.60).
[g] The value at sample mean is 0.44. The 10th, 50th, and 90th percentiles within the sample are (0.20, 0.35, 0.61).
[h] The pooled regression includes year dummies to account for the year-specific price and other effects. The pooling hypothesis is rejected based on the log-linear model. However, the log-linear model is misspecified. The pooling hypothesis is not rejected when non-linearities are accounted for. See the text for the results.

are included, the pooling hypothesis is no longer rejected. The estimated *elasticity* schedules based on the pooled data set are:

$$\frac{\partial \ln(V11)}{\partial \ln(HINC)} = - \underset{(1.11)}{3.02} + \underset{(0.11)}{0.34}\ \ln(HINC) - \underset{(0.08)}{0.30}\ \ln(HSIZE)$$

$$- \underset{(0.003)}{0.01}\ Eduhh2 - \underset{(0.10)}{0.25}\ Eduhh5$$

$$\frac{\partial \ln(V11)}{\partial \ln(HSIZE)} = \underset{(0.78)}{3.84} - \underset{(0.08)}{0.30}\ \ln(HINC) - \underset{(0.08)}{0.18}\ \ln(HSIZE)$$

$$- \underset{(0.02)}{0.12}\ Agehh1 - \underset{(0.02)}{0.05}\ Agehh2 - \underset{(0.03)}{0.11}\ Agehh5$$

(11)

where the variable *V*11 is the household consumption expenditure on food, *HINC* and *HSIZE* are the household's income and size, *Eduhh2* is a dummy variable that is 1 if the head of the household has only primary school education and 0 otherwise, and *Eduhh5* is a similar dummy indicating that the head of household has had higher vocational education.[13] The age categories indicated by the $Agehh1$, $Agehh2$, and $Agehh5$ dummies are 12–34 years, 35–44 years, and 65 and older, respectively. These schedules imply mean income elasticities of 0.29 for 1980 and 0.34 for 1988, and mean family size elasticities of 0.46 for both years. To give an idea of how variable these elasticities are over the population of households, the 10th, 50th and 90th percentiles of the income elasticity are (0.06, 0.25, 0.49) in 1980 and (0.14, 0.35, 0.58) in 1988, and the corresponding values for the family size elasticities are (0.22, 0.39, 0.71) in 1980 and (0.17, 0.35, 0.68) in 1988. Our conclusion from this section is that the non-log-linearity of the micro consumption function and non-constancy of the conditional variance over the population are quite robust and do not disappear, even when controlling for household characteristics. However, the conclusion that the micro schedule is non-constant over time seems to fade away once we control for household characteristics other than income and size. This suggests to us that the apparent changes in the US micro consumption function documented in the previous section may not be so much due to the result of change in the behavioural parameters of different categories of households but rather of shifts in the distribution of households over categories. Proper investigation of this conjecture is not possible with the available data in this experiment.

5.3. Forecasts

We used a standard modern time-series approach based on a multivariate error correction model to develop our forecasts of aggregate consumption. Such an approach is largely atheoretical and not strongly tied to any theory about a (representative) consumer, but given our earlier conclusion that there are, at best, only weak relationships between this theory and macroeconomic aggregates, we felt that it was appropriate to simply model and forecast the aggregates directly from the data. Our information set included the (natural logarithms) of per thousand capita real expenditure on food consumption ($\ln RFC$), per thousand capita nominal income ($\ln Y$), the food price index ($\ln FP$), and a non-food price index ($\ln NFP$)[14] for 1948–88. We modelled real consumption expenditures rather than nominal expenditures so as to maintain comparability with the rest of this report.

---

[13] Perhaps the only curious result here is the effect of higher vocational training on the income elasticity. We are not familiar with the education system in the Netherlands and do not know what higher vocational training really entails to be able to explain this finding.

[14] We did not consider family consumption because of missing data on the number of households. The given nominal expenditures on food consumption were converted to the logarithms of real per thousand capita expenditures by the transformation

$$\ln RFC = \ln \left(\frac{v11}{p11^* POP} \right)$$

income was left in nominal terms and was converted to a log per capita measure by the transformation

$$\ln Y = \ln \left(\frac{AGGY}{POP} \right)$$

and the food price measure was $\ln FP = \ln(p11)$. Our non-food price index was 'backed out' from the total expenditures price index and the food price index using 1951 quantity weights, i.e.

$$\ln NFP = \ln \left[\frac{14\,424 \times p1 - 5502 \times p11}{8922} \right].$$

Table III. Cointegration analysis based on Johansen's procedure, the Netherlands, 1948–88

Null hypothesis	Test statistic	5% critical value
Cointegration rank is $r \leq 3$	$trace_3 = 4.96$	8.07
Cointegration rank is $r \leq 2$	$trace_2 = 11.64$	17.86
Cointegration rank is $r \leq 1$	$trace_1 = 31.88$	31.54
Cointegration rank is $r = 0$	$trace_0 = 68.87$	48.88

The analysis is based on a VAR(2) in levels, in which the intercept has not been restricted. Critical values for Johansen's tests are those given by Microfit 4.0.
Estimated error correction terms

$$\ln NFP + \underset{(0.08)}{0.86} \ln RFC - \underset{(0.03)}{1.49} \ln FP + 6.78$$

$$\ln Y - \underset{(0.16)}{1.94} \ln RFC - \underset{(0.07)}{1.11} \ln FP - 5.30$$

See footnote 14 in the text for the definition of each variable.

Preliminary tests on the data suggested that all four variables are integrated of order 1 and a cointegration analysis based on Johansen's (1988) test on a VAR(2) in levels found two cointegrating, or linear long-run relationships between the aggregate variables.[15] The results of the Johansen (1988) procedure are presented in Table III together with the estimated cointegrating relationships.

Renormalizing these estimated relationships shows that

$$\ln RFC - 1.72 \ln FP + 1.16 \ln NFP \text{ and}$$

$$\ln RFC - 0.52 \ln Y + 0.57 \ln FP$$

are stationary in the long run, and one might choose to interpret these relationships as 'supply' and 'demand', respectively, although caution is required with this interpretation because other linear combinations of these relationships are also stationary. We note that if one *does* interpret the second relation as an aggregate demand for food, then the implied income and price elasticities are 0.52 and −0.57, respectively, and the sum of the coefficients of the nominal variables is 0.05, which is close to the zero required by the homogeneity postulate.

The associated vector error correction model of $\Delta \ln RFC$, $\Delta \ln Y$, $\Delta \ln FP$ and $\Delta \ln NFP$ is presented in Table IV, together with a wide selection of model diagnostics. An interesting feature of this model is that the error correction has little direct influence on the growth of food consumption, although it clearly influences the growth rates of other variables in the system, which in turn influence consumption. While the model does not explain a large proportion of consumption growth (in that the consumption equation R^2 is only about 0.33), it does well given the limited information set used, and all diagnostics are favourable for making forecasts. Important features of the model include no evidence of residual serial correlation (suggesting that the model has well captured the dynamics

---

We did not directly calculate the non-food price index from the given non-food indices and expenditures because of an apparent rebasing 'glitch' in the clothing price index between 1950 and 1952. Our resulting index still has an 'outlier' in 1951, but this is much less pronounced than that in a directly calculated index.

[15] We also found weak evidence for the presence of a non-linear long-run relationship between the variables. However, we did not pursue this matter further, because of the difficulties associated with forecasting with non-linear models.

Table IV. Error correction model for the Netherlands (1948–88)

Explanatory variable	$\Delta \ln RFC$	Endogenous variable		
		$\Delta \ln Y$	$\Delta \ln FP$	$\Delta \ln NFP$
Estimated coefficients (with standard errors)				
Constant	0.023 (0.009)	0.070 (0.132)	0.037 (0.009)	0.036 (0.015)
$ECT1_{t-1}$	−0.011 (0.119)	0.410 (0.169)	0.732 (0.113)	0.431 (0.188)
$ECT2_{t-1}$	−0.120 (0.082)	−0.465 (0.116)	0.009 (0.078)	−0.205 (0.129)
$\Delta \ln RFC_{t-1}$	−0.469 (0.213)	−0.436 (0.302)	−0.067 (0.203)	−0.429 (0.337)
$\Delta \ln Y_{t-1}$	0.314 (0.116)	0.361 (0.150)	−0.114 (0.101)	0.010 (0.167)
$\Delta \ln FP_{t-1}$	−0.196 (0.169)	0.308 (0.239)	0.438 (0.161)	0.397 (0.267)
$\Delta \ln NFP_{t-1}$	−0.347 (0.147)	−0.615 (0.209)	−0.110 (0.140)	−0.062 (0.233)
Regression R^2	0.329	0.668	0.722	0.488
P-values for selected diagnostic tests				
H_0 : No 1st order SC	0.117	0.393	0.404	0.243
H_0 : No 2nd order SC	0.207	0.279	0.558	0.073
H_0 : No 3rd order SC	0.256	0.467	0.747	0.124
H_0 : No 1st order Arch	0.950	0.971	0.374	0.004
H_0 : Normal residuals	0.910	0.215	0.614	0.007
H_0 : No heteroscedasticity	0.846	0.340	0.830	0.063
H_0 : No omitted $(\Delta \ln Y)^2$	0.256	0.410	0.530	0.745
Reset test	0.139	0.637	0.116	0.470
Forecast Chow (1981–8)	0.670	0.962	0.503	0.993

See footnote 14 in the text for definitions of the variables. The error correction terms are those presented in Table III.

The apparent problems with the $\Delta \ln NFP$ equation are due to an outlier at the beginning of the sample. This outlier is due to the problem related to the rebasing of the index in 1951 (discussed in footnote 14 in the text). Since this relates to the beginning of the sample, it should not influence forecasts based on the model.

of the system, despite our failure to account for the possible long-run non-linearity noted above), and no evidence of parameter instability. The forecasting Chow tests all show that the model has predictive power towards the end of the sampled period. LM tests which look for evidence that the short-run dynamics of the system are non-linear fail to find any such evidence, and these, together with the other diagnostics, suggest that this simple VECM(1) has well captured the important features that characterize the dynamics of this system of interrelated aggregates.

We assumed that a food manufacturer would best understand forecasts of nominal per-capita expenditures on food consumption, or aggregate expenditures on food consumption, so we chose to forecast these, rather than simply present forecasts of $\Delta \ln RFC$. To develop such forecasts, we firstly reparameterized the estimated VECM(1) into the equivalent (restricted) VAR(2) in log-levels, and then used this to generate a sequence of one- to twelve-steps-ahead forecasts for each of $\ln RFC$, $\ln Y$, $\ln FP$, $\ln NFP$, and $\ln NFC = \ln RFC + \ln FP$. We estimated the standard errors associated with these forecasts by a simulation procedure based on 10 000 iterations.[16] The resulting forecasts, standard errors and 95% confidence intervals for $\ln RFC$ are presented in Table V. The model predicts that real food consumption per capita will grow over the next twelve years.

The forecasts and standard errors associated with $\ln NFC$ were then converted to levels to obtain the set of forecasts of per-capita expenditure on food, which are also presented

---

[16] Our estimates accounted for variation in the model's errors only, and did not allow for additional variation arising from the fact that the model parameters were estimated rather than known.

Table V. Consumption forecasts for the Netherlands (1989–2000) (with standard errors)

Year	ln RFC (log of real food consumption)	Variable Nominal per-capita expenditure on food (thousands of guilders)	Total nominal expenditure on food (millions of guilders)
1989	−4.61 (0.01)	4.13 (0.09)	61 065 (1394)
1990	−4.60 (0.02)	4.29 (0.14)	63 848 (2084)
1991	−4.58 (0.03)	4.56 (0.20)	66 614 (2960)
1992	−4.57 (0.04)	4.64 (0.26)	69 735 (3956)
1993	−4.55 (0.05)	4.85 (0.35)	73 187 (5226)
1994	−4.53 (0.05)	5.08 (0.44)	76 912 (6688)
1995	−4.52 (0.06)	5.33 (0.54)	80 899 (8273)
1996	−4.50 (0.06)	5.59 (0.66)	85 161 (10 040)
1997	−4.48 (0.07)	5.87 (0.78)	89 701 (11 936)
1998	−4.47 (0.07)	6.17 (0.91)	94 523 (13 978)
1999	−4.45 (0.07)	6.42 (1.05)	99 635 (16 155)
2000	−4.43 (0.08)	6.81 (1.20)	105 047 (18 488)

in Table V. These latter forecasts predict that per-capita expenditure on food will increase by about 70% over the 12-year forecasting period. Food prices (which are predicted to rise by about 42%) account for much of this increase.

We needed population projections to estimate total expenditure on food, and based these projections on a simple trended autoregression of the population growth rate, i.e.

$$\Delta \ln POP_t = \underset{(0.002)}{0.008} - \underset{(0.00005)}{0.0001T} + \underset{(0.144)}{0.509} \Delta \ln POP_{t-1} + \hat{\varepsilon}_t. \qquad 12$$

This regression fitted the data well (with an R^2 of 0.79), and showed no evidence of dynamic misspecification. Forecasts and standard errors associated with the per capita expenditures were then multiplied by the population estimates to obtain the forecasts for total consumption expenditures contained in Table V. Standard errors and confidence intervals were not adjusted to account for the uncertainty associated with the estimated population growth rate equation.

The resulting forecasts predict that total expenditures on food will increase over the 1989–2000 period, and will be around 100 000 million guilders by the year 2000. There is, of course, much uncertainty associated with these forecasts, particularly those relating to the latter half of the forecasting period, so that point estimates should be used with caution.

6. DIRECTIONS FOR FURTHER RESEARCH

Previous sections have documented that there are significant non-linearities in the conditional mean and/or the conditional variance of the micro consumption function. This raises the interesting question of what the implied functional form of the aggregate relationship would be, given these non-linearities in the micro functional form. The answer depends, of course, on the distribution of income. Given the functional form of the micro consumption function and the distribution of income, the functional form of the aggregate relationship can, in theory, be derived. We think this is of particular importance, since it will suggest how aggregate variables might be non-linearly cointegrated, a possibility that has been posed by Granger (1995), and which has not yet been satisfactorily explored, in our opinion.

We assume a simple parametric distribution function for income, namely a Gamma distribution. The Gamma density is usually expressed as a function of two parameters (θ_t, λ_t) and has a density given by

$$g(y_{it}; \theta_t, \lambda_t) = \frac{\lambda_t^{\theta_t}}{\Gamma(\theta_t)} (y_{it})^{\theta_t - 1} e^{-\lambda_t y_{it}} \qquad y_{it} > 0, \qquad\qquad 13$$

a mean of θ_t/λ_t and variance of θ_t/λ_t^2. Reparameterizing this density in terms of θ_t and the mean income Y_t we obtain:

$$g(y_{it}; \theta_t, Y_t) = \frac{1}{Y_t} \left[\frac{\theta_t^{\theta_t}}{\Gamma(\theta_t)} \left(\frac{y_{it}}{Y_t} \right)^{\theta_t - 1} e^{-\theta_t(y_{it}/Y_t)} \right] = \frac{1}{Y_t} g(z_{it}; \theta_t, \theta_t) \qquad 14$$

where $z_{it} = y_{it}/Y_t$ is the relative income of individual i to the mean income at time t. This shows that the Gamma distribution is mean-scaled. We find that this simple parametric form fits the Dutch data reasonably well.[17] Now suppose that the micro relation is log-quadratic:

$$\ln c_{it} = \alpha + \beta \ln y_{it} + \gamma (\ln y_{it})^2 + \varepsilon_{it} \qquad\qquad 15$$

implying:

$$c_{it} = e^{\alpha + \varepsilon_{it}} y_{it}^{\beta + \gamma \ln y_{it}} \qquad\qquad 16$$

which after some algebraic manipulations can be written as:

$$c_{it} = e^{\alpha + \varepsilon_{it}} z_{it}^{\gamma \ln z_{it}} z_{it}^{\beta + 2\gamma \ln Y_t} Y_t^{\beta + \gamma \ln Y_t}. \qquad\qquad 17$$

In previous sections we showed that the conditional variance of ε_{it} also depends on income, and we showed how that would introduce additional terms in the aggregate equation. Here, for the sake of exposition, we assume that higher moments of ε_{it} are independent of income. With that assumption, if we integrate the above equation over the entire population, we get the approximate[18] relationship:

$$C_t \simeq A(\theta_t) \Gamma(\beta + 2\gamma \ln Y_t + \theta_t) \theta_t^{-(\beta + 2\gamma \ln Y_t)} Y_t^{\beta + \gamma \ln Y_t} \qquad 18$$

which gives rise to the aggregate equation:

$$\ln C_t \simeq f(\theta_t) + \ln(\Gamma(\beta + 2\gamma \ln Y_t + \theta_t)) + (\beta - 2\gamma \ln \theta_t) \ln Y_t + \gamma (\ln Y_t)^2. \qquad 19$$

This indicates that the aggregate equation will have non-linear terms in addition to the log-quadratic terms, where the additional non-linear terms involve the other parameter of the income distribution θ_t. Even if the distribution of relative incomes does not change over time, i.e. $\theta_t = \theta$ for the period of study, the above relationship shows that the functional form of the aggregate relationship would be different from the micro consumption function.

---

[17] We considered a log-normal distribution first, but log-normality is strongly rejected by the Dutch data.
[18] The approximation is a result of ignoring the dependence of the covariance between $z_{it}^{\gamma \ln z_{it}}$ and $z_{it}^{\beta + 2\gamma \ln Y_t}$, on Y_t.

We estimated a Gamma density for the distribution of household income in 1980 and 1988 for the Netherlands. In these estimations, we also used the top-coded information. The top-code value is the average of income, given that income is greater than a threshold. The exact distribution of the average of truncated Gamma random variables is not available, and we used a normal approximation to this distribution. The mean and the variance of this normal approximation are:

$$E(\bar{y}_n | y > c) = \frac{\theta}{\lambda} \frac{1 - G_{\theta+1,\lambda}(c)}{1 - G_{\theta,\lambda}(c)}$$

$$\text{Var}(\bar{y}_n | y > c) = \frac{1}{n} \times \left\{ \frac{\theta(\theta+1)}{\lambda^2} \frac{1 - G_{\theta+2,\lambda}(c)}{1 - G_{\theta,\lambda}(c)} - \frac{\theta^2}{\lambda^2} \left[\frac{1 - G_{\theta+1,\lambda}(c)}{1 - G_{\theta,\lambda}(c)} \right]^2 \right\} \qquad 20$$

where $\bar{y}_n$ denotes the average of a random sample of n observations, θ is the parameter of interest, $\lambda = \theta/Y$, c is the top-code threshold, and $G_{\theta,\lambda}(c)$ stands for the cumulative density of a Gamma distribution with parameters θ and λ evaluated at c. The estimated parameters are $\hat{\theta}_{1980} = 4.8$ and $\hat{\theta}_{1988} = 4.4$, and these estimates strongly reject the null hypothesis that θ_{1980} and θ_{1988} are equal.

Time variation in θ_t, lack of correspondence between the available cross-section and time-series data (the weighted average of the cross-section income is more than 10 000 guilders less than the time-series data for that year), and other complications regarding the heteroscedasticity of errors and the joint distribution of household size and household income made us cease work on this project at this point. However, we think that outside of this experiment, the quality and the extent of data available to econometricians makes the idea of extracting the functional form of the macro equation from the estimates of the cross-section relation and the income distribution a feasible and worthwhile exercise.

7. CONCLUSION

In this project we have investigated whether we should expect the individual household and the aggregate consumption functions for food to have the same function form, or even if they have the same functional form, whether we should expect their parameters to be exactly the same. Like Tobin (1950), we have focused our investigation on the assumptions necessary for the micro–macro correspondence, rather than on the statistical tests of poolability of micro and macro data sets.

Our main conclusion is that there is no simple correspondence between the micro and macro consumption schedules for food. The reason is that there is no single constant food income elasticity for the entire population: the elasticity changes with income and household size, as well as other household characteristics. In addition, the dispersion of food consumption for households with the same characteristics also varies with their income. This complicated pattern of dependence of food consumption on income, breaks the exact micro–macro correspondence, even if Tobin's assumption about the income distribution is correct.

Throughout this research, we have tried, as much as possible, to choose macro variables which correspond more closely to the micro variables. In our analysis of the cross-section data we have either incorporated the heterogeneity of the variances in the estimation or used heteroscedasticity-consistent covariance matrices to make sure that our inferences are valid. In the analysis of time-series data we have paid special attention to the order of integration of our variables and the residuals of our regressions to safeguard against spurious regressions. Finally, we have subjected our models to a battery of specification tests to ensure that they capture the dynamic properties of the data and are sufficiently stable to be used for forecasting.

APPENDIX: SUMMARY OF THE LOGBOOK

We used our logbook to record our theoretical derivations, our data transformations, our experimental regressions, our calculations, and our various notes. It includes printouts of every regression that we ran, and every graph that we looked at, be it the plot of the actual series, the plot of estimated residuals, or the plot of the squares of estimated residuals. The process of compiling it was definitely useful, but we doubt that anyone other than us would have any practical use for it, because it would be too difficult for them to find their way through our jungle of annotated printouts and scrawled notes.

Our paper is the summary of the results of all of the analysis that is contained in the logbook, and we do not repeat these results here. Instead, we explain some of the more important decisions that shaped our research, and influenced the types of data analysis we chose to emphasize in this work.

Planning Stage

From the *Experiment Information Pack*, and in particular from the fact that only Chetty (1968), Maddala (1971), and Izan (1980) were cited from the voluminous literature on estimating consumption functions, we sensed that the organizers wanted participants to concentrate on statistical tests of whether the income elasticity estimated from the cross-sectional data is the same as that estimated from the time-series data sets. However, we felt that the concentration on such tests would be meaningless unless we had first established that they should theoretically be the same. Hence we decided to concentrate on examining whether the necessary conditions for aggregating micro specifications into analogous macro specifications were satisfied. Moreover, since many experts in time series and applied demand analysis were listed among the participants, we decided to leave comparisons of different methodologies and estimation methods to others, and make the correspondence of micro and macro functional forms the main theme of our research. We have high hopes that this line of research will be fruitful for the empirical investigation of non-linear cointegration among aggregate variables.

Task 1: Redoing Tobin's Work

In the cross-sectional work we were surprised that heteroscedasticity due to cell size was not suspected by Tobin, Maddala (1971) and Izan (1980). We also suspected heteroscedasticity due to income. We had to derive the LM tests of heteroscedasticity due to income, maintaining the hypothesis of heteroscedasticity due to cell size. Establishing the form of heteroscedasticity was necessary for correct inference about the omitted non-log-linear terms in the specification. Given the limited number of observations in the budget survey, we decided to test the log-linear specification against the log-quadratic alternative only. That was sufficient to reject the log-linear model. In the time-series work on Tobin's data set (1913–41), we explicitly concentrated on accounting for log-quadratic non-linearities which might have been present because of changes in the distributions of log family size and log income. We used exactly the same data as Tobin, and like Tobin, used base 10 for all logarithmic transformations.

Task 2: Using the Extended US Data

With the cross-sectional data the steps of analysis were the same as in Task 1: first test for heteroscedasticity, and, when appropriate, account for it when making inference about the omitted quadratic terms. Since data from three additional budget surveys were provided, we investigated whether the micro relationship was constant over time. We had to decide whether to use the additional socio-demographic variables that were available for these budget surveys. The addition of such conditioning variables, which are not independent of income in the micro equation, complicates the aggregation issue. Since different socio-demographic variables were provided for different budget surveys, many of these variables had missing values, and the number of observations in each budget survey was not sufficiently large, we decided not to put too much emphasis on socio-demographic influences. Table I shows that the inclusion of these variables in the regressions did not account for the evidence of non-log-linearity of the specification.

There were more decisions to be made with the time-series data. We had to choose which series to use first. The food disappearance index was provided from 1912 to 1976, while aggregate expenditure on food was provided from 1929 to 1989. We decided to use the latter since it corresponded more closely to the cross-section measure of food consumption in the budget surveys. For the same reason, we decided to use per-household rather than per capita variables. For reasons that we have discussed in the text, we concentrated on data from 1948 to 1989. While we looked at system methods using a Johansen procedure, we abandoned this because we found evidence of only one cointegrating relationship, we were interested in only one of the equations, and we did not have a long data series. Our choice of one lag and one lead in the dynamic OLS regression was dictated by the small sample size.

Task 3: Measurement with Related Information

Household level data was available for the Netherlands, which made the investigation of micro–macro correspondence of functional forms more precise. We had to deal with top-coded income and consumption data, which we eventually did not use in our consumption regressions. The large number of available observations allowed a more detailed investigation of the effects of the household's socio-demographic characteristics on its food consumption behaviour. We constructed binary variables corresponding to different levels of education and age categories of the head of the household, and we investigated the effect of these characteristics on the intercept and the slope coefficients of the food equation by entering these dummy variables and their products with income and household size in the regression. The availability of household level data also allowed us to explicitly study the shape of the income distribution over households. The derivation of the functional form of the aggregate equation implied by aggregating log-quadratic micro equations with respect to this income distribution was what we assigned to ourselves as our 'own task'.

Task 4: Forecasting

For forecasting, we simply concentrated on building a conventional VECM which was consistent with the limited data we had at hand. Given that we knew very little about food consumption in Netherlands, and that we were explicitly told not to look at other data, we felt that this sort of general multivariate time-series approach was the most appropriate. A VAR(2)/VECM(1) with two cointegrating vectors was chosen on the basis of data; restrictions were not imposed on the constants because we saw no *a-priori* reason to do this. We were concerned that our forecasts for nominal consumption were high, but noted that the standard errors were wide, and that we had no reason not to believe our predictions, given our lack of knowledge about food consumption behaviour and population dynamics in the Netherlands. Due to time constraints and our ignorance about what we were trying to forecast, we did not allocate further time to the development of alternative forecasts.

ACKNOWLEDGEMENTS

We thank Jan Magnus, Mary Morgan and the *Journal of Applied Econometrics* for organizing 'The Experiment in Applied Econometrics'. We also thank Genevieve Peters, (Kelsey) Dan Wei, and Jingze Xi for research assistance. The US data are compiled from various US government publications (see the organizers' data chapters for details). We thank Statistics Netherlands for use of the Dutch data.

REFERENCES

Benus, J., J. Kmenta and H. Shapiro (1976), 'The dynamics of household budget allocation to food expenditures', *The Review of Economics and Statistics*, 129–38.
Breusch, T. S. and A. R. Pagan (1979), 'A simple test for heteroscedasticity and random coefficient variation', *Econometrica*, 47–58.
Chetty, V. K. (1968), 'Pooling of time series and cross section data', *Econometrica*, **36**, 279–90.
Deaton, A. (1992), *Understanding Consumption*, Oxford University Press, Oxford.
Engle, R. F. (1984), 'Wald, likelihood ratio and Lagrange multiplier tests in econometrics', in Z. Griliches and M. Intriligator (eds), *Handbook of Econometrics*, Vol. 2, North-Holland, Amsterdam.
Granger, C. W. J. (1995), 'Modelling non-linear relationships between extended-memory variables', *Econometrica*, **63**, 265–80.
Granger, C. W. J. and T. Teräsvirta (1993), *Modelling Dynamic Nonlinear Relationships*, Oxford University Press, Oxford.
Jarque, C. M. and A. K. Bera (1987), 'A test for normality of observations and regression residuals', *International Statistical Review*, **55**, 163–72.
Johansen, S. (1988), 'Statistical analysis of cointegration vectors', *Journal of Economic Dynamics and Control*, **12**, 231–54.
Izan, H. Y. (1980), 'To pool or not to pool: a reexamination of Tobin's food demand problem', *Journal of Econometrics*, **13**, 391–402.
Lewbel, A. (1992), 'Aggregation with log-linear models' *Review of Economic Studies*, **59**, 635–42.
Maddala, G. S. (1971), 'The likelihood approach to pooling cross-section and time-series data', *Econometrica*, **39**, 939–53.
Magnus, J. R. and M. S. Morgan (1995), 'An experiment in applied econometrics: call for participants', *Journal of Applied Econometrics*, **10**, 213–16.
Pakes, A. (1982), On the asymptotic bias of Wald-type estimators of a straight line when both variables are subject to error', *International Economic Review*, **23**, 491–7.
Stock, J. H. and M. W. Watson (1993), 'A simple estimator of cointegrating vectors in higher order integrated systems', *Econometrica*, **61**, 783–820.

Stoker, T. M. (1986), 'Simple tests of distributional effects on macroeconomic equations', *Journal of Political Economy*, **94**, 763–95.

Stoker, T. M. (1982), 'The use of cross-sectional data to characterize macro functions', *Journal of the American Statistical Association*, **77**, 369–80.

Tobin, J. (1950), 'A statistical demand function for food in the USA', *Journal of the Royal Statistical Society, Series A*, **113**, Part II, 113–41 [reprinted in Chapter 2, this volume].

White, H. L. (1980), 'A heteroscedasticity-consistent covariance matrix and a direct test for heteroscedasticity', *Econometrica*, **48**, 817–38.

COMMENTS BY PROFESSOR PETER SCHMIDT *(Michigan State University)*

This is a nice paper. The analysis shows thought and care, and the authors use 'modern' techniques so that one does get a feel for the difference that it makes to have available the results of forty-five years of econometric innovation since Tobin's paper.

This paper focuses on the micro relationship as the economically meaningful one. Because the model is not found to be log-linear, and because the error in the micro-equation is not independent of income (due to income-related heteroscedasticity), it is argued that the aggregate time-series model implied by the micro-model will not be of the same form as the micro-model and will not have the same values for elasticities or other parameters. This discussion is a partially successful attempt to explain one of the major puzzles in Tobin's paper, namely, the lack of correspondence between the micro and macro-income elasticities. It might be noted, however, that the paper shows that the effect of conditional heteroscedasticity would be to make the macro-elasticity greater than the micro-elasticity, the opposite of what occurs in the data, if $\omega_1 > 0$ (greater variance with higher income).

Section 6 also addresses the temporal aggregation question. The macro relation is derived for the case that the micro-relation is log-quadratic and the distribution of income is gamma. The macro-relation is not log-quadratic and the parameters would change if the parameter of the distribution of income changes. Can these results or similar ones be put into a positive form, to explain (or 'encompass') the estimated macro-relationships actually found? That would constitute a more convincing explanation of the puzzle in Tobin's results.

The authors make repeated use of a battery of specification tests, in the form of LM tests. Not everyone will like such extensive testing, without regard to questions like overall size, but I find that it increases my faith in the final models. For example, I like the reanalysis of the Tobin cross-section using formal specification tests. The interaction of family size and income and the non-log-linearity with respect to family size are believable and of some importance, (e.g. with respect to the aggregation question). Also, the conclusion about Izan's outliers not being outliers when heteroscedasticity is taken into account is interesting.

In the time-series data, a stable macro-relationship is found. Because of the aggregation question, it is viewed as atheoretical, and useful mainly for forecasting purposes. It is interesting that Tobin's time-series relationship fails a cointegration test (though it passes it if the cross-sectional elasticity is not imposed). By 1950, strong error autocorrelation should have been noticed and should have been regarded as important, even without modern cointegration theory to suggest what to do about it.

For the extended US time-series data, the authors use only the post-WWII data. The testing and imposition of the common factor restriction is neat, and something one would not have thought about in 1950. The same is true, obviously, of the unconstrained 'dynamic regression'. But the authors don't report a 1950-style regression, so I don't know if it makes a difference. That might have been interesting.

Analysis of the Dutch cross-sections is at the individual level. The paper argues, correctly, that grouping is not a successful solution to the problem of measurement error (current income instead of permanent income). I believe the literature, especially in development economics, does provide some guidance on how measurement error in consumption and income can be accommodated. However, this paper (like the other papers) did not really pursue this topic.

The Dutch data from 1980 and 1988 could not be pooled with a simple specification, but could have been with a more complicated specification that included household characteristics like age and education of head of household, and lots of interactions. The average income elasticities (0.29 for 1980 and 0.34 for 1988) are lower than for the USA. The reason is not clear. I would be curious to see what elasticities would be produced if the Dutch data were grouped.

The forecasting exercise is a relatively straightforward exercise in the estimation and interpretation of a cointegrated VAR. Unit-roots are relevant for forecasting, for two reasons, namely (i) the obvious one that innovations are persistent, and (ii) the fact that estimation of deterministic trend is potentially seriously biased if unit-roots are not taken into account. I can't tell how much this matters, empirically. The forecasts seem within reason. Since forecasts begin with 1989 and it is now 1997, we could violate the rules of the Experiment slightly and see how the forecasts have done so far. I presume that, if the rules of the Experiment did not forbid use of other data, we might try to improve the forecasts in some ways. For example, demographers certainly can make very accurate forecasts of population size by age; they would not use an AR model.

COMMENTS BY PROFESSOR J. S. CRAMER (University of Amsterdam)

This paper is distinguished by the great care taken by the authors to explain and justify their every move, and by their resolve to meet the central challenge of the experiment heads-on. As they see it, this is the explicit reconciliation of food demand equations at the micro- and the macro-economic level by theoretical arguments rather than by a direct comparison of actual estimates from either type of evidence. Their strategy is to start at the micro-level and to perfect the analysis of the cross-section data before attempting the construction of the corresponding macro-relation. But it turns out that it is impossible to obtain in this way a specification of the aggregate relation that is sufficiently simple to permit estimation by the usual methods.

Data limitations and some curious oversights restrict this venture. At the micro-economic level, the authors virtually use all the available information, but they do not discuss such obvious deficiencies of the data as the measurement of family size by the number of persons; still these might have thrown some light on the non-linearities they find. There is also very little discussion of actual consumer behaviour or of the values of the elasticity estimates obtained. At the macro-level, more attention could have been paid to the mixture of real and nominal variables in the same regression equations, this in view of the vast increases in the price level over the last fifty years.

When the authors find that the aggregate relation is too complicated for estimation, they do not pursue the matter but abandon it rather suddenly for something entirely different

(Section 4.2). A similar shift occurs when they tackle the forecasting task by a method that bears almost no relation to the earlier results (Section 5.3). In this they have probably been hampered by time constraints: they dutifully perform the tasks set by the organizers, and this may have prevented more reflection about the unity of the various parts.

The final paragraph, where the authors are on their own, is a very interesting attempt to give empirical substance to an aggregate relation derived from a micro-model. It is a pity that the authors have been here discouraged too soon by technical problems. Even when it is too difficult to *estimate* an aggregate relation with the requisite properties, it should be feasible to use the theoretical aggregate relation derived from the budget studies to track the actual movement of food consumption.

COMMENTS BY PROFESSOR M. HASHEM PESARAN (Trinity College, Cambridge)

The main focus of this paper is on non-linearities in the cross-sectional specification of the food consumption function, and the implications that such non-linearities may have for aggregate time-series models. The other aggregation problems, namely aggregation over commodities and aggregation across individuals with different income (expenditure) elasticities, are not addressed.

The section on aggregation of log-linear models considers the log-linear micro equations

$$\ln(c_{it}) = \alpha + \beta \ln(y_{it}) + \varepsilon_{it} \qquad \text{C1}$$

across individuals (or households) $i = 1, 2, \ldots, N$, and over time periods $t = 1, 2, \ldots, T$. It also assumes that

$$\varepsilon_{it}|y_{it} \sim N(0, \omega_0 + \omega_1 \ln(y_{it})). \qquad \text{C2}$$

Using the above formulation the authors then show that even under the 'mean scaling' assumption, the aggregate income elasticity of demand is not equal to β, but is rather given by $\beta + \frac{1}{2}\omega_1$. Hence, they conclude that the estimates of income elasticities obtained from the micro- and macro-studies need not in general coincide. There are two points that I wish to raise with respect to this conclusion:

- In the above simple set up the main reason for the disparity between the micro (β) and macro ($\beta + \frac{1}{2}\omega_1$) value of the income elasticity lies in the way income elasticity is defined, and does not solely arise because of aggregation. Due to the stochastic nature of (C1), special care needs to be exercised when deriving income elasticity of demand in terms of the parameters of the model. The traditional method where the presence of the stochastic term is ignored is appropriate only when income elasticity is defined as

$$\eta_i = \frac{\partial E(\ln(c_{it})|y_{it})}{\partial \ln(y_{it})} = \beta$$

where $E(\cdot|y_{it})$ denotes the conditional expectations operator. However, it is equally plausible to define the (micro) income elasticity as

$$\eta_i^* = \frac{\partial \ln\{E(c_{it}|y_{it})\}}{\partial \ln(y_{it})}.$$

In the deterministic case both definitions yield the same result. But in the stochastic context it is easily seen that

$$\eta_i^* = \beta + \tfrac{1}{2}\omega_1.$$

Therefore, in general these two definitions will not be the same, even at the micro level. It is this difference between the two definitions of income elasticity which is responsible for the disparity between the micro and macro income elasticities reported in the paper.

• The second point concerns the size and the direction of the bias of the macro-estimate as compared to the micro-estimate. Tobin and others have found the time-series estimates of income elasticity to be generally smaller than the ones obtained using cross-sections. If one accepts the paper's argument this would imply a negative value for ω_1, which may not be compatible with the cross-section evidence on the relationship between $V(\varepsilon_{it}|y_{it})$ and y_{it}.

Using Tobin's original data the authors claim to have identified an important non-linearity in the relationship between aggregate per capita food consumption and per capita disposable income, and suggest that there are no statistically significant dynamics in this relationship. (See the regression estimates reported in Equations (7) and (8).) However, this conclusion is subject to two important caveats. Firstly, important dynamics are found if one uses the revised Tobin data provided in the information pack. Estimating their preferred per capita equation using natural logarithms (denoted by ln) and over the full sample period (1915–1976) I obtained

$$\ln(\widehat{PCFC}_t) = \begin{array}{l} 1.105 + 0.5682 \ln(PCFC_{t-1}) + 0.3197 \ln(PCY_t) \\ (0.316)\quad (0.084) \qquad\qquad\qquad (0.064) \end{array}$$

$$- \begin{array}{l} 0.1497 \ln(PCY_{t-1}) + 0.0726 \ln(PCY_{t-2}) \\ (0.042) \qquad\qquad\quad (0.026) \end{array}$$

$$- \begin{array}{l} 0.0108 \,(\ln(PCY_t))^2 - 0.0943 \ \ln(FP_t) \\ (0.0036) \qquad\qquad (0.0218) \end{array}$$

$$+ \begin{array}{l} 0.018 \ \ln(NFP_t) \\ (0.028) \end{array}$$

$$\bar{R}^2 = 0.97, \quad \hat{\sigma} = 0.0135, \quad \text{Durbin's } h = 1.34$$

$$\chi_{SC}^2(1) = 0.75, \quad \chi_{FF}^2(1) = 2.27, \quad \chi_N^2(2) = 0.72, \quad \chi_H^2(1) = 0.004.$$

The χ^2 statistics refer to tests of residual serial correlation ($\chi_{SC}^2(1)$), functional form ($\chi_{FF}^2(1)$), non-normal errors ($\chi_N^2(2)$), and heteroscedastic errors ($\chi_H^2(1)$). Clearly there are important $\ln(PCY_{t-1})$ dynamics, interacting with the non-linear effects. The coefficients of the lagged values of the food expenditures and the income variable, $\ln(PCY_{t-1})$, $\ln(PCY_{t-2})$ and $\ln(PCFC_{t-1})$, are statistically highly significant.

However, the non-linear specification reported in the paper (Equation (7)) and its dynamic generalization given above suffer from a major shortcoming; namely that by construction they are unlikely to satisfy the homogeneity restrictions (in the short-run as well as in the long-run). For example, the non-linear demand function reported in Equation (7) will be homogeneous of degree one in nominal income and prices if the following condition is satisfied:

$$\beta_1 + \beta_2 + \beta_3 + \beta_4(2\ln y_t + \ln \lambda) = 0 \quad \text{for all } t$$

where β_1, β_2, β_3 and β_4 are the coefficients of $\ln(TOBPCY_t)$, $\ln(TOBFP_t)$, $\ln(TOBNF_t)$, $(\ln(TOBPCY_t))^2$, respectively, and λ is an arbitrary fixed constant. It is clear that only for certain values of y_t and λ can this restriction be satisfied.

The appropriate method of allowing for non-linear effects in demand equations is through real (rather than nominal) per capita income. But the evidence of a non-linear income effect disappears altogether if instead of $\ln(TOBPCY_t)$ one uses a per capita real income variable, such as $\ln(TOBPCY_t/P_t)$ where P_t is a general price index which for Tobin's data could be computed as

$$\ln(P_t) = 0.27\ln(TOBFP_t) + 0.73\ln(TOBNF_t).$$

For the longer US time-series, the authors correctly point out the possibility of a structural break in the food demand equation and confine their analysis to the 1948–1989 period (see Section 4.2 and my comments on the report of the CBS team). There is, however, a clear break in the authors' approach to modelling food consumption. They seem to abandon the 'economic theory' and opt for a purely data-driven strategy. For example, they drop the non-food price variable from the analysis, which is difficult to justify on *a priori* grounds. Given the authors' emphasis on non-linear effects, it is also surprising that they do not pursue this topic further.

The interpretation of the two cointegrating relations obtained in Section 5.3 as 'demand' and 'supply' equations is also problematic, particularly considering that only point estimates of the long-run elasticities are provided.[C1] Also for forecasting purposes identification of the cointegrating relations is unnecessary if the identifying restrictions are exactly identifying, as happens to be the case in this paper. Forecasts from cointegrating VAR models are invariant to alternative exactly identifying restrictions imposed on the cointegrating relations. Once again the long-run relations do not seem to satisfy the homogeneity restrictions.

The forecasts computed for the level of food consumption do not allow for the effect of uncertainty of the regression equation. This point is easily seen in the context of the following simple log-linear equation

$$\ln c_t = \alpha + \beta \ln y_t + \varepsilon_t, \quad \varepsilon_t \sim N(0, \sigma^2).$$

The optimal forecast of c_t conditional on y_t is given by

$$E(c_t|y_t) = (e^{\alpha+\beta \ln y_t})e^{1/2\sigma^2}.$$

The forecasts reported in the last columns of Table V do not seem to have allowed for the effect of the term $\exp(\frac{1}{2}\sigma^2)$.

[C1] I have been unable to exactly replicate the cointegration test results provided in Table III. For example, using Microfit 4.0, for $trace_0$ statistic I obtained the value of 65.61 instead of 68.87 reported in this table. Also, as argued in Pesaran, *et al.* (1997), given the trended nature of the underlying variables a VAR model containing linear trends with restricted coefficients would have been more appropriate. Using such a model the test results support the existence of only one cointegrating vector among the five variables.

REFERENCE

Pesaran, M. H., Shin, Y. and Smith, R. J. (1997), 'Structural analysis of vector error correction models with exogenous I(1) variables', *DAE Working Paper No. 9706*, Department of Applied Economics, University of Cambridge.

REPLY BY HEATHER M. ANDERSON AND FARSHID VAHID

We thank our assessors, Professors Schmidt, Cramer and Pesaran, and for their many insightful comments on our paper. After reflecting on what we think is a general weakness in our paper, we reply to the specific points raised by our assessors. For ease of reference, our reply is organized according to the sections in our paper.

1.   Data Considerations

In retrospect, we think that a major shortcoming of our paper is that it lacks a thorough investigation of data definitions, and a discussion of what our estimated elasticities are really measuring, given the data used. It is particularly important to note that our time-series measure of real consumption, $AGGEXPF/FP * NOH$, incorporates *quality* changes as well as *quantity* changes, in contrast to the variables $TOBPCFC$ and $PCFC$ which measure the 'disappearance' of the physical quantity of food. Clearly our results must be viewed in this light, and we share Cramer's view that one of the main effects of the upward trend in income on food consumption in the post-war era has been a quality upgrading in food consumption, rather than a quantity increase.[R1] Another related shortcoming, also mentioned by Cramer, is our failure to discuss the implications of using the $AHSIZE$ variable, which counts the number of people in a household without accounting for age structure.

2.   Aggregation of Log-Linear Models with Heteroscedasticity

Pesaran brings up an interesting point when he notes that one could derive our expression for aggregate income elasticity in Equation (3) by defining elasticity to be

$$\frac{\partial \ln\{E(c_{it}|y_{it})\}}{\partial \ln(y_{it})} = \left(\beta + \frac{1}{2}\omega_1\right)$$

rather than

$$\frac{\partial\{E(\ln c_{it}|y_{it})\}}{\partial \ln(y_{it})} = \beta.$$

This was something we had not considered. We note, however, that although the former expression provides a reasonable definition of elasticity in a stochastic setting, it is the latter definition which is implicitly assumed in the literature on pooling individual and aggregate demand functions. Regardless of which definition of elasticity is better,

---

[R1] Cramer elegantly elaborated on this point in his comments during the Workshop, but unfortunately he did not include it in his written comments. When we later investigated this by making an index of quality of food consumed by forming the ratio of $AGGEXPF/FP * POP$ to $PCFC$, we found that apart from the period between 1942 and 1947, this index has grown very steadily during 1929–1976.

our theoretical result simply says that in the presence of income related heteroscedasticity, the *coefficients of log-income* in log-linear micro- and macro-demand specifications will be different.

Both Pesaran and Schmidt felt our finding that the empirical micro-income coefficients were larger than their macro counterparts, contradicted their intuition that $\beta < (\beta + \frac{1}{2}\omega_1)$. Such intuition, which was also ours at first, assumes that the conditional variance is *positively* related to income, (i.e. $\omega_1 > 0$). However, if we assume that conditional variance is a *linear* function of income, then we find a *negative* slope. Although a negative relationship between variance and income may seem strange at first, a careful examination of the data shows why this is the case in our particular data set. A plot of squared residuals against log-income (not included here), suggests a quadratic relationship, with higher variance at the two income extremes than at average incomes. Noting that (i) the low income households are mostly one or two person households who are either very young or senior citizens, and (ii) our real food consumption variable measures quality and not just the physical intake of food, it becomes easy to see that there can be a higher dispersion around the conditional mean in the low income group than in the high income group. This then translates into a negative relationship between variance and income, if a linear approximation is used.

Following Schmidt's suggestion that we put the results of the paper in a positive form, we estimated income elasticity based on the pooled 1950 and 1960 budget surveys for the USA,[R2] subject to the restriction that conditional variance and log-income were linearly related.[R3] Our maximum likelihood estimate of the coefficient of log-income (which allowed for differences in cell size) was $\hat{\beta}_m = 0.527$, with a s.e. of 0.008, and in the variance equation, we found that $\hat{\omega}_1 = -0.172$, with a s.e. of 0.052. This implied an estimated aggregate income coefficient of 0.441, with a 95% confidence interval of (0.385, 0.497). Turning to the US time-series for 1948–68, the estimated macro income coefficient was $\hat{\beta}_M = 0.355$, with a 95% confidence interval of (0.249, 0.461). While the confidence intervals for β_m and β_M do not overlap, the ones for $(\beta_m + \frac{1}{2}\omega_1)$ and β_M do, supporting our argument that when income related heteroscedasticity characterizes a cross-sectional equation, then in the aggregate equation, the income coefficient will be $\beta_M = \beta_m + \frac{1}{2}\omega_1$.

3. Preliminary Measurement Exercise

Pesaran raises an important issue when he suggests that our non-linear functional forms should have allowed for possible homogeneity. To examine this issue further, we redid our analysis, deflating income using his suggested measure of price level. Like Pesaran, we found that if *homogeneity was imposed*, then the non-linear term drops out. However, if we then use this equation in real variables to test homogeneity by adding in the nominal variable $\log(TOBPCY_t)$, we find that homogeneity is strongly rejected with a p-value of 0.0002. We further find that a $(\log(TOBPCY_t))^2$ variable is also statistically significant. This leads to a specification which is simply a reparameterized version of our Equation (7). Fortunately our oversight did not matter in this case because the homogeneity restriction

---

[R2] Recall that we could not reject log-linearity of the conditional mean in either of the 1950 and 1960 surveys, and we also found that for these two surveys, the pooling restriction was accepted.

[R3] The details of the results given in this paragraph can be found in Anderson, H. M., and F. Vahid (1997), 'A Note on Log-linear Aggregation', mimeo, Texas A & M University.

was clearly rejected. However, this does not excuse us from discussing the possible causes and consequences of over-reaction of aggregate consumption to the nominal variables, and Cramer was right to point out that we should have done so.

Pesaran's other comment about misspecification of dynamics in our Equation (7) is not convincing, given that his equation for $\ln PCFC$ is based on pooled pre-war and post-war data, and he later agrees with us that there was a possible structural break in the food demand equation (see also footnote 8 in our paper). We tested the null of no structural break at 1948 in his equation, and rejected this with a p-value of 0.002. Recall that our diagnostic tests failed to find any evidence of dynamic misspecification in our Equation (7).

4. Measurement for the Extended US Data Set

Schmidt asks us to report the results of a '1950-style' regression with the extended time series data. If we are correct in assuming that a '1950-style' regression is just a static OLS regression, the results are:

$$\ln\left(\frac{AGGEXPF}{FP*NOH}\right)_t = -7.02 + 0.36\ln\left(\frac{AGGY}{NOH}\right)_t - 0.47\ln(FP)_t + \hat{u}_t,$$

$$R^2 = 0.89 \quad DW = 0.82$$

which are quite different from our estimated elasticities in Section 4.2. However, if one estimates this equation with the Cochrane-Orcutt procedure, allowing for first-order serial correlation in the errors, one gets results which are very close to our estimated Equation (10), which suggests that endogeneity is not a problem in this example.

Each of our assessors expressed concern about changes in our modelling philosophy/strategy as we moved from our cross-sectional analysis to our time-series analysis. This shift was, to some extent, unavoidable, given the page restrictions and the multitude of tasks that were assigned in the experiment. It was also partly deliberate, because, having established from our cross-section analysis that there was no simple correspondence between micro- and macro-parameters, we were avoiding any micro-behavioural interpretation of our macro-economic coefficients.

We did, however, test for homogeneity, and we never omitted a theoretically relevant variable unless we failed to find evidence that it was significant. We started with an unconstrained regression of real food consumption on nominal explanatory variables because homogeneity was an issue to be investigated. After establishing that homogeneity was rejected (with or without restricting the non-food price coefficient to be zero), and concluding that a model with real income and relative prices on the right-hand-side would therefore be misspecified, we reported our results with nominal right-hand-side variables. We could have reparameterized our final model, and presented our results with logarithms of real income and food price, or with logarithms of real income and nominal income on the right-hand-side, but such alternative reparameterizations can be readily deduced from our reported results. We restricted the real food consumption elasticity with respect to the relative price to be zero, because it was statistically insignificant. Leamer finds a similar result using a different methodology, and concludes that 'there isn't much evidence in the data about the price elasticity'.

5. Measurement with Related Information

Schmidt asks to see how grouping the Dutch cross-section data would have affected the results. We grouped the Dutch data by household size and divided each group into eight income categories: less than 20, 20 to 30, 30 to 40, 40 to 50, 50 to 60, 60 to 70, 70 to 80, and more than 80 thousand guilders. The cell size weighted least-squares regression of the logarithms of the *geometric* averages of food consumption and income in each cell, results in income and size elasticity estimates of 0.30 and 0.45 for the 1980, and 0.42 and 0.44 for the 1988 budget surveys. These are very similar to the estimates from the individual data reported in Table 2. The same regressions with the logarithms of the *arithmetic* averages produce more distorted size elasticity estimates: the estimates of income and size elasticities are 0.28 and 0.41 for the 1980, and 0.40 and 0.41 for the 1988 budget surveys.

As Pesaran and Schmidt point out, our failure to consider restrictions on the deterministic trends in our forecasting VECM was inappropriate. The trend restrictions are not rejected (in sample), with a p-value of 0.29, and imposing these restrictions leads to forecasts for 2000AD of -4.54 (with a s.e. of 0.14) for $\ln RFC$, 5.56 thousand guilders (with a s.e. of 1.32) for nominal per capita expenditure on food, and 85 372 million guilders (with a s.e. of 20 400) for total nominal expenditure on food. These point forecasts are lower than those reported in Table V. Forecasts for nominal consumption are not corrected for transformation bias, but since the standard errors associated with $\ln RFC$ are small, the multiplicative bias terms of $e^{1/2\sigma^2}$ are so close to one that such bias corrections would make little difference.

With respect to whether our cointegration test statistics are correct, we could reproduce Pesaran's cointegration statistic of 65.61 in his footnote 1 only if we used the originally supplied Dutch population data, which were subsequently corrected by the experiment organizers. All of our results are based on the corrected data. On the interpretation of the normalized cointegrating vectors as 'supply' and 'demand', we were careful to caution our readers about such interpretation, and we never implied that this normalization had any bearing on the forecasts generated by our model.

CHAPTER 4

THE DEMAND FOR FOOD IN THE UNITED STATES AND THE NETHERLANDS: A SYSTEMS APPROACH WITH THE CBS MODEL*

HANS VAN DRIEL, VENUTA NADALL AND KEES ZEELENBERG

1. INTRODUCTION

In 1950 Tobin published his analysis of the demand for food in the USA during the pre-war period. For this empirical analysis he used both budget-survey data, mainly for 1941, and time-series data for 1913–41. Using the same data as well as more extensive data, provided by 'The Experiment in Applied Econometrics', we will analyze the demand for food, using a complete demand system, the so-called CBS model[1] (Keller and Van Driel, 1985), which, in a comparative study of several demand systems, Barten (1993) found to perform as the best. For comparisons with Tobin (1950) we will focus on the income and price elasticities. Tobin's results on this point can be summarized as follows. In the 1941 budget-survey data he found an income elasticity of 0.56 with a standard error 0.03 (Tobin, 1950, p. 119, Equation 8), and in the time-series data he found an income elasticity of 0.27 with a 95% confidence interval of (0.24, 0.35), and an own-price elasticity of −0.28 with a 95% confidence interval of (−0.38, −0.23) (Tobin, 1950, p. 134, Equation 28). When making comparisons one should bear in mind that we do not estimate true income elasticities, but rather total-expenditure elasticities. These two are identical only if we assume a constant savings rate. This assumption is probably not true in the data sets we have used, but to incorporate savings to our analysis we would, with the approach taken, at least need data on the interest rate, which were not made available.

In Section 2 we summarize our research process. In Section 3 we set out the CBS model, and how it is to be applied to cross-section data and time-series data. In Section 4 we discuss the estimation results for the US data and in Section 5 those for the Dutch data.[2] In Section 6 we give some conclusions.

2. LOGBOOK

We started our research with the CBS demand system. We chose the course of demand systems, because our own work and experience with demand analysis has been mainly in

---

* Reprinted from the *Journal of Applied Econometrics*, **12**, 509–532 (1997).

[1] CBS = Central Bureau voor de Statistiek, the Dutch name of Statistics Netherlands.

[2] The US data are compiled from various US Government publications (see organizers' data section for details). We thank Statistics Netherlands for use of the Dutch data. The computations have been done with Limdep.

Methodology and Tacit Knowledge: Two Experiments in Econometrics
Jan R. Magnus and Mary S. Morgan © 1997 John Wiley & Sons Ltd

this area. Although the basics of the model were already known (Keller and Van Driel, 1985), several adaptations had to be made, first, because the model is developed for the individual household, whereas several data sets were for aggregated units, and second, because the model is a differential model, whereas for cross-sections the model has to be formulated in levels. To solve these problems we followed more or less the corresponding solutions for the Rotterdam model, although they could not be used straightforwardly owing to the differences between the CBS model, which is a quantity share model, and the Rotterdam model, which is a value share model. Our solutions are described in Sections 3.4–3.6.

Meanwhile we had started applied work with the analysis of the US budget data of 1941. This took some time, because we tried to reduce the within-group entropy, which appears in the group demand equation, to a form that could be estimated from the data along with the other parameters. The resulting forms were highly non-linear, and we failed to get any meaningful results. Therefore we adopted a more simple course, and modelled the entropy as a linear function of the number of households.

We then started work on the estimation of the US time-series data. First, we constructed from Tobin's price and quantity data a series on aggregate food expenditure; the movement in this series was very unlike the new series *AGGEXPF*. Since, moreover, we could not find a way to compute a series for aggregate total expenditure, we decided to use only the new series, which starts in 1929. This was the only point at which we felt seriously hampered by the requirement that only data from the *Information Pack* was to be used; if not for this requirement we would have gone back to Tobin's data sources and tried to obtain the data needed from these sources. The actual estimations were then straightforwardly executed on the basis of the aggregate model of Section 3.6.2.

Thereafter we began to work on the Dutch budget data. The analysis of the 1965 survey was performed in the same way as that of the US budget surveys. The 1980 and 1988 surveys posed more difficulties, mainly because they contained individual household date. At so late a stage we noticed that not only the income data had been truncated but also the expenditure data, that we could only eliminate these 'weird' cases, and were not able to try a more satisfying solution.

Finally we turned to the Dutch time-series. Estimation of the model on these data was straightforward, and we tested for homogeneity and symmetry.

To summarize our research strategy and tactics, one might say that we took a theoretical model as starting-point and estimated the model on the available data.

3. THE DEMAND SYSTEM

3.1. Introduction

For estimating price and income elasticities of consumer demand many demand systems have been developed in the past. In this paper we focus our attention on the CBS System, which was developed at Statistics Netherlands (Keller and Van Driel, 1985). It is a so-called consumer demand differential system, based on the differential equation for the budget shares of the consumer goods. Parts of this equation (derivatives or functions of derivatives) are assumed to be constant, in order to obtain estimable expressions. Depending on which *constancy assumptions* are made, we get different 'parameterizations' of this differential equation, so that we have a whole family of differential consumer demand systems. Other models belonging to this family are the Rotterdam Model (Theil, 1975) and the differential version of the Almost Ideal Demand System (Deaton and Muellbauer, 1980a).

3.2. The CBS Model

The CBS model describes the differential change in the quantity share as a function of changes in real total expenditure and prices:

$$w_i \mathrm{d} \log \frac{q_i}{Q} = \beta_i \mathrm{d} \log Q + \sum_{j=1}^{K} \pi_{ij} \mathrm{d} \log p_j \quad (i = 1, 2, \ldots, K) \qquad 1$$

where the parameters β_i and π_{ij} are assumed to be constant, q_i is the quantity demanded of good i, p_j is the price of good j, Q is total real expenditure implicitly defined by

$$\mathrm{d} \log Q = \sum_{j=1}^{K} w_j \mathrm{d} \log q_j = \mathrm{d} \log x - \sum_{j=1}^{K} w_j \mathrm{d} \log p_j$$

with x the value of total expenditure, $w_i = p_i q_i / x$ is the budget share of good i, and K is the number of goods. The coefficients π_{ij} of the prices are called the *Slutsky* coefficients.

Neoclassical consumer theory imposes some well-known restrictions on the parameters of these equations:

1. Adding up: $\Sigma_{i=1}^{K} \beta_i = 0$ and $\Sigma_{i=1}^{K} \pi_{ij} = 0$.
2. Homogeneity: $\Sigma_{j=1}^{K} \pi_{ij} = 0$.
3. Utility maximization: the matrix Π is symmetric and negative semidefinite of rank $K - 1$.

The income elasticities η_i and the uncompensated price elasticities η_{ij} of good i with respect to price j are:

$$\eta_i = \frac{\beta_i}{w_i} + 1 \qquad 2$$

$$\eta_{ij} = \frac{\pi_{ij}}{w_i} - \eta_i w_j. \qquad 3$$

3.3. The CBS Model in Finite Changes

The CBS model (1) reads in differentials. In order to arrive at estimable equations it has to be converted to finite changes. We follow the method used by Theil (1975) for the Rotterdam model, which is essentially an application of the Trapezoid rule.

Defining

$$\overline{w}_{it} = (w_{i,t-1} + w_{it})/2 \qquad 4$$

and the log-difference operator D as

$$\mathrm{D} y_t = \log y_t - \log y_{t-1} \quad (t = 2, \ldots, T), \qquad 5$$

the finite change expression becomes, after adding a disturbance term ε_{it},

$$\bar{w}_{it}\mathrm{D}\frac{q_{it}}{Q_t} = \beta_i\mathrm{D}Q_t + \sum_{j=1}^{K}\pi_{ij}\mathrm{D}p_{jt} + \varepsilon_{it} \qquad\qquad 6$$

where $\mathrm{D}Q_t$ is calculated as $\Sigma_j\bar{w}_{jt}\mathrm{D}q_{jt}$, which ensures adding-up (Theil, 1975, p. 40), and which differs only to the third order from $\mathrm{D}x_t - \Sigma_j\bar{w}_{jt}\mathrm{D}p_{jt}$.

3.4. The CBS Model in Levels

The CBS model introduced in the preceding sections is a micro-economic equation for one individual household. It is a differential demand system, developed for measuring the influence of *changing* prices and expenditure on the budget shares. Therefore it is particularly suitable for time-series analysis. For a cross-sectional analysis, a demand model in *levels* is more appropriate. Van Driel (1982) has investigated for several differential demand systems on which demand systems in levels they could be based. He showed that for a utility-maximizing consumer the constancy assumptions of the CBS model imply a degenerated demand system with constant budget shares, and so linear Engel curves belonging to a Cobb–Douglas utility structure. This, of course, is far too restrictive for practical applications.

The same property, by the way, was found by Theil (1975) for the Rotterdam Model. Theil (1975) suggests a way out, stating that the Rotterdam Model should be seen as an *approximation* of a demand system based on a utility function. A similar argument may be applied to the CBS model. Nevertheless, we still have to solve the question as to the demand equations underlying the CBS model. A natural choice which leads to a model that can be used for cross-section analysis is to base ourselves only on the constancy assumption for the β_i and to disregard the constancy assumption for the π_{ij}. Van Driel (1982) shows that in this case

$$w_i = \beta_i\log x + h_i(p). \qquad\qquad 7$$

In cross-sections, where prices can be considered to be constant, the price term $h_i(p)$ is a constant. Then the model passes into the well-known model of Working (1943) and Leser (1963, 1976) with Engel curves of the PIGLOG type (see Deaton and Muellbauer, 1980b). In time-series analysis, however, prices are usually not constant so neither is the price term $h_i(p)$. Where it occurred we have solved this by specifying different constants for different time periods.[3]

3.5. Equivalence Scales in the Model

Apart from total expenditure and prices some other, usually demographic, variables like household composition should be incorporated into the demand equations, as they influence the preferences of the household and consequently its expenditure pattern. Pollak

---

[3] Another possibility, suggested by Barten (1989) is to specify the function $h(p)$, which can be done by using an idea developed by Theil, Suhm, and Meisner (1981) for international consumption comparisons; see Van Driel *et al.* (1996, Section 3.5) for more details.

and Wales (1979) discuss several methods to do this. We have used their concept of an 'unconditional equivalence scale' which has a welfare-analytic interpretation: the ratio of the expenditures for households h with certain demographic characteristics (e.g. with z children) to obtain a particular utility level u and the expenditures for a reference household R (e.g. an adult couple without children) to obtain the same utility level. So we have

$$c^h(u, p, z) = m(u, p, z)c^R(u, p) \qquad \qquad 8$$

where $c^R(u, p)$ is the expenditure function of the reference household, $c^h(u, p, z)$ the cost function of household h and $m(u, p, z)$ the compensation function or equivalence scale, which may depend on the demographic variables, but also on the prices and the utility level of the household.

A problem with this method is, that usually knowledge of the household cost function $c^R(u, p)$ is required in order to derive the demand equations of household h. For the CBS model (just as for the Rotterdam model, but as opposed to the Almost Ideal Demand System) this cost function is unknown by lack of an underlying utility function, as was discussed in Section 3.4. This problem can be solved if we make the *simplifying assumption* that the compensation function $m(u, p, z)$ does not depend on the utility level and the prices, but only on the demographic variables, so $m = m(z)$. In that case the method reduces to the well-known method of Engel (see Deaton and Muellbauer, 1980b). Then the demand equations for a household h can be obtained from the equations for the reference household R by dividing the quantities consumed q and total expenditure x by the equivalence scale $m(z)$, so that, for instance, the CBS model (6) becomes:

$$\bar{w}_{it} \mathrm{D} \frac{q_{it}}{Q_t} = \beta_i \mathrm{D} \frac{Q_t}{m(z)} + \sum_{j=1}^{K} \pi_{ij} \mathrm{D} p_{jt} + \varepsilon_{it}. \qquad \qquad 9$$

3.6. Towards Estimation

3.6.1. Cross-section Model

As we have seen in Subsection 3.4 the CBS model passes into the Working–Leser model when it is applied to budget survey data. For a given good we have, omitting the subscript for the good,

$$w_h = \alpha + \beta \log \frac{x_h}{m_h} + \varepsilon_h \qquad \qquad 10$$

where h is household, m_h the equivalence scale for this household, and ε_h a disturbance term with expectation 0 and variance σ^2. The equivalence scale is specified as

$$m_h = \exp(\rho \, \mathrm{hsize}_h) \qquad \qquad 11$$

where 'hsize' is the size of the household; other determinants may be specified in a similar way.

For grouped data the model has to be aggregated to group levels. For group g we have

$$w_g = \sum_{h \in g} \frac{x_h}{x_g} w_h = \alpha - \beta H_g + \beta \log x_g - \beta_\rho \, \mathrm{hsize}_g + \varepsilon_g \qquad \qquad 12$$

where x_g is total expenditure of group g and H_g is the entropy of the expenditure of the households in group g. If the size of the households within the group is not constant, which may be caused by changing sizes during the year, the *average* household size of the group is used as an explanatory variable, which will hardly induce an error. The entropy of the distribution of total expenditures is apparently an explanatory variable in aggregated equations (see also Deaton and Muellbauer, 1980b, p. 157). Unfortunately no data on this distribution is available.

Van Driel (1996) shows for the entropy H_{ab} of a continuous distribution on an interval (a, b) that

$$H_{ab} = \log N_{ab} + \log \ \mathrm{E}(x) - \frac{\mathrm{E}(x \log x)}{\mathrm{E}(x)} \tag{13}$$

so the entropy varies with the number of households $\log N_{ab}$ within the group. The other terms in Equation (13) do not depend on the number of households, but on the bounds of the income classes. An option could be to assume that the second and third term in Equation (13) do not show much variation, which is the case, for instance, if income distributions over the classes do not differ very much. The effect of this assumption on the model is

$$w_g = \alpha + \beta \log \bar{x}_g - \beta \rho \ \mathrm{hsize}_g + \varepsilon_g \tag{14}$$

where $\bar{x}_g$ is per household expenditure in group g.

According to these considerations we estimate the model

$$w_g = \alpha + \beta_1 \log \bar{x}_g + \beta_2 \ \mathrm{hsize}_g + \beta_3 \log n_g + \varepsilon_g \tag{15}$$

where n_g is the number of households in group g, and test the assumption $\beta_3 = 0$.

Finally, we investigate the error term ε_g:

$$\mathrm{var} \, \varepsilon_g = \sigma^2 \frac{\sum_h x_h^2}{x_g^2} = \sigma^2 \left(\frac{1}{n_g} + \frac{s_{x_g}^2}{\bar{x}_g^2 n_g} \right). \tag{16}$$

Unfortunately $s_{x_g}^2$, the variance of total expenditures of the households in group g, is unknown. Therefore we assume that the coefficients of variation of total expenditures in the groups are approximately equal, reducing Equation (16) to

$$\mathrm{var} \, \varepsilon_g = \frac{\tau^2}{n_g}. \tag{17}$$

Consequently we expect heteroscedastic group error terms, inversely proportional with the numbers of households in the groups. The model can be tested for this heteroscedasticity by specifying $\mathrm{var} \, \varepsilon_g = \tau^2 / (n_g)^\phi$ and testing whether $\phi = 1$.

3.6.2. *Time-series Model*

For estimating the CBS model on macro-economic time-series data the micro CBS model has to be aggregated to a macro model. Following the lines developed by Barnett (1981) we aggregate the differential model (1). For some good i, the micro equation for household h is

$$w_h \mathrm{d} \log \frac{q_h}{Q_h} = \beta_h \mathrm{d} \log Q_h + \pi_h' \mathrm{d} \log p. \tag{18}$$

Then the macro equation for that good is obtained by multiplying with $x_h/\Sigma_h x_h$, summing and rearranging:

$$wd\log\frac{q}{Q} = \beta d\log Q + \pi'd\log p + \frac{\displaystyle\sum_h k_h v_h}{\displaystyle\sum_h x_h} - \frac{\displaystyle\sum_h l_h d\log Q}{\displaystyle\sum_h x_h} \qquad 19$$

where variables without subscript are macro variables, $\beta = \mu^* - w^*$, $\mu^* = E(x_h\mu_h)/E(x_h)$, $w^* = E(x_h w_h)/E(x_h)$, $v_h = d\log Q_h$, $k_h = x_h(\mu_h - \mu^*)$, and $l_h = x_h(w_h - w^*)$. Barnett (1981) shows that the probability limit of the first remainder term $\Sigma_h k_h v_h/\Sigma_h x_h$ is equal to cov $(k_h, v_h)/E(x_h)$ and generally can be neglected. The probability limit of the second remainder term is 0. The differential macro equation is consequently

$$wd\log\frac{q}{Q} = \beta d\log Q + \pi'd\log p \qquad 20$$

and, in finite changes, for good i

$$\overline{w}D\frac{q}{Q} = \beta DQ + \pi'Dp. \qquad 21$$

For estimation we have added an error term to Equation (21) and, in order to test for possible time trends, a constant term.

4.   ANALYSIS OF US DATA

First, we checked that we could reproduce the results of Tobin (1950). This was indeed the case, apart from the estimates for the constant terms; probably in Tobin's computations a scaling different from the data in his article has been used.

4.1.   Estimation on Budget Data

The model discussed in Section 3.6.1 has been estimated on the US budget data of 1941, 1950, 1960, and 1972. Data are needed on food consumption (variable *FOODCON*), on total consumption (*TOTCON*), on the number of households (*ESTPOPH* in 1941 and 1972, and *SAMPSIZE* in 1950 and 1960), and on the size of the households in the groups (*AHSIZE*). In terms of these variables Equation (15) becomes

$$\frac{FOODCON_g}{TOTCON_g} = \alpha + \beta_1\log TOTCON_g + \beta_2 AHSIZE_g + \beta_3\log SAMPSIZE_g + \varepsilon_g \quad 22$$

where in 1941 and 1972 *ESTPOPH* is used as proxy for *SAMPSIZE*, and var $\varepsilon_g = \tau^2/(SAMPSIZE_g)^\phi$.[4]

---

[4] We are grateful to W. K. Siegert for pointing out an error in Equation (22), now corrected.

For 1941 some groups had to be combined because the number of households in the groups was known only for the combination. The consumption data for these combined groups were constructed as arithmetic means of those in the underlying classes. Thus, 27 observations were available.

In Table I we present the results of the estimation of 1941. The income elasticity η is calculated using the average budget share in the population (weighting with total expenditures). First, the full model (15) was estimated and tested for (multiplicative) heteroscedasticity. Next we estimated the reduced model (with the restriction $\beta_3 = 0$). Then we estimated the full model under the restriction $\phi = 1$ (so with weighted least squares) and finally we did the same with the reduced model. The log-likelihood of the homoscedastic full model is 71.8219. From this we see that the hypothesis of homoscedasticity cannot be rejected ($\chi^2 = 2(73.1412 - 71.8219) = 2.64$ with 1 df). ϕ, however, could as well be 1 ($\chi^2 = 2(73.1412 - 72.8360) = 0.61$ with 1 df). The hypothesis $\beta_3 = 0$ need not be rejected, too ($\chi^2 = 2(73.1412 - 72.3413) = 1.60$ with 1 df), so the hypothesis of an entropy which varies mainly with the number of households in the group seems to be not very restrictive. The simultaneous hypothesis $\phi = 1$ and $\beta_3 = 0$ was neither rejected ($\chi^2 = 2(73.1412 - 72.2839) = 1.71$ with 2 df).

It is remarkable that the estimates are very insensitive to the method that is chosen. With respect to the results an income elasticity of 0.74 looks reasonable, just like a household scale factor of $\exp(0.24) = 1.27$, which implies that an additional person in the household requires 27% additional income in order to maintain the welfare level. Note that the income elasticity is much higher than the 0.56 found by Tobin.

In Table II we present the results for the 1950 budget data. The number of observations is 54. The log-likelihood of the full model under homoscedasticity is 133.8174. So this hypothesis is clearly rejected ($\chi^2 = 30.97$ with 1 df). The other results of the estimation look very much like those of 1941.

Table III contains the results for the year 1960. In that year 59 observations were available (one observation is missing). The log-likelihood of the full model under homoscedasticity is 134.9296. Again, the results look much like those of the preceding data sets.

In Table IV the 1972 results can be found. The number of observations is 72. For model 2 no estimation results could be obtained due to the fact that the estimation algorithm for the multiplicative heteroscedasticity did not converge. The log-likelihood of the full model under homoscedasticity was 189.8380. Though it is obvious that β_3 is unequal to

Table I. Estimation results for the 1941 US data

Method	α	β_1	β_2	β_3	ϕ	ρ	η	Log-likelihood
			Estimates					
1. Full model, multipl.hetero-scedasticity	0.93 (0.04)	−0.081 (0.006)	0.019 (0.002)	−0.008 (0.006)	0.69 (0.32)	0.24 (0.02)	0.74 (0.02)	73.1412
2. Reduced model, multipl.hetero-scedasticity	0.90 (0.04)	−0.085 (0.005)	0.020 (0.002)	—	0.89 (0.32)	0.24 (0.02)	0.73 (0.02)	73.3413
3. Full model, WLS	0.92 (0.05)	−0.081 (0.006)	0.019 (0.002)	−0.007 (0.007)	—	0.23 (0.02)	0.74 (0.02)	72.8360
4. Reduced model, WLS	0.90 (0.05)	−0.084 (0.006)	0.020 (0.002)	—	—	0.24 (0.02)	0.73 (0.02)	72.2839

In this table, and in the following tables, figures in parentheses denote standard errors.

Table II. Estimation results for the 1950 US data

Method	Estimates							Log-likelihood
	α	β_1	β_2	β_3	ϕ	ρ	η	
1. Full model, multipl.hetero- scedasticity	0.89 (0.03)	−0.076 (0.004)	0.019 (0.001)	−0.000 (0.002)	0.87 (0.13)	0.25 (0.02)	0.75 (0.01)	149.3041
2. Reduced model, multipl.hetero- scedasticity	0.88 (0.03)	−0.076 (0.004)	0.019 (0.001)	—	0.87 (0.13)	0.25 (0.01)	0.75 (0.01)	149.2956
3. Full model, WLS	0.88 (0.03)	−0.076 (0.004)	0.020 (0.001)	0.000 (0.002)	—	0.26 (0.02)	0.75 (0.01)	148.9307
4. Reduced model, WLS	0.88 (0.03)	−0.076 (0.004)	0.020 (0.001)	—	—	0.25 (0.01)	0.75 (0.01)	148.9275

Table III. Estimation results for the 1960 US data

Method	Estimates							Log-likelihood
	α	β_1	β_2	β_3	ϕ	ρ	η	
1. Full model, multipl.hetero- scedasticity	0.71 (0.02)	−0.065 (0.002)	0.019 (0.001)	0.005 (0.002)	1.05 (0.14)	0.29 (0.01)	0.73 (0.01)	179.5780
2. Reduced model, multipl.hetero- scedasticity	0.74 (0.02)	−0.064 (0.003)	0.018 (0.001)	—	1.01 (0.14)	0.28 (0.01)	0.73 (0.01)	176.6068
3. Full model, WLS	0.71 (0.02)	−0.064 (0.003)	0.019 (0.001)	0.005 (0.002)	—	0.29 (0.01)	0.73 (0.01)	179.4809
4. Reduced model, WLS	0.74 (0.02)	−0.064 (0.003)	0.018 (0.001)	—	—	0.28 (0.01)	0.73 (0.01)	176.6005

Table IV. Estimation results for the 1972 US data

Method	Estimates							Log-likelihood
	α	β_1	β_2	β_3	ϕ	ρ	η	
1. Full model, multipl.hetero- scedasticity	0.80 (0.04)	−0.067 (0.004)	0.022 (0.001)	−0.007 (0.002)	0.73 (0.19)	0.33 (0.02)	0.71 (0.02)	196.2060
3. Full model, WLS	0.77 (0.04)	−0.064 (0.004)	0.022 (0.001)	−0.007 (0.002)	—	0.34 (0.02)	0.71 (0.02)	195.5128
4. Reduced model, WLS	0.71 (0.04)	−0.063 (0.004)	0.023 (0.001)	—	—	0.37 (0.02)	0.72 (0.02)	191.3216

0, it is remarkable that the results of model 4 do not differ very much of those of the other models.

The results of the four surveys show a lot of similarity. The equivalence scale is in all four years approximately 30%, which is not implausible. Also the income elasticity has a plausible value of approximately 0.73 in all years. The estimated constant term α shows more variation, but that could be expected, since this term depends on the prices.

4.2. Estimation on Time-series Data

Model (21) has been estimated on two sets of aggregate US data: the data for 1929–41 and the complete set for 1929–89. The original Tobin data give income instead of total expenditure: for both periods we have therefore used the 'new' data set. We had to take 1929 as start of the estimation period, because for earlier years there were no data on both expenditure and prices. We have used data on food consumption (*AGGEXPF*), total consumption (*AGGEXP*), non-food consumption (*AGGEXP* less *AGGEXPF*), all three converted to per capita, and on the price index of food (*FP*) and the price index of non-food (*NFP*). From these data the budget shares and the quantity index numbers for food and non-food have been calculated.

Table V gives the estimation results for the period 1929–41. From the last column we see that the assumption of homogeneity cannot be rejected. The income elasticity of food, evaluated at the average budget share over the period 1929–41, appears to be 0.75, with a standard error of 0.18, so that the 95% confidence interval ranges from 0.3 to 1.1. As for the budget data, this is much higher than the value found by Tobin (1950). The own-price elasticity of −0.22 agrees more with the one found by Tobin.

Table VI gives the corresponding results for the period 1929–89. Again, homogeneity and symmetry cannot be rejected. Note that the estimated income elasticities are nearly the same as those for 1929–41, although the standard errors may be biased because of the apparent residual autocorrelation. So in the time-series, 1929–41 as well as 1929–89, there appears to be a strong indication for an income elasticity of food that lies between

Table V. Time-series estimates, United States 1929–1941

	Without restrictions		With homogeneity restrictions	
	Food	Non-food	Food	Non-food
Estimates				
Constant (α_i)	0.006	−0.006	0.006	−0.006
	(0.002)	(0.002)	(0.002)	(0.002)
Real expenditure (β_i)	−0.069	0.069	−0.076	0.076
	(0.050)	(0.050)	(0.038)	(0.038)
Price of food (π_{ij})	−0.005	0.005	−0.003	0.003
	(0.039)	(0.039)	(0.036)	(0.036)
Price of non-food (π_{ij})	−0.014	0.014	0.003	−0.003
	(0.074)	(0.074)	(0.036)	(0.036)
$\bar{R}^2$	0.40	0.40	0.46	0.46
Durbin–Watson statistic	2.04	2.04	2.03	2.03
t-statistic for $\Sigma_j \pi_{ij} = 0$	0.2	0.2		
Income elasticity (η_i)	0.75	1.28	0.72	1.28
	(0.18)	(0.18)	(0.14)	(0.14)
Own-price elasticity (η_{ii})	−0.22	−0.29	−0.21	−0.36
	(0.18)	(0.28)	(0.16)	(0.11)
Marginal budget share (μ_i)	0.20	0.80	0.20	0.80
	(0.05)	(0.05)	(0.04)	(0.04)

Table VI. Time-series estimates, United States 1929–89

Estimates	Without restrictions		With homogeneity restrictions	
	Food	Non-food	Food	Non-food
Constant (α_i)	0.001	−0.001	0.000	−0.000
	(0.001)	(0.001)	(0.001)	(0.001)
Real expenditure (β_i)	−0.062	0.062	−0.060	0.060
	(0.026)	(0.026)	(0.026)	(0.026)
Price of food (π_{ij})	−0.063	0.063	−0.070	0.070
	(0.023)	(0.023)	(0.022)	(0.022)
Price of non-food (π_{ij})	0.032	−0.032	0.070	−0.070
	(0.038)	(0.038)	(0.022)	(0.022)
$\bar{R}^2$	0.31	0.31	0.30	0.30
Durbin–Watson statistic	1.04	1.04	0.95	0.95
t-statistic for $\Sigma_j \pi_{ij} = 0$	1.2	1.2		
Income elasticity (η_i)	0.75	1.25	0.76	1.24
	(0.11)	(0.11)	(0.11)	(0.11)
Own-price elasticity (η_{ii})	−0.44	−0.44	−0.47	−0.59
	(0.11)	(0.15)	(0.11)	(0.08)
Marginal budget share (μ_i)	0.19	0.81	0.19	0.81
	(0.03)	(0.03)	(0.03)	(0.03)

0.5 and 1. For 1929–89 the own-price elasticity for food appears to be around −0.45, with a standard error of 0.1, much lower than for 1929–41.

5. ANALYSIS OF DUTCH DATA

5.1. Estimation on Budget Data

5.1.1. 1965 Budget Survey

Model (15) has been estimated on the Dutch budget data of 1965, which are grouped. Data are needed on food consumption (variable $V11$), on total consumption ($V1$), on the number of households ($NUMH$), and on the size of the households in the groups ($HSIZE$). We followed the same procedures as for the US budget data. In Table VII we present

Table VII. Estimation results for the 1965 Dutch data

Method	Estimates							Log-likelihood
	α	β_1	β_2	β_3	ϕ	ρ	η	
1. Full model, multipl.hetero-scedasticity	1.85	−0.189	0.027	0.014	−0.27	0.14	0.34	82.4554
	(0.15)	(0.017)	(0.019)	(0.004)	(0.55)	(0.11)	(0.06)	
2. Reduced model, multipl.hetero-scedasticity	1.72	−0.166	0.024	—	0.45	0.15	0.42	78.6564
	(0.17)	(0.019)	(0.002)		(0.55)	(0.16)	(0.07)	
3. Full model, WLS	1.79	−0.181	0.026	0.012	—	0.15	0.37	80.5056
	(0.17)	(0.020)	(0.002)	(0.006)		(0.01)	(0.07)	
4. Reduced model, WLS	1.70	−0.165	0.024	—	—	0.15	0.42	78.1901
	(0.18)	(0.020)	(0.002)			(0.02)	(0.07)	

the estimation results of the model. The log-likelihood of the full *homo*scedastic model is 82.3682.

As with the US results, it is remarkable that the estimates are very insensitive to the method that is chosen. The income elasticity of 0.42 seems rather low in comparison with the US results, although it agrees rather well with the Dutch time-series results in the next subsection. The household scale factor equals $\exp(0.15) = 1.16$, which implies that for an additional member the household requires 16% additional income in order to maintain the welfare level. The sign of ϕ in the full model is suspect, but note that its standard error is rather large; in the reduced model, ϕ could well be equal to one.

5.1.2.   *1980 and 1988 Budget Surveys*

Because of the truncation of the data (Magnus and Morgan, 1995, p. 44, fn. 11), we have simply eliminated all cases where one or more of the expenditure data was equal to the maximum value. This left us with the numbers shown in the first row of Table VIII.

For each budget survey we have estimated an equation with the same variables as in the grouped data, i.e. total expenditure and household size.

The models have been estimated with a multipicative-heteroscedastic error term with total expenditure as explanatory variable. A comparison of the log-likelihoods shows that in all cases the hypothesis of a homoscedastic error term must be rejected.

The income elasticity has a value of about 0.65, which is rather high compared to the 1965 result and the time-series results of the next subsection. We have also estimated a model with all possible explanatory variables. The estimates of the income elasticity are 0.63 with a standard error of 0.02 for 1980, and 0.65 with a standard error of 0.03 for 1988. The fact that these estimates do not differ much from those in Table VIII gives some confidence that the estimates of Sections 4.1 and 5.1.1 did not suffer much from omitted-variable bias.

Table VIII. Estimation results for the 1980 and 1988 Dutch data

	1980 budget survey	1988 budget survey
Number of observations	2266	1526
Estimates		
Constant	0.954	0.721
	(0.041)	(0.046)
Total real expenditure	−0.078	−0.055
	(0.004)	(0.005)
Household size:		
1–4	0.023	0.018
	(0.001)	(0.002)
≥5	0.099	0.077
	(0.006)	(0.006)
Log-likelihood	3156.934	2255.811
Log-likelihood with homoscedastic error	3055.932	2199.963
(degrees of freedom)	(1)	(1)
Income elasticity	0.63	0.69
	(0.02)	(0.03)

5.2. Analysis of Aggregate Data

The differential version of the CBS model has been estimated on the Dutch time-series, which cover the years 1948–88. We need data on consumption of Food ($V11$), Housing ($V22$), Clothing and footwear ($V33$), Hygiene and medical care ($V44$), Education, recreation and transport ($V55$), Other consumption ($V66$), total consumption ($V11 + V22 + V33 + V44 + V55 + V66$) and on the price index numbers ($P11$, $P22$, $P33$, $P44$, $P55$, and $P66$). The estimation has been done for three, progressively more restrictive, models:

1. The model with only the adding-up restriction
2. The model with the homogeneity restriction $\Sigma_i \pi_{ij} = 0$
3. The model with the symmetry restriction $\pi_{ij} = \pi_{ji}$, which encompasses the homogeneity restriction.

The log-likelihood of the first model is 881.880; for model 2 it is 878.234, so that homogeneity is not rejected ($\chi^2 = 7.3$ with 5 df). The log-likelihood of model 3 is 866.546, so that symmetry is on the edge of rejection ($\chi^2 = 30.7$ with 15 df). The estimated Slutsky

Table IX. Estimates under homogeneity and symmetry, Netherlands 1948–88

Commodity group	α_i	β_i	Slutsky coefficients π_{ij}					
Food	0.003	−0.208	−0.017	−0.028	0.014	−0.014	0.012	0.033
	(0.001)	(0.026)	(0.039)	(0.020)	(0.021)	(0.015)	(0.027)	(0.016)
Housing	0.001	−0.001		−0.080	0.032	0.037	0.020	0.020
	(0.001)	(0.018)		(0.020)	(0.015)	(0.011)	(0.016)	(0.010)
Clothing and	−0.005	0.146			−0.064	0.002	0.009	0.007
footwear	(0.002)	(0.036)			(0.032)	(0.011)	(0.018)	(0.010)
Hygiene and	0.001	0.010				−0.072	0.108	−0.001
medical care	(0.001)	(0.014)				(0.012)	(0.034)	(0.010)
Education,								
recreation	−0.001	0.027					−0.108	0.017
and transport	(0.001)	(0.021)					(0.027)	(0.013)
Other consumption	0.001	0.026						−0.076
	(0.001)	(0.013)						(0.013)

Table X. Income and own-price elasticities, Netherlands 1948–88

Commodity group	Income elasticity η_i	Own-price elasticity η_{ii}
Food	0.35	−0.24
	(0.08)	(0.13)
Housing	1.00	−0.59
	(0.08)	(0.08)
Clothing and footwear	2.08	−0.72
	(0.26)	(0.24)
Hygiene and medical care	1.07	−0.76
	(0.13)	(0.11)
Education, recreation and transport	1.11	−0.93
	(0.13)	(0.15)
Other consumption	1.41	−1.22
	(0.20)	(0.21)

matrix appears to be negative semidefinite of rank 5, as it should be according to the theory. The estimation results for the third model are given in Table IX.

In Table X the income and own-price elasticities are given for the third model; they are evaluated at the average budget share of the estimation period. Most elasticities do not change very much as additional restrictions are imposed, and always remain within the 95% confidence intervals of each other. Thus the model with homogeneity and symmetry restrictions gives a quite reasonable description of the data. The income elasticity of food is in the most restricted model equal to 0.32 and in the least restrictive model equal to 0.40, so that with some confidence one might say that it is about 0.35.

6. CONCLUSION

Using the CBS consumer-demand system, which is based on the microeconomic theory of consumer behaviour, we have analyzed the demand for food in the USA and the Netherlands in the years 1929–88 and compared our results with those of Tobin (1950), whose findings were:

1. For the grouped US budget-survey data of 1941 the income elasticity is about 0.55.
2. For the US time-series of 1913–41 the income elasticity is about 0.25 and the own-price elasticity is about −0.3.

Our main findings are:

1. For the grouped US budget-survey data of 1941, 1950, 1960, and 1972 the income elasticity lies between 0.7 and 0.75.
2. For the aggregate US time-series data of 1929–41 the income elasticity lies between 0.7 and 0.75, and the own-price elasticity is about −0.2.
3. For the aggregate US time-series of 1929–78 the income elasticity is about 0.75, and the own-price elasticity is about −0.45.
4. For the grouped Dutch budget-survey data of 1965 the income elasticity is about 0.4.
5. For the individual Dutch budget-survey data of 1980 and 1988 the income elasticity is about 0.65.
6. For the aggregate Dutch time-series data of 1948–88 the income elasticity is about 0.35 and the own-price elasticity is about −0.20.

Comparing Tobin's results and ours one might say that, in general, the income elasticity is smaller in time-series data than in cross-section data. But in our case there are two exceptions: first, the US budget-survey of 1941 and the US time-series 1929–41, and second, the Dutch budget-survey of 1965 and the Dutch time-series of 1948–88. In particular, the first exception is remarkable, in view of the fact that it covers more or less the same period as Tobin's.

ACKNOWLEDGEMENTS

We wish to thank George van Leeuwen for his help with the computations and Anco Hundepool for converting the manuscript into LATEX.

The views expressed in this paper are those of the authors and do not necessarily reflect the policies of Statistics Netherlands.

REFERENCES

Barnett, W. A. (1981), *Consumer Demand and Labor Supply*, North-Holland, Amsterdam.

Barten, A. P. (1989), 'Towards a levels version of the Rotterdam model and related demand systems', in *Contributions to Operations Research and Economics*, MIT Press, Cambridge, MA, 441–65.

Barten, A. P. (1993), 'Consumer allocation models: choice of functional form', *Empirical Economics*, **18**, 129–58.

Deaton, A. and J. Muellbauer (1980a), 'An almost ideal demand system', *American Economic Review*, **70**, 312–26.

Deaton, A. and Muellbauer (1980b), *Economics and Consumer Behavior*, Cambridge University Press, Cambridge.

Driel, J. van (1982), *Demand Equations Underlying Consumer Demand Differential Systems*, Internal CBS report, Statistics Netherlands, Voorburg.

Driel, J. van (1996), *The Entropy for Grouped Data*, Internal CBS report, Statistics Netherlands, Voorburg.

Driel, J. van, Nadall, V. and Zeelenberg K. (1996), *The Demand for Food in the United States and the Netherlands: a Systems Approach with the CBS Model*, Internal CBS report, Statistics Netherlands, Voorburg.

Keller, W. J. and J. van Driel (1985), 'Differential consumer demand systems', *European Economic Review*, **27**, 375–90.

Leser, L. E. V. (1963), 'Forms of Engel functions', *Econometrica*, **31**, 694–703.

Leser, L. E. V. (1976), 'Income, household size and price changes 1953–1973', *Oxford Bulletin of Economics and Statistics*, **38**, 1–10.

Magnus, J. R. and M. S. Morgan (1995), *The Experiment in Applied Econometrics: Information Pack*, CentER, Tilburg University.

Pollak, R. A. and Wales T. J. (1979), 'Welfare comparisons and equivalence scales', *American Economic Review*, **69**, 216–21.

Theil, H. (1975), *Theory and Measurement of Consumer Demand*, North-Holland, Amsterdam.

Theil, H., Suhm F. E. and Meisner J. F. (1981), *International Consumption Comparisons*, North-Holland, Amsterdam.

Tobin, J. (1950), 'A statistical demand function for food in the USA', *Journal of the Royal Statistical Society*, Series A, **113**, 113–41 [reprinted in Chapter 2, this volume].

Working, H. (1943), 'Statistical laws of family expenditure', *Journal of the American Statistical Association*, **38**, 43–56.

COMMENTS BY PROFESSOR MICHAEL R. WICKENS *(University of York)*

My first reaction upon reading about this experiment in the *Journal of Applied Econometrics* was one of alarm. It promised to be a high profile exercise in data-mining which would only serve to further discredit econometrics. I was greatly relieved, therefore, when I read the paper of the CBS team. More than anything else they have put the underlying economic theory at the forefront of their analysis and avoided the temptation to data-mine. Ironically, and to my surprise, my main concerns about the paper relate to traditional econometric issues.

The main focus of the experiment is on the values of two parameters: the price and income elasticities of the demand for food. This is such a modest request, and the experiment is so well intentioned — it gives us an unusual opportunity to examine what the last nearly fifty years of econometrics has contributed — that, perhaps, I should comment briefly on the reasons for my methodological misgivings.

After a mere thirty years as an applied econometrician (a lowly sub-species rarely to be found in the halls of fame of *Econometrica*) I am still wrestling with the problem of how to combine theory with evidence. Methodology is, of course, a young person's problem. Following a, usually embarrassing, attempt to instruct the world in this age-old, and intractable, issue, most of us quickly move on to the less turbulent waters of being a practitioner, adopting current professional conventions. This is probably wise. On occasions like this however we do need to take more notice than usual of methodological considerations.

The aim of this experiment is to see how far econometrics has 'progressed'. It is clear that in the last fifty years there has been an explosion of knowledge in econometric theory and a revolution in computing power, as a result of which our ability to estimate and test models has improved considerably. Even so, it is still relatively easy to demonstrate the lack of robustness of these findings to small changes in the model such as an additional variable, to new data, or to acting on the findings (the Lucas critique). Partly as a result of this, econometricians have focused increasingly on what they can do well rather than the issues that are of importance in economics. Examples of this are the use of VAR analysis as a substitute for structural models, the focus on whitening the errors as a model selection criterion, and the use of semi-parametrics to improve within sample fit.

It would seem from this that econometrics has not progressed very far, but I do not share this view. I would rather say that there is a widespread misperception of the role of econometric analysis, which I think should be to assist the underlying economics. Econometrics should be used to provide good estimates of the key parameters of the economic model, and to find out how robust the economic model is. The focus here is on learning about the economic theory and how consistent it is with the data. Persistent and significant empirical failures should prompt a revision of the theory rather than an attempt to fix up the model to improve its empirical properties. Paying too little attention to the economic origins of the model, and focusing instead on statistical criteria, is likely to lead to a good estimate of an uninterpretable, useless coefficient. This could prove particularly dangerous for policy analysis. An exception may be made for forecasting where the appropriate economic theory is often unnecessary, even though it may still be helpful.

As the focus of this experiment is on economically well-defined parameters, it is not open to the full extent of these strictures. Nevertheless, the spread of estimates obtained in these studies suggests to me, not a failure of econometric technique, but a lack of theoretical foundations for various of the models. Indeed, I would even be so bold as to claim that the different results can be attributed directly to the models estimated.

Although the experiment is about the price and income elasticities of the demand for food, the precise theoretical framework (and hence model) in which to embed these parameters is an open question. It is not clear, for example, whether other variables need to be taken into account, what the functional form should be, what stochastic structure to use, and whether the elasticities are constant, or vary across time, or are due to other variables. Most of the studies keep fairly closely to Tobin's original model, but it is by no means obvious that this is adequate. The CBS team are an exception in deriving their econometric model from a well-articulated economic theory, the CBS model. This results in them explaining quantity shares, i.e. the share in the total quantity demanded for each item. The model is derived from the definition of expenditure shares and is constrained by the imposition of the usual additivity, homogeneity and Slutsky symmetry conditions, but is not obtained directly from an explicit theory of consumer behaviour. The final model is expressed in terms of differentials. For application to the time-series data the differentials are interpreted as the proportional change over time of the corresponding cross-section aggregates. Due to data constraints the data period begins in 1929 instead of 1913, where Tobin's data began.

The cross-section model for each individual is given in Equation (6):

$$\overline{w}_{it} D\frac{q_{it}}{Q_t} = \beta_i DQ_t + \sum_{j=1}^{K} \pi_{ij} Dp_{jt} + \varepsilon_{it}$$

where $\overline{w}_{it} = (w_{it} + w_{it-1})/2$, w_{it} is the ith expenditure share, q_{it} is the demand for the ith good, Q_t is total demand (and is calculated as total expenditure x_t, divided by the general price level, P_t), p_{it} is the ith price, ε_{it} is the error term and D is the differential operator such that $Dx_t = \log(x_t) - \log(x_{t-1})$. The income elasticity is $\eta_i = 1 + \beta_i/w_i$ and the (uncompensated) own price elasticity is $\eta_{ii} = (\pi_{ii}/w_i) - \eta_i w_i$. This is then applied to groups of households after adjusting from the individual to a group of households and taking account of the problem of not being able to take time differences by integrating the model. The final model estimated for each household group is

$$w = \alpha + \beta_1 \log x - \beta_2 h + \beta_3 \log n + \varepsilon$$

where h is an equivalence measure for a household and n is the number of households in each group.

The time-series model is obtained by aggregating over individuals and the final estimating equations for each year is stated as

$$\overline{w}_i D\frac{q_i}{Q} = \beta_i DQ + \sum \pi_{ij} Dp_j.$$

This was implemented by estimating

$$\overline{w}_{it} \Delta \log \frac{q_{it}}{Q_t} = \alpha_i + \beta_i \Delta \log Q_t + \sum \pi_{ij} \Delta \log p_{jt} + \varepsilon_{it}.$$

Estimates of the price and income elasticities can be obtained from estimates of β_i, π_{ij} and w_i using the formulae above.

The advantages of this approach, and they are considerable, are that it delivers a precise model to estimate and it relates the parameters of the model directly to the parameters of interest. It will be noted, for example, that the model is not the same as Tobin's. The disadvantage for the researcher seeking to publish the results is that this approach highlights all too clearly the large number of implicit and explicit assumptions that need to be made along the way to arrive at an equation to estimate. For example, the theory does not predict that, in general, the elasticities will be constant; this is an extra assumption made for convenience. Although the additional assumptions may be inimical to getting the paper accepted for publication, they have the merit of identifying the probable cause of any empirical short-comings, and of pointing to how the model can be revised. Given the need to make these additional assumptions, it is easy to criticize this approach. Though, perhaps, such restrictions should be recognized as a strength, not a weakness, of the approach. My criticism should be seen in this context.

I shall focus mainly on the time-series estimates for the USA in my comments. My first concern relates to the choice of economic theory and the way it has been used. Although the model to be estimated has not been derived from an explicit theory, it is clear that it is broadly consistent with neoclassical consumer theory. As a result the final model ignores the distinction between non-durables and durables, and abstracts from intertemporal considerations, a time dimension not present in consumer theory.

The absence of a clearly articulated theory means that it is not obvious what is endogenous and what is exogenous. It appears from the results of other studies that this is an important consideration. It also worth noting that the estimating equation is based on quantity shares. To obtain these the total quantity demanded is derived indirectly by deflating total nominal expenditures by a price index. It means that the quantity share $q/Q = Pq/x = [pq/x]/[p/P]$ is an expenditure share divided by the price of the good relative to the general price level. I would guess that the expenditure share was relatively constant and that most of the variation in the quantity share comes from the relative price term. Thus variations in the dependent variable would be largely due to prices, but in consumer theory, prices are taken as exogenous. If the dependent variable is exogenous, there would then be concerns about the possibility of biases in the estimates.

I am also unhappy about formulating the time-series model in first differences, especially when the disturbances appear to be white noise and not a moving average. Even though it goes against the spirit of this approach, which is concerned with decisions on the margin, it is more natural to specify the model in levels. A levels version of the model would need to take into account the findings of the 'Dundee' team that the levels data are integrated. If the model is well specified in levels then the error term should be stationary. This means that taking first differences would generate a moving average error, and not white noise. One possible explanation for this anomaly is that by taking first differences the long-run solution has been lost and the estimates just reflect short-run dynamics contaminated by omitted deviations from long-run equilibrium.

A possible solution to this would be to integrate the time-series model so that it is expressed in levels. This would give

$$w_i \log \frac{q_{it}}{Q_t} = \alpha_i + \beta_i \log Q_t + \sum \pi_{ij} \log p_{jt} + e_{it}.$$

Noting that $\eta_i = 1 + \beta_i/w_i$, and $\eta_{ij} = \pi_{ij}/w_i - \eta_i w_j$ and using Tobin's notation for both the parameters and the variables, which means among other things converting the CBS model to per capita terms, the long-run CBS model can be written

$$\ln S_t = \alpha + \eta \ln(Y_t/\Pi_t) + (\beta + w\eta) \ln P_t + [\gamma + (1-1)\eta] \ln Q_t + (\eta - 1) \ln N_t + e_t$$

$$= \alpha + \eta \ln Y_t + \beta \ln Y_t + \beta \ln P_t + \gamma \ln Q_t + (\eta - 1) \ln N_t + e_t$$

where S is an index of the quantity of food per capita, Y is nominal total consumption per capita, P is the food price index, Q is the non-food price index, $\ln \Pi_t = w_t \ln P_t + (1 - w_t) \ln Q_t$ is a general consumption price index and w_t is assumed constant. β has been redefined as minus the own price elasticity of food and γ as the cross-price elasticity. This model is similar to Tobin's except that it has an extra term, $\ln N$.

To be consistent with the theory, the 'income' variable should be total consumption expenditure per capita and the dependent variable should be real aggregate expenditure on food per capita. Using these data definitions, rather than Tobin's, also enables the data set to be extended from 1929–1941 to 1929–1976.

In Tables V and VI, the CBS team report estimates based on the differential model and the new variable definitions for both time periods, and both with and without homogeneity restrictions. A satisfying feature of these results is that the unrestricted income

Table C1. Cointegrating regressions
of long-run versions of the CBS
model 1929–1976

ln S	1	2
constant	−5.811	−0.652
	(44.08)	(−0.81)
ln(Y/Π)	0.528	0.617
	(61.77)	(40.91)
ln P	0.213	0.160
	(12.42)	(10.84)
ln Q	−0.015	0.109
	(−1.14)	(5.05)
ln N	—	−0.353
		(−6.46)
R^2	0.999	0.999
CRDW	0.510	0.586
se	0.0123	0.0089

t-statistics are in parentheses

elasticity is 0.75 for both time periods, and this is very similar to both the corresponding restricted estimates, and to the cross-section estimates. This compares with an estimate of around 0.51 obtained by Tobin using different variables and a levels equation with dynamics.

It is interesting to compare these estimates with those obtained using a cointegrating regression on the levels data. These results are reported in Table C1. Looking first at column 1 — Tobin's model — the estimate of the income elasticity is lower than that obtained by the CBS team and much closer to that obtained by Tobin. Column 2 has the estimates for the long-run CBS model. It will be noted that the coefficient of ln N is significant as predicted by the theory. Subtracting this from the income elasticity gives 0.97 which is close to the theoretical prediction of unity. The price coefficients are Slutsky elasticities and not compensated price elasticities. The implied own price elasticities are −0.074 for column 1 and −0.118 for column 2 which are a little lower than those obtained by the CBS team. These results are generally consistent with the theory, though the low value of the Durbin–Watson statistic suggests that the model may still be misspecified possibly due to omitting long-run variables. For further discussion of the long-run CBS model and the possibility of including short-run dynamics see my comments on the Dundee paper (Chapter 7).

To sum up, the CBS team have approached the problem in a way that I approve of by starting with economic theory, and carefully deriving their model to estimate from this. Their results have the attractive feature of being similar for the cross-section and time-series data. My main criticism is the use of differenced data for the time-series analysis. When the model is integrated to levels it is found to differ from Tobin's, and estimates of this model lie between those obtained by Tobin and the CBS team.

COMMENTS BY PROFESSOR M. HASHEM PESARAN (Trinity College, Cambridge)

This paper reports on the application of the demand system approach developed at the Central Bureau of Statistics (CBS) of the Netherlands to the USA and the Netherlands data. The CBS approach is closely related to the Rotterdam model developed originally by Theil and Barten.

It is difficult to compare the elasticity estimates given in this paper with those originally obtained by Tobin (1950). This is partly due to the use of total expenditure rather than per capita disposable income. The two sets of estimates based on 'expenditure' and 'income' will be identical only under a constant saving rate which is unlikely to hold across households and/or over time. Also, as was pointed out by Richard Stone in his discussion of Tobin's paper, the dependent variable in Tobin's time-series regression analysis does not take full account of 'the amount of services rendered by caterers or any retail outlets, nor in all cases does it measure the amount of processing involved' (Tobin (1950, p. 141)), while the food expenditure data used by the CBS team does take account of the cost of food processing and restaurant services. From this, together with the fact that income elasticity of demand for outdoor food consumption is much higher than food consumption at home, one would then expect the use of a more comprehensive measure of food data as used by the CBS team to yield a much higher income elasticity estimate. It is therefore important that the estimate obtained by the CBS team is compared, not with the original Tobin estimate, but rather with the time-series estimate reported by Stone, which was approximately 0.62 (See Tobin (1950, p. 142)).

The authors clearly state that the time-series regressions are based on Equation (21), but they do not fully set out the discrete time version of Equation (21) actually estimated. I can only speculate that the equation they estimate (in terms of the available time-series) is given by

$$
\begin{aligned}
y_t &= \tfrac{1}{2}(w_t + w_{t-1})[\Delta \log(q_t/Q_t)] \\
&= \beta \Delta \log Q_t + \pi_{11} \Delta \log(FP_t) + \pi_{12} \Delta \log(NFP_t) + \varepsilon_t
\end{aligned}
\tag{C1}
$$

where

$$ w_t = AGGEXPF_t/AGGEXP_t, \qquad q_t = AGGEXPF_t/FP_t $$

$$ \Delta \log Q_t = \Delta \log(AGGEXP_t) - \Delta \log(P_t) $$

$$ \Delta \log q_t = \Delta \log(AGGEXPF_t) - \Delta \log(FP_t) $$

$$ \Delta \log P_t = w_{0t} \log(FP_t) + (1 - w_{0t}) \log(NFP_t). $$

The variables FP_t, NFP_t, etc. are as defined in the organizers' data chapters. The values chosen for weights w_{0t} are not specified in the paper and in my own empirical analysis I set them equal to w_{t-1}. It is also unclear whether the expenditure figures ($AGGEXP$ and $AGGEXPF$) were deflated by population, the number of households or neither? On the assumption that the expenditure figures where not deflated by the CBS team, I managed to replicate the results in Table V. Notice, however, that the regressions in this table are estimated over the period 1930–1941. Also for the estimates with the homogeneity restrictions imposed, using the appropriate critical values from the t-distribution with nine degrees-of-freedom, the 95% confidence interval for the expenditure elasticity of food lies between $0.403(= 0.72 - 0.14 \times 2.262)$ and $1.037(= 0.72 + 0.14 \times 2.262)$, and not 0.5–1.0, stated by authors (end of Section 4).

Turning to the aggregate US time-series estimates for the 1930–1989 period, I was unable to exactly replicate the estimates given in Table VI. I obtained an estimate of -0.0582 for β, in the case of the specification with the homogeneity restriction imposed, as compared to the estimate of -0.060 reported in Table VI. More importantly, the regressions for this period failed the tests of residual serial correlation, normality and heteroscedasticity. These failures could be due to a variety of factors. I investigated two possibilities: omitted dynamics and structural change. Adding a lagged dependent variable among the regressors turned out to be highly significant and lowered the point estimate of the 'income' elasticity from 0.75(0.11) to 0.56(0.247). The standard errors are given in brackets.

To investigate the possibility of structural change, I estimated the restricted version of the model (with the homogeneity restriction imposed) over the two sub-periods 1930–1949 and 1950–1989. The estimated standard errors of these regressions turned out to be 0.0117 and 0.0025, a five-fold decline, suggesting a massive change in the model's error variances over the two sub-periods. More importantly, the sub-period regressions now satisfy the various diagnostic tests for residual serial correlation, functional form mis-specification, non-normal errors and heteroscedasticity. Based on the regression estimated over the sub-period 1950–1989, the expenditure elasticity of food is estimated to be 0.41 (0.083), which is well below the estimate of 0.76 (0.11) obtained by the CBS team for the 1929–1989 period (see Table VI).

In summary, the substantially larger estimates of income elasticity of food obtained by the CBS team can be traced to the choice of the sample period and the fact that they use total expenditure as the proxy for the income variable. Differences in techniques used seem to have had only a marginal effect on the differences between the estimates obtained by the CBS team and the other investigators.

COMMENTS BY PROFESSOR ARIE KAPTEYN (Tilburg University)

The authors adopt a demand systems approach, which implies, among other things, that they estimate total expenditure elasticities rather than income elasticities. This in itself already makes if difficult to compare their estimates of 'income elasticities' (i.e. expenditure elasticities) with those of others. Yet, within a structural model with intertemporally additive preferences, their estimates may make more sense than estimates of true income elasticities.

The reason for this is simple. In a rational expectations life-cycle type of model, there is no direct role for income in the explanation of food consumption. Current income influences total consumption only insofar as it conveys information about the life-time budget constraint. This in turn depends on the assumed income process. For instance, if income follows a random walk the informational content of current income with respect to life-time resources is much larger than when income exhibits very low serial correlation. The income elasticity of the demand for food can therefore only be understood as some sort of reduced form parameter which mixes the total expenditure elasticity of the demand for food with a specification of the income process and the ensuing relationship between current income and total expenditures. Since there is no reason to believe that the income process remains the same over time (for example, institutional changes or changes in labour market status would affect it), nor that it will be the same across countries, we would not expect the income elasticities to exhibit any form of constancy.

To summarize: the authors are estimating a parameter which makes sense from a theoretical viewpoint, but not the parameter the organizers of the experiment are after. But then the latter parameter probably does not exist in a meaningful way.

The demand system is a differential system for the time-series data, whereas for the cross-sections, a Working–Leser type of system emerges. Ample consideration is given to aggregation and grouping problems that arise if the model for individual households is applied to time-series or grouped data. I do not understand the discussion in Section 3.5 about equivalence scales. It is stated that, in contrast with for instance the AID system, no underlying utility function exists. But for the specification in levels the associated cost function (corresponding with Working-Leser) does exist. Why the existence of utility functions matters for the specification of the equivalence scales is not quite clear to me. It is well known that one cannot identify equivalence scales from demand data alone, whether one has an underlying cost function or not. Imposing an independence of base assumption on the function $m(.)$ simplifies matters, but is arbitrary by necessity.

I like the paper for its consistent attempts to derive demand function specifications from utility theory and its head on tackling of aggregation problems. Sometimes the specification appears to be a bit simple and I would have liked to see some more specification search and diagnostic tests. The most serious omission from an econometric viewpoint may be that endogeneity of total expenditures has been ignored.

Interestingly, the authors find 'income elasticities' equal to roughly 0.75 for both the US time-series data and all four US cross-sections. For the Netherlands the 'income elasticities' are much lower: 0.35 for the time-series, 0.4 for the 1965 grouped data, and 0.65 for the individual data from 1980 and 1988.

Unfortunately, no attempt is made to explain these different outcomes. It would appear that either the elasticity of the demand for food with respect to total expenditures is not a well defined concept or the model estimated is incomplete. Both possibilities seem realistic.

REPLY BY HANS VAN DRIEL, VENUTA NADALL AND KEES ZEELENBERG

Reply to Wickens

1. We agree with Wickens that econometrics should assist the underlying economic model. That is why we started from neo-classical micro-economic theory and have based our estimates of the income and price elasticity of food on the CBS model.
2. Wickens seems to imply that in the CBS model the income and price elasticities are assumed to be constant. However, this is not the case. In the CBS model the parameters β_i and π_{ij} are assumed to be constant; the income and price elasticities are functions of these parameters and of the budget share w_i. Since the budget shares are not assumed to be constant, neither are the income and price elasticities.
3. Wickens suggests that the budget share (expenditure share) is relatively constant, and that most of the variation in the quantity share comes from the relative price term. He uses this constancy in his derivation of his levels model. Certainly for food, the budget share has not remained constant over the long periods that are considered in this experiment (1929–1989 for the US and 1948–1988 for the Netherlands), as can be seen from the data. Thus we do not think that most of the variation in the quantity share is due to the price.
4. We agree with Wickens that it would be better to integrate the time-series model so that it is expressed in levels. The derivation, however, of a levels version of the CBS model is very intricate (see Van Driel et al. (1996), Section 3.5). The levels model

suggested by Wickens seems to be inappropriate. Differencing the left-hand-side of his equation we obtain $\Delta w_i \log(q_i/Q)$, which is unequal (even as an approximation) to the left hand side $\overline{w}_i \Delta \log(q_i/Q)$ of the CBS model.

Moreover, the derivation of Wickens 'long run model' requires the assumption of a constant budget share of food, which we reject (see point 3); therefore we do not think that the levels model can be consistent with the data, so that the estimation results as presented in Table C1 are to be viewed with suspicion.

We could solve the question which variables are exogenous or endogenous by modifying Wickens' suggestion to solve the equation $\mathrm{d} \log S = \mathrm{d} \log \overline{q}$, but this still leads to a model in first differences so it does not solve the anomaly in the error structure. We do, however, agree with Wickens that the construction of a long-run model and the inclusion of short-run dynamics in it are important challenges.

Reply to Pesaran

1. Pesaran notes the differences between the concept of food expenditure used by Tobin and the one used in the data sets of the Experiment. We agree that our estimation results should be compared not with those of Tobin, but with those of Stone, who has obtained a much higher income elasticity than Tobin. Thus most of the difference between Tobin's results and ours is explained by differences in the concept of food expenditure.
2. Pesaran asks whether the expenditure data were deflated. Following Theil (1975) we have converted the expenditure data to per capita, i.e. deflated by population.
3. Pesaran raises the questions of omitted dynamics and structural change. As mentioned above in our reply to Wickens, we agree that the introduction of dynamics is important. The structural break around 1950 may be caused by the fact that we have converted all expenditure data to per capita, so that population size is in fact a variable in our model, with a coefficient restricted to be equal to minus that of total expenditure. Omitting population size may give more consistent results for the whole period.

Reply to Kapteyn

1. Kapteyn (as Pesaran) raises the question of expenditure elasticities versus income elasticities. He argues that the latter may be not very useful (even in an intertemporal context). He may be right, but since the requirement that we should stick to the Experiment's Information Pack deprived us of the possibility to use data on interest rates and build an intertemporal model, we could not investigate this.
2. As to Kapteyn's question about the equivalence scale we make the following remarks. Pollak and Wales (1981) discuss several methods (scaling, translating) to incorporate household composition in demand equations, allowing the parameters to be functions of household composition. These 'conditional equivalence scales' enable us to estimate the parameters of the demand system by pooling data from households with different composition. Knowledge of the utility or cost function on the background is not needed. We, however, prefer the concept of the 'unconditional equivalence scale'

which is defined in terms of the cost function. Such an unconditional scale may depend on household composition, utility levels and prices. A particular specification of this scale, combined to the cost function of the reference household, leads to a household cost function from which the demand equations are derived by Shephard's lemma. Kapteyn is right when he mentions the fundamental identification problem in this approach. Van Driel (1988) shows, however, that leaving prices out of the scale is identifying. Therefore we would have preferred an equivalence scale that depends on household composition *and* the utility level. Unfortunately for the CBS model the cost function of the reference household is not known, so neither is the household cost function which belongs to this type of scale. Therefore the household demand equations which belong to the CBS model with this scale cannot be derived. Therefore we had to confine ourselves to an equivalence scale depending only on household composition. For such a scale it can be shown that knowledge of the cost function is not needed for deriving the demand equations, since it is equivalent to Engel's method.

ADDITIONAL REFERENCES

Driel, J. van (1988), *Identification of Family Equivalence Scales*, Internal CBS Report, Statistics Netherland, Voorburg.
Pollak, R. A. and Wales T. J. (1981), Demographic variables in demand analysis, *Econometrica*, **49**, 1533–51.

CHAPTER 5

REVISITING TOBIN'S 1950 STUDY OF FOOD EXPENDITURE*

EDWARD E. LEAMER

1. GRAPHS

Tobin (1950) includes some informative data displays, but soon after 1950 graphical displays of data were put on the endangered species list. In the intervening half-century, the economics profession has been deluged by estimates and t-values. But we don't 'internalize' all these numbers. We walk through the mist as if it weren't there at all. Our intellectual lives are driven mostly by the manipulation of words in our offices. Some of the words are English, most of them are Mathematics.

There are probably many reasons why numbers don't much affect us. One important reason is that humans were not designed by evolution to process numbers. As a species we first learned to process images. Words and language came later. Numbers came last. As children we recapitulate our evolution, first learning to process images, then words and last of all numbers.

In the formal analysis of data, images also preceded numbers. J. N. Keynes (1891) wrote: 'In the use of statistics, considerable assistance may often be derived from the employment of diagrams.' Although graphical displays were common in the early days of econometrics from Keynes the elder in 1891 to Tobin the laureate in 1950, graphs went out of style in the 1950s. One reason is that graphs didn't seem to work well for the complex multi-dimensional non-experimental problems that econometricians were solving at that time. What kind of data display is appropriate for instrumental variables estimation? Frisch's (1934) bunch maps seemed more confusing than illuminating. Movement away from graphical analysis in the 1950s for intellectual reasons was amplified by technological advances in the 1960s that greatly lowered the cost of numerical processing with comparatively modest reductions in the cost of graphs. Monroe calculators and early electronic devices were strictly numerical. Printers until the 1980s allowed only primitive displays that were unsuited to publication. Most importantly, perhaps, the batch mode of processing forced analysts to wait for hours or even days to see the output. This delay worked against the use of graphs because the psychic costs of waiting are more severe for images than for numbers. Images evoke an emotional, creative response that depends greatly on the state of mind of the observer. Waiting can lower the psychic preparedness of the observer, and limit the value of the image. Numbers, by contrast, are typically processed in the preprogrammed part of the brain, and we can access these programs virtually at any time. Thus waiting doesn't matter as much for numbers. The phenomenal

* Reprinted from the *Journal of Applied Econometrics*, **12**, 533–561 (1997).

Methodology and Tacit Knowledge: Two Experiments in Econometrics
Jan R. Magnus and Mary S. Morgan © 1997 John Wiley & Sons Ltd

improvements in computing over the last decade have pushed the relative price of images compared to numbers in the opposite direction, greatly lowering the cost of graphs with little real reduction in the cost of computing numbers. At the touch of a button or two, desktop computers and printers can produce beautiful and persuasive graphs. This allows economists an entirely new language in which to discuss the issues. This visual language taps into our most primitive and most powerful information-processing systems. But graphs by themselves will not do. We need to be multi-lingual. We need to speak Images, English, Mathematics and Numbers. If we can say the same thing in all four languages, maybe someone will get the message.

2. ISSUES

You might imagine that it is hard to have a conversation without a topic, but when outsiders listen carefully, they have a difficult time unscrambling what exactly economists are discussing. Most of the conversation seems like a parlour game to decide who is the most clever of them all. (Do you remember 'Name That Tune'? First contestant: 'I can reject the hypothesis of cointegration with an F of 2.' Second contestant: 'I can reject it with an F of 4.' First contestant: 'OK, I challenge you to do it!!')

The real issues of economics are public policy questions. It is important to be explicit about them. If we are not, it is easy to turn economics into a parlour game.

3. OVERPARAMETERIZATION AND AMBIGUITY

Our data sets are not nearly strong enough to carry the heavy burdens of the models that we heap upon their shoulders. They need some kind of assistance. Here are the possibilities.

Assistant	Method
Classical monk	Include all the variables
Robot	Stepwise (a.k.a. unwise) regression
1000-pound economist	Any way he or she wants to
Bayesian monk	Fictional prior data
Sensitive Bayesian	Fuzzy prior data

The classical monk spends days copying tomes that explain how to do econometrics in Asymptopia. The classical monk's answer to every question is: 'Wait.' We let the classical monk determine the language that we use for discussing data analysis (t-values, standard errors, etc.) but we ignore altogether the monk's rules for the holy sacrament of data analysis. We sin, and we sin wantonly. Some of us use robots for assistance in our sin. These robots are preprogrammed to omit variables that have low t-values and to add new variables that have high t-values. Most of us prefer to do the discarding and adding ourselves. We analyze data the same way that the 1000-pound gorilla makes love: 'Any way she wants to.' Whatever the robots or gorillas produce, we carry the results up to the monastery of the classical monks for their blessing. We get the blessing, but only because we don't admit that we spent the night with robots and gorillas.

A small sect of Bayesian monks has rebelled against this hypocrisy. They express sympathy for our problems. They understand that real data are not strong enough to carry our huge models. They realize that we cannot wait for the age of Asymptopia. They know that if the data gets stronger, we will overwhelm them again by adding to their load a new parameter or two. These Bayesian monks tell us the solution is simple: Make up some more data. Call it your 'prior'. The prior can help carry the load. When hearing this advice, the classical monks fall to the floor and shake violently, and their mouths spew forth the epithet 'UNSCIENTIFIC'. 'Be calm,' counsel the Bayesian monks, 'The sin is Deceit. There is nothing at all deceitful about fictitious data. Actually, it is the gorilla and the robot who are unscientific, since they delude us into thinking that their estimates are based on the data alone, when we all know the data cannot carry the load.'

Conversion to Bayesianism soothes the consciences of those data analysts who have them. But I have to tell the truth here. Everyone I know who has converted to Bayesianism has retreated to monasteries. The Bayesian monasteries are not all that different from the sampling-theory monasteries. Instead of Asymptotic chants, the Bayesian monks swap stories about parameters coming from distributions. These stories are very unfamiliar and seem pretty preposterous. I hope nonetheless that you will listen to some of mine. I think that you will feel better if we explore the implications of several different stories, in other words, a sensitivity analysis. Perturb the prior a bit, and if the inferences change a lot, draw the conclusion that these data are not useful. If the inferences don't change very much, it doesn't matter that you are not too comfortable with the first story.

4. WHAT IS THE QUESTION?

A theme that I developed in Leamer (1996) is that economics needs questions, theory and data. These three need to be explicit, integrated and balanced. When one of these three is missing, when the three are otherwise imbalanced or poorly integrated, we do poor economics.

By a question I do not mean: Do the theory and the data fit together adequately? Some may be interested in economics for purely scientific reasons, but I prefer to think that the discipline derives from a set of policy questions such as: 'Should the government intervene in marketplaces to try to control the greed that drives us all?' 'No', is the answer. As if by an invisible hand, greed drives us to work for the greater good.

I have searched through the Tobin (1950) article to try to find exactly what is the question. I am afraid that I cannot find one. Tobin's apparent purpose is to fire off some practice rounds from shiny new econometric cannons. Never mind the target for now; let's see if these cannons work. From the vantage point of 1996, these cannons look remarkably modern, well worth testing. But in the intervening fifty years, econometricians have been rolling out designs for bigger and bigger cannons, most of which are not even constructed let alone test fired. Today it seems wise to aim at as 'real' a target as we can 'imagine'.

4.1. My Question

'How should we design public assistance programmes to ensure that all Americans have a minimal level of nutrition?' Specifically: *'How should food price subsidies vary by family composition and income level to ensure that families spend at least $150 on food (1941$) per family member?'* Of course, I cannot pretend to address this question in an entirely serious way within the scope of this econometric exercise. For example, I will ignore economies of home production that accrue to families of different composition; I will assume that subsidies are not transferable from poor to rich. And so on. In other words, the question is not entirely real. My point is not to solve a real problem but to show how a question can affect the analysis. The point of the exercise is to find the non-linear function of the parameters that is the subsidy rate needed to attain the target food consumption level.

5.   TOBIN'S 1941 DATA[1]

5.1.   1941 Data: Traditional Processing

Figure 1 displays the 1941 Tobin budget study data in a way that reveals much of what there is to be learned from these data. This figure compares food expenditure per family member with household income per family member, both using a logarithmic scale. The points are labelled by family size. The data for family size 1, 3 and 5+ are connected with line segments. Here are the clear messages that these data are sending:

1.   There are two outliers. Food expenditures for the poorest family 3 is too high, and food expenditures for the wealthiest family 2 is too low. More on this below.
2.   Food consumption is neutral to changes in family composition in the sense that per capita expenditure is mostly determined by per capita income except:

    (a)   Single individuals spend relatively more on a per capita basis at low levels of total family income. The single expenditure pattern conforms better with the

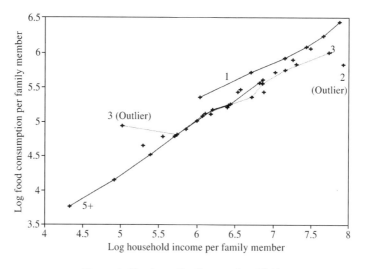

Figure 1. Food per family member 1941

---

[1] The data are compiled from various US government publications (see organizers' data section for details). Robert Murdock is thanked for able research assistance. The regressions reported below were all run with E-views. The Bayesian analyses were done with SEARCH-PC, a program of my own, and with a Gauss version, Micro EBA, written by Richard Fowles, University of Utah.

per capita expenditure pattern of other families at higher levels of income. This means that expenditures are less income elastic for these single families.

(b)   Large families with five or more members constitute all the data at low levels of family income per capita. These large poor families spend less on a per capita basis than is suggested by the income elasticity implied by the rest of the data. These families conform well with the pattern at higher levels of per capita income and therefore the apparent income elasticity is greater.

We should expect that numerical data analysis yields similar conclusions. Tobin's equation is

$\log(FOODCON) = 1.9 + 0.56 \log(HINC) + 0.25 \log(AHSIZE)$ where the variables are
$FOODCON =$ average family expenditures on food and beverages including that which is consumed away from home
$HINC =$ average household disposable income net of taxes, exclusive of net asset changes
$AHSIZE =$ average family size equal to an integer up to 4 and an average approximately equal to 6 for the 5+ families. (Taken from the Tobin write-up. Note that this is missing for the larger-income categories which were omitted by Tobin, which limits the sample.)

A residual plot (not shown) from this Tobin regression reveals the two outliers and also suggests greater sensitivity to income than the OLS estimate (0.56) for family sizes 2, 3 and especially 6. Both of the outliers have low values for $ESTPOPH$, the estimated number of households in the class. The correspondingly low cell counts could fully explain the apparent outliers which should be treated with weighted regression. The original data dissemination did not include the cell counts and I mistakenly thought these were unavailable. Weighting by $ESTPOPH$ would have forced a substantial reduction in the sample because of missing values. I chose instead the brute-force approach that just omits these rogue observations.

Table I reports a regression with these two outliers omitted and with a functional form that is allowed to vary by family size. This equation includes the family dummy variables

$FAMi =$ dummy variable taking on the value one if the family is size i. The family size 5+ has been lumped together into a single size which below will be taken to be 6.

In this regression, I have made no attempt to distinguish the average size of the cells corresponding to 5+ families, but these families are almost the same size on average. Next, statistically insignificant variables have been trimmed sequentially to produce the 'final' result reported in Table II. The fit of this equation is extraordinary for one like myself who is used to looking at very noisy scatters. Averaging across families has eliminated most of the noise, and what is left is a problem in curve fitting more than econometric inference.

As we already learned from an examination of the data in Figure 1, the estimated income elasticity for the family size 5+ is 'measurably' large, using a t-value of at least one as the definition of 'measurable'. This higher income elasticity is offset by a smaller constant, meaning that these large families consume less food at low levels of income but more at higher levels. What is interesting in this table is that a high income elasticity

Table I. Least squares regression, 1941 data, 35 observations (outliers omitted).
Dependent variable: LOG(*FOODCON*)

Variable	Coefficient	std. error	t-Statistic	Prob.
C	1.89	0.23	8.07	0.00
FAM1	0.02	0.33	0.05	0.96
FAM2	−0.53	0.32	−1.67	0.11
FAM4	0.25	0.33	0.76	0.45
FAM6	−0.73	0.29	−2.51	0.02
LOG(HINC)	0.59	0.03	19.67	0.00
FAM1*LOG(HINC)	−0.03	0.04	−0.62	0.54
FAM2*LOG(HINC)	0.06	0.04	1.49	0.15
FAM4*LOG(HINC)	−0.02	0.04	−0.38	0.71
FAM6*LOG(HINC)	0.13	0.04	3.40	0.00
R-squared	0.99	Mean dependent var.		6.39
Adjusted R-squared	0.99	S.D. dependent var.		0.50
S.E. of regression	0.05	Akaike info criterion		−5.79
Sum squared resid	0.06	Schwarz criterion		−5.35
Log likelihood	61.69	F-statistic		385.81
Durbin–Watson stat	2.97	Prob (F-statistic)		0.00

Table II. Least squares regression, 1941 data, 35 observations.
Dependent variable: LOG(*FOODCON*)

Variable	Coefficient	std. error	t-Statistic	Prob.
C	1.94	0.13	14.84	0.00
FAM2	−0.58	0.25	−2.35	0.03
FAM4	0.13	0.03	5.07	0.00
FAM6	−0.78	0.21	−3.67	0.00
LOG(HINC)	0.59	0.02	34.94	0.00
FAM1*LOG(HINC)	−0.03	0.00	−6.59	0.00
FAM2*LOG(HINC)	0.07	0.03	2.09	0.05
FAM6*LOG(HINC)	0.13	0.03	4.86	0.00
R-squared	0.99	Mean dependent var.		6.39
Adjusted R-squared	0.99	S.D. dependent var.		0.50
S.E. of regression	0.05	Akaike info criterion		−5.90
Sum squared resid	0.06	Schwarz criterion		−5.54
Log likelihood	61.58	F-statistic		532.12
Durbin–Watson stat	2.95	Prob(F-statistic)		0.00

and a low constant also applies to families of size two, although these effects are a bit smaller than for family size 5+. This is something that we didn't notice initially from the graph (Figure 1). A graph like Figure 1 with only the data for family sizes 2 and 3 requires one to look very hard to see why the numerical processing is making us think that family 2 has a greater income elasticity than Family 3. If one included the two outliers the picture would be much fuzzier, and anyway the numerical processing is driven very much by a commitment to log-linearity, an assumption which your eyes feel freer to discard.

After this numerical processing, we are now in a position to revise finding 2:

2. Food consumption is not neutral to changes in family composition. There are econo-
    mies of family size in the sense that doubling income and number of family members
    increases expenditures by less than 100%. The increase is roughly 80%.
3. A simple economies of scale adjustment is not enough to explain the differences in
    food consumption among families of different size:

    (a) After adjusting for the 'economies of scale', large families with five or more
         members spend less at low levels of income and more at high levels of income.
         In other words, their food expenditures are relatively income elastic.
    (b) Numerical processing suggests that single individuals are income insensitive and
         that couples are more income sensitive than families of size 3, but a close look
         at the graphs does not make this conclusion transparent.

5.2. Confession of Sin

Goodness, I have just done a 'specification search' (Leamer, 1978). I started with the
Tobin simple model and then enlarged it to allow behavioural differences among families of different composition and then shrunk the model again to eliminate statistically
unmeasurable differences among families. I looked at lots of graphs and used eyeball
estimation to choose a log-linear equation from a much larger set of possibilities. This is
forward and backwise stepwise, a.k.a. unwise, regression; e.g. Leamer (1978, 1983). I am
embarrassed about this sinful methodology since I have spent a large chunk of my career
preaching against it. From the pulpit, I have sermonized that there are two problems with
forward and backward stepwise:

1. Stepwise regression is based implicitly or explicitly on prior information, but the
    outcome of the specification search is an unknown and almost certainly inappropriate
    mixture of prior and data.

The regression in Table II is based partly on the data information regarding functional
form, family compositional effects and outliers, and partly on the prior. How much of
each is a total mystery. The regression reported in Table II thus suffers from the usual
pre-testing problem that it is based on a complete commitment to the particular final
model that popped mysteriously from the analysis, when the process of analysis reveals
that there is no such commitment. We can take care of that problem by being clear about
our level of commitment to these restrictions — in other words to write down a prior
distribution.

2. The 'prior' is often formulated after a preliminary examination of the data and the
    data thus are used inappropriately twice: once to form the prior and a second time
    to analyze the data. This double-counting of the prior makes us think the support for
    data-instigated hypotheses is greater than it really is.

The Bayesian treatment of pretesting is quite straightforward — be explicit about your
prior. But there is an additional problem. There is no way to access your 'prior' after

looking at graphs and running some preliminary regressions, since your current state of mind is a hopelessly confused mixture of prior and data. When you see curvature in the data, you think you had a prior of curvature; when you don't see curvature you think the opposite. Leamer (1974) proposes a way to discount the results (enlarge the standard errors) to allow for this kind of hypothesis/prior discovery. He proposes to act as if the researcher were solving implicitly a formal sequential observation problem in which a subset of potential explanatory variables is first observed and then a decision is made whether it is advantageous to observe some additional variables. This formal decision-theoretic problem generates a sequence of 'discount' factors. If the initial result is not much discounted then the researcher reveals a strong commitment to the irrelevance of additional variables, and when new variables are added, a high discount factor applies to the expanded model. If, on the other hand, the analyst is willing to discount heavily the initial results, knowing that there may well be important omitted variables, then the discount factor applicable to later results can be smaller.

But to follow Leamer's (1974) rules is a major headache. Better to avoid the problem by spending more time in advance thinking about the possibilities. The scarce commodity is not economists' time; it is the data. Better not waste the data with a mindless specification search. After all, neither outliers nor family compositional effects nor non-linearities are genuine discoveries and it is better to plan in advance how to handle them. In other words, expand the parameter space explicitly in the beginning and deal with the data inadequacies by formulating at the outset a prior distribution on this higher-dimensional parameter space.

5.3. Priors for Family Composition Effects

That's the sermon. The realities are very different, indeed. It is very difficult to do a persuasive Bayesian data analysis with a high-dimensional model because, the more parameters, the more arbitrary will seem the prior. I therefore choose to stick with the assumption of log-linearity because I am pretty sure a Bayesian analysis of more complicated functional forms would lead to pretty much the same conclusion. (Take a look at Figure 1!) I also choose to discard the two outliers, because I am pretty sure the Bayesian analysis of outliers would lead to pretty much the same conclusion. Remember that Bayesian methods are about combining prior and data. When the data overwhelm, no sense bothering. When the prior overwhelms, no sense bothering. I choose instead to use Bayesian thinking to study family compositional effects. Here the data and the prior seem roughly balanced, and I would like to be clear how much is prior and how much is data.

A Bayesian analysis needs a prior distribution. This requires a set of constraints on the model and measure of how 'hard' the constraints should be imposed. A 'natural' constrained model has family food consumption independent of family composition in the sense that if a family were split apart and if the income were split equally, then total food consumption would remain unchanged. In terms of an equation this means that

$$\log(FOODCON/AHSIZE) = \alpha + \beta \log(HINC/AHSIZE) \qquad 1$$

or equivalently

$$\log(FOODCON) = \alpha + \beta \log(HINC/AHSIZE) + \log(AHSIZE). \qquad 2$$

In selecting a parameterization for a more complete model it is essential to allow this constrained model to be a clear special case. Here is a form that will work:[2]

$$\log(FOODCON) = \alpha + \beta \log(HINC/AHSIZE) + \gamma \log(AHSIZE)$$

$$+ \sum_{i=1,2,4,6} \delta_i \log(HINC/AHSIZE)FAM_i + \sum_{i=2,4,6} \alpha_i FAM_i. \qquad 3$$

Note that the summations are defined to take the family size 3 (two adults and one child?) as the benchmark. This equation reverts to (2) if the coefficients satisfy $\gamma = 1$, and $\delta_i = 0$, $\alpha_i = 0$. These constraints will be imposed weakly by acting in Bayesian fashion as if the parameters came from independent normal distributions with means and standard errors reported in the first columns of Table III. The standard error of 0.5 for γ allows the family size elasticity considerable freedom to depart from its most probable value of one. A one standard error departure from zero for the family means α_i allows family composition to alter food consumption by 10%: $\exp(0.1) = 1.1$. The standard error of 0.1 for the income elasticity differences δ implies that the income elasticities are not likely to vary across family composition by more than 0.1. The prior means seem right, you may acknowledge, but what about the standard errors? Where did those numbers come from? Moreover, what about the covariances? If one of the prior constraints were badly violated, wouldn't that affect your opinions about the others? Never mind; we are going to do a sensitivity analysis to find out how much the standard errors and covariances matter.

Once the priors are announced they seem pretty transparent, but formulating them requires more effort than you might realize. I had to think carefully what are sensible values for the parameters, and I consequently had to be creative in selecting a felicitous and transparent functional form. Thus I chose formulation (3), not the one reported in Table I, which represents one of my first passes at these data. These models are statistically identical, but I found (3) a better setting in which to think about my priors. This brings us to the most important Bayesian advice: *Patience.* If, when you paint, you don't mind spending hours preparing the surface, then you would be a happy Bayesian. But if you are like most of us, who are impatient to see the result and prefer to slap on the paint long before the surface is really ready, then you will find it hard to be a virtuous Bayesian.

Understanding is the reward for patient preparation. If you rush to the data you will not be prepared to hear the softer messages. Thoughtful contemplation of your prior creates a prepared state of mind that can lead to real discoveries. You will be forced to choose a parameterization that can accommodate your priors and you will have to think a bit about what are reasonable estimates. This can facilitate the interpretation of the results, whether or not you use a formal Bayesian analysis. Compare the ordinary least squares estimates in the third from the last column of Table III with the prior means and standard errors in the first two columns. The OLS family size elasticity (0.53) is almost one prior standard error from the prior mean and the family size intercepts are several prior standard errors from their prior means. Except for family 6, the family effects on the income elasticity are not large compared with the prior standard errors. In other words, the data seem to be saying that there is a 'surprising' family composition effect on the intercepts but not the income elasticities. Here the word 'surprising' is a reference to our prior state of mind, which reference is facilitated by being formal about the prior.

---

[2] The reader may verify that the second summation cannot start at $i = 1$ without causing perfect collinearity.

Table III. Bayesian analysis of Tobin 1941 food consumption

	Prior Mean	Prior S.E.	Prior uncertainty multiplier 0	0.25	0.5	1	2	4	OLS Est.	OLS S.E.	t-stat.
Constant	1	0.5	0.87	1.25	1.48	**1.83**	1.92	1.94	1.94	0.22	8.86
Log(ahsize)	0	0.1	1.00	0.92	0.75	**0.49**	0.48	0.52	0.53	0.25	2.13
FAM2	0	0.1	0.00	0.00	0.00	**−0.07**	−0.35	−0.48	−0.49	0.25	−1.95
FAM4	0	0.1	0.00	0.00	0.01	**0.10**	0.29	0.28	0.27	0.31	0.86
FAM6	0		0.00	0.00	−0.01	**−0.07**	−0.27	−0.39	−0.41	0.38	−1.09
Log(hinc/ahsize)	0		0.69	0.64	0.63	**0.62**	0.61	0.60	0.60	0.03	20.51
fam1*log(hinc/ahsize)	0	0.1	0.00	0.01	0.00	**−0.04**	−0.04	−0.04	−0.04	0.04	−0.88
fam2*log(hinc/ahsize)	0	0.1	0.00	0.00	0.00	**−0.01**	0.04	0.06	0.06	0.04	1.45
fam4*log(hinc/ahsize)	0	0.1	0.00	0.00	0.01	**0.01**	−0.02	−0.02	−0.02	0.04	−0.44
fam6*log(hinc/ahsize)	0	0.1	0.00	0.00	0.03	**0.07**	0.10	0.12	0.12	0.04	3.13

Income elasticities

	0	0.25	0.5	1	2	4	OLS Est.
FAM1	0.69	0.65	0.62	**0.58**	0.56	0.56	0.56
FAM2	0.69	0.64	0.63	**0.61**	0.64	0.65	0.65
FAM3	0.69	0.64	0.63	**0.62**	0.61	0.60	0.60
FAM4	0.69	0.64	0.64	**0.63**	0.59	0.58	0.58
FAM6	0.69	0.64	0.66	**0.69**	0.71	0.72	0.72

Family 3 estimated per capita consumption at low income: $350 income per family member; log(inc) = 5.85

$	0	0.25	0.5	1	2	4	OLS Est.
	135.1	134.7	132.2	**132.9**	134.3	135.4	135.6

Scale effects: Per capita consumption at $350 income per family member compared with family 3

	0	0.25	0.5	1	2	4	OLS
FAM1	0%	19%	29%	**37%**	38%	37%	37%
FAM2	0%	6%	10%	**11%**	7%	5%	5%
FAM3	0%	0%	0%	**0%**	0%	0%	0%
FAM4	0%	−1%	1%	**1%**	3%	2%	2%
FAM6	0%	−4%	−2%	**−2%**	−3%	−4%	−4%

Bounds for estimates of income elasticity: Doubling and halving prior uncertainty
(1) Scalar multiplier: multiplying or dividing prior covariance matrix by a factor of two
(2) Matrix neighbourhood: covariance matrix bounded from above and below

	Scalar multiplier Lower	Upper	Matrix neighbourhood Lower	Upper
Log(hinc/ahsize)	0.61	0.63	0.58	0.66
fam1*log(hinc/ahsize)	0.00	−0.04	−0.09	0.04
fam2*log(hinc/ahsize)	0.00	0.04	−0.06	0.09
fam4*log(hinc/ahsize)	0.01	−0.02	−0.08	0.07
fam6*log(hinc/ahsize)	0.03	0.10	0.004	0.13

5.4. Bayesian Estimates

The bold column in the middle of Table III reports Bayesian estimates of Equation (3) using the reference prior defined at the left. The columns to the right and left of this bold column report estimates based on prior distributions that are either more concentrated or less concentrated in the sense that the prior standard errors are all multiplied by the 'prior uncertainty multiplier' reported in the first row of the table. If this 'prior uncertainty multiplier' is increased to infinity, the prior is completely diluted and the estimates revert to their unconstrained least-squares values. Thus the column in Table III with 'prior uncertainty multiplier' equal to infinity has the OLS estimates. If the 'prior uncertainty multiplier' is reduced to zero, the prior constraints are imposed exactly and the column at the extreme left thus is a constrained least squares estimate conforming to Equation (2). In that case, other than the constant there is only an income elasticity to estimate, which turns out to be 0.69. The bold Bayes estimates are a compromise between the unconstrained OLS estimates at the right and the constrained estimates at the left.

The middle panel of Table III translates these estimates into numbers that are most understandable, namely income elasticities for the five different family sizes and family scale effect which are comparisons of per capita expenditures at low family per capita income of \$350 per person ($\log(HINC/AHSIZE) = 5.85$). The Bayes income elasticities increment slowly with family size up to family size 4 and then take a larger jump up for family 6. The estimated per capita expenditure for this poor family is greatest for single individuals, 37% more than for a family of three with the same per capita income. Couples spend 11% more than families of size 3; families of size 4 spend 1% more. The largest families spend 2% less.

Using this Bayesian analysis we have thus arrived at somewhat different conclusions compared with the conclusions from the graphical and interactive numerical processing described above. The Bayesian conclusions are:

1. Income elasticities increment slightly with family size beginning at 0.58 for single individuals and incrementing to 0.63 for families of size 4 and 0.69 for families greater than 5.
2. At low levels of income per family member, families of size 3 and 4 have just about the same predicted food expenditures per family member. Single individuals have 37% more expenditure, couples 11% more and large families (5+) have 2% less.

These Bayesian conclusions are not compelling if they are excessively fragile, that is, if minor changes in the prior lead to substantially different conclusions. If the prior is weakened by multiplying the standard errors by a factor of 2, the conclusions do change a bit. It remains the case that the income elasticity is greatest for *FAM6* but the second highest income elasticity now applies to *FAM2*. This is very close to the unconstrained OLS results reported at the right. The pattern of predicted per capita consumption levels is not much affected by diluting the prior. Indeed the OLS results and the Bayesian results are very similar.

Varying the prior uncertainty multiplier changes the prior distribution in a special way: the whole covariance matrix is multiplied by a constant. This leaves unchanged the prior correlations. The third panel in Table III helps to answer the question: 'What about prior correlations?' This question is answered with a sensitivity analysis that allows all elements of the prior covariance matrix to vary independently. The results from the first sensitivity analysis are reported in the table under the heading 'scalar multiplier', meaning that the prior covariance matrix has been altered by a scalar multiplier, $V = \sigma_1^2 V_0$, with $1/4 < \sigma_1^2 < 4$. The bounds labelled 'Matrix Neighbourhood' allow the prior covariance matrix greater freedom, restricting the prior covariance matrix only to lie between an upper bound and a lower bound, $V_0/4 < V < 4V_0$, where the inequalities refer to positive-definite matrix orderings. The income elasticity for family 3 lies in the interval from 0.61 to 0.63 if the prior is varied by a scalar factor, but from 0.58 to 0.66 if a neighbourhood of matrices is allowed. Family 2 is estimated to have an income elasticity larger than family 3 if the scalar multiplier is used, but this inference breaks down if a neighbourhood of priors is allowed. The conclusion that the income elasticity for *FAM6* is greater than the income elasticity for *FAM3* survives this increased sensitivity analysis, but just barely. The other income elasticities cannot be distinguished from the *FAM3* elasticity.

These Bayesian sensitivity analyses are often worth-while, but in this case the results are about the same as the estimates and standard errors from the OLS estimates reported in the last columns of Table III: the *t*-value for the *FAM6* variable interacted with the income variable is 3.13. The *t*-value for the *FAM2* variable is less — 1.45. The other interactions are statistically insignificant. In other words, a formal Bayesian treatment of the compromise between data and prior doesn't lead to conclusions that conflict substantially with informal compromises, based solely on the inspection of *t*-values.

6. TOBIN TIME-SERIES

The budget studies don't have meaningful price variability across observations and therefore cannot be used to estimate the price elasticity, a task that Tobin performed using US time-series. Tobin's log-linear demand equation is

$$\log(C_t) = \log(K) + \alpha_1 \log(Y_t) + \alpha_2 \log(Y_{t-1}) + \beta \log(P_t) + \gamma \log(Q_t) \qquad 4$$

where C is per capita food consumption in constant dollars, Y is disposable income, P is a food price index, and Q is the non-food price index. An assumption that food supply S is fixed (no international trade, no inventories?) allows Tobin to invert this system to solve for price as a function of variables assumed to be exogenous:

$$\log(P_t) = [\log(S_t) - \log(K) - \alpha_1 \log(Y_t) - \alpha_2 \log(Y_{t-1}) - \gamma \log(Q_t)]/\beta \qquad 5$$

where S is per capita supply of food $=$ per capita consumption. Tobin's budget study allows him to constrain the sum of the income elasticities $\alpha_1 + \alpha_2$ to equal 0.56. Our reanalysis suggests an income elasticity more like 0.6. Another constraint considered by Tobin is homogeneity of degree zero, $\alpha_1 + \alpha_2 + \beta + \gamma = 0$, which means that an equi-proportional change in all prices has no real effect. A third constraint is that lagged income doesn't matter: $\alpha_2 = 0$. The Tobin equation can be rewritten to allow these constraints to be imposed by the omission of variables:

$$\log(P_t/Q_t) = [\log(S_t) - 0.6 \log(Y_t/Q_t) - \log(K) - (\alpha_1 - 0.6) \log(Y_t/Q_t)$$
$$- \alpha_2 \log(Y_{t-1}) - (\alpha_1 + \alpha_2 + \beta + \gamma) \log(Q_t)]/\beta, \qquad 6$$

the constrained form of which is

$$\log(P_t/Q_t) = [\log(S_t) - 0.6 \log(Y_t/Q_t) - \log(K)]/\beta. \qquad 7$$

A fourth piece of prior information used by Tobin concerns the correlation pattern of the residuals. Tobin's discussion centres on estimates uncorrected for autocorrelation in the residuals, but he does discuss the problem. By this ordering of the results he reveals his 'prior' that the autocorrelation coefficient is probably small. Most analysts today would have a different prior for the autocorrelation coefficient, possibly with a mode at one. For purposes of illustration, I will use the Tobin prior and treat autocorrelation as doubtful.

The time-series data used by Tobin are displayed in Figure 2. [3] This display, suggested by Equation (7), compares the relative price of food to non-food with per capita expenditure on food, controlling for real per capita income with an income elasticity of 0.6. The bivariate regression applicable to this display has a coefficient on the income variable equal to -1.26 implying a price elasticity equal to $1/-1.26 = -0.79$. The residual plot and the Durbin—Watson statistic in this regression scream out for help. Figure 2 suggests one kind of help: discard the observations after 1936. But maybe a more complete model can help pull these rogue observations back into the middle of the scatter.

The full regression model reported in Table IV includes current value of real per capita income ($TOBRPCY = TOBPCY/TOBNFP$), the lagged value of the per capita nominal income, the non-food price and an autoregressive error term. This allows four departures from the simple scatter Figure 2:

1. Lagged income affects food demand.
2. The income elasticity is different from the budget study estimate of 0.6.
3. Demand is not homogeneous of degree zero in prices. (Demand depends on absolute prices, not just relative prices.)
4. There are excluded determinants of demand with an autoregressive structure.

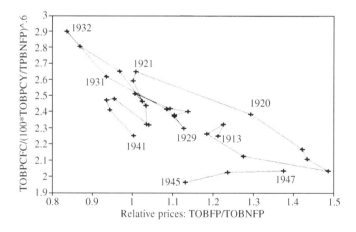

Figure 2. Food demand function (per capita consumption adjusted for income)

---

[3] Historians be alert. The version of the paper presented at the Tilburg conference had words that called for the use of real income but both the data display and the data analysis were based incorrectly on nominal data. When the nominal data are used, the 1914–19 data form a group of outliers and the sensitivity analysis is much affected by the data subset used. That error made me think that the information about the price elasticity in the time-series is much weaker than I now believe.

Table IV. Least squares regression. Dependent variable LOG($TOBFP/TOBNFP$), annual data
1914–1947

Variable	Coefficient	Std. error	t-Statistic	Prob.
C	0.13	2.59	0.05	0.96
LOG($TOBPCFC$) – 0.6* LOG($TOBRPCY$)	–1.45	0.64	–2.27	0.03
LOG($TOBRPCY$)	–0.06	0.32	–0.19	0.85
LOG($TOBPCY(-1)$)	–0.07	0.12	–0.61	0.55
LOG($TOBNFP$)	0.43	0.22	1.95	0.06
AR(1)	0.88	0.10	8.86	0.00

R-squared	0.92	Mean dependent var.		0.09
Adjusted R-squared	0.91	S.D. dependent var.		0.15
S.E. of regression	0.05	Akaike info criterion		–6.00
Sum squared resid	0.05	Schwarz criterion		–5.72
Log likelihood	51.88	F-statistic		56.51
Durbin–Watson statistic	1.75	Prob(F-statistic)		0.00

Coefficient correlation matrix					
LOG($TOBPCFC$) – 0.6* LOG($TOBRPCY$)	1.00				
LOG($TOBRPCY$)	**0.96**	1.00			
LOG($TOBPCY(-1)$)	**0.37**	0.33	1.00		
LOG($TOBNFP$)	**–0.35**	–0.31	–0.75	1.00	
AR(1)	**0.45**	0.46	0.30	–0.37	1.00

Included observations: 29
Excluded observations: 5 after adjusting endpoints
Note: $TOBRPCY = TOBPCY/TOBNFP$

In terms of the t-statistics reported in the top panel, the data support 3 and 4: demand is not homogeneous of degree one and the residuals are strongly autocorrelated. (*Warning*: E-views has omitted the 1945–47 data because of the lack of the war years for linking data.)

A menu of alternative estimates is reported in Table V. Here the four doubtful effects are discarded from the model in all possible ways. The results are then ordered by one measure of fit: the standard error of the regression. The best regression in that sense omits real per capita income, $RPCY$, and the lagged per capita income, $PCY(-1)$. This is perfectly predicted by the standard result that the adjusted R^2 increases or decreases depending on whether you omit a variable with a t-value less than or larger than one. The next best regression includes all the variables. The worst regressions of all fail to control for serial correlation, which is another way of saying the t-statistic for the first-order autocorrelation parameter reported in Table IV is 8.86. At the bottom of this table is a scatter diagram comparing the estimate price elasticity with the measure of model fit. *For the best-fitting models, the price elasticity varies from –0.69 to –0.92.*

This *ad hoc* sensitivity analysis depends on two features of these data: (1) the correlation matrix of coefficients reported at the bottom of Table IV and (2) the t-values of the constraints reported at the top. The correlation matrix reveals that the coefficient that determines the estimate of the price elasticity, that is, the coefficient on log($TOBPCFC$) – 0.6* log($TOBRPCY$), is highly positively correlated with the AR(1) effect. Thus, if one wants to make this coefficient more negative, and the implied price elasticity lower, constrain the AR(1) coefficient to a number less than 0.88. Indeed this is exactly what happens when the AR(1) coefficient is set to zero — see Table V. On the other hand, the

Table V. Estimates sorted by standard error of regression. Dependent variable LOG(TOBFP/TOBNFP)

C	-0.64	0.13	0.16	-0.41	-1.40	0.47	1.27	0.24	7.73	7.63	7.60	6.10	1.49	1.48	1.18	1.44
LOG(TOBPCFC) − 0.6* LOG(TOBRPCY)	-1.36	-1.45	-1.19	-1.34	-1.10	-1.25	-1.35	-1.09	-3.19	-3.21	-3.20	-2.54	-1.46	-1.45	-1.27	-1.25
LOG(TOBRPCY)		-0.06	0.15		0.12	0.01		0.13	-0.95	-0.93	-0.90	-0.61	-0.02	-0.02		
LOG(TOBPCY (−1))		-0.07		0.35	0.35	0.10			0.17	0.13	0.19			-0.01		
LOG(TOBNFP)										0.05						-0.06
AR(1)	0.82	0.88	0.82	0.81	0.83	0.84	0.73	0.76								
Elasticity	-0.73	-0.69	-0.84	-0.75	-0.91	-0.80	-0.74	-0.92	-0.31	-0.31	-0.31	-0.39	-0.68	-0.69	-0.79	-0.80
R-squared	0.93	0.92	0.92	0.92	0.92	0.91	0.90	0.90	0.87	0.87	0.83	0.79	0.74	0.74	0.66	0.67
Adjusted R-squared	0.92	0.91	0.91	0.91	0.90	0.90	0.89	0.89	0.85	0.85	0.81	0.77	0.72	0.71	0.65	0.65
S.E. of regression	0.04	0.05	0.05	0.05	0.05	0.06	0.05	0.05	0.06	0.06	0.06	0.07	0.08	0.08	0.09	0.09
Sum squared resid	0.04	0.05	0.05	0.05	0.05	0.06	0.07	0.07	0.09	0.09	0.11	0.14	0.17	0.17	0.22	0.22
Log likelihood	51.8	51.9	48.5	52.2	52.3	49.4	49.0	49.1	47.0	47.1	44.9	41.7	35.0	35.0	34.2	34.5
Durbin–Watson stat	1.52	1.75	1.33	1.39	1.34	1.53	1.17	1.16	1.15	1.10	1.06	0.78	0.39	0.39	0.37	0.41
Schwarz criterion	-5.94	-5.72	-5.83	-5.86	-5.76	-5.66	-5.77	-5.66	-5.43	-5.32	-5.21	-5.12	-4.83	-4.72	-4.76	-4.67

Scatter plot: Price elasticity (vertical axis, ranging 0.0 to −1.0) versus Model Standard Error (horizontal axis, ranging 0.04 to 0.09).

large t-value for the AR(1) parameter tells us that the data don't like setting it to zero. Again, take a look at Table V.

The problem with the sensitivity analysis reported in Table V is that it is both too extreme and not extreme enough. It is too extreme because it allows only one of two options: let the parameter be completely determined by the data, or let the parameter be completely determined by the prior. It is not extreme enough because it doesn't allow other linear constraints, say constraining to zero some linear combination of the coefficient on lagged per capita income and the AR(1) parameter. A Bayesian analysis treats both of the shortcomings. Its main goal is to help us interpret the correlation matrix and the t-values reported in Table IV.

The prior means for the doubtful variables are, of course, all zero. The prior standard errors have all been set to 0.1. A big issue in this analysis is whether the cross-section estimate of the income elasticity is properly transferred into the time-series analysis.[4] The transferability question is here addressed by erecting a 'permeable firewall' between cross-section and time-series. The firewall takes the form of a prior distribution that allows the cross-section and time-series estimates to be similar, but not identical. The degree of similarity is determined by the prior standard errors for the current and lagged income elasticities. If these standard errors are set to zero, then the constraints are hard and the transfer perfect. With prior standard errors greater than zero, the cross-section income elasticity estimate is only partially transferred into the time-series. Then, if the time-series information were informative enough, the cross-section estimate would be ignored altogether.[5]

Choosing prior standard errors for the regression coefficients is particularly difficult because they are ratios of parameters about which we are most likely informed, for example the lagged income elasticity divided by the price elasticity. I have set all the prior standard errors to 0.1 on the assumption that the price elasticity is around 1 and doesn't contribute much to the uncertainty about the regression coefficients. Thus I am thinking about the homogeneity constraint (within 0.1 of 1) and the lagged income elasticity (within 0.1 of 0) and the current income elasticity (within 0.1 of 0.6). If you thought the price elasticity is close to zero, you need to enlarge these prior standard errors dramatically.

Table VI reports Bayesian bounds that extend the sensitivity analysis reported in Table V to allow the 'partial' imposition of homogeneous linear constraints not just the complete omission/inclusion of variables. A homogeneous constraint would be that the sum of the coefficients on current and lagged income is equal to zero. Partial imposition of this constraint would occur if this linear combination is assumed to have a prior mean of zero but a non-zero standard error. Two kinds of Bayesian bounds are reported in Table VI. The limited bounds allow the prior covariance matrix to vary over an interval of matrices with lower bound equal to the original prior covariance V_0 divided by 4 and upper bound multiplied by 4. The extreme bounds let the prior covariance matrix be anywhere. Compared with Table V, the limited bounds in Table VI are narrower because they allow only 'partial' omission of variables but the bounds are larger because all linear constraints are allowed. The table has five columns, each corresponding to a different subset of doubtful variables. In the first column all four variables are treated as

---

[4] Two pertinent references that emerged from the Tilburg conference are Izan (1980) and Maddala (1971).

[5] Incidentally, the transfer should be operating also in the opposite direction informing the cross-section analysis of the time-series income elasticity. But the information about the income elasticity from the time-series is so minor compared with the cross-section that it is hard to imagine much transfer in that direction.

Table VI. Bounds for Bayesian estimates. Coefficient on
LOG(*TOBPCFC*) − 0.6* LOG(*TOBRPCY*)

Doubtful variables	(1)	(2)	(3)	(4)	(5)
LOG(*TOBRPCY*)	d	d	d		
LOG(*TOBPCY* (−1))	d		d	d	d
LOG(*TOBNFP*)	d		d	d	d
AR(1)	d	d		d	
Estimates					
Extreme bounds					
Lower	−4.82	−4.52	−2.10	−4.13	−1.59
Upper	2.13	1.68	−0.64	−0.68	−1.01
Limited bounds					
Lower	−3.82	−3.70	−1.80	−3.78	−1.46
Upper	1.14	0.80	−0.82	−0.91	−1.02
Corresponding price elasticity					
Extreme bounds					
Lower	−0.21	−0.22	−0.48	−0.24	−0.63
Upper	0.47	0.59	−1.56	−1.47	−0.99
Limited bounds					
Lower	−0.26	−0.27	−0.56	−0.26	−0.68
Upper	0.88	1.25	−1.22	−1.10	−0.98

Notes:
The prior means are all zero and the prior standard errors used to form the limited bounds are all 0.1.
The limited bounds restrict the prior covariance in an interval around its initial value. The initial matrix is multiplied and divided by 4 (the standard errors adjusted by 2).
The bounds for the price elasticities in the first two columns point away from zero because the mapping by $1/x$ of an interval that overlaps the origin is two open intervals excluding zero.

doubtful, which is the prior defined above. The extreme bounds for the coefficient on the adjusted consumption variable, log(*TOBPCFC*) − 0.6* log(*TOBRPCY*), are −4.82 and 2.13, meaning that there are homogeneous linear constraints on the doubtful variables that can produce any estimate in this range, but it is impossible to find estimates outside this range. Unfortunately, this range is very large, particularly when the estimates are inverted to solve for the estimate of the price elasticity. Moving from full to partial imposition of constraints — the limited bounds — doesn't help much. The interval of estimates still includes zero. The next four columns in the table reveal the source of the problem. If both the AR(1) correction and the real per capita income are treated as doubtful, the bounds are wide, but if only one of these is doubtful the bounds are narrow. In other words, it is constraints that jointly involve the AR(1) correction and the importation of the cross-section estimate that cause the problem. Since joint constraints on these two effects do not seem very plausible and since most of us think that dynamics are important, the bounds reported in column (3) with AR(1) a free parameter are probably the best way to enlarge the results reported in Table V. Here the interval of price elasticities varies from −0.48 to −1.56 if full imposition of constraints is allowed. *If only partial imposition is allowed then the interval shrinks to* −0.56 *to* −1.22. This is the set of estimates that I will live with. If you choose to let the time-series determine its own income elasticity and also let the data speak freely regarding the AR(1) variable, then the limited bounds reported in column (5) in Table VI shrink to the interval from −0.68 to −0.98, which conforms well with the informal inspection of Table IV.

7. DOES IT MATTER?

The stated purpose of this exercise is to solve for price subsidy rates to achieve a targeted level of food consumption per family member. Table VII reports four different tables of subsidy rates based on the different estimates so far determined. The results in the upper left-hand corner are the base against which the others are compared. These results are based on Tobin's cross-section equation and Tobin's estimate of the price elasticity. Moving to the right in the table are results that use the extreme Bayes estimate of the price elasticity. Moving downward are results based on models with more complex family-composition effects.

The Tobin subsidy rate for a family of size 2 with a very low income of $50 is 26%. To encourage this family to spend $300 on food, the government must bear 26% of the cost. A family of size 6, with the same very low income of $500, needs a subsidy rate of 85% to get its food expenditure up to 6 times 150 = $900. These subsidy rates depend substantially on the price elasticity as can be seen in the display on the right. If the price elasticity is -1.22 instead of -0.51, then the subsidy to this very poor family of two drops from 26% to 12%. The subsidy for the large poor family drops from 85% to 55%. Limited knowledge of the price elasticity is a major problem for the design of a subsidy programme.

Family composition effects also matter. The OLS estimates of the full model suggest a subsidy rate for a very poor family of size two equal to 40% in contrast to the Tobin subsidy of 26%. But it doesn't much matter whether one uses the OLS estimates or the Bayes estimates of this full model. One big difference implied by the full model is that the high income elasticity for large families makes the subsidy rates decline sharply with income. Also, compared with the Tobin subsidies reported in the first panel, there should be higher subsidy rates for the small poor families.

Table VII. Subsidy rates to attain targeted food consumption per family member. Target food consumption: $150 per family member

1: Tobin equation from Table I and two price elasticities							
Family size	Price elasticity: -0.51 Family income ($)				Price elasticity: -1.22 Family income ($)			
	500	1000	1500	2000	500	1000	1500	2000
1	0%	0%	0%	0%	0%	0%	0%	0%
2	26%	0%	0%	0%	12%	0%	0%	0%
3	59%	12%	0%	0%	31%	5%	0%	0%
4	73%	42%	10%	0%	42%	21%	4%	0%
5								
6	85%	68%	51%	32%	55%	38%	25%	15%
2: Full equation, price elasticity = -0.51								
Family size	OLS estimates: full equation Family income ($)				Bayes estimates: full equation Family income ($)			
	500	1000	1500	2000	500	1000	1500	2000
1	0%	0%	0%	0%	0%	0%	0%	0%
2	50%	0%	0%	0%	38%	0%	0%	0%
3	64%	18%	0%	0%	67%	24%	0%	0%
4	74%	42%	8%	0%	76%	44%	8%	0%
5								
6	84%	56%	23%	0%	86%	63%	36%	6%

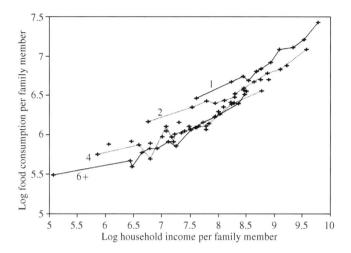

Figure 3. Food per family member 1972

8.   1950, 1960, 1972 DATA

I have chosen to concentrate this report on a re-analysis of Tobin's data in an effort to send my messages as clearly as possible. The message about graphics can be sent one more time. Scatters like Figure 1 for the 1950, 1960, and 1972 data are remarkably similar, even in the positioning of the large and small families. But the 1972 scatter depicted in Figure 3 suggests pretty clearly some non-linearity in the log-log relationship. It appears that the necessity nature of food forces low-income families to concentrate their income on food expenditures. I had expected to discover an S-shaped relationship with minimum food consumption levels at low incomes and saturation effects at high incomes. Except for the 1972 data there is no apparent departure from log-linearity. The concave shape of the scatter for the 1972 data seems right at low income levels but doesn't exhibit the saturation effects that I expected. I am left in a state of suspicion about the 1972 data.

9.   CONCLUSIONS

9.1.   Methodological Conclusions

1.   Graphs can help persuade ourselves and our audiences. Figures 1 and 2 pretty much tell the whole story.
2.   Questions should drive a data analysis. By keeping at least in the back of my mind the thought that I am trying to design a food subsidy programme, I haven't allowed myself to wander too far off-course.
3.   Bayesian methods are a lot of hard work, and by being so transparent seem pretty suspicious. Sometimes I think life with the 1000-pound economist is a lot more appealing. But Bayesian methods offer some new tools for doing sensitivity analyses which are more powerful than traditional *ad-hoc* searches.
4.   The spectre of data mining continues to haunt us all. The witch doctors who have befriended and endorsed data mining chant in indecipherable tongues, but I fear the translation of their message is: 'It must be right, I've been doing it since my youth.'

9.2. Empirical Conclusions

1. The income elasticity of food consumption of very large families is higher than Tobin realized.
2. The evidence in the 1913–41 time-series about the price elasticity is pretty fragile and depends on how the income elasticity from the cross-section budget study is imported into the time-series analysis and also on how the dynamics are controlled for. Lack of knowledge of the price elasticity is a major problem for the design of food subsidies.
3. The 1972 budget study data gives clear evidence of departures from log-linearity.

9.3. Things I Worry About, Some of Which I Have Explored

1. Heteroscedasticity/weighting of observations
2. Family composition effects beyond family size
3. Errors in measurement
4. Endogeneity in the time-series analysis.

9.4. Finale

Keep in mind the three most important aspects of real data analyses: compromise, compromise and compromise.

APPENDIX: LOGBOOK

January 1996 My first step is to read through the Tobin article to try to figure out its purpose. My impression is that the paper is primarily an exercise in econometrics that is lacking a clear issue. The econometric problems seem to fall into two groups — overparameterization and errors-in-variables including aggregation. The homogeneity postulate can be treated softly in a Bayesian way. Likewise the pooling of cross-section and time-series estimates. I am worried about the lack of data on lagged income — the permanent income hypothesis — in the budget study. I am also worried about the effects of grouping of the data, particularly in the extreme income classes.

A residual plot of the 1972 data with family size dummies suggests non-linearity in the log-log consumption function and also family size dependence. The full parameterization thus is a non-linear log-log model separately estimated for each family size. This is clearly a lot of model for this small data set to carry. Some kind of smoothing/prior seems necessary. I explored non-linear forms of the Tobin equation, even a cubic spline at one point to try to capture the apparent twists in the partial regression plot of food consumption controlling for family composition versus in $\log(HINC)$.

February 1996 After satisfying myself that I have learned all that is obvious about the 1972 data I move to the 1960 data. I am particularly trying to find saturation effects and also minimum consumption effects — an S-shaped consumption curve. In principle this is a big pooling problem with regressions indexed by family size and year. To carry this out would be a lot of work, but it may be interesting. I am focusing on choice of functional form but am keeping in the background errors-in-variables questions and including other family compositional controls like age distribution. The family size indicator for large families is sometimes limited.

July 1996 After a long hiatus because of other commitments, I am back at this project. Today I select the question. I explore the possibility of tying all the budget studies together, which is made difficult by changes in prices over time. I explore different deflation methods. I make some interesting graphs of the cumulative distributions of food expenditure per person. The 1972 database allows one to distinguish between children, adults, and the elderly. I will define the effective number of adults as $AHSIZE - ANCHILD - ANOVA65 + C(3)^*CHILDANY + CHILDANY + C(4)^*ANCHILD + C(5)^*ANOVA65$ where $CHILDANY$ equals 1 if $ANCHILD > 0$ and is zero otherwise. Finally, I do the Bayesian analysis of the Tobin budget study.

Now for an examination of the time-series data. The first step is to estimate a general dynamic model using the complete data set with $\log(FP)$ as the dependent variable and with $\log(REALFOODPC)$, $LOG(PCY)$, $LOG(NFP)$, all variables lagged two years. Next I do the more restricted model. The economics of demand is influencing my choice of equation.

At this point, I have to decide how to write up the article. I am imagining a great deal of overlap between what I have done and what others will report at the Tilburg conference, and I decide not to try to cover all the things that crossed my mind but to focus my write up on three messages.

Tilburg conference Egad, I think I have used nominal income in the time-series analysis when I wrote real income. (Blame that on the research assistant!!)

REFERENCES

Frisch, R. (1934), *Statistical Confluence Analysis by Means of Complete Regression Systems*, University Institute of Economics, Oslo.

Izan, H. Y. (1980), 'To pool or not to pool: a reexamination of Tobin's food demand problem', *Journal of Econometrics*, **13**, 391–402.

Keynes, J. N. (1981), *The Scope and Method of Political Economy*, Macmillan, London, excerpted in D. F. Hendry and M. S. Morgan (eds) (1995), *The Foundations of Econometric Analysis*, Cambridge University Press, Cambridge.

Leamer, E. E. (1974), 'False models and post-data model construction', *Journal of the American Statistical Association*, **69**, 122–31.

Leamer, E. E. (1978), *Specification Searches*, John Wiley, New York.

Leamer, E. E. (1982), 'Sets of posterior means with bounded variance priors', *Econometrica*, **50**, 725–36.

Leamer, E. E. (1983), 'Lets take the con out of econometrics', *American Economic Review*, **73**, 31–43.

Leamer, E. E. (1986), 'A Bayesian analysis of the inflation/unemployment tradeoff, in D. A. Belsley and E. Kuh (eds), *Model Reliability*, MIT Press, Cambridge, MA, 62–89.

Leamer, E. E. (1996), 'Questions, theory and data', in S. J. Medema and W. J. Samuels (eds), *Foundations of Research in Economics: How do Economists do Economics?*, Edward Elgar, Cheltenham, 175–90.

Maddala, G. S. (1971), 'The likelihood approach to pooling cross-section and time-series data', *Econometrica*, **39**, 939–53.

Tobin, J. (1950), 'A statistical demand function for food in the USA', *Journal of the Royal Statistical Society*, Series A, **113**, Part II, 113–41 [reprinted in Chapter 2, this volume].

COMMENTS BY PROFESSOR MICHAEL McALEER (University of Western Australia)

This is a typically controversial, challenging and highly readable paper by Ed Leamer, which will undoubtedly be seen by many as interesting and entertaining; will probably be seen by some as highly commendable and persuasive; and will definitely be seen by others, especially those who do not have the same Bayesian leanings as has Leamer, as misleading and irresponsible.

Regardless of one's methodological perspective, there are several strengths to the paper. Leamer's empirical research on Tobin's study of food expenditure deserves serious attention because he provides a prescriptive alternative to classical (time-series) econometric modelling, which can be deficient if it is applied without careful thought to non-experimental data. Although a Bayesian approach is carefully constructed, Leamer also presents, contrary to one's prior expectations, the results of a specification search, that is, a standard econometric modelling exercise which uses diagnostic test statistics, and hence involves a considerable amount of pretesting. More on this below.

The motivation for the paper is clear and concise. In the brief introductory comments, and again in his concluding remarks, Leamer makes three points, namely that graphs are a powerful device for discovery and for communication, the issues should be clearly identified so that questions should drive a data analysis ('the real issues of economics are public policy questions'), and that Bayesian methods are preferable to data-mining. It is not clear from his opening comments whether data-mining is perceived as the disease or the treatment, but he argues that the message of the witch doctors is: 'It must be right, I've been doing it since my youth'. As it so happens, Leamer also engages in a considerable amount of data-mining (any amount of data-mining is probably excessive for him), or a specification search, and admits that he is 'embarrassed about this sinful methodology since I have spent a large chunk of my career preaching against it.' It is probably better late than never to join the ranks of the realists.

Since graphs are widely used and accepted in applied econometrics, an emphasis on their use is not novel. Nevertheless, it should be noted that there are areas of concern associated with an excessive concentration on the use of graphs. It is well known that eyes can play tricks, even in a two-dimensional world! How does one measure dynamic relationships, appropriate functional forms, differences between short and long-run effects, standard errors and higher moments, the effects of auxiliary assumptions, and so on, through graphical analysis, especially in a multi-dimensional framework? Indeed, are these skills transferable or reproducible? These concerns notwithstanding, Leamer's emphasis on the use of graphs is worth comparing and contrasting with the presentations by other participants at the conference in Tilburg (the revised versions of these papers might have a different graphical content from the numbers presented here). Of the eight teams of participants at the conference, two participating teams did not present any graphs at all, two relatively parsimonious teams presented five graphs in three figures and eight graphs in three figures, one team presented 12 figures, and then all hell broke loose, with three teams presenting 26 graphs in three figures, 27 graphs in eight figures, and 46 graphs in 21 figures. It would seem that the use of graphs is alive and well in applied econometrics!

The presentation by Leamer of several detailed tables of empirical results and figures permits a number of interesting empirical economic questions to be answered. A brief, clear and precise summary of the empirical conclusions is given. There is a detailed and credible logbook, which enables an appreciation of the sequential nature of the modelling exercise undertaken. The honesty of the author (whether forced upon him or not) comes out in footnote 3: 'Historian be alert. The version of the paper presented at the Tilburg conference had words that called for the use of real income but both the data display and the data analysis were based incorrectly on nominal data.' and in the logbook: 'Egad, I think I have nominal income in the time-series analysis when I wrote real income.

(Blame that on the R.A.!!)'. The willingness on the part of the research assistant to accept responsibility for the data gremlin might well depend on which of the five types of assistant given by Leamer best describes the R.A., namely Classical Monk, Robot, 1000 Pound Economist, Bayesian Monk, or Sensitive Bayesian. For some reason, Leamer appears to think that monks (a community of men!) can be male or female, while a gorilla is necessarily a female. This reminds me of the way in which the world has been led to think of Mozart as Austrian and Hitler as German, when it is, in fact, the reverse! Moreover, can Leamer provide any evidence (other than a self-citation) that the Classical Monks give their blessing because 'we don't admit that we spent the night with robots and gorillas'?

Considerable thought is given by Leamer on developing the question to be answered by his data analysis. It is interesting that Leamer fails to find the serious economic question in Tobin's original article, but he nevertheless uses Tobin's model to answer his own question, which is 'to solve for price subsidy rates to achieve a targeted level of food consumption per family member.' However, in view of the strong assumptions that are necessarily imposed on the analysis, Leamer admits that: 'the question is not entirely real. My point is not to solve a real problem but to show how a question can affect the analysis.' Although the qualification is understood, the implication that the problem is somehow no longer real is unfortunate.

The empirical analysis involves a largely uncritical use of Tobin's (1950) original Cobb–Douglas family food demand function (including 'Q' as the non-food price index), the dynamics in the time-series version of which are very basic. There is little discussion of the use of the logarithmic (or log-linear) functional form. Since an emphasis of the paper is the sensitivity of the empirical estimates of elasticities and forecasts outside the sample to the assumptions of the model, it would have been useful to examine the issue of functional form at greater length. Scattered and cursory exceptions occur in the text and the logbook, including: 'the numerical processing is driven very much by a commitment to log-linearity, an assumption which your eyes feel freer to discard' (Section 5.1), 'I therefore choose to stick with the assumption of log-linearity because I am pretty sure a Bayesian analysis of more complicated functional forms would lead to pretty much the same conclusion. (Take a look at Figure 1!)' (Section 5.3), 'the 1972 scatter depicted in Figure 3 suggests pretty clearly some nonlinearity in the log-log relationship' (Section 8), which is repeated as 'except for the 1972 data there is no apparent departure from log-linearity' (Section 8), and 'the 1972 budget study data gives clear evidence of departures from log-linearity' (Section 9.2). Leamer's reaction to the finding of an apparently inappropriate functional form is as follows: 'I am left in a state of suspicion about the 1972 data.' it is also unclear whether Leamer's allusion to the Bayesian analysis of functional form refers to an extremely strong prior or to a rejection of data analysis.

Two outliers are 'detected' (Section 5.1), whereupon it is argued that 'a brute force approach just omits these rogue observations', 'if one included the two outliers the picture would be much fuzzier', and 'I also choose to discard the two outliers, because I am pretty sure the Bayesian analysis of outliers would lead to pretty much the same conclusion' (Section 5.3). It would have been instructive to have seen such a demonstration of a Bayesian approach to examining outliers, although it is not clear whether Leamer's allusion to the Bayesian analysis of outliers refers to an extremely strong prior or to a rejection of data analysis. Moreover, there are also several standard classical procedures available for testing outliers, but these have not been considered.

It is stated that 'statistically insignificant variables have been trimmed sequentially to produce the 'final' result in Table II' (Section 5.1). Regardless of one's views on stepwise regression, this procedure relies on the use of standard asymptotic test statistics, which are unlikely to be valid. No evidence is reported as to the adequacy of the formulae for the standard errors in Tables I–III (the Durbin–Watson statistic generally lies in the inconclusive region, so an adjustment to the standard errors and the corresponding t-ratios should at least be considered). In the absence of any diagnostics regarding the adequacy of the auxiliary assumptions underlying the conventional formulae for the standard errors, some caution is warranted.

As an aid in communication, how were the priors in Section 5.3 developed? Leamer asks the following questions: 'The prior means seem right, you may acknowledge, but what about the standard errors? Where did those numbers come from? Moreover, what about the covariances?' His answer to these questions is: 'Never mind; we are going to do a sensitivity analysis to find out how much the standard errors and covariances matter' (Section 5.3). Apparently, it does not matter from where these priors came! It is also not particularly helpful to be told that: 'I had to think carefully what are sensible values for the parameters, and I consequently had to be creative in selecting a felicitous and transparent functional form' (Section 5.3). Such careful planning notwithstanding, it would be useful to examine the sensitivity of the empirical results to the assumption of the logarithmic specification.

There is surprisingly no discussion of non-stationarity, with or without deterministic trends, of the time-series data. Modern developments in time-series econometrics, one of the more important issues in applied econometrics in recent years, are ignored entirely by Leamer. Indeed, non-stationarity frequently leads to high R-squared values and serial correlation, as is observed in some of the empirical results in the paper. Leamer also seems to ignore his own recommendation that 'I like to try to identify the feature or features of a data set that lead to an inference. The feature might be a trend...' (Leamer (1988, page 331)). Such an omission might have been comprehensible had Leamer been concerned about the extremely small numbers of time-series observations used in the data analysis, for which the available small sample corrections might not be suitable, or because tests of unit-roots and cointegration are not known to be robust to a wide range of non-linear data transformations, which can affect the outcomes of the tests. In cases such as these, it can be far more enlightening to highlight the sensitivity of the empirical results to the use of alternative data transformations, rather than to ignore the problem altogether.

A diagnostic statistics is used to suggest there might be problems in some regression results: 'The residual plot and the Durbin–Watson statistic in this regression scream out for help' (Section 6). Why is only the Durbin–Watson statistic used to test for serial correlation? Moreover, whatever happened to Leamer's (1988, page 322) lament that 'there are too many diagnostics. One is too many as far as I am concerned.'? Has he finally realized the folly of such an extreme position?

Leamer accommodates an AR(1) error process in the regression model on the basis of the Durbin–Watson test. This decision is consistent with Leamer's (1983, page 39) incorrect assertion that ' 'diagnostic' tests with explicit alternative hypotheses such as the Durbin–Watson test for first-order autocorrelation do not truly ask if the horizon should be extended, since first-order autocorrelation is explicitly identified and clearly in our field of vision.' Sadly, Leamer (1983) is confusing the roles of the null and alternative hypotheses: the null states that there is zero correlation, whereas the alternative is that there is not zero correlation. It is well known that there are numerous specifications which are consistent with the alternative, of which Leamer's chosen AR(1) process is but one. Where are Leamer's priors as regards, for example, higher-order AR processes, moving average processes of any order, non-linear processes, omitted variables, incorrect functional form, incorrect dynamics, incorrect transformation of variables, and structural change? How would an accommodation of any of these alternatives affect the empirical analysis?

Leamer's finale is: 'Keep in mind the three most important aspects of real data analyses: compromise, compromise, compromise.' This is in marked contrast to Hendry's (1980, page 403) exhortation: 'The three golden rules of econometrics are test, test, test.' (Footnote 6: 'Notwithstanding the difficulties involved in calculating and controlling type I and II errors.') Of course, Hendry's emphasis on the use of diagnostic tests (also known as specification searching) classifies him as a pre-tester, which involves estimation and not statistical testing. [Litmus test: How many models does Hendry have at the end of a specification search? A statistical tester should have zero models at least some of the time!] Thus, Hendry's golden rules are, in effect, 'estimate, estimate, estimate'.

What import should be made of Leamer's concerns about the specification search/pre-testing problem? He argues that 'the outcome of the specification search is an unknown and almost certainly inappropriate mixture of prior and data' (Section 5.2). A method has been proposed for discounting the results of so-called statistical tests, but Leamer admits that to follow his own rules 'is a major headache. Better to avoid the problem by spending more time in advance thinking about the possibilities. The scarce commodity is not economists' time; it is the data. Better not waste it with a mindless specification search' (Section 5.2). Such a lament, however accurate, is not new, having been made by Friedman (1940) in his insightful review of Tinbergen (1939), anticipating the objections to the specification search procedures involved in applied econometric modelling. Friedman (1940, page 659) criticized the lack of validity of statistical inferential procedures as follows: 'Tinbergen's results cannot be judged by ordinary tests of statistical significance. The reason is that the variables with which he ends up... have been selected after an extensive process of trial and error because they yield high coefficients of correlation'.

The above cautionary comments notwithstanding, it must be emphasized that specification searching does not affect the probability of truth of a particular theory. However, this is a question that is discussed far more frequently in the philosophy of science literature than it is in economics.

REFERENCES

Friedman, M. (1940), 'Review of Tinbergen (1939)', *American Economic Review*, **30**, 657–60.
Hendry, D. F. (1980), 'Econometrics — alchemy or science?' *Economica*, **47**, 387–406.
Leamer, E. E. (1983), 'Let's take the con out of econometrics', *American Economic Review*, **73**, 31–43.
Leamer, E. E. (1988), 'Things that bother me', *Economic Record*, **64**, 331–5.
Tinbergen, J. (1939), *Statistical Testing of Business-Cycle Theories*, 2 volumes, League of Nations, Geneva.

COMMENTS BY PROFESSOR ANTON P. BARTEN (Catholic University of Leuven)

The paper is fun to read. Ed Leamer is not afraid of strong, sometimes provocative, statements. Still it is not always convincing. The title is appropriate in the sense that the paper does not bother itself with the Netherlands part of the experiment nor with the additional budget-survey and time-series data for the United States. It is concentrated on the original Tobin data set. One may deplore this because data are still in very short supply and should not be too easily discarded. Still, the paper is already rather long as it stands.

The paper starts off with singing the praise of graphical analysis. It is true that a first look at a graphical representation of the data can reveal some properties otherwise not detected. It may seem very simple in the two-dimensional case, but becomes already complicated when three variables are involved. Leamer's Figure 1 is a nice example of a reduction of a three-dimensional problem to the two-dimensions of a sheet of paper. Graphs may be misleading. The outliers in Leamer's Figure 1 turn out to be quite regular after all.

The statement that applied econometrics should be problem driven is open for discussion. It is obviously self-defeating if each time a problem arises one should start collecting the data, develop the adequate hardware and software, set up the conceptual framework and finally conduct the empirical analysis. A specific policy question may add a special flavour to the empirical exercise, but to require a policy issue for each piece of applied work is going far too far. In fact, in the Leamer paper there is very little that is inspired by the policy question as formulated by the author. Actually, that question has been formulated *post factum* to fit more or less the empirical exercise. This simply demonstrates that empirical work can be useful even when not designed to answer a specific question of policy.

Is there an alternative to specification search? Leamer uses the help of no less than four assistants, each fundamentally different, but eventually leans most heavily on the 1000 Pound Economist/Gorilla. Among the assistants I miss the person that carefully specifies his regression equations and null hypotheses on the basis of economic theory and is not using a t-test to select relevant variables. Not being able to measure a coefficient with great precision does not mean that the variable does not belong in the explanatory scheme.

The author does not dwell on the issue of the difference in the estimates of the income elasticity between the budget-survey data and the time-series data. One reason could be that the income elasticity is not a fundamental constant, that it is variable and that the double-log specification is not correct. Another cause might be the aggregation over individuals implied by the time-series, which can cause such a divergence. Then there are the dynamics. The budget survey may be not adequately representing the long run effect of an income change. Most probably, it may be a matter of omitted variables, that vary over time in about the same way as income does, which therefore takes over their influence. Of course, all these possibilities may be at work at the same time. We should clearly be aware of the dangers involved in the use of results of micro-econometric analysis to market or nationwide applications and vice versa.

COMMENTS BY PROFESSOR PETER SCHMIDT (Michigan State University)

This paper reanalyzes Tobin's cross-sectional and time-series data. It also gives a rather perfunctory look at the later USA cross-sections. The author says that he makes three main points: (1) Graphs are useful, (2) Analysis of data requires clear issues, (3) Overparameterization is a universal problem; the solution is Bayesian.

I believe that the paper's results support the usefulness of graphs. A good example would be Figure 1, which reveals an interaction between the effects of income and family size, and Figure 2, which reveals the unusual nature of some of the 1914–47 data. The paper also shows the inherent limitation of graphics: they don't deal well with more than two-dimensions. For truly multivariate relationships graphs can be misleading. The paper's approach is to look at graphs of relationships that control (via regression) for non-graphed variables. This is hard to argue with, but it actually illustrates the negative point that graphs aren't of much use without a model.

Point (2) above, that clear issues are good to have in mind, is almost tautologically true. But, empirically, it is an open question for what class of problems the ultimate issue does or does not drive the modelling effort. An accurate model of the solar system allows rockets to go to Mars, and also allows prediction of eclipses, alignments of planets in the sky, etc.; and I'm not sure to what extent the modelling effort really should differ depending on the end aim of the exercise. In this paper the author declares his purpose: to calculate food price subsidies that ensure a given level of food consumption, for various types of families. However, I frankly don't see any indication that this ultimate purpose really influenced the data analysis in an important way.

With respect to point (3), I would agree that it is hard to resist the temptation to overparameterize models. Whether the solution should be self-restraint or a Bayesian prior is an arguable point. This is probably not the proper forum for a debate on the merits of Bayesian and non-Bayesian approaches. It may be more pertinent to ask whether, in the particular empirical exercises done here, Leamer's Bayesian approach made much difference relative to a classical approach. In my view it didn't in the cross-section, where the usual estimates are quite precise, and it made a larger difference in the time-series, where the usual estimates are less precise. This is not surprising, of course.

I believe that one can make a connection (perhaps not one that Leamer would approve of) between the first and third of these points. The use of graphical methods can tend to encourage overfitting; that is, adding features to the model to 'explain' minor features of the data. In the cross-section data, there clearly is an interaction between income and family size. For example, one of the other papers added a multiplicative interaction. This paper's use of dummy variables for family size adds more parameters than that, and we can have as many as 10 dummies plus interactions, which is a lot of extra parameters with only 37 data points. Of course, not all get used, but one still might accuse the author of overfitting. Is there any defense (other than just that it's an unconstitutionally vague charge)?

Interestingly, one of the clearest things to come out of this paper is a very nice demonstration of the usefulness of specification searches (or at least, of thoughtful specification searches). That's so, whether or not one feels the need to atone for one's 'sins' through a Bayesian sensitivity analysis.

Leamer provides an 'old style' reanalysis of the time-series data, focusing on a sensitivity analysis with respect to the prior. It is certainly surprising and maybe shocking to see time-series results like these without any reference to unit roots or cointegration, which I regard as one of the fundamental econometric advances (or at least changes) since 1950. I assume that the relevant series would have unit-roots. Even without a formal unit-root and cointegration analysis, a recognition of the relevance of the spurious regression phenomenon could be expected. Many of the regressions in Table V have very low Durbin–Watson values, and hence large values of the AR(1) coefficient in their transformed versions, and might not be cointegrated. If so, the proper response is not an AR(1) correction, but some more fundamental change in specification. Perhaps, even though Table V does not give Bayesian results, this is a Bayesian/classical issue. But personally I don't see it as such.

I might have expected a bit more in the paper about the relationship between micro and macro relationships (i.e. the aggregation question). Without certain restrictions on the income distribution and/or its change (e.g. the mean scaling condition), there is no reason to think that the cross-section and time-series results should be the same. Tobin imported his cross-sectional income elasticity of 0.56 into his time-series regression, despite the fact that the unconstrained time-series estimate was significantly lower than that. Leamer imports an estimate of 0.6, and does not find significant evidence against this value. I am puzzled both by the difference in results from Tobin's and by why Leamer thought that the income elasticity equal to its cross-sectional value was an interesting restriction to contemplate.

REPLY BY EDWARD E. LEAMER

I feared that my three distinguished assessors would chastise me for some failure to uncover an important feature of the data. I breathed a sigh of relief, since they have chosen to focus instead on the rhetoric, not the substantive conclusions. In other words, they are behaving like econometricians.

I used the brief space available to me to try to convey three messages: that graphs are useful, that pretesting is still our biggest problem and that clear issues can help keep the enterprise from wandering off in technically amusing but largely irrelevant directions. It is the last of these points that seems most doubtful to all three commentators. They complain that they don't see any evidence in my paper of my proposed question concerning the design of a food subsidy program. But, I reply, it is not what I did, but what I didn't do, that matters. I didn't use unit roots and cointegration, which brought complaints from McAleer and Schmidt. I didn't extensively explore alternative functional forms or more complicated dynamics, which also brought complaints. These things I didn't do because I am highly doubtful that addressing them would have any discernible effect on the design of a food subsidy program. These comments afford me the opportunity to make a complaint: The professional preoccupation with unit roots and cointegration has created an enormous diversion of intellectual resources toward issues that are very unimportant for three reasons:

1. The sharp hypotheses of unit roots and cointegration are completely uninteresting from the standpoint of economics. By the time that there is any difference between one and 0.99, numerous changes in the economy will have occurred, rendering the original model completely irrelevant. My advice: Don't test for unit roots and cointegration. Estimate dynamic relationships.
2. Energy spent looking for unit-roots would be better spent trying to understand the myriad unique events that we call history, thus generating an appreciation of why the future is a lot more blurry than most of our simple time-series models admit. For example: what about the rise in the divorce rate and the disappearance of the nuclear family, fast food franchises, school lunch/breakfast programs, frozen foods/refrigeration, and so on and so on??

3. The statistical sampling theory supporting the search for unit-roots is misguided. The likelihood function corresponding to dynamic models has no special pathologies and requires no special treatment, except possibly the initial observation.

The preoccupation with unit-roots is supported by an important shift in the foundation of macroeconomics. The source domain of our metaphors used to be biology and medicine: we spoke of depression, and animal spirits. Now the most common source is engineering and physics: the business 'cycle', the laws of motion of the system, the data generating process. As for me, I prefer not to think of the laws of motion of my life or the data generating process that compelled me to buy an airline ticket to come to the Netherlands in December. Nor do I worry whether my income and GDP are cointegrated.

Thus, for me, the metaphor of a 'sample' applied to macro time-series seems silly. I am happier accepting the subjective basis of probability applied to macro systems. Like Haavelmo (1944), I think that 'This is nothing but a convenient way of expressing opinions about real phenomena.' Then from the subjective definition of probability and Bayes Rule, come the likelihood principle — the likelihood function fully summarizes all the information in the data. But a likelihood function of a dynamic process is just the same as a static sample and is completely unaffected by unit roots. In other words, ordinary least squares will do for me. Unit-roots or not.

If the message of this literature on unit-roots and cointegration is that we need to be careful when we model the dynamics, I say 'Great, I agree'. If the message of this literature is that the authors have a monopoly on how to wander through the thicket of dynamic models, I say 'No way'. If the message of this literature is that the statistical problems of overparameterization and ambiguity are unique with time-series data, again I say 'No way'... Exactly the same remedies apply to overparameterized problems, no matter what are the names of the parameters.

Frankly, I remain worried that my somewhat perfunctory treatment of the dynamics in the time-series analysis may have led me astray. Schmidt expresses this point in an elliptical way: 'Even without a formal unit root and cointegration analysis, a recognition of the relevance of the spurious regression phenomenon could be expected.' That kind of comment is appropriate to a specification with no dynamics at all, not to the one that I used. I don't of course claim to have the best dynamical model. What I do conclude is that these data leave a lot of doubt about the price elasticity, so much doubt that it is very difficult to design a food subsidy program. I think that more elaborate dynamics are only going to add to the confusion. If Schmidt could show otherwise, then I am unhappy to be corrected.

Schmidt properly points out that graphical approaches raise pretesting issues that are far more profound than numerical treatments, to which I agree wholeheartedly. But I haven't the slightest idea what can be done about it. My point about graphs is very personal. I spend a lot more time looking at data displays today than I did 20 years ago. Naturally, I think that is a good thing to do, otherwise I wouldn't do it.

Both Schmidt and Barten wonder why more care is not taken with issues relating to pooling a cross-section with a time-series. As I explained in my paper, the Bayesian approach does deal with this issue by creating a 'permeable firewall' between the cross-section and the time-series, through which some information can transfer, but not all. I think this very well captures the spirit of the problem. Theoretically, the cross-section and time-series income elasticities need not conform, but still we need to use the cross-section result to help support the time-series analysis.

McAleer's long comment complains about everything but my parents. In addition to the gender of gorillas and monks, McAleer is very concerned with issues of priority, correctly pointing out that I did not invent graphs nor am I the first to object to pretesting. He doesn't offer his estimate of the date of the first graph, which may well have been made by Aborigines in Australia, but he does cite Friedman as the original source on pretesting. It wouldn't surprise me if the Aborigines had something to say about that too. But I cannot say that I am dazzled by McAleer's argument that neither Friedman nor I need worry; 'The above cautionary comments notwithstanding, it must be emphasized that specification searching does not affect the probability of truth of a particular theory.' I wish I had the slightest idea what that kind of sentence means. I can tell you that listening to words like these spoken by the mellifluous voice of McAleer's messiah, David Hendry, are soothing indeed, not because they mean anything, but only because they sound like they must. The song doesn't sound quite so soothing when the background switches from violin to digirido. In other words, pretesting really does matter, song or no.

McAleer continues to be confused about the difference between estimation and hypothesis discovery, both of which could give rise to exactly the same sequence of estimated models. The Friedman quotation to which McAleer alludes refers to a step-wise method of estimating a high dimensional parameter vector: '... the variables... have been selected after an extensive trial and error process because they yield high coefficients of correlation.' Hypothesis discovery is an entirely different phenomenon which is explicitly outside the scope of traditional statistical theory. (It was of course an Aborigine who first noticed that boys are more likely to be conceived when the moon is full.) Diagnostic statistics as part of an estimation process are a bad idea — the 1000 pound gorilla at work. Diagnostic statistics for hypothesis discovery are wrong-headed. It is not the job of a statistician to tell us if the model isn't working. It is the job of the practitioners. A great defect of this 'experiment' is that it included not a single person who has had any substantive interest in the demand for food. The assessment of the results therefore misses the mark. The proper measure of success of these data analyses is how many heads of food analysts we turn, not how many heads of econometricians.

ADDITIONAL REFERENCE

Haavelmo. T. (1944), 'The probability approach in econometrics', *Econometrica*, **12**, Supplement.

CHAPTER 6

EMPIRICAL ECONOMETRIC MODELLING OF FOOD CONSUMPTION USING A NEW INFORMATIONAL COMPLEXITY APPROACH*

PETER M. BEARSE, HAMPARSUM BOZDOGAN AND ALAN M. SCHLOTTMANN

1. INTRODUCTION

At the heart of empirical econometric modelling of economic data is the selection of an appropriate model on which economic theories can be studied. Over the past twenty years, modern statistical and econometric modelling activity has been moving away from formal methodologies using sampling distribution-based test theory. Traditional methodologies based on narrowly specified hypotheses have become difficult in solving large-scale real-world problems. Practitioners are beginning to question whether the classical techniques are capable of addressing complex economic and social issues. What is required is the ability in real time to identify the best-fitting model among a portfolio of competing models for a given complex data structure. In this paper, we accomplish this with computational ease, interpretability, and elegance using a new and novel information-theoretic, or in short, informational approach. This richer approach links statistics as an experimental science with high-speed computation and supercomputer technology, and bridges the frequentist and Bayesian schools of thought in statistics. With this new approach traditional table look-up is eliminated. Total flexibility and versatility are provided to practitioners, researchers, and students in solving their modeling problems (see Bozdogan, 1994a–c).

This paper is concerned with empirical econometric modelling of the classic food consumption data set used by Tobin (1950), a revised US data set, and data of a similar type, but from the Dutch economy, using a novel informational modelling approach. The efficacy of the informational approach will be studied on these data sets by introducing new and efficient statistical techniques in empirical econometric modeling of economic data. To our knowledge, some of the modelling techniques in this paper have not been previously introduced to analyse such data structures in a systematic fashion.

As aptly put by Hendry (1995, p. 3), we believe that 'all models are not born equal, and we seek those which are useful in practice for understanding economic behaviour, for testing economic theories, for forecasting the future, and analysing economic policy'. We feel that our measure of success is based on the merit of our findings using objective information-based model selection criteria. These procedures provide us 'figures of merit' for the evaluation of models which take into consideration both the fit and complexity of the model. Such procedures tend to select a parsimonious model for the underlying reality

* Reprinted from the *Journal of Applied Econometrics*, **12**, 563–592 (1997).

Methodology and Tacit Knowledge: Two Experiments in Econometrics
Jan R. Magnus and Mary S. Morgan © 1997 John Wiley & Sons Ltd

of the data to ascertain the truth status of the fitted empirical models without any subjectivity, and under very minimal assumptions (see Sakamoto *et al.*, 1986; Bozdogan, 1987).

The format of our paper is as follows. In Section 2 we discuss statistical model selection: an informational approach and introduce Akaike's (1973) Information Criterion (AIC) and its variants, and Bozdogan's (1988, 1990a,b) Informational Complexity ICOMP(IFIM) Criterion. In Section 3, we estimate the relationship between food consumption and income and test whether food demand is homogeneous of degree zero. We break this section into four parts. In Section 3.1, we consider the original Tobin data. In Section 3.2, we study the revised US data in isolation from the Netherlands data. In Section 3.3, we examine the Netherlands data in isolation from the US data. Finally, in Section 3.4, we consider whether gains can be achieved by pooling the US and Netherlands data. We forecast food consumption in the Netherlands through the year 2000 conditional on information available through 1988 in Section 4. Then, in Section 5, we analyse US Budget Data using multisample cluster analysis, a combinatorial grouping of samples developed by Bozdogan (1981, 1986), to see which data sets can be combined without forcing any particular clustering on the multisample data. We then cast the celebrated seemingly unrelated regressions (SUR) model of Zellner (1962) on the chosen multisample cluster and use the genetic algorithm (GA) to select the optimal predictors which separate the chosen partitioning of the groups (Luh, Minesky, and Bozdogan, 1996). In Section 6, we present our conclusions. The Appendix summarizes our logbook. In this paper all computations were performed on a personal computer using the statistical programming languages MATLAB and GAUSS.

2. STATISTICAL MODEL SELECTION: AN INFORMATIONAL APPROACH

In recent years, the statistical literature has placed increasing emphasis on model-evaluation criteria. The problem is posed as the choice of the *best approximating* model among a class of competing models by a suitable model evaluation criteria given a data set. Model evaluation criteria are *figures of merit*, or *performance measures*, for competing models. That model which optimizes the criterion is chosen to be the best.

Throughout this paper we introduce and utilize information-based model-selection criteria to seek the truth status of our empirical models and for comparative purposes. We classify these criteria into two categories: (1) Akaike's (1973) Information Criteria (AIC) and its variants; and (2) Bozdogan's (1988, 1990a,b) new Informational Complexity (ICOMP) Criterion.

2.1. Akaike's Information Criterion (AIC) and its Variants

Akaike's (1973) Information Criterion (AIC) is a sample estimate of the expected log likelihood or, equivalently, the expected Kullback–Leibler (1951) (K–L) information in a set of data. Thus, AIC can be used to compare the models in a set of competing models, as stated in the following proposition (Bozdogan, 1987):

Proposition 2.1: *Akaike's Information Criterion (AIC):* Let $\{M_k : k = 1, 2, \ldots, K\}$ be a set of competing models indexed by $k = 1, 2, \ldots, K$. Then the criterion

$$\text{AIC}(k) = -2 \log L(\hat{\theta}_k) + 2k \qquad\qquad 1$$

which is minimized to choose a model M_k over the set of models is sample estimator of $2E[I(\theta; \theta_k)]$ or $-2E[\log f(\mathbf{x}|\theta_k)]$ of the true distribution with respect to a model with the parameters determined by the method of maximum likelihood. For proof, see Bozdogan (1987).

The first term in Equation (1) provides us with a measure of model inaccuracy (*badness of fit* or *lack of fit*) when the maximum likelihood estimators of the parameters in the model are used. The second term serves as a penalty for bias induced in the first term when additional free parameters are included in the model. Since the decision rule is to minimize AIC over the set of competing models, the 'best approximating' model is chosen to be the one with the highest information gain. The application of AIC emphasizes the comparison of the goodness of fit of the competing models while taking into account the principle of parsimony. For the general theory and many applications of AIC, we refer the reader to Bozdogan (1987, 1994a–c).

In the literature, other penalties have been proposed to penalize overparameterization more stringently. For example, Schwarz (1978), assuming that the data is generated from an exponential family of distributions (see e.g. Cox and Hinkley, 1974, p. 27) and using the Bayes' procedure for the choice of a model, suggested the criterion

$$\text{SBC}(k) = -2\log L(\hat{\theta}_k) + k \log n \qquad 2$$

for large samples, where $\log(n)$ denotes the natural logarithm of the sample size n.

Rissanen (1978, 1979) proposed a criterion based on information-theoretic shortest code length for the data together with the parameters of a model. His criterion is called the *minimum description length* (MDL) and is defined by

$$\text{MDL} = -2\log L(\hat{\theta}_k) + k \log(n). \qquad 3$$

We note that the MDL is identical to SBC. However, its derivation is quite different. Unlike AIC, SBC and MDL are consistent model-selection criteria.

Bozdogan (1987) extended AIC to make it consistent without violating Akaike's (1973) underlying principles. He proposed

$$\text{CAIC} = -2\log L(\hat{\theta}_k) + k[\log(n) + 1] \qquad 4$$

and

$$\text{CAICF} = -2\log L(\hat{\theta}_k) + k[\log(n) + 2] + \log|\hat{\mathcal{F}}| \qquad 5$$

where $\hat{\mathcal{F}}$ is the estimated Fisher information matrix (FIM), and $|\cdot|$ denotes the determinant.

The above criteria all give a mathematical formulation of the principle of parsimony. The difference between these variants of AIC and AIC itself is the penalty term. In passing, we note that Phillips' (1996) Posterior Information Criterion (PIC) is an independent rediscovery of Bozdogan's (1987) CAICF. In fact, it is a special case of CAICF. However, PIC is not, technically speaking, an information-theoretic criterion. Instead, PIC is based on Bayesian asymptotics similar to Kashyap's (1982) general Bayesian criterion (KC). Further, PIC is also a special case of KC. For more on these criteria, we refer the readers to Bozdogan (1997a).

2.2. Bozdogan's Informational Complexity (ICOMP) Criterion

As an alternative to AIC, SBC, MDL, CAIC, and CAICF, Bozdogan (1988, 1990a,b) developed a new entropic statistical complexity criterion called ICOMP for model selection in general multivariate linear and non-linear structural models. Analytic formulation of ICOMP takes the 'spirit' of AIC, but it is based on the generalization and utilization of an entropic covariance complexity index of van Emden (1971) for a multivariate normal distribution in parametric estimation. For example, for a general multivariate linear or non-linear structural model defined by

$$\text{Statistical model} = \text{Signal} + \text{Noise}. \qquad 6$$

ICOMP is designed to estimate a loss function:

$$\text{Loss} = \text{Lack of Fit} + \text{Lack of Parsimony} + \text{Profusion of Complexity} \qquad 7$$

in two ways. This is achieved by using the additivity property of information theory and the developments of Rissanen (1976) in his *Final Estimation Criterion* (FEC) for estimation and model identification problems, as well as Akaike's (1973) AIC, and its analytical extensions in Bozdogan (1987). Here, we discuss the most general second approach which uses the *complexity of the estimated inverse-Fisher information matrix* (IFIM) $\hat{\mathcal{F}}^{-1}$ *of the entire parameter space of the model*. In this case ICOMP is defined as

$$\text{ICOMP(IFIM)} = -2 \log L(\hat{\theta}_k) + 2C_1(\hat{\mathcal{F}}^{-1}) \qquad 8$$

where $C_1(\hat{\mathcal{F}}^{-1})$ represents an information-theoretic maximal measure of complexity of $\hat{\mathcal{F}}^{-1} \equiv \text{Est. Cov}(\hat{\theta}_k)$. From van Emden (1971) and Bozdogan (1990a), the maximal complexity of IFIM of the model is defined as:

$$C_1(\hat{\mathcal{F}}^{-1}) = s/2 \log[\text{trace}(\hat{\mathcal{F}}^{-1})/s] - 1/2 \log |\hat{\mathcal{F}}^{-1}| \qquad 9$$

where $s = \dim(\hat{\mathcal{F}}^{-1}) = \text{rank}(\hat{\mathcal{F}}^{-1})$.

A model with minimum ICOMP(IFIM) is chosen to be the best model among all possible competing alternative models. For more on the C_1 measure as a 'scalar measure' of a non-singular covariance matrix of a multivariate normal distribution, we refer the reader to the original work of van Emden (1971). This approach takes into account the accuracy of the estimated parameters and implicitly adjusts for the number of free parameters included in the model.

The first component of ICOMP(IFIM) in Equation (8) measures the lack of fit of the model, and the second component measures the complexity of the estimated inverse-Fisher information matrix (IFIM), which gives a scalar measure of celebrated *Cramér–Rao lower bound* matrix of the model which has several rather attractive features. The trace term in Equation (9) involves only the variances of the parameter estimates, while the determinant involves the covariances as well. The greatest simplicity, i.e. zero complexity, is achieved when IFIM is proportional to the identity matrix. In this case the parameters are orthogonal and can be estimated with equal precision.

If we let $\lambda_1, \lambda_2, \ldots, \lambda_s$ be the eigenvalues of $\hat{\mathcal{F}}^{-1}$ and further let $\bar{\lambda}_a = 1/s \Sigma_{j=1}^{s} \lambda_j$ be the arithmetic mean and $\bar{\lambda}_g = (\Pi_{j=1}^{s} \lambda_j)$ be the geometric mean of the eigenvalues, then the complexity of $\hat{\mathcal{F}}^{-1}$ can be written as $C_1(\hat{\mathcal{F}}^{-1} = s/2 \log(\bar{\lambda}_a/\bar{\lambda}_g)$. Hence,

$$\text{ICOMP(IFIM)} = -2 \log L(\hat{\theta}_k) + s \log(\bar{\lambda}_a/\bar{\lambda}_g) \qquad 10$$

where $s = \dim(\hat{\mathcal{F}}^{-1} = \text{rank}(\hat{\mathcal{F}}^{-1})$. We note that ICOMP(IFIM) now looks like the CAIC of Bozdogan (1987), Rissanen's (1978) MDL, and Schwarz's (1978) Bayesian criterion SBC, except for using $\log(\bar{\lambda}_a/\bar{\lambda}_g)$ instead of using $\log(n)$.

With ICOMP(IFIM), complexity is viewed not as the number of parameters in the model, but as the *degree of interdependence* (i.e. the *correlational structure* among the parameter estimates). By defining complexity in this way, ICOMP(IFIM) provides a more judicious penalty term than AIC and SBC. The lack of parsimony is automatically adjusted by $C_1(\hat{\mathcal{F}}^{-1})$ across the competing alternative portfolio of models as the parameter spaces of these models are constrained in the model-selection process. The use of the $C_1(\hat{\mathcal{F}}^{-1})$ in the information-theoretic model evaluation criteria takes into account that fact that as we increase the number of free parameters in a model, the accuracy of the parameter estimates decreases. Hence, ICOMP(IFIM) chooses models that provide more accurate and efficient parameter estimates. It takes into account parameter redundancy, stability, and the error structure of the models. If scale invariance is an issue in the model selection procedure, one can use the correlational form $\hat{\mathcal{F}}_R^{-1}$ or $\hat{\mathcal{F}}^{-1}$ in Equation (8).

ICOMP(IFIM) is obtained as an approximation to the sum of two K–L distances. Other general forms of ICOMP are obtained by maximizing a posterior expected utility in Bayesian modelling. Consistency properties and several theoretical justifications of ICOMP have been studied and shown by Bozdogan and Haughton (1996) and Bozdogan (1997b), where the probabilities of underfitting and overfitting a model as n tends to infinity have been established.

In this paper, we shall only utilize AIC, SBC, and ICOMP(IFIM) in what follows.

3. MEASUREMENT

The purpose of this section is to estimate the relationship between food consumption and income and to test whether food demand is homogeneous of degree zero. In performing this exercise, we decided to focus solely on the time-series data. In particular, our analysis employs the variables per capita food consumption (C), per capita disposable income (Y), a food price index (FP), and a non-food price index (NP). The advantage to restricting our analysis in this way is that it lends itself to comparisons between the USA and Netherlands. Similar to Tobin (1950), we assume the dynamics of food consumption can be adequately described by the model

$$\ln C_t = k + \sum_{i=1}^{u} \rho_i \ln C_{t-i} + \sum_{i=0}^{v} \beta_i \ln Y_{t-i} + \sum_{i=0}^{w} \delta_i \ln FP_{t-i}$$

$$+ \sum_{i=0}^{x} \gamma_i \ln NP_{t-i} + \varepsilon_t \quad \varepsilon_t \sim \text{i.i.d. } N(0, \sigma^2) \tag{11}$$

which is an autoregressive distributed lag model of order **u, v, w, x** (i.e., an ADL(**u, v, w, x**) model of the logarithm of per capita food consumption). Pesaran and Shin (1995) develop the distributions of OLS estimators for ADL models with a cointegrating relationship. Further, based on finite sample simulations, they advocate a return to the ADL approach to time-series econometric modelling.

Economic theory tells us that income, food prices, and non-food prices should each be components of the demand for food. Since one of our goals is to test the homogeneity postulate, we include these variables in every ADL model considered. Our task is then to identify appropriate values of the lag lengths **u**, **v**, **w**, and **x**, to estimate the relationship between food consumption and income, and to test the homogeneity postulate.

An advantage to the ADL approach is that it lends itself naturally toward answering particular questions of interest. For example, Tobin (1950, p. 115) states the homogeneity postulate as requiring that '... the sum of elasticities of demand with respect to variables of a monetary dimension be identically zero'. We use information-theoretic criteria to identify the appropriate lag lengths **v**, **w**, and **x** in Equation (11), thereby identifying an appropriate order for a test of the homogeneity postulate. We exploit the equivalence between ADL and error correction models (ECMs) to examine the long-run relationship between food consumption and income (Davidson *et al.*, 1978).

A disadvantage to using the ADL approach is that it is a single-equation method which does not account for potential endogeneity between contemporaneous food consumption and food prices. This shortcoming could be remedied by applying, say, an instrumental variables approach, although we chose not to pursue this here.

We break this section into four subsections. In Section 3.1 we consider the original Tobin data. In Section 3.2 we study the revised US data in isolation from the Netherlands data. In Section 3.3 we examine the Netherlands data in isolation from the US data. Finally, in Section 3.4 we consider whether gains can be achieved by pooling the US and Netherlands data.

3.1. The Original Tobin Data

In this subsection, we use the original data available to Tobin from 1913 to 1947. In particular, the variables we use include per capita food consumption (*TOBPCFC*, denoted by *C*), per capita disposable income (*TOBPCY*, denoted by *Y*), a food price index (*TOBFP*, denoted by *FP*), and a non-food price index (*TOBNFP*, denoted by *NP*). Since the values for 1942–4 are missing from the original data set, we interpolated values for these years. In particular, we constructed a value for C_{1943} through a simple average of the values of C_{1941} and C_{1945} which is often used in statistical literature to impute the missing observations. We then obtained a value for C_{1942} and C_{1944} by averaging the values of C_{1941} and C_{1943} and those of C_{1943} and C_{1945}, respectively. Analogous operations were performed to fill in the missing values of Y, FP, and NP.

Using this as our data set, we next searched for an appropriate ADL model. When constructing our model portfolio, the maximum lag length we considered was four. Since we do not restrict the lag lengths to be equal, our model portfolio consists of 256 ADL models (i.e. 4 raised to the 4th power). We scored AIC, SBC, and ICOMP(IFIM) across all the 256 ADL models. We choose among these models using the ICOMP(IFIM) criterion. To ensure that we compared each model in the portfolio over the same sample of observations, we conditioned on the first four observations when evaluating each model. Our sample size for each model entertained then consists of 31 usable observations running from 1917 to 1947.

Table I presents the results of our model selection efforts for the original Tobin data set. *Ex ante*, we would expect AIC to overfit and SBC to underfit. In this case, both AIC and SBC choose an ADL(3,3,3,1) model, while ICOMP(IFIM) chooses the more parsimonious ADL(1,2,1,1). As always, the more heavily parameterized the model, the better the fit to the in-sample data. While AIC, SBC, and ICOMP(IFIM) each penalize lack of parsimony,

Table I. ADL model selection for the Tobin data. Best models according to model-selection criteria

Criterion	Order of ADL				Criterion value	Lack of fit	C_1
AIC	3	3	3	1	−196.61	−226.61	42.88
SBC	3	3	3	1	−175.10	−226.61	42.88
ICOMP(IFIM)	1	2	1	1	−147.85	−208.37	30.26

Sample: 1917–47 (Conditioning on 1913–16) (1942–4 interpolated).

ICOMP(IFIM) also penalizes the profusion of complexity among the parameter estimates. Using a large-scale Monte Carlo experiment, Bozdogan and Haughton (1996) demonstrate that ICOMP(IFIM) tends to perform better than either AIC or SBC in the usual multiple regression model when the entertained true model is not among the set considered under different configurations of error variances and the sample sizes (small to large). Thus, we decided to use the ADL(1,2,1,1) as our optimal model.

Having identified an appropriate ADL model, we next test the homogeneity postulate similar to Tobin (1950, pp. 132–3). The homogeneity postulate can be expressed as

$$\beta_0 + \beta_1 + \beta_2 + \delta_0 + \delta_1 + \gamma_0 + \gamma_1 = 0. \qquad 12$$

We impose this restriction on the ADL(1,2,1,1) model and evaluate the ICOMP(IFIM) score. With the restriction, the ICOMP(IFIM) score is equal to -140.8016 which is larger than the unrestricted score of -147.8509. We conclude that imposing the homogeneity postulate is not warranted based on our ICOMP(IFIM) results.

We next studied the long-run relationship between food consumption and income. Notice that the ADL(1,2,1,1) model has an equivalent ECM representation of the form

$$\Delta \ln C_t = (\rho_1 - 1)(\ln C_{t-1} - K - \lambda_1 \ln Y_{t-2} - \lambda_2 \ln FP_{t-1} - \lambda_3 \ln NP_{t-1}) + \beta_0 \Delta \ln Y_t$$
$$+ (\beta_0 + \beta_1)\Delta \ln Y_{t-1} + \delta_0 \Delta \ln FP_t + \gamma_0 \Delta \ln NP_t + \varepsilon_t \qquad 13$$

where

$$K = \frac{k}{1 - \rho_1} \quad \lambda_1 = \frac{\beta_0 + \beta_1 + \beta_2}{1 - \rho_1} \quad \lambda_2 = \frac{\delta_0 + \delta_1}{1 - \rho_1} \quad \lambda_3 = \frac{\gamma_0 + \gamma_1}{1 - \rho_1}. \qquad 14$$

We tested for unit roots in each series individually using augmented Dickey–Fuller (1979) (ADF) t-tests. The augmentation lag orders were chosen via ICOMP(IFIM) from a portfolio containing lag lengths 1–4. A constant and linear time trend were included in the fitted models. Our results are given in Table II.

Table II indicates that in no case can we reject the hypothesis of a unit root at the 5% level of significance. Interestingly, when we constructed a portfolio containing both I(0)

Table II. Unit root test results for Tobin data

Series	Augmentation lags	ICOMP(IFIM)	ADF t	5% critical values	Accept/reject
$\ln C_t$	4	−1816.51	−1.31	−3.46	Accept
$\ln Y_t$	1	−1964.55	−1.92	−3.46	Accept
$\ln FP_t$	1	−2001.63	−2.01	−3.46	Accept
$\ln NP_t$	3	−1954.31	−3.11	−3.46	Accept

and I(1) representations, ICOMP(IFIM) always chose an I(1) specification, indicating that the unit root representation provides the best approximating univariate model.

If the series $\ln C_t$, $\ln Y_{t-1}$, $\ln FP_t$, and $\ln NP_t$ are cointegrated, then the error correction term is I(0). We could then estimate the long-run elasticity of food consumption with respect to income from a cointegrating regression of $\ln C_t$ on a constant, $\ln Y_{t-1}$, $\ln FP_t$, and $\ln NP_t$. If the series are not cointegrated, this is a 'spurious' regression meaning that no stable, linear long-run relationship exists (see e.g. Granger and Newbold, 1974; Phillips, 1986).

We tested the null hypothesis of no cointegration between $\ln C_t$, $\ln Y_{t-1}$, $\ln FP_t$, and $\ln NP_t$ using Phillips's (1987) Z_α and Z_t statistics, Said and Dickey's (1984) ADF_t statistic, and Johansen's (1988) λ_{trace} statistic of zero cointegrating relationships against a general alternative. We included a constant and used three covariance lags for the Z tests, three augmentation lags for the ADF test, and one lag for the λ_{trace} test. The test statistics equalled -23.49, -4.18, -0.002, and 70.97, respectively. The 5% critical values for these statistics are -29.39, -4.22, -4.22, and 47.18, respectively. Thus, the λ_{trace} statistic rejects no cointegration at the 5% level, while the other three do not. However, Z_t is significant at the 10% level. It should be noted that we used ICOMP(IFIM) in selecting the lag lengths for Said and Dickey's (1984) and Johansen's (1988) tests.

Given some evidence of cointegration, we estimate the cointegrating regression

$$\ln C_t = K + \lambda_1 \ln Y_{t-1} + \lambda_2 \ln FP_t + \lambda_3 \ln NP_t + v_t \quad v_t \sim I(0) \qquad 15$$

using Phillips and Hansen's (1990) fully modified OLS estimator. (In this and the following subsections, when estimating the spectrum at frequency zero we use a Parzen (1962) kernel with four autocovariance terms.) The long-run elasticity of food consumption with respect to income is given by λ_1. We estimate this elasticity to equal 0.275 with a standard error 0.023. This says that, in long-run equilibrium, a 1% increase in income is associated with a 0.275% increase in food consumption. Here, we are abstracting from behavioural responses that might obscure such an inference. For example, see Lucas (1976).

Finally, notice that our test of the homogeneity postulate based on Equation (12) is equivalent to a test of

$$\lambda_1 + \lambda_2 + \lambda_3 = 0 \qquad 16$$

provided $\rho_1 \neq 1$ in Equation (14). In this sense, our specification of the homogeneity postulate in Equation (12) involves the long-run behaviour of food demand. However, testing Equation (16) based on Equation (15) requires that the variables in the error correction term are cointegrated, while testing Equation (12) based on the optimal ADL(1,2,1,1) model does not.

3.2. The Revised US Data

Here we use the revised US data from 1913 to 1976. In this case, C corresponds to *PCFC*, Y to *PCY*, *FP* to *FP*, and *NP* to *NFP*. Conditioning on the observations for 1913–16, we constructed a portfolio of 256 models with a maximum lag length of four analogously to that described in Section 3.1 above. Table III presents the models chosen by AIC, SBC, and ICOMP(IFIM) for the revised US data.

Table III. ADL model selection for the revised US data. Best models according to model selection criteria

Criterion	Order of ADL				Criterion value	Lack of fit	C_1
AIC	4	4	4	3	−349.46	−389.46	38.27
SBC	1	1	1	3	−322.00	−367.03	25.92
ICOMP(IFIM)	1	2	2	3	−317.02	−372.82	27.90

Sample: 1917–76 (Conditioning on 1913–16).

The results in Table III turned out to be consistent with our priors of AIC overfitting and SBC underfitting. In particular, the ADL(1,1,1,3) model chosen by SBC is a restricted (and, hence, less heavily parameterized) version of the ADL(1,2,2,3) model chosen by ICOMP(IFIM) which is, in turn, a restricted version of the ADL(4,4,4,3) model chosen by AIC. We chose the ADL(1,2,2,3) model as the best of the models in our portfolio.

We tested the homogeneity postulate by restricting the optimal ADL(1,2,2,3) model. In particular, we express the homogeneity postulate as the restriction

$$\beta_0 + \beta_1 + \beta_2 + \delta_0 + \delta_1 + \delta_2 + \gamma_0 + \gamma_1 + \gamma_2 + \gamma_3 = 0. \qquad 17$$

We impose this restriction on the ADL(1,2,2,3) model and evaluate the ICOMP(IFIM) score. With the restriction, the ICOMP(IFIM) score equals −314.8594 which is larger than the unrestricted score of −317.0155. As with the original Tobin data set above in Section 3.1, we again conclude that imposing the homogeneity postulate is not warranted based on our ICOMP(IFIM) results.

We next studied the long-run relationship between food consumption and income. The ADL(1,2,2,3) model has an equivalent ECM representation of the form

$$\Delta \ln C_t = (\rho_1 - 1)(\ln C_{t-1} - K - \lambda_1 \ln Y_{t-2} - \lambda_2 \ln FP_{t-2} - \lambda_3 \ln NP_{t-3}) + \beta_0 \Delta \ln Y_t$$
$$+ (\beta_0 + \beta_1)\Delta \ln Y_{t-1} + \delta_0 \Delta \ln FP_t + (\delta_0 + \delta_1)\Delta \ln FP_{t-1} + \gamma_0 \Delta \ln NP_t$$
$$+ (\gamma_0 + \gamma_1)\Delta \ln NP_{t-1} + (\gamma_0 + \gamma_1 + \gamma_2)\Delta \ln NP_{t-2} + \varepsilon_t \qquad 18$$

where

$$K = \frac{k}{1 - \rho_1} \quad \lambda_1 = \frac{\beta_0 + \beta_1 + \beta_2}{1 - \rho_1} \quad \lambda_2 = \frac{\delta_0 + \delta_1 + \delta_2}{1 - \rho_1} \quad \lambda_3 = \frac{\gamma_0 + \gamma_1 + \gamma_2 + \gamma_3}{1 - \rho_1}. \qquad 19$$

We tested for unit roots in each series individually using augmented Dickey–Fuller (1979) (ADF) t-tests. The augmentation lag orders were chosen via ICOMP(IFIM) from a portfolio containing lag lengths 1–4. A constant and linear time trend were included in the fitted models. Our results are given in Table IV. The table indicates that in no case can we reject the hypothesis of a unit root at the 5% level of significance. Again as in Section 3.1, when we constructed a portfolio containing both I(0) and I(1) representations, ICOMP(IFIM) always chose an I(1) specification as the best univariate model.

We tested the null hypothesis of no cointegration between $\ln C_t$, $\ln Y_{t-1}$, $\ln FP_{t-1}$, and $\ln NP_{t-2}$ using Z_α, Z_t, ADF_t, and λ_{trace} statistics. We included a constant and used two covariance lags for the Z tests, two augmentation lags for the ADF test, and one lag for the λ_{trace} test. The test statistics equalled −24.08, −3.96, 0.66, and 41.24, respectively. The 5% critical values for these statistics are −29.39, −4.22, −4.22, and 47.18, respectively. Again, we used ICOMP(IFIM) in selecting the lag lengths for the ADF_t, and the λ_{trace}

Table IV. Unit root test results for the revised US data

Series	Augmentation lags	ICOMP(IFIM)	ADF t	5% critical values	Accept/reject
$\ln C_t$	4	-3713.15	-2.79	-3.46	Accept
$\ln Y_t$	3	-3930.63	-1.61	-3.46	Accept
$\ln FP_t$	4	-3974.10	-1.47	-3.46	Accept
$\ln NP_t$	2	-3962.24	-2.02	-3.46	Accept

tests. Thus, in this case, we find no compelling evidence of cointegration between the variables as specified by the error correction term in the ECM associated with the optimal ADL(1,2,2,3) model.

Bearing in mind that we may in fact be performing a spurious regression, we went ahead and estimated the 'cointegrating' regression

$$\ln C_t = K + \lambda_1 \ln Y_{t-1} + \lambda_2 \ln FP_{t-1} + \lambda_3 \ln NP_{t-2} + v_t \qquad 20$$

using Phillips' and Hansen's (1990) fully modified OLS estimator. We estimate that the long-run elasticity of food consumption with respect to income is 0.213 with a standard error of 0.028.

3.3. The Netherlands Data

Now we examine the Netherlands data from 1948 to 1988. In this case, C corresponds to $1000 \cdot V11/POP$, Y to $1000 \cdot AGGY/POP$ and FP to $P11$. We constructed the non-food price index, NP, as follows. We defined weights, denoted s_i for $i = 2, \ldots, 6$, such that

$$s_i = Vii/(V22 + V33 + V44 + V55) \qquad 21$$

for expenditures in 1951. The non-food price index with $1951 = 100$ is then

$$NP_t = \sum_{i=2}^{6} s_i Pii_t, \quad t = 1948, \ldots, 1988. \qquad 22$$

It is important to emphasize that C, as defined in this subsection, corresponds to per capita food consumption *expenditures*. As was aptly pointed out by an assessor at the workshop, per capita food consumption is the theoretically appropriate measure.

Conditioning on the observations for 1948–51, we constructed a portfolio of 256 models with a maximum lag length of four analogously to that described in Sections 3.1 and 3.2. Table V presents the models chosen by AIC, SBC, and ICOMP(IFIM) for the Netherlands data. In this case, AIC, SBC, and ICOMP(IFIM) all choose the ADL(3,1,1,1) model.

The homogeneity postulate can be expressed as the restriction

$$\beta_0 + \beta_1 + \delta_0 + \delta_1 + \gamma_0 + \gamma_1 = 0. \qquad 23$$

We impose this restriction on the ADL(3,1,1,1) model and evaluate the ICOMP(IFIM) score. With the restriction, the ICOMP(IFIM) score equals -171.3664 which is smaller than the unrestricted score of -169.7632. Thus, we accept the homogeneity postulate when applied to the Netherlands time-series data.

Table V. ADL model selection for the Netherlands data. Best models according to model selection criteria

Criterion	Order of ADL				Criterion value	Lack of fit	C_1
AIC	3	1	1	1	−188.53	−210.53	20.38
SBC	3	1	1	1	−170.81	−210.53	20.38
ICOMP(IFIM)	3	1	1	1	−169.76	−210.53	20.38

Sample: 1952–88 (Conditioning on 1948–51).

We next studied the long-run relationship between food consumption and income. The ADL(3,1,1,1) model has an equivalent ECM representation of the form

$$\Delta \ln C_t = (\rho_1 + \rho_2 + \rho_3 - 1)(\ln C_{t-3} - K - \lambda_1 \ln Y_{t-1} - \lambda_2 \ln FP_{t-1} - \lambda_3 \ln NP_{t-1})$$
$$+ (\rho_1 - 1)\Delta \ln C_{t-1} + (\rho_1 + \rho_2 - 1)\Delta \ln C_{t-2} + \beta_0 \Delta \ln Y_t + \delta_0 \Delta \ln FP_t$$
$$+ \gamma_0 \Delta \ln NP_t + \varepsilon_t \qquad 24$$

where

$$K = \frac{k}{1 - \rho_1 - \rho_2 - \rho_3} \qquad \lambda_1 = \frac{\beta_0 + \beta_1}{1 - \rho_1 - \rho_2 - \rho_3}$$
$$\lambda_2 = \frac{\delta_0 + \delta_1}{1 - \rho_1 - \rho_2 - \rho_3} \qquad \lambda_3 = \frac{\gamma_0 + \gamma_1}{1 - \rho_1 - \rho_2 - \rho_3}. \qquad 25$$

We tested for unit roots in each series individually using augmented Dickey–Fuller (1979) (ADF) t-tests. The augmentation lag orders were chosen via ICOMP(IFIM) from a portfolio containing lag lengths 1–4. A constant and linear time trend were included in the fitted models. Our results are given in Table VI. The table indicates that in no case can we reject the hypothesis of a unit root at the 5% level of significance. Again, when we constructed a portfolio containing both I(0) and I(1) representations, ICOMP(IFIM) always chose an I(1) specification as the best univariate model.

We tested the null hypothesis of no cointegration between $\ln C_{t-2}$, $\ln Y_t$, $\ln FP_t$, and $\ln NP_t$ using the Z_α, Z_t, ADF$_t$, and λ_{trace} statistics. We included a constant and used four covariance lags for the Z tests, four augmentation lags for the ADF test, and one lag for the λ_{trace} test. The test statistics equalled −20.74, −3.84, 0.33, and 91.74, respectively. Again, we used ICOMP(IFIM) to select lag lengths for the ADF$_t$ and the λ_{trace} tests. The 5% critical values for these statistics are −29.39, −4.22, −4.22, and 47.18, respectively.

Given some evidence of cointegration, we went ahead and estimated the cointegrating regression

$$\ln C_{t-2} = K + \lambda_1 \ln Y_t + \lambda_2 \ln FP_t + \lambda_3 \ln NP_t + v_t \quad v_t \sim I(0) \qquad 26$$

Table VI. Unit root test results for the Netherlands data

Series	Augmentation lags	ICOMP(IFIM)	ADF t	5% critical values	Accept/reject
$\ln C_t$	1	−2173.67	−0.68	−3.46	Accept
$\ln Y_t$	1	−2216.94	−0.85	−3.46	Accept
$\ln FP_t$	1	−2337.10	−1.53	−3.46	Accept
$\ln NP_t$	1	−2280.25	−1.72	−3.46	Accept

Table VII. Elasticity of food consumption with respect
to income

Data set	Short-run	Long-run
Original Tobin	0.162 (0.030)	0.275 (0.023)
Revised US	0.175 (0.032)	0.213 (0.028)
The Netherlands	0.351 (0.103)	0.385 (0.055)

Standard errors in parentheses.

using Phillips and Hansen's (1990) fully modified OLS estimator. The long-run elasticity of food consumption with respect to income is given by λ_1. We estimate this elasticity to be 0.385 with a standard error of 0.055.

Before analysing whether to pool the data, we summarize our long-run income elasticity estimates from Sections 3.1–3.3. Additionally, for comparative purposes, we also report our estimates of the short-run (i.e. contemporaneous) income elasticity parameter β_0. These estimates are reported in Table VII. Our short-run estimate for the Tobin data is smaller than Tobin's estimate of 0.56 (see Tobin, 1950, p. 119) since Tobin's estimate involved both contemporaneous and once-lagged income. Also, the 'original' Tobin data used in our paper includes all data available to Tobin at the time he wrote his paper, whereas Tobin's estimate was based on data through 1941. Note that Table VII is consistent with Friedman's classic permanent income hypothesis (PIH), namely, consumption responds more strongly to changes in long-run income than short-run income. Technically, the PIH applies to consumption not necessarily expenditures. Thus our estimates for the Netherlands based on food consumption expenditures do not directly apply to our claim.

3.4. To Pool or Not to Pool

Here we examine whether better results can be obtained by combining the revised US data in Section 3.2 with the Netherlands data of Section 3.3. To do this, we begin by considering the most general ADL(4,4,4,4) model in a seemingly unrelated regressions (SUR) framework (see Zellner, 1962) for both the revised US and the Netherlands data. That is, we estimate the *unrestricted* model

$$\begin{bmatrix} \ln C_{US} \\ \ln C_{NL} \end{bmatrix} = \begin{bmatrix} \ln X_{US} & 0 \\ 0 & \ln X_{NL} \end{bmatrix} \begin{bmatrix} \beta_{US} \\ \beta_{NL} \end{bmatrix} + \begin{bmatrix} \varepsilon_{US} \\ \varepsilon_{NL} \end{bmatrix} \qquad 27$$

where $\ln C_{US}$ and $\ln C_{NL}$ denote the revised US and Netherlands time series on per capita food consumption running from 1917 to 1976 and 1952 to 1988, respectively. The data matrices $\ln X_{US}$ and $\ln X_{NL}$ include a constant term and four lags of the C, Y, FP, and NP for a total of 17 columns each. The unrestricted model in (27) is equivalent to the model (or hypothesis) $M_u : \beta_{US} \neq \beta_{NL}$, which allows intercept and slopes to be different in the two equations.

One problematic aspect to the set-up in (27) is that we have an unequal number of observations in the revised US and the Netherlands data sets, although work has been done in estimating SUR systems with unequal numbers of observations. For this see e.g. Schmidt (1977). In such a case, the general question is how to estimate the off-diagonal elements of the contemporaneous covariance matrix for the disturbance vectors ε_{US} and ε_{NL} in order to perform feasible generalized least squares (FGLS) estimation.

Since the data series do overlap during the years 1952–76, one approach for us would be to estimate the contemporaneous covariance matrix of the disturbances over this joint subsample. However, for ease of working, we decided to simply treat the off-diagonal elements equal to zero, and performed FGLS under this restriction. When we do this, for the unrestricted model in (27), we find the ICOMP(IFIM) score to equal -395.8988.

We next pooled the data and estimated the *restricted* model

$$\ln \mathbf{C}_{(US,NL)} = \ln \mathbf{X}_{(US,NL)} \boldsymbol{\beta}_{(US,NL)} + \boldsymbol{\varepsilon}_{(US,NL)} \qquad 28$$

using OLS. Comparing the restricted model in (28) with the unrestricted model in (27), we see that the $\mathbf{X}_g$ matrices ($g = 1, 2$) are now combined. This set-up is now equivalent to the model (or hypothesis) $\mathbf{M}_r : \boldsymbol{\beta}_{US} = \boldsymbol{\beta}_{NL}$, and that the variances of ε_{US} and ε_{NL} are common. The ICOMP(IFIM) score for this restricted model equals -434.8274 which is smaller than the score of -395.8988 for the more general unrestricted SUR-ADL model given in (27). Based on this evidence, we conclude that pooling the data can be useful.

Conditioning on the observations 1913–16 for the revised US data and 1948–51 for the Netherlands data, we constructed a portfolio of 256 ADL models with a maximum lag length of four analogously to that described in Sections 3.1–3.3. Based on the ICOMP(IFIM) scores, we found the optimal model for the pooled data to be an ADL(1,1,2,1).

We next tested the homogeneity postulate on the pooled data by restricting the optimal ADL(1,1,2,1) model. In particular, we express the homogeneity postulate as the restriction

$$\beta_0 + \beta_1 + \delta_0 + \delta_1 + \delta_2 + \gamma_0 + \gamma_1 = 0. \qquad 29$$

The ICOMP(IFIM) score for the optimal ADL model with this restriction imposed equals -438.8692, which is larger than the unrestricted score of -443.0359. We conclude that imposing the homogeneity postulate is not warranted based on our ICOMP(IFIM) results for the pooled data.

4.   FORECASTING FOOD CONSUMPTION IN THE NETHERLANDS

In this section, we forecast food consumption in the Netherlands through the year 2000 conditional on information available through 1988. We construct an autoregression involving the ($p \times 1$) vector process $\mathbf{x}_t$ which contains C_t and, possibly, Y_t, FP_t, and NP_t. Here, C, Y, FP, and NP are as defined in Section 3.3. An advantage of using vector autoregression (VAR) to forecast food consumption is that the fitted VAR provides forecasts of all variables on the right-hand-side of the food consumption equation.

We postulate that the dynamic behaviour of $\mathbf{x}_t$ can be approximated as

$$\mathbf{x}_t = \boldsymbol{\Phi} D_t + \boldsymbol{\Pi}_1 \mathbf{x}_{t-1} + \cdots + \boldsymbol{\Pi}_k \mathbf{x}_{t-k} + \boldsymbol{\varepsilon}_t \quad t = 1, \ldots, T \qquad 30$$

where $\mathbf{D}_t$ is a $m \times 1$ vector of deterministic terms containing a constant term and, possibly, a linear time trend, and $\boldsymbol{\varepsilon}_t$ is a Gaussian vector white-noise process with mean vector zero and contemporaneous covariance matrix $\boldsymbol{\Omega}$. We condition on the first k observations of $\mathbf{x}_t$ so that T is the *number of usable observations*. A more compact matrix notation for the VAR model is

$$\mathbf{Y} = \mathbf{Z}\boldsymbol{\Pi} + \mathbf{E} \qquad 31$$

where we have the $(T \times p)$ matrix $\mathbf{Y} = [\mathbf{x}_1', \ldots, \mathbf{x}_T']'$, $T \times (m + kp)$ matrix $\mathbf{Z} = [\mathbf{z}_1', \ldots, \mathbf{z}_T']'$ with the $(pk + m)$-vector $\mathbf{z}_t = (\mathbf{D}_t', \mathbf{x}_{t-1}', \ldots, \mathbf{x}_{t-k}')'$, and the $(T \times p)$ matrix $\mathbf{E} = [\boldsymbol{\varepsilon}_1', \ldots, \boldsymbol{\varepsilon}_T']'$.

When specifying the VAR, we limit our analysis in several ways. We maintain throughout that each equation contains the same set of regressors, and we allow for, at most, four lags. Since the goal of this section is forecasting and not the estimation of a structural model, we specify the VAR in levels of the variables (Sims, 1980; Enders, 1995, p. 301). However, because we maintain that ε_t is Gaussian, we entertain the possibility that a transformation of $\mathbf{x}_t$ may be necessary to induce normality of the residuals in Equation (30). In particular, we consider two possibilities: raw data versus log transformed data.

Our model-selection strategy relies on using information theoretic criteria to determine appropriate choices of the variables included in the VAR, $\mathbf{x}_t$, the deterministic terms, $\mathbf{D}_t$, the lag length, k, and whether to log transform the data. In particular, we examine how different models score on the basis of multivariate versions of the Akaike's (1973) Information Criterion (AIC), the Schwarz (1978) Bayesian Criterion (SBC), and the ICOMP(IFIM) criteria proposed by Bozdogan (1990a, 1994d, 1996, 1997a,b).

Analytical expressions for multivariate versions of these criteria are given by

$$\text{AIC} = \text{Lack of fit} + 2(\text{Numparms}) \qquad 32$$

$$\text{SBC} = \text{Lack of fit} + (\text{Numparms}) \ln (\text{Nobs}) \qquad 33$$

$$\text{ICOMP(IFIM)} = \text{Lack of fit} + 2C_1(\text{IFIM}) \qquad 34$$

where

$$\text{Lack of fit} = (\text{Nobs})p \ln(2\pi) + (\text{Nobs}) \ln |\hat{\boldsymbol{\Omega}}| + (\text{Nobs})p \qquad 35$$

where Nobs $= T =$ Rows of $\mathbf{Y}$ (i.e. the number of usable observations), $p =$ number of variables in the VAR and Numparms equals the number of estimated parameters (i.e. $p(pk + m) + p(p + 1)/2$ — the number of coefficients in the VAR plus the number of distinct elements in the contemporaneous covariance matrix $\boldsymbol{\Omega}$).

Bozdogan (1990a, 1997b), following Magnus and Neudecker (1988) for the VAR model in Equation (31) under the assumption of Gaussianity, gives IFIM as

$$\text{Cov}(\text{vec}(\hat{\boldsymbol{\Pi}}), v(\hat{\boldsymbol{\Omega}})) = \mathcal{F}^1(\hat{\boldsymbol{\Theta}}) = \begin{bmatrix} \hat{\boldsymbol{\Omega}} \otimes (\mathbf{Z}'\mathbf{Z})^{-1} & \mathbf{0} \\ \mathbf{0}' & (2/\text{Nobs})D_p^+(\hat{\boldsymbol{\Omega}} \otimes \hat{\boldsymbol{\Omega}})D_p^{+'} \end{bmatrix} \qquad 36$$

where D_p^+ is the Moore–Penrose inverse of the duplication matrix D_p; i.e. $D_p^+ = (D_p'D_p)^{-1}D_p'$. In Equation (36), $\text{vec}(\hat{\boldsymbol{\Pi}})$ denotes the vec operator which transforms a matrix into a vector by stacking the columns, $v(\hat{\boldsymbol{\Omega}})$ denotes the $p(p + 1)/2 \times 1$ vector obtained from $\text{vec}(\hat{\boldsymbol{\Omega}})$ by eliminating all supradiagonal elements of $\hat{\boldsymbol{\Omega}}$. D_p is a unique $p^2 \times \frac{1}{2}p(p + 1)$ duplication matrix which transforms $v(\hat{\boldsymbol{\Omega}})$ into $\text{vec}(\hat{\boldsymbol{\Omega}})$.

Proposition 4.1   For the VAR model in (31) ICOMP(IFIM) is

$$\text{ICOMP(IFIM)} = -2 \log L(\hat{\boldsymbol{\Pi}}, \hat{\boldsymbol{\Omega}}) + 2C_1(\hat{\mathcal{F}}^{-1})$$

$$= (\text{Nobs})p \ln(2\pi) + (\text{Nobs}) \ln |\hat{\boldsymbol{\Omega}}| + (\text{Nobs})p$$

$$+ (\text{Numparms}) \log \left\{ \frac{\text{tr}(\hat{\boldsymbol{\Omega}})\text{tr}(\mathbf{Z'Z})^{-1} + \dfrac{1}{2\,\text{Nobs}}}{\left[\text{tr}(\hat{\boldsymbol{\Omega}}^2) + (\text{tr}\hat{\boldsymbol{\Omega}})^2 + 2 \displaystyle\sum_j \hat{\boldsymbol{\Omega}}_{jj}^2 \right]} \middle/ (\text{Numparms}) \right\}$$

$$- (pk + m) \log |\hat{\boldsymbol{\Omega}}| - (p+1) \log |\hat{\boldsymbol{\Omega}}| - p \log |(\mathbf{Z'Z})^{-1}| - p \log(2)$$
$$+ p(p+1)/2 \log (\text{Nobs}). \tag{37}$$

Proof: See Bozdogan (1990a, 1997b).

Our set of candidate models includes eight possible specifications for $\mathbf{x}_t$; i.e. $(C_t Y_t FP_t NP_t)'$, $(C_t Y_t FP_t)'$, $(C_t Y_t NP_t)'$, $(C_t FP_t NP_t)'$, $(C_t Y_t)'$, $(C_t FP_t)'$, $(C_t NP_t)'$, and C_t. For each of the possible choices of $\mathbf{x}_t$, we consider two possible transformations, raw versus logarithmic, and two possible choices of $\mathbf{D}_t$, constant versus constant and linear time trend. For a given lag length k, we then have 32 possible models. Since we consider lag lengths 1,2,3, and 4, our model portfolio contains 128 possible VAR models. We condition on the observations of 1948–51 each time we evaluate a model. Our sample then has 37 p-dimensional usable observations running from 1952 to 1988.

Table VIII reports the optimal models chosen by AIC, SBC, and ICOMP(IFIM). Two interesting points gleaned from Table VIII are that all three model-selection criteria prefer a model in logs to one with the raw data, and each criterion chooses a pure autoregression of consumption alone. Based on AIC, the best model is deemed a second-order autoregression, whereas both SBC and ICOMP(IFIM) pick a first-order autoregression. In the light of Hall's (1978) theoretical result that consumption will follow a random walk, we imposed a unit coefficient on the first-order autoregression chosen by SBC and ICOMP(IFIM). The SBC value for this random walk with drift model is 400.41 while that for ICOMP(IFIM) is 398.05. Comparing these results with those of Table VIII, we see that both criteria prefer the random walk with drift model to the unrestricted first-order autoregression. Thus, the model chosen by both SBC and ICOMP(IFIM) corresponds to a model based on an established economic theory. This means that model-selection criteria also have the virtue of being able to validate the theoretical and empirical findings of an expert researcher. We emphasize that Hall's (1978) theoretical result applies to consumption, while the Netherlands data are in terms of consumption expenditures.

The results of some diagnostic tests of the residuals from the random walk with drift model are such that Mardia's (1970) tests of Estimated Skewness $= 0.66$ (against the

Table VIII. Best VAR models according to model-selection criteria

Criterion	Subset	Log	Trend	Lags	Criterion value	Lack of fit	C_1
AIC	C	Yes	No	2	396.82	388.82	11.96
SBC	C	Yes	No	1	403.18	392.35	8.29
ICOMP(IFIM)	C	Yes	No	1	408.93	392.35	8.29

Sample: 1952–88 (Conditioning on 1948–51).

true value of zero) with P-value $= 0.04$, and Estimated Kurtosis $= 3.61$ (against the true value of 3) with Z-Statistic $= 0.76$ and P-value $= 0.45$ (two-sided). The Jarque–Bera (1987) test of normality is equal to 4.37, with a P-value of 0.11. Figure 1 plots a kernel density estimate of the standardized residuals which indicates no severe departure from normality. As a whole, then, the hypothesis that the residuals are normally distributed is tenable. A plot of the sample autocorrelation function does not indicate strong evidence of a problem with serial correlation (see Figure 2). Figure 3 reports our forecast of per capita food consumption from 1989–2000 in the Netherlands.

To construct our forecast of per capita food consumption, we began by forecasting the log of per capita food consumption using the fitted VAR. Let $f_{t,h}$ denote the forecast of $\ln(C_{t+h})$ conditional on information available at date t, and $\sigma_{t,h}^2$ denote the forecast error variance. Our working assumption is that, conditional on information available at date t, $\ln(C_{t+h})$ is distributed $N(f_{t,h}, \sigma_{t,h}^2)$. Under this assumption, C_{t+h} is distributed Lognormal abbreviated as $LN(f_{t,h}, \sigma_{t,h}^2)$ so that

$$E_t C_{t+h} = \exp(f_{t,h} + \sigma_{t,h}^2/2). \tag{38}$$

Thus, we simply forecast the logarithm of per capita food consumption for dates 1989 through 2000 conditional on information available at date 1988 to obtain the sequence $\{f_{1988,h}, \sigma_{1988,h}\}_{h=1}^{12}$. From this, we construct our point forecast of per capita food consumption as

$$f_{1988,h}^c = \exp(f_{t,h} + \sigma_{t,h}^2/2), \quad h = 1, \ldots, 12. \tag{39}$$

Additionally, conditional on information available at date t,

$$\text{Prob}\left\{-1.96 \leq \frac{\ln(C_{t+h}) - f_{t,h}}{\sigma_{t,h}} \leq 1.96\right\} = 0.95 \tag{40}$$

so that

$$\text{Prob}\{\exp(f_{t,h} - 1.96\sigma_{t,h}) \leq C_{t+h} \leq \exp(f_{t,h} + 1.96\sigma_{t,h})\} = 0.95 \tag{41}$$

thereby also providing an interval forecast of per capita food consumption.

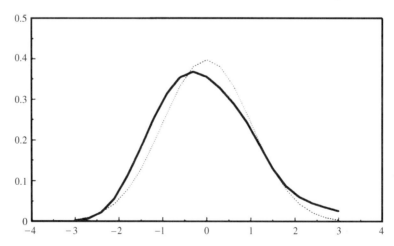

Figure 1. Kernel density estimate of the standardized one-step forecast errors. The solid line indicates density estimate and the dotted line the theoretical standard normal density

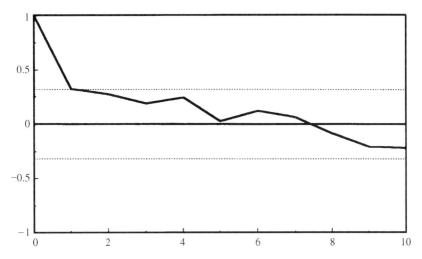

Figure 2. Sample autocorrelations of the one-step forecast errors at lags zero to ten years. Dashed lines indicate asymptotic 95% confidence intervals

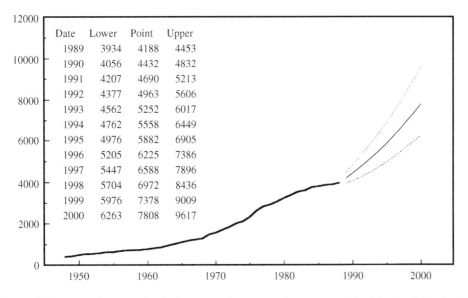

Date	Lower	Point	Upper
1989	3934	4188	4453
1990	4056	4432	4832
1991	4207	4690	5213
1992	4377	4963	5606
1993	4562	5252	6017
1994	4762	5558	6449
1995	4976	5882	6905
1996	5205	6225	7386
1997	5447	6588	7896
1998	5704	6972	8436
1999	5976	7378	9009
2000	6263	7808	9617

Figure 3. Forecast of per capita food consumption expenditures (in guilders) in the Netherlands from 1989 to 2000. Dotted lines indicate asymptotic 95% confidence intervals

5. ANALYSIS OF US BUDGET DATA

Many practical situations require the presentation of multivariate data from several structured samples for comparative inference and the grouping of the heterogeneous samples
into homogeneous sets of samples. While many multiple comparison procedures (MCPs)
have been proposed in the literature in the univariate case, in the multivariate case there
are few MCPs available in practice. Little or no work has been done under covariance heterogeneity for comparative simultaneous inference and on variable selection. The

general problem of multisample cluster analysis (MSCA), developed by Bozdogan (1981) using AIC, arises when we are given a collection of groups, profiles, or samples. For this, see e.g. Bozdogan (1981, 1986) and Bozdogan and Sclove (1984). The problem here is to cluster groups, samples, or data matrices into homogeneous groups, whether these are formed naturally or experimentally.

The goal of cluster analysis is to put the K groups or samples into k homogeneous groups, samples, or classes where k is unknown and varying, but $k \leq K$. Thus, we seek the smallest number k to achieve a parsimonious grouping of samples, and to reduce the number of given K groups.

We take the US budget data set and treat the budget year 1950 as our group G_1, budget year 1960 as our group G_2, and budget year 1972 as our group G_3 on jointly multinormal distributed random variables *FOODCON*, *AHSIZE*, *AGEHH*, *NONWHITE*, *HOMEOWN*, *HINC*, *NETASSCH*, and *ACCBAL* as our multivariate data. We carry out MSCA on these three budget groups using the information-based model selection criteria when the mean vectors and covariance matrices across these $K = 3$ groups are varying. Using the Stirling number of secondkind partitioning, the five multisample clustering alternatives in this case are: $\{G_1, G_2, G_3\}$, $\{G_1, G_2\}\{G_3\}$, $\{G_1, G_3\}\{G_2\}$, $\{G_2, G_3\}\{G_1\}$, and $\{G_1\}\{G_2\}\{G_3\}$. The results obtained from this analysis indicate based on the minimum value of ICOMP(IFIM) = 16 659 (on the raw data) and ICOMP(IFIM) = 9524 (on the transformed data containing log of food consumption and income) are such that, if we must cluster any one of the two budget years, we should cluster G_1 = budget year 1950 and G_2 = budget year 1960 as one homogeneous group, and leave G_3 = budget year 1972 alone in its own singleton cluster. That is, we have the partitioning $\{G_1, G_2\}\{G_3\} \equiv \{1950, 1960\}\{1972\}$. This partitioning seems consistent both with the expanded coverage of the 1972 data to include rural areas as well as the truly significant changes affecting American agriculture over the period as outlined in APAC (1995).

Using this result from the MSCA, we now cast the celebrated seemingly unrelated regressions (SUR) model of Zellner (1962) on the US budget years 1950 and 1960 data sets combined, and US budget year 1972 data set alone. We use Food Consumption (*FOODCON*) as our dependent variable, and *AHSIZE*, *AGEHH*, *NONWHITE*, *HOMEOWN*, *HINC*, *NETASSCH*, *ACCBAL* as our independent or predictor variables in the SUR system. We subject the SUR model to the Genetic Algorithm (GA) to select the best predictors using the information-based criteria as our fitness function. For this, see e.g. Luh, Minesky, and Bozdogan (1996). A GA is a random search algorithm which is based on concepts of biological evolution and natural selection. Using this new technique on the SUR system:

$$\mathbf{y} = \mathbf{X}\beta + \varepsilon \qquad\qquad 42$$

where

$$\begin{bmatrix} \mathbf{y}_{1950, 1960} \\ \mathbf{y}_{1972} \end{bmatrix} = \begin{bmatrix} \mathbf{X}_{1950, 1960} & \mathbf{0} \\ \mathbf{0} & \mathbf{X}_{1972} \end{bmatrix} \begin{bmatrix} \beta_{1950, 1960} \\ \beta_{1972} \end{bmatrix} + \begin{bmatrix} \varepsilon_{1950, 1960} \\ \varepsilon_{1972} \end{bmatrix} \qquad 43$$

under the usual assumptions, and treating the covariances of the disturbances of the equations to be equal to zero, since the sample sizes across these two SUR systems are unequal and for computational ease, we entertained several classes of models. These models are: M_1 = no transformation baseline model, M_2 = transform y's but no transformation of X's, M_3 = log transformed y on log transformed *HINC* (household income) but no transformation of the other predictors, and M_4 = log transformed y on log transformed first five predictors (since the last two variables had negative values). According to the minimum value of ICOMP(IFIM), we choose model M_3 as our best-fitting model with an ICOMP(IFIM) value equal to -209.82. The best subset of predictors for the first SUR system is: {Constant, *AHSIZE*, *NONWHITE*, log((*HINC*)}. For the second SUR system, the best subset is: {Constant, *AHSIZE*, *NONWHITE*, log(*HINC*)}. The intersecting best predictor set is {Constant, *AHSIZE*, log(*HINC*)}. So the non-intersecting predictor singleton set is {*NONWHITE*} between the two SUR systems. This is distinguishing the budget years 1950 and 1960 combined from budget year 1972 as our best predictor. We find this quite interesting since both the Civil Rights Act as well as related legislation (e.g. food stamps) were passed beginning in 1964, considerably changing the (legal) socio-economic status of minorities in the USA. We also obtain an estimate of the contemporaneous income elasticity of food consumption. Based on the US budget studies, the estimated coefficient of log(*HINC*) is equal to 0.3751 (for the first SUR system with a standard error of 0.0216), and the estimated coefficient of log(*HINC*) is equal to 0.3312 (for the second SUR system with a standard error of 0.0177).

6. CONCLUSION

In this paper we apply a new information-theoretic technique to the modelling of food consumption in the USA and the Netherlands. In the context of autoregressive distributed lag (ADL) models, we examine the relationship between food consumption and income. We use the information criterion ICOMP(IFIM) to select appropriate lag lengths. We use ADL models to study whether food consumption obeys the homogeneity postulate. Our conclusions on this point are mixed. Based on the revised US time-series data and the pooled data, we reject the homogeneity postulate. However, when examining the Netherlands time-series data in isolation, we accept the homogeneity postulate. Since our analysis of pooling in Section 3.4 indicates that the pooled sample is superior to the more general unrestricted SUR framework, we feel the evidence leans against the homogeneity postulate. We exploit the equivalence between ADL and error correction models (ECMs) to study the long-run relationship between food consumption and income. Based on cointegrating regressions, we find the long-run elasticity of food consumption with respect to income to equal 0.213 in the USA and 0.385 in the Netherlands. The Netherlands estimate is based on food consumption expenditures, while the US estimate is based on food consumption. These estimates should be interpreted cautiously since we find no evidence of cointegration for the revised US data and limited evidence for the Netherlands data. If the data are not in fact cointegrated, the regressions producing these results will be spurious.

We perform a forecast of food consumption in the Netherlands for the years 1989–2000 conditional on information available through 1988. Using a multivariate version of the ICOMP(IFIM) criterion, we select a drifting random walk in log-consumption as the optimal forecasting model. Finally, we applied the technique of multisample cluster analysis to a set of variables common to the 1950, 1960, and 1972 US budget studies. We find that the years 1950 and 1960 form a single cluster, and that the variable distinguishing 1972 from the earlier years is the percentage of households that are non-white. The analysis demonstrates a number of ways that information-theoretic modelling can be useful to applied econometricians. For example, we found information criteria to be useful for selecting the order of autoregressive distributed lag models (ADLs) and the number of augmentation lags in residual-based cointegration tests. We illustrated that information criteria can be useful for identifying the lag length, information set (i.e. subset of variables), transformation, and matrix of deterministic terms in VAR models. We further showed that information-theoretic modelling can be used to test whether distinct data sets can be pooled, and also how it can be applied to aid in the choice of regressors with cross-sectional and panel data settings.

Our analyses demonstrate the utility of information-theoretic model-selection and evaluation procedures in approximating the underlying structure of economic data. In contrast to the classical statistical procedures, these new methods avoid the use of sampling distributions. In particular, they do not require any arbitrarily specified level of significance or table look-up in the decision-making process. We believe the set of potential applications of informational modelling in applied econometrics is vast, and it is our hope that future research will explore some of these avenues.

APPENDIX: SUMMARY OF PARTICIPANTS' LOGBOOK

Throughout this experiment we maintained a logbook of our thought process, hoping that it will be helpful in future applied econometric projects. This appendix summarizes our logbook.

One of our first conclusions was that our primary contribution to this experiment would be to illustrate how information-theoretical model-selection techniques can be useful to applied econometricians. The *Experiment Information Pack* provided to participants in the experiment specifies the tasks we could include in our report. Our early meetings were consumed with discussions of which of these tasks we would attempt and which techniques would be most appropriate. We decided to put off discussions on task 4 (policy analysis), and concentrate on tasks 1, 2, 3, and 5 where we felt our information-theoretic approach could be best demonstrated. We began by analysing the US time-series data with ADL models of food consumption and using the Genetic Algorithm (GA) to select optimal predictors for Netherlands food consumption in a static regression framework. Our thinking was that, since the US time-series data is considerably more aggregated than the Netherlands data, we would focus on correlations over time among a few variables to model US food consumption. Since the Netherlands time-series data has a finer breakdown of expenditures and prices, we would exploit this richness in a static regression setting. While lags could in theory also have been included for the Netherlands, we had access to only 41 years of annual data. Attempting to examine both contemporaneous correlations between the disaggregated data and correlations over time would exhaust our degrees of freedom. We became disappointed with this approach because we found it hard to compare our results between the USA and the Netherlands, not to mention the issues that would be raised in attempting to integrate the analysis in task 2(b) of the *Experiment Information Pack*. So we decided to aggregate the Netherlands time-series data to construct variables similar to those available in the USA, and to handle tasks 1 and 2 focusing on the time-series data using autoregressive distributed lag (ADL) modelling techniques. We felt this symmetry of variables would allow us to examine the USA in isolation, the Netherlands in isolation, and the USA and Netherlands as a whole in a consistent manner. After using information criteria to select optimal ADL models for food consumption in the USA and the Netherlands, we next considered how we would decide whether to pool the US and Netherlands data. Initially, we took the residual series from the USA and Netherlands optimal ADL models, treated these as two groups, and performed multisample cluster analysis on these residual series to determine whether they constituted a single cluster. We found they did, but soon had reservations concerning what this finding actually meant. Since a successful ADL model will eliminate serial correlation from the residuals, we felt that the multisample clustering analysis here was merely testing whether the variances of the two residual series were equal. But what we really wanted was to know if pooling the data would improve our test of the homogeneity postulate. It was at this point that we decided to analyse the pooling issue in the context of a seemingly unrelated regressions (SUR) framework using the MSCA approach.

Initially, we had planned to complete task 3 by forecasting Netherlands food consumption using the optimal ADL model identified in task 2(a) of the *Experiment Information Pack*. Forecasting in this framework, however, necessitated that we obtain forecasts of income, food prices, and non-food prices from 1989 through 2000. We debated using ARIMA techniques on these variables or a VAR of income, food prices, and non-food prices to obtain such forecasts. However, this would raise issues concerning the generation of interval forecasts that we felt were beyond the scope of this paper. Instead, we decided to break away from the ADL formulation, and forecast food consumption using a VAR of food consumption, income, food prices, and non-food prices.

When formulating task 5, we decided that this would be a good place to show that information-theoretic modelling techniques are not limited to time-series data. In particular, information-theoretic model selection techniques can be applied with cross-sectional and panel data sets. With the help of the Genetic Algorithm (GA), information-based model selection can be practically implemented even when the number of variables considered is very large. Since a number of variables in the Netherlands budget data sets were categorical in nature, we found it difficult to construct data sets for the USA and the Netherlands that were comparable. We decided that we would focus on choosing optimal predictors of food consumption using just the US budget data, and, in particular, examining only those variables common to the 1950, 1960, and 1972 budget years. Having completed tasks 1, 2, 3, and 5, we realized that we would be facing space constraints reporting just these tasks within the 25-page limit. At this point, we regretfully decided to omit task 4. The issues concerning policy makers today relating to high-technology industry growth versus primary manufacturing, social programmes (such as food stamps) were not structural characteristics of the economy in the early budget periods. For example, the number of tractors on American farms did not exceed the number of horses and mules for the first time until the 1960 budget data (APAC, 1995). To a significant extent, we felt that this task 4 (policy analysis) was worthy of a separate paper or competition.

ACKNOWLEDGEMENTS

We extend our deep appreciation to Professor Jan Magnus for encouraging Professor Hamparsum Bozdogan to participate in this experiment by forming an 'Informational Modelling Team'. We benefited immensely by participating in this competition individually and as a team. The US data are compiled from various US government publications (see organizers' data chapters for details). We thank Statistics Netherlands for use of the Dutch data.

REFERENCES

Akaike, H. (1973), 'Information theory and an extension of the maximum likelihood principle', in B. N. Petrov and F. Csaki (eds), *Second International Symposium on Information Theory*, Academiai Kiado, Budapest, 267–81.

APAC (1995), 'An analytical database of US agriculture, 1950–1992', Agricultural Policy Analysis Center, The University of Tennessee, Knoxville, TN, USA.

Bozdogan, H. (1981), *Multi-sample cluster analysis and approaches to validity studies in clustering individuals*, PhD thesis, Department of Mathematics, University of Illinois at Chicago, Chicago, Illinois 60680.

Bozdogan, H. (1986), 'Multi-sample cluster analysis as an alternative to multiple comparison procedures', *Bulletin of Informatics and Cybernetics*, **22**, No. 1–2, 95–130.

Bozdogan, H. (1987), 'Model selection and Akaike's information criterion (AIC): The general theory and its analytical extensions', *Psychometrika*, **52**, No. 3, Special Section (invited paper), 345–70.

Bozdogan, H. (1988), 'ICOMP: A new model selection criterion', in H. H. Bock (ed.), *Classification and Related Methods of Data Analysis*, North-Holland, Amsterdam, April, 599–608.

Bozdogan, H. (1990a), 'On the information-based measure of covariance complexity and its application to the evaluation of multivariate linear models', *Communications in Statistics, Theory and Methods*, **19**(1), 221–78.

Bozdogan, H. (1990b), 'Multisample cluster analysis of the common principal component model in K groups using an entropic statistical complexity criterion', invited paper presented at the International Symposium on Theory and Practice of Classification, 16–19 December, Puschino, Soviet Union.

Bozdogan, H. (ed.) (1994a), *Theory & Methodology of Time Series Analysis*, Volume 1, Proceedings of First US/Japan Conference on The Frontiers of Statistical Modeling: An Informational Approach, Kluwer Academic Publishers, Dordrecht.

Bozdogan, H. (ed.) (1994b), *Multivariate Statistical Modeling*, Volume 2, Proceedings of First US/Japan Conference on The Frontiers of Statistical Modeling: An Informational Approach, Kluwer Academic Publishers, Dordrecht.

Bozdogan, H. (ed.) (1994c), *Engineering & Scientific Applications of Informational Modeling*, Volume 3, Proceedings of First US/Japan Conference on The Frontiers of Statistical Modeling: An Informational Approach, Kluwer Academic Publishers, the Netherlands.

Bozdogan, H. (1994d), 'Mixture-model cluster analysis using model selection criteria and a new informational measure of complexity', in H. Bozdogan (ed.), *Multivariate Statistical Modeling*, Vol. 2, Proceedings of the First US/Japan Conference on the Frontiers of Statistical Modeling: An Informational Approach, Kluwer Academic Publishers, Dordrecht, 69–113.

Bozdogan, H. (1996), 'A new informational complexity criterion for model selection: The general theory and its applications', invited paper presented in the Session on Information Theoretic Models & Inference of the Institute for Operations Research & the Management Sciences (INFORMS), Washington, DC, 5–8 May 1996.

Bozdogan, H. (1997a), *Statistical Modeling and Model Evaluation: A New Informational Approach* (forthcoming).

Bozdogan, H. (1997b), *Informational Complexity and Multivariate Statistical Modeling* (forthcoming).

Bozdogan, H. and S. L. Sclove (1984), 'Multisample cluster analysis with varying parameters using Akaike's information criterion', *Annals of Institute of Statistical Mathematics*, **36**, No. 1, B, 163–80.

Cox, D. R. and D. V. Hinkley (1974), *Theoretical Statistics*, Chapman and Hall, London.

Davidson, J. E. H., D. F. Hendry, F. Srba and S. Yeo (1978), 'Econometric modelling of the aggregate time-series relationship between consumer's expenditure and income in the United Kingdom', *Economic Journal*, **88**, 661–92.

Dickey, D. A. and W. A. Fuller (1979), 'Distribution of the estimators for autoregressive time series with a unit root', *Journal of the American Statistical Association*, **74**, 427–31.

Enders, W. (1995), *Applied Econometric Time Series*, John Wiley, New York.

Granger, C. W. J. and P. Newbold (1974), 'Spurious regressions in econometrics', *Journal of Econometrics*, **2**, 111–20.

Hall, R. (1978), 'Stochastic implications of the life cycle permanent income hypothesis: theory and evidence', *Journal of Political Economy*, **86**, 5, 971–87.

Haughton, D. and H. Bozdogan (1996), 'Informational complexity criteria for regression models', under review in *Computational Statistics and Data Analysis*.

Hendry, D. F. (1995), *Dynamic Econometrics*, Oxford University Press, Oxford.

Jarque, C. M. and A. K. Bera (1987), 'A test for normality of observations and regression residuals', *International Statistical Review*, **55**, 163–72.

Johansen, S. (1988), 'Statistical analysis of cointegration vectors', *Journal of Economic Dynamics and Control*, **12**, 231–54.

Kashyap, R. L. (1982), 'Optimal choice of AR and MA parts in autoregressive moving average models', *IEEE Transactions on Pattern Analysis and Machine Intelligence*, **4**, 99–104.

Kullback, S. and R. A. Leibler (1951), 'On information and sufficiency', *Annals of Mathematical Statistics*, **22**, 79–86.

Lucas, R. E. (1976), Econometric policy evaluation: a critique', in K. Brunner and A. H. Meltzer (eds), *The Phillips Curve and Labor Markets*, North-Holland, Amsterdam, 19–46.

Luh, H.-K., J. J. Minesky and H. Bozdogan (1996), 'Choosing the best predictors in regression analysis via the genetic algorithm with informational complexity as the fitness function', under review in *Communications in Statistics, Theory and Methods*.

Magnus, J. R. and H. Neudecker (1988), *Matrix Differential Calculus with Applications in Statistics and Econometrics*, John Wiley, New York.

Mardia, K. V. (1970), 'Measures of multivariate skewness and kurtosis with applications', *Biometrika*, **57**, 519–30.

Parzen, E. (1962), 'On estimation of a probability density function and mode', *Annals of Mathematical Statistics*, **33**, 1065–76.

Pesaran, M. H. and Y. Shin (1995), 'An autoregressive distributed lag modelling approach to cointegration analysis', working paper, University of Cambridge.

Phillips, P. C. B. (1986), 'Understanding spurious regressions in econometrics', *Journal of Econometrics*, **33**, 311–40.

Phillips, P. C. B. (1987), 'Time series regression with a unit root', *Econometrica*, **55**, 277–301.

Phillips, P. C. B. (1996), 'Econometric model determination', *Econometrica*, **64**, 763–812.

Phillips, P. C. B. and B. E. Hansen (1990), 'Statistical inference in instrumental variables regression with I(1) processes', *Review of Economic Studies*, **57**, 99–125.

Rissanen, J. (1976), 'Minmax entropy estimation of models for vector processes', in R. K. Mehra and D. G. Lainiotis (eds), *System Identification*, Academic Press, New York, 97–119.

Rissanen, J. (1978), 'Modeling by shortest data description', *Automatica*, **14**, 465–71.

Rissanen, J. (1989), *Stochastic Complexity in Statistical Inquiry*, World Scientific Publishing Company, Teaneck, NJ.

Said, S. E. and D. A. Dickey (1984), 'Testing for unit roots in autoregressive-moving average models of unknown order', *Biometrika*, **71**, 599–607.

Sakamoto, Y., M. Ishiguro and G. Kitagawa (1986), *Akaike Information Criterion Statistics*, D. Reidel, Dordrecht.

Schmidt, P. (1977), 'Estimation of seemingly unrelated regressions with unequal numbers of observations', *Journal of Econometrics*, **5**, 365–77.

Schwarz, G. (1978), 'Estimating the dimension of a model', *Annals of Statistics*, **6**, 461–4.

Sims, C. A. (1980), 'Macroeconomics and reality', *Econometrica*, **48**, 1–48.

Tobin, J. (1950), 'A statistical demand function for food in the USA', *Journal of the Royal Statistical Society*, Series A, **113**, Part II, 113–41 [reprinted in Chapter 2, this volume].

Van Emden, M. H. (1971), *An Analysis of Complexity*, Mathematical Centre Tracts, **35**, Amsterdam.

Zellner, A. (1962), 'An efficient method of estimating seemingly unrelated regressions, and tests for aggregation bias', *Journal of the American Statistical Association*, **57**, 348–68.

COMMENTS BY PROFESSOR M. HASHEM PESARAN (Trinity College, Cambridge)

This paper is primarily concerned with the application of information theoretic methods to a number of log-linear specifications of demand for food in the USA and the Netherlands.

In particular it emphasizes the use of the Information Complexity (ICOMP) criterion proposed in the statistical literature by one of the authors (H. Bozdogan).

Three model selection criteria (namely AIC, SBC and ICOMP) are used to select the orders of the following ARDL(p, q_1, q_2, q_3) model:

$$\phi(L, p)y_t = \alpha + \sum_{i=1}^{3} \beta_i(L, q_i)x_{it} + \varepsilon_t$$

$$\phi(L, p) = 1 - \phi_1 L - \phi_2 L^2 \cdots - \phi_p L^p$$

$$\beta_i(L, q_i) = \beta_{i0} + \beta_{i1}L + \beta_{i2}L^2 + \cdots + \beta_i q_i L^{qi}, \quad i = 1, 2, 3$$

where y_t denotes the logarithm of (nominal) consumption expenditures on food, and x_{1t}, x_{2t} and x_{3t} stand for the logarithms of per capita income, food price and non-food price indices, respectively.

In selecting the lag orders (p, q_1, q_2, q_3), the authors only consider non-zero values for these integers, which is likely to be restrictive and in particular does not nest the dynamic specification considered by Tobin (1950), namely ARDL(0,1,0,0). This is particularly problematic in the case of the SBC and the ICOMP criteria that impose a relatively high cost on complexity. For example, relaxing the restriction that $p > 0$, $q_i > 0$, but using the same data set as employed by the authors, the SBC criterion selected the specification ARDL(1,4,0,0) which is very different from the ARDL(1,1,1,3) selected in the paper.

I am not familiar with the ICOMP(IFIM) criterion, but it is not difficult to show that in the case of the stationary processes it is asymptotically equivalent to Schwartz's criterion. It is therefore likely to be subject to similar shortcomings of the SBC.[C1] The SBC (and hence ICOMP(IFIM)) is a consistent model selection criterion, but only if one is prepared to assume that the 'true' model belongs to the set over which the search for the 'best' model is carried out. In the present application the consistency property of SBC or ICOMP is relevant only if we believe that the data generation process for y (conditional on x_1, x_2 and x_3) is given by a finite order ARDL specification.

The task of selecting the (optimal) order of the underlying ARDL model is separated from the problem of testing for the existence of a long-run relationship between y, x_1, x_2 and x_3, and the estimation of the long-run parameters. For example, when testing for the existence of a long-run (or cointegrating) relationship between these variables, the authors apply the various cointegration tests proposed in the literature and then estimate the long-run coefficients using the Phillips–Hansen modified OLS procedure that deals with dynamics in a semi-parametric manner. The cointegration tests also pre-assume that the variables are I(1), (which may not be so, particularly in the case of the short time-series used in Tobin's original study), and do not require that the analysis be conditioned on x_1, x_2 and x_3. Such a dichotomy between the task of selecting the preferred ARDL model and testing on and estimation of long-run parameters is unnecessary. For example, using the ARDL approach recently developed in Pesaran and Shin (1997) and Pesaran, Shin and Smith (1996) a unified treatment of the three tasks (selection of the orders, testing for the existence of a long run relationship and the estimation of long-run parameters) can be achieved. Once again for the revised Tobin data and using the ARDL(1,4,0,0) model

---

[C1] When the sample is small, as is the case with the original data analysed by Tobin, none of the model selection criteria is likely to be satisfactory.

selected by the SBC, the long-run estimate of the income elasticity of demand turned out to be 0.248 (0.036), which is somewhat larger than the one reported in the paper (the standard error is in brackets).

In a number of cases the authors can not reject the hypothesis of no cointegration among the variables under analysis, but nevertheless go ahead with estimation of the 'long-run' parameters and also give standard errors for these parameters. As the authors themselves are aware this is rather problematic and needs further discussion, and could be due to the low power of cointegration tests that they use. The low power of the residual-based test is particularly well known.

In Section 4, 128 VAR models are estimated. Since the purpose of this analysis in this section is forecasting, it would have been interesting if the range of forecasts obtained across all of these models were also reported. Such an approach is more likely to reflect the effect of model uncertainty on forecasts rather than the forecast standard errors presently reported in the paper which are conditional on the selected model.

Given the emphasis of the paper on the use of model selection procedures, it would have been interesting also to report the elasticity estimates and the test results obtained if one had chosen to rely on SBC or AIC instead of the ICOMP criterion.

For purposes of comparability of the results in this paper and those reported in Tobin (1950) and the other researchers taking part in this experiment, it would be useful if the authors also confined their analysis to the period 1913–41. The interpolation carried out for the War years 1942–44 is also likely to be problematic given the rather unusual nature of these years.

REFERENCES

Pesaran, M. H. and Y. Shin (1997), 'An autoregressive distributed lag modelling approach to cointegration analysis', in S. Strom, A. Holly and P. Diamond (eds), *Centennial Volume of Ragnar Frisch*. Econometric Society Monograph, Cambridge University Press, Cambridge.

Pesaran, M. H., Y. Shin and R. J. Smith (1996). 'Testing for the existence of a long-run relationship', *DAE Working Paper No. 9622*, Department of Applied Economics, University of Cambridge.

COMMENTS BY PROFESSOR MICHAEL McALEER (University of Western Australia)

The purpose of this interesting paper by the authors from Tennessee is to provide a systematic approach to the empirical econometric modelling of food consumption in the USA and the Netherlands using some novel information theoretic model selection and evaluation techniques. Clear and concise motivation is provided in the paper. The authors illustrate how information theoretic model selection techniques can be useful to applied econometricians by identifying lag lengths, choosing subsets of variables, determining the appropriate transformations of variables, calculating the matrix of deterministic terms in VAR models, examining the pooling of alternative data sets, and choosing regressors for both cross-sectional and panel data sets.

This approach to econometric modelling appears to be quite different from the standard approach to econometric modelling based on classical statistical techniques, and provides an alternative strategy for undertaking applied data analysis. It deserves attention because the classical approach is well-known to be deficient when it is applied uncritically to nonexperimental data. The strength of the paper is its emphasis on a sustained use of informational criteria, although classical test statistics are also used in various parts of the paper.

In addition to presenting an interesting approach to data analysis, the reference list includes several useful contributions to the literature by one of the authors. The strengths and limitations of the techniques used seem to be generally well-understood and appreciated. There is a detailed and credible logbook, which enables an appreciation of the sequential nature of the modelling exercise undertaken by the authors.

The paper is primarily concerned with statistical and econometric techniques rather than with economics or the modelling of economic relationships. Economic variables are taken as given and functional forms are examined only briefly. It is stated in the Conclusion (and emphasized throughout the text) that: 'In contrast to the classical statistical procedures, these new methods avoid the use of sampling distributions. In particular, they do not require any arbitrarily specified level of significance or table look-up in the decision making process.' This statement, however disarmingly simple it might appear to be at first sight, is potentially misleading by way of what is left unstated. Information theoretic criteria are statistics with standard deviations and appropriate asymptotic distributions, and hence can be used in an entirely classical manner. The fact that practitioners generally choose not to use information theoretic criteria as classical statistics does not mean that they cannot be used in such a manner. Moreover, the arbitrary use of conventional significance values can be avoided by using probability values instead of levels of significance. In any event, even though the authors might appear to have a preference for not wishing to use the classical testing approach, they nevertheless do use standard (that is, classical) tests of unit-roots and cointegration with arbitrary levels of significance throughout the text.

Section 2 of the paper provides a brief but useful synthesis of the informational theoretic approach to statistical model selection. The Akaike information criterion (AIC), Schwarz's Bayesian criterion (SBC), and Rissanen's minimum description length criterion, which is identical to SBC but is derived from a different perspective, are compared with Bozdogan's informational complexity (ICOMP) criterion. Each of these criteria is a function of the goodness-of-fit and a penalty term which differs according to the criteria. One of the many reservations I have always had with both AIC and SBC, particularly from a practical perspective, is that the penalty term is identical for both autoregressive and moving average processes of the same order, so that the only discriminating criterion between these processes is the goodness-of-fit. Although it might appear that 'complexity' is equated with parsimony, or the number of parameters, it is, in fact, defined for ICOMP as 'the degree of interdependence, (i.e. the correlational structure among the parameter estimates)'. This would appear to provide a more judicious penalty function than those according to AIC and SBC. At least ICOMP is capable of awarding a penalty to autoregressive and moving average processes of the same order. In addition, Monte Carlo experiments would seem to suggest that the penalty function imposed by the ICOMP criterion is more accurate than those of AIC and SBC.

The basic model in the measurement Section 3 involves a dynamic autoregressive distributed lag, in logarithms, which is an uncritical extension of Tobin's (1950) original Cobb-Douglas family food demand function. At this stage, there is no discussion of the use of the logarithmic (or log-linear) functional form, but it would have been useful to examine this issue, especially regarding the sensitivity of the estimated elasticities and the forecasts outside the sample. The properties of the error term are assumed to be classical. Little guidance is provided as to the statistical adequacy of this assumption.

The arithmetic mean approach used to obtain missing values for 1942–44 is rather primitive, to say the least. This is not to say that the constructed data are necessarily incorrect, but the construction of data for war years is particularly problematic. Consequently, it would have been useful to have examined some alternatives, and to have evaluated the sensitivity of the estimated elasticities and forecasts to these alternatives.

Although the augmented Dickey–Fuller test was used to determine the orders of integration of the various series, the ICOMP criterion was also used in determining the orders of integration, as well as in selecting the lag lengths for the Said and Dickey, and Johansen, test statistics. Since the ICOMP criterion is not especially well known in econometric circles, it would have been useful to have presented some experimental evidence as to the usefulness of the criterion in such circumstances.

In a brief discussion of whether to pool or not to pool the data for the USA and the Netherlands, the seemingly unrelated regressions framework is considered. The contemporaneous covariance matrix of the two countries is imposed as being diagonal. Since the purpose of the exercise is to increase the efficiency of the estimates, it would have been useful had this restriction been tested empirically rather than imposed.

Normality of the errors of the VAR is assumed for purposes of forecasting. Two data transformations are examined to ensure that normality is an adequate statistical assumption, namely the linear and logarithmic transformations. Since alternative functional forms are considered only in the section on forecasting, it is somewhat curious that these alternatives were not considered earlier when the original logarithmic model specification was introduced.

A pure autoregression of the logarithm of consumption is determined to provide the optimal forecasting rule. Subsequently, a unit-root with drift is determined to be appropriate. Some diagnostic test statistics are reported for the random walk with drift model. Reference is made in this context to the classical Hall's consumption function as 'an established economic theory'. Although it may be established as a theoretical result, it is unfortunate to see an uncritical reference to Hall's consumption function in an empirical modelling exercise. There are many empirical reasons as to why consumers do not behave according to the rational expectations life-cycle, permanent income hypothesis, not least of which are the presence of liquidity constraints and uncertainty.

COMMENTS BY PROFESSOR ARIE KAPTEYN (Tilburg University)

The paper uses various model selection procedures to find the right model for the various data sets provided. The authors have tried to adhere to the rules rather strictly and provide a logbook. Specification search in time-series concentrates on lag structures (and sometimes on functional forms), and on the possibility to pool datasets from the USA and the Netherlands or to pool cross-sections from different years. In the cross-sectional analyses also various functional forms are considered and selected on the basis of genetic algorithms. The possibility of endogeneity of explanatory variables in macro models is mentioned, but not pursued.

The original Tobin time-series data are partly interpolated for 1942–44. How does this affect test outcomes (on lag length for instance)? Unit-roots are found in the individual series, but not always cointegrating regressions.

An attempt was made to pool the time-series data for the USA and the Netherlands. This was tested within a SUR framework. It is not quite clear what the use of such a framework is, given that correlations in error terms across countries are assumed away. A priori, I would have thought that pooling does not make sense, if only for the fact that in the USA homogeneity is rejected, but not for the Netherlands. Nonetheless, and somewhat to my surprise, pooling appears to be justified.

Since some, though not very strong, evidence is found for the existence of co-integrating relationships, a cointegrating regression of food consumption on a number of other variables is run. From this the long run income elasticity of the demand for food is found to be 0.28. As noted by the authors, such an estimate may be subject to the Lucas critique. After all, as I have argued in my comments on the CBS paper, there may not be such a thing as an income elasticity of the demand for food.

Next the USA budget data are analysed. On the basis of multisample clustering it is concluded that 1950 and 1960 may be clustered, but 1972 should remain separate. I must say that I do not quite see why this exercise is relevant. The pertinent question here would seem to be if the income elasticity is the same across samples, whether they are homogeneous or not.

The most interesting finding in the forecasting section is that the authors 'rediscover' Hall's conjecture that consumption is a random walk.

As in other papers estimates for the income elasticity of food vary quite a bit across datasets. The ultimate question should be: 'why?'. It appears to me that in the end the answer to such a question cannot come from statistical techniques alone. We should exploit our knowledge of theory and of institutional details to shed light on the differences observed. Yet, having said this, the techniques applied by the authors appear to be quite powerful.

REPLY BY P. M. BEARSE, H. BOZDOGAN, AND A. M. SCHLOTTMANN

We appreciate the careful comments of Professors Hashem Pesaran, Michael McAleer, and Arie Kapteyn as the three reviewers of our paper for the workshop on 'The Experiment in Applied Econometrics'. In general, we agree with the spirit of their observations if not always to the letter. Some confusion may have resulted from our attempt to carefully follow both the rules of the experiment as well as the conventions in the Tobin (1950) paper. In what follows, we respond to several conjectures made in the comments.

In our view, there is a general misunderstanding in the literature regarding asymptotic properties and inferential error rates of information-theoretic model selection criteria. It is well known that the classical theory of hypothesis testing is concerned with the following problem: 'Is a given data set consistent with some stated hypothesis or is it not?' In the hypothesis testing tradition, frequently ignoring power considerations, we choose an arbitrary significance level such as the celebrated 5%, 2.5%, or 1%. We then determine (at least approximately) a critical value for the test statistic to make our decision. Almost automatically, we also apply hypothesis testing procedures to situations involving multiple decisions. However, this involves the choice of a number of dependent significance levels without knowing what the overall error rate might be. Also, test procedures do not have the provision to penalize overparameterization since usually an unstructured saturated model is used as a reference (Akaike, 1987).

On the other hand, when we use the information theoretic model selection criteria, we do not specify what the arbitrary significance level is or should be. This is due to the fact that in using model selection criteria, the situation is totally the opposite of the classical inferential procedures. In this case, we are concerned with the following: 'Choosing a critical value that then determines, approximately, what the significance level is or might be.' Therefore, the significance level is implicitly incorporated within a model selection criterion that depends on the specific functional form of the penalty component and on the number of observations. For more on this, we refer readers to Bozdogan (1987). In this regard, information criteria should not be viewed in terms of classical test statistics. In general, the closed analytic forms of finite sampling distributions of information criteria are not known. Connotation of the large sample distributions are at best asymptotic. In some cases such as the non-linear regression model it is difficult even to conjecture what finite sampling distribution of the model selection criteria is or might be. In the literature of model selection, a few unsuccessful attempts have been made to put confidence sets on models chosen by the information criteria as a supplemental guide or yard stick for model selection in finite samples in the same manner as the confidence interval in the regular point estimation framework. For this, see e.g. Shimodaira (1995, 1996).

Such approaches are either based on the bootstrap approach or based on asymptotic approximations of the proposed test statistic under the normality assumption, and they do not provide any new insight on the models chosen by the minimum value of the information criteria. For example, a bootstrap approach is very computationally intensive. Therefore, an important question arises — 'Are we going to bootstrap the distribution of one's favourite information criterion each time we wish to use it in different modeling set ups or environments?' Also, 'How well should we trust on the asymptotic approximations to finite sampling distributions of the information criteria?' 'How do we define the critical values; analytically or via simulations?' 'What is (or are) the asymptotic sampling distribution(s) of the information criteria in regression analysis, in vector autoregressive (VAR) models, in factor analysis, in cluster analysis, etc., to mention but a few?' These are difficult questions to address. Therefore, it is a mistake to relate, to think, or cast the role of information criteria purely in the same vein as the classical test theory. Furthermore, it is simply not the case that ICOMP(IFIM) is equivalent (even asymptotically) to SBC. This is true even for the theoretical (if not particularly useful) case where the variables are mutually statistically independent. More importantly, the relevant issue here involves the frequent allegation that information-theoretic measures such as AIC are inconsistent while SBC is not. In this regard, we refer the reader to the recent work by Forster (1997). Forster argues (to us, convincingly) that too much stock has been placed on limiting properties. Specifically, he points out that AIC is consistent in the sense that, for a sufficiently large sample size and an exhaustive model portfolio, the true model is nested within the model chosen by AIC. For finite samples, Forster (1997) concludes that the information-theoretic framework is the appropriate method to investigate issues of model selection. We might add that in reality the model portfolio rarely, if ever, contains the true data generating process. In this regard, analysis of model selection criteria conditional on the true data generating process being contained in the model portfolio is misguided.

When examining the long run relationship between food consumption and income, we employed a classical hypothesis testing approach to examining unit-roots and cointegration. It is true that, in so doing, we condition our analysis on arbitrarily chosen levels of significance. However, both testing for unit roots and cointegration could have been carried out in the context of the information theoretic model selection approach. Additionally, we believe that the interpertation of unit-root/cointegration exercises is more sensible in this context. For instance, we could frame our question as follows: 'Given a data series, does a unit-root specification provide the best univariate model of the series given a portfolio of reasonable alternatives?' In contrast, the classical hypothesis testing approach would frame the question: 'Does the series have a unit root?' This latter question is unanswerable based on a finite data set. We plan to examine the performance of the ICOMP(IFIM) criterion in dynamic modeling of non-stationary data using Monte Carlo simulations.

In a similar vein, we agree that we did not perform an analysis of functional form when constructing ADL models of food consumption. This important omission was due primarily to space and time constraints. However, the information-theoretic approach to model selection is ideally suited to carrying out such an analysis. The reason is that the model portfolio need not be restricted to nested models, and the conclusions are not subject to uncertainties in inferential error rates induced by sequential hypothesis testing.

Finally, it is true that we imposed at least one lag of food consumption, income, food prices, and non-food prices in our ADL modeling exercise. In retrospect, we agree that it would have been better to incorporate less heavily parameterized versions directly into our model portfolio. The reason we made the ADL(1,1,1,1) model the simplest in our portfolio related to concerns regarding 'spurious regressions' in the sense of Granger and Newbold (1974) and Phillips (1986). In particular, Hamilton (1994, pp. 561–2) points out that ADL models with at least one lag of each variable 'cure' the spurious regression problem in the sense that OLS can always choose parameter estimates that imply a stationary error term. Further, as opposed to simply first differencing the data, such a specification allows for the possibility that the data are cointegrated. Notice, however, that Tobin's (1950, Equation 21) model is nested within our modelling framework. It merely involves appropriate zero restrictions on coefficients in our framework.

In concluding, we again thank all three of our reviewers for taking the time and energy to assess our results. We agree that the techniques presented in our paper are powerful enough to be recommended for use in empirical econometric modeling. We await future research efforts and challenges in this direction.

ADDITIONAL REFERENCES

Akaike, H. (1987), 'Factor analysis and AIC', *Psychometrika*, **52**(3), Special Section (invited paper) 317–32.

Forster, M. R. (1997), 'The new science of simplicity', in Michael McAleer and Arnold Zellner (eds), *Proceedings of the Tilburg Conference on Simplicity*, Hugo Keuzenkamp, forthcoming.

Hamilton, J. D. (1994), *Time Series Analysis*, Princeton University Press.

Shimodaira, H. (1995), 'Assessing the error probability of the model selection test' (unpublished manuscript).

Shimodaira, H. (1996), 'An application of multiple comparison techniques to model selection' (unpublished manuscript).

CHAPTER 7

A COMPARATIVE STUDY OF MODELLING THE DEMAND FOR FOOD IN THE UNITED STATES AND THE NETHERLANDS*

HAIYAN SONG, XIAMING LIU AND PETER ROMILLY

1. INTRODUCTION

Tobin's (1950) paper on food demand analysis makes systematic use of both cross-section and time-series data to derive a demand function for food in the USA. Tobin first estimates the income elasticity of demand for food from the budget survey data and the income elasticity is then used to estimate a reduced form time-series model.

Tobin's method of pooling the cross-section and time-series data was subsequently criticized by Chetty (1968), Maddala (1971), and Izan (1980). Chetty (1968) proposes a simultaneous data pooling system estimated using the Bayesian approach. Chetty's proposal is questioned by Maddala (1971) who suggests that a pre-estimation test should be considered to test the hypothesis that the income elasticities in the two types of models are equal before the data is pooled. Izan (1980) argues that the failure to account for the existence of outliers in the budget survey data, and the presence of serially correlated residuals in the time-series data, invalidates both the Chetty and Maddala conclusions. Izan uses a weighted least squares (WLS) method to correct for the presence of the outlier problem and finds that the cross-section and time-series income elasticities are not different from each other, so that the pooling of the two types of data is appropriate.

In Section 2 we undertake Task 1 set by Magnus and Morgan (hereafter MM) and extend the study by Tobin (1950) using the budget survey data of 1950, 1960, and 1972. A WLS method suggested by Izan (1980) is used to estimate the demand models and obtain unbiased efficient estimates of the income elasticities. Section 3 relates to Task 2 of MM and focuses on the estimation of aggregate time-series demand for food models for the USA. Using the general to specific approach we examine the long-run equilibrium relationship between consumers' expenditure on food and related variables for the USA and the corresponding error correction models. Section 4 carries out the remaining part of Task 2 by estimating similar models for the Netherlands. A disaggregate time-series model is also constructed for the Netherlands. Section 5 tackles our own selected task (i.e. Task 5 of MM), that of an alternative modelling strategy using the time-varying parameter (TVP) approach to examine changes in the various demand elasticities over time. The forecasting exercise (Task 3) specified by MM is undertaken in Section 6. Section 7 provides conclusions. A brief summary of the logbook is provided in the Appendix.

* Reprinted from the *Journal of Applied Econometrics*, **12**, 593–613 (1997).

2. THE MODEL OF DEMAND FOR FOOD IN THE USA: ESTIMATES FROM THE BUDGET SURVEY DATA

This and the following section deal with Task 1(a) specified by MM, namely to estimate the income elasticity of food demand in the USA using the 1950, 1960, and 1972 budget survey data sets and compare the results with that of Tobin (1950) for the 1941 budget survey data. There are a number of household-related variables which could be added to our model specification, but we retain Tobin's model for the following reasons.

First, although the composition of households (such as average number of children and average number of persons over 65 years per household) may affect food consumption, data are not complete for all the years 1950, 1960, and 1972. Furthermore, even if we reassess the size of households using so-called 'equivalent adult scales' (e.g. the 'Amsterdam scale' assigned a weight of 0.9 to an adult female) there can be no guarantee that households plan their budgets on the basis of such an assumption. Second, food consumption may also be influenced by other household variables such as the percentage of homeowning households (*HOMEOWN*). Inclusion of the homeowner variable in the model, however, shows that its coefficient is significant for 1960, but not for 1950 and 1972. Third, adopting the same model as Tobin allows direct comparisons to be made with our results.

The Tobin (1950) demand for food specification based on the budget survey data is:

$$\log \overline{c}_i = k + \alpha \log \overline{Y}_i + \delta \log n_i + u_i \qquad 1$$

where $\overline{c}_i$ is the average consumption of food for the ith group of families ($i = 1, 2, \ldots, N$), $\overline{Y}_i$ is the average disposable income, n_i is the size of family, and u_i is an error term with $u_i \sim \mathrm{ND}(0, \sigma_{u_i})$.

We re-estimate the Tobin model (1) using his data and the budget survey data for 1950, 1960, and 1972. The results are presented in Table I. The table shows problems of heteroscedasticity in all the regressions. Scatter diagrams (contained in the full logbook) of income against consumer expenditure on food indicate that the data sets for 1950,

Table I. Parameter estimates based on US budget survey data

Parameter	Tobin	1950	1960	1972
k	0.823	2.867	2.262	3.958
	(8.57)[a]	(17.96)	(10.660)	(31.422)
α	0.561	0.485	0.531	0.330
	(18.88)	(25.70)	(21.510)	(23.881)
δ	0.254	0.261	0.308	0.455
	(6.93)	(10.28)	(9.174)	(27.100)
R^2	0.93	0.94	0.910	9.950
S.E.	0.109	0.120	0.165	0.091
χ^2 white (4)[b]	9.811[c]	22.69[c]	11.22[c]	13.790[c]
Obs.	37	54	59	72

[a]The figures in parentheses are t-statistics.
[b]The White test for heteroscedasticity, where the value in parentheses is the degree of freedom. The critical value of χ^2 (4) at the 5% level is 9.488.
[c]The statistic is significant at the 5% level.

1960, and 1972 appear to have outlier observations. Moreover, the diagrams show that the pattern of the relationship between income and food consumption in 1972 appears to be different from that of 1950 and 1960. This may be an indication of structural change in the food demand function.

One option is to eliminate the outliers from the data. But although the outlier observations are undesirable they may still contain valuable information, so that their complete elimination may result in biased estimates of the elasticities. In order to remedy the outlier problem without losing too much information, a WLS method suggested by Izan (1980) is used to obtain the estimates of the demand elasticities. The variables in the demand model are weighted by $(|\hat{u}_i|1/2 + \gamma)^{-1}$ where $|\hat{u}_i|$ is the absolute value of the residual obtained from the estimated cross-section regression model without considering the outlier problem. γ is a scalar greater than 0, and is included because some values of the residuals are close to zero. The estimated results based on different γ values are shown in Table II. The table shows that for a given year the demand elasticities with the outlier corrections are generally higher than those without the corrections, although Tobin's δ is lower. The heteroscedasticity problem is eliminated in all cases. The values of the elasticities appear sensitive to the choice of γ, however, and there is some variation in them over time.

Table II. Parameter estimates after correcting for the outlier problem

	γ	k	α	δ	R^2	F
			Parameters			
1941	0.5	0.981	0.658	0.212	0.950	328.0
		(0.167)	(0.027)	(0.041)		
	0.7	0.834	0.630	0.220	0.940	292.0
		(0.124)	(0.028)	(0.040)		
	1.0	0.662	0.607	0.228	0.940	272.0
		(0.089)	(0.028)	(0.038)		
1950	0.5	1.308	0.697	0.386	0.987	1970.0
		(0.178)	(0.014)	(0.038)		
	0.7	1.267	0.671	0.373	0.983	1565.7
		(0.123)	(0.015)	(0.035)		
	1.0	1.177	0.641	0.358	0.981	1283.5
		(0.097)	(0.015)	(0.032)		
1960	0.5	0.841	0.728	0.304	0.982	1495.7
		(0.175)	(0.015)	(0.040)		
	0.7	0.872	0.704	0.309	0.976	1151.4
		(0.150)	(0.016)	(0.039)		
	1.0	0.866	0.673	0.312	0.970	903.4
		(0.121)	(0.017)	(0.036)		
1972	0.5	1.538	0.646	0.470	0.952	694.1
		(0.241)	(0.019)	(0.048)		
	0.7	1.580	0.608	0.463	0.937	513.9
		(0.207)	(0.021)	(0.046)		
	1.0	1.558	0.559	0.456	0.921	403.0
		(0.164)	(0.022)	(0.041)		

Notes:
1. Figures in parentheses are standard errors.
2. Numbers of observations for the estimation of the four models are the same as those given in Table I.

3. DEMAND FOR FOOD MODELS IN THE USA: ESTIMATES FROM THE TIME-SERIES DATA

In this section we use general to specific methodology in conjunction with cointegration analysis to estimate the short- and long-run relationships between income and food consumption. The MM information pack provides the four revised time-series used in Tobin's (1950) study, which are $PCFC$ (Tobin's S), PCY (Tobin's Y), FP (Tobin's P) and NFP (Tobin's Q), respectively. Since Tobin indicates that his quantity series (food and income) are not strictly comparable to those used in budget studies, three alternative series, $AGGEXPF$, $AGGEXP$ and $AGGY$, are supplied by MM. These represent aggregate consumers' expenditure on food, aggregate total consumers' expenditure and aggregate personal disposable income, respectively, all measured in current US dollars. This data has to be transformed into variables measured in real terms. Since the data set does not supply an overall price index such as the retail price index, we use the existing indexes to create a price index which approximates the general price index. A new index $\log P^*$ is created based on Stone's (1953) weighted index:

$$\log P_t^* = (w_t^f \times \log p_t^f) + (w_t^{nf} \times \log p_t^{nf}) \qquad\qquad 2$$

where w_t^f and p_t^f are the share of food expenditure and the price index of food, respectively, and w_t^{nf} and p_t^{nf} are the share of other expenditure and the non-food price index, respectively. $AGGEXPF$ and $AGGY$ in log form are then deflated by $\log P^*$ creating the real variables $\log TS_t^* (= \log(AGGEXPF_t) - \log P_t^*)$ and $\log TY_t^* (= \log(AGGY_t) - \log P_t^*)$, respectively. The corresponding per capita data are calculated as $\log S_t^* = \log TS_t^* - \log(POP_t)$ and $\log Y_t^* = \log TY_t^* - \log(POP_t)$, where POP_t is the estimated total population at time t. The integration order of the time-series is determined prior to modelling the demand for food relationships. Applying the Dickey–Fuller type tests and the Perron (1989) outlier test for unit roots, we find that $\log PCFC_t$, $\log TS_t^*$, $\log S_t^*$, $\log PCY_t$, $\log TY_t^*$, $\log Y_t^*$, $\log FP_t$ and $\log NFP_t$ are all I(1) variables. The average family size variable $\log \overline{N}_t$ is obtained from $\log \overline{N}_t = \log(POP_t) - \log(NOH_t)$, where NOH_t is the number of households at time t. This series is found to be trend stationary. Details of these test procedures are given in the full logbook.

The demand for food relationship is modelled in terms of the following (log-linear) specifications:

$$\log PCFC_t = f(\log FP_t, \log PCY_t, \log NFP_t, \log \overline{N}_t) \qquad\qquad 3$$

$$\log S_t^* = f(\log FP_t, \log Y_t^*, \log NFP_t, \log \overline{N}_t) \qquad\qquad 4$$

$$\log TS_t^* = f(\log FP_t, \log TY_t^*, \log NFP_t, \log \overline{N}_t). \qquad\qquad 5$$

The reasons for using a log-linear model specification are discussed in Tobin (1950). The variables in Equation (3) are those used by Tobin, while those in Equations (4) and (5) are defined above. Per capita consumption and income data are used in Equations (3) and (4), while total income and consumption data are used in Equation (5). For all three equations a cointegration relationship is tested for both with and without the inclusion of the family size variable, giving six equations in total. The Engle–Granger (1987) two-step method is initially used to test for cointegration, and the results are shown in Table III.

Table III. Cointegration regression results

Variable	log $PCFC_t$		log S_t^*		log TS_t^*	
	(3i)	(3ii)	(4i)	(4ii)	(5i)	(5ii)
Sample	(1913–76)		(1929–89)		(1929–89)	
Constant	4.547	3.902	−2.810	−4.199	2.667	−0.688
log FP_t	−0.091	−0.155	0.620	0.637	0.596	0.638
log PCY_t	0.131	0.195	—	—	—	—
log Y_t^*	—	—	0.530	0.685	—	—
log TY_t^*	—	—	—	—	0.640	0.755
log NFP_t	−0.408	−0.026	−0.987	−0.779	−0.923	−0.737
log $\bar{N}_t$	−0.276	—	−1.683	—	−1.774	—
R^2	0.943	0.925	0.969	0.958	0.992	0.987
CRDW[a]	0.741	0.595	0.324	0.210	0.410	0.258
S.E.	0.019	0.021	0.053	0.061	0.0470	0.057
ADF(p)[b]	−3.66(1)	−3.321(0)	−5.001(2)[c]	−3.382(2)	−5.197(2)[c]	−3.890(2)

[a]CRDW is the cointegration regression Durbin–Watson statistic.
[b]ADF(p) is the Dickey–Fuller test for unit roots in the cointegration residuals.
The values in parentheses are the lag lengths of the augmented terms. The critical values of ADF(p) are from MacKinnon (1991).
[c]Significance at the 5% level.

The results from Table III are mixed. Equation (3) has negative own-price elasticities, but the corresponding values from (4) and (5) are positive.[1] All the cross-price elasticities are negative, implying complementarity between the food and non-food categories. The income elasticities are all positive, and the values in Equations (4) and (5) are reasonably close to the cross-section estimates given in Table II. All the family size elasticities are negative.

Interpreting the equations as long-run relationships, it seems reasonable to test for the non-existence of money illusion, i.e. to test for homogeneity of degree zero. Imposing the appropriate restrictions gives Chi-square values (with one degree of freedom) of 0.323, 0.827, 3.242, 225.549, 23.922, and 1510.230, respectively for each of the six equations. These results show that we cannot reject the assumption of no money illusion at the 5% significance level for the first three equations, but that the assumption is clearly rejected for the remaining three. The finding of homogeneity in three of the six aggregate times series is encouraging, since this finding tends to be the exception rather than the rule in many demand models (see, for example, Deaton and Muellbauer, 1980a, p. 78). The ADF statistics in Table III show that there is a cointegration relationship for (4i) and (5i). The ADF statistic for (3i) is only just insignificant, however. Thus (4i) is the only equation which exhibits a long-run equilibrium relationship and satisfies the homogeneity requirement. The Johansen (1991) cointegration test procedure is then applied to the above equations. The test detects one cointegration relationship for Equation (3) with and

---

[1] In fact, the own and cross-price coefficient values in Tables III–V are not elasticities corresponding to those in the Tobin model, and need to be transformed according to a suggestion of Professor Wickens. This transformation delivers the expected negative own-price elasticities: details are given in our reply to the comments following this paper (see Table R1). We retain the untransformed values in our paper in order to keep within the spirit of the experiment.

Table IV. The cointegration vectors from the Johansen
procedure

Variable	Cointegration vectors			
	$\log PCFC_t$	$\log S_t^*$	$\log TS_t^*$
Constant	4.629	4.105	−6.469	−3.232
$\log FP_t$	0.013	−0.035	0.563	0.778
$\log PCY_t$	0.171	0.260	—	—
$\log Y_t^*$	—	—	0.253	—
$\log TY_t^*$	—	—	—	0.583
$\log NFP_t$	−0.245	−0.302	−0.799	−0.580
$\log \overline{N}_t$	−0.249	—	−1.587	1.172

Normalized coefficient values. The lag length is 2 for all cases and
the sample sizes are the same as those in Table III.

without the family size variable. But for Equations (4) and (5) the test shows that there
is no cointegration relationship when the family size variable is excluded. The relevant
estimated cointegration vectors are given in Table IV.

The Engle–Granger and Johansen approaches both detect a cointegrating relationship
in (4i) and (5i), but give conflicting results for the other equations (although (3i) is close
to the borderline). The corresponding error correction models are now specified in order
to examine the short-run dynamics. For comparison purposes all six error correction
models are estimated, and insignificant variables are dropped from the specification. The
estimation results are based on the Engle–Granger two-step procedure and presented
in Table V. The error correction models provide a reasonable fit to the data, although
Equations (4) and (5) have problems of heteroscedasticity and ARCH. Apart from (3ii)
all the overall own-price elasticities are positive, a result similar to that for the long-
run elasticities from the cointegration regressions in Table III. All the overall cross-price
elasticities are negative, as in Table III. In Equations (4) and (5) the family size variable
has an overall positive effect on food demand, although in the cointegration regressions
in Table III the sign of the coefficient is negative. All the overall income elasticities are
positive, as in Table III. The short-run income elasticities based on Equations (4) and
(5) in Table V are about 0.30, although this value is only about 0.15 for Equation (3).
These short-run elasticities are lower than the long-run elasticities given in Table III, as
economic theory suggests.

4. DEMAND FOR FOOD MODELS IN THE NETHERLANDS: THE TIME-SERIES ESTIMATES

This section estimates time-series models of demand for food in the Netherlands, and
compares the results with those of the USA. The Netherlands data contains information not
only on overall food expenditure and the price index of food but also on consumers' expenditure and price indexes for sub-categories of foods and other commodities. This permits
the use of demand-system as well as single-equation time-series modelling. Although the
focus of this paper is on the use of single-equation demand analysis, the almost ideal
demand system (AIDS) of Deaton and Muellbauer (1980b) is used in Section 4.1 to
derive estimates of income, price and family size elasticities and to test the homogeneity
postulate.

Table V. Results of error correction models

Variable	$\Delta \log PCFC_t$		$\Delta \log S_t^*$		$\Delta \log TS_t^*$	
	(3i)	(3ii)	(4i)	(4ii)	(5i)	(5ii)
Sample	(1916–76)		(1931–89)		(1931–89)	
Constant	0.003	0.002	0.006	0.005	0.009	0.007
	(0.002)	(0.002)	(0.005)	(0.004)	(0.005)	(0.005)
$\Delta \log PCFC_{t-1}$	0.517	—	—	—	—	—
	(0.143)					
$\Delta \log PCFC_{t-2}$	0.289	—	—	—	—	—
	(0.108)					
$\Delta \log S_{t-1}^*$	—	—	0.512	0.432	—	—
			(0.117)	(0.107)		
$\Delta \log TS_{t-1}^*$	—	—	—	—	0.507	0.422
					(0.116)	(0.107)
$\Delta \log FP_t$	0.224	−0.105	0.488	0.416	0.499	0.433
	(0.061)	(0.034)	(0.089)	(0.080)	(0.085)	(0.078)
$\Delta \log FP_{t-1}$	—	0.071	−0.227	−0.163	−0.220	−0.160
		(0.045)	(0.095)	(0.077)	(0.093)	(0.077)
$\Delta \log PCY_t$	0.077	0.152	—	—	—	—
	(0.026)	(0.035)				
$\Delta \log PCY_{t-1}$	0.138	−0.067	—	—	—	—
	(0.043)	(0.036)				
$\Delta \log PCY_{t-2}$	—	0.057	—	—	—	—
		(0.028)				
$\Delta \log Y_t^*$	—	—	0.485	0.551	—	—
			(0.074)	(0.072)		
$\Delta \log Y_{t-1}^*$	—	—	−0.174	−0.147	—	—
			(0.096)	(0.095)		
$\Delta \log TY_t^*$	—	—	—	—	0.491	0.555
					(0.070)	(0.072)
$\Delta \log TY_{t-1}^*$	—	—	—	—	−0.189	−0.148
					(0.094)	(0.090)
$\Delta \log NFP_t$	−0.209	—	−0.638	−0.425	−0.650	−0.441
	(0.064)		(0.217)	(0.164)	(0.207)	(0.162)
$\Delta \log NFP_{t-1}$	−0.309	−0.255	0.251	—	0.230	—
	(0.078)	(0.076)	(0.188)		(0.179)	
$\Delta \log NFP_{t-2}$	0.339	0.142	—	—	—	—
	(0.062)	(0.058)				
$\Delta \log \overline{N}_t$	—	—	−0.447	—	−0.539	—
			(0.462)		(0.448)	
$\Delta \log \overline{N}_{t-1}$	—	—	0.807	—	0.859	—
			(0.468)		(0.449)	
EC_{t-1}	−0.614	−0.259	−0.210	−0.133	−0.259	−0.158
	(0.091)	(0.081)	(0.063)	(0.054)	(0.068)	(0.059)
R^2	0.613	0.572	0.859	0.841	0.866	0.843
S.E.	0.012	0.012	0.022	0.022	0.209	0.022
χ^2_{auto} (2)	0.880	0.371	0.539	0.581	2.713	1.159
χ^2_{ARCH} (1)	0.221	0.002	6.380[b]	7.901[c]	8.200[c]	7.534[c]
χ^2_{hetro} (d.f.)	9.50	16.21	23.90[b]	24.98[b]	30.10[b]	28.08[b]
F_{Chow}[a]	1.503	1.126	0.328	0.305	0.333	0.270

Notes:

Figures in parentheses underneath the coefficient values are standard errors.

χ^2_{auto} (2), χ^2_{ARCH} (1), χ^2_{hetro} (d.f.) and F_{Chow} are Breusch–Godfrey's serial correlation, Engle's ARCH, White's heteroscedasticity and Chow's predictive failure tests respectively.

[a]The starting date for forecasting failure is 1972 for the first two models and 1982 for the last four models.

[b]Significance at the 10% level.

[c]Significance at the 5% level.

4.1.   The AIDS Model

Developed by Deaton and Muellbauer (1980b), the AIDS model is based on the Engel
function:

$$w_{it} = \alpha_i' + \beta_i' X_t \tag{6}$$

where w_{it} is the budget share of the ith commodity consumed at time t and X_t is the
aggregate household expenditure at time t. Using the PIGLOG cost function, the AIDS
model is derived as

$$w_{it} = \alpha_i + \beta_i \log(E/P)_t + \sum_j \gamma_{ij} \log p_{jt} \tag{7}$$

where E is representative expenditure on commodity i, α_i, β_i, $\gamma_{ij}(i, j = 1, 2, \ldots, n)$ are
constant parameters, and P_t is an overall price index derived from

$$\log P_t = \alpha_0 + \sum_i \alpha_i \log p_{it} + 1/2 \left(\sum_i \sum_j \gamma_{ij} \log p_{it} \log p_{jt} \right). \tag{8}$$

Demand theory requires that the following conditions are satisfied:

$$\sum_i \alpha_i = 1, \sum_i \beta_i = 0, \sum_i \gamma_{ij} = 0 \quad \text{(adding-up condition)} \tag{9}$$

$$\sum_j \gamma_{ij} = 0 \qquad\qquad \text{(homogeneity condition)} \tag{10}$$

$$\gamma_{ij} = \gamma_{ji} \qquad\qquad \text{(symmetry condition).} \tag{11}$$

Following Ray (1980) Equation (7) can be further developed by including a family size
variable which allows for the effect of economies of household size:

$$w_{it} = \alpha_i + \beta_i \log(E/P)_t + \sum_j \gamma_{ij} \log p_{jt} + \theta_i \log \bar{n}_t. \tag{12}$$

The Netherlands data set includes all the series necessary to estimate the demand
system equations denoted by Equation (12). The system equations include total household
consumer expenditure (*VI*) and expenditure on the following commodities: Food (*V11*),
Housing (*V22*), Clothing (*V33*), Hygiene and medical care (*V44*), Education (*V55*) and
Other consumption (*V66*). The appropriate price indexes, *P1*, *P11*, *P22*, *P33*, *P44*, *P55*,
and *P66*, are also provided. In estimating Equation (12), we use the general price index
provided by MM rather than that derived from Equation (8). A time trend is also added to
the specification to capture the effect of changes in consumers' tastes. Table VI presents
the estimation results for the unrestricted equations.
    In Table VI the Wald test implies that the homogeneity restriction is accepted for the
demand equations for Food, Education, and Other commodities, but rejected for Housing,
Clothing, and Hygiene and medical care. The family size variable is significant in the
Food, Housing and Other consumption equations, although the sign is negative in this last

Table VI. The unrestricted parameter estimates for the Netherlands (AIDS). Estimation Sample: 1960–88

Parameter	Commodity					
	$V11$	$V22$	$V33$	$V44$	$V55$	$V66$
α_i	0.873[b]	−0.019	0.408[a]	−0.288[b]	0.100	−0.073
	(0.141)	(0.129)	(0.160)	(0.107)	(0.165)	(0.101)
β_i	−0.148[b]	−0.023[a]	−0.011	0.067[b]	0.036[b]	0.078[b]
	(0.015)	(0.014)	(0.016)	(0.011)	(0.017)	(0.011)
γ_{i1}	0.172[b]	−0.053	−0.054	−0.100[b]	0.069	−0.033
	(0.039)	(0.035)	(0.044)	(0.029)	(0.045)	(0.027)
γ_{i2}	−0.029	0.046[b]	−0.025	0.082[b]	−0.099[b]	0.026
	(0.023)	(0.021)	(0.027)	(0.018)	(0.027)	(0.017)
γ_{i3}	−0.037	0.002	0.039	−0.085[b]	0.109[b]	−0.028
	(0.031)	(0.029)	(0.035)	(0.024)	(0.037)	(0.023)
γ_{i4}	0.010	−0.004	−0.082[b]	0.102[b]	−0.042	0.018
	(0.025)	(0.023)	(0.029)	(0.019)	(0.029)	(0.018)
γ_{i5}	−0.091[b]	0.010	−0.033	0.099[b]	−0.037	0.052[b]
	(0.032)	(0.030)	(0.037)	(0.025)	(0.038)	(0.024)
γ_{i6}	−0.043	0.027	0.101[b]	−0.072[b]	0.017	0.030
	(0.031)	(0.013)	(0.034)	(0.023)	(0.035)	(0.021)
θ_i	0.220[b]	0.136[b]	0.053	−0.072	−0.126	−0.210[b]
	(0.078)	(0.071)	(0.089)	(0.059)	(0.091)	(0.056)
R^2	0.998	0.994	0.993	0.997	0.956	0.992
DW	2.287	2.102	2.901	2.434	2.190	2.149
χ^2_{Wald} (d.f.)	1.743	4.579[b]	12.13[b]	5.00[b]	1.234	0.178

Notes:
Figures in parentheses are the standard errors. In reporting the results, the estimated coefficients of the time trends are omitted.
[a]Significance at the 10% level.
[b]Significance at the 5% level.

case. The coefficients of own-price for Housing, Clothing, Education, and Other consumption are not significant and, apart from Hygiene and medical care, most of the cross-price coefficients are not significantly different from zero. The expenditure coefficients are all significant except for that of Clothing.

Based on Equation (12) the expenditure, own-price, cross-price, and size elasticities $(ex_i, ep_{ii}, ep_{ij}$ and $e\bar{n}_i)$ can be calculated from:

$$ex_i = 1 + \beta_i/w_i \qquad\qquad 13$$

$$ep_{ii} = -1 + \gamma_{ii}/w_i - \beta i \qquad\qquad 14$$

$$ep_{ij} = \gamma_{ij}/w_i - \beta_i w_j/w_i \qquad\qquad 15$$

$$e\bar{n}_i = \theta_i/w_i. \qquad\qquad 16$$

The resulting own-price, expenditure and size elasticities are presented in Table VII.

The own-price and expenditure elasticities for all commodities have the expected signs and plausible magnitudes. The results for the family size elasticity are rather interesting

Table VII. Unrestricted elasticity estimates for the Netherlands (AIDS)

Commodity	Own-price	Expenditure	Size
Food	−0.290	0.516	0.719
Housing	−0.769	0.896	0.615
Clothing	−0.706	0.920	0.130
Hygiene and medical care	−0.131	1.614	−0.661
Education	−1.189	1.219	−0.767
Other consumption	−0.595	2.254	−3.376

in that they can be given an intuitively appealing interpretation. The positive coefficients for the first three commodities, and the negative coefficients for the remaining three, are consistent with the interpretation that, in order to feed extra mouths from a limited budget, spending patterns must be changed. As family size increases for a given level of expenditure and prices, families are forced to adjust their pattern of demand towards 'essential' commodities such as Food, Housing, and Clothing, and away from 'less essential' commodities such as Hygiene and medical care, Education, and Other consumption.

4.2. A Single-Equation Demand for Food Model

In this sub-section the demand elasticities for the Netherlands are estimated using a single equation approach. The purpose of this analysis is to compare the results with those of the US demand function. The proposed demand model is based on: $\log TS_t^* = f(\log TY_t^*, \log P11_t, \log NFP_t^*, \log \overline{N}_t)$, in which $\log TS_t^* = \log(V11_t/P1_t)$ and $\log TY_t^* = \log(AGGY_t/P1_t)$ are real total food expenditure and income, i.e. the nominal food expenditure and income variables ($AGGY$) deflated by the price index of total consumers' expenditure in their log forms. Total rather than per capita data is used since the estimation results from the Netherlands per capita data are not satisfactory. The price index of non-food items is not given in the information pack, so the non-food price index is constructed as: $\log NFP_t^* = \sum_i w_{it} \log PI_t$, where w_{it} is the share of the ith non-food commodity in relation to total non-food expenditure at time t ($i = 2$, 3, 4, 5, 6 representing Housing Clothing, Hygiene and medical care, Education, and Other consumption, respectively) and PI_t is the price index for the ith non-food commodity ($I = 22, 33, 44, 55$, and 66).

All variables are tested for their order of integration. The non-food price variable is a trend stationary series, real food expenditure, real income, and household size are I(1), and the food price variable is I(2). The long-run equilibrium relationship is tested using the Engle–Granger two-step cointegration test as well as the Johansen cointegration approach, and both tests support the assumption of cointegration. The Johansen approach detects one cointegration vector. The results are presented in Table VIII.

Comparing the Netherlands cointegration results from Table VIII with those for the equivalent US model (5i) in Tables III and IV, it is apparent that the signs on the income, cross-price, and family size variables are the same, i.e. positive, negative, and negative, respectively. The long-run income elasticity for the Netherlands is 0.792 and that of the USA is 0.755, so that the two income elasticity estimates are very similar. The coefficient on the Netherlands price variable in Table VIII is the food demand elasticity with respect

Table VIII. The Netherlands cointegration test results. Estimation Sample: 1960–88

Engle–Granger two-step cointegration estimates:

$$\log TS_t^* = \begin{array}{c} 2.460 \\ (0.567) \end{array} + \begin{array}{c} 0.792 \\ (0.046) \end{array} \log TY_t^* + \begin{array}{c} 0.571 \\ (0.165) \end{array} \Delta \log P11_t$$

$$- \begin{array}{c} 0.329 \\ (0.050) \end{array} \log NFP_t^* - \begin{array}{c} 0.703 \\ (0.244) \end{array} \log \overline{N}_t \qquad\qquad 17$$

$R^2 = 0.988$ S.E. $= 0.018$ $CRDW = 1.28$ ADF(4) $= 3.94^a$ χ^2_{wald} (1) $= 57.8$

Johansen cointegration estimates (normalized based on the coefficient of $\log TS_t^*$):

$$\log TS_t^* = 1.879 + \begin{array}{c} 0.574 \\ (0.023) \end{array} \log TY_t^* + \begin{array}{c} 0.870 \\ (0.182) \end{array} \Delta \log P11_t$$

$$- \begin{array}{c} 0.085 \\ (0.028) \end{array} \log NFP_t^* - \begin{array}{c} 0.149 \\ (0.109) \end{array} \log \overline{N}_t \qquad\qquad 18$$

Notes:
The statistics in Table VIII are the same as those in Table III. Figures in parentheses are the standard errors.
[a]Significance at the 10% level.

to the change in the price level, and thus not directly comparable with the price coefficient for the US price variable in Tables III and IV.

Given the existence of cointegration, the corresponding error correction model is estimated and insignificant variables are deleted from the general specification. This procedure yields the following model:

$$\Delta \log TS_t^* = \begin{array}{c} 0.011 \\ (0.008) \end{array} + \begin{array}{c} 0.336 \\ (0.198) \end{array} \Delta \log TS_{t-1}^* + \begin{array}{c} 0.389 \\ (0.182) \end{array} \Delta \log TS_{t-2}^*$$

$$+ \begin{array}{c} 0.478 \\ (0.182) \end{array} \Delta \log TY_t^* - \begin{array}{c} 0.324 \\ (0.177) \end{array} \Delta \log TY_{t-1}^*$$

$$+ \begin{array}{c} 0.752 \\ (0.194) \end{array} \Delta\Delta \log P11_t - \begin{array}{c} 0.697 \\ (0.252) \end{array} \Delta \log NFP_t^*$$

$$+ \begin{array}{c} 0.509 \\ (0.286) \end{array} \Delta \log NFP_{t-1}^* - \begin{array}{c} 0.751 \\ (0.214) \end{array} EC_{t-1} \qquad\qquad 19$$

$$R^2 = 0.768 \quad S.E. = 0.015 \quad \chi^2_{\text{auto}}(2) = 0.583 \quad \chi^2_{\text{ARCH}}(1) = 3.017$$

$$\chi^2_{\text{Hetro}}(16) = 21.29 \quad F_{\text{Chow}} = 1.497$$

where the statistics are the same as those in Table IV. The break point for the Chow (1960) forecasting failure test is 1982.

Once again, the income and cross-price elasticities are positive and negative, respectively. The overall income elasticity ($= 0.163$) is very close to the average of the income elasticities ($= 0.15$) for (3i) and (3ii) in Table V. Similarly, the overall cross-price elasticity ($= -0.188$) is very close to the average of the cross-price elasticities ($= -0.146$) for the same models. The family size variable is also insignificant.

5.   TIME-VARYING PARAMETER MODELS FOR THE USA AND THE NETHERLANDS

This section deals with our own chosen task (i.e. Task 5 of MM) of constructing time-varying parameter (TVP) models for the USA and the Netherlands. The rationale underlying our use of TVP modelling is that, particularly where long periods of time are involved, it seems reasonable to assume that the parameters in the food demand models may not be stable. Engle and Watson (1987) suggest that a TVP model can be applied in a number of circumstances including behavioural changes, unobserved variables and model misspecification. TVP modelling in the context of cointegration analysis is discussed in Granger (1991) and Granger and Lee (1991). Song, Liu, and Romilly (1996) provide an application of these ideas to the relationship between aggregate consumption and income in China.

Our emphasis is on the estimation of TVP models for the USA, since there are consistent annual observations available for the whole of the period 1929–89. This period covers the Second World War, during which one would expect significant changes in consumer behaviour and consequently in parameter values such as that of the income elasticity of demand for food. The equivalent data set for the Netherlands is smaller, running from 1960 to 1988, and consequently less appropriate to the task in hand. The US model is based on Equation (4i) from Table III, and uses real per capita food expenditure and income. The Netherlands model is based on Equation (17) from Table VIII and uses real total food expenditure and income. Following Engle and Watson (1987), the time variation in the model parameters is specified as a random walk and the Kalman (1960) filter algorithm is used for estimation. Details of the estimation procedures and results for both countries are given in the full logbook.

Figure 1 shows the Kalman filter estimates of the time paths of the US income elasticities of food demand. Figure 1(a) is derived by allowing the income elasticity to vary over

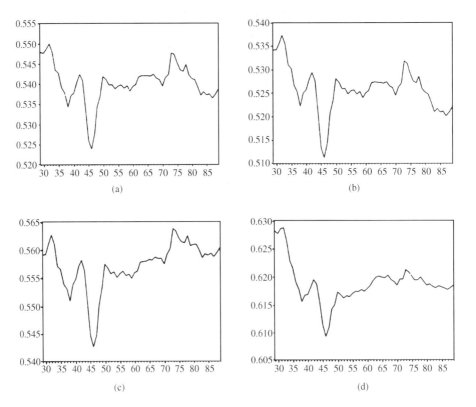

Figure 1. Kalman filter estimates of the income elasticities (USA)

time, *ceteris paribus*. Figure 1(d) shows the time path when all parameters (including the constant) are allowed to vary. The intermediate cases are given in Figures 1(b) and 1(c).

The pattern of variation across the four panels is similar, showing a strong downward trend in the period 1929 to 1946, and another downward trend from the mid-1970s. Our tentative hypothesis is that the 1930s recession and the Second World War created a 'feel-bad' factor which increased precautionary savings from a given income and reduced spending on food, particularly on luxury items. Food rationing is also likely to have depressed food expenditures. The overall effect is to reduce the income elasticity of demand for food. After the Second World War, increasing prosperity creates a 'feel-good' factor which reduces precautionary saving and increases the income elasticity. A similar explanation would apply to the effects of the oil-price shocks of 1973/74.

Time variations in the US own-price, cross-price, and family size elasticities are smaller and less amenable to a straightforward explanation. In the case of the Netherlands results, the time variation in the income, cross-price, and family size elasticities is very small, although the time variation for the own-price elasticity is relatively large. Our regrettable ignorance of the history of the Netherlands prevents us (perhaps fortunately) from suggesting explanations for these findings. For both the USA and the Netherlands the TVP income, own-price, cross-price, and family size elasticities are always positive, positive, negative and negative, respectively. The Netherlands income elasticity is always somewhat higher than that of the USA. It is possible that alternative specifications of the way in which the parameters vary over time could produce significantly different results. This is a lengthy undertaking, however, and time constraints did not permit the exploration of alternative specifications to the random walk process used above.

6. FORECASTS FOR FOOD DEMAND IN THE NETHERLANDS

This section deals with Task 3 set by MM. Our approach is to provide forecasts for the demand for food in the Netherlands for the period 1989–2000, using both fixed and time-varying parameter models under four sets of assumptions. The forecasts for the Netherlands' real total food expenditure (in log form) are presented in Table IX. Series 1, 3, 5, and 7 are the forecasting results from the fixed parameter model (17). Series

Table IX. Food demand forecasts for the Netherlands 1989–2000[a]

Year	Series 1	Series 2	Series 3	Series 4	Series 5	Series 6	Series 7	Series 8
1989	5.00387	4.98775	5.07235	5.06088	4.96128	4.95602	5.02975	5.02915
1990	5.11019	5.08692	5.18004	5.16152	5.02417	5.02282	5.09402	5.09742
1991	5.21864	5.18808	5.28098	5.26414	5.08830	5.09095	5.15953	5.16702
1992	5.32925	5.29126	5.38133	5.34687	5.15375	5.16047	5.20582	5.21608
1993	5.44209	5.39651	5.55791	5.52020	5.22050	5.23137	5.33631	5.35506
1994	5.55717	5.50385	5.61170	5.56208	5.28854	5.30366	5.34306	5.36189
1995	5.67458	5.61337	5.75172	5.69574	5.35802	5.37746	5.43515	5.45983
1996	5.79431	5.72504	5.87296	5.80903	5.42882	5.45267	5.50747	5.53667
1997	5.91644	5.83895	5.99667	5.92464	5.50105	5.52941	5.58128	5.61509
1998	6.04101	5.95515	6.12285	6.04255	5.57474	5.60768	5.65658	5.69508
1999	6.16808	6.07367	6.25155	6.16282	5.64987	5.68750	5.73334	5.77664
2000	6.29770	6.19457	6.38284	6.28550	5.71887	5.76732	5.86334	5.87077

[a]Real total food expenditure (in logs).

2, 4, 6, and 8 are for the corresponding time-varying parameter model. The estimation sample is 1960–88 and the forecasting starts from 1989. Series 1 and 2 (Scenario 1) show the forecasting results assuming that income increases by an annual rate of 2%, *ceteris paribus*. Series 3 and 4 (Scenario 2) are derived on the assumption that both income and food price increase by 2% annually, *ceteris paribus*. Series 5 and 6 (Scenario 3) assumes that income and non-food price increase by 2% annually, *ceteris paribus*. Series 7 and 8 (Scenario 4) are based on the assumption that income, food and non-food prices increase by 2% annually, *ceteris paribus*. These assumptions are of course somewhat arbitrary.

Table IX shows that in Scenarios 1 and 2 (series 1, 2, 3, 4) the forecasts generated from the fixed parameter model are higher than the TVP model over the whole forecasting period. In Scenarios 3 and 4 (series 5, 6, 7, 8), the pattern is generally reversed, with the TVP model forecasts higher apart from 1989 and 1990 (series 5 and 6) and 1989 (series 7 and 8).

7. CONCLUSIONS

Our results indicate that the income elasticities of food demand for the USA and the Netherlands are of the same order of magnitude for both cross-section and time-series data, where the time-series elasticity is derived from long-run models. This order of magnitude is 0.5 to 0.8. The shortrun time-series income elasticities are around 0.15 to 0.30. These results are reasonably encouraging, although the range of the values suggests that parameter instability may be a problem.

The results for the own-price, cross-price, and family size elasticities are less encouraging. Their values are subject to considerable variation, and the sign on the own-price food elasticity is invariably positive for the aggregate time-series models (4) and (5). This contrasts with the negative value of the own-price food elasticity derived using the Tobin specification (3). In the case of the AIDS model for the disaggregate time-series Netherlands data the sign on the own-price food elasticity is negative. The overall results from our static AIDS model seem satisfactory, although estimation of a dynamic AIDS model would have provided an interesting point of comparison.

The results of the TVP modelling of the aggregate data do not add much to these conclusions. Similar income elasticities are produced and the sign on the own-price elasticity remains positive in every time period. The forecasts for Netherlands food demand produced by the fixed and time-varying parameter specifications show some degree of variation between specifications and over time.

APPENDIX: A SUMMARY OF THE LOGBOOK

This appendix attempts to condense the full logbook of this experiment, numbering over 40 pages and 122 equations split into six chapters, into a very short summary which concentrates on the problems encountered in the modelling process.

First, we duplicated Tobin's results from the 1941 US budget survey data and tested for heteroscedasticity using White's test. The results differed according to the form of the test. In one case the null hypothesis of homoscedasticity was rejected, in the other it was accepted. This ambivalent result was a warning of further difficulties to arise when all four US budget survey data sets were considered. The (incorrect) use of Izan weights to remedy heteroscedasticity suggested that the cross-sectional income elasticities were not significantly different from each other, while the use of the $\sqrt{m}$ treatment indicated that the 1972 income elasticity was significantly different from the others. But the way in which we applied this latter treatment did not eliminate heteroscedasticity from the 1941 and 1960 budget survey data, so it was decided to rely on the results from the Izan weightings in writing Section 2 of this paper. Details of these procedures are contained in Chapters 1 and 2 of the full logbook.

We then turned to an analysis of the revised time-series data for the Tobin variables using the same model specification as Tobin. Our primary concern was to determine the integration and cointegration properties of the data. Considerable effort was expended in establishing the appropriate lag lengths for the ADF test for each variable, and the Perron test was implemented to allow for the possibility of structural breaks. The results from the cointegration tests were not clear-cut: the Engle–Granger two-step test did not find a cointegrating relationship between the variables, but the Johansen test did. We were also concerned with the possible existence of a simultaneity problem in our model specification, and used Hausman and other tests to determine the extent of this problem. As a further check, different model specifications were also examined. Once again, the results were not clear-cut, although the own-price variable in the Tobin specification did exhibit weak exogeneity and so provided a justification for the use of the single-equation approach. None of these results are reported in our paper, although details are given in the full logbook in Sections 3.1 to 3.5.

Our next step was to use similar procedures for the alternative US time-series data set provided by MM. After extensive data analysis, a cointegrating relationship was found which also satisfied the homogeneity requirement. But we were puzzled by the fact that the sign on the own-price coefficient, both short- and long-run, was positive rather than negative. This outcome also occurred when we specified and estimated a similar model for the Netherlands time-series data (this puzzle was later solved at the Tilburg workshop; see our reply to the comments following this paper). The greater disaggregation of the Netherlands data set allowed us to estimate an AIDS model in which all the income and own-price coefficients had the expected sign. This was some consolation for our disappointment at the single-equation results. Details are given in Section 3.6 and Chapter 4 of the full logbook.

At this stage we were not satisfied with the overall results of our modelling procedures. Although the estimated income elasticities were not too dissimilar given the differences in data sets and estimation procedures, the other coefficient estimates showed considerable variation and the persistence of the positive sign for the own-price coefficient was a particular concern. Perhaps our assumption of parameter stability was questionable, especially in view of the long time span covered by the US data? It was decided to use an alternative methodology, that of the time-varying parameter approach, to examine whether a more consistent set of results could be obtained. Details of the estimation procedures and results are given in Chapter 5 of the full logbook.

Finally, we attempted to forecast food demand in the Netherlands using both the fixed and time-varying parameter models developed earlier. This was not a task we approached with any degree of conviction, mainly because of our uncertainty regarding the likely future values of the exogenous variables in our forecasting models. The set of assumptions eventually used was determined more by the impending deadline (given 'holy' status by MM) rather than a detailed assessment of the Netherlands' economic prospects. Details are provided in Chapter 6 of the full logbook.

ACKNOWLEDGEMENTS

The authors would like to express their appreciation of the efforts of Jan Magnus and Mary Morgan in organizing 'The Experiment in Applied Econometrics', and also for the referees' comments on this paper. Remaining errors are the responsibility of the authors. The US data are complied from various US government publications (see organizers' data chapters for details). We also thank Statistics Netherlands for permission to use the Dutch data. The empirical estimates of the demand models are carried out using the EVIEWS-2.0 and FORECAST MASTER computer packages.

REFERENCES

Chetty, V. K. (1968), 'Pooling of time-series and cross-section data', *Econometrica*, **36**, 279–90.

Chow, G. (1960), 'Tests of equality between sets of coefficients in two linear regressions', *Econometrica*, **28**, 591–605.

Deaton, A. and J. Muellbauer (1980a), *Economics and Consumer Behaviour*, Cambridge University Press, Cambridge.

Deaton, A. and J. Muellbauer (1980b), 'An almost ideal demand system', *American Economic Review*, **70**, 312–26.

Engle, R. F. and C. W. J. Granger (1987), 'Cointegration and error correction: representation, estimation and testing', *Econometrica*, **55**, 251–76.

Engle, R. F. and M. Watson (1987), 'The Kalman filter: applications to forecasting and rational expectations models', in T. F. Bewley (ed.), *Advances in Econometrics*, Fifth World Congress, Cambridge University Press, Cambridge.

Granger, C. W. J. (1991), 'Developments in the study of cointegrated economic variables', in R. Engle and C. W. J. Granger (eds), *Long-Run Economic Relationships: Readings in cointegration*, Oxford University Press, Oxford.

Granger, C. W. J. and S. H. Lee (1991), 'An introduction to time-varying parameter cointegration', in P. Hackl and A. Westlund (eds), *Economic Structural Change*, Springer-Verlag, Berlin.

Izan, H. Y. (1980), 'To pool or not to pool? A re-examination of Tobin's food demand problem', *Journal of Econometrics*, **13**, 391–402.

Johansen, S. (1991), 'Estimation and hypothesis testing of cointegration in Gaussian vector autoregressive models', *Econometrica*, **59**, 1551–80.

Kalman, R. E. (1960), 'A new approach to linear filtering and prediction problems', *Journal of Basic Engineering*, **82**, 35–45.

MacKinnon, J. (1991), 'Critical values for cointegration tests', in R. Engle and C. W. J. Granger (eds), *Long Run Economic Relationships: Readings in Cointegration*, Oxford University Press, Oxford.

Maddala, G. S. (1971), 'The likelihood approach to pooling cross-section and time-series data', *Econometrica*, **39**, 939–53.

Perron, P. (1989), 'The crash, the oil price shock and the unit root hypothesis', *Econometrica*, **57**, 1361–1401.

Ray, R. (1980), 'Analysis of a time-series of household expenditure surveys for India', *The Review of Economics and Statistics*, **62**, 595–602.

Song, H., X. Liu and P. J. Romilly (1996), 'A time varying parameter approach to the Chinese aggregate consumption function', *Economics of Planning*, **29**, 185–203.

Stone, J. R. N. (1953), *The Measurement of Consumers' Expenditure and Behaviour in the United Kingdom, 1920–1938*, Cambridge University Press, Cambridge.

Tobin, J. (1950), 'A statistical demand function for food in the USA', *Journal of the Royal Statistical Society*, Series A, **113**, 113–41 [reprinted in Chapter 2, this volume].

COMMENTS BY PROFESSOR MICHAEL R. WICKENS (University of York)

In analyzing the US data, the Dundee team have focused on the purely econometric aspects without considering the underlying economic theory. (Curiously they only introduce theoretical considerations when they analyze the Netherlands' data.) Their aim has been to see what estimates the new techniques produce, and they perform this analysis very competently. Since I have already commented in general terms on this approach to econometric modelling in my discussion of the CBS team's results, I shall not repeat those remarks here. I will simply add that, even if statistical problems are found with Tobin's estimates, and the new estimates have 'acceptable' statistical properties, it is not clear what the results mean without considering whether the models estimated, and the variable definitions used, are theoretically appropriate.

The main thrust of the Dundee team's paper is a time-series analysis of the United States' and Netherlands' data using cointegration analysis and time-varying parameter models. This follows a brief consideration of the US cross-section data based on Tobin's original model. The cross-section evidence is of a declining income elasticity over time ranging from 0.56 to 0.33 (see Table I), a significant elasticity with respect to family size which is increasing over time, and significant residual heteroscedasticity. Weighted least-squares estimation to take account of outlier residuals has the effect of raising all of the income elasticities approximately to the interval $\{0.6, 0.7\}$, and removing the heteroscedasticity. This makes the income elasticities quite close to those obtained from the CBS model.

The aim of the time-series analysis is to re-cast Tobin's model into a framework that takes account of the non-stationarity of the data and allows for time-varying parameters. I shall focus my comments on the analysis of the US data. A comparison is made between using Tobin's original definitions of the data and alternative definitions that deflate expenditures and total income by the general price level, and as a further variant the use of per caput variables by deflating also by population. The cointegration analysis is carried out using both the Engle–Granger two-step error correction method and the Johansen estimator of a VECM. The former uses a cointegrating regression to estimate the long-run elasticity, and the latter uses a cointegrating vector. The general conclusions to emerge from this are, first, that the biggest cause of differences in the estimates of the income elasticities arises from the different definitions of the variables. The Tobin definitions give the lowest values (around 0.2), and the deflated series give the highest (0.58 for the cointegrating regression and 0.76 from the cointegrating vector). Second, the own price elasticity is negative (between −0.01 and around −0.16) using Tobin's definitions, but *positive* using the other definitions (between +0.60 and +0.78). Third, there is strong evidence of more complex dynamics than that considered by Tobin.

As already noted, there is almost a complete absence of discussion of the appropriate theoretical framework in which to conduct the analysis. This is typical of the way cointegration analysis is carried out. I agree that one should take account of the non-stationarity of the data, but one should also seek some theoretical justification for the models estimated. Cointegration analysis does not absolve one from this. For example, how can one justify including dynamics in consumer demand functions when neoclassical consumer theory predicts that in the absence of durability, learning, intertemporal decisions, or evolving preferences, there should be none? Since the choice of definition for the variables has the greatest impact on the estimates, consideration must also be given to the theoretical consequences of these choices.

To take up the last point, suppose that we begin with Tobin's model in the long run

$$\ln S_t = \alpha + \eta \ln Y_t + \beta \ln P_t + \gamma \ln Q_t + e_t$$

where S is an index of the quantity of food per capita, Y is nominal disposable income per capita, P is the food price index and Q is the non-food price index. The Dundee team provide estimates of Tobin's model using both his variable definitions and new definitions which allow the data set to be extended beyond 1941 to 1976. They consider two definitions for the dependent variable. The first is total expenditure on food deflated by a general consumption price index Π, where $\ln \Pi_t = w_t \ln P_t + (l - w_t) \ln Q_t$ and w_t is the share of food in total consumption expenditure. The second is the first expressed in per capita terms by deflating it by the size of the population. They also consider two income variables: real disposable income, and real disposable income per capita.

The cointegrating regression estimates obtained using the different definitions of the variables vary considerably, as shown in Table III. The estimates of the income elasticity using Tobin's data are much smaller than when the new data are used. Whether the new data are expressed in per capita terms, or not, has little impact. It is not clear whether this difference can be attributed to the change in the measure of the dependent variable, or the income variable.

Also, the interpretation of the coefficients of the price variables based on the new data seems to be a problem. For example, Equation (4ii) of Table III in the Dundee paper uses the per capita definitions and can be written in Tobin's notation as

$$\ln(P_t S_t / \Pi_t) = \alpha^* + \eta^* \ln(Y_t / \Pi_t) + \beta^* \ln P_t + \gamma^* \ln Q_t + e_t^*.$$

If the original Tobin equation were re-written with these variable definitions it would be

$$\ln(P_t S_t / \Pi_t) = \alpha + \eta \ln(Y_t / \Pi_t) + [1 + \beta - w_t(1 - \eta)] \ln P_t$$
$$+ [\gamma - (1 - w_t)(1 - \eta)] \ln Q_t + e_t^*.$$

Thus whilst the coefficient of the income variable has the interpretation of the income elasticity, the coefficients of the two price terms need careful interpretation. The sign of the estimated own price coefficient is positive and not negative. The Dundee team originally comment that this is by no means unusual, though one gets the impression that, as an estimate of the own price elasticity, they expect it to be negative. It is clear, however, that it is by no means obvious what the sign of β^* should be. For example, if the Tobin model is correct with $\beta = -0.22$, $\eta = 0.75$ (the values found by the CBS team) and $w = 0.26$ (its average value) then $\beta^* = 0.72$, which is not far from the value found by the Dundee team. The apparent puzzle is therefore not a puzzle at all and can be cleared up using a little theory.

It is well-known, of course, that cointegrating regression results are liable to show considerable small sample biases if there are dynamics and adjustment is slow. This is why cointegration analysis has largely replaced the Engle–Granger two-step procedure. A better procedure in my view would be to estimate the equation in the form

$$y_t = \alpha' x_t + \beta_1 \Delta y_t + \gamma' \Delta x_t + e_t$$

instrumenting Δy_t by y_{t-1} (or when y_t is a vector, by including reduced form equations for Δy_t and using sub-system IV) and treating the x_t variables as exogenous. A super-consistent point estimate of the long-run coefficient vector α is then obtained directly. Adding higher order differences does not alter this. With a lag of one the additional variables are not very significant and the previous cointegration estimates are not greatly altered. This suggests that there is little to be gained by introducing dynamics, which is what consumer theory would predict.

The Dundee team complete their analysis of the US data with a time-varying parameter estimation of Tobin's model in which they assume that the long-run coefficients are random walks. Once sufficient observations are used, the coefficient estimates settle down and are fairly stable, except in 1946 when they are all temporarily perturbed downwards. This is almost certainly a statistical phenomenon with no economic content, and has nothing to do with any time-varying response to changes in the explanatory variables. It is significant that in the constant parameter model 1946 has the largest (positive) residual, reflecting the fact that food consumption has a temporary peak in this period. This illustrates a general problem with Kalman filtering of this sort. Whenever there is an outlier in the residuals in the constant coefficient model, the Kalman filter will tend to re-attribute the shock to a temporary change in the coefficient values even if the coefficients really are constant. This is a classic illustration of data-mining. My own view is that Kalman filtering should be used either when there is a good theoretical reason to do so, or as a form of misspecification test.

In summary, the Dundee team have used modern time-series techniques to answer the questions posed, and they have carried out the analysis very competently. Their results, which are based on models very similar to Tobin's do not, however, differ substantially from those obtained by Tobin using less sophisticated econometric methods and a different data set.

COMMENTS BY PROFESSOR KENNETH F. WALLIS (University of Warwick)

The general approach of the teams assigned to me for comment was to stay in the spirit of Tobin's original formulation but apply more modern econometric methods. Although there are differences at the implementation level, these are not fundamental differences in 'approach/methodology' as I imagine the organizers of the experiment conceive of them. The debate about different research methods in empirical macro-economics, for example, is at a completely different level than how to analyze a given dataset and estimate an elasticity. In turn staying in the same general approach, I have three comments about the Dundee team's implementation.

(1) The income elasticities for US budget survey data presented in Table II are higher than those reported by other teams. In an attempt to reproduce these results for a comparative analysis described below, it appears that they are in error, weighted least-squares having been carried out without weighting the regression constant. Instead, a constant (a dummy variable that is identically equal to one for all observations) and weighted ln(income) and ln(family size) were used as regressors, which is incorrect: see, for example, Cramer, J. S. (1969), *Empirical Econometrics*, North Holland, Amsterdam, p. 86.

(2) Unlike most other participants, the Dundee team exploit the richness of the Dutch time-series data by estimating a demand system, choosing the AIDS specification. This represents a different functional form than the log-linear specification used in most of the time-series analyses, which again seem to follow Tobin's lead, although the suitability of this specification was already questioned in the discussion of Tobin's paper. Following their AIDS modelling, the Dundee team return to the single-equation log-linear form for

the Dutch data, so as to compare with the US data. An opportunity that is missed is a comparison of the competing specifications on the same dataset.

(3) As their 'own task' the Dundee team address time variation in elasticities by applying Kalman filter methods to both time-series datasets. The underlying models have already passed Chow break-points tests, however, so one's expectations may not be very high. Indeed, the results in Figure 1 show rather little variation over time. No measures of statistical significance are provided, but careful attention to the scale of the plots indicates that the economic importance of the reported variation is small.[C1]

COMMENTS BY PROFESSOR J. S. CRAMER (University of Amsterdam)

This is a workman-like empirical analysis of the data that were provided and it faithfully follows the formula of the experiment. I like the full and explicit reporting of what the authors did and why they did it. The authors must also be complimented for the original idea to apply an almost ideal demand system to the Dutch data.

While the considerations taken into account in the calculations are spelled out, there is a curious reticence about the implications of the results. The analysis of USA budget study data is an example. Here the authors correct for heteroscedasticity in Izan's way, eschewing the standard correction for cell size in the use of cell means (and this is not justified). Upon comparing Table II and Table I it is found that Izan's technique has spectacular effects; it leads all round to higher income elasticities and lower family size elasticities, and it brings the 1972 survey in line with the others. But the elasticities vary with the parameter γ, which governs the correction. All this is only *very* briefly noted below Table II, and there is no discussion of how it comes about and what are the best elasticities from the three sets reported in Table II.

In the same way, we have a wealth of different income elasticities from the time-series, all obtained by different methods, and it is not quite clear what specification (and what estimates) the authors prefer in the end.

The final conclusion at the start of Section 7 makes curious reading. Few participants conclude that the income elasticity of food from BS and TS data are 'of the same order of magnitude'. This suggests that pooling of this evidence is legitimate. Surely the participants, who are not afraid of computational efforts, should have proceeded to provide a pooled analysis!

REPLY BY HAIYAN SONG, XIAMING LIU AND PETER ROMILLY

1. The Estimated Income Elasticities from the Cross-Sectional and Time-Series Models

The near-constancy of the income elasticity over the four budget data sets given in our report was indeed in error, as noted by Professors Cramer and Wallis. This result arose from the incorrect application of the Izan treatment of heteroscedasticity. However, our cross-sectional estimation using the $\sqrt{m}$ treatment (where m = the number of households

---

[C1] *Note by the Editors*: Professor Wallis makes further comments on the Dundee results in his discussion of the Maastricht report by de Crombrugghe, Palm and Urbain.

within a particular class) reported in our full logbook did indicate that the income elasticity estimates for 1941, 1950 and 1960 were very close, whilst there was a substantial fall in the estimate for 1972 (see column 2 of Table C1 of the comments on the Maastricht report by de Crombrugghe *et al.*). This result is consistent with those for other studies in this experiment, and confirmed by Professor Wallis. If the Izan treatment had been applied correctly, the conclusion that the income elasticities of the cross-section and time-series models are 'of the same order of magnitude' (as noted by Professor Cramer) would not have been reached. Given the ambiguity in our results, we were not convinced that a pooled analysis was justifiable.

2. Parameter Constancy and the TVP Elasticities

The introduction of a time-varying parameter model in our comparative study was based on the hypothesis that the parameters in the food demand models may not be stable, particularly over the relatively long time period in the USA data set. In response to Professor Wallis' comment about our Chow break-point test results indicating that the TVP approach was inappropriate, it should be borne in mind that these were Chow tests for predictive failure carried out on the short-run models. We also carried out Chow tests for parameter instability on the long-run cointegration models (not reported in our paper but available from the authors on request) which indicated that parameter instability was a problem. Although the changes in the elasticities are not particularly significant in terms of 'scale', the pattern of change can be given an economic interpretation as outlined in our paper. Although Professor Wickens argues that the pattern of change may simply result from 'a statistical phenomenon with no economic content', food consumption in 1946 was very high and there must have been economic (and other) factors causing this. Unfortunately, we did not have time to explore alternative models of time variation in the parameters, and it is possible that some of these alternative specifications might not be open to the 'statistical phenomenon' objection.

3. Positive Own-Price Elasticities

Professor Wickens provides the solution to the problem of the positive own-price elasticities reported in our paper. Our model can be regarded as a transformation of Tobin's model such that $\eta^* = \eta$, $\beta^* = [1 + \beta - w_t(1 - \eta)]$, $\gamma^* = [\gamma - (1 - w_t)(1 - \eta)]$. Since the average value of w_t in our study is 0.248, we can obtain the following long-run elasticities for Equations (4i), (4ii), (5i) and (5ii) from the estimated cointegration coefficients given in Table III:

Table R1. Long-run demand elasticities for the United States

Elasticity	Equation (3i) (1913–76)	Equation (3ii) (1913–76)	Equation (4i) (1929–89)	Equation (4ii) (1929–89)	Equation (5i) (1929–89)	Equation (5ii) (1929–89)
Income η	0.131	0.195	0.530	0.685	0.640	0.755
Own-price β	−0.091	−0.155	−0.263	−0.285	−0.315	−0.302
Cross-price γ	−0.048	−0.026	−0.634	−0.542	−0.652	−0.553

Now all the equations have negative own-price elasticities, as expected by theory. Using similar methods we can obtain demand elasticities with expected signs from the regression coefficients in the corresponding error correction models.

4. Theoretical Framework

One of Professor Wickens' criticisms of our paper is that the study lacks an appropriate theoretical framework. However, we did emphasize in our paper that demand theory requires the satisfaction of the adding-up, homogeneity and symmetry conditions. As suggested by Deaton (1987), the demand functions of an individual consumer can be derived by maximizing a utility function subject to a budget constraint, and the above three conditions as well as negativity essentially exhaust the implications of utility maximization. In addition, basic economic theory indicates that demand for food is determined by income, food and non-food prices, and family size. We included all these explanatory variables in our models, and believe that this was our implicit theoretical framework.

Though an explicit and systematic review of standard theories may be desirable, it would reduce the space available for the presentation of new results from our comparative study of different econometric methods. As a static approach, neo-classical consumer theory is only one of a number of competing theories. Since consumption habits can be persistent, it may be necessary to introduce dynamics in the food demand model. We remain to be convinced that the analysis of demand should be based on neoclassical theory only.

5. The Application of the Engle–Granger Two-step Cointegration Approach

We take the point made by Professor Wickens concerning the small sample bias present in the Engle–Granger two-step procedure. Indeed, the estimates of the Netherlands' model may well suffer from this problem, although those for the USA model are estimated on a relatively large sample and should be statistically acceptable. The alternative of estimating the short and long-run relationships for the USA and the Netherlands using a single equation model proposed by Wickens and Breusch (1988) would certainly be desirable for future investigation.

ADDITIONAL REFERENCES

Deaton, A. (1987), 'Consumers' expenditure', in J. Eatwell, M. Milgate and P. Newman (eds), *A Dictionary of Economics*, Macmillan Press, London, pp. 592–604.
Wickens, M. R. and T. S. Breusch (1988), 'Dynamic specification, the long-run and the estimation of transformed regression models', *Economic Journal*, **98** (Conference), 189–205.

CHAPTER 8

STATISTICAL DEMAND FUNCTIONS FOR FOOD IN THE USA AND THE NETHERLANDS*

DENIS DE CROMBRUGGHE, FRANZ C. PALM AND JEAN-PIERRE URBAIN

1. INTRODUCTION

This paper reports the results of an extensive analysis of statistical demand functions for food using household expenditure survey data and aggregate time-series data on food consumption in the USA and the Netherlands (see Magnus and Morgan, 1995, hereafter denoted as MM). Our aim has been to analyse and assess the model put forward by Tobin (1950) applying recently developed econometric methods to both the original Tobin data and the additional data provided to us by MM. More specifically, we analysed the survey data separately and jointly and tested whether the impact of other socioeconomic variables (see e.g. Schokkaert, 1983) than those included by Tobin in his model is significant. We assessed the stability through time of the findings for the various surveys. Because the Dutch survey data were censored, we also estimated the food demand functions for the Netherlands using the Tobit estimator. When analysing aggregate food consumption through time, we paid attention to the non-stationarity of the series which were generally found to be integrated of order one with the exception of food prices and the deflator of income in the Netherlands which were found to be integrated of order two. For the USA the post-World War II data suggest that there is one cointegration relationship between food consumption, income, food prices, and the deflator of income. Weak exogeneity of the two price series with respect to the parameters of the cointegration vector has to be rejected, whereas consumption and income were found to be weakly exogenous with respect to the long-run parameters. The structural stability of the model for the four variables, consumption, income and the two price series, has to be rejected. Homogeneity of degree zero of the food demand functions has to be rejected as well. For the Netherlands, similar conclusions were reached with the exception that the two price series appear as I(2) processes. After transforming into an I(1) model, there is some evidence in favour of a single cointegration relationship interrelating consumption, income, relative prices, and the change in food prices. Structural stability has to be rejected for the Netherlands as well. There are some signs that the instability concerns the short-run dynamics parameters rather than the long-run relationship.

The findings of the analysis of aggregate time-series corroborate the results for the survey data in the sense that the latter also yield different results for different surveys. The income elasticity estimated from the survey data for the USA decreases from about 0.61 to approximately 0.39 over a period ranging from 1941 to 1972. For the Netherlands

---

* Reprinted from the *Journal of Applied Econometrics*, **12**, 615–645 (1997).

Methodology and Tacit Knowledge: Two Experiments in Econometrics
Jan R. Magnus and Mary S. Morgan © 1997 John Wiley & Sons Ltd

the income elasticity is found to increase from 0.34 to 0.47 between the surveys of 1980 and 1988. Socioeconomic variables others than household size and income appeared not to be significant in the analysis of survey data.

The paper is organized as follows. In Section 2, we report the results of the analysis of the survey data. Section 3 contains the findings of the time-series analyses. Also, a comparison of the survey and time-series analyses is given and forecasts based on the time-series models are reported. Section 4 presents conclusions. A summary of the logbook is given in an appendix.

2. ANALYSIS OF SURVEY DATA

2.1. The Model

The basic model used to analyse the survey data is Tobin's (1950) original family food demand function which reads as follows

$$\ln c_{it} = \beta_0 + \beta_1 \ln y_{it} + \beta_2 \ln n_{it} + \varepsilon_{it} \qquad\qquad 1$$

where c_{it} denotes the quantity of food consumed by family i in year t, y_{it} is disposable family income, n_{it} is the number of persons in the family (household size), and ε_{it} is a disturbance term. The β_j's are unknown parameters assumed to be constant.

Our choice of specification was based both on prior criteria (including matters of convenience) and on data-analytic criteria. *A priori*, we required a parameterization invariant with respect to arbitrary measurement units. In view of the tasks set by MM, and for the sake of comparability with Tobin's own work, the parameterization should preferably include the income elasticity and allow for a natural formulation of the 'homogeneity postulate' as a restriction on the parameter space. Log-linearity of the specification was especially attractive to preserve Tobin's aggregation logic, and also in prevision of the cointegration analyses of the time-series. Since Tobin's log-linear demand equation satisfied all these prior requirements we decided to tentatively adopt it as a working hypothesis.

This basic specification was subjected to a data-analytic control. We investigated its stability, and found shifts across surveys and over time. We tested for non-linearity and omitted factors by augmenting the regressions with socioeconomic (mostly categorical) variables as well as square and cubic income terms, and with RESET tests. The additional regressors did not significantly improve the statistical fit and did not resolve the shifts of parameters over time. As contending models we investigated the semilogarithmic model of Prais and Houthakker (1955), and the Working (1943) and Leser (1963) Engel curve relating the budget share of food to the logarithm of income. The statistical fit of those models was similar to that of the log-linear specification, and in spite of allowing for a non-constant (mostly decreasing) income elasticity they still revealed similar instability over time. Unfortunately, no income growth or wealth data were available in the surveys; cf. Tobin's Figure 1. This precluded the integration of permanent income/life cycle theory, and is probably the single most important shortcoming of the surveys.

In sum, we found that Tobin's specification, slightly adapted and extended, was *a priori* more convenient and empirically not worse (in particular, not less stable) than the other specifications envisaged. We therefore maintained Tobin's specification as our working hypothesis, splitting the sample period into two subperiods when necessary to resolve instability. We note that although our specification search was partly data-instigated, it did not amount to post-data model construction, since hypotheses instigated by an earlier data set were systematically tested on later data sets.

2.2. The US Budget Surveys

We begin with the US budget surveys (BSs) from 1941, 1950, 1960–61, and 1972–3. In obvious notation we call them BS41, BS50, BS60 and BS72. The data are grouped by household size and income class, with the number of income classes varying from 6 to 12. The actual number of households sampled is given per group for BS50 only; for the three other surveys, simple approximations are based on the total sample size and on the estimated distribution of incomes and household sizes provided. Our cross-sectional analysis was carried out in four major steps. First, we reproduced and reworked Tobin's original calculations for BS41. Second, we estimated similar regressions for all four BSs, with only slight extensions. Third, we evaluated the adequacy of Equation (1) by variable addition tests. Fourth, to test the constancy of the income elasticity, we re-estimated the models for the four BSs jointly as a system of independent equations linked by a coefficient constraint.

The first step in our analysis was, naturally, to reproduce Tobin's calculations (which, as was the practice at the time, used logarithms to the base 10). Tobin excluded the open-ended upper income classes from his analysis, to account for the fact that 'the reported observations are arithmetic rather than geometric means' (p. 117). Thus he kept to 37 observations rather than the total of 40 available from BS41.

There are two possibly related problems with Tobin's regression. First, the data are in the form of sample averages for household groups of very different sizes. This calls for a heteroscedasticity correction by weighted least squares (WLS). Second, there are two unmistakable outliers. Izan (1980) suggested deleting or unweighting them. One notable development since the time of Tobin's paper is that of diagnostic checks. For instance, Tobin's OLS regression yields a White test statistic of 13.470 (0.019) (asymptotic p-value from χ^2 (5) in parentheses); and a Jarque–Bera statistic of 19.939 (0.000) (asymptotic p-value from χ^2 (2)). Both tests bear out the non-conformity of the OLS residuals with the standard assumptions. But a straightforward application of WLS, with the square root of group sample size as the weight, resolves the excessive diagnostics and brings the estimates remarkably close to Izan's (1980) estimates with the outliers left out. For instance, the WLS income elasticity is 0.615, compared to Tobin's value of 0.561 (OLS with outliers in) and Izan's estimate of 0.628 (OLS with outliers out); White's statistic becomes 10.076 (0.344) (asymptotic p-value from χ^2 (9)); Jarque-Bera's statistic is down to 0.349 (0.840) (asymptotic p-value from χ^2 (2)). We conclude that WLS renders the exclusion of outliers (or Izan's scheme for unweighting them, for that matter) unnecessary. More diagnostics, based on the full data set, will be presented in Table I.

Tobin was troubled not only by the top income classes but also by those at the bottom. He remarked (p. 122) 'the erratic nature of the lowest-income observations' in some surveys, and attributed it to the treatment of food received in kind by poor families. As a more modern explanation we suggest the lack of proxies for permanent income or wealth. Savings and other reserves are resources of special importance to households experiencing a temporary gap in earnings and therefore reporting unusually low current incomes. In his own data, Tobin did not find it necessary to treat the lowest-income class differently from the rest. Nevertheless, it turns out that large positive residuals mostly correspond to

Table I. Estimates of Tobin's model for US budget surveys

Survey	BS41	BS50	BS60	BS72
(a) Constant	1.532	2.246	2.134	3.440
	(0.187)	(0.081)	(0.069)	(0.127)
ln *HINC*	0.610	0.551	0.543	0.386
	(0.025)	(0.011)	(0.009)	(0.014)
ln *HSIZE*	0.236	0.292	0.332	0.454
	(0.023)	(0.015)	(0.008)	(0.013)
*CLASS*1	0.076	0.140	0.060	0.118
	(0.066)	(0.086)	(0.048)	(0.047)
(b) Sample size	40	54	58	72
R^2	0.9987	0.9998	0.9998	0.9995
Ramsey RESET $\chi^2(1)$	0.000	1.079	1.879	8.397
	(0.996)	(0.299)	(0.171)	(0.004)
Jarque–Bera $\chi^2(2)$	0.697	17.510	2.087	1.121
	(0.706)	(0.000)	(0.352)	(0.571)
White (all terms) $\chi^2(13)$	7.036	47.075	40.428	31.444
	(0.900)	(0.000)	(0.000)	(0.003)
*LM*1 (fitted values) $\chi^2(1)$	0.557	1.138	4.735	1.822
	(0.455)	(0.286)	(0.030)	(0.177)
*LM*2 (*CLASS*1) $\chi^2(2)$	1.843	44.885	25.078	14.117
	(0.398)	(0.000)	(0.000)	(0.001)

Dependent variable: ln *FOOD*.
Weighting variable: square root of group size.
Restriction across surveys: none.
Panel (a): estimated coefficients (heteroscedasticity-consistent standard errors in parentheses).
Panel (b): diagnostics (asymptotic *p*-values in parentheses when applicable).

the lowest-income groups. These observations led us to include a dummy variable for the lowest-income class in subsequent regressions.

Starting on a second major step of cross-sectional analysis, we unsealed the more recent data and estimated similar regressions for all four BSs with both OLS and WLS. WLS visibly reduced but did not wholly eliminate heteroscedasticity. The WLS estimates are reported in Table I. *HINC* and *HSIZE* denote household income and household size; *CLASS*1 denotes the dummy variable for the lowest income class. The coefficients have the expected signs and magnitudes. A striking feature is the evolution of the income elasticity through time. It decreases monotonically in the successive surveys, from 0.61, through 0.55, 0.54, to 0.39. Conversely, the elasticity with respect to household size almost doubles, from 0.24 to 0.45, indicating a fall in the economies of family scale.

From the diagnostics reported in Table I, it appears that WLS does not eliminate heteroscedasticity altogether. Therefore the standard errors are made heteroscedasticity-consistent à la White (1980). In addition to White's test, we report two more Lagrange Multiplier statistics calculated only *after* the Tilburg conference following a suggestion by M. McAleer. The first, *LM*1, is a 'one-degree-of-freedom' test of significance of a regression of the squared residuals on the squared fitted values. The second, *LM*2, is the analogous significance test for the two 'White' terms representing the regressor *CLASS*1 (weighted and weighted-squared). Both illustrate that heteroscedasticity mainly takes the form of a few extreme residuals in the lowest-income groups.

In the third step of our analysis, adequacy of specification was tested further by variable addition. One-term Ramsey RESET tests are reported in Table I; high-order terms mattered

Table II. Testing equality of income elasticities in
different US budget surveys

	$\varepsilon_{41} = \varepsilon_{50}$	$\varepsilon_{50} = \varepsilon_{60}$	$\varepsilon_{60} = \varepsilon_{72}$
$\varepsilon_{41} = \varepsilon_{50}$	0.0367	0.0374	0.0000
$\varepsilon_{50} = \varepsilon_{60}$		0.6122	0.0000
$\varepsilon_{60} = \varepsilon_{72}$			0.0000

Entries are the p-values of the χ^2-statistics testing the
equalities indicated in both margins; ε_t represents the income
elasticity for BS_t ($t = 41, 50, 60, 72$).

little. Additional regressors considered are the percentage of home owners, and the average age and years of education of household heads. These variables are available for three surveys, BS50 to BS72. Dummies for the upper (open-ended) income classes and for the upper family-size groups were also tried out. None of these additional explanatory variables was retained, as they were found to have no consistent and significant effects (even when tested jointly). Furthermore, to test the sensitivity of the estimates, income was replaced by total consumption. Total consumption gives a higher elasticity and a closer fit, but does not seem to alter other coefficients in important ways.

Finally, joint weighted estimation was carried out, treating the four BSs as a system of independent equations (with uncorrelated disturbances and different residual variances). Constraining the income elasticities to be equal across the four BSs then yielded a common estimate of 0.53, and a likelihood ratio statistic of 267.8 (0.000) ($\chi^2(3)$ under the null). The equality restriction is rejected at any sensible level of significance. In view of the strength of this rejection, no attempt was made at testing the equality of the other coefficients. Table II presents p-values of tests of the equality of income elasticities in successive pairs of BSs. Whereas BS50 and BS60 are rather close, BS41 and BS72 are clearly different.

2.3. The Budget Surveys for the Netherlands

The three Dutch budget surveys present rather different data problems. The 1965 survey data are grouped by urbanization degree, household size, and income class. There are only two income classes, and no income data are available. We therefore had to use total consumption expenditures as a proxy for disposable income. The variable *HSIZE* was not well defined, and was replaced by the number of adult-equivalents (*ADULTEQ*). In addition to the variables in model (1), we included a dummy variable for rural areas. A second dummy variable for urban areas (there is a third category of households living in the three largest cities Amsterdam, Rotterdam, and The Hague) did not have a significant effect. The WLS total expenditure elasticity is 0.41, a value which comes close to a simple average of the income elasticities for BS60 and BS72 for the USA. A similar comment can be made about the effect of household size on consumption, estimated at 0.42. Somewhat surprisingly, living in a rural area appears to have a positive impact (0.071) on the level of food expenditures.

The 1980 and 1988 survey data sets (henceforth BS80 and BS88) are much richer. They provide ungrouped data for, respectively, 2859 and 1950 households. Unfortunately, for privacy reasons, the income and consumption data are censored. In the BS80 and BS88, income is censored above Dfl. 80 000 and replaced by the average of higher incomes (Dfl.

97 300 in 1980 and Dfl. 100 800 in 1988). As to consumption, the upper five percentiles are censored and replaced by the average of higher consumption. For BS80 and BS88, the 95th percentiles are Dfl. 13 030 and Dfl. 14 686.6, respectively, whereas average consumption in the upper five percentiles is Dfl. 17 670 and Dfl. 17 078.3, respectively. Scatter plots for BS80 and BS88 given in Figures 1 and 2 (not in logs) show how the data are censored. Two lines are drawn in the figures: the 45° line, on which all income is consumed for food, and the overall OLS regression line, which is suggestive of the downward bias of the overall OLS slope.

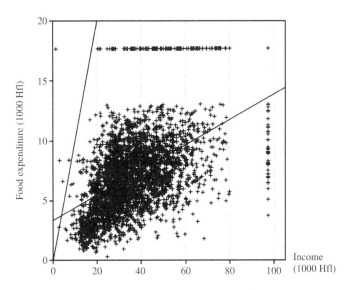

Figure 1. Dutch 1980 budget survey, scatter plot

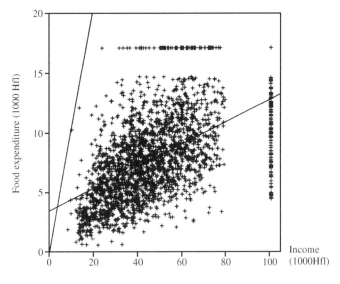

Figure 2. Dutch 1988 budget survey, scatter plot

In BS80 and BS88, negative food consumption expenditures are reported in some instances whereas in many other cases food consumption expenditures are incredibly low. One explanation offered is that consumption differs from consumption expenditure because of inventory holding or domestic production. In our analysis, for obvious practical reasons non-positive consumption expenditures have been treated as missing. Unfortunately, with respect to food, no information is provided on whether the household is involved in farm production or food trading. Identification of farmers might be useful to explain some extreme negative residuals in the food expenditure-income relationship.

To deal with the censoring of the consumption data, we use the Tobit estimator (see Tobin, 1958). The households with censored income (or censored income and consumption) are excluded from the sample. Estimation results are presented in Table III. The Tobit estimates of the income elasticity are 0.34 in 1980 and 0.47 in 1988. Fortunately, the differences between the Tobit and the corresponding OLS estimates are very small. Therefore, the bias resulting from censoring appears to be small, a finding which is likely to be due to the fact that the data for only a small number of households were actually censored. The proportionality of the probability limits for the different coefficients established by Greene (1981) and Chung and Goldberger (1984) is visible in the estimates, but not, however, in the value of the proportional correction. Under multivariate normality, this should amount to the inverse of the sample proportion of non-limit observations, increasing the coefficients by 4 to 5%. Actual changes are of the order of 1%.

The variable $MIDAGE$ denotes a dummy variable which is equal to one if the age of the head of household is between 35 and 64 years. Arguably it measures the effect on food consumption of the age of the children, rather than the effect of the age of the household head herself.

We note that specifications including as additional regressors dummy variables for the age class, education level, and socioeconomic status of the head of household have been investigated. These variables were not found to have highly significant effects

Table III. Estimates of Tobin's model for Dutch budget surveys

Survey	BS80	BS88
Constant	4.709	3.445
	(0.186)	(0.255)
ln $HINC$	0.340	0.467
	(0.019)	(0.025)
ln $HSIZE$	0.473	0.441
	(0.016)	(0.020)
$MIDAGE$	0.095	0.070
	(0.015)	(0.019)
Sigma	0.367	0.379
	(0.005)	(0.006)
Number of included observations	2801	1810
Number of non-limit observations	2674	1737
% non-limit	95.5	96.0
$FOOD$ censoring limit (Hfl.)	13 030	14 686.60
OLS — R^2	0.475	0.502

Estimation method: 'TOBIT' maximum likelihood.
Dependent variable: ln $FOOD$.
Household inclusion condition: $0 < HINC \leq 80\,000$.
Asymptotic standard errors in parentheses.

on food consumption expenditures in BS80 and BS88. Therefore, the results are not reported here.

2.4. Conclusion

From the investigation of both the American and Dutch BSs, we conclude first that the income elasticity of food expenditures has changed over time. In the USA it decreased between 1941 and 1972. In the Netherlands it increased between 1980 and 1988. The Dutch figure for BS65 is not comparable. (In other instances, figures based on total expenditures were higher than those based on income.) Estimated values of the income elasticity range between 0.33 and 0.61 for the different specifications used and for the different BSs.

Second, besides household income and size, few other socioeconomic variables were found to be of importance for explaining food consumption expenditures. These findings corroborate the model put forward by Tobin (1950) in the cross-sectional dimension.

Like Maddala (1971), and in contrast to Tobin (1950), Chetty (1968) and Izan (1980), we must conclude that it is not in this analysis advisable to pool the cross-sections and time-series information. Rather, since many more BSs have taken place than those available here (in the Netherlands, one every year since 1978), it would be possible to study the temporal evolution of Tobin's model in much further detail and, perhaps, with more information concerning the income dynamics.

In the next section, a closer look at the temporal stability of the food demand relation will be taken based on the aggregate time-series data.

3. TIME-SERIES ANALYSIS

3.1. The Model

The discussion of household surveys in the previous section naturally focused on the income elasticity of food expenditure. With time-series the emphasis partly shifts toward price elasticities and the 'homogeneity postulate'. Our line of attack is first to study the dynamic properties of the most relevant series. Considering that Tobin's food consumption was measured as a quantity index, and that the aggregation is with respect to both households and goods, we opted for relating food consumption to 'real' (or deflated) income and the corresponding general price index (or deflator). Depending on the exact specification of the consumer's constrained optimization problem, the income deflator ideally takes the form of some weighted average of all prices. Unfortunately, the series I_t mentioned by Tobin (see his notes to Table 5, p. 131) is not available for the purposes of the experiment nor is there information about the weight of food prices in I_t (Tobin's w, *ibid.*). After examining the share of food in total expenditures for the years in which expenditure data were available (1929–41), we decided to approximate the series I_t by the following fixed-weights average of food prices $pf_t = FP_t/100$ and non-food prices $pnf_t = NFP_t/100$ (in terms of the MM series):

$$pya_t = 0.25 \cdot pf_t + 0.75 \cdot pnf_t \quad (t = 1913, \ldots, 1941)$$

$$= 0.25(FP_t/100) + 0.75(NFP_t/100).$$

The weight 0.25 is a value which seems representative of the food expenditure share when it becomes available in 1929. (It also equals the average food expenditure share for the extended sample period 1929–89.) The series pya_t will be used as the income deflator for the period 1913–41 in the next subsection. It is constructed within the information set available to Tobin in 1950, but without doubt Tobin would rather have used the proper I_t series.

Fixed weights ignore shifts in the relative importance of food and non-food goods, like those bound to occur in wartime. It would be preferable to take account of such shifts. Indeed, from 1929 onwards the MM information pack provides aggregate expenditure data relevant for weighing food and non-food prices. We define

$$py_t = w_t \cdot pf_t + (1 - w_t) \cdot pnf_t \quad (t = 1929, \ldots, 1989) \qquad 3$$

where (in terms of the MM series) $pf_t = FP_t/100$, $pnf_t = NFP_t/100$, and

$$w_t = \frac{AGGEXPF_t/FP_t}{AGGEXPF_t/FP_t + (AGGEXP_t - AGGEXPF_t)/NFP_t}. \qquad 4$$

In words, w_t measures the share of (deflated) aggregate food expenditures in (deflated) aggregate total expenditures. The constructed series py_t will be used in Section 3.3 as the best available income deflator for the period 1949–89.

From time plots of the different series, it appears quite implausible that they represent stationary variables. Our empirical analysis will therefore be conducted in the framework of cointegrated systems, more specifically, in the Gaussian maximum likelihood framework of Johansen (1991, 1995).

In the case where all the series are I(1), we consider the vector autoregressive error correction model (VECM) of finite order p for the $(k \times 1)$ vector time-series x_t

$$\Delta x_t = \sum_{i=1}^{p-1} \Gamma_i \Delta x_{t-i} + \Gamma x_{t-1} + \mu_0 + \mu_1 t + \varepsilon_t \quad (t = 1, \ldots T) \qquad 5$$

where ε_t denotes a k-dimensional normal variate with mean zero and non-singular, p.d.s. covariance matrix Σ, μ_0 is a vector of constant terms, and μ_1 denotes the slope coefficients of the linear trend. We assume (1) that rank $(\Gamma) = r \le k$ so that Γ can then be written as $\alpha\beta'$ where both α and β are $(k \times r)$ matrices of full column rank, and (2) that $\alpha'_\perp (I - \Gamma_1 - \cdots - \Gamma_p)\beta_\perp$ has full rank, with $\alpha_\perp$ and $\beta_\perp k \times (k - r)$ matrices of full rank which are orthogonal to α and β, respectively. The second assumption rules out I(2) processes, a point to which we shall return later. The r rows of β' are the r *cointegrating vectors* while the elements of α are the *factor loadings*, i.e. the weights of the different cointegrating vectors in the different equations.

Once the number of cointegrating relationships has been determined using likelihood ratio tests proposed by Johansen (1991), particular hypotheses on α and/or β can be tested using χ^2 LR tests. If the cointegrating space is of dimension one, then the normalization is sufficient to ensure identification, and the hypothesis of long-run price homogeneity is a testable restriction, namely that the price coefficients in the cointegrating vector sum to zero. If more than one cointegration vector is found among I(1) variables, then the identification of a *long-run food demand relation* requires some identification restrictions (see, for example, Johansen and Juselius, 1994). If price homogeneity is used as an identifying restriction, it is no longer a testable hypothesis.

Note that in an I(1) system the issue of weak exogeneity with respect to the long-run parameters can also be addressed, using likelihood ratio or LM tests (see, *inter alia*, Johansen, 1992; Boswijk and Urbain, 1996; Urbain, 1992). This will enable us to evaluate the decision of Tobin to retain food prices as the endogenous variable and to treat food expenditures as exogenous. Finally, following Hansen and Johansen (1993), we will use the VECM framework to investigate the parameter constancy of the long-run relationships found in our analysis.

A word of caution is in order concerning the small samples that are used in these time-series analyses. Although some (conflicting) Monte Carlo evidence exists in the literature, it must be stressed that the behaviour of the estimators and test statistics we use may be seriously affected by the smallness of the available samples. One should always bear this in mind and we will as often as possible recognize the problem by using small-sample corrections which have been argued to provide less distorted versions (in terms of empirical size and power) of the test statistics we use.

3.2. The Tobin Time-Series Data: 1913–41

The empirical analysis is first conducted on the data of Tobin (1950), except that his non-food price index (Q_t) is replaced by the fixed-weights income deflator pya_t defined in Equation (2). In this subsection, the c_t will denote the quantity index of *per capita* food consumption (MM's series TO BPCFC, Tobin's S_t); y_t per capita disposable income (MM's *TOBPCY*, Tobin's Y'_t); and pf_t the food price index (MM's *TOBFP*, Tobin's P_t).

The vector of variables to be analysed is thus given by the four-dimensional vector

$$x_t = \left(\ln c_t, \ln \frac{y_t}{pya_t}, \ln pf_t, \ln pya_t \right)'$$

and the sample period covers the years 1913–41. Given the extremely small sample available unit root tests are not reported in detail, although we point out that the two price terms may be I(2) series according to Dickey–Fuller tests, while Phillips–Perron statistics favour the I(1)ness of all the retained series.

After some preliminary investigation a VECM with $p = 2$ was retained as providing the best description of the dynamic interrelationships in the data. Given that the series clearly exhibit linear trend components, the specification of the deterministic part is retained as an unrestricted (drift) constant in the short-run dynamics and a linear trend in the cointegration space, excluding herewith the existence of quadratic trends in the data.

We first investigate the presence of I(2) components in this system using the sequences of likelihood ratio test statistics recently proposed by Paruolo (1996) which provide a way to determine simultaneously the cointegration rank (r), the number of I(1) common trends (s_1) and the number of I(2) common trends (s_2). These tests are found to reject all I(2) hypotheses at the 5% level.

Our analysis will thus be based on an I(1) system. Although the likelihood ratio tests corrected for the small-sample effect do not detect a single cointegrating vector, the uncorrected trace test and maximum eigenvalue test are significant at a 5% and 10% level, respectively. We opted for assuming one cointegrating vector. Since deterministic cointegration could not be rejected, the model was specified with an unrestricted constant term in the short-run dynamics. The results are presented in Table IV.

Table IV. I(1) Analysis — Tobin data set (1913–41)

H_0	Eigenvalue	λ_{max}	*Trace*	λ_{max}^{corr}	*Trace*^{corr}
$r = 0$	0.6216	26.24[b]	48.73[a]	18.46	34.29
$r \leq 1$	0.4979	18.60[b]	22.49	13.09	15.83
$r \leq 2$	0.1132	3.24	3.89	2.28	2.74
$r \leq 3$	0.0238	0.65	0.65	0.46	0.46
	$\ln c_t$	$\ln(y_t/py_t)$	$\ln pf_t$	$\ln py_t$	
Coint. Vect.: β	1.000	−0.306	0.295	−0.410	
α-vector	−0.330	1.402	2.030	0.956	
t-value	(−1.50)	(1.49)	(1.86)	(1.47)	
Diagnostics	$\ln c_t$	$\ln(y_t/py_t)$	$\ln pf_t$	$\ln py_t$	
AR(1–2)	0.99	1.08	0.51	0.06	$F(2,16)$
ARCH(1)	1.52	0.16	0.00	1.59	$F(1,16)$
Jarque-Bera	0.41	3.42	1.13	1.34	$\chi^2(2)$
Hypothesis tests					
Homogeneity H_0^H			7.11	p-value: 0.01	$\chi^2(1)$
Weak exo. $\ln c_t$ H_0^{wel}			1.73	p-value: 0.19	$\chi^2(1)$
Renormalized coint. vect.					
	$\ln c_t$	$\ln(y_t/py_t)$	$\ln pf_t$	$\ln py_t$	
β	2.826	−0.935	1.000	−1.394	
α-vector	0.000	0.577	0.825	0.457	
t-value	—	(2.26)	(2.89)	(2.72)	

Notes: [a]Significant at the 5% level.
[b]Significant at the 10% level.
Critical values for both the *Trace* and the λ_{max} tests are taken from Johansen (1995).
Trace^{corr} and λ_{max}^{corr} are computed using the small sample correction advocated by Boswijk and Franses (1992) which consists of premultiplying the usual statistics by $(T - kp)/T$ where T is the sample size, k the number of equations in the VECM, and p the lag length.

In spite of the similar magnitudes of the two price coefficients, price homogeneity is rejected statistically at the 1% significance level. What causes this rejection must remain an open question here. A further interesting result is that the LR test for the weak exogeneity of $\ln c_t$ reinforces Tobin's hypothesis that food consumption may be treated as exogenous. Indeed, $\ln c_t$ appears weakly exogenous in this system with respect to the long-run parameters and the loadings. We re-estimate the long-run relationship under this hypothesis and normalize it on the food price to get results that can be directly compared to Tobin's original findings (last panel of Table IV). The long-run relation can also be renormalized on food expenditures $\ln c_t$; however, because of our finding that $\ln c_t$ is weakly exogenous, we are reluctant to give the ordinary economic interpretation to the elasticities in the resulting equation. (The implied values are 0.33 for the income, −0.35 for the food price, and 0.49 for the general price level elasticities.)

3.3. The Post-war US Data Set: 1949–89

The same analysis is now conducted on the extended US data set, which covers the period 1929–89. The notation is changed as little as possible, but the series used in this subsection differ somewhat from Tobin's and are defined as follows: for c_t, deflated per capita personal food expenditures (MM's series *AGGEXPF* divided by *POP* and deflated by *FP*); for y_t, per capita disposable personal income (MM's *AGGY* divided by *POP*); and for pf_t, the food price index (MM's *FP*/100). The series py_t is the variable-weights income deflator defined in Equation (3).

The basic vector of variables is now

$$x_t = \left(\ln c_t, \ln \frac{y_t}{py_t}, \ln pf_t, \ln py_t \right)'.$$

Some preliminary analyses suggested a split in two rather different subperiods: 1929–48 and 1949–89. The suggestion of a shift in the behaviour of the series is so strong, and the estimates for the complete period so implausible, that we only report results for the post-war subsample, 1949–89.

Unit root tests are ambiguous but tend to favour I(1) processes. As in the previous analysis, a lag length of two periods was retained in the VECM and a linear but no quadratic trend was allowed in the model. Paruolo's likelihood ratios tests for integration indices show that if we base our analysis strictly on the 5% level asymptotic critical values, the hypotheses $r = 1$ and $s_2 = 1$ cannot be rejected, which would imply the existence of one common I(2) trend. However, with a slightly higher significance level all I(2) hypotheses would be rejected as in the pre-war data set. Although this issue might deserve further investigation we pursued the analysis under the assumption that the series are well described as I(1) processes. The I(1) system is therefore estimated and Table V reports the outcome of the standard I(1) analysis. Contrary to the results for the pre-war data set, the absence of a linear trend in the cointegration space, e.g. the hypothesis of deterministic cointegration H_0^{DC}, is easily rejected. The price homogeneity assumption, H_0^H, is again rejected statistically although the price coefficients have similar magnitudes. It is interesting to note that income and food consumption have equal coefficients with opposite signs, which could be interpreted as a unit long-run income elasticity. This stands in sharp contrast to the pre-war results, and substantiates the splitting of the extended sample. The estimated long-run relation renormalized on the food prices is also reported.

Note that the weak exogeneity of both price terms with respect to the long-run parameters is rejected, while $\ln c_t$ and $\ln(y_t/py_t)$ appear as the weakly exogenous variables in the system. As in the pre-war data, a dynamic conditional model for food expenditure given the remaining variables will not have a significant error correction term, and is therefore not the best basis for the analysis of any long-run relationships involving food expenditures. Accordingly, the cointegration vector reported in the bottom panel of Table V is normalized on the food price variable. (Renormalizing on food expenditures in any case, one gets elasticities of 1.00 for income, −0.59 for food prices, and 0.49 for the general price level.)

One issue which up to now has not been explicitly addressed is the issue of parameter constancy. As was pointed out in the analysis of the budget surveys, the US income elasticity did not seem to remain constant over the years. Although one should be very careful, given the apparent weak exogeneity of food expenditures, when comparing these time-series results with those for the budget surveys, it may be important to analyse the potential parameter non-constancy of our time-series results and particularly of our final estimates of the cointegration parameters. The simplest approach would be to estimate the model for several *a priori* fixed subsamples. It may appear more natural to investigate

Table V. I(1) Analysis—extended US data set (1949–89)

H_0	Eigenvalue	λ_{max}	*Trace*	λ_{max}^{corr}	*Trace^{corr}*
$r = 0$	0.7083	50.51[a]	78.77[a]	40.66[a]	63.39[a]
$r \leq 1$	0.3350	16.72	28.26	13.46	22.75
$r \leq 2$	0.1816	8.22	11.54	6.61	9.29
$r \leq 3$	0.0778	3.32	3.32	2.68	2.68
	$\ln c_t$	$\ln(y_t/py_t)$	$\ln pf_t$	$\ln py_t$	Trend
Coint. Vect.: β	1.000	−1.072	0.616	−0.734	0.019
α-vector	−0.214	−0.037	−1.550	−0.993	
t-value	(−1.09)	(0.82)	(1.51)	(2.02)	

Diagnostics	$\ln c_t$	$\ln(y_t/py_t)$	$\ln pf_t$	$\ln py_t$	
AR(1–2)	0.30	3.60[a]	1.91	4.60[a]	$F(2,29)$
ARCH(1)	0.57	0.29	0.04	0.24	$F(1,29)$
Jarque-Bera	0.88	1.43	2.57	1.80	$\chi^2(2)$

Hypothesis tests

Det. coint H_0^{DC}			24.51[a]	p-value: 0.00	$\chi^2(1)$
Homogeneity H_0^H			19.31[a]	p-value: 0.00	$\chi^2(1)$
Unit inc. el. H_0^U			1.04	p-value: 0.31	$\chi^2(1)$
Weak exo. $\ln c_t$ H_0^{we1}			0.87	p-value: 0.35	$\chi^2(1)$
Weak exo. $\ln(y_t/py_t)$ H_0^{we2}			0.02	p-value: 0.89	$\chi^2(1)$
Weak exo. $\ln pf_t$ H_0^{we3}			14.36[a]	p-value: 0.00	$\chi^2(1)$
Weak exo. $\ln py_t$ H_0^{we4}			13.26[a]	p-value: 0.00	$\chi^2(1)$

Renormalized Coint. Vect.

	$\ln c_t$	$\ln(y_t/py_t)$	$\ln pf_t$	$\ln py_t$	Trend
β	1.705	−1.705	1.000	−1.178	0.029
Sd. err.	(0.099)	(0.099)	—	(0.017)	(0.0001)
α	0.000	0.000	−1.094	−0.664	
t-value	—	—	(−5.15)	(−4.87)	

the potential parameter non-constancy by considering a recursive analysis of the VECM such as proposed by Hansen and Johansen (1993). The analysis can be conducted in two different model representations: one representation where all the parameters are allowed to change, a second where the likelihood function is concentrated with respect to the short-run dynamics parameters so that only the long-run parameters are allowed to change over time.

We use the subsample 1948–64 for initialization so that the reported recursive analysis covers the sample 1965–89. A first informative graphical representation is provided by the recursively computed (significant) eigenvalues which determine the cointegrating rank. Figure 3 reports the time path of the largest eigenvalue with its 95% confidence bounds computed using a non-parametric Bartlett kernel estimator. It appears that although there is some slight downward trend in its evolution, this eigenvalue remains significantly different from zero for the entire sample, reinforcing the evidence in favour of a unique cointegrating vector.

A further interesting procedure is to test for the within-sample constancy of the long-run parameters for a given (and fixed) cointegration rank. For this purpose we use recursively

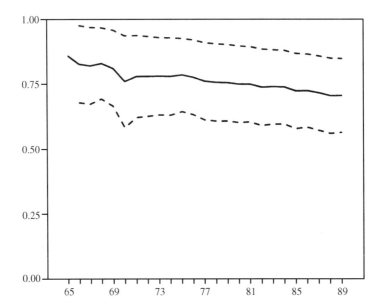

Figure 3. Recursive eigenvalue — post-war US data set

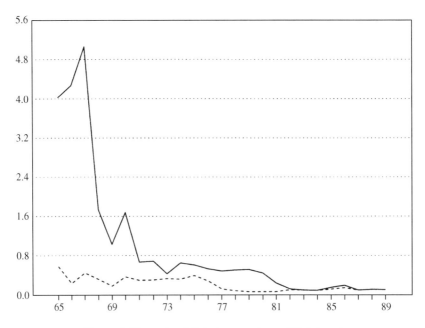

Figure 4. Recursive LR tests — post-war US data set

computed approximate likelihood ratio statistics for known cointegration vectors, as proposed by Johansen and Juselius (1992), where the full sample estimates are chosen as the known vector. Figure 4 presents the time path of these LR tests scaled by their 95% critical values. The dashed line is the sequence of LR tests computed when short-run dynamics are fixed at their full sample estimates and the cointegration relations are recursively estimated, whereas the solid line represents the LR tests when all parameters are recursively estimated. One interesting conclusion from this analysis is that although parameter constancy can be rejected for our model, it seems that fixing the short-run dynamics parameters and then estimating recursively the long-run parameters generates a situation in which the parameter constancy can no longer be rejected. It is tempting to interpret this as a situation where the observed non-constancy mainly originates from the short-run dynamics of the system.

Finally, we also computed the recursive estimates of the cointegrating vector components and the loadings. Parameter constancy cannot be maintained although we found a fairly constant behavior in the last part of the sample, namely the period 1977–89. The weak exogeneity of $\ln c_t$ and $\ln(y_t/py_t)$ appears as a constant feature over the whole sample since their loadings remain insignificant throughout.

3.4. The Dutch Data: 1948–88

A similar analysis is now conducted using the time-series data for the Netherlands covering the period 1948–88, that is, a sample of 41 observations. The construction of deflated per capita series from the available data set is relatively straightforward: MM series $p11_t$ is used as a deflator for food consumption $v11_t$, and $p1_t$ is used as an approximate deflator for income $AGGY_t$; both are expressed per capita using POP_t. Thus we define $c_t = 100 \cdot v11_t/(p11_t \cdot POP_t)$; $y_t = AGGY_t/POP_t$; $pf_t = p11_t/100$; and $py_t = p1_t/100$.

As previously, unit root tests yield ambiguous results but tend to favour I(1) processes although again the price terms could be equally well characterized as I(2) processes. The integration indices of the series are therefore analysed using Paruolo's likelihood ratio tests. The results are reported in Table VI and are based on a VECM with two lags. The two lags are necessary to eliminate signs of dynamic misspecification. For the deterministic part of the model we again allow for linear but no quadratic trends in the data. The LR tests have been calculated for all values of r and $s_1 = k - r - s_2$. Testing sequentially increasingly less restricted hypotheses by starting from the most restricted case ($r = 0$, $s_1 = 0$ and $s_2 = 5$) the calculated statistics show that we cannot reject, at the 5% level, the presence of I(2) series in our system. In particular the hypothesis that $r = 2$,

Table VI. I(2) Indices — Dutch data series (1948–88)

$k - r$	r	$Q(s_2, r)$			
4	0	183.86	130.33	90.54	79.40
		(116.3)	(91.4)	(73.0)	(58.0)
3	1	—	106.38	57.97	45.07
			(70.9)	(51.4)	(38.8)
2	2	—	—	33.25	20.57
				(36.1)	(22.6)
1	3	—	—	—	14.28
					(12.9)
s_2		4	3	2	1

Notes: $Q(s_2, r)$ are Paruolo's (1996) LR tests for integration indices. 95% asymptotic critical values in parentheses.

$s_2 = 2$, $s_1 = 0$ cannot be rejected, which suggests the existence of two non-cointegrated I(2) common trends.

From a graphical inspection the two price series are suspected to be I(2). Different routes are therefore worth considering. Either we pursue the analysis of the I(2) system in terms of multicointegration or we modify our framework. We opted for the pragmatic alternative. Since prices are likely to be I(2) series with relative prices being I(1), we redefine our vector of variables as

$$x_t^* = \left(\ln c_t, \ln \frac{y_t}{p y_t}, \ln \frac{p f_t}{p y_t}, \Delta \ln p f_t \right)'$$

which can be reasonably assumed to be a vector of I(1) series. The practical advantage of this formulation is that it enables us to test for price homogeneity in the long run without imposing it in the short-run dynamics, thanks to the inclusion of both the relative price index $\ln(p f_t / p y_t)$ and food price inflation $\Delta \ln p f_t$.

Computing Paruolo's LR tests for the integration indices shows that all I(2) hypotheses can now be rejected at the 5% level so that we may proceed with the analysis of the Dutch data set in an I(1) framework, allowing for linear trends and excluding quadratic trends. Results are reported in Table VII.

Fixing the lag length of the VECM to two, there is some evidence of, at most, one cointegrating vector, and the computed LR test statistic for the deterministic cointegration hypothesis H_0^{DC} does not reject that hypothesis. Imposing this restriction, we obtain coefficients with economically meaningful signs and magnitudes. The results are reported in the bottom panel of Table VII, where it is also shown that price homogeneity (i.e. excluding $\Delta \ln p f_t$ from the long-run relation) is firmly rejected by the data.

The reader will notice that, once again, the weak exogeneity of food expenditures ($\ln c_t$) with respect to the long-run parameters cannot be rejected; in fact, only the food price inflation $\Delta \ln p f_t$ is clearly not exogenous. So once again, we avoid normalizing the reported cointegration vector on food expenditures in Table VII. (Renormalizing on $\ln c_t$ in any case, one obtains elasticities of 0.48 for income, and -0.17 for the relative food price.)

The last issue we want to investigate before the forecasting exercise is the issue of parameter constancy. The tools are the same as for the extended US data set. We use the subsample 1948–64 for initialization so that the reported recursive analysis covers the sample 1965–89. The recursively computed (significant) eigenvalue which determines the cointegrating rank, the recursively computed trace test statistics, the recursively computed approximate likelihood ratio statistics for known cointegration vectors, and the evolution of the recursive estimates of the cointegrating vector components and the loadings yield strong evidence of parameter instability. The cointegrating rank appears to be one over the whole sample period but the first eigenvalue displays an important shift around 1976.

3.5. Forecasting the Demand for Food in the Netherlands (1989–2000)

The third task assigned by MM was to provide forecasts for the post-sample period 1989–2000. In constructing these forecasts, we tried as far as possible to take into account the empirical findings of the preceding subsection. These are essentially related to the non-stationary food expenditures (which seem well characterized as an I(1) process), the possible presence of cointegration and the evidence of parameter non-constancy in our

Table VII. I(1) Analysis — Dutch data set (1948–88)

H_0	Eigenvalue	λ_{max}	Trace	λ_{max}^{corr}	$Trace^{corr}$
$r = 0$	0.5138	27.40[b]	59.23[b]	21.63	46.76
$r \leq 1$	0.3456	16.11	31.83	12.72	25.13
$r \leq 2$	0.2098	8.95	15.72	7.06	12.41
$r \leq 3$	0.1632	6.77	6.77	5.34	5.34

	$\ln c_t$	$\ln(y_t/py_t)$	$\ln(pf_t/py_t)$	$\Delta \ln pf_t$	Trend
Coint. Vect.: β	1.000	−0.299	−0.103	−1.179	−0.007
α-vector	0.083	0.373	−0.011	0.728	
t-value	(0.56)	(1.72)	(−0.08)	(4.29)	

Diagnostics	$\ln c_t$	$\ln(y_t/py_t)$	$\ln(pf_t/py_t)$	Δpf_t	
AR(1−2)	0.77	2.28	5.10[a]	5.47[a]	$F(2,26)$
ARCH(1)	0.004	0.06	5.66[a]	0.15	$F(1,26)$
Jarque-Bera	0.33	3.38	3.82	2.67	$\chi^2(2)$

Hypothesis tests

Det. coint H_0^{DC}		3.69	p-value: 0.05	$\chi^2(1)$
Homogeneity H_0^{H}		10.99[a]	p-value: 0.00	$\chi^2(1)$
Weak exo. $\ln c_t$ H_0^{we1}		0.22	p-value: 0.64	$\chi^2(1)$
Weak exo. $\ln(y_t/py_t)$ H_0^{we2}		1.51	p-value: 0.22	$\chi^2(1)$
Weak exo. $\ln pf_t/py_t$ H_0^{we3}		0.0001	p-value: 0.94	$\chi^2(1)$
Weak exo. $\Delta \ln py_t$ H_0^{we4}		7.46[a]	p-value: 0.01	$\chi^2(1)$

Restricted and renormalized Coint. Vect.

	$\ln c_t$	$\ln(y_t/py_t)$	$\ln(pf_t/py_t)$	$\Delta \ln pf_t$	Trend
β	−1.168	0.557	−0.203	1.000	0.000
Sd. err.	(0.187)	(0.093)	(0.098)	(0.000)	—
α	0.000	−0.545	0.000	−0.459	
t-value	—	(−2.86)	—	(−2.51)	

Notes: See Table IV. We have corrected one typographical error in the first line of this table (27.40 instead of 27.10). We are grateful to W. K. Siegert for bringing this error to our attention.

recursive analysis. The issue of whether one can really gain much, in terms of forecast accuracy, by imposing cointegration restrictions for forecasting purposes has been often discussed in the literature; see Clements and Hendry (1995) who, for instance, report Monte Carlo results showing that the advantage of imposing cointegration restrictions is inversely related to the sample size.

We computed forecasts of the natural log of per capita food consumption expenditures in the Netherlands. The models used are a VAR(1) for the first differences with an intercept and a trend, a VAR(1) for the first differences with an intercept only, a VECM(2) with an unrestricted intercept and a VECM(2) with an unrestricted intercept and a linear trend restricted to lie in the cointegration space. For comparison purposes, and given that our results for the Dutch data set were not clear-cut, we also computed forecasts based on a simple univariate random walk with drift and an ARIMA(1,1,1) process. In Figure 5 and Table VIII we present the forecasts for the period 1989–2000.

For both the VARs and the VECM the vector of variables retained is

$$x_t^* = \left(\ln c_t, \ln \frac{y_t}{py_t}, \ln \frac{pf_t}{py_t}, \Delta \ln pf_t \right)'.$$

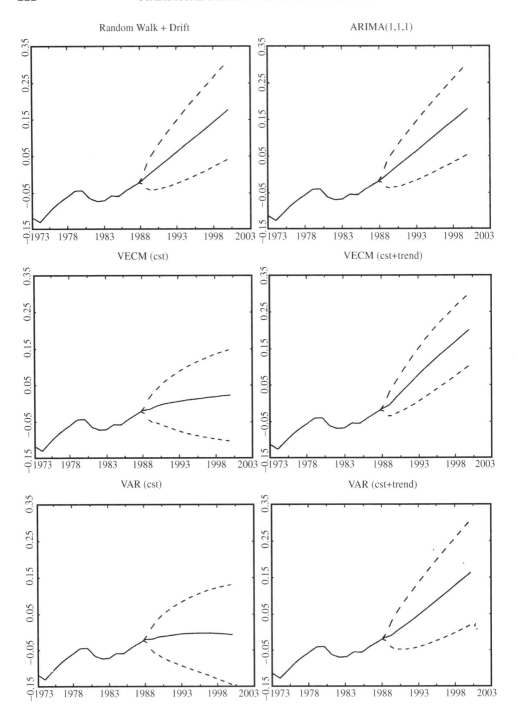

Figure 5. Forecasting Dutch food expenditures: 1989–2000

Table VIII. Forecasting Dutch demand for food: 1989–2000

	R.W.	ARIMA (1,1,1)	VECM(2)$_{cst}$	VECM(2)$_{trend}$	VAR (1)$_{cst}$	VAR(1)$_{trend}$
1989	0.9960	0.9954	0.9827	0.9907	0.9804	0.9868
	(0.96, 1.04)	(0.96, 1.03)	(0.95, 1.02)	(0.96, 1.02)	(0.95, 1.02)	(0.95, 1.02)
1990	1.0124	1.0122	0.9919	1.0127	0.9869	1.0027
	(0.96, 1.07)	(0.96, 1.07)	(0.95, 1.04)	(0.97, 1.06)	(0.94, 1.04)	(0.95, 1.06)
1991	1.0291	1.0285	0.9972	1.0333	0.9894	1.0169
	(0.96, 1.10)	(0.96, 1.09)	(0.94, 1.06)	(0.98, 1.09)	(0.93, 1.06)	(0.95, 1.09)
1992	1.0460	1.0456	1.0012	1.0546	0.9924	1.0328
	(0.97, 1.13)	(0.97, 1.12)	(0.93, 1.07)	(0.99, 1.12)	(0.92, 1.07)	(0.95, 1.12)
1993	1.0632	1.0626	1.0047	1.0764	0.9947	1.0494
	(0.97, 1.16)	(0.98, 1.15)	(0.93, 1.09)	(1.00, 1.16)	(0.91, 1.08)	(0.96, 1.15)
1994	1.0807	1.0802	1.0076	1.0972	0.9962	1.0661
	(0.98, 1.19)	(0.99, 1.18)	(0.92, 1.10)	(1.01, 1.19)	(0.90, 1.10)	(0.96, 1.18)
1995	1.0985	1.0978	1.0104	1.1177	0.9973	1.0834
	(0.99, 1.21)	(1.00, 1.21)	(0.92, 1.11)	(1.03, 1.21)	(0.90, 1.11)	(0.97, 1.21)
1996	1.1166	1.1159	1.0131	1.1378	0.9976	1.1009
	(1.00, 1.24)	(1.01, 1.23)	(0.91, 1.12)	(1.04, 1.24)	(0.89, 1.11)	(0.98, 1.23)
1997	1.1349	1.1341	1.0155	1.1576	0.9974	1.1188
	(1.01, 1.27)	(1.02, 1.26)	(0.91, 1.13)	(1.06, 1.27)	(0.88, 1.12)	(0.99, 1.26)
1998	1.1536	1.1528	1.0178	1.1775	0.9966	1.1369
	(1.02, 1.30)	(1.03, 1.29)	(0.91, 1.14)	(1.07, 1.29)	(0.88, 1.13)	(1.00, 1.29)
1999	1.1726	1.1717	1.0198	1.1973	0.9951	1.1554
	(1.03, 1.33)	(1.04, 1.32)	(0.91, 1.15)	(1.09, 1.32)	(0.87, 1.13)	(1.01, 1.32)
2000	1.1919	1.1910	1.0218	1.2172	0.9931	1.1742
	(1.04, 1.36)	(1.05, 1.35)	(0.90, 1.16)	(1.10, 1.34)	(0.86, 1.14)	(1.02, 1.35)

Note: The table reports the implied forecasts for the mean food expenditure per capita in 1000 HFL (constant 1951 prices) per year. Corresponding 95% confidence intervals are provided in parentheses. These are computed by appropriately transforming the point and interval forecasts obtained from our models for the natural logs of the variables. The one-step-ahead forecast of the level of food expenditure is for example given by $\tilde{c}_{T+1|T} = \exp(\widetilde{\ln}c_{T+1|T} + (\hat{\sigma}^2/2))$ where $\widetilde{\ln}c_{T+1|T}$ is the one-step-ahead point forecast of the natural log of food expenditures and $\hat{\sigma}$ its associated standard error.

Notice that in each case the forecasts were based on per capita expenditures transformed into natural logarithms. We also present 95% forecast intervals taking into account only the variance of the error process. Although these are wide they still underestimate the uncertainty of our forecasts.

4. CONCLUSIONS

In this paper we have analysed household budget survey and aggregate time-series information on the demand for food in the USA and the Netherlands using econometric models put forward by Tobin (1950). After some specification testing, we decided to maintain throughout the analysis Tobin's basic functional form with only slight extensions. The conclusions from the empirical analyses are as follows.

First, Tobin's model relating the logarithm of food consumption to that of income and household size (extended by including a dummy variable for the lowest income class) performs remarkably well. Other socioeconomic variables were found not to improve significantly the explanation of household food consumption. The use of weighted least squares suffices to solve the outlier problem exposed by Izan (1980).

Second, the income elasticities vary through time. For the USA, the estimated income elasticity is found to decrease over time. For the Netherlands there is also evidence of time-dependence, but the pattern of the time-variation is less clear-cut. This finding is much in line with the structural instability of the parameters of the time-series models. Therefore it does not seem at this point wise to pool time-series and BS data.

Third, the sign and size of income elasticity estimates from BSs and time-series information are similar.

Fourth, while requiring appropriate methodological treatment — at least in principle — the censoring of the food consumption and income data in the BSs for the Netherlands turns out to lead to only a small bias in practice.

Fifth, the aggregate time-series were found to be non-stationary. With the exception of the two price series for the Netherlands, the time-series appear to be integrated of order one. Price series for the Netherlands were found to be I(2), but relative prices appear to be I(1), so that the model for the Netherlands was formulated in terms of relative prices.

Sixth, for the data originally used by Tobin (1950) one cointegration relationship is found and the long-run homogeneity hypothesis of food demand with respect to prices is statistically rejected. Food consumption may in fact be considered as weakly exogenous for the long-run parameters, a finding which corroborates an assumption made by Tobin (1950).

Seventh, for the extended set of data for the USA (1929–89), the analysis was restricted to the post-war period. One cointegration relationship was found. Long-run price homogeneity was statistically rejected. Again, food consumption and real income may be considered as being weakly exogenous whereas weak exogeneity of prices has to be rejected. Parameter constancy has to be rejected as well. When we fix the parameters of the short-run dynamics, the constancy of the long-run parameters is no longer rejected. The conclusion about the structural instability of the parameters in the time-series models is in line with the finding of a varying income elasticity across BSs.

Eighth, to account for the integration of order two of prices for the Netherlands, the time-series model was formulated in terms of relative prices and food price inflation. The conclusions are similar to those for the USA. At most one cointegration relationship was found. Price homogeneity in the long run was statistically rejected. Weak exogeneity of food consumption with respect to the long-run parameters cannot be rejected. Parameter stability appears to be an issue as well for the Netherlands.

Ninth, the forecasts obtained using various time-series models are rather similar and unprecise.

Finally, we look back on a very instructive experiment in applied econometrics with appreciation for the organizers and also admiration for the meticulous and lucid quality of the empirical work that Professor James Tobin did almost half a century ago.

APPENDIX: LOGBOOK

Our aim was to follow the list of tasks set by MM as closely as practically feasible and we projected the following plan. First (1), we had to reproduce and perhaps elaborate further upon Tobin's estimates. Second (2) came the separate and joint analyses of all four US budget surveys. Third (3), we would investigate the relationship between food consumption and income in the longer US time-series. The fourth intended step (4) was to check on the realism of pooling the cross-sectional and time-series information and, in the affirmative, to evaluate the benefits of pooling. Next, steps (2)–(4) were to be repeated for the Netherlands (MM Task 2(a)) and the findings were to be compared to those for the USA (MM Task 2(b)). Finally, we planned to produce the requested forecasts and to conduct policy-relevant analysis as indicated (MM Tasks 3 and 4). The outline of the paper still partly reflects our initial intentions, although due to unfavourable outcomes (on the question of pooling) and data limitations (especially with regard to the policy questions), some steps were somewhat curtailed. In practice, we proceeded as follows.

January–February 1996

Reproduction of Tobin's estimates for both BS41 and time-series 1912–48. For BS41, re-estimation of Tobin's model with slightly corrected and/or extended data; application of WLS, resolving Izan's outliers. For Tobin's time-series data, exploratory estimation of simple conditional dynamic models of food expenditures. No stable and significant (both economically and statistically) long-run equilibrium relationship was found. Construction of an income deflator series for Tobin's time-series data for the purpose of testing the homogeneity hypothesis. System-cointegration analysis of Tobin's time-series data, tests of price homogeneity, tests of weak exogeneity. Comparison with alternative approaches to cointegration.

March–April 1996

Estimation of Tobin's model for all four US BSs (separately), with OLS and WLS. Weighting variable is the square root of either the number of households sampled (BS50) or an approximation thereof (BS41, BS60, BS72). WLS clearly reduces heteroscedasticity. Regular peaks remain in the residuals, corresponding to the extreme (esp. lowest) income classes. Introduction of dummy $CLASS1$ for the lowest income class. Additional regressors tried but not retained: $HOMEOWN$ (% homeowners at year end), $EDUHH$ (average years of education of household head), $AGEHH$ (average age of household head) (these three not available for BS41); dummies for the upper (open-ended) income classes and for the largest household size. Final regressions were rerun with $TOT(al)CON(sumption)$ replacing income to test the sensitivity of the coefficients. Joint estimation of the same model for all four US BSs with the income elasticities restricted to be equal across surveys. Strong rejection of the restriction. Exploratory analysis of the extended US time-series data set (single-equation ECM/ADL models), without much success on the long-run equilibrium front. Oddities keep emerging from the series $Q_t(= NFP)$; hence, inquiry with MM concerning the availability of more original information (since Tobin, p. 131, in his notes to Table 5, mentions an initial series I_t and quantity weights w and $1 - w$ which are not part of the data provided). Construction of income deflator series for the longer US time-series data set for the purpose of testing the homogeneity hypothesis. Cointegration analysis of the full US time-series data. Investigation of practical issues such as lag length and specification of the deterministic components. Tests of weak exogeneity, homogeneity and analysis of parameter constancy. In view of lack of time invariance, decision to work on a subsample covering the period 1949–89. Using the (as yet uncorrected) Dutch time-series: exploratory conditional modelling of food expenditures (single-equation ECM/ADL models); these were rather unsuccessful in the same sense as before. System cointegration analysis, tests of weak exogeneity, homogeneity, parameter constancy.

May–July 1996

Dutch BS65: Tobin's model is estimated with income (which is unavailable) replaced by total consumption ($v1$), household size (which is not well defined) replaced by *ADULTEQ* *(univalent)*, and a dummy *RURAL* (for $URB = 3$) included as a regressor. Additional dummies used but not retained: *DURBAN* (for $URB = 2$) and DHINC (for $HINC = 2$). Dutch BS80 and BS88: discovery that incomes and food expenditures are censored (the data concern individual households). Estimation of Tobin model by OLS with and without the censored observations, with relatively small differences. For BS80, various dummies for the age, education level, and socioeconomic status of the head of household were tried, but not found to be significant, with one exception: *MIDAGE* (for $1 < AGEHH < 5$). Finally, only *MIDAGE* was retained (arguably measuring the effect on food consumption of the age of the children, rather than the effect of the age of the household head herself). Dutch BS80 and BS88: Tobit 'ML' estimation of the model including *MIDAGE* (with outcomes almost identical to OLS). Receipt of corrected Dutch time-series. New cointegration analysis and formal comparison of alternative dynamic specifications. Discovery of the possible I(2)-character of the price series. I(2) analysis of the Dutch time-series data. Issue of weak exogeneity of food expenditures and homogeneity for the Dutch case. Parameter constancy analysis. Similar I(2) analyses for both the extended US and the original Tobin time-series data which led us to maintain the assumptions of I(1) prices for these data sets. Forecasting exercise using both univariate and multivariate models. Examination of policy issues. Production of the final report.

The computations on the budget surveys were carried out with the econometric programs EVIEWS 1.0, LIMDEP 6.0 and TSP 4.3; for the time-series analyses, use was made of four packages: PCGIVE/PCFIML 8.0, RATS420, GAUSS 3.2.14, and EVIEWS 1.0.

ACKNOWLEDGEMENTS

We gratefully acknowledge helpful comments by A. P. Barten, A. Buse, M. McAleer, M. Peeters, and K. F. Wallis as well as other participants at the conference 'The Experiment in Applied Econometrics'. We enjoyed the enthusiastic computational assistance of Erwin Lambrix. Thanks are due to J. Magnus and M. Morgan for organizing 'The Experiment in Applied Econometrics' and for supplying the data. The US data are compiled from various US government publications (see organizers' data chapters for details). We thank Statistics Netherlands for use of the Dutch data.

REFERENCES

Boswijk, H. P. and P. H. Franses (1992), 'Dynamic specification and cointegration', *Oxford Bulletin of Economics and Statistics*, **54**, 369–81.
Boswijk, H. P. and J.-P. Urbain (1997), 'Lagrange multiplier tests for weak exogeneity: A synthesis', *Econometric Reviews*, **16**, 21–38.
Chetty, V. K. (1968), 'Pooling of time-series and cross-section data', *Econometrica*, **36**, 279–90.
Chung, Ch.-F. and A. S. Goldberger (1984), 'Proportional projections in limited dependent variable models', *Econometrica*, **52**, 531–4.
Clements, M. and D. F. Hendry (1995), 'Forecasting in cointegrated systems', *Journal of Applied Econometrics*, **10**, 127–46.
Greene, W. H. (1981), 'On the asymptotic bias of the ordinary least squares estimator of the Tobit model', *Econometrica*, **49**, 505–13.

Hansen, H. and S. Johansen (1993). 'Recursive estimation in cointegrated VAR-models', Preprint 1, Institute of Mathematical Statistics, University of Copenhagen.

Izan, H. Y. (1980), 'To pool or not to pool: a reexamination of Tobin's food demand problem', *Journal of Econometrics*, **13**, 391–402.

Johansen, S. (1991), 'Estimation and hypothesis testing of cointegration vectors in Gaussian vector autoregressive models', *Econometrica*, **59**, 1551–80.

Johansen, S. (1992), 'Cointegration in partial systems and the efficiency of single-equation analysis', *Journal of Econometrics*, **52**, 389–402.

Johansen, S. (1995), *Likelihood-Based Inference in Cointegrated Vector Autoregressive Models*, Oxford University Press, Oxford.

Johansen, S. and K. Juselius (1992), 'Testing structural hypotheses in a multivariate cointegration analysis of the PPP and UIP for UK', *Journal of Econometrics*, **53**, 211–44.

Johansen, S. and K. Juselius (1994), 'Identification of the long run and short run structure: An application to the ISLM model', *Journal of Econometrics*, **63**, 7–36.

Leser, C. E. V. (1963), 'Forms of Engel functions', *Econometrica*, **31**, 694–703.

Maddala, G. S. (1971), 'The likelihood approach to pooling cross-section and time-series data', *Econometrica*, **39**, 939–53.

Magnus, J. R. and M. S. Morgan (1995), *The Experiment in Applied Econometrics: Information Pack*, CentER for Economic Research, Tilburg University.

Paruolo, P. (1996), 'On the determination of integration indices in I(2) systems', *Journal of Econometrics*, **72**, 313–56.

Prais, S. J. and H. S. Houthakker (1955), *The Analysis of Family Budgets*, Cambridge University Press, Cambridge, 2nd edition, 1971.

Schokkaert, E. (1983), 'The introduction of sociological variables in Engel curve analysis', *Tijdschrift voor Economie en Management*, **28**, 409–36.

Tobin, J. (1950), 'A statistical demand function for food in the USA' (with discussion), *Journal of the Royal Statistical Society*, Series A, **113**, 113–41 [reprinted in Chapter 2, this volume].

Tobin, J. (1958), 'Estimation of relationships for limited dependent variables', *Econometrica*, **26**, 24–36.

Urbain, J.-P. (1992), 'On weak exogeneity in error correction models', *Oxford Bulletin of Economics and Statistics*, **54**, 187–208.

White, H. (1980), 'A heteroscedasticity-consistent covariance matrix estimator and a direct test for heteroscedasticity', *Econometrica*, **48**, 817–38.

Working H. (1943), 'Statistical laws of family expenditure', *Journal of the American Statistical Association*, **38**, 43–56.

COMMENTS BY PROFESSOR KENNETH F. WALLIS (University of Warwick)

The Maastricht team do a very thorough job within the general approach I noted above (on the Dundee Report[1]), and have also revised their paper after the Tilburg conference to a greater extent than other teams, so several of my initial comments no longer apply. In this comment I focus on the task assigned to me as an assessor, namely 'to understand why paper A gets different results from paper B', and compare the analyses of the USA budget surveys by Dundee and Maastricht. I gratefully acknowledge the assistance of Marga Peeters in this exercise.

For the years 1941, 1950, 1960 and 1972, Maastricht report decreasing income elasticities and reject the hypothesis of constancy. Dundee present a range of income elasticities for each year, for $\gamma = 0.5$, 0.7 and 1.0 in the Izan weighting scheme (they comment that 'there is some variation in them over time'), but this is less than Maastricht find, and constancy is not tested. Both teams indicate that heteroscedasticity is apparent in the data:

---

[1] Note by Editors: These comments refer to both this report and to the Dundee Report by Song, Liu and Romilly.

Maastricht initially look at OLS-residual graphs; Dundee apply the White test; both then use weighted least squares (WLS). Their analyses differ in that: (i) different weighting schemes are used and (ii) a dummy variable is included for the lowest income class by Maastricht. We assess whether these two differences are the (only) reason for the different findings, and undertake some diagnostic checking on heteroscedasticity.

Seven sets of regression results, obtained with STATA, are presented in Table CI. Column (1) contains OLS results. Columns (3) and (5) reproduce the main WLS results reported by Maastricht and Dundee, who respectively use $\sqrt{m}$ and Izan weights. Column (2) presents the $\sqrt{m}$-WLS results reported by Dundee in their logbook, which are similar to the Maastricht results in column (3), but without the dummy variable *CLASS*1. In reproducing the Dundee results in column (5), it appears that they carried out WLS without weighting the constant, as noted above (see my comments on the Dundee Report), and corrected results for the Izan weighting scheme are presented in column (4). Column (6) presents corresponding WLS results with the inclusion of the *CLASS*1 dummy variable found to be important by Maastricht.

Concentrating on the income elasticities, the pattern over the four years is 0.585, 0.517, 0.534 and 0.348 in column (2) and 0.605, 0.551, 0.542 and 0.386 in column (3). This comparison shows that the monotonically declining pattern emphasized by Maastricht is due to the inclusion of the *CLASS*1 dummy. In column (2), where the dummy variable is omitted, the decline is not monotonic. This result also holds under the Izan scheme: income elasticities decreases monotonically when the dummy is included (0.596, 0.553, 0.549 and 0.366 in column (6)), but not otherwise (0.586, 0.496, 0.541 and 0.337 in column (4)). Comparison between the two weighting schemes (take (2) and (4) or (3) and (6)), shows that the elasticity patterns are quite similar across schemes. After all, 'wrong' weights, including the case of equal weights as in OLS, nevertheless produce unbiased estimators in the classical linear regression model.

To test the constancy of the income elasticity over the four years, we estimate pooled regressions. First the hypothesis that the income elasticity is the same across all four years is clearly rejected by a likelihood ratio test against the alternative of four different income elasticities. This result is obtained irrespectively of the different weighting schemes and whether or not the *CLASS*1 dummy is included. As the results in Table CI indicate that parameter estimates for 1941, 1950 and 1960 are rather close in almost all cases, a constant income elasticity for these three years, but not for 1972, is next tested. Likelihood ratio statistics do not reject this model against the general model, again irrespective of weighting scheme or the dummy variable, although conventional critical values may not be appropriate since the formulation of this hypothesis is clearly the result of a prior peek at the data. The common income elasticity is about 0.57 across the first three surveys, considerably higher than the 1972 value of 0.38. These results add some precision to the Maastricht result, rejecting constancy over the four years. In summary, the difference in findings of the two teams seems not to be due to differences in weighting schemes or the inclusion of a dummy variable. Results reported by Dundee that indicate near-constancy seem to be in error.

Let us finally return to the question of heteroscedasticity. Table CI includes the 'vener-able' Goldfeld-Quandt test statistic, which seems to have become unfashionable. Ordering the data by income, the error variance at high incomes is compared with that at low incomes (with about 20 observations in each group). This ordering in any event seems more informative than the ordering in the supplied datafile, and it was difficult to see in

Table CI. Comparison of the Dundee (D) and Maastricht (M) USA budget survey regressions

	(1) OLS	(2) WLS ($\sqrt{m}$)	(3) WLS ($\sqrt{m}$)	(4) WLS (Izan)	(5) WLS (Izan)	(6) WLS (Izan)	(7) OLS
1941							
k	1.806	1.727	1.570	1.711	0.592	1.635	1.488
	(0.192)	(0.146)	(0.184)	(0.160)	(0.217)	(0.192)	(0.132)
α	0.572	0.585	0.605	0.586	0.760	0.596	0.618
	(0.026)	(0.021)	(0.025)	(0.022)	(0.021)	(0.025)	(0.018)
δ	0.260	0.227	0.226	0.249	0.190	0.248	0.230
	(0.038)	(0.022)	(0.022)	(0.028)	(0.051)	(0.028)	(0.025)
*CLASS*1			0.072			0.055	
			(0.053)			(0.075)	
R^2	0.95	0.99	0.99	0.99	0.98	0.99	0.98
s.e.	0.14	1.70	1.68	0.14	0.25	0.18	0.09
G-Q(14, 15)	1.05	0.61	0.59	1.11	1.69	1.06	1.87
White	11.70	11.75	13.51	5.84	6.71	24.94	19.62
# obs	40	40	40	40	40	40	38
reported	D/M	D	M		D		
1950							
k	2.864	2.529	2.246	2.759	1.316	2.272	2.823
	(0.160)	(0.102)	(0.118)	(0.137)	(0.145)	(0.151)	(0.158)
α	0.486	0.517	0.551	0.496	0.696	0.553	0.493
	(0.019)	(0.013)	(0.015)	(0.016)	(0.014)	(0.018)	(0.019)
δ	0.260	0.291	0.292	0.269	0.381	0.262	0.239
	(0.025)	(0.016)	(0.015)	(0.020)	(0.038)	(0.017)	(0.023)
*CLASS*1			0.140			0.252	
			(0.037)			(0.052)	
R^2	0.94	0.99	1.00	0.99	0.99	0.99	0.94
s.e.	0.12	0.84	0.75	0.13	0.23	0.10	0.10
G-Q(18, 18)	1.03	0.40	0.35	0.92	1.12	0.67	1.09
White	27.86	3.98	44.50	28.01	11.71	29.55	27.39
# obs	54	54	54	54	54	54	51
reported	D	D	M		D		
1960							
k	2.263	2.206	2.140	2.160	0.838	2.088	1.947
	(0.212)	(0.082)	(0.089)	(0.138)	(0.176)	(0.159)	(0.152)
α	0.531	0.534	0.542	0.541	0.728	0.549	0.573
	(0.025)	(0.010)	(0.011)	(0.016)	(0.015)	(0.018)	(0.018)
δ	0.308	0.335	0.333	0.317	0.303	0.318	0.269
	(0.034)	(0.012)	(0.011)	(0.020)	(0.040)	(0.021)	(0.024)
*CLASS*1			0.072			0.064	
			(0.041)			(0.069)	
R^2	0.91	1.00	1.00	0.99	0.98	0.99	0.96
s.e.	0.17	1.16	1.13	0.14	0.27	0.14	0.11
G-Q(17, 18)	0.46	0.49	0.42	0.55	0.56	0.28	0.50
White	26.83	18.10	23.64	42.67	10.30	43.24	29.55
# obs	59	59	59	59	59	59	57
reported	D	D	M		D		

(continued overleaf)

Table CI. (*Continued*)

	(1) OLS	(2) WLS ($\sqrt{m}$)	(3) WLS ($\sqrt{m}$)	(4) WLS (Izan)	(5) WLS (Izan)	(6) WLS (Izan)	(7) OLS
1972							
k	3.958	3.792	3.440	3.892	1.538	3.617	3.824
	(0.126)	(0.101)	(0.134)	(0.105)	(0.241)	(0.112)	(0.130)
α	0.330	0.348	0.386	0.337	0.646	0.366	0.346
	(0.014)	(0.012)	(0.015)	(0.011)	(0.019)	(0.012)	(0.015)
δ	0.455	0.453	0.454	0.457	0.470	0.462	0.445
	(0.017)	(0.015)	(0.014)	(0.013)	(0.048)	(0.012)	(0.017)
CLASS1			0.118			0.169	
			(0.032)			(0.038)	
R^2	0.95	0.99	0.99	0.99	0.95	0.99	0.96
s.e.	0.09	2.07	1.90	0.10	0.38	0.09	0.09
G-Q(24, 24)	1.24	0.72	0.57	1.20	0.73	0.93	1.12
White	20.37	3.96	18.65	32.88	4.97	34.99	20.36
# obs	72	72	72	72	72	72	70
reported	D	D	M		D		

Notes:
'Izan' weights are $(|u_i|^{1/2} + 0.5)^{-1}$
'G-Q' is the Goldfeld-Quandt F-statistic based on the indicated (lower income, higher income) subsample sizes. The error variance of the higher income subsample is always in the numerator of the statistic.
'White' is his χ^2 heteroscedasticity test statistic, as used by Dundee, but also including the cross-product term and the dummy variable where relevant. The degrees-of-freedom are six in columns (3) and (6) and five elsewhere.

plots previously presented by Maastricht that WLS 'visibly reduces heteroscedasticity', as was claimed. Indeed, the use of the $\sqrt{m}$ weights is seen to drive the G-Q statistic further away from one in all four years. In general, it indicates less heteroscedasticity than does the White statistic, a result that can be reconciled by recalling that White's test is a more general test of misspecification, sensitive to a range of departures including wrong functional form. Inspection of Dundee's scatter diagrams of log C against log Y for the three later years, referred to in Section 2 of their paper, suggests that there is scarcely a heteroscedasticity problem at all — at least, none that remains after the log transformation — but there may be a small number of outliers, and these are deleted in the final column of Table CI. The general evidence of the White statistic, which contrasts with that of the G-Q statistic, suggests that alternative functional forms should be investigated. In the version of their paper presented at the Tilburg conference, the Maastricht team agreed that such a study 'might be worthwhile'.

COMMENTS BY PROFESSOR MICHAEL MCALEER (University of Western Australia)

The purpose of this valuable paper by the authors from Maastricht is to report the 'results of an extensive analysis of statistical demand functions for food using household expenditure survey data and time-series data on aggregate food consumption in the USA and The Netherlands.' Indeed, the nature of the analysis is extensive, and there is much to commend in this paper. The approach to econometric modelling is predominantly classical, with extensive use of graphical analysis, tests and diagnostics to examine the auxiliary assumptions. Clear and concise motivation is provided in the paper. There are careful discussions of the choice of functional form, use of alternative explanatory variables, including dummy variables (there seems to have been a judicious and abundant use of dummy variables in the paper, even though not all of the dummy variables were subsequently found to be significant), checking for outliers and heteroscedasticity, testing for unit roots and cointegration, examining parameter constancy, and pooling of data. The strengths of the paper far outweigh any weaknesses.

The paper uses modern econometric time-series methods, the reference list is current, and the strengths and limitations of the various techniques are clearly understood and appreciated by the authors. In addition to presenting a sophisticated time-series approach to data analysis, there is a detailed and credible logbook, which enables an appreciation of the sequential nature of the modelling exercise undertaken by the authors. The presentation of a substantial number of tables of empirical results, a reasonably wide range of diagnostics, and figures for the USA and Dutch budget surveys, and USA and Dutch post-war time-series data, permit a number of important questions to be answered empirically.

Sensible warnings about the small sample limitations of some of the modern time-series methods are also provided, with useful suggestions regarding small sample corrections (some of the samples used are extremely small). [Having said that, the authors demonstrate a preference for the uncorrected trace and maximum eigenvalue likelihood ratio test statistic results for cointegration over their small sample corrected counterparts in Section 3.2 because of a preference for having one cointegrating vector over none.] Although the paper is concerned with statistical and econometric techniques, the modelling of short-run and long-run economic relationships is also examined carefully. Economic variables are taken as given, but the statistical significance of socio-economic information of households is also investigated. The issue of appropriate functional forms is examined, albeit briefly. A clear and precise summary of the empirical conclusions is given. Moreover, a highly readable presentation by the three co-authors suggests the research was a joint effort.

Six econometric and time-series computer software packages have been used in the empirical analysis, three for the computations on the budget surveys and four for the time-series analysis (one package was used for both sets of data). Such a large number probably sets some kind of record for use of software packages on a single research paper.

The basic model (2.1) involves a largely uncritical use of Tobin's (1950) original Cobb-Douglas family food demand function. The authors explain their choice of specification in terms of prior criteria and data-analytic criteria. These criteria include convenience (by which is presumably meant computational considerations), ease of interpretation of the coefficients as elasticities, ease in the formulation and testing of the homogeneity postulate, a need to preserve Tobin's aggregation logic, strict comparability with Tobin's original formulation, and 'also in prevision of the cointegration analyses of the time-series'. Convenience would not seem to be a major issue when there are numerous equivalently simple models available, each with ease of interpretation of coefficients as elasticities (although perhaps not in terms of testing homogeneity). Since tests of unit roots and cointegration are not known to be robust to alternative data transformations, the choice of data transformation can also have significant effects on the outcomes of such tests.

Emphasizing that 'One notable development since the time of Tobin's paper is that of diagnostic checks', various diagnostics, such as the addition of polynomials of income and Ramsey's RESET test of functional form misspecification, are presented by the authors to check the specific functional form used. Perhaps surprisingly, the range of diagnostics provided does not include direct and computationally simple tests of the linear and logarithmic functional forms against each other (perhaps due to their not being available on the numerous software packages used?) The authors also investigated the semilogarithmic model and report that they found the statistical fit to be similar to that of the logarithmic specification. Given the emphasis in the paper on the sensitivity of the empirical results to the assumptions made, it would have been useful to examine this issue at greater length.

An important issue is raised by the authors regarding the absence of income and wealth data in the surveys, which 'precluded the integration of permanent income/life cycle theory, and is probably the single most important shortcoming of the surveys'. With reference to Tobin's concerns with the top and bottom income classes in the surveys, the authors suggest, as a more modern explanation, 'the lack of proxies for permanent income or wealth'. There has been much theoretical and empirical research in the area of the rational expectations life-cycle, permanent income hypothesis, and substantial empirical results from cross-section and time-series studies point to there being an excess sensitivity of consumption to current disposable income. However, it is not entirely clear whether these empirical results arise because of the failure of the perfect capital markets assumption, which leads to liquidity constrained consumers being unable to smooth out their consumption plans over time, or through a lack of certainty leading to consumers being unable to behave according to the life-cycle, permanent income hypothesis. It is, therefore, still an unresolved issue from an empirical perspective. The data needed to resolve this issue are far more than income growth and wealth, and include consumer debt and effective tax rates, which are not readily available either in national income accounts or consumer surveys.

The construction of a (seemingly arbitrary) fixed-weights average of food prices and non-food prices used in constructing the price deflator yields a variable which replaces Tobin's non-food price index, 'Q' (not to be confused with Tobin's 'q'). Although 'pya' might not provide the most appealing abbreviation, it is probably far more clear than 'Q', at least to economists.

In concluding, the authors state their 'admiration for the meticulous quality of the empirical work that Tobin did almost half a century ago'. It is impossible for anyone who has had the pleasure of reading the original Tobin article to disagree with such sentiments.

COMMENTS BY PROFESSOR ANTON P. BARTEN (Catholic University of Leuven)

This paper reads with pleasure. The authors apply the tools of modern econometrics to the Tobin experiments of about half a century ago with great care. Basically, their results are not that much different from Tobin's, which is a comforting thought for the elderly and somewhat disappointing for the young.

One of the issues which leaves the reader somewhat unhappy is that of the order of integration of the variables in the case of the time-series applications. After some experimentation the authors consider their time-series to be I(1). The exception is the series of the prices which is (perhaps) I(2), which is consistent with the I(1) nature of relative prices. Why should economic time-series be I(1)? No explanation is offered. Is this because the fundamental relationships are in terms of changes rather than levels? Is it because of the I(1) nature of exogenous entities like population or the accumulation of knowledge? Or are our data taken from a time-series with very large wavelengths? In the latter case the I(1) nature is just an optical illusion. For someone educated in a deductive approach to applied econometrics, merely taking the I(1) nature of the time-series as a matter of fact is too inductive. One lacks a theoretical justification.

Another source of worry is the rejection of the homogeneity of demand, i.e. the property that demand in physical terms does not change if income in money terms and the prices change by the same (positive) factor. The rejection of the homogeneity postulate is not unique for the present exercise. The homogeneity property of demand derives from the invariance of the budget set for equiproportional changes in income and prices because it is defined in the y/p space. Invariance is almost a tautology. Its rejection is puzzling. Is it an optical illusion, i.e. are the test statistics too easily rejecting? Is it a consequence of incomplete specification? Otherwise said, is it the econometrics that is wrong or is it the economics that is incorrect? Perhaps a microeconomic experiment might shed some light on this dilemma.

A final remark. The authors have done a fine job which does justice to the high quality of the original paper by Tobin.

REPLY BY D. DE CROMBRUGGHE, F. C. PALM AND J.-P. URBAIN

First of all, we want to thank the discussants for their thoughtful comments on the initial and the current version of our paper. The comments on the previous version allowed us to clarify a number of issues and to reduce the length of the paper by focusing it more on features which were found to be of importance by the discussants and which differentiate our paper from those of other teams. We agree with many comments made by the discussants. Issues of disagreement and questions raised in the discussion will be addressed in this reply.

We appreciate the precision added to our results by Ken Wallis' extensive comparative analyses which confirm our conclusion that the equality of income elasticities across USA surveys has to be rejected at any sensible level of significance.

On the question of heteroscedasticity, however, we continue to believe that correcting for group size adds precision to the results and can be motivated on both theoretical and empirical grounds. A priori, one expects that weighted least squares (WLS) correcting for group size accounts for heteroscedasticity arising from the use of group averages. Empirically, this correction leads to the expected reduction in heteroscedasticity as Figure R1 illustrates. Figure R1 is the plot to which Ken Wallis refers in his comment. It exhibits the WLS residuals for the 1941 USA budget survey, unweighted as well as weighted. The series are plotted in the order in which they were provided by MM, that is, first by increasing household size and second by increasing income class. The bands in the graph R1 correspond to ±1 standard error of regression (SER). The graph of the unweighted residuals shows, in particular, two very conspicuous outliers (about five SERs), which are precisely those that bothered Izan (1980) so much. When weighted these 'outliers' are much less conspicuous and only one attains twice the value of the SER. It is also useful to point out that the White test statistic for heteroscedasticity and the Bera-Jarque test statistic for normality are not significantly different from zero when based on WLS, whereas based on OLS both statistics allow but for one conclusion, i.e. to reject the model.

In the later surveys, WLS also seems to alleviate heteroscedasticity somewhat. Although homoscedasticity is rejected (and for BS50 normality too), this rejection is less extreme

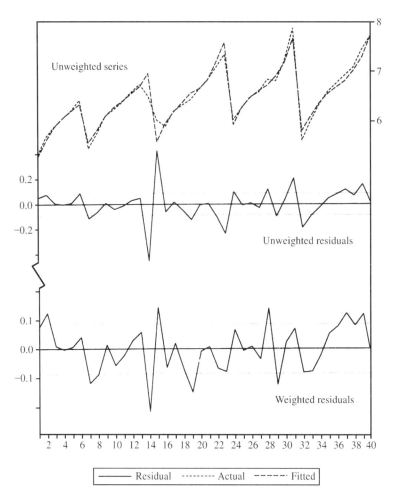

Figure R1. USA 1941 budget survey. Actual, fitted and residual series calculated by WLS (MM's corrected and extended BS41 data, cf. Table 1)

than with OLS. Recall that the numbers of households sampled were not generally available but approximated.

The White statistics reported by Wallis differ from ours for computational reasons. Wallis included respectively five and six regressors in the auxiliary regressions while we include all thirteen non-collinear regressors, squares and cross-products (only *CLASS*1 could not be squared). There is one more source of discrepancy: we have one observation less than Wallis in BS60 (58 rather than 59), because we treat the negative income figure as a missing value.

Mike McAleer's impression of an abundant use of dummy variables possibly originates in our extensive account (in the spirit of the experiment) of dummies used throughout the many analyses needed to check the appropriateness of our model. We entirely agree with him that a thorough analysis of the consumption behaviour of households possibly facing liquidity and other constraints requires data which are not readily available in national income accounts or consumer surveys. While we find his suggestion appealing and worthwhile to pursue in order to better understand consumer behaviour, we would like to point out that we had a much more modest extension of the model in mind, namely to investigate to what extent a dynamic version of the model would explain some of the outliers. It is a stylized fact in budget surveys that 'survey data often show households, particularly poor households, spending more than they earn. [....] Such an effect is predicted by random measurement error; the slope of the regression function of consumption on mismeasured income is biased towards zero, generating apparent dissaving at low incomes, and apparent saving at high incomes.' (Deaton (1992, pp. 138–139)). It would be worthwhile to study these issues in a more thorough way, going beyond the use of dummy variables for some income classes.

In response to Anton Barten's concern about the I(1)-ness of the variables expressed in real terms we emphasize that we carried out detailed statistical and graphical analyses of the time-series. These analyses support the hypothesis that the variables expressed in real terms have a unit root. On theoretical grounds, the I(1) property follows from some present-value and inter-temporal optimization models. For instance, for a utility function with constant absolute risk aversion parameter under normality and income uncertainty, consumption follows a random walk with drift parameter. Similarly, as shown by Hall (1978), if the interest rate is constant and equal to the discount rate, consumption follows a martingale. Deaton (1992) discusses several models of consumption involving the martingale property.

Also, the literature (see e.g. Banerjee *et al.* (1993, p. 96)) lends support to the view that in the presence of some doubts between the appropriateness of the (sharp) unit root or the near-unit root assumption, asymptotics relying on the unit-root hypothesis provide better guidance than the standard asymptotics for stationary (near-unit root) processes. The problem of whether or not to rely on the assumption of I(1)-ness may be circumvented by adopting statistical methods that do not require an accurate classification of the variables in the model into I(1) and I(0) variables (see e.g. Phillips (1995), among others).

Finally, we share Anton Barten's concern about the rejection of the price homogeneity of demand. We do not have a good explanation that goes beyond the reasons for this finding mentioned in the many studies that lead to the same puzzling conclusion. We agree with Barten that a microeconomic experiment might shed some light on this dilemma. Price homogeneity seems to be an issue that deserves more attention than it presently gets. For the time-series data, the aggregation issue might deserve further attention in this respect too.

ADDITIONAL REFERENCES

Banerjee, A., J. J. Dolado, J. W. Galbraith and D. F. Hendry (1993), *Co-Integration, Error Correction, and the Econometric Analysis of Non-Stationary Data*, Oxford University Press, Oxford.
Deaton, A. S. (1992), *Understanding Consumption*, Clarendon Press, Oxford.
Hall, R. (1978), 'Stochastic implications of the life cycle permanent income hypothesis: Theory and evidence', *Journal of Political Economy*, **86**, 971–87.
Phillips, P. C. B. (1995), 'Fully modified least squares and vector autoregression', *Econometrica*, **63**, 1023–78.

CHAPTER 9

THE DYNAMICS AND STATICS OF FOOD CONSUMPTION AND WELFARE: TOBIN REVISITED

RUNE HÖGLUND, MARKUS JÄNTTI, JOHAN KNIF, LEIF NORDBERG AND GUNNAR ROSENQVIST

1. INTRODUCTION

In his classic paper 'A Statistical Demand Function for Food in the USA' published in 1950, James Tobin estimated an aggregate demand function for food using both family-budget and time-series data. The main methodological novelty was the idea of combining information from household budget surveys and national accounts in the same analysis. The pooling technique used by Tobin has since been discussed in Chetty (1968) and Maddala (1971). Also, Izan (1980) reanalyzed Tobin's data, paying special attention to the effects of possible outliers among the observations and autocorrelations in the residuals. However, all these studies are based on the same model for family food demand.

Although Tobin fully realized the necessity of using models allowing lag-effects he, as most econometricians at that time, seems to have been largely unaware of the problems with modelling dynamic relationships between non-stationary time series. In fact, he clarified most of the difficulties by assuming that the change in geometric mean income had been the same in all income classes. Today, econometricians, due to the work of, among others, David Hendry and his colleagues, know that one should be very careful in the specification and estimation of models for non-stationary variables. Thus, we will start the analysis with a discussion of the specification and estimation of vector-autoregressive distributive-lag models. In Section 3, we present the empirical results. The forecasts of food consumption in the Netherlands are in Section 4. We round up with a summary and some general conclusions in Section 5.

2. CONSUMPTION AND FOOD DEMAND FUNCTIONS

The modelling of consumption behaviour is one of the most intensively researched topics in both macro- and micro-econometrics. There has also been a lot of discussion about why one often gets very different estimates of, e.g. price and income elasticities from time-series and cross-section data (see, e.g. Spanos, 1989). However, despite the extensive theoretical and empirical research in this area, we still seem to lack a firm theoretical basis for the specification of consumption functions or systems of consumption functions. Most researchers today seem to agree that much more attention should be payed to the dynamic features of the interplay between income, consumption and price streams than has usually been the case (for an excellent review of recent research on consumption and

Methodology and Tacit Knowledge: Two Experiments in Econometrics
Jan R. Magnus and Mary S. Morgan © 1999 John Wiley & Sons Ltd

saving see Deaton, 1992). A clear distinction between short and long-term effects is called for in modelling and estimation. Unfortunately, standard consumer theory does not tell us much about the dynamics of consumption processes. For example, economic theory offers no hypothesis about how long it will take before consumption has fully reacted to a change in the income level. Thus, when specifying models for empirical analyses, we are largely dependent on *ad hoc* considerations and statistical criteria. Also, our modelling will be largely data-driven as we try to develop a model that fits the data. On the other hand, with access to data from two countries, we have an opportunity to analyze the stability of the model.

Another much discussed question in empirical econometrics is the relationship between 'micro' and 'macro' models, e.g. the aggregation problem. It is obvious that if the consumers can be split into groups using different decision rules, e.g. on how much to spend on food consumption, we will easily run into great difficulties in combining results from independent micro and macro sources (Hall and Mishkin, 1982). At least we ought to have some information about possible changes in the relative sizes of the groups. What we really need for more comprehensive studies of consumer behaviour is access to sufficiently large panel data sets. Further problems are created if the decision rules are changing during the observation period. Thus, in the empirical analysis, it is also important to pay attention to the stability of the coefficients.

We will start the analysis on the macro level. The principal reason for this is that, as we are mainly interested in the dynamics of food consumption, we need time-series data, which in this case means that we have to stick to the aggregated series. However, we are painfully aware of all the problems with interpreting the macro-model parameters in a situation where we may have considerable heterogeneity in consumer behaviour. Also, as we intend to use quite long time series, the assumption of constant parameters seems rather dubious. At least we would have liked access to data making it possible to check the stability of the model for changes in the demographic structure of the population and in the income distribution.

If $\mathbf{x}_t$ denotes the vector of the means of the log of food consumption per capita C_t' and of the log of the food price index P_t during period t and $\mathbf{z}_t$ is a vector of variables which are exogenous in the sense of not being Granger-caused by $\mathbf{x}_t$, let us assume that

$$\mathbf{B}_0\mathbf{x}_t + \mathbf{B}_1\mathbf{x}_{t-1} = \Gamma_0\mathbf{z}_t + \Gamma_1\mathbf{z}_{t-1} + \Phi\mathbf{q}_t + \mathbf{u}_t, \quad t = 1, 2, \ldots, T, \qquad 1$$

where $\mathbf{q}_t$ represents a set of deterministic variables (constants, dummies, etc.), $\mathbf{B}_0$, $\mathbf{B}_1$, Γ_0, Γ_1 and Φ are matrices of model coefficients, and $\mathbf{u}_t \sim \text{IN}(0, \Sigma)$. To make the model complete we also assume that the exogenous variables are I(1) variables.

We could, of course, include more 'lags' in the model, but this model is already fairly general. The model is basically the same as used by Tobin. However, embedded in the model are also many variants of models based on the life cycle or on the permanent income hypothesis. In the empirical analysis we will use as exogenous variables the logs of per capita disposable income Y_t', non-food price Q_t and mean household size N_t. Thus $\mathbf{B}_0$ and $\mathbf{B}_1$ are matrices of dimension 2×2 and Γ_0 and Γ_1 of dimension 2×3. Like Tobin we searched for ways of reducing the simultaneity in the model and ended up with specifying $\mathbf{B}_0$ and $\mathbf{B}_1$ as lower-triangular (see, e.g. Hendry, 1995, pp. 333–335). The assumption that the system is recursive is obviously questionable, but testing for Granger causality did not produce convincing evidence against it. In fact we also used the full model, but the estimates of income elasticity did not change significantly.

We further assume that the system is stable (see Davidson and Hall, 1991) guaranteeing that the endogenous variables also follow an I(1) process and that $\mathbf{x}_t$ and $\mathbf{z}_t$ completely cointegrate. Then, as shown, e.g. by Davidson and Hall (1991), the model can be reparametrized into the following 'vector equilibrium correction' form (VECM):

$$\mathbf{B}_0\Delta\mathbf{x}_t = \Gamma_0\Delta\mathbf{z}_t - \mathbf{H}(\mathbf{x}_{t-1} - \Psi\mathbf{z}_{t-1} - \Phi^*\mathbf{q}_t) + \mathbf{u}_t, \qquad\qquad 2$$

where $\mathbf{H} = \mathbf{B}_0 + \mathbf{B}_1$ is lower triangular, $\Psi = \mathbf{H}^{-1}(\Gamma_0 + \Gamma_1)$, and $\Phi^* = \mathbf{H}^{-1}\Phi$. This reparametrization of the basic model makes it possible to separate the short-run and long-run effects from each other. We also note that under the assumptions stated above, all the stochastic variables in (2) are I(0) allowing us to use standard techniques to estimate the parameters in the model. As pointed out by, e.g Hendry (1995), the VECM parametrization also has several other advantages when compared with the basic specification. One major advantage is that the last period's deviations from the equilibrium values of the endogenous variables can often be assumed to be only moderately correlated with the current changes in the levels of the variables, making the estimation and interpretation of the parameters easier. Of course, before applying the model described above to real data, it is appropriate to first test the model assumptions.

Our system model consists of two equations, one for food consumption and one for food price. Writing these out explicitly (in the ECM parametrization) we get

Food Consumption Model:

$$\Delta C_t' = \gamma_{0,11}\Delta Y_t' + \gamma_{0,12}\Delta Q_t + \gamma_{0,13}\Delta N_t - \eta_{11}ECC_{t-1} + u_{1,t}, \qquad\qquad 3$$

Food Price Model:

$$\Delta P_t = -\beta_{0,21}\Delta C_t' + \gamma_{0,21}\Delta Y_t' + \gamma_{0,22}\Delta Q_t + \gamma_{0,23}\Delta N_t - \eta_{21}ECC_{t-1} - \eta_{22}ECP_{t-1} + u_{2,t}. \quad 4$$

Here, $\Delta C_t'$ denotes the change in the log of food consumption per capita and $\Delta Y_t'$ the change in the log of disposable income per capita. For the equilibrium correction terms ECC_{t-1} and ECP_{t-1} we have the expressions

$$ECC_{t-1} = C_{t-1}' - \psi_{11}Y_{t-1}' - \psi_{12}Q_{t-1} - \psi_{13}N_{t-1} - \phi_1^*,$$

and

$$ECP_{t-1} = P_{t-1} - \psi_{21}Y_{t-1}' - \psi_{22}Q_{t-1} - \psi_{23}N_{t-1} - \phi_2^*,$$

assuming that the deterministic components in the model are constants (ϕ_1^* and ϕ_2^*).

We still seem to know very little about the relationship between 'micro' and 'macro' VAR- and VEC-models. Also, the data available for this study does not allow us to test for consumer heterogeneity or for other problems caused by the behaviour of individual consumers (e.g. nonlinearities). Thus we have chosen the 'representative consumer' approach and assume that the same log-linear model that explains food consumption on the macro level, can also be applied to individual households. The price equation is, of course, relevant only on the macro level.

The cross-section budget surveys allow specification of models only in levels, not in differences. The question then arises how we can use data from budget surveys within the framework of Equations (3) and (4). To shed some light on this, let $c_{i,t}'$, $y_{i,t}'$ and $n_{i,t}$ denote the logs of food consumption per capita, disposable income per capita and household size of household i in year t respectively, and let us assume that model (1) applies to individual households as well. Then,

$$c'_{i,t} = -\beta_{1,11} c'_{i,t-1} + \gamma_{0,1} \mathbf{z}_{i,t} + \gamma_{1,1} \mathbf{z}_{i,t-1} + \phi_1 + u_{i,t} \quad i = 1, 2, \ldots, N, \ t = 1, 2, \ldots, T, \quad 5$$

where $\gamma_{0,1}$ and $\gamma_{1,1}$ denote the first rows in Γ_0 and Γ_1 respectively and ϕ_1 is a constant. Using the fact that $c'_{i,t} = c'_{i,t-1} + \Delta c'_{i,t}$ and $\mathbf{z}_{i,t} = \mathbf{z}_{i,t-1} + \Delta \mathbf{z}_{i,t}$, we see from model (5) that

$$c'_{i,t} = \psi_1 \mathbf{z}_{i,t} + \phi_1^{**} + \delta \beta_{1,11} \Delta c'_{i,t} - \delta \gamma_{1,1} \Delta \mathbf{z}_{i,t} + \delta u_{i,t}, \quad 6$$

where ψ_1 denotes the first row in ψ, ϕ_1^{**} is a constant, and $\delta = (1 + \beta_{1,11})^{-1}$, assuming that $\beta_{1,11} \neq -1$. Thus, only a part of the systematic variation in the food consumption among the households at a certain time is explainable by the variation in disposable income during the same time period and the household size. If we have a cross-section model with the contemporaneous level values of the exogenous variables as regressors and estimate the parameters by OLS techniques, we may get biased estimates of the parameters due to the correlation between the regressors and the 'error' term. On the other hand, assuming that the correlation between the 'levels' and 'the changes' is negligable, we get asymptotically unbiased estimates of the long-term income and household size elasticities by fitting the model

$$c'_{i,t} = \alpha + \psi_{11} y'_{i,t} + \psi_{13} n_{i,t} + u_{i,t} \quad 6'$$

to the cross-sectional data.

To sum up, cross-sectional data is of interest mainly for the purpose of estimating the parameters in the ECM-term of the dynamic model. It should, however, be stressed that the possibility to use also cross-section data to estimate the long-term effects critically depends on what we assume about the dynamics of the consumption processes. We can get seriously biased estimates if the upper part of the income distribution is 'overcrowded' with households which have recently experienced high increases in their incomes, or if the opposite situation occurs in the bottom half of the income distribution.

Of the many problems connected with the assumption that the same model that works for individual households can also be used on the macro-level (see, e.g. Lewbell, 1992), one is that we know only the logs of the means and not the means of the logs of the variables concerned. Tobin (1950) gives one example of a situation where exactly the same model that is valid for individual households also works on the aggregated level. Another way out of this dilemma is to assume that the (micro) variables concerned are log-normally distributed. Namely, if v_t is lognormally distributed then

$$\log E(v_t) = E(\log(v_t)) + \text{Var}(\log(v_t))/2, \quad 7$$

which implies that at least for large samples the difference between $\log \bar{v}_t$ and $\overline{\log v_t}$ is almost constant, if we assume that the variance of the distribution does not change.

3. EMPIRICAL ANALYSIS

The data[1] used in order to estimate[2] the vector equilibrium model for the USA, is the revised Tobin data covering the years 1924 to 1976, in all 53 usable time-series

---

[1] The USA data are compiled from various US Government publications (see organizers' data chapters for details). We thank Statistics Netherlands for use of the Dutch data.

[2] For the estimation we have used the program packages LIMDEP and RATS, and for the forecasts SHAZAM.

observations. Hence, the chosen series for the USA starts after the confusing period following the First World War. If we want to include also the average household size, complete time-series data is available for the Netherlands only for the years 1960 to 1988, amounting to 29 observations. For the Netherlands we construct a non-food price index as a weighted average of the available non-food price indices, $P22, \ldots, P66$, using the corresponding expenditure variables, $V22, \ldots, V66$, as weights. An application of standard unit root and cointegration tests (e.g. Holden and Perman, 1994, Banerjee et al., 1993) suggests that the series are random walks and cointegrated.

Regarding the budget surveys, we restrain from using the 1965 survey for the Netherlands, because the central income variable in that survey is only a dichotomy. That leaves us with four budget surveys for the USA and two for the Netherlands.

Table I reports the results of an Engle-Granger (1987) two-step estimation of the recursive VECM-system. The corresponding estimates of the long-run relations are given in columns 2, 3, 5 and 6 of Table II. In Table I, we report results for both a 'full' system as well as for a restricted version where the most insignificant variables have been dropped. In the latter case, the standard errors of estimated coefficients are reduced, although the estimated coefficients of the main variables are not altered in any serious degree. All the long-run relations are significant, with the exception of the estimated long-term consumption relation in the price equations, especially in the price equation for the Netherlands.

Table I. Engle-Granger type estimates of the recursive VECM-system for the US and the Netherlands

Variable	USA Full system		USA Restricted system		The Netherlands Full system		The Netherlands Restricted system	
Dependent	$\Delta C'_t$	ΔP_t	$\Delta C'_t$	ΔP_t	$\Delta C'_t$	ΔP_t	$\Delta C'_t$	ΔP_t
Intercept	0.001	−0.006	0.002	−0.008	0.0011	−0.013	−0.000	−0.014
	(0.003)	(0.007)	(0.002)	(0.005)	(0.014)	(0.008)	(0.008)	(0.007)
$\Delta C'_t$		−0.85		−0.87		0.44		0.42
		(0.37)		(0.36)		(0.12)		(0.083)
$\Delta Y'_t$	0.09	0.51	0.10	0.51	0.73	−0.028	0.77	
	(0.03)	(0.08)	(0.03)	(0.08)	(0.16)	(0.13)	(0.097)	
ΔQ_t	−0.11	0.76	−0.11	0.76	0.043	0.30		0.28
	(0.07)	(0.18)	(0.07)	(0.18)	(0.17)	(0.11)		(0.091)
ΔN_t	−0.15	0.53			0.13	−1.04		−1.07
	(0.29)	(0.72)			(0.91)	(0.56)		(0.53)
ECC_{t-1}	−0.46	0.71	−0.45	0.68	−0.67	0.18	−0.70	0.16
	(0.12)	(0.36)	(0.12)	(0.35)	(0.23)	(0.16)	(0.19)	(0.13)
ECP_{t-1}		−0.14		−0.14		−0.47		−0.47
		(0.07)		(0.07)		(0.21)		(0.20)
Observations	53	53	53	63	28	28	28	28
Adj. R^2	0.28	0.78	0.29	0.78	0.67	0.86	0.70	0.86
F-value	6.1	32.0	8.1	38.7	14.7	27.7	31.9	34.8
Durbin-Watson	1.84	1.81	1.86	1.81	1.82	1.70	1.82	1.71
Ljung-Box Q(15-0)	14.5	11.0	15.1	11.5	—	—	—	—

$\Delta C'_t = \text{Dlog}(PCFC)$, $\Delta P_t = \text{Dlog}(FP)$, $\Delta Y'_t = \text{Dlog}(PCY)$, $\Delta Q_t = \text{Dlog}(NFP)$, $\Delta N_t = \text{Dlog}(POP/NOH)$ for USA. $\Delta C'_t = \text{Dlog}(V11/POP)$, $\Delta P_t = \text{Dlog}(P11)$, $\Delta Y'_t = \text{Dlog}(AGGY/POP)$, $\Delta Q_t = \text{Dlog}(\text{non-food price index})$, $\Delta N_t = \text{Dlog}(POP/NOH)$ for the Netherlands. We have used time-series information for the long-run coefficients of family income and size in the ECC and ECP variables. Standard errors in parentheses. (The corresponding estimates of the long-run relations are presented in Table II.)

Table II. Pooled cross-section and time-series regressions for estimating long-run relations

	USA			The Netherlands		
	1.	2.	3.	4.	5.	6.
Data	cross	time	time	cross	time	time
Dependent	c_i'	C_t'	P_t	c_i'	C_t'	P_t
Intercept	1.01	4.39	−1.76	4.05	−0.22	2.97
	(0.05)	(0.16)	(0.75)	(0.13)	(0.55)	(0.43)
Income per	0.52	0.15	0.38	0.41	0.84	0.18
capita; Y_t', y_t'	(0.01)	(0.02)	(0.09)	(0.013)	(0.058)	(0.045)
Household size	−0.14	−0.12	0.46	−0.12	−0.12	−0.22
N_t, n_t	(0.02)	(0.08)	(0.255)	(0.013)	(0.21)	(0.16)
Q_i		−0.19	0.61		−0.13	0.41
		(0.03)	(0.15)		(0.081)	(0.063)
Observations	221	54	54	4802	29	29
Adj. R^2	0.91	0.94	0.98	0.32	0.999	0.999
F-value	1142.1	277.4	701.4	1114.1	6866.9	6974.2

$C_t' = \log(PCFC)$, $P_t = \log(FP)$, $Y_t' = \log(PCY)$, $Q_t = \log(NFP)$, $N_t = \log(POP/NOH)$ for USA time series data;
$c_{ti}' = \log(FOODCON/AHSIZE)$, $y_{ti}' = \log(HINC/AHSIZE)$, $n_{ti} = \log(AHSIZE)$ for USA cross-sectional data;
$C_t' = \log(V11/POP)$, $P_t = \log(P11)$, $Y_t' = \log(AGGY/POP)$, $Q_t = \log(\text{non-food price index})$, $N_t = \log(POP/NOH)$ for the Netherlands' time-series data; and
$c_{ti}' = \log(V11/HSIZE)$, $y_{ti}' = \log(HINC/HSIZE)$, $n_{ti} = \log(HSIZE)$ for the Netherlands' cross-section data. All variables are logs base 10. Standard errors are in parentheses.

The short and long-term estimates of the income elasticity are 0.09 and 0.15 for the USA, and 0.73 and 0.84 for the Netherlands. Based on these figures, most of the effect of a change in income on food consumption takes place during the first year; the long-term effect does not add very much to the short-term effect. Compared to previous studies for these two as well as for other countries, the estimated income elasticities in Table I seem rather low for the USA and correspondingly rather high for the Netherlands.

Surprisingly, the changes in the log of non-food prices and the log of average family size have, in some cases, opposite signs for the USA and the Netherlands; these coefficients are, however, not significant. Moreover, the change in the log of the average family size is obviously very close to a constant and is accordingly not significant in any of the regressions. The effect of incorporating non-food prices in the equations as a proxy for inflation does not change the coefficients in the table in any significant way; for the USA the changes are not even seen in the two decimals reported for the coefficients in the table.

The length of the US series makes diagnostic testing possible. The estimated models in Table I all pass a battery of diagnostic tests, checking for residual autocorrelation, heteroscedastcity with time and with the dependent variable as well as with the regressors. No ARCH-effect was found in the residuals. Furthermore, parameter stability was confirmed using a Chow-type test as well as an Engle-Watson-type test for stationary AR variability in the coefficients. Incorporating the period before 1924 would alter the results of the parameter stability tests, for the USA series. Finally, the residuals of the equations were found to be stationary and cross-uncorrelated.

As an experiment, we also estimated the long-run relations from pooled cross-sections. This did not alter the main results. We also estimated the whole model using straight-forward OLS in one step. Finally, a two-step experiment was performed utilizing for the

USA the long-run relations estimated from Dutch times-series data, and vice versa. This last mentioned attempt to evaluate the possibility to use long-run equilibrium information from one country in estimation of the VECM model for the other country, showed somewhat smaller degrees of determination, but in many respects similar results. The detailed results of these alternative estimation experiments were presented in our original report and are available from the authors on request. Although stationarity conditions are violated in some of these experiments, it is interesting to see that a certain degree of consistency appears in the results from the various estimations. Table III presents a summary of estimated income elasticities obtained by various estimation procedures.

We also estimated the same model as in Table I for the time period used by Tobin for his original data set as well as for the revised US data. In both cases the results were close to those for the US in Table I, differing, however, somewhat from the original estimates obtained by Tobin. With our model the long-run income elasticity estimates are around 0.15 for Tobin's time period, whereas Tobin himself produced an estimate of 0.27 from his time-series data and an estimate of 0.56 from the cross-section data. The latter figure is close to what we obtain for the US cross section in Table II (0.52).

Table II reports long-run relationships for the consumption function estimated from time-series data (the *ECC* relation referred to in Table I) as well as from pooled cross-sections. For both countries the difference between cross-section (e.g. 0.52 for USA) and time-series (0.15 for USA) estimates of the income elasticity of food demand is striking. For both countries the model differs significantly over the cross sections. We experimented however, with a pooling of the cross-sections for mainly two reasons. First, there was no clear trend found to be modelled over the different cross-sections. Secondly, in the time-series analysis we allow for dynamics within the VECM-framework but assume constancy of the coefficients in the dynamic structure. As price information on household level is not available for the cross-sections, the corresponding *ECP* equation is estimated from time-series data only. Table II also offers interesting information about the limits of what would have been obtained if for each country the cross-section and the time-series regressions had been pooled with a dominating larger weight given to either of the two data sets. Of course, the pooling of cross sections and time series is debatable. Nevertheless, we experimented with such pooling as well as with the utilization of long-run relationships

Table III. Estimated income elasticities obtained by various procedures

	USA		The Netherlands	
Procedure	Long-run coefficient	Short-run coefficient	Long-run coefficient	Short-run coefficient
Engle-Granger two-step estimation	0.15	0.09/0.10	0.84	0.73/0.77
Two-step estimation with long-run relations for consumption estimated from pooled cross sections and long-run relations for prices from time series	0.52	0.11	0.41	0.47
One-step OLS	0.18/0.19	0.09	0.61	0.61/0.73
Two-step estimation utilizing long-run relations from the other countries time-series data	0.41	0.10	0.52	0.33

estimated from one country in the error correction models for the other country. Over various data combinations, however, our results show clear consistency, giving some promise to the potential of pooling.

4. FORECASTING OF FOOD CONSUMPTION IN THE NETHERLANDS 1989–2000

The Dutch series for food consumption is a pretty smooth curve, suggesting that maybe a trend curve could be used to predict future consumption. However, even though we may get a good fit to the series in the estimation period, the forecasts are more or less peculiar. Other simple univariate techniques do not seem to be appropriate either. An alternative could be a changing growth model, and, indeed, a model with a decreasing increase, seems a plausible simple model for the end-period of the series. However we are not going to dwell on this issue here, because our intention is to use the models discussed in the previous sections also in forecasting. Let us just note that the simple model

$$\Delta C'_t = 0.85 \Delta C'_{t-1} \qquad\qquad 8$$

gives a forecast for year 2000 for the consumption of food per capita of 4.34 ($= 4340$ guilders per person), with a starting value in 1988 of 3.97. According to the analysis in previous sections, food consumption can be modelled with an equilibrium correction model. For forecasting we write the model in a level formulation. Generally, if the estimated model is of the form

$$\Delta C'_t = \hat{\alpha}_0 + \hat{\alpha}_1 \Delta Y'_t + \hat{\alpha}_2 \Delta P_t + \hat{\beta}(C'_t - \hat{\delta}_1 Y'_{t-1} - \hat{\delta}_2 P_{t-1}), \qquad 9$$

where the last component on the right hand side is the equilibrium correction term, it can be written as

$$C'_t = \hat{\alpha}_0 + (1 + \hat{\beta})C'_{t-1} + \hat{\alpha}_1 Y'_t - (\hat{\alpha}_1 + \hat{\beta}\hat{\delta}_1)Y'_{t-1} + \hat{\alpha}_2 P_t - (\hat{\alpha}_2 + \hat{\beta}\hat{\delta}_2)P_{t-1}. \qquad 10$$

This model is then used for forecasting. In order to get interval forecasts, taking account of the parameter uncertainty, we compute these by Monte Carlo simulations. To produce forecasts for consumption we have to forecast the values of the regressor variables as well. One possibility would be to see what happens under different more or less realistic scenarios for the evolution of the regressors. Here we illustrate what happens when we use the random walk assumption (compare Section 3), and when we use an AR(1) model of the same kind as above for consumption itself for some of the regressors. The forecasting model for food consumption in the Netherlands is based on the second procedure in Table III. The log-consumption per capita can be expressed in levels as

$$C'_t = -0.8875 + 0.55C'_{t-1} + 0.47Y'_t - 0.2875Y_{t-1} + 0.46Q_t - 0.31Q_{t-1} - 0.054N_{t-1}. \quad 11$$

The first alternative specifications for the input variables, Y'_t, Q_t and N_t are random walk models of the form

$$\Delta y_t = \alpha + \varepsilon_t. \qquad\qquad 12$$

The estimated equations, based on observations from 1960 onwards, are:

$$\begin{array}{ccc} \Delta Y'_t = 0.076889, & \Delta Q_t = 0.060240, & \Delta N_t = -0.013039. \\ (0.007333) & (0.006494) & (0.0009298) \end{array} \qquad 13$$

Table IV. Point forecasts and 95% forecast intervals for the consumption of food per capita in the Netherlands, 1989–2000.

Year	1989	1990	1991	1992	1993	1994	1995	1996	1997	1998	1999	2000
Upper	3.93	3.94	3.96	3.98	4.02	4.06	4.10	4.15	4.20	4.25	4.31	4.37
Point	3.93	3.92	3.93	3.95	3.97	3.99	4.01	4.03	4.06	4.08	4.10	4.13
Lower	3.92	3.92	3.91	3.91	3.92	3.92	3.92	3.92	3.92	3.91	3.91	3.90

The consumption of food for capita is given by $V11/POP$, in thousands of guilders per person, nominal values.

The point forecast, using this specification, for year 2000 is 7.39. This seems an unrealistic result as it would imply an 86% increase in the food consumption per capita. The second alternative specification for the input variables are simple AR(1) models of the form

$$\Delta y_t = \hat{\beta} \Delta y_{t-1}. \qquad\qquad 15$$

The AR(1) models used are:

$$\Delta Y'_t = 0.90 \Delta Y'_{t-1}, \qquad \Delta Q_t = 0.92 \Delta Q_{t-1}, \qquad\qquad 16$$

while for the household size we use the same random walk model as above.

Forecasts produced with this specification, which is the one we prefer, are summarized in Table IV. The forecast intervals are based on 1000 Monte Carlo simulations for each forecast period.

5.   CONCLUSIONS

We have found the task to combine information from static and dynamic data both intriguing and exciting. In the spirit of Tobin, we have tried to use all the available information and the best econometric methods, paying special attention to the dynamic features of consumption processes. We have emphasized the difficulties of combining cross sections and time series. Obviously, we have left some open ends, especially as the empirical results are far from satisfactory in all cases. We have deliberately chosen to make a coherent analysis as far as possible within a unified methodology, answering in some cases the tasks formulated by the organizers only implicitly. All in all, we think that our analyses clearly show that in order to formulate and estimate realistic models of consumer behaviour we need access to large panel data sets.

APPENDIX: LOGBOOK

The group started with a critical appraisal of the original Tobin paper and previously published comments on it. The following topics were identified as problematic and open for improvements: the specification of the demand function; the modelling of the dynamics; the treatment of the aggregation problem; and the estimation strategy.

Several researchers have stressed the importance of decomposing the income concept and of allowing for consumer heterogeneity. However, in order to fully implement these ideas in empirical studies, one obviously needs access to panel data or fairly detailed time-series data, which was not the case in this study. A lot of time was used to discuss the philosophy behind data pooling, the correct weighting of the observations and the use of survey and country 'dummies'. Many experiments with differents methods for pooling the cross sections were made. As regards incorporating both short-run and long-run aspects in the specification of the demand functions, the Equilibrium Corrections Model specification (ECM) seemed to be the best choice. Also, empiricial analyses seemed to support the usefulness of this specification.

The aggregation problem was discussed repeatedly and even if the 'representative consumer approach' looked questionable, especially in the ligth of several recent analyses based on panel data, the data did not allow other, preferable, approaches. Some indicators of changes in the demographic structure of the population would have been helpful, but information of this kind was not included in the data set.

The group agreed on using an ECM-type model not only as the base for the estimation of the price and income elasticities, but also as the starting point for solving the forecasting task. Experiments with varying the observation periods were made as well.

The stability of the parameters seemed questionable, especially as the estimate for the long-term income elasticity seemed to change significantly from cross section to cross section. In fact, the whole task seemed a little outdated, since many of the problems that the group encountered were problems that could have been solved if only we would have had access to panel data, which is usually the case today.

REFERENCES

Banerjee, A., J. Dolado, J. W. Galbraith and D. F. Hendry (1993), *Co-integration, Error Correction, and the Econometric Analysis of Non-Stationary Data*, Oxford University Press, Oxford.

Berg, L. (1994), 'Household savings and debts: the experience of the nordic countries', *Oxford Review of Economic Policy*, **10**, 42–53.

Campbell, J. Y. and N. G. Mankiw (1991), 'The response of consumption to income. A cross-country investigation', *European Economic Review*, **35**, 723–767.

Chetty, V. K. (1968), 'Pooling of time series and cross section data', *Econometrica*, **36**, 279–290.

Davidson, J. E. H. and S. Hall (1991), 'Cointegration in recursive systems, *Economic Journal*, **101**, 239–251.

Deaton, A. (1992), *Understanding Consumption*, Clarendon Press, Oxford.

Engle, R. F. and C. W. J. Granger (1987), 'Co-integration and error correction: representation, estimation, and testing', *Econometrica*, **55**, 251–76.

Ericsson, N. R. and D. F. Hendry (1985), 'Conditional Econometric Modeling: an application to new house prices in the United Kingdom', in: A. C. Atkinson and S. E. Fienberg (eds), *A Celebration of Statistics. The ISI Centenary Volume*, Springer-Verlag, New York.

Hall, R. E. and F. S. Mishkin (1982), 'The sensitivity of consumption to transitory income: estimates from panel data on households', *Econometrica*, **50**, 461–481.

Hendry, D. F. (1995), *Dynamic Econometrics*, Oxford University Press, Oxford.

Holden, D. and R. Perman (1994), 'Unit roots and cointegration for the economist', in: B. B. Rao (ed.), *Cointegration for the Applied Economist*, St.Martin's Press, New York, Chapter 3.

Izan, H. Y. (1980), 'To pool or not to pool: a reexamination of Tobin's food demand problem', *Journal of Econometrics*, **13**, 391–402.

Jonsson, B. (1996), 'On how to use forecasts of a regressor when making predictions with a regression model', *Research Report*, **6**, Uppsala University, Department of Statistics, Uppsala.

Lewbell, A. (1992), 'Aggregation with log-linear models', *Review of Economic Studies*, **59**, 391–402.

Maddala, G. S. (1971), 'The likelihood approach to pooling cross-section and time-series data', *Econometrica*, **39**, 939–953.

Spanos, A. (1989), 'Early empirical findings on the consumption function, stylized facts or fiction: a retrospective view, *Oxford Economic Papers*, **41**, 150–169.

Theil, H., C.-F. Chung and J. L. Seale Jr. (1989), 'International evidence on consumption patterns', *Advances in Econometrics, Supplement 1*, JAI Press Inc, London.

Thomas, J. J. (1989), 'The early econometric history of the consumption function', *Oxford Economic Papers*, **41**, 131–149.

Tobin, J. (1950), 'A statistical demand function for food in the USA', *Journal of the Royal Statistical Society*, **113**, 113–141 [reprinted in Chapter 2, this volume].

COMMENTS BY PROFESSOR ANTON BARTEN (Catholic University of Leuven)

The authors have approached their task carefully, while keeping the paper clear and concise. They are very much aware of current time-series analysis, which they apply in a creative manner.

The special point of the authors is the combination of the time-series data and the budget-survey data. They consider the budget-survey data as specifically relevant for the estimation of the long-run income elasticity and use the cross-section estimate of that entity in the error term of their time-series model. They are aware of the possible conflict between the income elasticity as measured from a cross section and the one as implied by a time-series approach with macro data. Knowledge of (some of) the problems is no excuse for simply ignoring it. However they are in (good?) company, because to my knowledge very little work has been done on this score.

The authors are also not greatly worried about the best choice of functional form. They follow without any hesitation the example of Tobin. The very low values of the income elasticity for the United States (0.09 and 0.15) and the very high values of it for the Netherlands (0.73 and 0.84) suggest that something is wrong. A very rudimentary determination of size and rate of change can be achieved by using the relation that the income elasticity is one minus the rate of change in the budget share of food divided by the rate of change in income.

A feature of the paper which causes me some problems is the omission of the food price as explanatory or dependent variable in the food consumption model (3) and in the corresponding *ECC* term. It contrasts with the presence of the non-food price. Its omission makes the model recursive, which is fine from a purely technical point of view but which does not impress an economist educated with the quantity-price relationship as the central one of economics. At best one may consider (3) a reduced form expression, with (4) being a structural equation. Mixtures of such relations occur — e.g. in the case of LIML — but then the focus is on the structural relation, while in the paper discussed the two relations are treated symmetrically. A lagged price term would have saved the recursiveness but allowed some price effect surely in the long run.

COMMENTS BY PROFESSOR PETER SCHMIDT (Michigan State University)

This paper takes the point of view that the dynamic macro relationship is the meaningful one, and that micro data are of use only to the extent that they are helpful in estimating the macro relationship. The authors 'are mainly interested in the dynamics of food consumption' and thus focus on the time-series data. This seems to be the reverse of Tobin's view, and of the (perhaps) conventional wisdom that the micro relationship is the fundamentally meaningful one. In any case, there really is no serious analysis of the cross-sectional data. Similarly, the paper does not fundamentally deal with the question of when the micro relationship and the macro relationship are the same (the aggregation question). Assuming a 'representative consumer' is not enough; for a consistent relationship over time we also need restrictions on how the distribution of income changes (the so-called 'mean scaling' condition). There is an extensive literature on this topic, which would be worth referring to.

The time-series estimates generally do not seem to reflect current standards of good practice in light of the recent literature on cointegration. The recursive vector error correction model was estimated by the Engle-Granger two-step method, which is some-what out of date. In particular, the first step of this method, ordinary least squares applied to the long-run equilibrium relationships, is consistent but not efficient, and does not lead to asymptotically valid inference. Some other unusual procedures were also employed, such as using the cross-sectional data to estimate the long-run relationship and the time-series data to estimate the short-run dynamics. It's hard to judge how much difference this might make, but it would have been interesting to see the results from an asymptotically efficient method of estimation, such as Johansen's quasi-MLE.

The forecasting exercise is the best and most interesting part of the paper. It yields three rather different sets of forecasts. Model 1 is an AR(1) model for C', the change in per capita consumption. The AR(1) coefficient of 0.85 implies that C' is almost I(2), a possibly questionable assertion. Models 2 and 3 use the VAR implied by the VECM, with exogenous variables forecasted in a first-step. Model 2 assumes that the exogenous variables are random walks with drift, while model 3 makes them AR(1). The AR(1) coefficients given in Equation (15) certainly suggest a unit root. I suspect that the very large difference in the long-run forecasts from models 2 and 3 is not a reflection of the unit root assumption, but rather the implicit assumption of a linear deterministic trend in the exogenous variables in model 2. The authors prefer the forecasts from model 3. The basis for this preference is not made very clear, however. Despite the rules of the experiment, which forbid the use of data other than that officially provided, I would be very curious to see how these models did from the beginning of the forecast period (1989) to the present.

Since VAR's are in some sense natural for forecasting, it is perhaps too bad that a large VAR that simultaneously includes and forecasts the exogenous and endogenous variables was not considered.

*REPLY BY RUNE HÖGLUND, MARKUS JÄNTTI, JOHAN KNIF, LEIF NORDBERG
AND GUNNAR ROSENQVIST*

We want to thank professor Barten and professor Schmidt both for their general and their more technical remarks. Both assessors point out that our analysis is mainly based on the time-series data. This is of course true, especially in the current version of our report. In fact, we also made a lot of studies concerning only the cross-section data, but in comparison with Tobin's original paper and the already published comments to it, we were unable to find anything really new and worth reporting. However, the basic reason why we chose to focus on the macro data was that we, in the light of recent development in consumption theory, saw it as necessary to pay much more attention to the dynamics of consumption than had previously often been the case. We fully agree with professor Schmidt's comment that the micro relationship is the fundamentally more meaningful one, and would definitely have liked to work with panel data, as most econometricians in this area do today. As this was not possible within the rules of the game, we tried to make the best of the situation by looking for a way to combine the information about the long-run relationships in the time-series and the cross-section data with the evidence of the short-run dynamics available only from the time series.

Of course, as soon as we try to combine information on micro and macro level we run into serious aggregation problems. This was pointed out already in Modigliani and Brumberg (1954). Also Deaton (1992), which we referred to in the paper, gives a fairly comprehensive review of the basic topics in this area. We could have been much more explicit on this point, but that would have made it still more problematic to keep within the size limit of the report.

We fully agree that an application of a more sophisticated method, like Johansen's quasi-MLE, would have been of interest. However, in our setup of the analysis where we, according to the tasks specified, are trying to compare the usefulness of the different information sets available, the simple Engle-Granger two-step method is a very convenient approach.

Also, we fully accept the argument that the estimated income elasticity for the USA is surprisingly low and correspondingly surprisingly high for the Netherlands. However, using the pooled data the estimates are more in line with what is to be expected. Regarding the recursive representation, we also state in our paper that it is debatable. We further point out in the paper that testing for Granger causality did not produce convincing evidence against the recursive representation and that the residuals from the two equations were found to be cross-uncorrelated. Alternative specifications of the simultaneity did not change the income elasticities significantly. For both countries, e.g. a lagged food-price variable, as suggested by professor Barten, was clearly found to be non-significant in the consumption equation. The non-food price seems to carry the long-run dynamics of price changes.

Regarding the comments on the forecasting exercise we motivate the AR(1) coefficient for model 1 by the assumption of decreasing change in per-capita consumption. The same comment also applies for the exogenous variables forecasts used in model 3. The coefficients in all cases are near one and suggest unit roots, implying I(2) processes for the variables. We have however considered the used estimates as reasonable for the latter part of the series and we assume that this pattern could be reasonable also in the forecasting period.

The difference in the long-term forecasts between models 2 and 3 is indeed the result of the deterministic trend in the exogenous variables for model 2. The models we really chose between were 2 and 3, because we wanted to utilize the models estimated in the preceeding section. Then we simply disqualified model 2 and chose model 3. Of course we could (and should) have evaluated the forecasts on more formal grounds, for instance by withholding a few of the last observations and comparing different forecasts for these with the realizations. The comment on the large scale VAR is certainly very relevant also in this context.

Finally, both commentators have given us a lot to think about. However, we find some comfort in professor Barten's remark that we are certainly not the only ones, who still have a lot to think about in this fascinating area of micro-macro econometric research.

ADDITIONAL REFERENCE

Modigliani, F. and R. Brumberg (1954), 'Utility analysis and the consumption function: an interpretation of the cross-section data, in: *Post-Keynesian Economics*. Rutgers University Press, New Brunswick.

CHAPTER 10

TOBIN'S STUDY ON THE DEMAND OF FOOD IN THE US REVISITED: AN EXAMINATION OF THE ISSUE OF POOLING INFORMATION FROM BUDGET STUDIES AND TIME SERIES

G. S. MADDALA, SHAOWEN WU AND YONG YIN

'If you go to one doctor, you get a prescription. If you go to two doctors, you get a consultation. If you go to three doctors, you get your own cremation.'

An old Indian proverb

1. INTRODUCTION

The purpose of the present paper is to re-examine the issue of pooling information from cross-sectional budget studies with the information in time-series data. We shall confine ourselves to an analysis of the US data. First, recalling the history of the problem, Tobin (1950) used the estimate of the income elasticity of demand from a cross-sectional (CS) budget study in a time-series (TS) equation and estimated the other parameters from the time-series model. There is, of course, the issue of taking the standard error of the CS estimate of income elasticity into account. In any case, since the TS data also provide an estimate of the income elasticity, the two equations can be estimated simultaneously. Chetty (1968) and Maddala (1971) argued that the evidence on the CS and TS estimates of the income elasticity suggests that the data should not be pooled. Izan (1980) argues that no diagnostics were employed to either equation, in particular outliers in the CS data and serial correlation in the TS regression and that allowing for these factors shows that pooling the data is not invalid as argued by Chetty and Maddala.

In the following sections, we shall first examine in Section 2, the conclusions of Izan. In Section 3 we review the developments in outlier detection. Section 4 discusses problems related to time series analysis and diagnostics. Needless to say we have to omit many but a few salient points. Section 5 discusses the relationship between the CS and TS estimates. The final section presents the conclusions.

2. A RE-EXAMINATION OF IZAN'S CRITICISM

The outlier problem that Izan raised is not a big issue, but we shall come to it later. Taking outliers into account actually increases the estimate of α, the income elasticity of

Methodology and Tacit Knowledge: Two Experiments in Econometrics
Jan R. Magnus and Mary S. Morgan © 1999 John Wiley & Sons Ltd

demand. In Maddala's study, the TS estimate of α was substantially below that of the CS estimate and there was no overlap in the 95% confidence intervals of α from the TS and CS data sets. This led him to conclude that the two data sets should not be pooled (a conclusion that was also substantiated by the LR test). There is also the problem that the variables used in the CS and TS data sets are different even if they go by the same name. Section 5 discusses some other related issues.

Izan *does not* report the TS estimates (only the pooled estimates). Hence, we computed the TS estimates allowing for first order serial correlation in the errors (we found the second order serial correlation to be not significant). The TS estimate of α is now higher, but more importantly, the confidence interval is very wide and hence the confidence interval for α from the CS data lies entirely within the CI interval from the TS data. This explains why Izan came to the conclusion that pooling is not invalid. But what this says is that there is hardly any information on α in the TS data (once we take into account serial correlation in the errors). This also explains why the estimate of α from the pooled data in Izan's study was very close to the CS estimate. Specifically, the following estimates of α are obtained (standard errors in parentheses):

$$\text{CS}: \quad 0.628(0.02) \qquad \text{Pooled}: \quad 0.625(0.02).$$

These results indicate that in fact, Tobin's procedure of substituting the CS estimate of α in the TS equation is not off the mark.

When we tried to replicate Izan's results *by using Tobin's original data series,* we obtained slightly different results. For the CS equation deleting the same two outliers, we got the estimate of α as (standard errors in parentheses):

$$\text{CS}^1: \quad \text{estimate of } \alpha : 0.60(0.027),$$

whereas the TS estimate allowing for AR(1) errors was

$$\text{TS}: \quad \text{estimate of } \alpha : 0.572(0.1736).$$

For the 95% confidence intervals, we shall use the approximate $\pm 2\sigma$ intervals. We get the confidence intervals:

$$\text{CS}: \quad 0.60 \pm 0.054 \text{ or } (0.546, 0.654) \qquad \text{TS}: \quad 0.572 \pm 0.347 \text{ or } (0.225, 0.919).$$

Thus, the CS interval lies within the TS interval. We did not compute the pooled estimates.

A more relevant issue is this. When the TS equation was estimated with AR(1) errors the coefficient of $\Delta \log Y_t$ dropped to -0.09062 with SE of 0.09139. Deleting this variable gave an estimate of α as 0.4556 with SE of 0.096. Now the 95% confidence interval of α is (0.4556 ± 0.192) or $(0.2636, 0.6476)$. We did not check it but we guess that the pooled estimate of α will not be as close to the CS estimate as in Izan's study. But what this shows is that the TS estimates are more sensitive to what variables are included in the TS regression than the CS estimates are to outliers.

Tobin estimated the inverse demand function (and so did Chetty, Maddala and Izan). This is given by

$$\log P_t = b_0 + b_1(\log S_t - \alpha \log Y_t) + b_2 \Delta \log Y_t + \varepsilon_t, \qquad 1$$

---

[1] Except where explicitly stated, all computations were done using GAUSS matrix language.

where P_t is the price index of food, Y_t is per capita disposable income, S_t is per capita food consumption and ε_t is the disturbance term. The standard errors for the estimates of income elasticity α and price elasticity $1/b_1$ that one gets are asymptotic. One can get the small sample standard errors using the bootstrap method but we did not pursue this. However, we decided to try the direct form of the demand function. Therefore, the following equation was estimated:

$$\log S_t = b_0 + \alpha \log Y_t + \beta \log P_t + \gamma \Delta \log Y_t + u_t. \qquad 2$$

In this form, the income elasticity is α, and the price elasticity is β. The estimates were:

$$\log S_t = \underset{(0.073)}{3.974} + \underset{(0.0282)}{0.2346} \log Y_t - \underset{(0.0230)}{0.2168} \log P_t + \underset{(0.290)}{0.004} \Delta \log Y_t. \qquad 3$$

Dropping the variable $\Delta \log Y_t$ which is not significant, we get

$$\log S_t = \underset{(0.074)}{3.984} + \underset{(0.0217)}{0.2532} \log Y_t - \underset{(0.0230)}{0.2043} \log P_t. \qquad 4$$

The DW statistic was 1.31 which is on the borderline. The important thing is to note that both the income and price elasticities are estimated with good precision and that the income elasticity of 0.253 is substantially lower than the CS elasticity.

The conclusions are not much different if we allow for AR(1) errors as done by Izan. The estimates were:

$$\log S_t = \underset{(0.0926)}{3.996} + \underset{(0.0270)}{0.2481} \log Y_t - \underset{(0.0293)}{0.1994} \log P_t. \qquad 5$$

These results show that pooling is not valid as argued in Maddala (1971).

The estimation of the inverse demand with the revised time-series data covering 1913–76 data, however, gave wide confidence intervals for α, as was noted earlier with the Tobin's *original* data. The implied estimate of α was 0.6571 with a SE of (0.1806). The $\pm 2\sigma$ interval is (0.2959, 1.0183). The CS results for the budget studies showed (deleting the outliers in each case):

Year	$\hat{\alpha}$	SE	$\pm 2\sigma$ intervals
1941	0.60	(0.027)	(0.546, 0.654)
1950	0.5617	(0.01355)	(0.5346, 0.5888)
1960	0.5583	(0.009376)	(0.5395, 0.5771)
1972	0.3441	(0.0136)	(0.3169, 0.3713)

Thus, *all* the CI intervals for α from the cross-section data lie entirely in the CI interval for α from the time series. However, again the TS confidence interval is so wide that the CS information completely dominates the TS information.

Apart from the statistical issues, there are also conceptual issues regarding the CS and TS estimates of the same parameter. These are discussed in Section 5.

There are also some defects in the procedures that Izan follows for outlier detection although the results are not different in this particular case. We shall discuss this in the next section, and clarify some points regarding recent developments in this area that have not been widely noticed.

3. OUTLIER DETECTION

Izan (1980) used a plot of the OLS residuals to determine the outliers (and says that these are confirmed by looking at the studentized residuals). As is well known, using the OLS residual plots for outlier detection is not a valid procedure. The OLS regression line can get tilted by including the outliers in the estimation and this can lead to identifying the wrong outliers. This is the reason why outlier detection is usually based on what is known as deletion methods. We would like to clarify the confusion regarding some outlier diagnostics, that are built into several computer programs (e.g. SAS).

In the regression model $y = X\beta + u$ where y is an $n \times 1$ vector, X is an $n \times k$ matrix of explanatory variables, define the 'hat matrix' H as $H = X(X'X)^{-1}X'$ and h_i as the i-th diagonal element of H. Then, if $\hat{u}_i$ is the i-th residual from the OLS regression, $\text{Var}(\hat{u}_i) = (1 - h_i)\sigma^2$. Also denote by $\hat{\beta}(i)$ as the estimator of β with the i-th observation deleted and $s^2(i)$, the corresponding estimator of σ^2. s^2 is the estimator of σ^2 from the entire sample.

The predicted residual $\tilde{u}_i$ is given by $\tilde{u}_i = y_i - x_i'\hat{\beta}(i)$ where x_i is the i-th row of X. It is the residual from a prediction of the deleted observation y_i using the estimator $\hat{\beta}(i)$. It is well known that $\tilde{u}_i = \hat{u}_i/(1 - h_i)$. The studentized residual u_i^* is just the predicted residual divided by its standard error. It is given by

$$u_i^* = \frac{\hat{u}_i}{s(i)(1 - h_i)^{1/2}}.$$
6

To compute $s(i)$ we do not have to recompute the regression equation deleting one observation at a time. Note that

$$(n - k)s^2 - (n - k - 1)s^2(i) = \hat{u}_i^2/(1 - h_i).$$
7

Thus, all the statistics for the row-deletion case can be computed using the OLS regression. (See, *inter alia*, Donald and Maddala, 1993, p. 665).

Belsley, Kuh and Welsch (1980), hereafter referred to as BKW, introduce another diagnostic $DFFITS_i$ defined by

$$DFFITS_i = \sqrt{\frac{h_i}{1 - h_i}}u_i^*.$$
8

This is supposed to test the change in prediction in y_i by deleting the i-th observation. A rough value of $DFFITS > 2\sqrt{k/n}$ is considered 'significant'. This criterion has been suggested to distinguish between outliers and influential observations. An outlier need not be influential (u_i^* significant but $DFFITS_i$ not) and a significant observation need not be an outlier ($DFFITS_i$ is significant but u_i^* is not).

Unfortunately, this criterion has been built into several computer programs (e.g. SAS) and it is in widespread use. However, *this criterion is not useful* and the supposed conflict it detects is spurious. To see this, examine how it was derived. BKW divide the change in prediction by what they call the 'scaling factor' which is the SE of $\hat{y}_i = x_i'\hat{\beta}$. Note that $\text{Var}(\hat{y}_i) = h_i\sigma^2$ and the change in prediction is $x_i'(\hat{\beta} - \hat{\beta}(i)) = h_i\tilde{u}_i$. If we divide this by the correct standard error, instead of the arbitrary 'scaling factor' used by BKW, we end up with the studentized residual. *Thus, DFFITS is a different criterion because the change in fit is divided by the wrong standard error.*

The same argument applies to another criterion suggested by BKW (and also incorporated in several computer programs). This is $DFBETAS_{ij}$. This is supposed to measure the influence of the i-th observation on the estimate of β_j, the j-th component of β. However, we have

$$\hat{\beta}_j - \hat{\beta}_j(i) = (X'X)_j^{-1} x_i \tilde{u}_i, \qquad 9$$

where $(X'X)_j^{-1}$ is the j-th row of $(X'X)^{-1}$. Again a test of significance of this is exactly equivalent to test of significance of $\tilde{u}_i$ and this is done by using the studentized residual. BKW arrive at a different answer because they use the wrong standard error (they use arbitrary 'scaling factor').

We used the SAS program to detect outliers in the budget studies for the years 1941, 1950, 1960 and 1972. The program gives the studentized residuals and also $DFFITS$. We ignored the latter because, as we argued, it is not useful. Since studentized residual is a 'delete one' diagnostic, we deleted one outlier at a time (the one with the largest significant studentized residual).

The results for the four budget studies are reported in Table I. The results show that for the 1941 urban US data the first two outliers were the ones detected by Izan but the last one is not. For both the 1941 and 1950 urban US data, the deletion of the outliers produced a higher estimate of α, the income elasticity but for 1960 and 1972 budget surveys outlier deletion had no effect. This means that the outliers were not 'influential observations' if by 'influential' we mean their influence on the estimate of α (we always have to ask the question: 'influence on what'?).

One other issue is as to what to do with the outliers. Legendre, in his first paper on least squares in 1805 suggested that the outliers be thrown out. So did Edgeworth in 1887. Donald and Maddala (1993) discuss three methods:

Table I. Outliers in the Budget Studies

Year	$\hat{\alpha}$	Observations Deleted
1941	0.57	None
$n = 39$	0.60	#15
	0.62	#15, 14
	0.64	#15, 14, 23
1950	0.49	None
$n = 54$	0.51	#28
	0.52	#28, 19
	0.54	#28, 19, 37
	0.56	#28, 19, 37, 10
1960–1	0.56	None
$n = 58$	0.54	#10
	0.56	#10, 11
	0.55	#10, 11, 9
	0.56	#10, 11, 9, 12
1972–3	0.33	None
$n = 72$	0.34	#30

Note: In 1941, 1950 and 1960–1 budget surveys, the last observation deleted did not have a significant studentized residual at the first stage but had a highly significant studentized residual (>3.6) after the deletion of the other outliers.

(i)   throw the rascals out;
(ii) leave them in but under control (robust methods);
(iii) listen to what the rascals are saying and change the model (often the outliers suggest that the model used is not appropriate).

Considering the course of action (ii), several methods have been suggested in the past two decades on robust methods to handle outliers. See Huber (1981) and Hampel et al. (1986). Huber presented a robust estimation method for the estimation of a location parameter in 1964 and this was extended to estimation of regression equations in 1968. But it was since Andrews' paper (1974) that robust regression became widely used. It has also been argued by Huber (1987) that L_1 estimators (and some other M-estimators) are not robust to outliers. It is not clear how robust to outliers the procedure used by Izan is. In any case there have been several other robust estimation methods that have been suggested. See Maddala and Yin (1997) for a survey.

Dodge (1996) gives an interesting account of 90 different studies done using a multiple regression on a famous data set called 'stack loss data' consisting of 21 observations and three explanatory variables. In this data set, observations (1, 3, 4, 21) were widely acknowledged as outliers. Andrews (1974) presented a robust estimation method using all the 21 observations which gave essentially the same estimates as those obtained using OLS with four outliers deleted. To demonstrate the diversity of conclusions by different investigations and different criteria about outliers, Dodge (1996) lists 26 studies which find different outliers using different techniques. He concludes that, if we take these sets as outliers, then 16 observations are outliers and only five are inliers.

We did not want to turn the budget data into a guinea pig and so we did not pursue the different robust methods. What the results presented in Table I suggest is that based on the budget studies of 1941, 1950 and 1960, the income elasticity is in the range of 0.56–0.64 but the budget study of 1972 shows it to be much lower around 0.33. Tests of significance applied to the estimates in the budget studies of 1941, 1950 and 1960 do show that the differences are 'statistically significant'. But the small discrepancies can as well arise from two budget studies in the same year. Of more concern is the 1972 figure. One question is: Do the time series data show a structural break between 1960 and 1972? We shall investigate this issue in the next section. Apart from this, an explanation has to come from a detailed examination of the changes in food consumption patterns, and the way the budget study has been conducted.

It should be noted that the definition of the variables did change between the years (as explained in the information pack). The definition of food consumption included alcoholic beverages in the data for 1941 and 1950 but not in the data for 1960 and 1972. Thus, the definition of the variables changed between 1950 and 1960 but the decline in income elasticity occurred between 1960 and 1972. One other possibility is that the surveys of 1940, 1951 and 1960 covered urban US but the survey of 1972 covered *both* urban and rural US.

4.   THE TIME SERIES EVIDENCE

In contrast to the CS results, the TS evidence is mixed. As noted earlier, the results are very sensitive to the inclusion and deletion of some variables, and the way the demand function is specified. Programs like the PC-GIVE by Hendry and MICROFIT by Pesaran and Pesaran, generate a lot of diagnostics but we decided against using them because we believe, as Friedman and Schwartz (1991, p. 47) say, that it is difficult to interpret the final results after 'treating' the data with so many tests. Leamer (1988, p. 332) also remarks: 'There are too many diagnostics. One is too many as far as I am concerned'. We shall, however, use a few diagnostics such as the tests for first order autocorrelation in the errors and give some ballpark figures on what the TS data say. Autocorrelation in the errors can arise due to a lot of misspecifications (see Chapter 6 of Maddala (1992) for instance). However, pursuing all these avenues will lead us too far away from the main issues we are concerned with here.

Time-series analysis has changed a lot in the last two decades. The latest fashion (or fad) is to start with unit-root tests and cointegration tests. The Augmented Dickey–Fuller (ADF) tests and the Phillips–Perron (PP) tests are no longer fashionable (we have more efficient tests, and we also have tests that reverse the roles of unit root and stationarity as null). In any case, the ADF tests (with lags 0–4) applied to $\log S_t$, $\log Y_t$, and $\log P_t$ revealed that we do not reject the unit root null for the Tobin's *original* data set (1913–41) or the *revised* data set (1913–76).

As with unit-root tests, there is now a vast array of cointegration tests (tests using the null of cointegration rather than the null of no cointegration and so on). To determine whether there is any cointegration and if so, the number of cointegrating vectors, we applied the Johansen tests. (Details are omitted for the sake of brevity.) These tests suggested one cointegrating vector (which is good news because if there are two we are in trouble, since any linear combination of the two cointegrating vector is also a cointegrating vector). This suggests that the regression of $\log S_t$ on $\log Y_t$ and $\log P_t$ is a cointegrating regression. The results we get for OLS are as follows (results from other estimation methods like the FM-OLS are presented in the next section):

Tobin's Original Data (1913–41)

$$\log S_t = \underset{(0.0736)}{3.9844} + \underset{(0.0217)}{0.2532} \ \log Y_t - \underset{(0.0230)}{0.2043} \ \log P_t; \qquad 10$$

Revised Data (1913–76)

$$\log S_t = \underset{(0.0232)}{3.8816} + \underset{(0.0159)}{0.1883} \ \log Y_t - \underset{(0.0262)}{0.1648} \ \log P_t. \qquad 11$$

Allowing for first order serial correlations gave the following results:

Tobin's Original Data (1913–41)

$$\log S_t = \underset{(0.0926)}{3.996} + \underset{(0.0270)}{0.2481} \ \log Y_t - \underset{(0.0293)}{0.1999} \ \log P_t; \qquad 12$$

Revised Data (1913–76)

$$\log S_t = \underset{(0.0503)}{3.889} + \underset{(0.0231)}{0.1693} \ \log Y_t - \underset{(0.0355)}{0.1344} \ \log P_t. \qquad 13$$

We also estimated simple partial adjustment models. The results were:

Tobin's Original Data (1913–41)

$$\log S_t = \underset{(0.1245)}{0.2768} \log S_{t-1} + \underset{(0.0303)}{0.2035} \log Y_t - \underset{(0.0277)}{0.1664} \log P_t; \qquad 14$$

Revised Data (1913–76)

$$\log S_t = \underset{(0.0830)}{0.6318} \log S_{t-1} + \underset{(0.0177)}{0.0858} \log Y_t - \underset{(0.0215)}{0.0876} \log P_t. \qquad 15$$

In both the equations, Durbin's h-test showed no significant serial correlation (of first order). The implied LR income and price elasticities from these models are:

	Income	Price
1913–41	0.2814	−0.2300
1913–76	0.2330	−0.2379

In both cases, these LR elasticities are higher than those obtained from the static regressions but the income elasticity is still well below that given by the budget studies.

The results presented in the previous section showed a decline in income elasticity in the latter period. To check this we applied structural change tests with the 1913–76 *revised* data. A search based on the Wald statistic showed a break in 1952. The results for the two regimes were (allowing for AR(1) errors)

1913–51

$$\log S_t = \underset{(0.0614)}{3.650} + \underset{(0.0219)}{0.2355} \log Y_t - \underset{(0.0308)}{0.1835} \log P_t; \qquad 16$$

1952–76

$$\log S_t = \underset{(0.0927)}{3.896} + \underset{(0.0345)}{0.1971} \log Y_t - \underset{(0.0548)}{0.1845} \log P_t. \qquad 17$$

Thus, the time-series evidence shows a lower (though not significantly lower) income elasticity in the latter period. Still this evidence is not as strong as that in the budget study of 1972. One possibility is that the latter period 1952–1976 covers the budget studies of 1960 as well as 1972 and since 1972 is almost at the end of the data points, the Wald statistic (which requires a minimum of four data points) would not be able to detect a structural change closer to 1972. Also, this difference is actually less than the one presented earlier for the periods 1913–41 and 1913–72. But it should be noted that the revised data cover revisions for also the period 1913–41, the time span of Tobin's original data.

We can summarize the results as follows:

(i) The time series evidence shows a lower income elasticity than that obtained in the cross-sectional budget studies.

(ii)   Estimation of a partial adjustment model yielded higher long-run elasticities but these are still lower than those given by the budget studies.
(iii)   If the results of the budget study of 1972 are taken seriously, there appears to be a decline in the income elasticity after 1960. The time-series evidence showed a break in 1952, and a slightly lower income elasticity in the latter period. The dating of the break is, however, questionable, because the Wald statistic cannot detect the break, if it occurred closer to 1972.

In the next section, we shall comment on the discrepancies between the time-series and cross-section estimates.

5.   DISCREPANCY BETWEEN THE CS AND TS ESTIMATES

The results presented in the preceding sections consistently show that the TS estimates are lower than the CS estimates from the budget studies. This is consistent with the argument advanced in the 1950s and 1960s that CS estimates from budget data typically measure long-run elasticities and the TS estimates measure short-term elasticities; and thus it is inappropriate to substitute estimates from the budget studies in the time series equation. See Kuh and Meyer (1957) and Kuh (1959) for early arguments in this vein. Since then it has been also observed that in panel data studies the CS (or 'Between Group') estimates are consistently higher in magnitude than the corresponding TS (or 'Within Group') estimates *from the same data set*, thus, invalidating the use of models like the fixed effects and random effects models which assume homogeneity of the slope coefficients across time and across cross-section units. For some discussion of this issue, see Mairesse (1990). What we have in our study is not a panel data set but separate CS and TS data sets. Also, in the case of Tobin's data the budget study (in 1941) is at the end of the time span (1913–41) of the time-series data, although for the *revised* data set covering 1913–76 the dates of the budget studies fall in between.

There are several ways of trying to reconcile the differences. One procedure is to estimate a partial adjustment or an error correction model and get the SR and LR elasticities and compare the LR elasticities so obtained with those from the budget studies. We tried this but it did not work (we are omitting the details for the sake of brevity). Deriving LR elasticities from DLR (dynamic linear regression) models did not prove promising. See Alogoskoufis and Smith (1991) for a similar experience. The discrepancies still persist. A DLR regression of $\log S_t$ on $\log S_{t-1}$, $\log Y_t$, $\log Y_{t-1}$, $\log P_t$ and $\log P_{t-1}$ is the same as a regression of $\log S_t$ on $\log Y_t$ and $\log P_t$ with AR(1) errors (with one common factor restriction). The results from the latter equation have been reported earlier. A LR test for the common factor restriction yielded a test statistic of 2.48 with a p-value of 0.71. Thus, we do not reject the common factor restriction and conclude that the serial correlation model reported earlier is alright.

One question that can be asked is, if the cointegration tests showed one cointegrating vector, and since estimates of the parameters in the cointegrating vectors give estimates of the LR parameters, aren't the OLS estimates we obtained those of LR parameters? It is now well known that although the Engle-Granger method of OLS applied to static relationships gives superconsistent estimates, as Banerjee *et al.* (1993, pp. 214–223) argue there can be substantial biases in the OLS estimates, and adding dynamic terms or using non-parametric adjustments as in Phillips and Hansen (1990) reduces these biases. But we have not yet been successful in reconciling the differences pursuing this approach. The conclusion remain unchanged. The results from Phillips–Hansen's FM-OLS are as follows:

Tobin's Original Data (1913–41)

$$\log S_t = \underset{(0.0767)}{3.892} + \underset{(0.0215)}{0.2742} \log Y_t - \underset{(0.0224)}{0.2121} \log P_t; \qquad\qquad 18$$

Revised Data (1913–76)

$$\log S_t = \underset{(0.0538)}{3.861} + \underset{(0.0361)}{0.1940} \log Y_t - \underset{(0.0595)}{0.1680} \log P_t. \qquad\qquad 19$$

In summary, we have to live with the discrepancy between the estimates of the income elasticity α from the CS budget studies and the TS estimates. But as argued earlier, this discrepancy is to be expected. One can invoke arguments of aggregation but this will make the error variance of the TS regression to be different form the error variance of the CS regression (because the time-series data are obtained by aggregating over individuals) and this should be taken into account when estimating a pooled regression. But this does not change the preceding arguments which are about the issue of whether pooling is valid or not.

6. CONCLUSION

The cross-section budget studies of 1941, 1950 and 1960 show an income elasticity in the range of 0.55–0.60. The budget study of 1972, however, gives an estimate in the low 30s. There are either aberrations in the data or a structural change (changes in the pattern of food consumption). The time-series evidence shows a decline in the income elasticity in the latter period but not of the magnitude as the one in the budget study of 1972.

Outliers made a slight difference in the estimates from the budget studies of 1941 and 1950, but not in the studies of 1960 or 1972. As is well known, least squares residuals should not be used in outlier detection. We used studentized residuals. We also clarify the important point that some measures like *DFFITS* and *DEFBATAS* suggested in the well known book by Belsley, Kuh and Welsch (BKW) and incorporated in several computer programs like SAS, are of no use. BKW made an error in computing the standard errors of their measures and when this is corrected, we end up testing the significance of the studentized residual.

One conclusion that emerges from the time-series data is that the income elasticities are lower than those from the budget studies. This result also holds true when serial correlation in the errors are taken into account and methods that estimate long-run and short-run elasticities are used. The estimate of long-run elasticity from the time-series data is still substantially lower than that given by the budget studies. Thus, it is not valid to use the cross-section estimate in the time-series estimation.

Apart from the statistical reasoning, there are also conceptual differences in the CS and TS parameters. Hence, one should not expect the estimates from the two data sets to be equal.

The conclusions of Maddala (1971) about pooling are still valid.

We would like to summarize the empirical results by saying that the time-series evidence suggests an income elasticity in the range (0.20, 0.30) and a price elasticity in the range $(-0.15, -0.25)$.

REFERENCES

Alogoskoufis, G. and R. Smith (1991), 'On error correction models: specification, interpretation, estimation', *Journal of Economic Surveys*, **5**, 97–128.

Andrews, D. F. (1974), 'A robust method for multiple linear regression', *Technometrics*, **16**, 523–31.

Banerjee, A., J. Dolado, J. W. Galbraith and D. F. Hendry (1993), *Cointegration, Error Correction, and the Econometric Analysis of Non-Stationary Data*, Oxford University Press, Oxford.

Belsley, D. A., E. Kuh and R. E. Welsch (1980), *Regression Diagnostics: Identifying Influential Data and Sources of Multicollinearity*, Wiley, New York.

Chatterjee, S. and A. S. Hadi (1986), 'Influence, observation, high leverage points and outliers in linear regression', *Statistical Science*. **1**, 379–416.

Chetty, V. K. (1968), 'Pooling of time series and cross-section data', *Econometrica*, **36**, 279–90.

Donald, S. G. and G. S. Maddala (1993), 'Identifying outliers and influential observations in econometric models'. In: G. S. Maddala, C. R. Rao and H. D. Vinod (eds) *Handbook of Statistics*. Vol. 11, 663–701.

Dodge, Y. (1996), 'The guinea pig of multiple regression', in H. Reider (ed) *Robust Statistics, Data Analysis and Computer Intensive Methods* (in honor of Peter Huber's 60th birthday), Springer Verlag, New York, 91–117.

Friedman, M. and A. J. Schwartz (1991), 'Alternative approaches to analyzing economic data', *American Economic Review*, **81**, 39–49.

Hampel, H. R., E. M. Ronchetti, P. J. Rousseeuw, and W. A. Stahel (1986), *Robust Statistics: The Approach Based on Influence Functions*, Wiley, New York.

Huber, P. J. (1981), *Robust Statistics*, Wiley, New York.

Huber, P. J. (1987), 'The place of the L_1-norm in robust estimation', in Y. Dodge (ed) *Statistical Data Analysis Based on the L_1-norm*, Elsevier, 23–33.

Izan, H. Y. (1980), 'To pool or not to pool: a reexamination of Tobin's food demand problem', *Journal of Econometrics*, **13**, 391–402.

Kuh, E. (1959), 'The validity of cross-sectionally estimated behavior equations in time series applications', *Econometrica*, **27**, 197–214.

Kuh, E. and J. R. Meyer (1957), 'How extraneous are extraneous estimates?', *The Review of Economics and Statistics*, **39**, 380–93.

Leamer, E. E. (1988), 'Things that bother me', *Economic Record*, **64**, 331–35.

Maddala, G. S. (1971), 'The likelihood approach to pooling cross-section and time-series data', *Econometrica*, **39**, 939–53.

Maddala, G. S. (1992), *Introduction to Econometrics*, 2nd Edition, Prentice Hall, New York.

Maddala, G. S. and Y. Yin (1997), 'Outliers, unit roots and robust estimation of non-stationary time series', in G. S. Maddala and C. R. Rao (eds) *Handbook of Statistics*, Vol. 15, Elsevier, Amsterdam, 237–66.

Mairesse, J. (1990), 'Time series and cross-sectional estimates on panel data: Why are they different and why should they be equal?' In J. Hartog, G. Ridder and J. Theeuwes (eds) *Panel Data and Labor Market Studies*, Elsevier, 81–95. Reprinted in G. S. Maddala (ed) *Econometrics of Panel Data*, Edward Elgar, 1992.

Phillips, P. C. B., and B. Hansen (1990), 'Estimation and inference in models of cointegration: A simulation study', In T. B. Fomby and G. F. Rhodes (eds) *Advances in Econometrics*, **8**, 225–48. JAI Press, London.

Tobin, J. (1950), 'A statistical demand function for food in the USA', *Journal of the Royal Statistical Society*, Series A, **113**, Part II, 113–41 [reprinted in Chapter 2, this volume].

COMMENTS BY PROFESSOR MICHAEL WICKENS (University of York)

This paper has a more limited focus than the others. It concentrates largely on a statistical reconciliation of the information contained in the US cross-section and time-series data, and operates exclusively within Tobin's framework with no discussion of consumer theory.

The cross-section estimates reported are based on the indirect rather than the direct demand function (price rather than quantity as the dependent variable). This was also used by Tobin and by most subsequent studies. It is interesting that this is not consistent with neo-classical demand theory where price is taken as given.

Estimates for both versions of the demand function are reported for the time-series data where it is found that the *direct* estimates of the income elasticity are much lower than the *indirect* and have much smaller standard errors. Assuming the model is correct, the traditional explanation of this difference would be the effect of biases arising from measurement errors. Nevertheless, there is some support for the indirect formulation in that the time-series estimate is similar to that from Tobin's original cross-section which was for 1941. But to set against this, the estimates of the income are found to decrease the more recent the date of the cross section. The Maddala team seem to interpret this finding as evidence that the income elasticity is falling over time. If correct, it would, however, imply that their time-series model is flawed.

Much of the paper is taken up with an analysis of possible outlier effects on the cross-section estimates. Following a discussion of the theory of outlier detection, it is shown that significant outliers exist for all of the cross-section data sets. After all of this, however, it is found that dropping the outliers has a negligible effect on the income elasticity estimates.

Another finding of the paper is that (based on the indirect formulation) the cross-section evidence produces much higher income elasticities than the time series. It is concluded from this that it is invalid to use the cross-section estimates in the time-series estimation. However, as the confidence intervals for the time-series estimates completely encompass those of the cross section, there is no statistical inconsistency between the two. Put another way, the time-series evidence is so imprecise that it seems to add little to the information contained in the cross-section data.

My general impression of the paper is that trying to reconcile the cross-section and time-series evidence is a sensible thing to do, and especially since it seems to be so easy. On the other hand, the emphasis on outliers turns out to be unproductive. It might have been far more profitable to have followed up the very interesting, but as yet unexplained, findings that the estimates of the income elasticity are greatly affected by the choice of formulation of the demand function and the date of the cross section.

COMMENTS BY PROFESSOR J. S. CRAMER (*University of Amsterdam*)

This lively and enjoyable contribution provides two articles for the price of one. One is a brief but vehement argument about criteria for detecting outliers, the other a comparison of income elasticity estimates from cross-section data and time series.

To begin with the latter, the authors show convincingly (1) that the dynamic specification of the time-series (TS) equation makes an appreciable difference to the income elasticity estimate; (2) that pooling seems justified because the TS evidence is so feeble that it agrees with any cross-section (CS) results; and (3) that there is a persistent difference in income elasticity estimates from the two sources.

The conclusions drawn from these findings are full of the contradictions and inconsistencies so typical of applied work. If the TS evidence is so sensitive to specification, great care should be taken in selecting a preferred form; yet no arguments are put forward for the change from indirect to the direct demand function. If the TS evidence is so feeble, this pleads for pooling, since it would strengthen the analysis by a shot of strong CS results. And if the TS evidence is so fickle and unreliable, little importance should be attached to their contrast with the CS estimates. Finally, the authors tell us belatedly (Section 5) that the two income elasticities are so conceptually different in the first place that there is really no reason to expect agreement. Without further qualifications this argument invalidates the entire exercise at a stroke; with such qualifications, a tenuous correspondence might be traced out. But the authors do not follow up the matter.

The central issues are thus resolved by a simple comparison of income elasticities. Little attention is paid to the other tasks set by the organizers. The Dutch evidence is ignored.

The article about outliers, while full of life, is irrelevant in the present context. The authors show that omitting outliers makes no appreciable difference to the CS estimates (even if the cell mean character of the observations is disregarded), so that it is a non-issue as far as the pooling issue is concerned.

The authors do worry about the 1972 budget survey which is a massive outlier by itself. At the end of Section 3 they argue that the reasons must be found in a detailed examination of the food consumption pattern and the budget study itself; but they do not follow up this admirable prescription.

COMMENTS BY PROFESSOR ARIE KAPTEYN (*Tilburg University*)

This is an interesting paper, but with a limited scope. The authors restrict themselves to the American data, do not provide a logbook, and essentially take Tobin's model for granted. The main emphasis is on whether the time series and budget data can be pooled in estimating parameters of a demand function for food. Variations considered are AR(1) errors, both direct and inverse macro demand functions, outlier detection, unit roots, cointegration, structural breaks (income elasticities appear to fall over time), outlier detection in the budget data.

Income elasticities based on time series are lower than those found for cross-section data. Removing outliers has some effect, but not a whole lot.

Within the self-imposed constraints chosen by the authors, I have little to offer by way of criticism. However, one could think of at least three issues that deserve more attention than they receive here. The first one is functional form. A log-linear specification is used throughout and no diagnostics are given to tell us that this is actually the right choice. Secondly, both direct and inverse demand functions are estimated. Although one can view these as different parametrizations of a co-integrating relationship, the income elasticity implied by the estimates of the two types of demand functions are quite different. The authors point at small sample biases, but a fuller analysis of the difference in estimates and attempts to reconcile them would have aided insight. Thirdly, and in contrast to Tobin's original article, there is no discussion of aggregation as a means of reconciling the CS and TS estimates, let alone an attempt to build aggregation into the estimation. If one builds from a micro-relationship, the macro-relationship would include variables that reflect distributions of micro quantities. These quantities are now ignored and in principle this would cause omitted variable bias affecting the macro-estimates. Since there is no reason why these omitted variables would exhibit a constant correlation with the included variables, this might be one reason why estimates vary by period.

REPLY BY G. S. MADDALA, SHAOWEN WU AND YONG YIN

We appreciate the comments by Wickens, Cramer, and Kapteyn. We are in full agreement with the points they raised but it is too late to do work in reply to their criticisms. We shall therefore give a brief explanation for the limited scope we chose.

The *Experiment Information Pack* (p. 6) said 'for example, Chetty (1968), Maddala (1971), and in particular Izan (1980) are the papers you might wish to consult.' Since Izan's paper was a scathing criticism of the papers by Tobin, Chetty, and Maddala, that they ignored simple diagnostics about outliers and serial correlation, we decided to prepare a reply to his criticism (we were sure nobody else would do it). We considered only the two diagnostics he mentioned and did not consider other diagnostics (functional form, inverse vs. direct formulation of the demand function, etc.). Our conclusion was that Izan's criticisms were unfounded.

Regarding the outliers issue, we concentrated on it, not that it makes a difference in this case, but that there is a lot of confusion caused by the book by Belsley, Kuh, and Welsch. In particular, their criteria *DFFITS*, *DFBETAS*, etc. built into such popular programs as SAS are useless, if not downright misleading. This needs to be pointed out and we used this opportunity (offered by Izan's criticism on the basis of outliers) to do just this. This is an important point that deserves attention whether or not it is directly relevant to this problem.

CHAPTER 11

MY 1950 FOOD DEMAND STUDY IN RETROSPECT

JAMES TOBIN

(ADDRESS TO THE WORKSHOP, 17 DECEMBER 1996)

Christmas is upon us. For our three-and-a-half year old grandson, my wife found a wonderful video tape. It's a Disney-type adventure in which the boy himself is the central character. You first send the seller of the video his picture, and somehow the child becomes the character in the film. As he looks at it, he will see himself in the drama. I felt like that at this conference. It is a rare and odd experience.

I have recently encountered a fashionable idea in economic theory. (Theory is full of fashions that come and go.) This idea starts from the current emphasis in modern economic theory on intertemporal choices, for example life-cycle consumption decisions. Some young theorists think they detect, if only by common introspection and observation, dynamic inconsistency in individual time preferences. People seem to have a decisive preference for doing onerous things tomorrow rather than today. Yet looking into the distant future, they don't discount, say, 30 years from now significantly more than 29 years. But when 29 and 30 become zero and one, then they will discount 30 to 29 as they now discount 1 to 0.

Theorists who worry about this fancy the notion that different individuals with different utility functions are involved. Here I am in this video tape where all of a sudden the participant is not I, a 78-year old guy, but another James Tobin, only 29–30 years old. As I reread this article I thought 'that earlier J. T. wrote a pretty good paper'. Well, anyway, it's a very interesting experience, for which I am as grateful as I expect my grandson to be for his Christmas present.

I shall tell you about how I happened to write this paper in the first place. I had been a graduate student at Harvard from 1939 to 1941, just before the USA got into the Second World War. Then I was away from economics for almost five years, mostly in the US Navy on a destroyer. In January 1946 I went back to graduate school at Harvard, wrote my thesis, and earned my PhD in another year and a half. The thesis was on the consumption function. In it, I pragmatically combined information from the 1935–6 US national budget study with national income accounts time series. (Thanks to work relief in the United States in the depression, the country was able to carry out a large and detailed budget study.) This was a prelude to my 1950 paper on food demand.

Let me digress to tell you about statistics and econometrics at Harvard in those days. Mathematical statistics at Harvard was very good. I took a course from an eminent scholar and wonderful teacher, E. V. Huntington. But, there was not much econometrics around at

* Reprinted from the *Journal of Applied Econometrics*, **12**, 647–650 (1997).

Methodology and Tacit Knowledge: Two Experiments in Econometrics
Jan R. Magnus and Mary S. Morgan © 1997 John Wiley & Sons Ltd

Harvard. In what was called 'Business Cycles' Professor Edwin Frickey was decomposing time series into seasonal, cyclical and trend components. I never did understand how he was doing it, nor could he show us how to do it ourselves. The senior economic statistics teacher, Professor William Leonard Crum, thought that his duty was to warn us about all the 'booby traps', all the things that could go wrong. Those of us interested in econometrics had to study it on our own, reading the outputs of the Cowles Commission, then in Chicago. We did have one visitor, the Swiss econometrician Hans Staehle, who was interested in empirical demand analysis. That was very good, but on the whole there was little econometrics at Harvard in those days.

In America, beginning early in the century, statistical analysis developed in conjunction with agricultural economics, in the federal Department of Agriculture and in the state agricultural schools and experiment stations subsidized by the federal government at 'land-grant' universities, especially in the Midwest. These statisticians pioneered demand and supply analysis. Even before the First World War, they were quite conscious of identification problems. How could you tell whether you were getting a supply curve or a demand curve or some uninformative mixture of the two?

At Harvard there fortunately was a Professor of Agricultural Economics in the economics department, John D. Black. He had the only electrical-mechanical calculators around. I was not studying agricultural economics, but I did persuade Professor Black to let me use his facilities, and that's where my calculations for the thesis and for the food demand paper were done. As I recall, it took two or three days to do a regression with three regressors. That was an automatic incentive to think carefully in advance about your specification. You were not able to press a button and compute another specification a second later. Maybe nowadays we should impose a tax or a quota to play the same role! Anyway, there is quite a difference between the scarcity price of calculations reported in an article written in 1949–50 and in the papers written for this conference.

After I got my degree I was fortunate enough to get a post-doctoral fellowship, three years to do whatever I wanted. It helped me make up for the time I had missed during the war. One of the things I wanted to do was to try to write as good a paper as I could using the cross-section/time-series coalition. The reason for doing it on food was to avoid the complication of the durable goods included in aggregate consumption. I was not abandoning my interest in the consumption function, but the food paper was supposed to be a sort of baptism in econometric method.

I think it may surprise you how conscious I and my friends were about the paucity of information in economy-wide time-series data. Perhaps we were more conscious of it than practitioners are now. Why was that? One reason was some work of Richard Stone, a principal components analysis of US macroeconomic time series. Remember that the only time-series national accounts available in the late 1940s were annual data between the two wars. In Stone's principal components analysis, the first component is just the pervasive business cycle dominating 1920–40 macro fluctuations. It is quite pronounced, shows prosperity in the 1920s, then a deep depression, and then a recovery from the depression, ending in a 1939–41 military boom. More than 90% of variance in these series are 'explained' by this first component and there are really only one or two other identifiable components. The reason everything looked so good — the Keynesian consumption function looked great — is that consumption and income, and almost everything else, move with the pervasive business cycle. Back then, we were very conscious of this problem with time series, and that's one reason why we thought cross-sectional data would be a good idea, not to be used in place of, but in addition to, time-series data. Maybe things aren't so collinear now. We have longer series and more 'natural' experiments.

In the third year of my fellowship, I went to Dick Stone's Institute, the Department of Applied Economics, Cambridge, England. The food paper had been virtually completed beforehand. I had been in England for only three months when I gave it as a paper at the Royal Statistical Society in London, quite an awesome scene, quite formal, very non-American. The DAE was a great help in calculations and charts; I got good advice from Durbin and Watson and Stone himself. The whole year was an excellent experience. There was a great group of people: not only Durbin and Watson, but also Michael Farrell who, alas, died young, and Hendrik Houthakker. Orcutt and Cochrane had been there the year before.

My purpose in using cross-section data was to dodge the collinearity of aggregate time series. The criticism here in these meetings was that I overstressed that difficulty. Unfortunately, the issue is clouded by discrepancy in the definitions of consumption between my cross-section and time-series data, to which Dick Stone called attention. (Most of you read the discussion at the back of my 1950 paper.) Evidently, if the definitional discrepancy were rectified, then the difference in estimates of income elasticity, between the time series and the 1941 and subsequent budget studies, probably would be diminished. It is unfortunate that nobody has done that: it seems that it is not hard to do now.

At the same time, I don't agree in principle that if time-series regression gives a different number from the budget study estimate the time series is right and the budget study wrong. No. What worried me was that whatever number you assumed for the income elasticity, a regression estimate of the price elasticity would be that same number with a negative sign. I showed this collinearity in my paper by Frisch's confluence analysis, now an archaic technique no one would use. It was high-tech in the 1940s.

I realize that there are plenty of problems with cross-section data. For example, consider savings data. To understand them, you need a stock-flow mechanism, some relationship between the stock of wealth that an individual or family already has and the amount they save. The natural presumption is that the more wealth the consumer unit already has, the less saving it will do. On the other hand, a cross-section reflects persistent personality differences among people. Some are thrifty and some are not. Those who report a lot of wealth in the cross-section are the thrifty — that's why they have a lot of wealth. The chances are that they are going to continue to be thrifty. You are going to see saving apparently positively related to wealth. But that is not a cause-and-effect relationship. The economic theory says that the more wealth you have, the *less* you are going to add to it. The only escape is re-interviews or panels of identical respondents. The latent variable, the personality, remains the same, so that changes in individual saving over time can be attributed to wealth, income, and other determinants.

In the 1950s I became quite interested in analysis of cross-section data. After I returned to the United States, I spent some time at the Survey Research Center at the University of Michigan working with George Katona, James N. Morgan and Laurence Klein. They were re-interviewing their respondents, and eventually collected panel data. Now we have samples with plenty of observations in the Research Center's Panel Study of Income Dynamics. Unfortunately they do not obtain saving and wealth observations, but we can hope. Problems are better resolved by new data rather than by arguing about how to treat existing data.

One problem in my 1950 paper was to distinguish between changes in average income and in its distribution among households. I wanted to interpret aggregate time series as changes in average income with the distribution constant, defining 'constant distribution' as suggested by Jacob Marschak.

Despite the impression of some conflicts, disagreements, and chaos in the eight papers that I heard about over the last couple of days, I think there was a fair amount of agreement on the general specification of the demand function, and on what the explanatory variables are. And there was apparently little disagreement on the shapes of the functions. It was not a contentious couple of days. I didn't come away thinking that econometrics was in a crisis. I must admit that I am not adept at many of the new techniques and diagnostics commonplace in modern econometrics. Maybe I start out with a little more scepticism than most of the practitioners do, but on the whole I think the project was successful.

I congratulate Magnus and Morgan for the initiative in doing this experiment. Many talk about retrospective tests of econometric tools, without doing them. Here it has been done under your leadership.

Personally, I enjoyed the attention. I'm proud and grateful that my work of long ago was selected as a target and impetus. Thank you for bringing me here. I wish you success in your future studies of applied econometrics.

CHAPTER 12

COMPARATIVE ASSESSMENTS OF THE FIELD TRIAL EXPERIMENT

ANTON P. BARTEN, J. S. CRAMER, M. HASHEM PESARAN, PETER SCHMIDT AND MICHAEL R. WICKENS

1. EDITORS' INTRODUCTION

The eight assessors played a crucial role in the field trial experiment. Since there were eight reports and eight assessors, we decided to send each assessor three papers to read. Our assessors were most responsive and put in an amount of work much above our expectation. The assessors were (in alphabetical order): Anton Barten, J. S. Cramer, Arie Kapteyn, Michael McAleer, Hashem Pesaran, Peter Schmidt, Kenneth Wallis and Michael Wickens.

In August 1996, we sent each assessor: the information pack (54 pages), the data diskette (nine original files plus five ASCII files concerning the US data), the Tobin article, E-mail messages sent to participants (four pages of clarifications/corrections), and three reports to assess. We asked them (i) to act as referee for the three papers; (ii) to provide detailed comments for each report on how to improve the presentation, help the authors clarify their own ideas and suggest possible cuts; and (iii) to act as comparative assessor for the three reports, that is, to analyze how the three reports differ and possibly why.

The assessors' comments on each report separately are printed following the relevant report in Chapters 3–10. The comparative assessments are collected in the current chapter. Five of the eight assessors provided such a comparative assessment. Kenneth Wallis compared the Maastricht and the Dundee results in his comments on the Maastricht paper and did not prepare a separate comparative assessment. The five assessors who did are:

Assessors	Reports compared
Anton P. Barten	Leamer, Maastricht, Finland
J. S. Cramer	Texas, Maddala, Dundee
M. Hashem Pesaran	CBS, Texas, Tennessee
Peter Schmidt	Texas, Leamer, Finland
Michael R. Wickens	CBS, Maddala, Dundee

Their contributions follow below.

2. ANTON BARTEN'S COMPARATIVE ASSESSMENT: LEAMER, MAASTRICHT AND FINLAND

The three papers, but also the others at the conference, have several aspects in common which generate mixed feelings with their reader. First of all, the cross-section part of

Methodology and Tacit Knowledge: Two Experiments in Econometrics
Jan R. Magnus and Mary S. Morgan © 1999 John Wiley & Sons Ltd

Tobin's original contribution appears to be robust against recent developments of a methodological nature. That is a comforting thought. If our empirical results are very sensitive to the way the data are handled one would feel suspicious about the outcomes in general.

Another feature is the failure of the forecasting part of the experiment. The results show the impact of the within model lack of precision. To this, one should add the uncertainty about the conditioning variables. Is it, in general, true that our knowledge of the future is so inadequate? It is commendable of Magnus and Morgan to have formulated the prediction question, because its answer has revealed a weak spot in our empirical research.

Another worrying aspect is the shift towards a more inductive approach, a shift away from the economic underpinning in favour of more elaborate statistical methodology. The consequence is the absence of a question of intellectual interest. What does one try to prove with an empirical application? Surely not that it makes a difference applying statistical approach A rather than statistical approach B, unless that difference is crucial for the deeper question about what the 'true' state of the world looks like.

The consequence of ignoring the economics of the set up is demonstrated by the lack of stability of the point estimates of the income elasticity. These are not really comparable across time and across space (USA-Netherlands), while also the cross section results are not in line with the time-series outcomes. The idea of constant elasticities has to be rejected on first sight. It is common (theoretical) knowledge that a constant income elasticity causes problems away from the sample mean. There is no piece of economic theory that states that elasticities should be constant. If there is no reason for elasticities to be constant one should have looked for a parameterization that allows for more comparability. A non- or semiparametric approach could also have been attempted.

The discrepancy between the time-series and cross-section outcomes can be also due to differences in the nature of the data collecting processes, causing differences in results even if one had the correct functional form. The same is true in the case of international comparisons. The inability to deal adequately with dynamic features in a cross-section approach can be another reason why one could not expect the point estimates to be similar to the ones of an exercise with time-series data. Perhaps more attention should have been paid to these issues.

One of the interesting results of the experiment of Magnus and Morgan is the variety of approaches and outcomes. There is clearly no common standard of how one should go about such an exercise in applied econometrics. Is that an indication of immaturity, or of the stage preceding the emergence of a new paradigm, or simply a sign of creative variability that is healthy and worth stimulating? It might be that the 'clients' of the applied econometrician prefer stability to variability, and do not care so much about methodological finesse. That, however, is no reason to stop being creative.

3.   J. S. CRAMER'S COMPARATIVE ASSESSMENT: TEXAS, MADDALA AND DUNDEE

At first sight the Experiment in Econometrics of Morgan and Magnus is a dazzling and exciting enterprise that testifies to the brilliance of its authors. They have advocated their plans with great force, and once sufficient support was obtained they have executed the project with thoroughness, perseverance and considerable organizational abilities. The result is, however, disappointing, and in retrospect this can be traced to certain flaws in design which should be avoided if anyone thinks of repeating the experiment.

The experiment has yielded eight competent and interesting papers of good quality. What is disappointing is that little common conclusions of substance emerge. The experiment does not materially contribute to our knowledge of the demand for food, and it contributes only very little to the general methodology of pooling cross-section and time-series evidence. I doubt whether an analyst contemplating pooling CS and TS evidence in a study of investment would find fruitful suggestions in this volume, although it might put him off.

A major reason for these failures is that the authors of the experiment have not themselves attempted the tasks they set for the participants. How could they resist the temptation of this exciting challenge? Perhaps to the plodding analyst performing the work (and a great deal of work) the project was not as exciting and rewarding as it was made out to be. It certainly demanded a considerable amount of time and effort, probably underestimated by the authors when they were gaily listing the participants' 'tasks'. Many would-be participants must have concluded that their time and effort could be spent more profitably on other pursuits.

Because the analyses had not been tried out before, each participant had to find out for himself certain distracting technical issues, such as:

1. the nature of the CS data as cell means and the concomitant need to reweigh them;
2. the truncation of Dutch CS data in respect of income as well as food consumption;
3. the nature of the TS series as *nominal* variables, and its implications for the analysis.

These simple technical issues would not have frustrated the participants as much as they did if the authors had done their homework, if there had been an interim workshop soon after the start of the experiment, or free and frequent communication among the participants (e.g. by an 'Experiment Newsletter').

It was an unfortunate idea of the authors to treat the project as a competition by expressly forbidding the free exchange of ideas, collusion, and the use of other data, however sensible this would be. This exemplifies that neither the organizers nor the participants were particularly interested in the demand for food.

4. M. HASHEM PESARAN'S COMPARATIVE ASSESSMENT: CBS, TEXAS AND TENNESSEE

This note provides my comparative assessment of the three papers by Anderson & Vahid (Texas), Bearse, Bozdogan & Schlottmann (Tennessee), and van Driel, Nadall & Zeelenberg (CBS). I shall focus on two important issues raised by the experiment:

1. In view of the econometric methods employed in this paper, can we say whether econometrics has 'progressed' since Tobin's (1950) contribution?
2. An evaluation of the different approaches to the applied problems that Magnus and Morgan (hereafter MM) have set, namely
   (i) estimation of income elasticity of food demand in the US;
   (ii) testing the 'homogeneity postulate' in the US and the Netherlands;

(iii)   forecasting the demand for food in the Netherlands over the period 1989–2000;
(iv)   the policy issues concerning the relationship between income distribution and
         aggregate economic performance.

The participants were also expected to define a task of their own to be performed in the
context of the data sets provided. As it turns out, the three papers that I have been asked
to read primarily address the first three tasks, and do not concern themselves with explicit
policy issues and do not set out a task of their own.

4.1.   Estimates of Income Elasticity of Food Demand

All three papers consider the estimation of income elasticity of food expenditures in the
US using Tobin's data. The Texas team emphasize nonlinearities in the cross-sectional
specification of the food consumption function and examine the implications that such
nonlinearities may have for aggregate time-series models. Their analysis, perhaps not
surprisingly, leads them to be rather sceptical of the existence of simple relationships
between micro and macro parameters and their comparability. They nevertheless go
ahead and estimate a nonlinear specification of the original Tobin model but without any
dynamics, and obtain an income elasticity (calculated at the sample means of 0.25), which
falls within the unrestricted time-series estimate obtained by Tobin, namely 0.22–0.35.
In my separate report on this paper, I note a number of difficulties with this nonlinear
specification and in particular I note that by construction this specification cannot satisfy
the homogeneity restriction.

On the other hand, the Tennessee team use a simple log-linear specification but consider
the problem of dynamic specification in detail. In particular they emphasize the use of
Information Complexity criteria (ICOMP) proposed in the statistical literature by one of
the authors (H. Bozdogan). They estimate the long-run income elasticity to be around
0.275 with a standard error of 0.023. It is, however, important to note that the data they
use covers 1930–1947 with the war years 1942–1944 being interpolated. Despite these
slight differences in the data set used, this estimate is also very similar to the ones obtained
by the Texas team, and once again falls well within the range estimated by Tobin. It is
interesting that despite the use of much more sophisticated econometric techniques and
arguments the income elasticities obtained by the Texas and the Tennessee teams (which
are based on the same data set) are very similar to Tobin's original estimate. Another
reason for this similarity lies in the fact that they base their analysis on the same basic
log-linear specification employed by Tobin. Moreover, due to the non-stationary nature of
the underlying regressors of the demand equation, the introduction of different dynamics
(as the Tennessee team) is unlikely to have much impact on the point estimate of the
long-run parameters of the model. The square of the logarithm of per capita income used
in the specification by the Texas team could and does have an important implication for
income elasticities, but the point estimate computed at sample mean obscures the major
differences that exist between the log-linear and the quadratic log-linear specifications.
Note that with (nominal) per capita income rising steadily sooner or later income elasticity
based on the non-linear specification will become larger than unity, which is clearly
unsatisfactory.

In contrast to the other two studies, the CBS team obtain the much larger estimate of
0.75 (with a standard error of 0.18), which is well above the other estimates obtained for

the US. One reason for this difference seems to be due to the fact that the CBS team use total expenditures rather than per capita disposable income in estimating their model. One would expect the income elasticity estimates based on expenditure and income to be similar only under the restrictive assumption of a constant saving rate, both over time and across households. Also, as was pointed out by Richard Stone in his discussion of Tobin's paper, the dependent variable in Tobin's time-series regression analysis (which is the same as the one analyzed by the Texas and the Tennessee teams) does not take full account of 'the amount of services rendered by caterers or any retail outlets, nor in all cases does it measure the amount of processing involved' (Tobin 1950, p. 141), while the food expenditure data used by the CBS team does take account of the cost of food processing and restaurant services. This, together with the fact that income elasticity of demand for outdoor food consumption is much higher than food consumption at home, one would then expect that the use of a more comprehensive measure of food data as done by the CBS team to yield a much higher income elasticity estimate. It is therefore important that the estimate obtained by the CBS team is compared not with the original Tobin estimate but rather with the time series estimates reported by Stone, which was about 0.62 (see note 2 to Table I and Tobin 1950, p. 142). Also estimating the CBS model over the period 1950–1989 results in a significant reduction in the estimate of the expenditure elasticity of food (from 0.76 to 0.41) and substantially closes the gap between the elasticity estimates obtained by the three teams.

The cross-section estimates summarized in Table I are closer together (as compared to the dispersion of the time series estimates), which partly reflects the fact that they are based on similar data. Once again, we see that the CBS team's estimates tend to be larger than those reported in the other two papers.

Overall, it seems that the (average) elasticity estimates reported in these papers are much more affected by the data set used rather than the particular estimation procedure followed.

4.2. Homogeneity Postulate

The studies by the Texas team and by the Tennessee team that use log-linear specification tend to arrive at a mixed conclusion as far as the validity of the homogeneity postulate is concerned. The outcome seems to critically depend on the particular data set used and the econometric methodology employed. These results are once again in direct contrast with those obtained by the CBS team. In fact, in all of the applications, the CBS team fail to reject homogeneity (and symmetry) restrictions, which is quite interesting considering that their treatment of the dynamics does not always seem to be adequate.

Considering the substantial development in the theory and practice of consumer analysis over the past four decades, it is interesting that the Texas team and the CBS team both start from the log-linear specification originally analyzed by Tobin. It is quite clear that the main concern of these two papers is more with the econometric issues than the economic theory that underlie the specification of the demand function. On the other hand, the paper by the CBS team which does attempt to utilize modern developments in consumer theory in estimation of income elasticities, pays little attention to dynamics and other types of misspecifications. It is also interesting to note that none of these papers addresses the issue of the simultaneous determination of food consumption and food prices which was one of the main concerns of Tobin. In the case of the Netherlands this is understandable,

Table I. Estimates of Income and Price Elasticities of Food-Expenditure in the US

	Time Series		Cross-sections
	Income	Price	Income (Expenditure)
Tobin	0.22–0.35	−0.38 −0.23	0.56 (0.03)
Tobin-Stone[1]	0.62	−0.51	N/A
Texas team			
Tobin Data (1913–41)	0.25	−0.22	N/A
Expenditure Data (1948–89)	0.40	−0.51	
Tobin Urban (1941)	N/A	N/A	0.62
Various US Budget Surveys	N/A	N/A	0.52, 0.42, 0.54 0.35
Pooled Estimates	N/A	N/A	0.48 (0.02)
Tennessee team			
'Original' Tobin Data (1913–47)[2]	0.275 (0.023)	—	N/A
Tobin Revised Data (1913–76)	0.213 (0.028)		
CBS team			
Time Series			
1929–1941 (Expenditures)	0.75 (0.18)	−0.22 (0.18)	
1930–1978 (Expenditures)	0.75 (0.11)	−0.44 (0.11)	
Budget Surveys			
Urban 1941	N/A	N/A	0.74 (0.02)
1950	N/A	N/A	0.75 (0.01)
1960	N/A	N/A	0.73 (0.01)
1972	N/A	N/A	0.71 (0.01)
Pooled Estimate	N/A	N/A	0.72 (0.01)

but the case for the US is less clear cut, particularly when the sample period covers the pre-war period.

As far as the income elasticity of food expenditure in the Netherlands is concerned, the three studies, although using very different approaches, arrive at reasonably similar estimates. These are summarized in Table II. For example, the estimates obtained by the Tennessee team and the CBS team on time-series data are around 0.39–0.41. The Texas team estimate is slightly larger (0.52). However, the Texas team consider this to be a tentative estimate and do not even provide a standard error for it. The Tennessee team do

---

[1] This estimate is reported in Stone's discussion of Tobin's (1950, p. 142) paper, and uses a more comprehensive measure of expenditures on food. Stone also ran the regression of food expenditures on income and price rather than the reverse regression of price on income and food expenditures estimated by Tobin.

[2] The data for the years 1942–44 are interpolated.

Table II. Estimates of Income and Price Elasticities of Food-Expenditure in the Netherlands

	Time Series		Cross-sections	
	Income	Price	Income (Expenditure)	
Texas team				
Time Series (1948–1988)	0.52	−0.57	N/A	
Budget Surveys				
1980	N/A	N/A	0.34	0.30
			(0.03)	(0.03)
1988	N/A	N/A	0.42	0.37
			(0.06)	(0.06)
Pooled Estimate	N/A	N/A	0.39	
			(0.04)	
Tennessee team				
Time Series (1948–1988)	0.385	—	N/A	
	(0.055)			
CBS team				
Time Series (1948–1988)				
Unrestricted model	0.40	−0.17		
	(0.12)	(0.18)		
With homogeneity restrictions	0.41	−0.14		
	(0.08)	(0.14)		
With homogeneity and	0.32	−0.15		
symmetry restrictions	(0.08)	(0.13)		
Budget Surveys				
Grouped data (1965)			0.40	
Individual data			0.65	

not report a price elasticity. The Texas team's tentative price elasticity is −0.57, which is much larger than the estimate of around 0.15 given by the CBS team. However, in the CBS team's study the price elasticities for the Netherlands are not statistically significant.

The Tennessee team do not give any cross-section estimates of income elasticity for the Netherlands. The estimate based on group data reported by the Texas team and the Tennessee team are very similar and are around 0.4.

Among the cross-section estimates reported by the CBS team, their estimate of 0.65 based on data on individual consumers is considerably higher than the estimate of 0.4 obtained using group data. I have not been able to examine the reason for this large difference. Perhaps the authors could shed light on this matter.

4.3. Forecasting Food Demands in the Netherlands (1989–2000)

Both the Texas team and the Tennessee team provide forecasts. The Texas team provide per capita expenditure of food as well as total expenditure on food. The Tennessee team give per capita food consumption and not total food expenditure. The CBS team do not provide any forecasts, although from the estimates of the marginal budget shares they seem to imply that the level of real expenditures on food will remain constant in the Netherlands.

As to be expected, the two sets of predictions by the Texas team and the Tennessee team are quite similar for the initial years and start to depart considerably towards the end of the prediction period, with the Texas team's point predictions always exceeding those of the Tennessee team. Both sets of predictions are based on VAR models subject to different restrictions.

A priori it is very difficult to choose between the two forecasts. I would have preferred to see an ensemble of forecasts based on a number of different univariate and multivariate models, thus giving some indication of the degree of model uncertainty involved. As it is, both papers give interval predictions which at best can capture the parameter uncertainty of the selected model, and ignore the issue of model uncertainty.

4.4. A Final Remark

There is no doubt that there has been important progress in econometric methodology over the past three decades and these papers clearly reflect that. However, what seems to be lacking is a better integration of developments in economic theory and econometrics, an issue which was also of particular concern to Frisch and Tinbergen.

5.   PETER SCHMIDT'S COMPARATIVE ASSESSMENT: TEXAS, LEAMER AND FINLAND

This is a comparative assessment of the Finland, Leamer and Texas papers. According to the instructions, the aim of the Experiment is to 'assess ... the advantage (if any) of 45 years of econometric theory since Tobin's paper, the impact of new economic theories (e.g. the permanent income hypothesis), and, of course, the differences between several ways of doing econometrics in a practical application.' With this in mind, I will first ask what the notable and potentially relevant advances in economic and econometric theory have been, and to what extent they seem to have influenced these three papers and their results.

5.1.   Advances in Economic and Econometric Theory Since 1950

5.1.1.   The Permanent Income Hypothesis

Milton Friedman won the Nobel Prize for his observation that current income is a mismeasured version of permanent income, and that this causes a downward bias in the estimated income elasticity of consumption, with severity depending on the time span of the data. This is clearly relevant in the present setting. It is worth noting explicitly that Friedman's argument applies both to the cross-section and to the time-series case; in the time-series, however, it can be addressed by including appropriate dynamics that model expectations formation. Tobin clearly anticipated Friedman's permanent income argument, but it appears to me that he thought that it was not a problem in group-averaged data. As Texas notes, this optimistic thought is not justified. Finland does not really do much with the cross section, in part because of worries about permanent income. Neither Texas nor Leamer really make any serious accommodation empirically for the permanent income hypothesis. This is perhaps surprising. I think there is relevant literature, for example in development economics, for guidance.

5.1.2. Unit Roots and Cointegration

Several econometricians no doubt will win Nobel Prizes for their work on this topic. This theoretical work has caused a true revolution in the way time-series econometrics is carried out. One way to interpret this literature is in terms of the Granger–Newbold spurious regression: strong error autocorrelation is even more important than people thought. Another is in terms of inference: least squares and its variants don't lead to valid inference, even asymptotically, even if there is no error autocorrelation, if the regressors are integrated (unless unrealistically strong exogeneity conditions hold). Leamer's failure to acknowledge this literature in his empirical work is very surprising to me. I don't see this as a Bayesian versus classical issue, but I am often surprised at what is considered such an issue. Perhaps one could argue that unit root asymptotics are not reliable with so few observations; if so, such arguers should read Stock (1988) for evidence to the contrary. Finland clearly displays awareness of the relevance of cointegration, but does not use its literature to pick an efficient method of estimation. Only Texas uses results from this literature in a way that seems natural and appropriate to me.

5.1.3. Specification Analysis

Here I would include two somewhat different topics, namely (i) the methods of dynamic specification largely developed by David Hendry; and (ii) the tradition of formal specification tests that began with Theil and more recently led to a large battery of LM tests. Leamer mostly avoids formal specification tests. I think this is a mistake, personally, but it may not make much difference empirically because he clearly does look thoughtfully at diagnostics (graphical or otherwise) of the adequacy of the model. Finland reports that their estimated models pass a battery of diagnostic tests. However, one does not get the sense that there was a serious interplay between specification tests and the specification process; for example, there is no visible respecification in response to failures of specification tests. Texas uses the Hendry methodology only a little (they test for and impose a common factor restriction, yielding autocorrelation as a simplifying device), but they make extensive use of LM tests of model specification. Not everyone will like such extensive testing, without regard to questions like overall size, but I do. Simply put, it increases my faith in their models.

5.1.4. Aggregation

An obvious question is whether the cross-section and time-series data should be expected to yield the same results. This is related to the question debated in modern macroeconomics of whether the assumption of a representative consumer has any microeconomic virtue or content. Basically it is a question of aggregation. There is a very large literature on this question. Only Texas deals with the relevant literature. Their results are essentially negative: given what they find, you can't aggregate simply. They even give some formal analysis of their own. None of the papers attempts an 'encompassing' analysis that asks what features of the world would yield the same kinds of differences between micro and macro results that we observe. This seems to me to be a fruitful way to proceed, akin to Friedman's explaining the difference between short-run and long-run consumption functions on the basis of the permanent income hypothesis.

5.1.5. Practical Bayesianism

Since 1950, a large number of people (though a minority of the econometrics profession) have developed what I would call practical Bayesian methods; that is, methods that go beyond just quoting Bayes' theorem to allow its implementation in realistic applications. Only Leamer tries Bayesian methods in this exercise. That's too bad, because one can't readily tell whether he gets different results because he's Bayesian or because he's Leamer and not one of the other authors. Leamer does provide some non-Bayesian results, but it would be equally interesting to see alternative Bayesian analyses by others. For example, I can imagine an analysis by John Geweke that would look a lot different from Leamer's, but I don't have any feel for what his answers would be.

I will now turn from a discussion of methodological issues to the more purely empirical question of how different these papers' results are.

5.2. Cross-Sectional Results

Tobin found an income elasticity of food consumption of 0.56, using a simple log-linear model. Finland did not attempt a serious analysis of the cross section data. Leamer and Texas both did a thorough reexamination of Tobin's cross-section. They both found interactions between the effects of family size and income. Texas found significance for a multiplicative interaction of log family size and log income, and for the square of log family size. Leamer found significance for some dummy variables reflecting family size, and their interactions with log income. These strike me as different parameterizations of the same phenomenon. Leamer reports income elasticities of food consumption that range from 0.56 to 0.72 (non-Bayesian estimates) or from 0.58 to 0.69 (Bayesian estimates) for the various family sizes, with a specific income level assumed. Texas reports an income elasticity of 0.62 at the means of the data. If I interpret their results correctly, their elasticity depends on family size only (not income) and would range from 0.54 with family size of one to 0.81 with family size of five. I would say that Leamer and Texas found about the same thing, and both found a higher income elasticity than Tobin did.

5.3. Time-Series Results

For the time series, there was much more difference across authors in approach and results. Tobin used yearly US data from 1913–1941 and found a price elasticity of 0.53 when the income elasticity was constrained to equal 0.56. For the unconstrained case, he found a price elasticity of 0.28 and an income elasticity of 0.27. From the current perspective, his imposition of the cross-section value of 0.56 for the income elasticity seems clearly a mistake. The time-series value is significantly different from 0.56 and it is not sensible to criticize it (as he does) as unreliable due to multicollinearity.

Finland use the revised Tobin data for 1924–1976, omitting the post-World War I period but including World War II. They estimate a recursive VAR in log food consumption per capita and log food price index, with three exogenous variables, namely log real disposable income per capita, log nonfood price index and household size. Estimation is by the Engle-Granger two-step method, perhaps a mistake. They obtain a very low long-run income elasticity of 0.15. This is not due to the time period; for Tobin's choice of time period, they also obtain 0.15. For the Dutch data, 1960–1988, they obtain a much higher income elasticity of 0.84. They do not report price elasticities.

Texas does two separate and surprisingly different analyses of the US time-series. First they use Tobin's data. I presume they estimate by ordinary least squares, which is surprising unless they are deliberately trying to put themselves in Tobin's shoes. They report that Tobin's residuals are nonstationary, which is surprising because by 1950 strong error autocorrelation should have been noticed. With the income elasticity not constrained, and with a 'per family' function that includes family size and the square of log income, they obtain stationary residuals, an income elasticity (at the means) of 0.28, and a price elasticity of 0.26. Obviously, these results are very close to Tobin's. They later turn to the extended US data, but use only 1944–1989. Now they estimate by dynamic OLS and derive an error correction model. They test and impose a common factor restriction to get a simple specification with an income elasticity of 0.40 and a price elasticity of 0.51. Finally, for the Dutch time series, 1949–1988, they estimate a four-dimensional VAR. They find two cointegrating relationships, one of which they interpret as a demand curve; it gives an income elasticity of 0.52 and a price elasticity of 0.57.

I think that the motivation for the VAR for the Dutch data was to estimate a model that would be useful for the forecasting exercise. Other than that, I am puzzled by the use of different methods on different data. Only the analysis of the 'extended' US data seems to me to pay serious attention to empirical and econometric detail.

Leamer begins his analysis of the Tobin time-series with an 'unrestricted' Tobin-style regression that does not impose the cross-section income elasticity (which he takes to be 0.6), contains lagged income, does not impose homogeneity of degree zero in prices, and allows for AR(1) errors. This yields a price elasticity of 0.69, which is statistically significant by usual standards. He then goes on to consider all 15 possible restricted regressions that are gotten by imposing the income elasticity of 0.6, excluding lagged income, imposing homogeneity and/or not allowing AR(1) errors. The range of elasticity estimates is from 0.31 to 0.92. The AR(1) coefficients are all very large (ranging from 0.73 to 0.88) and I would discount the uncorrected regressions. Leamer's use of the standard error of regression to pick 'best fitting' regressions has the same effect, and lowers the range of estimates from 0.69 to 0.92. This would strike me as reasonable.

Leamer proceeds to do a sensitivity analysis on the choice of Bayesian priors. Changing the prior variance in a perhaps reasonable way changes the posterior a lot. Now the range of estimates is from 0.48 to 1.56, or from 0.56 to 1.22 if cross-parameter constraints involving the AR(1) coefficient are not considered. This is the range that Leamer 'would live with,' and it is slightly over twice as wide as the range from 0.69 to 0.92 given above. It is wider than I would consider reasonable because it corresponds to imposing cross-parameter constraints that I would not contemplate; that is, the extreme estimates do not come from regressions I would consider sensible.

It is hard to know what to make of all this. Clearly, there's a lot more variation across papers in the time-series results than in the cross-section results. This is presumably true because there's more difference in technique and because there are some differences across papers in the sample periods used. With some (considerable) extra work one could try to see what differences in procedures really drove the differences in results, but at this point I don't feel that I really would care to guess.

5.4. Forecasting

This part of the Experiment was much less satisfying to read about. Leamer did not do the forecasting exercise, and that's disappointing because 'judgement' has typically been introduced much more explicitly in forecasting problems than in estimation problems; I'd like to see judgement used in a formal Bayesian way. Texas and Finland did forecast, in each case using cointegrated VAR's, and came up with forecasts that do not seem very convincing to me.

A widely accepted general statement is that over medium to long horizons, the imposition or non-imposition of unit roots will make more difference than the treatment of short-run dynamics. Similarly, the treatment of deterministic trends will dominate the treatment of stochastic components of the data. In fact, following Nelson and Kang (1984) and others, one of the major reasons why unit roots matter is that they strongly affect the appropriate choice of method for estimating deterministic trends.

Finland considers a univariate AR model in first differences, without intercept, which is their model 1. They also estimate a two-variable VAR with three exogenous forcing variables. Using this model to forecast requires constructing forecasts of the forcing variables. They then consider two different ways of forecasting the forcing variables, leading to models 2 and 3. Model 2 assumes a random walk with drift while model 3 assumes an AR(1) without intercept for the forcing variables. These models lead to very different results: the forecasts for the year 2000 are 4.34, 7.39 and 4.13, respectively (with the 1988 value being 3.97). As the authors note, the middle value seems unrealistic. It seems clear to me that the reason that model 2 is so different from the others is that it explicitly assumes a linear deterministic trend in the forcing variables, which leads to a deterministic trend in the forecasts. Models 1 and 3 do not incorporate a deterministic trend in the forcing variables, and therefore do not have it in the forecasts. However, I would suspect that reasonable forecasts would require some accommodation of deterministic trend. I am not sure why model 2 does so poorly, frankly. We might consider an alternative simplistic univariate model, namely a random walk with drift model for food consumption per capita itself. For this model, we forecast simply by connecting the first and last in-sample data points with a straight line, and then extrapolate to 2000. When I do this, graphically, I get about 5.3. I am not sure what to conclude from this except that I approve of trying multiple models, but some systematic way of choosing which to believe is going to be necessary. If the choice is based simply on which results seem 'most reasonable,' we are essentially just making a 'reasonable' judgemental forecast and then using the chosen model to justify it.

Texas consider a four-variable VAR, in which they find two cointegrating vectors. Their forecasts then follow in a relatively straightforward manner from the VAR. They use a 'modern' approach that is probably what I would have done and what I would have expected most of the participants in the Experiment to do. A vague and perhaps unfair criticism is that their forecasting exercise seemed a bit mechanical and uncritical. There are lots of LM tests, but a shortage of sensitivity analyses and discussion of whether the results are reasonable.

When all is said and done, I do not think I would care to go to the Dutch food manufacturers with any of these forecasts. Maybe this reflects my 'old-fashioned' 1970's background, but the forecasts seem based on too small an information set and too little institutional knowledge. (This may be due to the rules of the Experiment, which prohibited use of any other information.) For example, to forecast population I'd hire a demographer.

To understand historical increases in the relative price of food and to make my forecasts, I would try to look at the relative price of wholesale (raw, unprocessed, . . .) food as well as the reported food price index. I suspect the reason people spend more on food now is mostly that they eat in restaurants more often than they used to, and that the substitution of restaurant food for home-cooked food is why the real price of food has risen so much. Data on restaurant visits and prices would be clearly relevant, then. A pure time-series approach may be a good way to generate forecasts from a very limited information set, but if the forecasting problem is really important there is no good reason to limit the information set.

6.   MICHAEL WICKENS' COMPARATIVE ASSESSMENT: CBS, MADDALA AND DUNDEE

Although I was impressed by the considerable efforts made both by the teams and the assessors at the conclusion of the presentation of the papers, it was clear that no consensus had emerged about how to model food consumption, about what the values of the two key parameters are, or about whether the time-series or cross-section results were the more reliable. So what have we learned from the experiment? Is it possible to explain why the various studies had obtained their results and can one recommend a preferred approach?

It is convenient to focus on the income elasticity. The general findings were that the cross-section estimates were higher than the time-series estimates, and were much more precisely estimated, but the estimates decreased the more recent the cross-section. Whether the demand function was estimated with quantity or price as the dependent variable was also found to be very important, as the 'direct' estimates of the income elasticity were much lower than the 'indirect', and had much smaller standard errors.

It is possible to identify four areas that are the main cause of the different results. These are the choice of variables in the equation, the choice of dependent variable, the measurement of the variables and the effect of including dynamics. It will come as little surprise to those who have read my comments on the CBS paper that the key to each of these choices is to be found more in the underlying economics than in the econometrics.

I shall take as my starting point for the relevant economic theory the neo-classical consumer demand theory used by the CBS team. As I have explained previously, in my view this is not strictly appropriate as it takes no account of inter-temporal considerations, or potential substitution across other consumer goods. Also, for empirical implementation on time-series data, the CBS model should be expressed in terms of levels and not as differentials. Nevertheless, with one amendment, I shall use this theory.

The theory tells us that quantity should be the dependent variable and price should be an explanatory variable on the grounds that prices are taken as given in the theory. This implies that the direct version should be estimated. Only much larger measurement errors in own price than quantity would justify using the indirect version on grounds of bias. The theory also indicates that quantity is probably best measured by aggregate nominal expenditure on food per capita deflated by the general consumption price level, and the income variable by deflated aggregate total consumption per capita. Tobin's variable definitions are not as consistent with the theory as he doesn't use a common price deflator. This choice of dependent variable and way of measuring the variables both contribute to producing larger estimates of the income elasticity.

There is some ambiguity about the level of aggregation that the theory should work at — the individual or household — and there are further problems about translating this for use with aggregate data. I have found that deflating aggregate expenditures by population and including population in the final equation seems to work best. Finally, although neo-classical consumer theory is static, it is clear that some dynamics are required in the time-series model. This finding indicates that neo-classical theory is not strictly appropriate, and suggests that some life-cycle element may be required as originally envisaged by Tobin. Again, taking account of both of these tends to raise the estimate of the income elasticity.

The accompanying Table III presents estimates of a number of different versions of the model which illustrate the above arguments. Column 1 is a static version of Tobin's original model and uses his variable definitions. The estimate of the income elasticity is the lowest of all and is not significantly different from zero. Column 2 uses the alternative variable definitions based on expenditures discussed above. The estimate of the income elasticity is dramatically different; it is close to the cross-section estimates and is as precisely estimated. Column 3 includes an extra variable, $\ln N$, which is highly significant. Column 4 adds the change in each variable as additional explanatory variables and uses GMM. This is equivalent to adding the lagged value of each variable, but has the advantage of allowing the estimates reported to retain their long-run interpretation, see Wickens and Breusch (1988). This equation gives my preferred estimate of the long-run income elasticity which is about 0.7. It will be noted that this is very close to the cross-section values.

To sum up, in my view the starting point of all good applied econometrics is economic theory. It is essential to derive the equation to be estimated carefully from this. Without

Table III. Long-run estimates, US data, 1929–76

	$\ln S$	$\ln(PS/\Pi)$	$\ln(PS/\Pi)$	$\ln(PS/\Pi)$
	1	2	3	4
constant	5.42	−5.81	−0.65	4.89
	(19.7)	(−4.08)	(−0.81)	(1.2)
$\ln(Y/N)$	0.07	—	—	—
	(2.99)			
$\ln(Y/\Pi)$	—	0.53	0.62	0.70
		(61.77)	(40.9)	(10.4)
$\ln P$	−0.08	0.21	0.16	0.14
	(−2.84)	(12.42)	(10.8)	(2.9)
$\ln Q$	0.10	−0.02	0.11	0.25
	(4.40)	(−1.14)	(5.1)	(2.3)
$\ln N$	—	—	−0.97	−0.75
			(−14.1)	(−2.6)
R^2	0.938	0.999	1.000	0.996
CRDW	0.67	0.51	0.59	—
se	0.016	0.012	0.009	0.024

Notes: (i)   col 1 uses *PCFC* and *AGGY* per capita
       (ii)   cols 2–4 use *AGGEXPF* and *AGGEXP* both per capita and deflated
       (iii) col 4 includes first differences of the variables and is estimated by IV
       (iv)   *t*-statistics in parentheses

the theory, econometrics is just data-mining, no matter how sophisticated the estimation or modelling procedures. New developments in econometric methods, estimation theory and inference have greatly improved applied econometrics over the years but they are no substitute for thinking about the economic theory first. This experiment is a good example. Those teams who emphasized econometric methodology to the virtual exclusion of economic theory were left at the end with an unclear picture of what their results implied and with different results from each other. And this was despite being able to draw heavily on Tobin's original formulation, which although not explicitly based on formal theory obviously drew carefully on theory.

REFERENCES

Nelson, C. R. and H. Kang (1984), 'Pitfalls in the use of time as an explanatory variable in regression', *Journal of Business and Economic Statistics*, **2**, 73–82.

Stock, J. (1988), 'A reexamination of Friedman's consumption puzzle', *Journal of Business and Economic Statistics*, **6**, 401–14.

Tobin, J. (1950), 'A statistical demand function for food in the USA', *Journal of the Royal Statistical Society*, Series A, **113**, Part II, 113–141 [reprinted in Chapter 2, this volume].

Wickens, M. R. and T. S. Breusch (1988), 'Dynamic specification, the long-run and the estimation of transformed regression models', *The Economic Journal* (Conference), **98**, 189–205.

CHAPTER 13

ANALYSIS OF THE FIELD TRIAL EXPERIMENT

JAN R. MAGNUS AND WIEBE K. SIEGERT

1. INTRODUCTION

In this chapter, we provide a summary and exploratory analysis of the results obtained by the eight teams who participated in the field trial experiment. We emphasize again that the experiment was never intended to be a competition, with a winner and a loser. We simply try to understand what each team has done and why this has resulted in different estimates than those obtained by another team.

In Section 2 we discuss the measurement tasks 1 and 2, where the questions were to estimate the income elasticity of food demand, to test the homogeneity postulate, and to comment on the results, both for the US and the Dutch data. Tables II–IV summarize the results obtained by the eight teams. It is interesting that even with the original Tobin data set, there is no agreement on whether homogeneity holds or not. Tobin accepts homogeneity, as does Dundee, but Leamer, Tennessee and Maastricht reject it.

In Section 3, we provide some further analysis of the estimated elasticities. Figures 1–3 summarize the estimates. We see that for both the extended US time series and the Dutch time series there is substantial disagreement between the teams. For the extended US time series we summarize the estimating equations for each of the teams. This provides some insight into the reasons why the estimates differ so much.

In Section 4, we discuss the forecasting task. Figure 4 provides graphs of the various forecasts provided. We have realizations until 1995 and we also calculated a naive Holt-Winters forecast, which serves as a benchmark. Texas and Maastricht are closest to the 'truth.'

In Section 5, we ask how well the teams' results for task 1 can be reproduced. We conclude that for three teams the results could be replicated exactly, for two teams there were some ambiguities, and for the remaining three teams we obtained different results than the authors.

A summary of the tasks completed is provided in Table I. On average, each team completed 10.5 of the 19 tasks, that is 55%. Leamer only attempted four tasks, while Maastricht attempted an impressive 15 tasks. None of the tasks was completed by all eight teams; part (i) of Task 1(b) was the most popular, Task 2(a) the least popular.

Our strong impression is that all participants resisted the 'exam-like' set-up of the experiment. In many of the papers, we had to search carefully to find answers in the text. Sometimes we had to read 'between the lines' and do our own calculations, based on the estimates provided. The number of instances where a question like: 'estimate the income elasticity of food demand' was answered by: 'the estimate is 0.59 (0.04)'—well, there were no such answers. One of the benefits of being an academic is to be able to ask one's

Methodology and Tacit Knowledge: Two Experiments in Econometrics
Jan R. Magnus and Mary S. Morgan © 1999 John Wiley & Sons Ltd

Table I. Summary of tasks completed

	Task	Texas	CBS	Leamer	Tennessee	Dundee	Maastricht	Finland	Maddala	Total
1a(i)	original budget data, USA	✓				✓	✓			3/8
1a(i)	original time series, USA	✓		✓		✓	✓		✓	5/8
1a(ii)	test homogeneity, USA	✓			✓	✓	✓			4/8
1a(iii)	comment on the difference, USA	✓		✓		✓	✓			4/8
1b(i)	extended 1941 data set, USA	✓	✓	✓		✓	✓			5/8
1b(i)	extended 1950 data set, USA	✓	✓		✓	✓	✓	✓	✓	7/8
1b(i)	extended 1960 data set, USA	✓	✓		✓	✓	✓	✓	✓	7/8
1b(i)	extended 1972 data set, USA	✓	✓		✓	✓	✓	✓	✓	7/8
1b(i)	extended time series, USA	✓	✓		✓	✓	✓	✓	✓	7/8
1b(ii)	test homogeneity, USA	✓	✓		✓	✓	✓			5/8
1b(iii)	comment on the difference, USA	✓	✓		✓	✓		✓		5/8
2a(i)–(ii)	Netherlands									0/8
2b(i)	1965 data set, Netherlands		✓				✓			2/8
2b(i)	1980 data set, Netherlands	✓	✓				✓	✓		4/8
2b(i)	1988 data set, Netherlands	✓	✓				✓	✓		4/8
2b(i)	time series, Netherlands	✓	✓		✓	✓	✓	✓		6/8
2b(ii)	test homogeneity, Netherlands		✓		✓	✓				3/8
3	forecast for food, Netherlands	✓			✓	✓	✓	✓		5/8
5	own task			✓						1/8

own questions (and try to answer them). To answer someone else's question is less exciting, and all eight teams, some more, some less, had difficulty in accepting, quite understandably of course, the 'exam-like' situation. This has seriously complicated the analysis.

2. THE MEASUREMENT TASKS

Tasks 1 and 2 asked each team to estimate the income elasticity of food demand, to test the homogeneity postulate of the family food demand function, and to comment on the results. Task 1(a) asked these questions for the original Tobin data set for the USA, task 1(b) for the extended (full) US data set, and task 2 for the Dutch data.

Task 1(a) was the simplest to perform. It was designed to find out whether Tobin's original questions, posed more than 45 years ago, would now be answered differently. The teams could only use the same data as were available to Tobin in 1950, but they could use a different model or method of estimation.

The results are summarized in Table II. Only three of the eight teams estimated the required income elasticity from the 1941 US budget survey; five from the Tobin time series. The variation between the estimates is within the bounds of credibility: 0.56–0.66 for the budget survey, about 0.15–0.20 for the time series (short run), and 0.20–0.29 for the time series (long run).

Texas provided two elasticities based on two different models, without favouring one model above the other. The CBS team did not answer the question. They mentioned that they were able to reproduce Tobin's results, 'apart from the estimates for the constant terms' (beginning of Section 4). This is the result of the fact that the CBS team used natural logarithms whereas Tobin used logarithms base 10. Leamer did not estimate the income elasticity from the time series. He used the cross-section estimate (0.62, rounded to 0.6) in his time-series analysis in the same way as Tobin's 0.56. Dundee answered 1(a) implicitly in their reply to 1(b) because, in answering 1(b) for 1941, they used the Tobin data set (by mistake?) instead of the extended data set. Maastricht reported that they could

Table II. Summary of answers to task 1(a), Tobin's US data

	'Original' Budget Survey 1941	'Original' Time Series	Homogeneity Test	Comments
Tobin	0.56	0.27	not rejected	
Texas	0.62	0.25 0.29		✓
CBS				
Leamer	0.62		(rejected)	✓
Tennessee		short run: 0.16 long run: 0.28	rejected	
Dundee	0.66 0.63 0.61	short run: 0.15 long run: 0.20	not rejected	✓
Maastricht		0.33	rejected	✓
Finland				
Maddala		short run: 0.20 long run: 0.28		

reproduce Tobin's results, but they didn't answer 1(a) for the budget data. Maddala's results have been extracted by us from his Equation (14) and his table in Section 4.

The homogeneity postulate, *not* rejected by Tobin, was rejected by Tennessee. Leamer's results (Section 6) were ambiguous and he didn't explicitly state whether or not homogeneity is rejected. There was an error in Leamer's Equation (6), where $-\alpha_2 \log(Y_{t-1})$ should be changed to $-\alpha_2 \log(Y_{t-1}/Q_t)$, meaning that both current and past income should be measured relative to today's prices. Using Leamer's Table IV, the estimate of $(\alpha_1 + \alpha_2 + \beta + \gamma)/\beta$ is $-(0.43 - 0.07) = -0.36$ and the estimate of $(\alpha_1 + \alpha_2 + \beta + \gamma)$ is $-0.36/ - 1.45 = 0.25$. Since Leamer also provided the coefficient correlation matrix, we find that the estimate -0.36 has a standard error of 0.15. Hence, standard econometrics would reject the hypothesis $(\alpha_1 + \alpha_2 + \beta + \gamma)/\beta = 0$.[1] The Maastricht team mentioned (Section 3.2) that price homogeneity is rejected at the 1% level and we interpret this as a rejection of the homogeneity postulate. Only Dundee did not reject homogeneity (Section 3). In summary, three of the four teams who attempted this question rejected homogeneity, contrary to Tobin's original conclusion, even though the same data were used.

The third part to question 1(a) asked the teams to comment on the differences between their results and Tobin's. None of the teams said: 'I have this answer, Tobin had that answer. The difference is caused by ...' However, four of the teams attempted some partial answer.

In Task 1(b) the teams could use the full 'extended' data sets for the US. The amount of variation in the estimates of the income elasticity of food demand is substantial. For example, in 1972 the elasticity estimate varies between 0.34 (Maddala) and 0.71 (CBS). The results are summarized in Table III.

Texas provided two estimates for the four budget surveys. The first number was based on Tobin's model with weighting; the second number was obtained by adding socio-demographic variables. The CBS team considered two subsets of the time-series data: 1929–1941 and 1929–1989. They used the same model for both subsets and found the same elasticity of 0.75. Leamer did not answer 1(b) since he concentrated fully on a re-analysis of Tobin's original data. Tennessee pooled the 1950 and 1960 data sets. Dundee gave various estimates for the cross-section elasticity. Maastricht found the very high estimate of 1.00 for the time-series elasticity.

The homogeneity postulate was rejected by Texas, Tennessee and Maastricht, was ambiguous in Dundee, and was not rejected by the CBS team.

We now come to task 2. Task 2(a) concerned the relationship between various pieces of relevant information. The question is based on the following observation. Suppose we wish to estimate the income elasticity of food demand in the Netherlands. There exists in the literature one closely related study, based on US data. How do we treat this US study? Clearly it contains some relevant information, but how can this information be properly incorporated in the Dutch study? A Bayesian approach might be the solution, although this approach has its own difficulties. But most of us are non- or semi-Bayesians. So, what do we do? The common procedure seems to be as follows. We read the other study, but since we want our own contribution to be as novel as possible, we do not copy exactly its model or estimation technique. Instead, we try something a little different. The US paper is mentioned

---

[1] We attempted to reproduce Leamer's Table VI in order to provide a similar analysis to the coefficient of $\log Q$, but were unsuccessful.

Table III. Summary of answers to task 1(b), 'extended' US data

	'Extended' Budget Surveys				'Extended' Time Series	Homogeneity Test	Comments
	1941	1950	1960	1972			
Texas	0.59	0.52	0.54	0.35	0.41	rejected	
	0.61	0.42	0.42	0.38			
CBS	0.74	0.75	0.73	0.71	0.75 / 0.75	not rejected	✓
Leamer							
Tennessee		0.38	0.38	0.33	short/long run: 0.18/0.21	rejected	✓
Dundee		0.70	0.73	0.65	short/long run: 0.30/0.76	rejected and not rejected	✓
		0.67	0.70	0.61			
		0.64	0.67	0.56			
Maastricht	0.61	0.55	0.54	0.39	1.00	rejected	✓
Finland	0.52	0.52	0.52	0.52	short/long run: 0.09/0.15		✓
Maddala	0.64	0.56	0.56	0.34	short/long run: 0.09/0.23		

Note: Tennessee pooled the 1950 and 1960 US Surveys, Finland pooled all four US Surveys.

in the introduction, but otherwise ignored until we come to the conclusion. Now there are two possibilities. Either our results are close to the previous study or they are not. If they are, we are happy and tell the reader that clearly our study was a good and solid one, confirming for the Netherlands what had already been found in the USA. If, on the other hand, our results are not close to the previous study, we are also happy and tell the reader that the result is no surprise, because our method is different and what our colleague did is clearly wrong.

This picture of econometric practice may be too black, and task 2(a) was designed to see if the teams had any suggestion on how to deal with this often occurring situation. Since none of the teams attempted an answer, we conclude that this important question is essentially unsolved!

Task 2(b) differed from 2(a) in that all US data are available, not just the resulting US estimates. The question was to estimate the income elasticity and test homogeneity for the Netherlands. All teams except Leamer and Maddala attempted the task for the Netherlands, but only two teams took any notice of the available US data set. Finland (their Table III) used the long-run estimate from the US cross sections to estimate the short-run elasticity for the Dutch time series, while Tennessee (Section 3.4) attempted to pool the two countries.

The results are summarized in Table IV. Finland provided three analyses: one cointegration analysis using only Dutch time-series data, one combined cross-section time-series analysis using Dutch data, and one combined US cross-section Dutch time-series analysis. The resulting estimates are far apart.

Three teams (CBS, Tennessee, Dundee) tested the homogeneity postulate. In each case the hypothesis could not be rejected. Texas did not formally test for homogeneity, but

Table IV. Summary of answers to task 2(b), Dutch data

	Budget Surveys			Time Series	Homogeneity Test
	1965	1980	1988		
Texas		0.34 0.30 0.35	0.42 0.37 0.44	0.52	(not rejected)
CBS	0.42	0.63	0.69	0.35	not rejected
Leamer					
Tennessee				short run: 0.35 long run: 0.39	not rejected
Dundee				short run: 0.15 long run: 0.79	not rejected
Maastricht	0.41	0.34	0.47	0.48	
Finland		0.41	0.41	short run: 0.73 long run: 0.84	
Maddala					

Note: Finland pooled the 1980 and 1988 Dutch Surveys.

mentioned (below their Table IV) that 'the sum of the coefficients of the nominal variables is 0.05, which is close to zero required by the homogeneity postulate.'

Although the question of pooling was not part of any of the tasks, Tobin himself used an estimate from the 1941 budget study in his time-series analysis and the *Experiment Information Pack* mentioned papers by Chetty (1968), Maddala (1971) and Izan (1980). Maybe this is one reason why many of the papers considered pooling the data. Leamer followed Tobin's example. There were four teams who attempted to combine different budget studies: Texas considered pooling the four US budget surveys, Tennessee pooled the 1950 and 1960 US budget surveys, Finland pooled the four US budget surveys and the 1980 and 1988 Dutch budget surveys, and Maastricht (Section 2.2) also considered pooling the cross-section data and found, like Tennessee, that 1950 and 1960 can be pooled, but no other years. In addition, Finland considered pooling the cross-section and time-series data.

In the next section we provide graphs of the estimated elasticities and try to understand the cause of the differences.

3. FURTHER ANALYSIS OF THE ESTIMATED ELASTICITIES

In this section we provide a further summary and analysis of the estimated income elasticities of food demand. In Figure 1 we summarize the estimates from the US budget surveys, including Tobin's own estimates on his original data set. For the 1941 budget surveys (both original and extended) the reported estimates are close, but for the 1950, 1960 and 1972 budget surveys, the estimates are not so close. If standard errors of the estimates are provided, we give a '95% interval,' namely the estimate plus/minus twice its standard error. If standard errors are not provided, we simply give the point estimate. On the whole, Texas reported the largest standard errors and CBS the highest estimates. Remarkable is the stability of the patterns. For example, the CBS team obtained a relatively high estimate from all four US budget surveys.

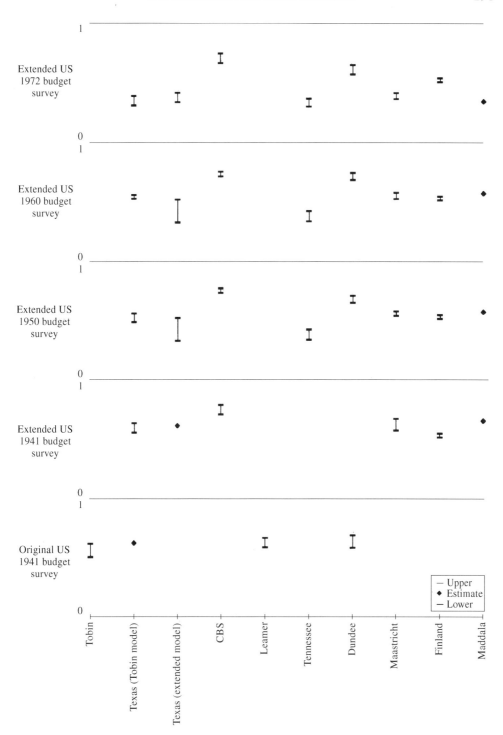

Figure 1. Estimates of the income elasticity of food demand, US budget surveys

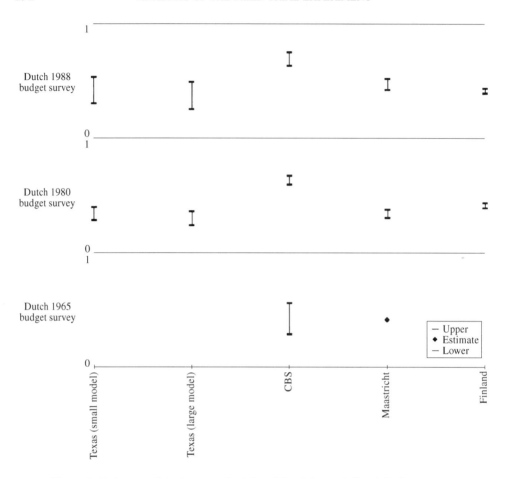

Figure 2. Estimates of the income elasticity of food demand, Dutch budget surveys

In Figure 2 we summarize the corresponding estimates for the Dutch budget surveys. The range is fairly wide, slightly wider than for the US budget surveys 1950, 1960, 1972.

In Figure 3 we consider the time-series results. In the original US time series, the estimates are close together. But for both the extended US time series and the Dutch time series the range of estimates is very wide. For this reason we analyze the extended US time series results a little further in the hope that we can perhaps understand why these results are so different.

All teams except Leamer analyzed the extended US time series. Hence, there are seven models to consider. Texas used an error correction model and imposed common factor restrictions until they arrived at

$$\log(FOOD_t) = \mu + \beta_0 \log(INCOME_t) + \gamma_0 \log(FP_t) \quad (t = 1948, \ldots, 1989),$$

where the disturbances follow an AR(1) process (their Equation (10)). Here, $FOOD$ and $INCOME$ are defined as

$$FOOD_t = \frac{AGGEXPF_t}{FP_t * NOH_t}, \quad INCOME_t = \frac{AGGY_t}{NOH_t}.$$

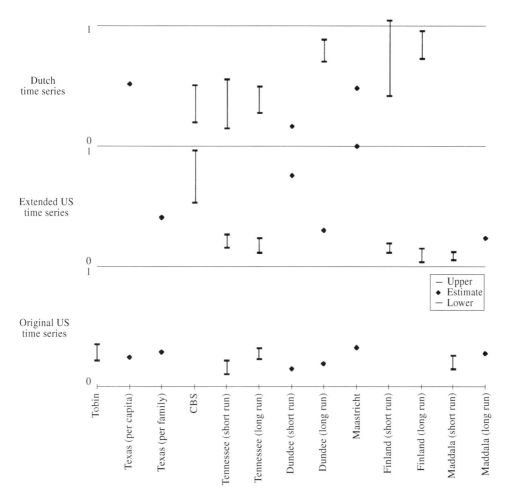

Figure 3. Estimates of the income elasticity of food demand, Dutch and US time series

Texas found a (short run = long run) elasticity of 0.41.

The CBS team considered the equation

$$\frac{1}{2}(w_t + w_{t-1})\Delta \log\left(\frac{q_t}{Q_t}\right) = \beta_0 \Delta \log Q_t + \gamma_0 \Delta \log(FP_t)$$

$$+ \delta_0 \Delta \log(NFP_t) \quad (1929, \ldots, 1989),$$

where

$$w_t = \frac{AGGEXPF_t}{AGGEXP_t}, \quad q_t = \frac{AGGEXPF_t}{FP_t},$$

$$Q_t = \frac{AGGEXP_t}{P_t}, \quad \Delta \log P_t = w_{t-1}\log(FP_t) + (1 - w_{t-1})\log(NFP_t),$$

see Pesaran's comments, Equation (C1). They found an elasticity of 0.75.

Tennessee estimated the following autoregressive distributed log model (Equation 18):

$$
\begin{aligned}
\log(FOOD_t) = {}& \mu + \alpha_1 \log(FOOD_{t-1}) \\
& + \beta_0 \log(INCOME_t) + \beta_1 \log(INCOME_{t-1}) + \beta_2 \log(INCOME_{t-2}) \\
& + \gamma_0 \log(FP_t) + \gamma_1 \log(FP_{t-1}) + \gamma_2 \log(FP_{t-2}) \\
& + \delta_0 \log(NFP_t) + \delta_1 \log(NFP_{t-1}) + \delta_2 \log(NFP_{t-2}) \\
& + \delta_3 \log(NFP_{t-3}) \quad (1913, \ldots, 1976),
\end{aligned}
$$

where $FOOD_t = PCFC_t$, $INCOME_t = PCY_t$. They obtained a long-run elasticity of 0.21 and a short-run elasticity of 0.18.

The Dundee team formulated a cointegration model:

$$
\begin{aligned}
\Delta \log(FOOD_t) = {}& \mu + \alpha_1 \Delta \log(FOOD_{t-1}) \\
& + \beta_1 \Delta \log(INCOME_t) + \beta_2 \Delta \log(INCOME_{t-1}) \\
& + \gamma_1 \Delta \log(FP_t) + \gamma_2 \Delta \log(FP_{t-1}) \\
& + \delta_1 \Delta \log(NFP_t) + \xi EC_{t-1} \quad (1931, \ldots, 1989),
\end{aligned}
$$

where

$$
FOOD_t = \frac{AGGEXPF_t}{P_t^*}, \quad INCOME_t = \frac{AGGY_t}{P_t^*},
$$

P_t^* is a geometrically weighted average of food and non-food price,

$$
P_t^* = (FP_t)^{w_t} (NFP_t)^{1-w_t},
$$

w_t denotes the share of food expenditures in total expenditures, and EC_{t-1} denotes an error correction term. They obtained a long-run elasticity of 0.76 and a short-run elasticity of 0.30.

Maastricht employed a vector error correction model:

$$
\begin{pmatrix} \log(FOOD) \\ \log(INCOME) \\ \log\left(\frac{FP}{100}\right) \\ \log(P^*) \end{pmatrix}_t = \begin{pmatrix} \mu_1 \\ \mu_2 \\ \mu_3 \\ \mu_4 \end{pmatrix} + \begin{pmatrix} v_1 t \\ v_2 t \\ v_3 t \\ v_4 t \end{pmatrix}
$$

$$
+ \begin{pmatrix} \alpha_{11} & \beta_{11} & \gamma_{11} & \delta_{11} \\ \alpha_{21} & \beta_{21} & \gamma_{21} & \delta_{21} \\ \alpha_{31} & \beta_{31} & \gamma_{31} & \delta_{31} \\ \alpha_{41} & \beta_{41} & \gamma_{41} & \delta_{41} \end{pmatrix} \begin{pmatrix} \log(FOOD) \\ \log(INCOME) \\ \log\left(\frac{FP}{100}\right) \\ \log(P^*) \end{pmatrix}_{t-1}
$$

$$
+ \begin{pmatrix} \alpha_{12} & \beta_{12} & \gamma_{12} & \delta_{12} \\ \alpha_{22} & \beta_{22} & \gamma_{22} & \delta_{22} \\ \alpha_{32} & \beta_{32} & \gamma_{32} & \delta_{32} \\ \alpha_{42} & \beta_{42} & \gamma_{42} & \delta_{42} \end{pmatrix} \begin{pmatrix} \log(FOOD) \\ \log(INCOME) \\ \log\left(\frac{FP}{100}\right) \\ \log(P^*) \end{pmatrix}_{t-2} \quad (1949, \ldots, 1989),
$$

where

$$FOOD_t = \frac{AGGEXPF_t * 100}{POP_t + FP_t}, \quad INCOME_t = \frac{AGGY_t}{POP_t * P_t^*},$$

$$P_t^* = (w_t FP_t + (1 - w_t)NFP_t)/100,$$

and w_t is the share of real food expenditures in real total expenditures. Maastricht obtained an income elasticity of 1.00.

Finland also estimated a vector error correction model:

$$\begin{pmatrix} \Delta \log(FP_t) \\ \Delta \log(FOOD_t) \end{pmatrix} = \begin{pmatrix} \mu_1 \\ \mu_2 \end{pmatrix} + \begin{pmatrix} \alpha_1 & \beta_1 & \delta_1 \\ 0 & \beta_2 & \delta_2 \end{pmatrix} \begin{pmatrix} \Delta \log(FOOD_t) \\ \Delta \log(INCOME_t) \\ \Delta \log(NFP_t) \end{pmatrix}$$

$$+ \begin{pmatrix} \xi_1 & \xi_2 \\ 0 & \xi_3 \end{pmatrix} \begin{pmatrix} ECP_{t-1} \\ ECC_{t-1} \end{pmatrix} \quad (1924, \ldots, 1976),$$

where $FOOD_t = PCFC_t$, $INCOME_t = PCY_t$ and ECP_{t-1} and ECC_{t-1} denote error correction terms. They found a long-run elasticity of 0.15 and a short-run elasticity of 0.10.

Finally, Maddala estimated a partial adjustment model,

$$\log(FOOD_t) = \alpha_1 \log(FOOD_{t-1}) + \beta_0 \log(INCOME_t)$$

$$+ \gamma_0 \log(FP_t) \quad (1913, \ldots, 1976),$$

where $FOOD_t = PCFC_t$ and $INCOME_t = PCY_t$. Maddala's equation does not contain a constant term. Their estimate of the long-run elasticity is 0.23 and of the short-run elasticity 0.09.

A comparison of these seven equations provides some insight into the differences between the teams in their elasticity estimates based on the extended US time-series data. A fully integrated model comparison, such as an encompassing exercise, is however beyond the scope of this chapter.

4. THE OTHER TASKS

Originally, there were five tasks. Tasks 1 and 2 relate to measurement (estimation), task 3 to forecasting, task 4 was a policy question, and task 5 was an 'own task.' Few teams attempted the policy question. At the Tilburg workshop in December 1996, the policy task was severely criticized by the teams as being vague and unsuitable. As a result, the organizers decided to drop task 4 and to ask the teams who had attempted this task to remove the relevant sections from their paper.

Task 3 consisted in providing forecasts for the years 1989–2000 for the demand for food in the Netherlands. Five of the eight teams attempted to answer this question: Texas, Tennessee, Dundee, Maastricht and Finland. Since the question was not sufficiently sharp, it could be answered either for nominal or real food consumption, and either per capita or not. This gives four possibilities and each of these was attempted by one or more teams. Texas provided forecasts for three of the four possible interpretations of the question, the other teams just one. Since three teams (Texas, Tennessee, Finland) provided forecasts for nominal per capita food consumption, we decided to interpret the question in this way.

As a result, we had to transform the Dundee and Maastricht forecasts. Dundee (Table IX) produced no less than eight series of forecasts for real total food expenditure (in logs). The bounds are determined by series 3 ('Dundee max') and 5 ('Dundee min'). Following Dundee's earlier remarks we assumed that the food price increases 2% annually. To this we added our own forecast of population (see Table V below), and scaled the forecast so that the 1989 forecast equals its realization.

The Maastricht forecasts were for real per capita food expenditure (Table VIII, VECM(2)$_{\text{trend}}$) and had to be multiplied by our own forecast of the food price. Our forecast for the food price ($P11$) and population (POP) are naive forecasts based on the Holt–Winters method (see Harvey, 1993) and are presented in Table V.

Table V also presents, as a naive benchmark, the Holt–Winters forecasts for the nominal per capita food consumption and the realized figures, 1989–1995. The resulting forecasts are given in Figure 4.

The bold solid line gives the realized food consumption (until 1995) and the light solid line gives our own naive Holt–Winters forecast, which appears to be a little below the realization. There are two peculiarities in the graphs. First, the Dundee max graph has a kink in 1993, probably due to a misprint in Dundee's Table IX, series 3. Secondly, the Finland forecast for 1989 is 3930 which is *smaller* than the observed food demand in 1988, which is $(58\,230*10^6)/(14\,715*10^3) = 3957$. The Dundee forecasts appear to be too large, while the other forecasts are all within the bounds of credibility. Texas and Maastricht appear to perform slightly better than the naive Holt–Winters forecasts.

Since task 4 was dropped, we now turn to task 5. The idea here was to give each team the opportunity to shine in its own speciality by raising a question which, within the data provided, they felt they could answer particularly well. Texas derived the functional form of the aggregate relationship from the functional form of the micro consumption function and the income distribution, and claimed this as their 'own task.' Similarly, Dundee used time-varying parameter models and Kalman-filter estimates. However, the use of modern or new techniques to answer one of the set tasks was the intention of the experiment in general, and not our idea of an 'own task.' Maybe the formulation of task 5 was ambiguous. In our view only Leamer set himself a task: 'How should food

Table V. Holt–Winters forecasts of Dutch food price, population and nominal per capita food consumption, 1989–2000, and realized nominal per capita Dutch food consumption, 1989–1995

Year	Food price (*P11*)	Population (*POP*)	Nominal food per capita (*V11/POP*)	Realized food consumption
1989	406.0	14810	4006	4132
1990	408.2	14910	4062	4309
1991	410.5	15010	4117	4505
1992	412.7	15110	4172	4737
1993	415.0	15210	4227	4786
1994	417.3	15310	4282	4928
1995	419.5	15410	4338	4993
1996	421.8	15510	4393	
1997	424.1	15610	4448	
1998	426.3	15700	4503	
1999	428.6	15800	4558	
2000	430.8	15900	4614	

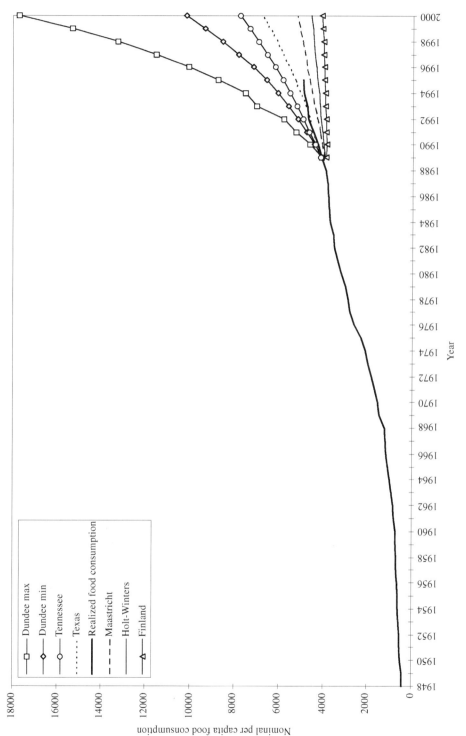

Figure 4. Forecasts of nominal per capita food consumption in the Netherlands, 1989–2000

price subsidies vary by family composition and income level to ensure that families spend at least $ 150 on food (1941 $) per family member.'

5. REPRODUCIBILITY

We were interested to know how well the results in the eight papers could be reproduced. Since task 1 was answered by all teams (at least partially), we decided to try and replicate the budget survey results of task 1 for each of the teams.

Three teams (Leamer, Tennessee, Finland) could be replicated exactly. All three are simple OLS regressions.

Texas produced nine elasticities in their Table I. Of these, six can be immediately reproduced. Of the remaining three elasticities, two ($BS50^a$, $BS60^a$) can be reproduced if the variable *HOMEOWN* is deleted from the regression. Texas included sociodemographic variables, but deleted *HOMEOWN* because the coefficient was insignificant. This is not mentioned in their text. The final elasticity ($BS72$, 9th row in Table I) could not be reproduced.

The CBS team made an error in the passage from Equation (15) to Equation (22). The variable $\bar{x}_g$ was written as $TOTCON_g/SAMPSIZE_g$, while it should have been $TOTCON_g$. This has been corrected in the current version of their paper. Fortunately, their estimation results were based on the correct specification. We could replicate the CBS weighted least squares results (their Methods 3 and 4) for the years 1950, 1960 and 1972. We could not replicate 1941, because 'for 1941 some groups had to be combined' and it was unclear how this had been done.

For the Dundee team, we could reproduce 1972 exactly. The estimates from the other three budget surveys could not be reproduced. We consulted the Dundee team and they sent us the data underlying the 1960 estimates. From this it became clear that they had made two data errors: the third observation on *FOOD* is 608 (Dundee: 606), and the negative number −984 on *HINC* at average household size 5 was changed by them into +984. With these two changes, we could reproduce the 1960 results. However, the 1941 and 1950 results could still not be reproduced, probably because of data errors. (The Dundee team copied the data from the tables provided and not from the diskette.) Our results for 1950 and 1972 correspond perfectly with those of Wallis in his comments on the Dundee team (see his comments following the Maastricht paper). Wallis also changed the negative number −984 on *HINC* to +984 in the 1960 data set. With this change we obtained exactly the estimates of Wallis for the 1960 data set. For the 1941 data set Dundee used 37 and Wallis used 40 observations. Thus, they obtained different results. If we set the last observation on *AHSIZE* to 6, then we obtain results that look like those of Wallis. Dundee carried out weighted least squares without weighting the constant term, as also observed by Wallis.

The Maastricht estimates could be exactly reproduced for 1950, 1960 and 1972. The 1941 estimates, however, could not be reproduced, probably because Maastricht filled in the missing values for *ESTPOPH* and we didn't know how; see their Section 2.2. Wallis also attempted to reproduce the 1941 results and obtained different estimates than Maastricht and also different estimates than ours. Wallis' 1950 and 1972 results correspond exactly with those of Maastricht. For the 1960 data set, Wallis used 59 observations and Maastricht 58 (Maastricht deleted the negative number −984 on *HINC*). Thus, they have different results.

Finally, Maddala concentrated on finding outliers. For this purpose, 'studentized residuals' were used. We agree with Maddala's results for 1941 and 1950. In 1960 we find consecutive outliers in observations 10, 11, 49 and 9, while Maddala found 10, 11, 9 and 12. In 1972 Maddala found one outlier at observation 30, whereas we find that observation 61 has a higher 'studentized residual.' Our results, therefore, disagree with two minor findings in the paper.

In summary, when checking the US budget survey results of task 1 for each of the eight teams, we could replicate three teams exactly (all simple OLS regressions), there were ambiguities in two papers, and disagreements between our results and the authors' in three papers. These results provide food for thought. It is 'well-known' that trying to reproduce the results of published applied econometrics papers often leads to estimates which are different from the authors'. The results in this section confirm this unfortunate situation.

REFERENCES

Chetty, V. K. (1968), 'Pooling of time series and cross section data,' *Econometrica*, **36**, 279–90.
Harvey, A. C. (1993), *Time Series Models*, 2nd edition, Harvester, Wheatsheaf, New York.
Izan, H. Y. (1980), 'To pool or not to pool: a reexamination of Tobin's food demand problem,' *Journal of Econometrics*, **13**, 391–402.
Maddala, G. S. (1971), 'The likelihood approach to pooling cross-section and time-series data,' *Econometrica*, **39**, 939–53.

CHAPTER 14

LESSONS FROM THE FIELD TRIAL EXPERIMENT

JAN R. MAGNUS AND MARY S. MORGAN

1. INTRODUCTION

To the best of our knowledge, our field trial experiment is the first experiment conducted to assess competing methodologies, not just in econometrics but in any discipline. Simulation experiments, however, have been undertaken within various fields to assess particular methods, or to analyze or assess competing methods, including at least one in econometrics with methodological concerns (see Hoover and Perez, 1997). Such simulation experiments, by their very nature, are provided with a set of rules and processes to generate results: the simulation has to be instructed and this provides a strong form of control. Our field trial experiment involved the applied scientist and real data in a design that asked the scientist to follow his/her own normal applied practices in dealing with these data. In other words, each participant relied on his/her own beliefs and personal knowledge, which cannot be reduced to rules. The design thus encouraged rather than controlled individual variety, and this created problems of assessment.

2. CONTROL PROBLEMS IN THE FIELD TRIAL EXPERIMENT

There were three major areas of the experiment which in retrospect we ought to have thought about more carefully before hand. The first was that we asked the experimenters to attempt too many tasks. This is no doubt one of the reasons why a large number of signed-up participants did not take part. Of the 39 original teams who signed up, only eight completed and participated in the Tilburg workshop. A small questionnaire among the 31 drop-outs produced 27 replies. In addition to father's eightieth birthday, a car accident destroying relevant research material, and family problems, most replies (20) indicated that lack of time or substitutable resources (e.g. suitable collaborators, student assistance, etc.) and pressure of other commitments were the main reason for withdrawing.

More seriously, our desire to ask too much meant that in the experimental reports so many different things were done that legitimate comparisons between our eight participating teams became more limited. This, of course, is a classic trap for the beginner — being over-optimistic and over-ambitious about what can be learnt from one experiment — and we fell into this trap.

The second problem was that our ability to build in controls proved insufficient. Recall from our discussion in the introductory chapter that the aspects we aimed to control were the data used, the tasks set, and to prevent both cross-contamination of knowledge between teams and local knowledge advantage. In practice, experimenters (unconsciously) circumvented these controls. They chose different periods from the time-series data. The tasks were not as clearly specified as we believed in advance. (And one of our tasks, the policy task, was found by all concerned to be thoroughly misconceived!) We had not allowed for (or even considered) the possibility, pointed out to us by one participating group, that experimenters would seek to differentiate their own contribution from others sharing the same methodology who were amongst those reported to be taking part (the experimental pack contained a list of all those who had originally committed themselves to the experiment). Local knowledge was clearly at work, but it was not clear that there was local advantage: we found that one of our Dutch teams knew far more about the events underlying the American time-series data than did one of the American teams.

The third problem was the extent to which personal knowledge, even within roughly shared methodological approaches, lead to different outcomes. The variability in the way tasks were undertaken and completed was the necessary outcome not only of our uncontrolled variables but of the breadth of experience and range of our participating teams. So, even with the simple first task of measurement, we had underestimated the ability of eight participating teams to produce different versions of the variables, different models, use different elements of the data sets and different measurement procedures. The 'methodological approaches' that we were trying to get at included a mix of econometric methods and software tools, specialization of interest and economic beliefs and theories as well as procedures for modelling, specific econometric methodologies and general scientific principles. This was a potent mix which lead to huge variability and made our task and that of the assessors, much more difficult.

It is fair to say that one reason that we did not foresee fully the problems caused by variety was that we had not adequately worked out before hand how we were going to assess the experiment. We were anxious to remain neutral in the assessment of the methodologies, so we appointed independent assessors for this, but we neglected to think through clearly enough how we were going to assess the experiment as a whole. We thus broke one of the cardinal rules of experimental design — that of thinking through what kinds of results might be obtained with our experimental set-up and refining the design until it was such that we could in principle be able to draw valid inferences about the subject of our experiment. Such an ideal experiment was never practically possible, of course, and a satisfactory solution for the problem of comparing different methodologies is almost equivalent to having an ideal methodology, but we should have given the assessment aspect more thought.

Nevertheless, we have learnt much about econometric methodology from undertaking the field trial experiment, both about the assessment of such an experiment and about the content of applied econometrics.

3. ASSESSING THE FIELD TRIAL EXPERIMENT

Different methodologies invoke different assessment criteria. Those methodologies which place high value on the role of economic theory in modelling invoke criteria associated with their economic theories whilst those which concentrate on statistical issues prefer to be judged by statistical criteria. There is no reason that these should be compatible. This was recognized most clearly in Pesaran and Smith's (1985) discussion of evaluating macro-econometric models where they point out the difficulty of reconciling, even in the sense of trade-offs, the three criteria of relevance (for users), consistency (for economists) and adequacy (for econometricians). We have clear examples of this within our eight experimental reports, where we might point to the difficulty of reconciling Leamer's desire to ask a policy-useful question with the CBS team's insistence on economic theory consistency with the Tennessee team's focus on statistical fit.

This problem was recognized in our design by our decision to appoint 'assessors' from various different methodological camps. Although our experiment asked assessors to assess the individual reports, and to make comparisons, it was nevertheless difficult to make any general assessment of the methodologies involved. These could not be assessed on matters of shared principle and there were too few of each type of methodology available within the set of eight reports to assess the characteristics of any one applied methodology in a sensible way. If there had been lots of examples for each general methodology, a pattern might have emerged in each such set of experimental results so that we might have been able to wash out some of the effects of variation in individual knowledge and ability. This would have made assessment of the practical level of the methodologies more feasible, but would have been likely to raise large costs in assessment time. (An alternative design, considered in our 1992–3 attempt to fund the experiment, was to have one experienced econometrician acting as a 'control' trying out each methodology in turn; this at least would have held individual variation of abilities and economic theoretical commitments constant.) It is difficult to see how this problem could have been overcome. We could phrase the outcome on this issue in another way by saying that assessors' priors as to the appropriateness of different methodologies was probably not changed by the experiment's outcomes.

The difficulty of determining an overall assessment principle relative to the experimental design (above) is somewhat separate from the practical difficulties of detailed comparative assessment which arose from the variety of results obtained. These variations were due not only to differences in methodological approach, but also to the many uncontrolled choices which have to be made in any applied econometrics project and which are made on the basis of different personal knowledge and ability.

One way to get at the size and implications of this problem of variation is to look at the most clearly defined task and consider the results obtained by our participants. This was the task which asked the participants to update Tobin by using the 1941 American budget data to calculate income elasticities and test the homogeneity constraint. At first, the workshop participants viewed their measurements as rather different, perhaps because of the range of methods they had used to obtain them. But by the end of the workshop, participants began to think that there was considerable agreement on the value of the parameter. (The estimates, including Tobin's original one, are given in Chapter 13, Tables II and III.) Although the elasticities are a little higher than Tobin's, the results for four of the five teams reporting results were closely aligned, if we omit the CBS team's results for the moment. They also reported relatively small standard error bands (shown in the bottom two rows of Figure 1, Chapter 13). Despite the battery of new statistical tests, the power of modern computers and the advances in both economic and econometric theory, and regardless of methodology, the consensus measurement of 1941 US income elasticity of food demand on budget survey data is only around 0.05 different from that obtained by Tobin's 1950 work (and with almost equivalent standard errors to his).

What can we conclude from the achievement of similar results in such an experiment? Two possibilities come to mind. If this had been the only task set in the experiment and the results were largely the same, we might conclude that method and approach don't matter very much—however you approach this particular measurement task, with whatever assumptions and whatever tools and methodologies, the question elicited the same measurement outcomes. But philosophers of science might suggest that we cannot thereby conclude that we have found the 'true elasticity' (if this is taken to mean the elasticity true of 1941 American consumption), for we have no neutral or outside criteria to judge the measurement against. We are restricted to statistical and economic criteria to judge the goodness of the measurement devices used to obtain the elasticity, and these criteria differ according to the methodologies and economic beliefs espoused by the participants. These criteria are certainly valuable (and they are discussed by the assessors of the reports), but they do not provide the same kind of independent test, or technological test, available in cases such as getting a laser to work as reported in Collins' (1985) tacit knowledge experiment. (Those who might be tempted to think this is the difference between natural and social science might look at another Collins' experiment (1990) in which it is not easy to judge whether a crystal has been grown successfully.) In some econometric tasks, we do have such independent knowledge, particularly in forecasting, when outcomes become available. This is surely the appeal of forecasting tests in econometrics and similar disciplines. Other philosophers of science, drawing on the pragmatist tradition, might argue, as Kevin Hoover did at the Tilburg workshop, that there is something like a true elasticity in the world and that is what we expect our beliefs to converge upon if we consistently throw out error (see Hoover, 1994).

But, even if we take Hoover's line and agree on the value of the income elasticity for 1941, we can not conclude from the observed consensus that methodology doesn't make a difference, because this was not the only task, and there is far less consensus in the results of the homogeneity test and in the estimates using the other budget data. That is, in nearly all the other tasks, we observe a considerable lack of consensus from those same methodologies which gave us consensus in the estimate of the 1941 income elasticities (see the comparative results shown in Chapter 13). Methodology, or at least some aspect of practice which incorporates methodology (see our introductory chapter) does matter, and makes a difference.

We had expected variety in the results on the tasks reported by our participants, though perhaps not necessarily of the order demonstrated. It was somewhat pleasing and a little unexpected to find the consensus on the income elasticity reported above. In comparison, the results reported by the CBS team (Chapter 4) were surprising. Their results are surprising in two respects. First, they reported an income elasticity for the 1941 results much higher than other participants, and even outside the top of the range reported by Leamer in his analysis. The second surprise is that the CBS measure of income elasticity remained at this high level throughout the rest of the US budget studies and was consistent with their measure from the US time series. (With the exception of the Texas team, other teams found their (macro) time-series measure outside the range of the cross-section measure (see Chapter 13, Table III). Both the consistency and the high level throughout might have stemmed from the fact that the CBS team measured expenditure elasticities rather than income elasticities (as one commentator pointed out). But even the CBS team were surprised by their outcome: 'it is remarkable' that even the 1972 results did not differ very much from the previous budget study measures. They also commented that their different ways of estimating the elasticity made almost no difference to their results. This was not so amongst other participants: for example note the differences between elasticity measurements in Tables I and II of Dundee and for a systematic Bayesian comparison,

Leamer's Table III. These differences are apart from those due to differences in modelling or form of variables used. (More of such results were reported in the original versions of experimental reports, but were omitted for space reasons in this volume).

On one view, we could take the remarkable stability of the CBS results as a sign of the 'success' of their approach, without troubling to separate out what contributed to this stability, whether it resulted from their methodology, their model, their form of variables, their treatment of outliers and so forth. But is consistency of results a virtue here? Again, we might consider two possibilities. On the one hand, we might argue that the CBS consistency of results stemmed from their strong attention to the theoretical grounding of their model (commented upon by one assessor) which they adopted for both time and cross-section measures, and note (as did another commentator at the workshop) that their approach successfully solved the apparent puzzle of Tobin's work which had reported the micro and macro results to be of different order.

On the other hand, what reason, theoretical or empirical, is there to suppose that the budget study measurements of income elasticity would be stable over this period? Apart from the CBS, other participating teams who measured from all four budget studies found variations or some evidence of decline. (We also noted a consistency in the relative values obtained between teams, as evidenced by the regularity of patterns in Figure 1 of Chapter 13.) One of the questions which arose was, naturally, whether the elasticity measurements from the four budget studies might be considered to represent the same stable behaviour, whether the four elasticities were in fact 'equal' or not. Maastricht's test rejected this hypothesis, but suggested that whereas 'BS50 and BS60 are rather close, BS41 and BS72 are clearly different' (their Section 2.2). Texas concurred, but more definitively, finding that BS50 and BS60 data could be pooled, but that BS41 and BS72 are 'different from each other, and different from the 1950–1960 schedule' (their Section 4.1).

What can be inferred from these findings of difference? One possibility is that the behaviour parameter that the elasticity measurements represent has indeed changed over the period. The year 1941 was a year when the US economy was in hangover from the Great Depression but had not yet become a war economy, and consumers might well reveal a marked difference in behaviour compared with the 1950–60 period of rapid growth and domestic stability, and with the more problematic situation in 1972, almost regardless of econometric methodologies used to measure the elasticities. Certainly, Texas and Maastricht interpret their results as implying a change in elasticity over the period; both groups also noted the increasing elasticity with respect to family size over the period. Dundee initially also suggested a 'structural change' between the 1950–60 and 1972 experience (from their Table I — but their evidence for this perhaps disappeared in their weighted least squares results of Table II). These inferences seem perfectly reasonable based on their methods — as reasonable as CBS' inferences that measured behaviour hasn't changed based on their methods!

Another possibility, perhaps less likely to be noticed by the participants, is that the difference in measured behaviour is due to the survey methods used in collecting the data. One of the advantages that the participants had was that they did not have to assemble their own data, but this was also a disadvantage. Although the main differences in design and execution of the budget studies were described in the experimental pack, none of the experimental participants had gained any tacit knowledge of the data from having to assemble it themselves. The prior held by the data 'collector' from such tacit knowledge (in this case Morgan, who spent many days struggling to make a consistent data set from the avalanche of available US data) was that there were sufficient differences in the way the 1972 budget study survey was constructed and data collected (it covered rural and urban population, whereas previous ones had covered only urban population; the 1972 survey used more interviews over the time period, but there was less attempt to make sure consumption data were consistent with the rest of the household accounts) to expect a marked difference between measured elasticity for BS72 compared to BS50 and BS60. Thus, the CBS result was a considerable surprise to at least one of the organizers of the experiment. Only Leamer, on the basis of his graphic analysis of the data (given more space in the original version of his report) was willing to blame the data, admitting to being 'left in a state of suspicion about the 1972 data'.

All this should come as no surprise to those who criticize econometrics on the grounds that one can draw no conclusions from such a method because there is no experimental closure in carrying out a piece of applied econometrics (see for example Lawson, 1997 and for a reply, Hoover, 1997). Nevertheless, few critics are in a position to compare results of econometricians working on the same task and with the same data — usually they attack one particular econometric exercise, or aim at a more abstract level. Our examination of applied econometrics is only possible because of the field trial experiment, where certain controls are in place. By exploring the results of one particular part of the experiment, we are in a position to explore examples of stability and of variation in results in a way which we hope has been illuminating despite its lack of clear conclusions. Our inability to draw more specific inferences arises because of the pervasiveness of tacit or personal knowledge in the application of abstract econometric methodologies, which we address further in Chapter 20.

4. CONCLUSION

All applied econometricians know how difficult it is to do good applied econometrics, but find it difficult to communicate this without critics accusing them of hand-waving or data mining or lacking scientific standards and so forth. What we have tried to do in this chapter is give the non-econometrician some sense of just how difficult the task is.

Given how difficult and time consuming it is to do good applied econometrics, both of us have been impressed by the commitment of those who participated in the field trial experiment, reported their results, and revised their reports to meet our exacting deadlines. We have also benefited enormously from the help of our band of assessors who worked hard to think about how and why the experimenters obtained different results. All of those involved genuinely entered into the spirit of the experiment and its success, if we can call it that, is largely due to their combined commitment.

REFERENCES

Collins, H. M. (1985), *Changing Order. Replication and Induction in Scientific Practice*, Sage, London.
Collins, H. M. (1990), *Artificial Experts. Social Knowledge and Intelligent Machines*, MIT Press, Cambridge, USA.
Hoover, K. D. (1994), 'Pragmatism, pragmaticism and economic method' in R. E. Backhouse (ed.), *New Directions in Economic Methodology*, Routledge, London.

Hoover, K. D. (1997), 'Econometrics and reality', University of California, Davis, Department of Economics, Working Paper.

Hoover, K. D. and S. J. Perez (1997), 'Data-mining reconsidered: encompassing and the general-to-specific approach to specification search', University of California, Davis, Department of Economics, Working Paper.

Lawson, T. (1997), *Economics and Reality*, Routledge, London.

Pesaran, M. H. and R. P. Smith (1985), 'Evaluation of macroeconometric models', *Economic Modelling*, April, 125–34.

Part II

The Tacit Knowledge Experiment

CHAPTER 15

ORGANIZATION OF THE TACIT KNOWLEDGE EXPERIMENT

JAN R. MAGNUS AND MARY S. MORGAN

1. INTRODUCTION

Tacit knowledge fills the gap between methodological treatises and successful applications. The distance between theory and practice has led some unsympathetic observers to claim that 'econometricians do not practise what they preach'! This is, of course, naive. Applied econometrics, like all applied science, involves craft skill, or tacit knowledge, which enables the master econometrician to get practical results from using his/her methodology where the unskilled worker flounders.

The role of tacit or personal knowledge in the practical methodology of science was first put under the microscope by Michael Polanyi (1958, 1967). During the 1980s, sociologists of science, particularly Harry Collins (1985, 1990), carried out a number of empirical investigations into tacit knowledge in science. We discussed the general components of tacit knowledge in our introduction and provide further comments in Chapter 20. Two points are worth restating here. First, a theoretical approach and its reasoning are embedded in the practice of applied econometrics: tacit knowledge includes 'methodological' knowledge. Secondly, tacit knowledge, which includes knowledge to make choices and judgements, is partly hidden and cannot be fully articulated and written down. Thus, Collins suggested that in order to practise science, students must not only learn theories and rules of scientific procedure along with an accepted body of knowledge in their field, but must also acquire 'tacit knowledge' or 'craft skill' by working alongside an already qualified professional.

We know little about such tacit knowledge in economics, although everyone is aware that it exists. For the most part, students acquire this kind of knowledge during their PhD time, or by working as research assistants. Advice from supervisors and working on their projects provides students with a training which is quite different from the book learning involved in course work. It also means that most students acquire the particular approach (called 'methodology') of their advisor.

2. THE EXPERIMENT

We wished to find out how important tacit knowledge is in applied econometrics by asking an 'apprentice' to undertake an analysis using the methodological approaches of some acknowledged 'master craftsmen' in the profession. The apprentice only had access to the articulated knowledge of each methodology — that written by each master or about each

Methodology and Tacit Knowledge: Two Experiments in Econometrics
Jan R. Magnus and Mary S. Morgan © 1999 John Wiley & Sons Ltd

master's methodology and that enshrined in software. He had no 'apprenticeship' contact (i.e. personal working experience, even at a distance) with the masters while working on the project. The object of the experiment was to access the tacit knowledge involved in each approach or equivalently to assess how complete and usable the written accounts of such methodologies are in the absence of direct and personal advice from the master craftsmen.

We selected David Hendry, Ed Leamer and Chris Sims as the master craftsmen, each with a distinctly different methodology, in part because a lot has already been written by and about them and their methodologies. Of course, we could have selected others, or chosen alternative experimental designs (as we suggested in the Introduction), but our resources were limited. In an interesting comment after the event, Ed Leamer suggested that each 'master' could have nominated his own 'star apprentice'. This would have been a different experiment in the sense that such disciples were likely to have had direct contact with and probably be trained by the relevant master. Thus, Leamer's suggestion would more likely have tested the importance of individual ability than tacit knowledge (see Pagan's concluding discussion in Chapter 19). A comparison of the results of the work done by the star disciples with the work done by an apprentice would have been another way to access tacit knowledge.

We asked Wiebe Siegert, a Master's student at Tilburg University, to be the apprentice for the experiment and perform a specific task and analysis according to the methodology of each chosen master econometrician, using as guidance only their writings and the papers of some commentators, particularly Pagan (1987). The three analyses, together with a historical and methodological introduction and some conclusions, constituted Siegert's Master's thesis. Siegert obtained his Master's degree from Tilburg University in August 1997. His Master's thesis was written during the Spring and Summer of 1997 under the supervision of one of us (Magnus), and an edited and shortened version of the thesis is printed as Chapter 16 below. Siegert followed a number of courses in econometrics during his six years at Tilburg University, both theoretical and applied. One optional course which he took was *Econometrics and Philosophy*, taught by Bert Hamminga, Hugo Keuzenkamp and Jan Magnus. In this course he conducted a re-analysis of Tobin's 1950 paper (Chapter 2) 'as if' he were Leamer.

3.   THE APPRENTICESHIP TASK

Siegert's task was to try and use each of the three 'methodological' approaches of the chosen masters on task 1 (the measurement question) from the field trial experiment. Specifically, his task was to use the full data set for the USA (with or without corrections, and with or without the additional data that Tobin could have used but didn't) to estimate the income elasticity of food demand. Siegert also used the Dutch time series in answering the question for Sims.

What Siegert tried to do is to answer the above question *as if* he were Hendry, Leamer or Sims. His instruction was to pretend that some agency had come to Hendry, Leamer or Sims with the request to investigate the above economic problem. Hendry (or Leamer or Sims) has no time to take on this task, but suggests Siegert as someone who can do it in his spirit. Of course, we would not expect Siegert to agree with everything that Hendry (or Leamer or Sims) has written on econometrics, but he was told as far as possible not to impose his own ideas on the project and always to remember that he acted as a stand-in for Hendry (or Leamer or Sims). Obviously, there were decisions to be made along the way and Siegert used his own judgment in following the master methodologies as well as he could.

The role of the supervisor (Magnus) was to guide Siegert by helping him find the relevant literature and software for each master econometrician, discuss problems with him as they came up and generally provide encouragement and support. The supervisor took great care not to push Siegert in any particular direction according to his own views.

For the sake of completeness and accurate reporting, we note that Siegert made use of Pagan's (1987) appraisal of the three methodologies as a helpful article in his attempt to understand the master approaches. We also note that Siegert did meet Leamer at the Tilburg workshop, and did have some limited E-mail contact with him, mostly after he had completed his work in the Leamer approach.

Siegert kept a meticulous logbook of his activities and, of course, this reveals that he made mistakes and did things that were wrong or useless. All of this formed an integral part of the experiment, for the logbook and its record of problems and mistakes could potentially reveal the difficult decision points the apprentice faced. (A brief version of the apprentice logbook is included in Chapter 16.) From the logbook we can gain some idea at which points the textbook account of the masters (taken to imply the set of text writings and software tools) was inadequate to guide the apprentice. The apprentice logbook provides one tool for us to access the tacit knowledge involved in each of the methodologies.

4.   THE THREE MASTER CRAFTSMEN

The second method of getting at and assessing the tacit knowledge involved in applied econometrics was designed to be via the reaction of the master econometricians to the apprenticeship work. The 'masters' Hendry, Leamer and Sims were informed of the project at an early stage in the hope to involve them in some way. We wrote to them again in July 1997 when Siegert had completed his analyses. Since two of the three 'masters' had requested maximum information, we sent them a very bulky package consisting of the *Experiment Information Pack* (Magnus and Morgan, 1995), the Tobin (1950) article (Chapter 2 of this volume), six of the eight reports (including comments and replies), the data diskette, organization of the field trial experiment (Chapter 1, this volume), and Siegert's analyses. We asked each of the three 'masters' to read through Siegert's analysis concerning their own approach, and to write about 3000 words as a comment. The same package was sent to Pagan, who had agreed to write a summary appraisal of the whole tacit knowledge project. We asked Hendry, Leamer and Sims to emphasize how they would have done things differently than Siegert and why, and, if possible, to suggest the reason for any misinterpretation of their writings. Leamer responded quickly (but, of course, as a participant of the field trial experiment he had already struggled with the data), Hendry needed a little persuasion (not least because Siegert's initial 'Hendry analysis' had been conducted on the cross-section data which he felt inappropriate — he willingly commented on Siegert's time-series work and undertook his own analysis of the data to do so). Sims regrettably decided not to comment. We considered briefly the possibility of asking a 'Simsian' to comment instead of Sims, but decided against it.

Siegert's three analyses can be found in shortened form in Chapter 16. Chapters 17 and 18 contain the responses by Hendry and Leamer, respectively. Chapter 19 contains an appraisal of the tacit knowledge experiment by Pagan. We are very grateful to our participating 'masters' and to Adrian Pagan for taking part in this second experiment. Without their time and effort, and their written contributions, the possibility of learning about tacit knowledge from this experiment would have been severely constrained. In Chapter 20, we use their contributions to link our experiment with the tacit knowledge literature and to draw some conclusions.

REFERENCES

Collins, H. M. (1985), *Changing Order. Replication and Induction in Scientific Practice*, Sage, London.

Collins, H. M. (1990), *Artificial Experts. Social Knowledge and Intelligent Machines*, MIT Press, Cambridge, USA.

Magnus, J. R. and M. S. Morgan (1995), *The Experiment in Applied Econometrics: Information Pack* (54 pages), CentER for Economic Research, Tilburg University.

Pagan, A. (1987), 'Three econometric methodologies: a critical appraisal', *Journal of Economic Surveys*, **1**, 3–24.

Polanyi, M. (1958), *Personal Knowledge: Towards a Post-Critical Philosophy*, Routledge, London.

Polanyi, M. (1967), *The Tacit Dimension*, Routledge, London.

Tobin, J. (1950), 'A statistical demand function for food in the USA', *Journal of the Royal Statistical Society*, Series A, **113**, Part II, 113–41 [reprinted in Chapter 2, this volume].

CHAPTER 16

AN APPLICATION OF THREE ECONOMETRIC METHODOLOGIES TO THE ESTIMATION OF THE INCOME ELASTICITY OF FOOD DEMAND*

WIEBE K. SIEGERT

1. INTRODUCTION

'Tacit knowledge' (or 'craft skill' or 'connoisseurship') refers to our ability to perform tasks without being able to articulate how we do them. The standard example is the skill involved in riding a bicycle. No amount of reading and study in the physics and dynamics of the bicycle will enable a novice to get on and ride immediately. Polanyi (1962, pp. 54–55) writes:

> Connoisseurship, like skill, can be communicated only by example, not by precept. To become an expert wine-taster, to acquire a knowledge of innumerable different blends of tea or to be trained as a medical diagnostician, you must go through a long course of experience under the guidance of a master. Unless a doctor can recognize certain symptoms, e.g. the accentuation of the second sound of the pulmonary artery, there is no use in his reading the description of syndromes of which this symptom forms part. He must personally know that symptom and he can learn this only by repeatedly being given cases for auscultation in which the symptom is authoritatively known to be present, side by side with other cases in which it is authoritatively known to be absent, until he has fully realized the difference between them and can demonstrate his knowledge practically to the satisfaction of an expert.
>
> Wherever connoisseurship is found operating within science or technology we may assume that it persists only because it has not been possible to replace it by a measurable grading. For a measurement has the advantage of greater objectivity, as shown by the fact that measurements give consistent results in the hands of different observers all over the world, while such objectivity is rarely achieved in the case of physiognomic appreciations. The large amount of time spent by students of chemistry, biology and medicine in their practical courses shows how greatly these sciences rely on the transmission of skills and connoisseurship from master to apprentice. It offers an impressive demonstration of the extent to which the art of knowing has remained unspecifiable at the very heart of science.

---

* This paper is a condensed version of my Master's thesis submitted to the Department of Economics at Tilburg University, written under the supervision of Professor Jan R. Magnus. I am grateful to Statistics Netherlands for use of the Dutch data. The US data are compiled from various US Government publications (see the data chapters for details).

Methodology and Tacit Knowledge: Two Experiments in Econometrics
Jan R. Magnus and Mary S. Morgan © 1999 John Wiley & Sons Ltd

In this chapter an attempt is made to study connoisseurship in econometrics. I have tried to answer one question (the measurement question) from the field trial experiment, using three different methodologies, namely the methodologies of Professors Edward E. Leamer, David F. Hendry and Christopher A. Sims. The only guide I had was the written work of the masters, while I used Pagan's (1987) comparison of the three methodologies as a starting point.

I have tried to ride Polanyi's bike after studying the written work of the masters. The masters will judge how hard I fell.

The question that must be answered using the three different methodologies is: estimate the income elasticity of food demand for the USA. Tobin (1950) answered this question as did all the eight participating teams in the field trial experiment. Section 2 contains my analysis *as if* I were Leamer. Section 3 contains my analysis à la Hendry, and Section 4 reports my VAR analysis following Sims. A summary is given in Section 5.

2.   THE METHODOLOGY OF EDWARD E. LEAMER

The setting is the linear regression model $y = X\beta + u$, where u is normally distributed with mean 0 and variance $\sigma^2 I$. There are prior linear constraints $R\beta = r$. The variables that are associated with the constraints are called 'doubtful'; the other variables are called 'free'. The free variables are the variables that definitely belong in the model. The doubtful variables are the variables that may be dropped. The particular coefficient (or linear combination) which has our primary interest is called the 'focus' coefficient. This focus coefficient may be doubtful or free. I chose the focus coefficient to be free. The extreme bounds are the largest and smallest values that can be obtained as estimates for the focus coefficient by different treatment of the prior constraints. The prior linear constraints have a prior mean (namely r), but no prior variance matrix. The distribution of the free variables remains diffuse. Chamberlain and Leamer (1976) provide a bound (extreme bound) for the posterior mean vector with prior mean given and prior variance free. Leamer (1982) provides a bound for the posterior mean vector with prior mean given but prior variance matrix bounded between a maximum and a minimum. See also Leamer (1983), Leamer and Leonard (1983) and Breusch (1985).

Leamer (1985) preaches sensitivity analysis. He suggests a form of organized sensitivity analysis which he calls 'global sensitivity analysis' in which a neighbourhood of alternative assumptions is selected and the corresponding interval of inferences is identified. Conclusions are judged to be sturdy only if the neighbourhood of assumptions is wide enough to be credible and the corresponding interval of inferences is narrow enough to be useful. But when an incredibly narrow set of assumptions is required to produce a usefully narrow set of conclusions, inferences from the given data set are reported to be too fragile to be believed. This sensitivity analysis is what I will try to do in this section of the experiment.

2.1.   Data Problems for the 1941, 1950, 1960 and 1972 US Budget Surveys

First, the variable N (Tobin's household family size) is constructed in the 1941 data set. The observations for the first four household sizes are simply the numbers 1 to 4. Estimates for the 567 household category are obtained with the use of the variable *AHSIZE*. The variable *AHSIZE* is dropped afterwards. Estimates for missing observations of the variable *ESTPOPH* are obtained with the use of the estimated sample sizes (*SAMPSIZE*).[1] The variables *ANCHILD*, *HOMEOWN*, *RENTER*, *AUTOOWN* and *NETASSCH* are, for each household size and for each income class, the average number which is available for all households. The last three income rows for the one-person household category and the last row for the two-person household category are dropped due to missing observations. The variable *TOTCON* is dropped because Leamer himself warned me that income is measured twice when both *HINC* and *TOTCON* are in the model. Therefore, *TOTCON* is dropped from every data set. Taking logarithms of the variable *NETASSCH* is not possible because it contains negative observations.

In the 1950 data set the following variables are dropped: *NONWHITE* because it has too many missing observations and *SAMPSIZE* because it isn't a household characteristic. The first row of the 678 household category is dropped because the observation for *ANFTEARN* was missing. The seventh row of the one-person household category and the first row of the five-person household category are dropped because the variable *%INPOPH* contains zeros for those households.

In the 1960 data set the variables *ANCHILD*, *NONWHITE* and *ANFTEARN* are dropped because there are too many missing observations. Also dropped is the variable *SAMPSIZE* (only given for each household size category and not a household characteristic). The row for the income category $>15\,000$ of the one person family is dropped because the observation for *HOMEOWN* is missing and the *ACCBAL* item is -3218, which suggests considerable inaccuracy in recording. The row for the lowest income category of the five-person family is dropped because the observation for *HINC* is negative and the *ACCBAL* item is 1081, which also suggests considerable inaccuracy in recording.

The variables *ANCHILD* and *ANOV65* of the 1972 data set are dropped because they contain several zeros which causes trouble with logarithms. A few observations of the variables *EDUHH*1 and *EDUHH*3 are missing. These cells are filled up so that *EDUHH*1, *EDUHH*2 and *EDUHH*3 add up to 100%.[2]

2.2. Idealistic Versus Materialistic Priors

We regress the logarithm of food consumption on all available variables (logarithms are taken when possible) left in the data set after the deletions described above. So the model for the 1941 data set is:

$$\log(FOODCON) = \beta_0 + \beta_1 \log(N) + \beta_2 \log(ESTPOPH) + \beta_3 \log(ANCHILD)$$
$$+ \beta_4 \log(HOMEOWN) + \beta_5 \log(RENTER) + \beta_6 \log(AUTOOWN)$$
$$+ \beta_7 \log(HINC) + \beta_8 NETASSCH. \qquad\qquad 1$$

Different people choose different variables to be free (F) or doubtful (D) in (1). The question is: how fragile is the inference on the income elasticity of food demand with respect to different subsets of doubtful variables? Different people have different eating habits.

---

[1] Magnus and Morgan provided the variable *SAMPSIZE* after a suggestion from Professor J. S. Cramer (E-mail message sent to all participants, 19 August 1995); see the data chapters for details.

[2] In household size 678 income class 20000–25000 *EDUHH*1, *EDUHH*2 and *EDUHH*3 add up to 101%. These observations are not changed.

We distinguish between 'idealistic' and 'materialistic' people. The 'idealistic' people eat macrobiotic and ecological food. They do not care about cars and houses. The other extreme are the 'materialistic' people. They are the careerists, the 'fast food eating, time-is-money' people. In between these two extremes exists a whole continuum of different people.

Each person can spend his/her money only once. Everyone has to ask: do I spend my money on houses, cars, food or something else? The materialistic people have a strong affinity with houses and cars, and hence the variables HOMEOWN, RENTER and AUTOOWN are labelled free for this prior. Of course, this holds only if the relevant variable is in the data set. The idealistic people choose these variables to be doubtful. By changing the variables HOMEOWN, RENTER and AUTOOWN from doubtful to free, we obtain priors 2, 3 and 4 (the materialistic prior) from the idealistic prior 1. The variable HINC is the focus variable and hence free in every prior. The variables NETASSCH and ACCBAL are free, because they are income related variables. The variables %INPOPH, ESTPOPH, ANFTEARN, AGEHH and EDUHH are doubtful because they do not influence the eating habit. The variables N, ANCHILD, and AHSIZE are chosen to be free because large households need more food than small households.

The variables HOMEOWN, RENTER and AUTOOWN are all in the 1941 and 1972 data sets. Therefore there are four different prior specifications for the 1941 and 1972 data sets; these are presented in Table I. It is a pity that the variables RENTER and HOMEOWN are not available in the 1950 data set. The only variable relevant for the idealistic versus materialistic setting is HOMEOWN. For this reason there are only two alternative prior specifications possible in the 1950 data set. The variables relevant for the idealistic versus materialistic setting in the 1960 data set are HOMEOWN and AUTOOWN. Within this setting there are four alternative prior specifications possible. Table I also reports the extreme and limited bounds and the posterior mean of the initial prior for the input covariance matrix.

2.3. Sensitivity Analysis of the 1950 Data Set

A complete sensitivity analysis is reported in Table II for the idealistic prior of the 1950 data set.[3] The sample covariance matrix is used as reference or initial prior for the input covariance matrix. The upper-left corner in Table II contains the restricted OLS estimate (all doubtful variables are omitted), the upper-right corner contains the unrestricted extreme bounds, and the lower-right corner contains the unrestricted OLS estimate for the income elasticity. The diagonal elements of the matrix contain estimates of the income elasticity as the prior covariance matrix is scaled up and down; these elements are also known as the contract curve. If the prior covariance matrix is set to zero, then the restricted OLS estimate is obtained. If the prior covariance matrix is infinity, then the unrestricted OLS estimate is obtained. The centre element(s) of the matrix is the estimate of the income elasticity based on the initial prior (0.30). Moving from this centre box to the upper-right adjacent box we find extreme bounds where the prior covariance matrix is restricted by $0.25V_0 < V < 4V_0$, where V_0 is the sample covariance matrix. These limited bounds are [0.26, 0.36]. In the upper right corner we find the extreme bounds where the

---

[3] My Master's Thesis contains sensitivity analyses for each prior and each data set.

Table I. Alternative prior specifications for the various data sets and bounds for focus coefficient on *HINC*

Data set	Prior	TOBIN'S N	%INPOP	ESTPOPH	AHSIZE	ANCHILD	ANFTEARN	AGEHH	EDUHH	EDUHH1	EDUHH2	EDUHH3	NONWHITE	HOMEOWN	RENTER	AUTOOWN	HINC	NETASSCH	ACCBAL	Extreme bounds	Limited bounds	Posterior mean
BS41US	Idealistic	F	D	D		F								D	D	D	F	F		[0.14,0.79]	[0.26,0.48]	0.31
	2	F	D	D		F								D	D	F	F	F		[0.14,0.63]	[0.23,0.47]	0.31
	3	F	D	D		F								D	F	F	F	F		[0.27,0.46]	[0.35,0.38]	0.37
	Materialistic	F	D	D		F								F	F	F	F	F		[0.29,0.34]	[0.34,0.34]	0.34
BS50US	Idealistic		D		F		D	D	D					D			F	F	F	[−0.03,0.85]	[0.26,0.36]	0.30
	Materialistic		D		F		D	D	D					F			F	F	F	[−0.02,0.83]	[0.28,0.36]	0.30
BS60US	Idealistic		D	D	F			D	D					D	D		F	F	F	[0.36,0.63]	[0.43,0.51]	0.47
	2		D	D	F			D	D					D	F	F	F	F	F	[0.38,0.62]	[0.43,0.51]	0.47
	3		D	D	F			D	D					F	D	F	F	F	F	[0.37,0.60]	[0.43,0.51]	0.46
	Materialistic		D	D	F			D	D					F	F	F	F	F	F	[0.41,0.59]	[0.43,0.51]	0.47
BS72US	Idealistic		D	D	F			D		D	D	D	D	D	D	D	F	F	F	[0.16,0.36]	[0.21,0.27]	0.21
	2		D	D	F			D		D	D	D	D	D	D	F	F	F	F	[0.19,0.32]	[0.22,0.24]	0.23
	3		D	D	F			D		D	D	D	D	F	F	F	F	F	F	[0.19,0.30]	[0.22,0.24]	0.24
	Materialistic		D	D	F			D		D	D	D	D	F	F	F	F	F	F	[0.19,0.28]	[0.22,0.24]	0.24

Table II. Bounds for estimates of the income elasticity of food demand. Prior variance matrix bounded between $V_0\sigma_L^2$ and $V_0\sigma_U^2$ where V_0 is the input variance matrix. Dataset: 1950, the idealistic prior

		σ_U								
		0	1/64	1/16	1/4	1	4	16	64	∞
	0	0.55	0.58	0.66	0.80	0.84	0.85	0.85	0.85	0.85
		0.55	0.51	0.37	0.10	0.01	−0.02	−0.03	−0.03	−0.03
	1/64		0.55	0.59	0.68	0.71	0.71	0.71	0.71	0.71
			0.55	0.43	0.21	0.14	0.11	0.11	0.11	0.11
	1/16			0.48	0.55	0.57	0.57	0.57	0.57	0.57
				0.48	0.28	0.21	0.19	0.19	0.19	0.19
	1/4				0.35	0.36	0.36	0.36	0.36	0.36
					0.35	0.28	0.26	0.26	0.26	0.26
σ_L	1					0.30	0.30	0.30	0.30	0.30
						0.30	0.28	0.27	0.27	0.27
	4						0.28	0.28	0.28	0.28
							0.28	0.27	0.27	0.27
	16							0.27	0.27	0.27
								0.27	0.27	0.27
	64								0.27	0.27
									0.27	0.27
	∞									0.27
										0.27

prior covariance matrix is unrestricted. These bounds are $[-0.03, 0.85]$ for the 1950 idealistic prior.

Whether the interval of inferences is narrow enough to be useful depends on the user who needs the income elasticity of food demand as an input for a further study. I think that the interval is narrow enough for the 1941, 1960 and 1972 data sets. The differences between the posterior means of the alternative prior specifications are small, and the maximum range of the intervals from the adjacent upper-right box is 0.24 (limited bounds of the 1941 second prior). Whether the neighbourhood of assumptions is wide enough to be credible depends on the interpretation of 'wide'. I have used only one functional form so in that sense the neighbourhood of assumptions isn't that wide. But four alternative prior specifications are used for the 1941, 1960 and 1972 data sets. Thus the neighbourhood of assumptions within this one functional form is wide. I think that conclusions for these data sets are not too fragile to be believed. The posterior means for the income elasticity of food demand are between 0.31 and 0.37 for the 1941 data set, about 0.47 for the 1960 data set and between 0.21 and 0.24 for the 1972 data set.

2.4. Extreme Bounds

The range of the extreme bounds is 0.88 for the 1950 idealistic prior and 0.85 for the 1950 materialistic prior. The extreme bounds both contain the origin. Here I think that the interval of inferences is narrow enough to be useful if the prior covariance matrix is bounded from below by $1/64 \, V_0$. If this is the case then the interval for the posterior means does not contain the origin. Is the neighbourhood of assumptions wide enough to be credible? Only one functional form is used. Within this functional form only two alternative prior specifications are used, because several social-economic variables were missing in the data set, and the prior covariance matrix must be bounded from below by $1/64 \, V_0$. I think that these conclusions are too fragile to be believed, but if the reader feels comfortable with the narrow set of assumptions, then the inference can be considered sturdy.

In Figures 1 and 2 the extreme bounds of the income elasticity for the idealistic and the materialistic prior are presented for the four available datasets. One glance at these figures shows that the income elasticity of food demand is not constant over time. Not much can be said about whether there is an increase or decrease over time. Tobin (1950) concludes that estimates from the budget data should not be inserted into the time-series equations as known quantities. I think that Figures 1 and 2 also lead to this conclusion, although I did not perform a time-series analysis. Figure 3 shows the extreme bounds of the income elasticity for the four alternative prior specifications of the 1941 data set.

2.5. Logbook

Sensitivity analysis is indeed, as Leamer (1985) says, a bitter pill to swallow. I did not have a computer package which produces the extreme bounds, such as Leamer's SEARCH package, and hence the functions that I had to write to calculate the tables were difficult and time consuming. I assumed wrongly that the word 'precision' meant variance instead of the inverse of the variance. This caused a lot of wrong and silly results in calculating the contract curve.

Leamer (1978) was amazed by the transmogrification of particular individuals who wantonly sinned in the basement of the University of Michigan (where the econometric modeling was done) and metamorphosed into the highest of high priests as they ascended

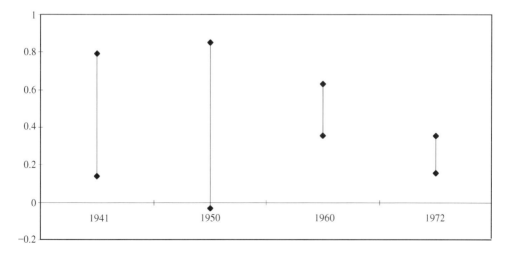

Figure 1. Extreme bounds of the income elasticity of food demand. The idealistic prior

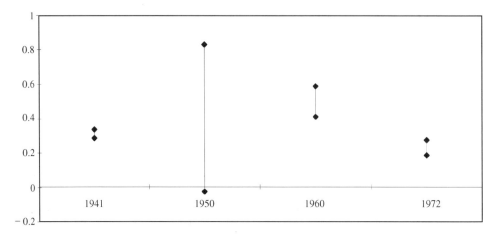

Figure 2. Extreme bounds of the income elasticity of food demand. The materialistic prior

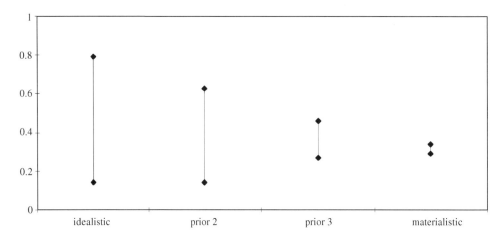

Figure 3. Extreme bounds of the income elasticity of food demand, 1941 data set

to the third floor (where the econometric theory courses were taught). The econometric courses I took came from the eighth, ninth and tenth floors of Tilburg University. Maybe I did go down a few floors but I hope I did not end in the basement.

3.   THE METHODOLOGY OF DAVID F. HENDRY

Hendry (1993) made it easy for the people who want to use his methodology, because he developed a computer package: PC-GIVE. The philosophy underlying PC-GIVE embodying its methodology is as follows. Economic time-series data are generated by a process of immense generality and complexity. The econometrician seeks to model the main features of the data generation process (DGP) in a simplified representation based on the observable data and related to prior economic theory. Hendry and Doornik (1996) distinguish three levels of knowledge potentially available in a theoretical analysis. Write the data set as $X_T^1 = (x_1 \ldots x_T)$ and denote the DGP by $D_x(X_T^1|\theta)$. Then:

1. Both $D_x(\cdot)$ and θ known corresponds to a probability theory course;
2. $D_x(\cdot)$ known and θ unknown corresponds to an estimation and inference course;
3. Both $D_x(\cdot)$ and θ unknown corresponds to a modelling course.

In empirical econometrics 3 is the realistic situation. Two important issues arise once the limited knowledge of 3 is granted: first, the postulated likelihood function for an empirical model will not coincide with the actual density function of the observations; and secondly, models will inevitably be simplifications, not facsimiles of the economic mechanism. Consequently, it is crucial to test empirical claims rigorously. A model is congruent when it matches the available evidence in all the dimensions examined (for example, has innovation, homoscedastic errors, constant parameters, etc.). Information criteria, which penalize for additional parameters more than the degrees of freedom adjustment to $\hat{\sigma}$, are often used but assume that many of the necessary criteria are satisfied. They are related to the use of R^2, $\overline{R}^2$ and $\hat{\sigma}^2$ as model-selection criteria, and in finite samples seem preferable to those.

Hendry preaches a 'general to specific' approach. Start with a general congruent model and move to a parsimonious and interpretable econometric model thereof, which is theory consistent and encompasses both the general and other competing models. This 'general to specific' approach is what I will try to do. Starting with a model which contains all the available variables in the data set and then test and reduce the model until it passes all the diagnostic tests. I shall follow Hendry's three main rules; test, test and test.

3.1. Data for the US Time Series

The variables listed in Table III are available for the time-series analysis. All variables are in logs. There are three income and food consumption variables available: the original Tobin series, the revised series and the aggregated series. All the original Tobin series are revised and hence the original series won't be used.

The variables that are considered important are aggregated income, aggregated food expenditure, food prices, non-food prices and population. Multiplying disposable income

Table III. US time series variables

TOBPCFC	Tobin's per capita food consumption (his S), 1912–1948 (1942–44 missing)
TOBPCY	Tobin's per capita disposable income (his Y'), 1912–1948 (1942–44 missing)
TOBFP	Tobin's food price index (his P), 1912–1948 (1942–44 missing)
TOBNFP	Tobin's non-food price index (his Q), 1912–1948 (1942–44 missing)
PCFC	revised *TOBPCFC* for 1912–1976
PCY	revised *TOBPCY* for 1912–1989
FP	revised *TOBFP* for 1913–1989
NFP	revised *TOBNFP* for 1913–1989
AGGEXP	aggregate personal expenditure in billion \$, 1929–1989
AGGEXPF	aggregate personal expenditure on food in billion \$, 1929–1989
AGGY	aggregate personal disposable income in billion \$, 1919–1989
POP	population in thousands
NOH	number of households in thousands

(*PCY*) with population (*POP*) gives aggregated personal disposable income (*AGGY*). Hence, if *AGGY* and *POP* are in the model than *PCY* can be left out. The same holds for food consumption (*PCFC*). If population is in the model than there is no need to include the number of households because the two variables are strongly related to each other. Aggregated total expenditure (*AGGEXP*) is left out, because income is measured twice when both *AGGY* and *AGGEXP* are in the model.

3.2. General-To-Specific

We first check whether the series are $I(0)$ or $I(1)$. All five series (logged) have a unit root according to the outcome of the augmented Dickey–Fuller tests. The series are all differenced to become stationary. Model 1 is a general model of food consumption (logged and differenced) regressed on all the variables in the data set, including two lags:

$$\log(AGGEXPF_t) = \mu + \beta_1 \Delta \log(AGGEXPF_{t-1}) + \beta_2 \Delta \log(AGGEXPF_{t-2})$$

$$+ \beta_3 \Delta \log(AGGY_t) + \beta_4 \Delta \log(AGGY_{t-1}) + \beta_5 \Delta \log(AGGY_{t-2})$$

$$+ \beta_6 \Delta \log(FP_t) + \beta_7 \Delta \log(FP_{t-1}) + \beta_8 \Delta \log(FP_{t-2})$$

$$+ \beta_9 \Delta \log(NFP_t) + \beta_{10} \Delta \log(NFP_{t-1}) + \beta_{11} \Delta \log(NFP_{t-2})$$

$$+ \beta_{12} \Delta \log(POP_t) + \beta_{13} \Delta \log(POP_{t-1}) + \beta_{14} \Delta \log(POP_{t-2}) + \varepsilon_t$$

2

Estimates of the parameters in model 1 are given in Table IV.

Table IV. OLS estimates, model 1

Variable	The present sample is: 1932 to 1989 Coefficient	Std. Error	Instab
Constant	0.03	0.01	0.19
DLAGGEXPF _1	0.45	0.15	0.06
DLAGGEXPF _2	−0.17	0.16	0.08
DLAGGY	0.48	0.09	0.20
DLAGGY _1	−0.16	0.11	0.08
DLAGGY _2	0.12	0.11	0.08
DLFP	0.48	0.12	0.18
DLFP _1	−0.13	0.14	0.02
DLFP _2	0.03	0.14	0.11
DLNFP	−0.07	0.20	0.03
DLNFP _1	−0.22	0.24	0.09
DLNFP _2	−0.01	0.18	0.05
DLPOP	−3.47	2.04	0.14
DLPOP _1	0.34	2.79	0.17
DLPOP _2	1.47	2.39	0.19

$R^2 = 0.91$ $F(14, 43) = 30.78$ [0.00] $\sigma = 0.02$ $DW = 2.15$
$RSS = 0.02$ for 15 variables and 58 observations

Variance instability test: 0.89**;   Joint instability test: 3.20
Information Criteria: $SC = -6.85$; $HQ = -7.17$; $FPE = 0.0006$

Note that the variance of the error term is not constant over time. The variance instability test statistic has a value of 0.89, with two stars. This means that it is significant at the 1% level. The hypothesis that all the parameters in model 1 are constant over time, is not rejected. The joint instability test outcome has no stars. Dynamic analysis is carried out on model 1. The solved static long run equation is

$$DLAGGEXPF = \underset{(0.02)}{0.04} + \underset{(0.14)}{0.60} \; DLAGGY + \underset{(0.24)}{0.53} \; DLFP$$

$$- \underset{(0.24)}{0.41} \; DLNFP - \underset{(1.14)}{2.29} \; DLPOP.$$

The hypothesis that all the coefficients of the solved static long run equation are zero is rejected. Table V presents significance tests on model 1.

The variables non-food price and population (with both lags) are insignificant. The second lag in model 1 is insignificant and the first lag is almost significant. The diagnostic tests are summarized in Table VI.

The diagnostic tests reveal that there may be a autocorrelation and/or a heteroscedasticity problem. Common factor analysis is carried out and shows that there may be common factors present. The variables 'population' and 'non-food price' (with both lags) are dropped from model 1 because they were insignificant. This gives model 2. Model 2 is estimated and the main result is that the variance of the error term is not constant over time. The variance instability test has an outcome of 1.35 and is marked with two stars.

Table V. Significance tests, model 1

Tests on the significance of each variable

Variable	F(num, denom)	Value	Probability		Unit Root t-test
DLAGGEXPF	F(2, 43) =	4.39	[0.02]	*	−4.36*
Constant	F(1, 43) =	5.61	[0.02]	*	2.37
DLAGGY	F(3, 43) =	11.37	[0.00]	**	3.25
DLFP	F(3, 43) =	6.01	[0.00]	**	1.85
DLNFP	F(3, 43) =	0.96	[0.42]		−1.61
DLPOP	F(3, 43) =	2.17	[0.11]		−1.85

Tests on the significance of each lag

Lag	F(num, denom)	Value	Probability
1	F(5, 43) =	2.10	[0.08]
2	F(5, 43) =	0.60	[0.70]

Tests on the significance of all lags up to 2

Lag	F(num, denom)	Value	Probability
1− 2	F(10, 43) =	1.68	[0.12]
2− 2	F(5, 43) =	0.60	[0.70]

Table VI. Diagnostic tests, model 1

AR 1− 2	F(2, 41) = 3.15	[0.05]		'Autocorrelation'
ARCH 1	F(1, 41) = 5.10	[0.03]	*	'Autoregressive Conditional Heteroscedasticity (ARCH)'
Normality	Chi^2 (2) = 0.75	[0.69]		'Normality'
Xi^2	F(28, 14) = 1.16	[0.40]		'Heteroscedasticity using squares'
RESET	F(1, 42) = 5.08	[0.03]	*	'Reset test'

Dynamic analysis is carried out on model 2 and the solved static long run equation is

$$DLAGGEXPF = \underset{(0.01)}{0.01} + \underset{(0.17)}{0.65}\ DLAGGY + \underset{(0.23)}{0.14}\ DLFP.$$

The static long run equation is not rejected. Table VII presents significance tests on model 2.

All the variables are now significant. The first lag is now significant and the second lag isn't. The diagnostic tests are in Table VIII.

The diagnostic tests reveal that there may be a heteroscedastic problem. Carrying out a common factor analysis shows that there may be common factors. The second lag is now dropped from model 2 because it was not significant. Model 3 is thus obtained. Estimating model 3 gives the results in Table IX.

Again, the variance of the error term is not constant over time. Dynamic analysis is carried out on model 3 and the solved static long run equation is

$$DLAGGEXPF = \underset{(0.01)}{0.01} + \underset{(0.17)}{0.63}\ DLAGGY + \underset{(0.20)}{0.24}\ DLFP.$$

The static long run equation is not rejected. Table X presents significance tests on model 3.

All the variables and lags are now significant. The diagnostic tests are presented in Table XI.

There is a heteroscedasticity problem in model 3. One way to deal with this is to shift from aggregated series to per capita series. Per capita series are, in general, smoother than aggregated series. The variables *AGGEXPF* and *AGGY* are divided by *POP* to obtain

Table VII. Significance tests, model 2

Tests on the significance of each variable				
Variable	F(num, denom)	Value	Probability	Unit Root t-test
DLAGGEXPF	F(2, 49) =	8.30	[0.00] **	−4.29**
Constant	F(1, 49) =	2.13	[0.15]	1.46
DLAGGY	F(3, 49) =	15.44	[0.00] **	3.14
DLFP	F(3, 49) =	8.68	[0.00] **	0.56
Tests on the significance of each lag				
Lag	F(num, denom)	Value	Probability	
1	F(3, 49) =	5.36	[0.00] **	
2	F(3, 49) =	1.31	[0.28]	
Tests on the significance of all lags up to 2				
Lag	F(num, denom)	Value	Probability	
1– 2	F(6, 49) =	4.00	[0.00] **	
2– 2	F(3, 49) =	1.31	[0.28]	

Table VIII. Diagnostic tests, model 2

AR 1– 2F(2, 47) = 1.65 [0.20]	
ARCH 1 F(1, 47) = 7.68 [0.01] **	
Normality Chi^2 (2) = 5.96 [0.05]	
Xi^2 F(16, 32) = 7.29 [0.00] **	
Xi*Xj F(44, 4) = 2.20 [0.23]	
RESET F(1, 48) = 1.17 [0.28]	

Table IX. OLS estimates, model 3

The present sample is: 1932 to 1989			
Variable	Coefficient	Std. Error	Instab
Constant	0.00	0.00	0.23
DLAGGEXPF _1	0.50	0.12	0.05
DLAGGY	0.52	0.08	0.22
DLAGGY _1	−0.20	0.10	0.07
DLFP	0.47	0.08	0.11
DLFP _1	−0.35	0.10	0.03

$R^2 = 0.88$ $F(5, 52) = 78.45$ [0.0000] $\sigma = 0.02$ $DW = 1.97$
$RSS = 0.03$ for 6 variables and 58 observations

Variance instability test: 1.44**;   Joint instability test: 2.03*
Information Criteria: $SC = -7.22$; $HQ = -7.35$; $FPE = 0.0005$

Table X. Significance tests, model 3

Tests on the significance of each variable

Variable	F(num, denom)	Value	Probability		Unit Root t-test
DLAGGEXPF	F(1, 52) =	16.95	[0.00]	**	−4.20*
Constant	F(1, 52) =	1.05	[0.31]		1.03
DLAGGY	F(2, 52) =	23.86	[0.00]	**	2.93
DLFP	F(2, 52) =	18.83	[0.00]	**	1.07

Tests on the significance of each lag

Lag	F(num, denom)	Value	Probability	
1	F(3, 52) =	6.56	[0.00]	**

Tests on the significance of all lags up to 1

Lag	F(num, denom)	Value	Probability	
1− 1	F(3, 52) =	6.56	[0.00]	**

Table XI. Diagnostic tests, model 3

AR 1− 2	F(2, 50) =	0.17	[0.84]
ARCH 1	F(1, 50) =	9.98	[0.00] **
Normality Chi^2(2)	=	2.50	[0.29]
Xi^2	F(10, 41) =	8.85	[0.00] **
Xi*Xj	F(20, 31) =	11.48	[0.00] **
RESET	F(1, 51) =	1.00	[0.32]

EXPFPC and *YPC*.[4] Model 4 is the same as model 1, except that the aggregated series is replaced by the *per capita* series and the variable *POP* is dropped:

$$\Delta \log(EXPFPC_t) = \mu + \beta_1 \Delta \log(EXPFPC_{t-1}) + \beta_2 \Delta \log(EXPFPC_{t-2})$$
$$+ \beta_3 \Delta \log(YPC_t) + \beta_4 \Delta \log(YPC_{t-1}) + \beta_5 \Delta \log(YPC_{t-2})$$
$$+ \beta_6 \Delta \log(FP_t) + \beta_7 \Delta \log(FP_{t-1}) + \beta_8 \Delta \log(FP_{t-2})$$
$$+ \beta_9 \Delta \log(NFP_t) + \beta_{10} \Delta \log(NFP_{t-1}) + \beta_{11} \Delta \log(NFP_{t-2}) + \varepsilon_t$$

3

---

[4] The variable *YPC* is exactly the same as *PCY*, but *EXPFPC* is surprisingly not equal to *PCFC*!

Model 4 is estimated and the most important result is that the variable non-food price is insignificant. Dropping non-food price then leads to model 5. In model 5, lag 2 is not significant. Hence we drop lag 2 and this leads to model 6:

$$\Delta \log(EXPFPC_t) = \mu + \beta_1 \Delta \log(EXPFPC_{t-1}) + \beta_2 \Delta \log(YPC_t) + \beta_3 \Delta \log(YPC_{t-1})$$
$$+ \beta_4 \Delta \log(FP_t) + \beta_5 \Delta \log(FP_{t-1}) + \varepsilon_t. \qquad\qquad 4$$

We see that measuring the data in per capita terms does not solve the problem. The variance of the error term is still not constant over time in models 4, 5 and 6. The diagnostic tests of model 6 are in Table XII.

Regretfully, the heteroscedastic problem is still present in model 6. Figure 4 demonstrates this graphically. The series $\log(AGGEXPF)$, $\log(AGGY)$ and $\log(FP)$ are graphed in the upper-left plot, the series $\log(EXPFPC)$ and $\log(YPC)$ in the upper-right plot, the series $\Delta \log(EXPFPC)$, $\Delta \log(YPC)$ and $\Delta \log(FP)$ in the lower-left plot and the scaled residuals of model 6 in the lower-right plot. An eyeball test reveals that the series can be split in two subseries, namely 1929–1951 and 1952–1989. Probably, this is the cause of

Table XII. Diagnostic tests, model 6

AR 1– 2F(2, 51)	=	0.06	[0.94]	
ARCH 1 F(1, 51)	=	7.51	[0.01]	**
Normality Chi^2(2)	=	3.11	[0.21]	
Xi^2 F(10, 42)	=	7.65	[0.00]	**
Xi*Xj F(20, 32)	=	11.69	[0.00]	**
RESET F(1, 52)	=	1.46	[0.23]	

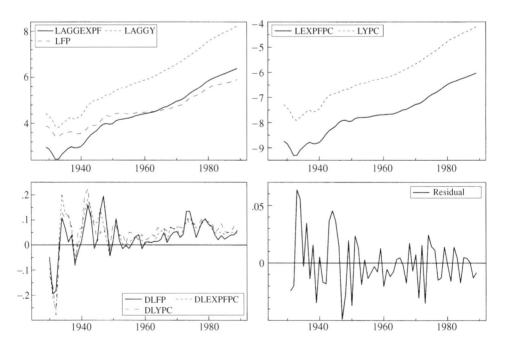

Figure 4. Time-series plots: US data and residuals from model 6

the instability in the error variance. Model 6 is now estimated twice, once for the years 1929–1951 and once for the years 1952–1989. This gives models 7 and 8. The results for model 7 are presented in Table XIII.

The variance of the error term is now constant over time. The estimate for the standard deviation of the error term is 0.037. The diagnostic tests are carried out for model 7 and presented in Table XIV. The diagnostic tests are now satisfactory.

Model 8 is estimated and the results are presented in Table XV.

Again, the variance of the error term is constant over time. The estimate for the standard deviation of the error term is 0.010 for the second subsample. The diagnostic tests on model 8 are in Table XVI, and are again satisfactory.

Table XIII. OLS estimates, model 7

Variable	The present sample is: 1931 to 1951 Coefficient	Std. Error	Instab
Constant	0.00	0.01	0.08
DLEXPFPC _1	0.53	0.21	0.08
DLYPC	0.57	0.13	0.26
DLYPC _1	−0.16	0.17	0.16
DLFP	0.48	0.15	0.38
DLFP _1	−0.48	0.18	0.06

$R^2 = 0.92$ $F(5, 15) = 36.82$ [0.00] $\sigma = 0.04$ $DW = 1.88$
$RSS = 0.0209$ for 6 variables and 21 observations

Variance instability test: 0.07;   Joint instability test: 1.53
Information Criteria: $SC = -6.04$; $HQ = -6.28$; $FPE = 0.002$

Table XIV. Diagnostic tests, model 7

AR 1– 2F(2, 13)	= 0.03	[0.97]
ARCH 1 F(1, 13)	= 0.26	[0.62]
Normality Chi² (2)	= 2.12	[0.35]
Xi² F(10, 4)	= 0.65	[0.74]
RESET F(1,14)	= 1.62	[0.22]

Table XV. OLS estimates, model 8

Variable	The present sample is: 1952 to 1989 Coefficient	Std. Error	Instab
Constant	−0.01	0.01	0.04
DLEXPFPC _1	−0.15	0.17	0.04
DLYPC	0.47	0.11	0.06
DLYPC _1	0.24	0.14	0.05
DLFP	0.36	0.08	0.10
DLFP _1	0.12	0.11	0.07

$R^2 = 0.89$ $F(5, 32) = 52.61$ [0.00] $\sigma = 0.01$ $DW = 2.18$
$RSS = 0.0035$ for 6 variables and 38 observations

Variance instability test: 0.23;   Joint instability test: 1.35
Information Criteria: $SC = -8.71$; $HQ = -8.88$; $FPE = 0.0001$

Table XVI. Diagnostic tests, model 8

AR 1–	2F(2, 30)	= 1.04	[0.37]
ARCH 1	F(1, 30)	= 0.91	[0.35]
Normality	Chi^2 (2)	= 0.64	[0.73]
Xi^2	F(10, 21)	= 0.49	[0.88]
Xi*Xj	F(20, 11)	= 0.25	[0.99]
RESET	F(1, 31)	= 3.06	[0.09]

The parameters are constant in both subsamples. The hypothesis

$$H_0 : \text{Var}\{\varepsilon_t\} = \sigma^2 \text{ for all } t,$$

can be tested against the alternative

$$H_1 : \text{Var}\{\varepsilon_t\} = \begin{cases} \sigma_1^2 & \text{if } 1929 \leq t \leq 1951 \\ \sigma_2^2 & \text{if } 1952 \leq t \leq 1989 \end{cases}$$

using the Goldfeld-Quandt test. The test statistic is

$$F(15, 32) = \frac{RSS_6}{RSS_7} = \frac{0.0209}{0.0035} = 5.93 \; [0.00]^{**}.$$

Hence homoscedasticity is rejected. The idea is now to estimate model 6 on transformed data. All the series are divided by the estimated standard deviation of model 7 (0.037) for the years 1929–1951 and by the estimated standard deviation of model 8 (0.010) for the years 1952–1989. Thus, model 9 is obtained. The results of model 9 are in Table XVII.

The variance of the error term is now constant over time and close to one. The diagnostic tests are in Table XVIII.

The heteroscedasticity problem is now solved. The reset test suggests that a variable must be added to the model. However, this sign is neglected at this stage. Dynamic analysis is carried out and the solved static long run equation is

$$WDLEXPFPC = \underset{(0.29)}{0.15} + \underset{(0.10)}{0.46} \; WDLYPC + \underset{(0.10)}{0.49} \; WDLFP.$$

Table XVII. OLS estimates, model 9

The present sample is: 1931 to 1989			
Variable	Coefficient	Std. Error	Instab
Constant	0.13	0.24	0.13
WDLEXPFPC _1	0.18	0.14	0.07
WDLYPC	0.44	0.08	0.16
WDLYPC _1	−0.06	0.10	0.03
WDLFP	0.48	0.07	0.14
WDLFP _1	−0.08	0.10	0.03

$R^2 = 0.90$ $F(5, 53) = 94.69 \; [0.00]$ $\sigma = 1.10$ $DW = 1.99$
$RSS = 64.37$ for 6 variables and 59 observations

Instability tests, variance: 0.12;   joint: 1.57
Information Criteria: $SC = 0.50$; $HQ = 0.37$; $FPE = 1.34$

Table XVIII. Diagnostic tests, model 9

AR 1– 2	F(2, 51)	=	0.18	[0.83]
ARCH 1	F(1, 51)	=	0.45	[0.51]
Normality	Chi^2 (2)	=	1.16	[0.56]
Xi^2	F(10, 42)	=	1.04	[0.43]
Xi^*Xj	F(20, 32)	=	1.20	[0.31]
RESET	F(1, 52)	=	5.09	[0.03] *

The hypothesis that all the coefficients of the solved static long run equation are zero, is not rejected. Table XIX presents significance tests on model 9.

The variables 'income per capita' and 'food-price' are significant. The variable 'lagged food consumption' is not significant. In fact, lag 1 is not significant for any of the variables. Common factor analysis is carried out and presented in Table XX. The outcome is that there is a common factor present.

Dividing both the left hand and the right hand side of model 9 by the common factor leads to a static model with an autoregressive error. Note that autocorrelation is rejected. Model 10 is now obtained. Model 10 is estimated and the results are presented in Table XXI.

The autoregressive error term is low (0.17) and not significantly different from zero. Dropping the autoregressive error term leads to static model 11. All the parameters in model 11 are constant over time. The standard deviation of the error term is close to one. There is no heteroscedasticity problem in model 11. The reset test suggests that a variable must be added. A test for omitted variables on 'non-food price' is performed. The

Table XIX. Significance tests, model 9

Tests on the significance of each variable				
Variable	F-test	Value	Probability	Unit-root t-test
WDLEXPFPC	F(1, 53) =	1.61	[0.21]	−5.96**
Constant	F(1, 53) =	0.29	[0.59]	
WDLYPC	F(2, 53) =	15.90	[0.00] **	3.57
WDLFP	F(2, 53) =	22.52	[0.00] **	3.88
Tests on the significance of each lag				
Lag	F-test	Value	Probability	
1	F(3, 53) =	0.55	[0.65]	

Table XX. Common factor analysis, model 9

Roots of the lag polynomials

WDLEXPFPC	lags 0 − 1
	0.18
WDLYPC	lags 0 − 1
	0.15
WDLFP	lags 0 − 1
	0.16

COMFAC WALD test statistic

Order	Chi^2df	Value	p-value
1	2	0.10	[0.95]

Table XXI. OLS estimates, model 10

Variable	The present sample is: 1931 to 1989 Coefficient	Std. Error
Constant	0.17	0.26
WDLYPC	0.46	0.07
WDLFP	0.49	0.07
Uhat_1	0.17	0.14

$\Sigma y(t)^2 = 639.34$ $\sigma = 1.08$
$\Phi = 64.49$ for 3 variables and 59 observations (4 parameters)

outcome is that 'non-food price' must not be added to the model. This is not surprising because it was removed in one of the steps above. There are no other variables available in the data set left. The estimate of the income elasticity of food demand is then 0.47 with a standard error of 0.06. Does this estimate differ much from estimates of the subsamples 1929–1951 and 1952–1989? In model 8 (the model estimated for the second subsample) the lagged variables are insignificant. Dropping this insignificant lag leads to model 12, which is the same as model 11, except that it is estimated for subsample 1952–1989. The results are in Table XXII.

The estimated income elasticity of food demand is now 0.49 with a standard error of 0.11. The diagnostic tests are in Table XXIII.

There is no heteroscedasticity problem present. Model 12 has, however, the same problem with respect to the reset test. What about the first subsample? In model 7 (the model estimated for the first subsample) the lagged income variable is insignificant. But the main difference is that lagged food consumption and lagged food price do now matter. Note

Table XXII. OLS estimates, model 12

Variable	The present sample is: 1952 to 1989 Coefficient	Std. Error	Instab
Constant	−0.00	0.01	0.09
DLYPC	0.49	0.11	0.03
DLFP	0.47	0.07	0.03

$R^2 = 0.87$ $F(2, 35) = 118.82$ [0.00] $\sigma = 0.01$ $DW = 2.30$
$RSS = 0.004$ for 3 variables and 38 observations

Instability tests, variance: 0.23;   joint: 0.88
Information Criteria: $SC = -8.83$; $HQ = -8.91$; $FPE = 0.0001$

Table XXIII. Diagnostic tests, model 12

AR 1–	2F(2, 33)	=	0.65 [0.53]
ARCH 1	F(1, 33)	=	0.06 [0.81]
Normality	Chi^2 (2)	=	2.56 [0.28]
Xi^2	F(4, 30)	=	1.27 [0.31]
Xi*Xj	F(5, 29)	=	1.12 [0.37]
RESET	F(1, 34)	=	5.95 [0.02] *

that there may be another unit root present in the variable food price! The final models for the whole sample and the second subsample differ only in the period selected, not in the model specification. For the first subsample the specification search leads to another specification. Since the second subsample is more interesting, because it is closer to today, the desired income elasticity of food demand is estimated from the second subsample. It has a value of 0.49 and comes from model 12.

3.3. Logbook

All results have been obtained using PC-GIVE 8.0. I also estimated equations on the budget surveys and on time series for the Netherlands. These results are not included in this paper.

PC-GIVE is very easy to use. Regressions are easily estimated and test statistics are very easily obtained. Maybe a little too easy — it is easier to try than to think. I am sure that I estimated a lot of redundant regressions and performed many unnecessary tests. Time-series analysis is very easy with PC-GIVE. Dynamic analysis and common-factor analysis help to reduce the general model to the parsimonious model. I did not encounter very serious problems with the time series for the US and the Netherlands. It is a pity that PC-GIVE can not perform weighted least squares estimation directly. I have estimated various models with WLS and each time I had to perform OLS on transformed data.

4.   THE METHODOLOGY OF CHRISTOPHER A. SIMS

The framework of Sims (1980) is the VAR(p) model:

$$y_t = \mu + \Phi_1 y_{t-1} + \cdots + \Phi_p y_{t-p} + v_t.$$

The most important aspect of Sims' method is the impulse response analysis. Consider a zero mean VAR(1) model,

$$\begin{pmatrix} y_{1,t} \\ y_{2,t} \end{pmatrix} = \Phi \begin{pmatrix} y_{1,t-1} \\ y_{2,t-1} \end{pmatrix} + \begin{pmatrix} v_{1,t} \\ v_{2,t} \end{pmatrix}. \qquad\qquad 5$$

Suppose at $t = 0$ a unit shock $[1 \; 0]^T$ in the residuals occurs. The response of the system is then

$$y_0 = \begin{pmatrix} y_{1,0} \\ y_{2,0} \end{pmatrix} = \begin{pmatrix} 1 \\ 0 \end{pmatrix},$$

$$y_1 = \begin{pmatrix} y_{1,1} \\ y_{2,1} \end{pmatrix} = \Phi y_0,$$

$$y_2 = \begin{pmatrix} y_{1,2} \\ y_{2,2} \end{pmatrix} = \Phi^2 y_0,$$

$$y_3 = \begin{pmatrix} y_{1,3} \\ y_{2,3} \end{pmatrix} = \Phi^3 y_0.$$

Hence, the response in period $t = i$ is $\Phi^i y_0$. Note that Φ^i is just the i-th coefficient matrix in the infinite moving average (MA) representation. The disturbances of (5) are assumed to have a white noise variance covariance matrix of Σ_v. The Choleski decomposition $\Sigma_v = PP'$ can be used to transform v_t. Model (5) can be rewritten in such a way that the residuals of different equations are uncorrelated:

$$y_t = \Phi y_{t-1} + Pu_t, \text{ where } v_t = Pu_t \text{ and } \text{var}\{u_t\} = I. \qquad 6$$

Impulse response analysis applied on (6) is called orthogonal impulse response analysis. The order in which the variables in (6) appear is now very important. Shocks at time zero in the first residual of the system are allowed to affect all the other variables in the system instantaneously. Shocks at time zero in the last residual of the system are only allowed to affect the last variable. The response function then is $y_i = \Phi^i P y_0$. Sims (1980) provides a way to locate the main channels of influence in the model. This method is called 'innovation accounting' and it asks the question: which variable accounts for most of the variance in the forecast error of one particular variable? In the end Sims (1980) checks whether the model is stationary with the use of the forecast standard error table. For a stationary process, forecast standard error tends to some upper bound as the horizon rises. This is the analysis which I shall try to do for time series in the USA and the Netherlands.

4.1. The US Time Series

The variables listed in Table III are available for the US time-series analysis. All variables are logged. There are three income and food consumption variables available: the original Tobin series, the revised series and aggregated series. Since we have annual data, a VAR(1) model seems to be appropriate. It is not likely that shocks from two years ago influence the present. Which variables of Table III do we wish to consider for inclusion in the VAR(1) model? All the original Tobin series are revised thus these numbers won't be used. Multiplying disposable income (*PCY*) with population (*POP*) gives aggregated personal disposable income (*AGGY*). Hence, if *AGGY* and *POP* are included in the VAR then *PCY* can be left out. The same holds for food consumption (*PCFC*). If population is in the VAR then there is no need to include the number of households because they are strongly related to each other. If food demand rises it is most likely that food prices will go up, so the revised food price index (*FP*) is included in the VAR. If the non-food demand rises it is most likely that non-food prices will go up too. But if the non-food demand (*AGGEXP* − *AGGEXPF*) is added to the VAR then income is measured twice, once through aggregated personal disposable income (*AGGY*) and once through aggregated food demand (*AGGEXPF*) plus aggregated non-food demand (*AGGEXP* − *AGGEXPF*). So non-food demand and non-food prices are left out. The variables are ordered as *AGGY*, *AGGEXPF*, *FP*, *POP*. Shocks in income disturb food consumption, food prices and population instantly, while shocks in the population are only allowed to affect the population itself.

The VAR(1) model then looks as follows:

$$\begin{pmatrix} AGGY_t \\ AGGEXPF_t \\ FP_t \\ POP_t \end{pmatrix} = \mu + \Phi \begin{pmatrix} AGGY_{t-1} \\ AGGEXPF_{t-1} \\ FP_{t-1} \\ POP_{t-1} \end{pmatrix} + u_t. \qquad 7$$

After estimating the VAR(1) and obtaining estimates for μ, Φ and P, the response of the system to an innovation in income can be calculated as follows:

$$(\text{response}_k) = \hat{\Phi}^k \hat{P} \begin{pmatrix} 1 \\ 0 \\ 0 \\ 0 \end{pmatrix}. \qquad\qquad 8$$

For the time series of the US the response of the system to an innovation in income is listed in Table XXIV. The table shows that an innovation of 0.0627 in income at time zero leads to an instantaneous response of 0.0591 in food consumption. One could say that the instantaneous income elasticity of food demand is $0.0591/0.0627 = 0.94$. The short-run elasticity is then $0.0599/0.0627 = 0.96$, the middle-run elasticity is $0.0585/0.0627 = 0.93$ and the long-run elasticity is then $0.0386/0.0627 = 0.63$.

Table XXV provides a type of summary which is useful in locating the main channels of influence in the model. A variable which was strictly exogenous would, if there were no sampling error in estimates of the system, have entries of unity in the diagonal cells, and zeros in all other cells. Exogeneity is equivalent to the condition that a variable's own innovations account for all of its variance. The income variable has more than 78% of its variance accounted for by own innovations at all time horizons shown. No other variables have so much variance accounted for by own innovations, indicating that interactions among variables are strong. Could the income variable now be removed from the VAR? The answer is no, because the main source of feedback into food consumption is income. Food consumption has only 20% of its one-step forecast error variance accounted

Table XXIV. Response of the system to an innovation in
AGGY, *k* years ahead: USA 1929–1989

k	AGGY	AGGEXPF	FP	POP
0	0.0627	0.0591	0.0409	−0.0007
1	0.0614	0.0599	0.0442	−0.0007
3	0.0579	0.0585	0.0478	−0.0005
9	0.0393	0.0386	0.0400	0.0003

Table XXV. Proportions of forecast error variance *k* years ahead produced by
each innovation: USA 1929–1989

forecast error in:	forecast horizon k	Triangularized innovation in:			
		AGGY	AGGEXPF	FP	POP
AGGY	1	1.00	0	0	0
	3	0.97	0.01	0.02	0.00
	9	0.78	0.02	0.20	0.00
AGGEXPF	1	0.80	0.20	0	0
	3	0.80	0.16	0.04	0.00
	9	0.66	0.09	0.25	0.00
FP	1	0.55	0.19	0.26	0
	3	0.68	0.18	0.14	0.00
	9	0.75	0.12	0.13	0.00
POP	1	0.08	0.00	0.01	0.91
	3	0.06	0.15	0.00	0.79
	9	0.01	0.50	0.08	0.42

for by own innovations and 80% is accounted for by innovations in income. Income, food consumption and food prices all have 0% of their variance accounted for by population innovations at all time horizons shown. Apparently the shocks in the population are too small to seriously influence the economy. In the long run the population has 50% of its variance accounted for by innovations in food consumption. If the US were a third world country this result could be credible. But it isn't and hence this effect can be marked as a negative point of the VAR model. If the population had 100% of its variance accounted for by own-innovations then population would be strictly exogenous and could be removed from the model. Now it stays in.

Table XXVI displays the forecast standard errors over various forecasting horizons. The forecast error rises steadily as the forecasting horizon lengthens, for every variable. For a stationary process, forecast standard error tends to some upper bound as the horizon increases. This indicates that the estimated system is very slowly damped.

4.2. The Dutch Time Series

For the Netherlands the same model as for the US is applied (equation (7)). Thus four variables are needed: aggregated disposable income, aggregated food consumption, food prices and population. For aggregated disposable income the series *AGGY* is used, for aggregated food consumption the series *V11*, for food prices the series *P11* and for population the series *POP*.[5] Again, all variables are logged. After estimating the VAR and obtaining estimates for μ, Φ and P, the response of the system to an innovation in income can be calculated as in (8).

For the time series of the Netherlands the response of the system to an innovation in income is listed in Table XXVII. We see that an innovation of 0.0258 in income at time zero leads to an instantaneous response of 0.0145 in food consumption. Thus the instantaneous income elasticity of food demand is $0.0145/0.0258 = 0.56$. The short-run elasticity is then $0.0158/0.0258 = 0.61$, the middle-run elasticity is $0.0146/0.0258 = 0.57$ and the long-run elasticity is then $0.0024/0.0258 = 0.09$.

Table XXVI. Forecast standard errors, k years ahead: USA 1929–1989

	k	USA
AGGY	1	0.063
	3	0.108
	9	0.187
AGGEXPF	1	0.066
	3	0.115
	9	0.202
FP	1	0.055
	3	0.092
	9	0.158
POP	1	0.003
	3	0.005
	9	0.011

---

[5] The series *POP* is the corrected series from the E-mail message of 1 May 1996. See the data chapters for details.

Table XXVII. Response of the system to an
innovation in *AGGY*, *k* years ahead: Netherlands
1948–1988

k	AGGY	FOOD	FP	POP
0	0.0258	0.0145	0.0090	−0.0002
1	0.0248	0.0158	0.0131	−0.0002
3	0.0206	0.0146	0.0156	−0.0004
9	0.0031	0.0024	0.0078	−0.0012

Table XXVIII. Proportions of forecast error variance, *k* years ahead
produced by each innovation: Netherlands 1948–1988

forecast error in:	forecast horizon k	Triangularized innovation in:			
		AGGY	FOOD	FP	POP
AGGY	1	1.00	0	0	0
	3	0.70	0.21	0.09	0.00
	9	0.45	0.28	0.25	0.01
FOOD	1	0.30	0.70	0	0
	3	0.33	0.62	0.05	0.00
	9	0.30	0.50	0.20	0.01
FP	1	0.17	0.48	0.35	0
	3	0.30	0.56	0.12	0.01
	9	0.32	0.53	0.14	0.01
POP	1	0.03	0.05	0.00	0.92
	3	0.02	0.05	0.06	0.87
	9	0.10	0.30	0.04	0.55

Table XXVIII is again useful in locating the main channels of influence in the model. The income variable has more than 45%, food consumption has more than 50% and the population has more than 55% of its variance accounted for by own innovations at all horizons shown. Interaction between the variables is again strong. Food consumption has 17% of its one-step forecast error variance accounted for by innovations in income (for the USA this was 80%). In the long run, population has 30% of its variance accounted for by innovations in food consumption. It is interesting that food consumption for both the Netherlands and the USA is the main source of feedback into population.

Table XXIX displays the forecast standard errors over various forecasting horizons. The forecast error rises steadily as the forecasting horizon lengthens, for every variable. This indicates that the system is very slowly damped.

4.3. Logbook

The results of the US and the Dutch time series show a lot of similarities. The Dutch and US elasticities reveal the same development over time, shown in Figure 5. They both first rise a bit and then drop a little and then both fall. The main difference between the US and the Netherlands is the instantaneous elasticity: 0.94 for the US and 0.56 for the Netherlands. Both time series have the strange phenomenon that the main source of feedback into the population is food consumption.

Table XXIX. Forecast standard errors,
k years ahead: Netherlands 1948–1988

	k	Netherlands
AGGY	1	0.026
	3	0.051
	9	0.082
FOOD	1	0.027
	3	0.046
	9	0.067
FP	1	0.022
	3	0.040
	9	0.070
POP	1	0.001
	3	0.003
	9	0.006

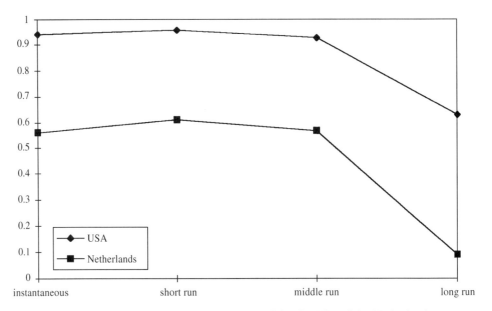

Figure 5. Income elasticities of food demand for the US and the Netherlands

One could ask: does food consumption cause food prices or do food prices cause food consumption? I have switched the food consumption and the food prices in the ordering for both the US and the Dutch dataset. This switch did not change the results.

I have used the formulas of Lütkepohl (1993) to compute the orthogonal impulse responses, the proportions of forecast standard errors and the forecast standard errors itself.

5. SUMMARY

Pagan (1987) concludes in his final section that there exists no complete general methodology. Sims explicitly deals only with time series, while Leamer's methodology is heavily based on the OLS estimator. Hendry's methodology covers time series and, to a certain degree, also cross sections. The first problem that arises when comparing the final results of this experiment is that the various elasticities can not be directly compared with each other. The second problem is the question asked in this experiment: estimate the income elasticity of food demand. This question can be more suitable for one methodology than for the other, and indeed favour one methodology above the others.

The question is right up Leamer's street. Leamer's methodology uses a focus variable/coefficient. This focus coefficient points out the inference of interest. Here, the focus coefficient is the income elasticity of food demand. Once the focus is set, then sensitivity analysis is carried out upon this focus variable. So the whole methodology is focused on the income elasticity of food demand.

Hendry also has a focus variable, but it is hidden in his methodology. His focus variable is not the inference of interest, but the residuals. Hendry is only satisfied when both the general congruent model and the parsimonious simplified model pass all the diagnostic tests. To simplify a model requires a criterion function or decision rule. Hendry's decision rule is based on the loglikelihood. So, Hendry answers a different question, namely: how can I explain one variable the best way in terms of other variables? If the criterion function would be adapted to the inference of interest it should be based on something like the mean squared error of the income elasticity of food demand.

Sims' methodology is designed for policy making. He is focused on the mutual dependence among the residuals of the different equations in the VAR. The main difference between Sims on the one hand and Leamer and Hendry on the other is the *ceteris paribus* condition. As Sims is not interested in *ceteris paribus* inferences, his methodology cannot focus on one inference of interest. Nevertheless, the inference of interest can be extracted afterwards from the impulse response analysis.

Applying the three methodologies I encountered certain problems. There were moments that I missed the presence of a master. During the workshop in December 1996 Leamer told me to get rid of total consumption in the model. Income is measured twice when both *HINC* and *TOTCON* are included. This is a general piece of information, not just suitable for his methodology. This is exactly one of the points where I needed the master. Each variable must be labelled 'doubtful' or 'free' in his methodology. I labelled the income-related variables *NETASSCH* and *ACCBAL* as free. But another choice would have been to simply drop these variables, which is equivalent to give the coefficients of *NETASSCH* and *ACCBAL* a prior mean and variance of zero. I did not have this much prior information. One could think, if a choice must be made between dropping variables or label them as 'free', the label 'doubtful' is appropriate. At this point I really would have liked to consult Leamer.

After the workshops I received an E-mail message from Leamer. I should make the reference prior as sensible as possible. Again, Leamer gave me a 'forbidden' push. In the spirit of the experiment I decided not to use this information. So, I just used my original prior, the sample covariance matrix, as reference prior. I think that Leamer would use $\mathrm{diag}(0.1^2 \ldots 0.1^2)$ as reference prior because he used this prior in the analysis he presented at the workshop. He just conjures this prior out of his magic hat. He never shows why his reference prior is the most sensible prior. Again, I would have liked to ask.

Another point where tacit knowledge is involved is in the interpretation of the words 'narrow' and 'wide'. Conclusions are judged to be sturdy only if the neighbourhood of assumptions is wide enough to be credible and the corresponding interval of inferences is narrow enough to be useful. Certain experience is needed to distinguish narrow from wide.

Using the methodology of Hendry I encountered the same problem. Is dropping a variable with a significant coefficient allowed? Or is it allowed to include a variable with an insignificant coefficient? Both the general and the parsimonious model need to be theory consistent. But what is the economic theory underlying this experiment? What about the signs of the coefficients? Should a significant coefficient with the wrong sign be removed from the model or not? In all these cases I would have liked to consult Hendry.

Using the methodology of Sims, I did not encounter the problems mentioned above. The only problem was the choice of lag length. I thought that a lag length of one should be enough when dealing with annual data. Sims uses a shrinkage estimator for non-stationary time series. This shrinkage estimator sets the prior mean of the first lag of each variable equal to one in its own equation and all other coefficients to zero. Then prior variances of the coefficients are chosen such that higher lags are less important. At this point exactly the same problem arises as with the methodology of Leamer. An arbitrary choice must be made for these prior variances.

REFERENCES

Breusch, T. S. (1985), 'Simplified extreme bounds', in: C. W. J. Granger (ed), *Modelling Economic Series*, Clarendon Press, Oxford.

Chamberlain, G. and E. E. Leamer (1976), 'Matrix weighted averages and posterior bounds', *Journal of the Royal Statistical Society*, Series B, **38**, 73–84.

Hendry, D. F. (1993), *Econometrics: Alchemy or Science?* Blackwell, Oxford.

Hendry, D. F. and J. A. Doornik (1996), *Empirical Econometric Modelling Using PcGive 9.0 for Windows*, International Thomson Business Press, London.

Leamer, E. E. (1978), *Specification Searches*, John Wiley and Sons, New York.

Leamer, E. E. (1982), 'Sets of posterior means with bounded variance priors', *Econometrica*, **50**, 726–36.

Leamer, E. E. (1983), 'Let's take the con out of econometrics', *American Economic Review*, **73**, 31–44.

Leamer, E. E. (1985), 'Sensitivity analyses would help', *American Economic Review*, **75**, 308–13.

Leamer, E. E. and H. Leonard (1983), 'Reporting the fragility of regression estimates', *Review of Economics and Statistics*, **65**, 306–17.

Lütkepohl, H. (1993), *Introduction to Multiple Time Series Analysis*, Second Edition, Springer-Verlag, Berlin.

Pagan A. R. (1987), 'Three econometric methodologies: a critical appraisal', *Journal of Economic Surveys*, **1**, 3–24.

Polanyi M. (1962), *Personal Knowledge: Towards a Post-Critical Philosophy*, Routledge and Kegan Paul, London.

Sims, C. A. (1980), 'Macroeconomics and reality', *Econometrica*, **48**, 1–48.

Tobin, J. (1950), 'A statistical demand function for food in the USA', *Journal of the Royal Statistical Society*, Series A, **113**, 113–41 [reprinted in Chapter 2, this volume].

CHAPTER 17

AN ECONOMETRIC ANALYSIS OF US FOOD EXPENDITURE, 1931–1989*

DAVID F. HENDRY

1. OVERVIEW

This chapter applies a 'general-to-specific' modelling approach to the US annual food expenditure time series in Magnus and Morgan (1995), denoted MM. It discusses how to model the updated data from Tobin (1950), given the questions MM seek to have answered.

After comments on the historical background and the data period, Section 1.2 considers scale factors (population, number of households, etc.), and Section 1.3 discusses cointegration and alternative measures of food time series ('disappearance', real expenditure, income share). Then, Section 1.4 turns to demand determinants (income and total expenditure), Section 1.5 to prices (of food and other goods), and Section 1.6 describes some long-run theory. Since it is essential to begin empirical analyses with data graphs to see what has to be modelled, and whether there are any data problems, such as transcription errors, many graphs are shown below. Then in Section 2, a cointegrated vector autoregressive system will be investigated and modelled via sequential simplification, followed by a conditional single-equation model in Section 3. Section 4 comments on the approach adopted by Siegert (1998), and Section 5 concludes.

1.1. Historical Background

This is always central to any empirical study, and requires knowledge of the main economic and political events. For the period 1912–89, we know that there was World War I (WWI); the 1920–21 flu' epidemic that killed even more people than the war; prohibition (affecting the drinks expenditure component); the Great Depression from 1929–35 (approximately, but lingering on to 1939); World War II (WWII); the Korean war (which dramatically spurred demand and inflation); the Vietnam war; and the oil crises of the mid and late 1970s. Throughout, there was a steady decline in family size, and an increase in average age of death. Such factors need to be handled to avoid contaminating inference.

An awkward consequence of commencing the sample in 1929 is that the initial observation coincides with the largest shock. It would be worth back-extending the sample pre-1929 before undertaking policy analyses. As truncation loses information about the

---

*This is both a report on the paper by W. Siegert acting 'as if' he were DFH, and a contribution to the Experiment in Applied Econometrics. I am grateful to Mary Morgan for advice about the data, to Adrian Pagan for helpful comments, and to the UK ESRC for financial support under grant R000234954.

Methodology and Tacit Knowledge: Two Experiments in Econometrics
Jan R. Magnus and Mary S. Morgan © 1999 John Wiley & Sons Ltd

period of greatest variation, I will first saturate the initial years with indicator variables (zero-one dummies) — in effect removing those observations — but later restrict the dummies from data evidence to allow a role for the early period. A similar treatment will be accorded WWII.

1.2.   The Scale Factor for Food Demand

Neither population (N) nor number of households (H) is an appropriate deflator — a better weighting system should allow for 'baby booms', changes in household composition, and aging effects. As Figure 1 records, average family size (A) fell from about 4.5 to about 2.5, so deflating by H is clearly inappropriate. Consider a thought experiment of an increase in divorce that doubled the number of households *ceteris paribus* the population: this will not have the same effect on demand for food as doubling the population. This suggested N as the scale deflator, including $a = \log A$ as a separate regressor, even though that does not correct for aging (e.g., pensioners may spend an above-average share of their budget on food).[1] Thus per capita variables were used.

However, there are problems with n and a — see the 1980 blips in Figure 1. These looked like recording errors, but the information pack from Magnus and Morgan (1995) noted the problem as due to revision after the census. Even so, indicators for 1980 and perhaps 1981 may be needed.

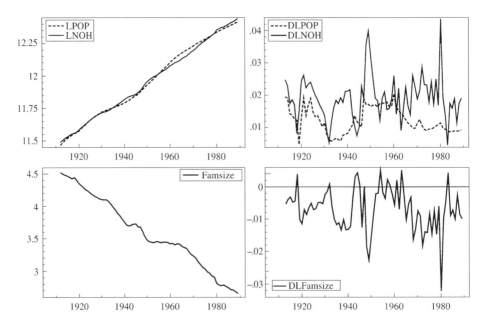

Figure 1. Time series of population measures and family size

---

[1] The experiment rules precluded collecting extra data. In the absence of an equivalence scale, one might assume two adults per household — albeit that is now false — so the remainder are children with a weight less than unity (e.g., ψ), hence:

$$(2 + \psi(A - 2))H = (2(1 - \psi) + \psi A)H = 2(1 - \psi)H + \psi N.$$

This weights both components, but goes wrong when $A < 2$, and has no convenient log approximation.

1.3. Cointegration

This is about the most important recent time-series development, and clearly differentiates modern work from that in Tobin. The multivariate methods in Johansen (1988) are attractive, but require a congruent vector autoregression (VAR) as a sound inferential basis. Once cointegration is established, long-run weak exogeneity can be tested, and hence one requirement for a valid conditional model investigated.

If the VAR is not congruent, a single-equation conditional model still merits analysis, though it is harder to check weak exogeneity. Using the approach in Banerjee and Hendry (1992) (embodied in PcGive: see Hendry and Doornik, 1996), the solved long-run will be used for the equilibrium correction, and a restricted model developed.

1.3.1. Alternative Measures of Food Demand

First, the time series used by Tobin (1950) (also discussed by MM)—which measures food 'disappearance', denoted by $pcfc$—and constant-price expenditure on food (e_f) need testing for cointegration. Investigating their bivariate relationship via a scalar autoregressive-distributed lag (AD) model, an AD(4,4) with a WWII dummy yielded the following long-run solution (over 1933–76, the model had $\hat{\sigma} = 0.010$):

$$pcfc = \underset{(0.4)}{9.2} + \underset{(0.03)}{0.38} \; e_f - \underset{(0.01)}{0.03} \; D4245.$$

The unit-root t-test (t_{ur}) was -3.66^* which rejects at the 5% level, but shortening to one lag, t_{ur} did not reject even though all longer lags were insignificant—all diagnostic tests were acceptable. When using expenditure on food, therefore, elasticity comparisons with Tobin's are suspect, given the long-run elasticity of $pcfc$ of 0.4 with respect to e_f.

Figure 2 shows the problem starkly: the Tobin measure is almost a straight line relative to the expenditure measure (scaled to match in mean), and the difference of the latter has vastly more variation to explain. Thus, measures of fit may be much worse for real expenditure despite the model being preferable.[2]

1.4. Alternative Measures of Resources

Selecting real expenditure on food still leaves open the choice of an income or expenditure 'deflator'. Logically, the choice is one of conditioning viewed as an 'allocation' of income (Y) to expenditure (E) and saving, then the former to categories; or of income to categories, with saving as a residual. I assumed the former, but included $s = \log Y - \log E$, (called the log of the savings ratio below, but really an approximation to the savings ratio) as a separate regressor. As Figure 3 shows, income and expenditure differed greatly during WWII, and the savings ratio was relatively constant otherwise. The WWII dummy is graphed in Figure 3 to highlight this.

---

[2] The mismatch of these two data series on per capita food consumption led me to discuss that issue with Mary Morgan, and decide not to use the Tobin measure. Related concerns were raised in discussion of his original paper, and his 'Reply'—I probably 'knew' that, but did not actively remember it—as were issues of equivalence scales, measurement of the data, simultaneity from the supply side, and the form of the demand function.

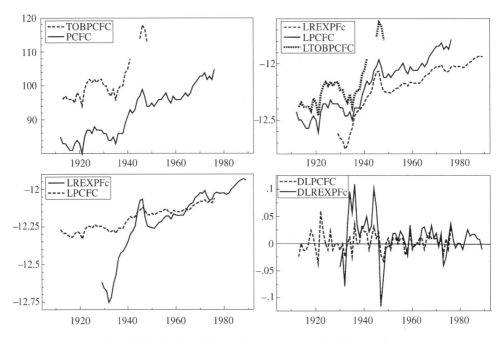

Figure 2. Alternative time-series measures of food expenditure

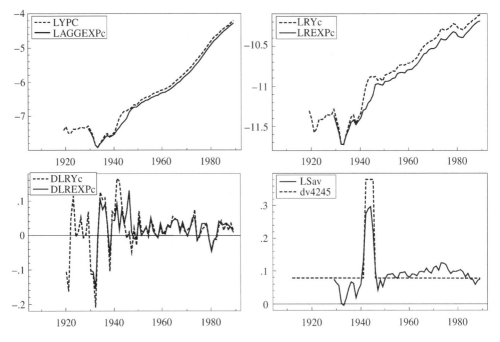

Figure 3. Alternative time-series measures of income and expenditure

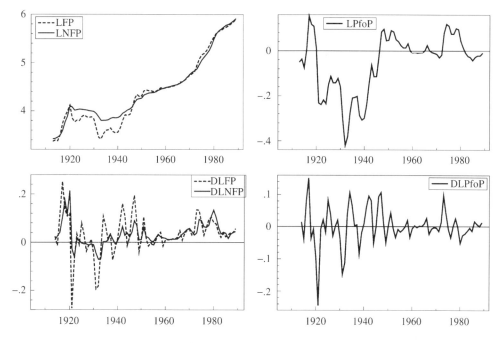

Figure 4. Food price series

1.5. Prices

Figure 4 reveals that $p_f - p$ had a sharp dip after WWI (perhaps the end of war production and the flu' epidemic), declines till the Great Depression, recovers, and stabilizes after WWII close to its initial value. The two series are dominated by inflation in the levels graph, with the greater volatility in p_f shown in their changes, and reflected in changes in $p_f - p$. Indeed, Figure 4 shows an odd time series for $\Delta(p_f - p)$, somewhat like a damped sine wave, with considerable heteroscedasticity.

1.6. Long-run Theory

Food shares in total expenditure tend to fall towards a lower bound as income rises; the bound depends on the definition of 'food expenditure', namely, type of food, how much human input is involved in its preparation etc., and on its quality, as well as on quality-adjustment of the price data used to deflate nominal expenditures. It may also depend on supply side factors such as the relative price of production, given biological determination of minimal intake. However, the need for a given nutrient intake does not constrain the demand function when expressed as expenditure. Finally, income distribution must matter, as food expenditure is a much larger budget share item for the very poor.

This suggests a logit long-run relation in the share of food expenditure relative to available resources as being data admissible. Let lower case temporarily denote real values, and capitals nominal, then:

$$\frac{E_f}{Y} = \frac{P_f e_f}{P y} = w,$$

so that w is the share of nominal food expenditure in nominal income. Thus, ignoring dynamics:

$$\log\left(\frac{w}{1-w}\right) = a - \frac{b}{y} - c\log\left(\frac{P_f}{P}\right) + \cdots \tag{1}$$

See, e.g. Hendry and Richard (1982). However, the parameterization in (1) needs thought once such a non-linear form is adopted.

Figure 5 records various measures of the share. Relative to total expenditure, the share rises till the end of WWII, then falls sharply, and steadily declines till the end of the sample. The rise during the period 1935–48 is out of line with expenditure, but is roughly associated with the rising relative price of food, albeit from a low level. The graph also shows that the logit and log are similar, so despite the 'admissibility' problem, I will use the log form for analysis, even though, relative to the 'question' posed, there is a substantive difference as (1) has a variable, not a constant, income elasticity.

Also, Figure 5 shows that the share is similar whichever deflator (income or expenditure) is used ($w_e = P_f e_f / Pe$). Note that P is a non-food price index, not all prices, but this should not greatly distort the analysis; indeed:

$$\log\left(\frac{w_e}{1-w_e}\right) = \log\left(\frac{P_f e_f}{Pe - P_f e_f}\right) = \log\left(\frac{E_f}{E - E_f}\right) = \log\left(\frac{E_f}{E_{nf}}\right) = \log\left(\frac{P_f e_f}{P_{nf} e_{nf}}\right)$$

which might help remove any price distortion. Thus, $\log w_e$ is the 'target' transformation (variables denoted LRWe on the graph are of the form $\log(e_f/e)$, etc.).

While a model of w_e is the target transform, one must not begin by modelling w_e directly, as that implicitly imposes common-factor restrictions, which may be invalid. Figure 5 also reports the shares in constant-price terms (e.g., $Rw_e = e_f/e$). Of course, all

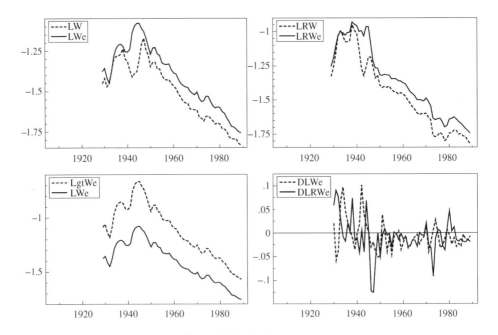

Figure 5. Food share series

these 'targets' impose homogeneity on the long-run relation, and this could be tested easily during the reduction in a single-equation analysis, and less easily in a system approach. Thus, $\log e_f$ is the regressand, with the other variables entered separately. For the rest of the paper, lower case will denote logs.

1.7. General Model

Careful formulation of the initial general model is needed when the Great Depression and WWII, etc. intervened in the sample. Recently, I have been 'saturating' potential outliers using zero-one dummies then condensing the outcome, and will use that approach here.

2. THE VAR AND A MODEL THEREOF

The main variables suggested by the above sketch are (all in logs and per capita): e_f, e, and $(p_f - p)$, with s and a as possible auxiliary variables. Together with two lags of the three stochastic variables, zero-one dummies for 1931–36, 1938, 1941–46, 1973, and 1980–81 were added (partly after a first estimate revealed several large outliers), and these plus a constant entered unrestrictedly, whereas a linear deterministic trend was restricted to the cointegration space. First and second lagged values of s and a were also entered unrestrictedly, but the latter dropped as irrelevant on testing. The resulting estimates are reported in the Appendix. Here we record summary statistics for 1931–89. The presence of the dummies, endogenously chosen to remove actual and potential 'outliers' is bound to affect inference, and does so even in cointegrated processes. A rigorous analysis would need to re-calibrate the relevant critical values accordingly, e.g. using Bent Nielsen's Disco program.

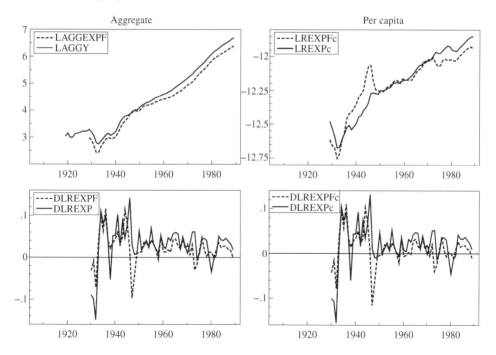

Figure 6. Food and total expenditure, and income time series

First, the system diagnostic tests were:

Table I. System goodness of fit and evaluation

statistic	e_f	e	$(p_f - p)$	VAR
$\hat{\sigma}$	1.5%	1.8%	1.7%	
$F_{ar}(2, 32)$	0.25	2.39	3.22	
$F_{arch}(1, 32)$	0.82	0.00	1.03	
$F_{het}(14, 19)$	0.79	0.57	0.42	
$\chi^2_{nd}(2)$	0.47	0.98	12.6**	
$F^v_{ar}(18, 74)$				0.91
$F^v_{het}(84, 84)$				0.34
$\chi^{2v}_{nd}(6)$				27.7**

The diagnostic tests are of the form $F_j(k, T - l)$ which denotes an F-test against the alternative hypothesis j for both scalar and vector (or system) tests (shown as $F^v_j(k, T - l)$) of the form: 2nd-order serial correlation (F_{ar}; see Godfrey, 1978), 1st-order autoregressive conditional heteroscedasticity (F_{arch}; see Engle, 1982), heteroscedasticity (F_{het}; see White, 1980), and a chi-square test for normality ($\chi^2_{nd}(2)$; see Doornik and Hansen, 1994): * and ** denote significance at the 5% and 1% levels respectively. Below we also report the RESET test (F_{reset}; see Ramsey, 1969). $\hat{\sigma}$ denotes a residual standard deviation, expressed as a percentage of the level of the associated variable. Non-normality in the equation for $p_f - p$ is the only problem, communicated to the system test.

Next, Table II shows the residual inter-correlations, which suggest there are interesting features to model in the relation between e_f, e and $p_f - p$.

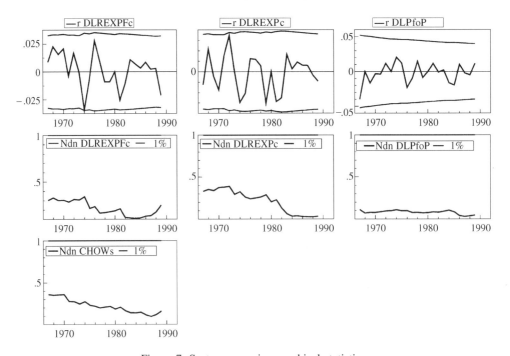

Figure 7. System recursive graphical statistics

Table II. System residual correlations and dynamics

$$\begin{bmatrix} & & e_f & e \\ e & & 0.66 & \text{—} \\ p_f - p & & -0.52 & -0.05 \end{bmatrix}$$

$$\begin{bmatrix} |\lambda_a| & 0.36 & 0.27 & 0.09 \\ |\lambda_b| & 0.90 & 0.70 & 0.57 & 0.28 & 0.28 & 0.20 \end{bmatrix}$$

The eigenvalues of the long-run matrix (denoted λ_a in Table II) reveal one large and one near zero so the rank is neither zero nor 3. This matches the eigenvalues of the dynamics (denoted λ_b), where one is near unity, and the remainder much smaller. Every dummy was significant in at least one equation. The second lagged endogenous variables were significant as a group (on a joint reduction F-test) though none is significant individually. As Figure 7 shows, to the extent that it can be evaluated, the system is constant, with the one-step residuals having constant 95% confidence bands (even slightly decreasing) and all break-point Chow (1960) tests lying well below their 1% critical values.

Being in levels, the fitted and actual values are barely distinguishable, so we turn to reductions to I(0). The cointegration analysis, using Doornik and Hendry (1997) with only the trend restricted to the cointegration space, yielded:

Table III. Cointegration analysis

$$\begin{bmatrix} r & 1 & 2 & 3 \\ \ell & 798 & 803 & 805 \\ \mu & 0.56 & 0.16 & 0.07 \\ Max & 48.2^{**} & 10.1 & 4.5 \\ Tr & 62.8^{**} & 14.6 & 4.5 \end{bmatrix}, \quad \begin{bmatrix} \hat{\alpha} & 1 & 2 & 3 \\ e_f & -0.55 & -0.13 & 0.01 \\ e & -0.32 & -0.07 & 0.03 \\ p_f - p & -0.09 & 0.20 & 0.01 \end{bmatrix}$$

$$\begin{bmatrix} \hat{\beta}' & e_f & e & p_f - p & t \\ 1 & 1 & -0.67 & 0.49 & 0.0057 \\ 2 & -0.19 & 1 & -0.90 & -0.0192 \\ 3 & 3.27 & -5.34 & 1 & 0.0837 \end{bmatrix}$$

For each value of the rank r of the long-run matrix in the Johansen (1988) procedure, Table III reports the log-likelihood values (ℓ), eigenvalues (μ) and associated maximum eigenvalue (*Max*) and trace (*Tr*) statistics together with the estimated cointegrating vectors (β) and feedback coefficients (α). There is one well-defined cointegration vector at conventional I(1) critical values.[3] It is potentially interpretable as a food-demand relation given the signs and magnitudes of the expenditure and price 'elasticities' of 0.7 and -0.5. When the trend is excluded from the cointegration relation, the coefficients become 0.4 and -0.4, respectively. However, the sizes of the feedback coefficients suggest a violation of weak exogeneity for total expenditure (of which food expenditure is a major component). Enforcing the weak exogeneity of $p_f - p$, testing yielded:

Table IV. Restricted cointegration analysis

$$\begin{bmatrix} & \hat{\alpha} & SE \\ e_f & -0.49 & (0.08) \\ e & -0.31 & (0.12) \\ p_f - p & 0 & (\text{—}) \end{bmatrix}, \quad \begin{bmatrix} & e_f & e & p_f - p & t \\ \hat{\beta}' & 1 & -0.40 & 0.33 & 0 \\ SE & 0 & (0.015) & (0.07) & (\text{—}) \end{bmatrix}$$

---

[3] The dummies effectively remove observations, but even using the degrees-of-freedom correction to the Tr statistic suggested by Reimers (1992), its value is 56.4^{**}.

Trend deletion and weak exogeneity of $(p_f - p)$ are jointly accepted as $\chi^2(2) = 5.92$ and imposing a long-run price 'elasticity' of -0.4 led to $\chi^2(3) = 6.9$. Using $e - e_f$ in place of e allowed its long-run weak exogeneity to be accepted conditional on deleting the trend from the cointegration relation, although the latter was rejected on a likelihood-ratio test. This evidence is somewhat equivocal, but suggests that a single-equation analysis may not be importantly distorted.

First, however, a small simultaneous model of the system was constructed by imposing a restricted cointegration vector (mean zero, with coefficients of 0.4 and -0.4), using differences for all other stochastic variables, and in each equation, eliminating the insignificant dummy variables, adding current Δe and $\Delta(p_f - p)$ to the food-demand equation. The equilibrium correction was constructed as:

$$c_{1,t} = e_{f,t} + 7.88 - 0.4e_t + 0.4(p_f - p)_t. \qquad 2$$

After sequential simplification, and retaining the 1980s for a constancy test, this yielded (dummies not shown) the following FIML model estimates:

$$\Delta e_{f,t} = + \underset{(0.10)}{0.41} \Delta e_t - \underset{(0.07)}{0.29} \Delta(p_f - p)_t + \underset{(0.05)}{0.31} \Delta s_{t-1} - \underset{(0.03)}{0.25} c_{1,t-1} + \underset{(0.003)}{0.007}$$

$$\Delta e_t = - \underset{(0.004)}{0.26} \Delta s_{t-1} - \underset{(0.11)}{0.27} c_{1,t-1} + \underset{(0.003)}{0.030}$$

$$\Delta(p_f - p)_t = + \underset{(0.08)}{0.71} \Delta e_{t-1} - \underset{(0.004)}{0.017}$$

$$c_{1,t} \equiv c_{1,t-1} + \Delta e_{f,t} - 0.4\Delta e_t + 0.4\Delta(p_f - p)_t.$$

These are basically descriptive equations beyond the first, as the system manifestly lacks the appropriate information to explain relative food prices or real total expenditure, but the test of 'over-identification' was $\chi^2_{oi}(15) = 24.1$. The residual cross-correlations are smaller as expected:

$$\begin{bmatrix} & e_f & e \\ e & 0.27 & - \\ p_f - p & -0.21 & -0.11 \end{bmatrix}$$

On the vector diagnostic tests, the model is congruent with the sample evidence, but the scalar autocorrelation tests are significant due to deleting some dummies which have t-values around 1.5 — even though the residual correlograms are small.

Table V. Model goodness of fit and evaluation

statistic	e_f	e	$p_f - p$	VAR
$\hat{\sigma}$	1.2%	1.9%	2.2%	
$F_{ar}(2, 32)$	5.29*	6.05**	7.23**	
$F_{arch}(1, 31)$	0.14	1.90	0.61	
$F_{het}(14, 19)$	0.79	0.57	0.42	
$\chi^2_{nd}(2)$	0.03	0.77	0.41	
$F^v_{ar}(18, 85)$				0.80
$\chi^{2v}_{nd}(6)$				4.60

The short-run income and price elasticities are 0.4 and -0.3, so are not far from their long-run values. The feedback coefficients in the food and expenditure equations are large at -0.25 and highly significant, strongly supporting cointegration. The over-identifying

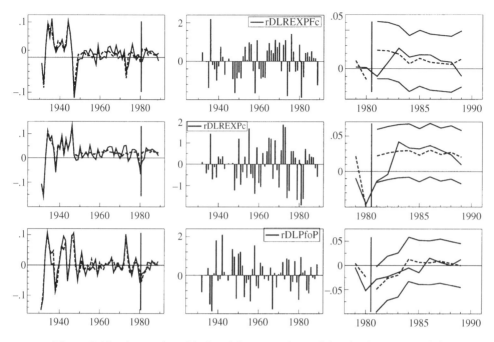

Figure 8. Fitted, actual, residual and forecast values of the simultaneous model

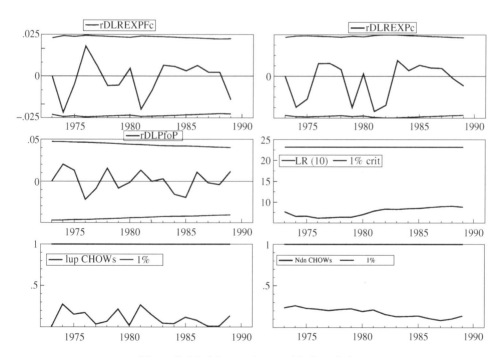

Figure 9. Model recursive graphical statistics

restrictions test here merely reflects that the reduction has not lost any information, since no prior theory is being tested. Interestingly, lagged $\Delta(p_f - p)$ was not significant.

The model is constant over the 1980s as Figure 8 shows (the middle column legend applies to all graphs in that row): the system-constancy F-test yielded $F(27,38) = 0.48$. However, the forecast period was quiescent compared to earlier, so that test is hardly demanding. The overall constancy statistics are similar to those of the system as Figure 9 records.

Overall, this model is sufficiently satisfactory to try a single-equation analysis, despite the apparent violation of weak exogeneity for e, noting that will distort inference on the cointegration coefficients if any tests are conducted thereon (see Hendry, 1995b). The proposed model will condition on the contemporaneous values of e and $p_f - p$, but allow stronger restrictions on the dummies than is easily achieved in a system.

3. A SINGLE-EQUATION MODEL

The analysis recommences with all variables in levels, and postulates the general model as the first equation of the above VAR with the addition of contemporaneous values of e and $p_f - p$. This is a unique conditional representation, but its validity depends on that of the conditioning variables, a proposition thrown into doubt by the system analysis rejecting long-run weak exogeneity of e for β. The initial unrestricted equation with two lags on stochastic regressors, and dummies for successive years created by lagging is reported in Table VI.

Table VI. Lag structure analysis of levels

Lag	0	1	2	3	4	Sum
e_f	−1 (—)	0.79 (0.15)	−0.09 (0.11)	—	—	−0.30 (0.07)
1	−2.41 (0.52)	—	—	—	—	−2.41 (0.52)
e	0.53 (0.07)	−0.39 (0.13)	−0.01 (0.11)	—	—	0.12 (0.04)
$p_f - p$	−0.40 (0.09)	0.37 (0.12)	−0.04 (0.08)	—	—	−0.11 (0.03)
a	0.06 (0.25)	−0.06 (0.24)	—	—	—	−0.00 (0.05)
s	0.22 (0.12)	0.14 (0.14)	−0.14 (0.14)	—	—	0.22 (0.14)
dv31	−0.09 (0.02)	−0.11 (0.03)	−0.02 (0.03)	0.01 (0.02)	−0.03 (0.02)	—(—)
dv42	−0.00 (0.02)	−0.03 (0.03)	0.03 (0.03)	0.04 (0.03)	0.04 (0.02)	—(—)
dv73	−0.02 (0.01)	—	—	—	—	−0.02 (0.01)
dv80	0.00 (0.01)	−0.01 (0.01)	—	—	—	—(—)

The diagnostic tests are:

$$R^2 = 0.9987 \quad F(26, 32) = 954.18 \quad \hat{\sigma} = 0.0096 \quad DW = 2.13 \quad SC = -8.05$$

$$F_{ar}(2, 30) = 0.30 \quad F_{arch}(1, 30) = 4.17 \quad \chi^2(2) = 10.5^{**} \quad F_{reset}(1, 31) = 0.33$$

and these are acceptable other than the excess number of zero residuals (owing to the many 0−1 dummies), leading to a rejection of normality. SC denotes the Schwarz criterion (see, e.g. Hendry, 1995a). Solving for the long-run solution yields:

$$e_f = -\ \underset{(0.53)}{7.93} + \underset{(0.07)}{0.40}\ e - \underset{(0.09)}{0.36}\ (pf - p),$$

with a unit-root test $t_{ur} = -4.55$ (which does not reject at 5%). However, eliminating the insignificant second lags of e_f, e and $p_f - p$ yielded the similar long run:

$$e_f = -\ \underset{(0.45)}{7.86} + \underset{(0.06)}{0.41}\ e - \underset{(0.07)}{0.39}\ (p_f - p),$$

and $t_{ur} = -5.8^{**}$ which rejects a unit root. The coefficients are, in the event, very close to those found by the vector analysis, so the selected equilibrium correction was the same as in (2). This has a sample mean of near zero, so the intercept can be interpreted as a net rate of growth. Note that a only enters the model as a difference. Also, the log of the savings ratio, s, seems stationary, so should not be in a cointegrating relation.

Table VII. ADF statistics for s

t_{adf}	$\hat{\beta} y_1$	$\hat{\sigma}$	t_{Dy_1}	t_{prob}	F_{prob}
-4.64^{**}	0.71	0.025	5.40	0.00	0.36

The Dickey and Fuller (1981) test outcome for s in Table VII supports the hypothesis of stationarity. A constant, but no trend, was included; $\hat{\beta}$ is the coefficient on y_{t-1} in levels; $\hat{\sigma}$ is the residual standard deviation; t_{Dy_1} is the coefficient on the longest lagged Δs that is significant at the 5% level; followed by its probability; and the F-test is against a longer lag on Δs.

The next major reduction is to switch to differences and the equilibrium correction, yielding Table VIII:

Table VIII. Analysis of Δe_f lag structure

Lag	0	1	2	3	4	Sum
1	−0.02 (0.01)	—	—	—	—	−0.02 (0.01)
Δe	0.53 (0.06)	—	—	—	—	0.53 (0.06)
Δs	0.17 (0.09)	0.13 (0.09)	—	—	—	0.31 (0.10)
$\Delta(p_f - p)$	−0.39 (0.06)	—	—	—	—	−0.39 (0.06)
Δa	0.11 (0.21)	—	—	—	—	0.11 (0.21)
$c_{1,t}$	—	−0.33 (0.05)	—	—	—	−0.33 (0.05)
s	—	0.26 (0.09)	—	—	—	0.26 (0.09)
dv31	−0.10 (0.02)	−0.13 (0.02)	−0.05 (0.02)	−0.00 (0.02)	−0.02 (0.02)	— (—)
dv42	0.01 (0.02)	−0.03 (0.02)	0.03 (0.02)	0.04 (0.02)	0.03 (0.02)	— (—)
dv80	0.01 (0.01)	−0.02 (0.01)	—	—	—	— (—)
dv73	−0.02 (0.01)	—	—	—	—	−0.02 (0.01)

With the following EqCM equation diagnostics:

$$R^2 = 0.969 \quad F(20, 38) = 44.9 \quad \hat{\sigma} = 0.0090 \quad DW = 1.82 \quad SC = -8.40$$

$$F_{ar}(2, 36) = 0.16 \quad F_{arch}(1, 36) = 4.47^* \quad \chi^2(2) = 11.2^{**} \quad F_{reset}(1, 37) = 0.93.$$

This I(0) transform also clarifies which dummies are irrelevant, that average family size, a does not matter, even in differences, and that the effects of the war dummies for 1944–46 are equal (denoted dv4446). The former were deleted and the restricted dummy substituted, to yield (3):

$$\Delta e_{f,t} = \underset{(0.07)}{0.28} \ s_{t-1} - \underset{(0.03)}{0.33} \ c_{1,t-1} - \underset{(0.01)}{0.02} + \underset{(0.07)}{0.13} \ \Delta s_{t-1} + \underset{(0.05)}{0.17} \ \Delta s_t$$

$$+ \underset{(0.05)}{0.52} \ \Delta e_t - \underset{(0.04)}{0.40} \ \Delta(p_f - p)_t - \underset{(0.01)}{0.10} \ dv31_t$$

$$- \underset{(0.02)}{0.12} \ dv31_{t-1} - \underset{(0.01)}{0.04} \ dv31_{t-2} - \underset{(0.01)}{0.02} \ dv31_{t-4}$$

$$- \underset{(0.01)}{0.03} \ dv42_{t-1} + \underset{(0.01)}{0.03} \ dv4446_t - \underset{(0.01)}{0.02} \ dv73_t - \underset{(0.01)}{0.02} \ dv80_{t-1} \quad 3$$

$$R^2 = 0.959 \quad F(14, 44) = 72.8 \quad \hat{\sigma} = 0.0084 \quad DW = 1.82 \quad SC = -8.79$$

$$F_{ar}(2, 42) = 0.16 \quad F_{arch}(1, 42) = 4.50^* \quad \chi^2(2) = 8.39^{**} \quad F_{reset}(1, 43) = 0.43$$

$$F_{het}(20, 23) = 0.24.$$

Successive reductions of the variables with the smallest t-ratios that were not significant at the 1% level yielded an overall reduction test of $F(17, 32) = 1.09$: several intermediate steps were rejectable at the 5% level or higher, suggestive of possible early overfitting. Finally, the dummies for 1931–32 are also roughly equal and twice that for 1933, and after implementing that (denoted $dv3133$) to allow computation of the variance-change and joint parameter-constancy tests from Hansen (1992) (denoted Jt and V), the resulting estimates were:

$$\Delta e_{f,t} = \underset{(0.04)}{0.27} \; s_{t-1} - \underset{(0.02)}{0.34} \; c_{1,t-1} - \underset{(0.004)}{0.019} + \underset{(0.05)}{0.24} \; \Delta s_t$$

$$+ \underset{(0.05)}{0.53} \; \Delta e_t - \underset{(0.04)}{0.46} \; \Delta(p_f - p)_t + \underset{(0.010)}{0.038} \; dv4446$$

$$- \underset{(0.01)}{0.12} \; dv3133 \hspace{6cm} 4$$

$$R^2 = 0.936 \quad F(7, 51) = 107.2 \quad \hat{\sigma} = 0.0098 \quad DW = 2.00 \quad SC = -8.85$$

$$F_{ar}(2, 49) = 0.18 \quad F_{arch}(1, 49) = 0.59 \quad \chi^2(2) = 0.21 \quad F_{reset}(1, 50) = 0.26$$

$$F_{het}(13, 37) = 0.47 \quad Jt = 0.63 \quad V = 0.08.$$

Thus, we have concluded with two data-based dummies only, allowing use of almost the whole sample period, with a residual standard error of just under 1%. All the diagnostic tests are insignificant, with the short-run income and price elasticities close to, but larger than, their long-run values. They are larger than the system-based estimates which endogenize e and $(p_f - p)$, suggesting some contemporaneity bias. However, fixing those coefficients at their FIML values has minimal effect on forecasts, but does worsen the fit ($\hat{\sigma} = 1.2\%$). Figure 10 reports the graphical statistics of fitted and actual values, residuals, and 'forecasts' over the 1980s for (4).

As noted, the forecast period was not demanding ($F_{Chow}(9, 42) = 0.56$). The overall constancy statistics are similar to those of the system model as Figure 11 records.

Clearly, there is no evidence against an unchanged model over the entire post-war sample from estimates using essentially very different pre-war data. Indeed, for 1948–89, $F_{Chow}(42, 9) = 0.82$ and Figure 12 shows the feasibility of describing the post-war period from the fit to 1947 alone.

3.1. A Net-Expenditure Model

The earlier long-run weak exogeneity failure suggests important feedbacks from e_f to e. Redoing the reduction using total net expenditure ($E - E_f = E_n$) in place of E, delivers a reduction $F(19, 33) = 0.98$, whereas against the initial Table VI model, $F(20, 32) = 1.85$ with $p = 0.06$. This is just not rejected at the 5% level, but a deterioration in fit was expected as e_f is a component of e. The resulting net expenditure and price elasticities

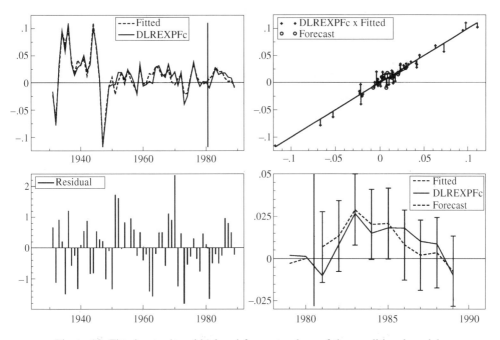

Figure 10. Fitted, actual, residual and forecast values of the conditional model

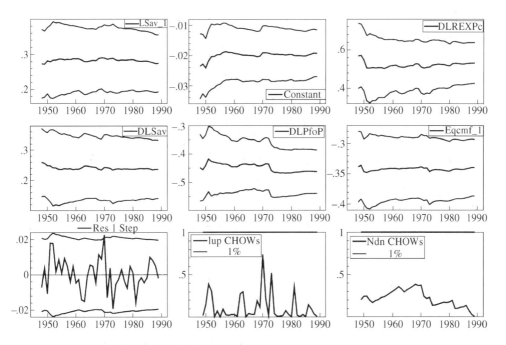

Figure 11. Conditional equation recursive graphical statistics

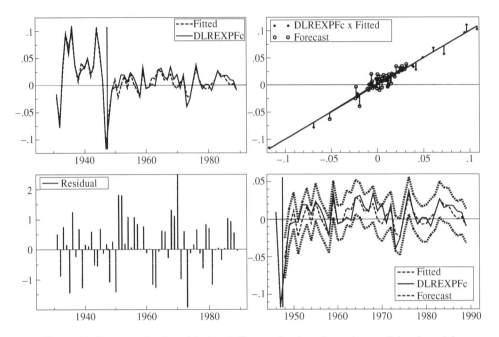

Figure 12. Post-war fitted, residual and 'forecast' values from the conditional model

become 0.34 and -0.45 in the long-run and 0.4 and -0.51 in the short:

$$\Delta e_{f,t} = \underset{(0.03)}{0.31} \ s_t - \underset{(0.02)}{0.38} \ c_{3t-1} - \underset{(0.16)}{3.21} + \underset{(0.05)}{0.40} \ \Delta e_{n,t}$$

$$- \underset{(0.05)}{0.51} \ \Delta(p_f - p)_t + \underset{(0.009)}{0.059} \ dv4446 - \underset{(0.01)}{0.15} \ dv3133$$

$$R^2 = 0.918 \quad F(6, 52) = 96.6 \quad \hat{\sigma} = 0.0110 \quad DW = 2.04 \quad SC = -8.65$$

$$F_{ar}(2, 50) = 0.56 \quad F_{arch}(1, 50) = 0.73 \quad \chi^2(2) = 0.31 \quad F_{reset}(1, 51) = 0.12$$

$$F_{het}(11, 40) = 0.36 \quad Jt = 0.63 \quad V = 0.07.$$

Replacing e by y makes no difference when s is allowed to enter, provided appropriate per-capita measures are used uniformly.

3.2. Encompassing

There are several potential 'rival' explanations to encompass: specifically, that by Anderson and Vahid (Chapter 3) and by Siegert (Chapter 16, considered in Section 4). To avoid an exact singularity, Δs in (4) was replaced by Δy noting that Δe is already a regressor.[4] Also, despite the apparently different definitions, the two EqCMs in Anderson and Vahid actually generate closely similar time series ($c_{2,t-1}$ is defined

---

[4] The singularity is in the joint model which includes Δn, and this change slightly biases the outcome against (4).

in their Equation (9)[5]). Then, re-expressing the Anderson and Vahid model in terms of Δe_f (real food expenditure *per capita*, which introduces changes in population and number of households), M_1 is Δe_f on Δy, 1, s_{t-1}, Δe, $\Delta(p_f - p)$ and $c_{1,t-1}$; and M_2 is Δe_f on Δh, 1, Δy, Δp_f, $c_{2,t-1}$, Δn. With all regressors used as instruments, we find $\hat{\sigma}_{M_1} = 0.00986$ $\hat{\sigma}_{M_2} = 0.0103$ $\hat{\sigma}_{\text{Joint}} = 0.00989$ delivering the test outcomes shown in Table IX.

Table IX. Encompassing test statistics versus Anderson and Vahid

M_1 v M_2	Form	Test	Form	M_2 v M_1
−0.839	N(0, 1)	Cox	N(0, 1)	−2.388
0.742	N(0, 1)	Ericsson IV	N(0, 1)	1.963
3.820	$\chi^2(4)$	Sargan	$\chi^2(4)$	6.642
0.949	F(4, 31)	Joint Model	F(4, 31)	1.815
(0.45)		Probability		(0.15)

The null that M_1 is valid is on the left; the null that M_2 is valid is on the right. If the left-side tests are insignificant, M_1 encompasses M_2, whereas if they are significant, M_1 fails to encompass M_2. Similarly for the right-side tests with models 1 and 2 interchanged. While not decisive, the tests favour M_1. In fact, the homogeneity restrictions on M_2 are rejected: it has $RSS1 = 0.0040$ for 4 variables and 41 observations, whereas the less restricted model has $RSS2 = 0.00374$ for 6 variables, so $F(2, 35) = 4.87^*$. Thus, a direct encompassing test would probably reject M_2.

4. COMMENTS ON W. SIEGERT

Not commencing by careful graphing of the relevant time series is perhaps his most significant failure to follow the methodology. This may be because many participants in the experiment had already graphed the principal series. Nevertheless, that should have allowed him to peruse the graphs and hence not make some of his mistaken claims later.

For example, a glance at Figure 1 shows that n and h are not substitutes and are not 'strongly related' in any useful sense: there was a major trend in family size. Only reduction from a general model can reveal whether or not this matters empirically. It may be tacit knowledge, but even if two levels time series are similar when graphed, graph the difference between them (properly scaled) to see if they will play the same role econometrically.

Next, the whole issue of cointegration discussed in Section 1.3 above is eschewed. It is neither necessary to difference to achieve stationarity (e.g. cointegration), nor is it sufficient (e.g. deterministic shifts). I have strongly argued against blanket differencing since 1975 — see Hendry (1993). How can this possibly mimic my approach? The arbitrary assumption of common factors of unity cannot be part of any 'general-to-specific' analysis, whether system or individual-equation based. Having made this mistake, the remaining analysis is otiose, but appears to contradict the assumption made that the differences are I(0), by continually testing for unit roots. Section 2 shows that

---

[5] There was a crucial misprint! — their coefficient sign on p_f should be +. The sample period used is theirs.

there is indeed one well-defined cointegrating relation, which enters the I(0) system as about its most significant explanatory variable, and is certainly that in the conditional equation.

Beginning with a conditional linear single-equation model ignores the arguments in Hendry and Doornik (1994) for system analysis at the start till the validity of weak exogeneity is established. This issue is especially important when there is potential simultaneity, as Tobin discussed. Further, model expansion occurs at several stages of the analysis (e.g. split sample) without returning to the general formulation to restart. Apart from the need to 'heteroscedasticity correct' when replicating the results in Friedman and Schwartz (1982) or estimating Monte Carlo response surfaces as in, e.g. Hendry (1984), when there is a theoretical basis for such transforms, where are empirical examples of my doing so, as against a dozen pleas not to camouflage mis-specification by 'sophisticated' estimation methods? Here, the tacit knowledge is that one can shed bad ideas taught in early econometrics courses in favour of approaches with a better basis.

Turning to encompassing his results, it is hard to test against his heteroscedasticity-weighted models. However, it is straightforward to test against his second-sample model, over 1952–89. Here the outcome is decisive. M_1 is as above, and M_2 is Δe_f on Δy, 1, and ΔP_f, with all regressors again used as instruments, such that $\hat{\sigma}_{M_2} = 0.01092$, $\hat{\sigma}_{\text{Joint}} = 0.009476$ with the test outcomes shown in Table X.

Table X. Encompassing test statistics versus Siegert

M_1 v M_2	Form	Test	Form	M_2 v M_1
−0.316	N(0, 1)	Cox	N(0, 1)	−5.552
0.286	N(0, 1)	Ericsson IV	N(0, 1)	4.098
0.314	$\chi^2(4)$	Sargan	$\chi^2(4)$	12.407
0.149	F(4, 31)	Joint Model	F(4, 31)	3.295
(0.86)		Probability		(0.017)

Thus, the non-cointegrated approach is clearly rejected. The two estimates of the short-run price and expenditure/income elasticities are very similar, although the long-run implications are dramatically different.

5. CONCLUSION

The 'general-to-specific' approach commenced from a VAR with two lags on three stochastic variables and with every dummy unrestricted, and concluded with a conditional model having eight regressors. Several reductions could be rejected on the information examined, specifically the long-run weak exogeneity of e and elimination of some 0–1 dummies could be rejected at the 5% level or higher. Otherwise, the resulting equation did not fail any diagnostic tests and encompassed two 'rival' models.

The final specification can be expressed as a share of food expenditure in total expenditure, and hence modified without loss to the target variable discussed in Section 1.6 above. Switching to a logistic then poses little technical difficulty, but is strongly rejected if the regressors are retained unaltered ($\hat{\sigma} = 1.36\%$). Despite the share not being fully admissible, its negative dependence on total expenditure and relative prices in both long-run and short-run suggests it will be violated only under a catastrophic collapse — at which point it becomes a trivial issue.

The dummies for the initial observations reflect the massive impact of the Great Depression, and could proxy income distribution and unemployment effects, given that the very poor have large food budget shares.

To test price homogeneity, p_t, Δp_t and Δp_{t-1} were added to (4), yielding $F(3, 48) = 1.08$, with no new regressor significant at even 5%, so that hypothesis is not rejected.

The long-run total expenditure and price elasticities were around 0.4 and -0.4 from both system and conditional analysis. However, the weak exogeneity failure suggested important feedbacks from e_f to e. Using income in place of total expenditure had little effect, but the model in Section 3.1 delivered somewhat lower net expenditure and larger (absolute) price elasticities in the long-run.

I could not delineate what aspects of the above were 'tacit knowledge' and what known explicitly, in that, almost every step has a precedent in earlier work. It is surprising that so many of the published recommended practices were not reflected in the study by Siegert. One problem may be the large volume of material that needs to be digested, but although it is long, Hendry (1995a) seeks to integrate the approach. Also, the 'methodology' remains progressive, such as using the recent research on dummies to guide how the empirical analysis was conducted here. At one level, that suggests it will be difficult to 'mechanize' the approach, but I have long argued for an investigators' own value added being crucial. In any case, restricting the analysis to post-war data would have obviated the need for any dummies. Conversely, Hoover and Perez (1996) show how well an automated reduction search works when multiple paths are followed, and the final model choice is based on encompassing and adequate diagnostics. This strongly supports the role of reduction approaches in empirical modelling.

APPENDIX: VAR

Reported coefficients are truncated to three digits.

	e_f coefficient	SE	e coefficient	SE	$(p_f - p)$ coefficient	SE
$(e_f)_{-1}$	0.731	0.249	-0.171	0.299	-0.352	0.268
$(e_f)_{-2}$	-0.242	0.170	-0.056	0.204	0.248	0.182
e_{-1}	-0.020	0.189	1.082	0.227	0.702	0.203
e_{-2}	0.232	0.155	-0.070	0.187	-0.475	0.167
$(p_f - p)_{-1}$	-0.138	0.158	-0.164	0.190	0.774	0.170
$(p_f - p)_{-2}$	-0.010	0.123	0.093	0.147	0.007	0.132
s_{-1}	0.175	0.194	-0.151	0.233	-0.196	0.208
s_{-2}	-0.081	0.151	0.286	0.181	0.334	0.162
$dv31$	-0.174	0.045	-0.187	0.054	-0.147	0.048
$dv31_{-1}$	-0.250	0.045	-0.260	0.054	-0.106	0.049
$dv31_{-2}$	-0.151	0.050	-0.122	0.060	0.051	0.054
$dv31_{-3}$	-0.060	0.030	-0.001	0.036	0.102	0.032
$dv31_{-4}$	-0.053	0.023	-0.004	0.028	0.050	0.025

(Continued)

	e_f coefficient	SE	e coefficient	SE	$(p_f - p)$ coefficient	SE
$dv34_4$	−0.027	0.016	−0.110	0.020	−0.094	0.018
$dv41$	0.029	0.018	0.053	0.022	0.045	0.019
$dv42$	0.011	0.024	−0.003	0.029	0.072	0.026
$dv42_1$	0.014	0.044	0.075	0.053	0.114	0.047
$dv42_2$	0.117	0.040	0.001	0.049	−0.080	0.043
$dv42_3$	0.095	0.043	0.036	0.051	−0.000	0.046
$dv42_4$	0.086	0.033	0.104	0.039	0.046	0.035
$dv73$	−0.032	0.016	0.034	0.019	0.069	0.017
$dv80$	−0.019	0.016	−0.065	0.019	−0.030	0.017
$dv80_1$	−0.036	0.016	−0.038	0.020	0.014	0.018
Constant	−3.920	0.965	−2.705	1.159	1.300	1.037
Trend*100	−0.017	0.207	0.165	0.249	−0.387	0.223

correlation of URF residuals

	e_f	e
e	0.658	1.000
$(p_f - p)$	−0.519	−0.053

standard deviations of URF residuals

e_f	e	$(p_f - p)$
0.0154	0.0185	0.0165

loglik = 805.05   log $|\Omega| = -27.29$ $|\Omega| = 1.4065e - 012$
$T = 59$ log $|Y'Y/T| = -16.93$
$R^2(LR) = 0.999$ $R^2(LM) = 0.898$

F-test on all regressors except unrestricted

$$F(21, 92) = 157.96 \ [0.0000]^{**}$$

F-tests on retained regressors, F(3, 32)

$(e_f)_1$	7.326 [0.0007]**	$(e_f)_2$	0.919 [0.4426]
e_1	13.357 [0.0000]**	e_2	2.734 [0.0598]
$(p_f - p)_1$	9.891 [0.0001]**	$(p_f - p)_2$	0.327 [0.8056]
Trend	2.756 [0.0584]		

correlation of actual and fitted

e_f	e	$(p_f - p)$
0.998	0.999	0.995

REFERENCES

Banerjee, A. and D. F. Hendry (1992), 'Testing integration and cointegration: An overview', *Oxford Bulletin of Economics and Statistics*, **54**, 225–55.

Chow, G. C. (1960), 'Tests of equality between sets of coefficients in two linear regressions', *Econometrica*, **28**, 591–605.

Dickey, D. A. and W. A. Fuller (1981), 'Likelihood ratio statistics for autogressive time series with a unit root', *Econometrica*, **49**, 1057–72.

Doornik, J. A. and H. Hansen (1994), 'A practical test for univariate and multivariate normality', Discussion paper, Nuffield College.

Doornik, J. A. and D. F. Hendry (1997), *Modelling Dynamic Systems using PcFiml 9 for Windows*, Timberlake Consultants Press, London.

Engle, R. F. (1982), 'Autoregressive conditional heteroscedasticity, with estimates of the variance of United Kingdom inflations', *Econometrica*, **50**, 987–1007.

Friedman, M. and A. J. Schwartz (1982), *Monetary Trends in the United States and the United Kingdom: Their Relation to Income, Prices, and Interest Rates, 1867–1975*, University of Chicago Press, Chicago.

Godfrey, L. G. (1978), 'Testing for higher order serial correlation in regression equations when the regressors include lagged dependent variables', *Econometrica*, **46**, 1303–13.

Hansen, B. E. (1992), 'Testing for parameter instability in linear models', *Journal of Policy Modeling*, **14**, 517–33.

Hendry, D. F. (1984), 'Monte Carlo experimentation in econometrics', in Z. Griliches and M. D. Intriligator (eds), *Handbook of Econometrics*, Vol. 2, Ch. 16, North-Holland, Amsterdam.

Hendry, D. F. (1993), *Econometrics: Alchemy or Science?*, Blackwell Publishers, Oxford.

Hendry, D. F. (1995a), *Dynamic Econometrics*, Oxford University Press, Oxford.

Hendry, D. F. (1995b), 'On the interactions of unit roots and exogeneity', *Econometric Reviews*, **14**, 383–419.

Hendry, D. F. and J. A. Doornik (1994), 'Modelling linear dynamic econometric systems', *Scottish Journal of Political Economy*, **41**, 1–33.

Hendry, D. F. and J. A. Doornik (1996), *Empirical Econometric Modelling using PcGive for Windows*, Timberlake Consultants Press, London.

Hendry, D. F. and J.-F. Richard (1982), 'On the formulation of empirical models in dynamic econometrics', *Journal of Econometrics*, **20**, 3–33 [reprinted in: C. W. J. Granger (ed) (1990), *Modelling Economic Series*, Clarendon Press, Oxford and in: D. F. Hendry (1993), *Econometrics: Alchemy or Science?* Blackwell Publishers, Oxford].

Hoover, K. D. and S. J. Perez (1996), 'Data mining reconsidered: Encompassing and the general-to-specific approach to specification search', Mimeo, Economics department, University of California, Davis.

Johansen, S. (1988), 'Statistical analysis of cointegration vectors', *Journal of Economic Dynamics and Control*, **12**, 231–54.

Magnus, J. R. and M. S. Morgan (1995), *The Experiment in Applied Econometrics: Information Pack*, Center for Economic Research, Tilburg University.

Ramsey, J. B. (1969), 'Tests for specification errors in classical linear least squares regression analysis', *Journal of the Royal Statistical Society B*, **31**, 350–71.

Reimers, H.-E. (1992), 'Comparisons of tests for multivariate cointegration', *Statistical Papers*, **33**, 335–59.

Siegert, W. K. (1998), 'An application of three econometric methodologies to the estimation of the income elasticity of food demand', Chapter 16, this volume.

Tobin, J. (1950), 'A statistical demand function for food in the USA', *Journal of the Royal Statistical Society, A*, **113**, 113–41 [reprinted in Chapter 2, this volume].

White, H. (1980), 'A heteroscedastic-consistent covariance matrix estimator and a direct test for heteroscedasticity', *Econometrica*, **48**, 817–38.

CHAPTER 18

IS THIS HOW I LOOK?

EDWARD E. LEAMER

1. INTRODUCTION

I am impressed and actually surprised by Wiebe Siegert's (1998) accomplishments in applying a kind of model sensitivity analyses that I have been suggesting for some time. He is very close to pleasing me completely, but there is, of course, room for improvement. What I think to be shortcomings in his analysis are lessons for us all: lessons for him and for others interested in this kind of sensitivity analyses, but also lessons for myself regarding the real value of my ideas and also the accuracy of their conveyance.

The biggest problem with any Bayesian analysis is, of course, the choice of prior. Indeed, if this were not the case, Bayesian analyses would be entirely routine. I have to confess that with the passage of time and with the benefit of hindsight, it is very rare that my own choices of prior distributions please me. It is even more rare for the choices made by others to seem sensible to me. I am afraid to report that I do not find the prior distribution used by Siegert to be compelling. At the least, this means that he has to devote more energy trying to persuade me. A serious concern is that, for much of the analysis, the sample covariance matrix is adopted as an initial prior covariance matrix. Though this is expedient and not uncommon, it is a bad idea. Rarely will the structure of prior information conform with the structure of data information. Indeed, the reason for using a prior is to support the data where they are weak, while letting the data speak where they are strong. In any case, more care needs to be exercised in the formulation and communication of the prior. Easier said than done, I must admit.

The second concern I have is with the technical limitations of the Bayesian bounds. The methods that I have suggested allow one in principle to distinguish uncertainty from ambiguity, the first having to do with the rough size of the prior standard error and the second with the width of the interval of 'indistinguishable' prior standard errors. For example, I can say that there is a small chance (1/32) that a coin will land heads up five times in a row. (Uncertain.) I can say also that there is a small but ambiguous chance of rain in LA tomorrow, between zero and 2/32. (Uncertain and ambiguous.) Though generally the methods allow one to distinguish uncertainty from ambiguity, the Extreme Bounds Analysis allows only two sets of variables, and thus collapses a two-dimensional continuous problem into a bivariate classification: FREE and DOUBTFUL. The more general bounds that Siegert reports in triangular displays do allow the analyst to distinguish uncertainty from ambiguity, but only if all variables are 'equally' ambiguous. Allowing different degrees of ambiguity is conceptually straightforward, though numerically complex.

Methodology and Tacit Knowledge: Two Experiments in Econometrics
Jan R. Magnus and Mary S. Morgan © 1999 John Wiley & Sons Ltd

2.   CHOICE OF PRIOR

The first and probably the most important benefit of a Bayesian analysis should be better psychic preparation for examining the data. If approached thoughtfully, the process of formulating a prior should improve the formulation of the model and should prepare the researcher for real discoveries — namely those that conflict with the prior and that require either a change of mind or a change of model. There is, however, nothing internal to the process that forces the analyst to be thoughtful. One can rush the construction of a prior distribution just as one can rush the examination of the data or the writing of the results. But there is something external that does force some care — one has to 'sell' the results in an intellectual marketplace. It is hard for a consumer of research to tell if the examination of the data has been careful, but problems with the writing or the prior are often transparent.

Thus, when I read a Bayesian bounds analysis such as this one by Wiebe Siegert, the prior gets my first and most intense examination. Of course, priors are neither 'right' nor 'wrong' — they are only 'mine' or 'yours.' But when 'you' use 'yours' and it is much different from mine, then 'your' results don't interest me much. Siegert's prior has some very important 'motivational' differences from mine, but the details are surprisingly similar. One big difference is that the cell count *ESTPOPH* or *%INPOPH* seems to me a very unlikely variable to affect food consumption of the family. I cannot understand why it is included at all. It certainly is not behavioral — no family knows how many other families are in the same cell defined by those who collect the data. Perhaps, this variable is tied in some way to issues of measurement error, but I haven't any clear idea what I should be expecting regarding its coefficient. Secondly, to include both *HOMEOWN* and *RENTER* in the 1941 analysis is to measure the same effect twice. This is allowable statistically only because the variables are measured with serious error. One reason is that *ANCHILD*, *HOMEOWN*, *RENTER*, *AUTOOWN* and *NETASSCH* are recorded only by income levels and do not vary with family size. This measurement problem renders these variables very doubtful. Except for measurement error problems, I think it is appropriate to let food consumption depend on total income, asset income plus non-asset income, *NETASSCH* + *HINC*. I also imagine that there are family composition effects that are not captured by the $\log(N)$ variable, but the most likely model allows food consumption per family member to depend on income per family member. The following is a pretty good summary of my initial state of mind.

Central, most likely model	$\log(FOODCON/N) = \theta_0 + \theta_1 \log(HINC/N)$
Not too doubtful variable	$\log(NETASSCH/N)$
Doubtful variables	$\log(ANCHILD/N)$, $\log(N)$, dummies for family size
Very doubtful variables	$\log(HOMEOWN)$, $\log(AUTOOWN)$
Extremely doubtful variables	$\log(RENTER)$, $\log(ESTPOPH)$

The problem confronting any data analysis is how to make use of opinions regarding the doubtfulness of (or other restrictions on the) variables. The advice not to use the prior opinion is routinely and properly ignored for one simple reason: our models have many more parameters than can be estimated from our weak data sets. The usual way to deploy prior opinion is via *ad hoc* specification searches in which many different equations are estimated and one or a few are selected for reporting. This *ad hoc* methodology has obvious deficiencies which I have complained about for a long time — to little effect, I might add; see, for example, Chamberlain and Leamer (1976), Leamer and Chamberlain (1976), Leamer (1973, 1978, 1982, 1983), and Leamer and Leonard (1983). I think an appealing alternative is a Bayesian analysis which begins with a prior probability distribution that is intended to represent as well as possible the prior opinion. The fundamental problem for a Bayesian analysis is how to translate the vague language 'not too doubtful' and 'very doubtful' into a prior probability distribution, or a family of distributions. A first pass is an Extreme Bounds Analysis which allows the widest possible range of priors. I think in this setting it would make sense to do EBA hierarchically, first with only the extremely doubtful variables treated as doubtful, then add the very doubtful variables to the doubtful list, then the doubtful and last the not-too-doubtful. It would make sense to me to repeat this hierarchy but with the extremely doubtful variables dropped altogether from the analysis.

Siegert does provide a hierarchy of priors that is close to the one I just suggested. The highest level 'idealist' prior allows *N*, *ANCHILD*, *HINC* and *NETASSCH* to be free and the other variables doubtful. Then *AUTOOWN* is freed, then *RENTER* leaving only *ESTPOPH* as doubtful. The most important difference between Siegert and myself is that his central, most likely model has *AHSIZE*, *HINC* and *NETASSCH* as free, while mine excludes *NETASSCH* and imposes a linear constraint on the coefficients of *AHSIZE* and *HINC*.

3. WHAT'S WRONG WITH EXTREME BOUNDS ANALYSIS?

Although this hierarchical approach captures an aspect of the ordering of doubtfulness of the variables, there is something fundamentally wrong about it. Each time the bounds are computed, the free variables are free, but the doubtful variables are allowed to be either free and doubtful. What I mean is that the sensitivity analysis produces an interval of estimates that includes estimates with the doubtful variable included in the equation, with the doubtful variable excluded, and everything in between. Expressed in Bayesian terms, the prior variance for a doubtful variable is allowed to be any number — it can be zero (completely doubtful) or infinity (completely free). Thus when we treat *ESTPOPH* always as a doubtful variable, it is allowed to have way too much freedom.

The fundamental problem with Extreme Bounds Analysis (EBA) is that it collapses two aspects of prior opinion into one. A variable can be doubtful meaning that it is unlikely to matter much. A variable can also be ambiguous, meaning that the analyst isn't sure about the degree of doubt. For doubtful variables, the treatment is to use a Bayesian analysis without a sensitivity analysis. Simply proceed as if you had observed another data set that yielded a zero estimate with a known standard error. But if you try to select a specific prior distribution as Bayesians imagine, you are going to feel pretty uncomfortable selecting a precise value for the prior standard error (not to mention the normality assumption!). To treat this kind of ambiguity, a Bayesian sensitivity analysis is required.

Technically, a Bayesian sensitivity analysis should make use of intervals of prior standard errors S, say $L < S < U$, where L is the lower bound and U is the upper bound. Doubt about the variable can be expressed by the choice of a small upper bound, $\text{DOUBT} = 1/U$. If a variable is very doubtful, the largest the standard error can be is a small number. Ambiguity on the other hand is measured by the length of the interval of prior standard errors: $\text{AMBIGUITY} = U/L$. This suggests a matrix of intervals for the prior standard errors of the following form.

| | AMBIGUITY | | | |
DOUBT	None	Some	Substantial	Complete
None	$S = \infty$	$S = \infty$	$S = \infty$	$0 < S < \infty$
Some	$S = 8$	$4 < S < 8$	$1 < S < 8$	$0 < S < 8$
Substantial	$S = 2$	$1 < S < 2$	$0.25 < S < 2$	$0 < S < 2$
Complete	$S = 0$	$S = 0$	$S = 0$	$S = 0$

Unfortunately, EBA collapses a two-dimensional family of priors into the binary classification of 'free' and 'doubtful' variables. There are 'free' variables that are entered into the equation without doubt. And there are doubtful variables that are all treated as completely ambiguous. In terms of the matrix above, only some of the cells are allowed:

| | AMBIGUITY | | | |
DOUBT	None	Some	Substantial	Complete
None	FREE	FREE	FREE	DOUBTFUL
Some				
Substantial				
Complete	Omitted	Omitted	Omitted	Omitted

Below is a matrix that captures my feelings about Wiebe Siegert's problem. Note that I think *ESTPOPH* is a very doubtful variable but not an ambiguous one — I am very confident that it doesn't belong. *HOMEOWN*, on the other hand, is also a very doubtful variable, but a much more ambiguous one. *ANCHILD*, on the other hand, is not so doubtful, and since I have a pretty easy time thinking about the coefficient that I expect to obtain, it is not very ambiguous. I have some doubt about whether *NETASSCH* belongs in the equation, but I have a lot of ambiguity about that opinion.

| | AMBIGUITY | | |
DOUBT	Little	Some	Substantial
Little	*HINC*		
Some		*ANCHILD*, N	*NETASSCH*
Substantial	*ESTPOPH*	*RENTER*	*HOMEOWN*,
			AUTOOWN

Although this matrix 'feels' right to me, there is a very big step from words like 'some' doubt and 'substantial' ambiguity to the choice of precise upper and lower bounds for the prior standard errors, $L < S < U$. In Leamer (1982) I have suggested that one begin with a 'best-guess' prior covariance matrix, say V_0, and explore bounds implied by families of priors built from intervals of prior covariance matrices V around this initial best guess: $\sigma_L^2 V_0 < V < \sigma_u^2 V_0$ with the upper and lower multipliers being powers of 2: 1/4, 1/2, 1, 2, 4. Siegert provides us with a large number of such intervals of estimates displayed in triangular arrays.[1] The problem with the numbers Siegert provides is that 'The sample covariance matrix is used as reference or initial prior for this input covariance matrix.' The use of the sample covariance matrix is a very bad idea, from my perspective, since the structure of information in the data may be quite unlike the structure of information in the prior. Indeed, the gains from using a prior are greatest when the prior information matrix is unlike the sample information matrix, that is when the prior can fill in the gaps left by the data. Although the use of the sample covariance matrix is, in my opinion, a bad idea, this is a choice that in my experience is quite common. There is a reason for this — what else can one do? The answer is you have to think. What percentage change in family *per capita* expenditures on food is likely to occur as a result of change in *RENTER* status? I think: 1% possibly, 5% at the outside, certainly not more than 50%. Thus a standard error between 0.01 and 0.5 on the *RENTER* dummy suits me pretty well.

4. SIEGERT'S CONCLUSIONS

The prior distribution that underlies the triangular displays of intervals of estimates in Siegert's tables is not appealing to me for reasons just discussed. A consequence is that all these numbers do not affect my opinions. The bounds displayed graphically are more comprehensible and worth (for me) a close look. If asset ownership — *HOMEOWN*, *RENTER*, *AUTOOWN*, are very doubtful and very ambiguous, Siegert shows that the analysis of the 1941 data is in trouble because linear combinations of these variables are sufficiently correlated with *HINC* that the *HINC* coefficient can be pushed around a lot. My guess is, however, that if I were careful to specify the doubt and ambiguity, the high doubtfulness of these variables would keep my interval of estimates for the *HINC* coefficient agreeable short. For the 1950 data, the variables *%INPOPH*, *ANFTEARN*, *AGEHH* and *EDUHH*, collectively can cause a lot of trouble for estimating the coefficient on *HINC*. The 1969 and the 1972 data set have a much lower degree of multicollinearity between *HINC* on the one hand and the collection of doubtful variables on the other. For that reason, the potential misspecification error is much less.

5. MY CONCLUSION

There is more to be squeezed from these data.

REFERENCES

Chamberlain, G. and E. E. Leamer (1976), 'Matrix weighted averages and posterior bounds', *Journal of the Royal Statistical Society*, Series B, **38**, 73–84.
Leamer, E. E. (1973), 'Multicollinearity: a Bayesian interpretation', *Review of Economics and Statistics*, **55**, 371–80.
Leamer, E. E. (1978), *Specification Searches: Ad Hoc Inference with Nonexperimental Data*, John Wiley and Sons, New York.
Leamer, E. E. (1982), 'Sets of posterior means with bounded variance priors', *Econometrica*, **50**, 725–36.
Leamer, E. E. (1983), 'Let's take the con out of econometrics', *American Economics Review*, **73**, 31–43.

---

[1] *Editors' remark*: Most of these triangular arrays are not reproduced in Siegert's chapter.

Leamer, E. E. and G. Chamberlain (1976), 'A Bayesian interpretation of pretesting', *Journal of the Royal Statistical Society*, Series B, **38**, 85–94.

Leamer, E. E. and H. Leonard (1983), 'Reporting the fragility of regression estimates', *Review of Economics and Statistics*, **65**, 306–17.

Siegert, W. K. (1998), 'An application of three econometric methodologies to the estimation of the income elasticity of food demand', Chapter 16, this volume.

CHAPTER 19

THE TILBURG EXPERIMENTS: IMPRESSIONS OF A DROP-OUT

ADRIAN R. PAGAN

1. THE FIELD TRIAL EXPERIMENT

I was a drop-out from the first of the Tilburg experiments. It is pleasing that others had more stamina and made the first of the experiments an important contribution to the literature on applied econometrics. In many ways the responses to it by the participants reflect tensions in applied econometrics more generally. To see this, consider what it involved. First, analysts were asked to measure a coefficient with a variety of data sets. Secondly, they were asked whether they thought that it would be worth pooling the data set to produce 'better' estimates of the parameter. Thirdly, they were instructed to seek a model that would be useful for forecasting. Finally, a policy problem was described which might be addressed with the research that had been done. Exactly what the connection was between the last of these and the preceding trio was never entirely clear, and it is not surprising that it was eventually dropped from the list of activities. Such an outcome is not uncommon; a lot of empirical research which is reported is ill suited to serve as inputs into policy decisions. Knowing what you want to do with a study is a key ingredient in determining how it is that you will proceed. Leamer's strategy of designing a policy issue which would depend upon the magnitude of an income elasticity shows this interdependence very well, even though his discussants felt that it hadn't impacted much upon what he had actually done.

Turning to the other themes, the first is the emphasis placed upon estimating a single parameter. *'Single parameter research'* has a long and distinguished history in econometrics. Recent examples would be the effects of the minimum wage on employment and the returns to schooling. However, it is not true that this is the only way to characterize applied work. Many questions that one seeks answers to pertain to *combinations* of parameters e.g. the impact of taxes upon quantities transacted depend upon both demand and supply elasticities. In those cases, a *systems perspective* needs to be taken.

One advantage of restricting attention to the estimation of a single parameter is that one can conduct a comparative study without being distracted by arguments about what the relevant combination of the parameters is. By using such a control, the Tilburg experiment might have been expected to shed light upon whether econometric work really is characterized by a diversity of approaches. In Leamer's language do we have a lot of 1000 pound gorillas? In the language of work on innovations do we have a lot of 'special purpose technologies' (SPTs) versus 'general purpose technologies' (GPTs)? We did see at least one SPT, in the form of a system of demand equations, but mostly those participating felt that they were working with GPTs, even if the domain of application was sometimes just to time series rather than cross section data. A question that didn't seem to come up is whether it is better to use SPTs rather than GPTs to do data analysis; putting it somewhat crudely, if I wished to hire a consultant to tell me about food expenditure, would I hire Leamer, Sims, Hendry or Deaton? Leamer referred to this tangentially in his final remark and I think it is a real issue.

The first Tilburg experiment was also fascinating for the absence of some approaches advocated for applied work. Given the amount of attention lavished on it in theoretical journals in the past decade, it seemed a bit surprising that one did not see a greater emphasis upon non-parametric methods. After all, the estimation of Engel curves is one of those areas sometimes invoked as justifying the amount of theoretical work. Perhaps the problem comes from the phrasing of the tasks, in that participants were asked to estimate a parameter rather than a relationship. Even then one might have expected to see some participants utilize non-parametric ideas when performing tests of whether the functional forms chosen to estimate the parameter were reasonable. Perhaps this tells us something about the impact of non-parametric methods upon applied work. The closest anyone came to non-parametrics was Leamer's graphical treatment, in that a lot of non-parametrics involves the averaging of data around points defined by a conditioning set and so is a way of formally doing something that Leamer was doing informally.

2. THE TACIT KNOWLEDGE EXPERIMENT

In the beginner's mind there are many possibilities but in the expert's mind there are few.

Zenmaster Shuniya Suzuki in *Zen Mind, Beginner's Mind*

Zenmaster Suzuki's contention is one that seemingly resonates with many workers in many fields. Casual reflection seems to validate it. We can think of many instances in our own experience in which we have been hopelessly confused over an issue until an authority on it has laid bare the essential issues with a few well chosen sentences. So it does not seem unreasonable to think that this could be a general principle that would arise within the area of econometric modelling. Indeed, it is such considerations that led to the addendum to the Tilburg experiment that goes under the heading of tacit knowledge. Unfortunately for the novice, Siegert, there were three masters, and he did not have the luxury of choosing to become a drop-out; see Siegert (1998).

How did he do? Leamer seemed satisfied with what Siegert had learned about his own style of research, and that was my reaction as well.[1] Leamer's main objection was not that Siegert had erred in thinking of too many ways of doing the analysis, but rather that he had come up with too few. Since Ed uses Bayesian language this translated into how to select a prior and how to recognize the uncertainty surrounding that choice. Still, I think that Siegert convincingly shows that the GPT associated with Leamer can be gleaned either from a reading of his writings or at least learned from some source. My caution here is that no student comes to such a task with a blank mind. During the time spent formally studying econometrics, he will have accumulated a store of knowledge and

---

[1] Of course, as the conference revealed, there is the new improved Leamer approach which revels in graphical analysis, so that it is 'old Leamer' which Siegert excels at.

attitudes from lecturers, text books, and exercises. These sources may have been such as to have provided a better training in some traditions than in others. So it is possible that his skills in this area have been learned in other ways than from just a reading of Ed's papers.[2]

The Hendry-Siegert interchange seems to reflect the Zen principle very well. In comparison to Siegert's somewhat rambling approach, Hendry's is well structured and comes up with some precise conclusions. Hendry is very unhappy with what Siegert has learned about how to implement the LSE methodology (LSEM). Siegert seems to have learned too little about it, concentrating upon the 'general to specific' and the 'test, test, test' lessons. In doing so he misses a vital ingredient of the LSEM, always entertain the possibility that the best model is an error correction model, thereby enabling one to simultaneously work with both differenced and levels data. Having missed this lesson, Siegert responds to non-stationarity in the variables by expressing all variables in differences. It is hard to see how one would miss this part of the LSEM. Hendry is right about the two decades he has spent preaching against an automatic use of differenced data when faced with evidence of non-stationarity. He has gone to some lengths to point out that all 'long-run' information is thereby lost. Indeed, I was somewhat taken aback with Siegert's references to 'static long-run equations' given his formulation of the model in terms of differences.

Even if Siegert had correctly started with an error correction model one might still ask whether he would have produced a piece of work like Hendry's. One reason for thinking that he might not have is the fact that Hendry sees the LSE approach as being 'progressive'. That raises the possibility of having to distinguish between 'early' and 'late' LSEM and it becomes important for the novice to know what to read. Are some of the differences between Hendry and Siegert due to this fact? To look at this precisely, I re-read my two pieces on methodology — Pagan(1987) and Pagan(1995) — and compared what I said there with what Hendry's piece showed about the LSEM today. There clearly were some changes.

Although in Pagan(1995) I pointed to the fact that Hendry was now augmenting the single equation analysis of the past with a VAR, I thought of the latter as a general model against which the single equation would be tested, i.e. the VAR was the source of a specification test for the validity of the single equation. Instead, it now seems as if a small simultaneous equations system is proposed as the beginning point of an analysis. Other developments in the LSEM have been an increasing emphasis on unit roots and co-integration testing; the addition to equations of a potentially large number of dummy variables to account for various historical events; and extensive testing of the stability of models. Although some of the elements were present in the papers that Pagan(1987) and Pagan(1995) were based upon, Hendry's presentation leaves little doubt that they have become much more prominent in the past five years.

Where would Siegert have found this material? David cites a paper in the *Scottish Journal of Political Economy* in support of the emphasis upon systems, but this is surely not one of the most widely read journals around.[3] Moreover, it is always hard to know

---

[2] My general impression was that Siegert was more comfortable when working with cross section rather than time series data.

[3] Hendry draws attention to the fact that Hendry (1995) would be an important source for understanding his approach, and a reading of it does confirm that most of the themes in his work with the Tobin data set are very closely related to the material of that book. Its length, however, makes it rather daunting to use as a text from which to teach a novice the fundamentals of the LSEM within a relatively short space of time.

whether a particular paper is a fundamental part of the canon or not. Tacit knowledge may be important here, in that serving with the master means that one learns what is important to him. Consequently, the critical parts of the canon can be precisely documented and the student does not need to make a decision about that. When a choice has to be made it is quite possible that a paper might be ignored because the student has his own ideas about the worth of the approach advocated in it. To assess this, I thought it might be useful for me to change places with Siegert and ask whether I would regard these new developments as a fundamental part of the LSEM. I am pretty certain that I am ambivalent about some of these new steps, either because I have little empathy with them or because they were never described clearly enough to be useful to me. Inclusion of dummy variables scores on both criteria. We all use dummy variables to handle some special events, and the earliest examples of the LSEM in action featured them. However, they have multiplied to such an extent in Hendry's paper that one really wonders how they are ever to be selected. David lists a lot of events in US history that might impact on consumption and income, but it doesn't take much thought to come up with others e.g. the Korean and Vietnam wars. So one is left to wonder why one particular set of dummies is chosen over an alternative one. Starting with a small system of structural equations also seems fine, but what principles govern the specification of its equations? In particular, how do we resolve the identification problem that is always present in such systems? Ex post it is clear from Hendry's paper that this is done by exclusion restrictions, but there is little discussion in his work, on the matter. Other papers representative of the LSEM are also vague about this step, e.g. Mizon (1995), Hendry and Doornik (1994) and Hendry and Mizon (1993). Although there has always been 'art' in the LSEM these new developments seem to be raising the art to science ratio to an uncomfortable level, and certainly make it harder to learn its principles from a reading of the literature around it. One cannot escape the feeling that Siegert should be absolved from any failure to absorb some of the elements in the 'new LSEM'.

I sometimes think that Sims is the closest thing we have to a Zen master. Leamer prefers metaphor to paradox; Hendry has the charisma of a Dalai Lama; but Sims' written and spoken work is frequently worthy of a Zen master. Things may be simple in Zen but they are never presented that way. Although Sims has not responded to Siegert's attempt to replicate his thought, I would be very surprised if Chris was happy with it. Siegert has the technology right but doesn't quite know how to use it. The problems reside in the fact that Sims always wants to answer questions that can only be asked with a system. Consequently, his work has a strong focus upon issues involving the extraction of information from and the judging of a system. Unless this point is grasped one is left to struggle with the problems that Siegert experienced.

First, he valiantly tries to find some measure that represents the 'income elasticity of food consumption' from the myriad of impulse responses that are in a VAR. Conceptually, this seems simple, as it merely requires an answer to the query of how much consumption would change if income changed and nothing else did. Unfortunately, such an experiment is very hard to perform. There are four shocks to Siegert's VAR, all of which affect income as well as the other variables of the system, at least after the first period. Siegert chooses one of these, that associated with the first equation of his system, but this choice seems arbitrary, except in the initial period when it is the only shock that affects income. Fundamentally, the concept of a single income elasticity becomes tenuous, and has to be replaced by elasticities with respect to the strongly exogenous variables in the system, namely the four shocks. Of course, for any named shock, the associated changes in income and consumption can be computed and these might be used to construct an 'income elasticity', but there can be up to four of these 'pseudo elasticities'. Only when income is strongly exogenous is there a single one. So, as I argued in Pagan (1987), Sims' analysis is really not what we would do if we wanted to conduct 'single parameter research'.

This systems feature creates problems in other dimensions. Sims has substituted a whole new terminology of 'orthogonalized residuals' and 'Choleski decompositions' (or Wold orderings) for the older term of 'recursive system' and thereby left the impression that one is not dealing with a simultaneous equations system. Like the master he is, Sims knows that this is not true, but many disciples have yet to figure it out. Every year I see papers that refer to Sims' work as 'a sort of simultaneous equations system'. This is absolute nonsense. It is neither more nor less. Does it matter that users of Sims' work don't quite appreciate this? It can matter a lot and Siegert's work shows why. If you don't see the simultaneous equation context then the ordering of the equations doesn't bother you much. But it should. In Siegert's preferred ordering the last equation in his system is a structural equation in which population depends (contemporaneously) on income, consumption and prices. It's not easy to see the sense of this (at least for yearly data). It would seem more logical to think of population as responding only with a lag to all of these variables, i.e. it should be the first equation of his system and not the last. A similar consideration applies to the price of food equation. Implicitly Siegert is adopting the approach, common in agricultural economics, of making the food price the dependent variable in a structural equation and having consumption of the commodity on the right hand side, rather than the more conventional demand function which normalizes on quantity. In agricultural economics this normalization seems to be justified by thinking of the quantity supplied as fixed, with prices adjusting to clear the market. In an auction market that makes sense, but in retail markets it is more likely that price smoothing will occur so that the standard demand formulation which normalizes on quantity may represent a better approximation.[4] Such considerations may point towards likely structural change in the VAR. In 1929 food prices may well have been determined closer to auction markets then they were in 1989. It's clear that these two views produce different structural relations and so different orderings. They both have the same reduced form and are therefore observationally equivalent, requiring extra information to discriminate between them. In Sims' work that extra information frequently comes from the signs and sizes of the whole collection of impulse responses within the system. If I adopt the sticky price idea, as well as the 'exogeneity' of population, a better ordering of the four variable system that Siegert uses would be (pop, fp, aggy, food) rather than (aggy, food, fp, pop). Then the impulse responses of (aggy, food) to an 'income' shock in this new system are (0.042, 0.025) (lag zero), (0.044, 0.033) (lag 1) and (0.047, 0.049) (lag 9) as compared with his results of (0.065, 0.061), (0.064, 0.062) and (0.041, 0.040).[5] To avoid trivial differences due to different sizes of income shocks, one can focus upon the ratios of the impulse responses, and these are clearly quite different in the short run.

---

[4] One might say that both are inaccurate. However, if the only option is a recursive system one must make a choice between them.

[5] I obtained these results using MICROFIT 4. Siegert's corresponding results are slightly different: (0.063, 0.059), (0.061, 0.060) and (0.039, 0.039), because he used the formulae in Lütkepohl (1993). The difference appears to lie in the number of degrees of freedom in estimating the residual covariance matrix.

3. FINAL THOUGHTS

When doing applied research we might distinguish between the relative contributions of common knowledge, tacit knowledge and, as Hendry emphasized, individual ability. In many ways what the second Tilburg experiment has shown is how hard it is to distinguish between the first two. What might have been thought of as common knowledge — published work — does not seem to have been that: Siegert clearly experienced difficulties in ascertaining modelling principles simply from a reading of such work. Perhaps it is here that working with a master is important. Proximity enables one to question the master about what he has written and to quickly correct wrong impressions. Moreover, it is likely that the student will be part of a milieu that constantly emphasizes the master's approach, and repetition is the key to a lot of learning. Even then, all this does is to ensure that the disciple has got the master's attitude correct. It does not mean that he could ever reproduce the same quality of work. This proviso brings to mind another Zen story. A Zen master presents his student with a stick and asks him what it is. The student responds with a description of its length and what it is made of, whereupon he is beaten with it. After a week of similarly precise answers and beatings, the student finally takes the stick and beats the master with it. As the student was meant to discover, it is not what you know about something which is important but rather how you use it. Our hope is always that the contribution of communicable knowledge to the process of applied work is high. Our fear is that individual ability is the dominant factor. In Pagan (1987) I wrote, 'Few would deny that in the hands of the masters the methodologies perform impressively, but in the hands of their disciples it is all much less convincing'. It is a little depressing that, a decade later, the Tilburg experiments have not lead me to discard this impression.

REFERENCES

Hendry, D. F. (1995), *Dynamic Econometrics*, Oxford University Press, Oxford.
Hendry, D. F. and J. A. Doornik (1994), 'Modelling linear dynamic econometric systems', *Scottish Journal of Political Economy*, **41**, 1–33.
Hendry, D. F. and G. E. Mizon (1993), 'Evaluating dynamic econometric models by encompassing the VAR', in: P. C. B. Phillips (ed), *Models, Methods and Applications of Econometrics*, Basil Blackwell, Oxford, 272–300.
Lütkepohl, H. (1993), *Introduction to Multiple Time Series*, Second Edition, Springer-Verlag, Berlin.
Mizon, G. E. (1995), 'Progressive modelling of macroeconomic time series: the LSE methodology', in: K. D. Hoover (ed), *Macroeconometrics, Developments, Tensions and Prospects*, Kluwer Academic Publishers, Boston, 107–70.
Pagan, A. R. (1987), 'Three econometric methodologies: a critical appraisal', *Journal of Economic Surveys*, **1**, 3–24.
Pagan, A. R. (1995), 'Three econometric methodologies: an update', in: L. Oxley, D. A. R. George, C. J. Roberts and S. Sayer (eds), *Surveys in Econometrics*, Basil Blackwell, Oxford, 30–41.
Siegert, W. K. (1998), 'An application of three econometric methodologies to the estimation of the income elasticity of food demand', Chapter 16, this volume.

CHAPTER 20

LESSONS FROM THE TACIT KNOWLEDGE EXPERIMENT

JAN R. MAGNUS AND MARY S. MORGAN

1. TACIT KNOWLEDGE IN THEORY AND PRACTICE

Our second experiment was concerned with assessing the contribution of tacit knowledge to applied econometrics. There was also an element in our first experiment concerned with getting at tacit knowledge. In order to draw these strands together, let us renew our discussion of Polanyi's concept of 'personal knowledge' (begun in the Introduction), and look also to the various empirical studies which have been made of tacit knowledge in other sciences, to help us assess what we have learnt about this element from the experiments.

Polanyi's concept of personal or tacit knowledge is not easy to characterize. One particularly difficult aspect is the extent to which such knowledge can be articulated. At one point Polanyi states that

'the aim of a skilful performance is achieved by the observance of a set of rules which are not known as such to the person following them.'

(Polanyi, 1958, p. 49)

At another point, he suggests that there are rules, which can be written down and shared, but are insufficient in themselves,

'they are maxims, which can serve as a guide to an art only if they can be integrated into the practical knowledge of the art. They cannot replace this knowledge.'

(Polanyi, 1958, p. 50)

Questions as to how far tacit knowledge can be turned into rules for procedure and how such rules are integrated into practice are obviously relevant for applied econometrics. Both questions can be easily understood through one of the standard examples used to illustrate the problem, namely the cooking recipe. A recipe gives ingredients and rules for combination and production, but such rules are both very difficult to follow, and insufficient to guarantee successful results, without the practical knowledge gained from experience of learning to cook with someone who does have practical knowledge. This certainly was the case in our tacit knowledge experiment where the written down instructions proved insufficient for the apprentice to follow on his own.

To what extent can rules of applied scientific practice be written down? Could a recipe for successful cake baking, let alone ones for successful applied econometrics, ever have accurate, sufficient and comprehensible written rules? One of the on-going debates about

Methodology and Tacit Knowledge: Two Experiments in Econometrics
Jan R. Magnus and Mary S. Morgan © 1999 John Wiley & Sons Ltd

tacit knowledge is whether it can in principle be something that, given sufficiently careful and exhaustive articulation, could be written down. According to Turner (1994, p. 8), Kant believed this to be the case, for practice amounted to 'following certain general principles of procedure' in which any failure of application must be due to inadequacies in the procedures (the theory). Even here it seems there is a catch, however, because one still needed 'judgement to apply the principles to particular cases' and judgement itself is very likely the domain of hidden knowledge.

Sociologists of science have tended to take the opposite view — that it is impossible to reduce everything to rules. First, since sociologists of science see science as a social process like any other, science can not be a practice of following purely mechanical rules (or principles), for then science would be both inhuman and asocial. The second reason is empirical: in practice, science is not rule-following. This is best seen in the work of Harry Collins, the most experienced researcher and perceptive commentator on tacit knowledge. His exploration of the tacit knowledge involved in growing crystals for semiconductor materials, reported in Collins (1990), provides some convincing cases in which neither the written down, field-specific principles given in text books, nor the 'rules' worked out for an 'expert system' rule book by eliciting knowledge directly from the applied scientist, were sufficient to decide what choice of process would be good for growing a particular type of crystal not previously grown.

Rules for making choices about materials and methods is one domain where tacit knowledge seems indispensable, particularly where, as is often the case, a combination of circumstances are involved so that the simple, single-circumstance, text-book rules do not apply. In applied econometrics, perhaps the most common situation of this type is where statistical and economic theory criteria have to be taken together in deciding the next step in procedure. Another set of circumstances where tacit knowledge is important are those requiring non-rule based judgements. This need arises with new situations, for example Collins' 1985 study of a new laser construction throws up many such problems of judgement (the size of electrodes, the length of leads). The need also arises with quality-based judgements, such as interpreting the character of the sound of certain reactions in the laser case. More critically, Collins (1990) suggests that the expert scientist judges (knows) when certain general principles of scientific experiment can be safely ignored and when not. For example, as reported in his 1990 book, the expert chemist knows when to measure ingredients accurately and when it doesn't matter; when it is imperative to have clean equipment and when it doesn't matter.

The fact that applied science can not be reduced to rule-following doesn't necessarily imply Polanyi's claim that tacit knowledge is knowledge which the expert does not know he/she possesses. How is it that expert econometricians, or indeed anyone else, can know things they don't know? Applied research requires making choices, using judgement and taking decisions in which many factors are involved at the same time. The expertise to do this grows from experience rather than that it is learnt from books or other formal sources. Just as an expert car driver relies on experience when making a decision in a complex situation, so too the scientist. As Collins puts it: 'the role of conscious choice and analysis becomes minimal' (Collins, 1990, p. 81). To some extent, a scientist can recreate and articulate the expertise involved in the choices made from experience, but only in a new and difficult case or in case of disagreement over a procedure. In this context it is instructive to read about the great difficulty that the chemist has in explaining his decisions to the layman and describing all the factors which made him decide to grow a particular crystal in a particular experimental set-up (reported in Collins, 1990, Chapter 11). Leamer's description in his comments on the tacit knowledge experiment (Chapter 18) of how he chooses whether to label variables 'doubtful' or 'free' exhibits a similar sense of someone trying to express beliefs which are both difficult to articulate accurately and involve decisions which are probably not normally subject to such conscious justification.

If science practice can not be reduced to rule following, and if some of the knowledge embedded in expertise is also hidden from the master practitioner, how does the student ever learn to be a master applied scientist? We might assume that these hidden knowledge elements are learned by unconscious emulation, usually in some kind of apprenticeship system by working with the skilled person. The literature here suggests that this is indeed the case, but perhaps this answer requires expansion.

2. TACIT KNOWLEDGE IN TRANSMISSION

Turner (1994) has considered the theory of such transmission mechanisms, which he divides into two: methods of imitation and methods of habitualization. The former can be understood either in terms of the learning that goes on in childhood or in terms of the apprenticeship process. The latter creates more of a problem for Turner, for the notion of habit implies that the same practices are transmitted, but why should this be so? This creates a conundrum for a social theory of transmission, for the same transmission mechanism might or might not lead to the same habit, and the same habits might or might not derive from the same transmission mechanisms. This may not seem of particular interest here, for we would not expect a PhD student to do exactly the same as the master scientist on the same job, any more that we would expect a master Bayesian econometrician to present exactly the same answers as another Bayesian econometrician. Nevertheless, we cannot dismiss the issue of sameness entirely, for our second experiment involved an apprentice whom we hoped would do the project 'in the same way' as did the master craftsman. The notion of sameness therefore acts as a benchmark to assess the extent of tacit knowledge involved. Indeed, the main thrust of Leamer's comments on Siegert's apprenticeship efforts are aimed at the sameness and difference in choice of prior. In doing so, Leamer articulates the complexity of the decision making going on in the mind of the master, and the subtlety of categories he uses, as he explains why his choices were not the same as those made by the apprentice.

Once again, in contrast to the theoretical work, the empirical research on the topic has been rather fruitful. Collins (1990, p. 8) claims that the reason that scientists (or any expert) knows how to act and how to do things, but cannot write down the rules of action is that 'we learn by being socialized, not by being instructed'. Intelligent machines are instructed: they follow rules. Applied scientists are socialized, they learn in part from experience and in part from working with others, as well as from more formal instruction. This implies that programmed methodologies will not be able to replace true apprenticeship systems.

Socialization involves not only imitation (enabling the apprentice to learn how to use tools and so forth), but also a process of coming to share assumptions, presuppositions and commitments. For example, pattern recognition, which appears at first sight to be a matter of cognitive training, also requires social consensus amongst scientists, according to the work of Collins (1985) and others. Being able to see certain patterns in the graphs given by Leamer (Chapter 5) for example is not just a matter of our perception; it also involves our commitment as econometricians about exactly what kinds of patterns we are likely to find in the graphs. The early twentieth century statistical studies on business cycles relied on graphical methods of analysis to the horror of later analysts who regarded such methods as entirely ad hoc. This was not because later investigators could not see the patterns, but rather because they had agreed among themselves that such graphical methods could not reveal true business cycles in such patterns (see Morgan, 1997).

Learning to be an applied econometrician apparently involves learning the appropriate rules of scientific procedure and when to ignore them, growing the expertise which enables choices, decisions and judgements to be made almost unconsciously, and learning the tacit skills to undertake the work. As we found in the Introduction, personal knowledge also involves acquiring a set of guiding pre-suppositions, a set of beliefs about the economic world and about the correct methodological principles for accessing it. Since much of this knowledge is hidden, and can not be provided as a set of rules, learning the practice of any science is likely to rely on an apprenticeship system.

3.   TACIT KNOWLEDGE IN THE APPLICATION OF ECONOMETRIC METHODOLOGIES

Our two experiments — the field trial experiment and the tacit knowledge experiment — tend to confirm the findings of other experimental studies of practice and tacit knowledge. In general, we found that the application of econometric methodologies involves a large element of choice and judgement decisions which rely on tacit knowledge rather than rule following. These findings emerge both from a study of the logbooks of the participants and workshop discussions of the field trial experiment and in the apprentice logbook and reactions of the masters in the tacit knowledge experiment. We count it a minor success of the experiment that the reports from the experiment participants do not follow the normal style of applied econometrics papers — reporting only finally successful results, and giving little idea of the process. It is not only the presence of the logbooks which add verisimilitude to the accounts — the contributions are experimental reports with a degree of immediacy and transparency which is unusual.

The importance of tacit knowledge can not be appreciated fully by describing it as the ability to make decisions in the absence of written rules. The decisions often involve situations where many different aspects of personal knowledge have to work together: methodological and procedural concerns about how to do applied science; econometric knowledge (part statistical, part economics) about how to do applied econometrics; economic theory knowledge (if modelling and interpretation are involved); knowledge of the data or raw material and knowledge of the tools (software, etc), and so forth. Situations within which practical decisions have to be made are usually extremely complex, and these are not single situations — applied econometrics requires a succession of such judgements to proceed through each step of the work.

These decisions depend on personal or tacit knowledge (a combination of intellectual knowledge, cognitive skills and more obviously tacit or manual skills), which is partly hidden even to the person who holds the knowledge and thus cannot easily be articulated into rules. Although the participants' logbooks did not show directly the personal knowledge (by definition it is hidden), they do give evidence of the difficulties in decision making marked by wrong turns and new starts, the consideration of the complex circumstances that go in to deciding how to proceed, and the difficulties of articulating the full reasons behind the judgement.

The difficulties of the decision making and the critical role of judgement was more clearly evident in the tacit knowledge experiment, where the gap between the apprentice and the master is assumed to be a combination of tacit knowledge and individual ability. In terms of our design, given the fact that our apprentice had to rely only on written versions of the methodologies and was relatively inexperienced in applied econometrics, we assume that the tacit knowledge gap swamped the individual ability gap. What emerged from this experiment was really how difficult it was to work out how to do applied work from a combination of abstract methodological statements and examples of applied work by the master. There is clearly a big problem of middle-level instruction. Abstract methodology has somehow to be turned into practical advice. Here it is significant that the apprentice in the tacit knowledge experiment relied partly on Pagan's (1987) articulation of the practical process involved in each of the methodologies as a way of getting started. Pagan's writings provided an essential connection between the master writings and the apprentice by helping him to acquire some of the tacit knowledge not available directly. Even so, there were still main elements of the methodologies which remained opaque to the appentice. For example, in his assessment of the tacit knowledge experiment (Chapter 19), Pagan pointed out that the apprentice failed to understand one of the main elements of Sims' approach, namely that it was a simultaneous systems approach and that this has important implications for the ordering of equations. But Pagan also noted that many professionals fail to grasp this point fully — it remains to some extent tacit knowledge rather than common knowledge.

To some extent, it might seem as if software which embodies some of the methodology in practice, like Hendry's GIVE program, should have overcome this gap between abstract principles and practice. In fact this did not seem to be the case in our experiment. Following Collins work on artificial intelligence, we should not expect it to be so. Software, like other intelligent machines, depends on instructions and rule following. Any aspect of the methodology where hidden judgement comes in may not be translatable into general instructions which can always apply. However, this was not the only problem experienced by the apprentice in working with Hendry's methodology. His main mistake, according to remarks from the master econometrician, Hendry, was not on issues of tacit knowledge judgement (as in the Leamer version of the task) but that the apprentice had failed to grasp the essential building blocks of his practical methodology which were explicit in the literature. Pagan noted this explicit knowledge gap with surprise (see Chapter 19), but he also partly defended the apprentice by suggesting that if he had put himself in the stance of the apprentice, he too would have been unsure how central some of the more recent elements were to Hendry's programme. Clearly some of the knowledge that the master thought was explicit remains in part tacit.

It may also seem as if methodologies which follow very clear and strict rules of scientific procedure or methodologies in which the subject-specific knowledge from economic theory dominates the decision process must minimize the importance of tacit knowledge in the practical sphere. Particularly it appears that such principle or theory following will have a great advantage when it comes to assessment. If the rules of scientific procedure are followed, then the results of the applied work can be claimed good on such grounds. Similarly, economic theory dominated applied work might lead the scientist to claims that s/he has found the 'true' measure — true in the sense that it is true to a theory concept.

Apart from the danger of operationalism implied by such a view, there is also the standard difficulty that the methodological and subject field rules may suggest conflicting steps (as for example when economic and statistical significance indicators are inconsistent; for the general point, see Pesaran and Smith, 1985). The field trial experiment suggests that the safety advantages of strong principles or theory are, in part, illusory.

While it is true that some methodologies used in the field trial experiment required more points of choice and judgement than others — for example, the Tennessee methodology (see Chapter 6) is relatively simple and has clear modelling rules and clear decision/assessment criteria in comparison with the Texas approach (see Chapter 3) which requires more judgement in modelling and decisions made according to multiple criteria — all methodologies required practical expertise and personal knowledge. This is evidenced by the nature of discussions at the Tilburg workshop reporting the experimental results from the field trial. Despite strongly held methodological and theoretical views, arguments and discussions amongst participants were quite often not about general principles, nor about specific results obtained, but about the justification for intermediate practical steps in the applied econometrics which were seen to embody methodology, assumptions or technical skills. This experience — that the specific decisions taken in the process of application have to be explained and justified to other professionals — is consistent with the empirical findings on tacit knowledge in other scientific contexts, and comes as no surprise.

Professor Tobin's 1950 article (Chapter 2) played an interesting role in this respect. The experience of the experiment and the workshop gave participants a rather stronger sense of, and higher regard for, the tacit knowledge involved in Tobin's applied work than one would normally expect to glean from reading an early paper in the field. It was one of the features of the Tilburg workshop discussion that participants often referred to a specific argument from Tobin's paper (or from Stone's discussion of the Tobin paper) in justifying something they had done in their own paper. By working on the same problem and studying his solution, Tobin's tacit knowledge had apparently been transmitted to the econometricians taking part and became a usable resource for them.

So, while strong methodological rules and subject field theories do put some limits on choice and thus imply stronger assessment claims, it does not seem as if any applied methodology can be entirely rule based. If any version of econometrics offered such an example, it would probably be unique in the scientific community. Applied economet-rics, like other applied disciplines, involves both subject criteria and scientific method criteria which are not necessarily consistent since they come from different domains. The inevitable practical requirement for personal knowledge within these rule-based constraints, means that decisions are also made on the basis of individual experience and judgement. The possibility of unambiguous assessment seems remote.

REFERENCES

Collins, H. M. (1985), *Changing Order. Replication and Induction in Scientific Practice*, Sage, London.

Collins, H. M. (1990), *Artificial Experts. Social Knowledge and Intelligent Machines*, MIT Press, Cambridge, USA.

Morgan, M. S. (1997), 'Searching for causal relations in economic statistics: reflections from history', in V. McKim and S. P. Turner (eds.), *Causality in Crisis*, University of Notre Dame Press, Notre Dame.

Pagan, A. (1987), 'Three econometric methodologies: a critical appraisal', *Journal of Economic Surveys*, **1**, 3–24.

Pesaran M. H. and R. P. Smith (1985), 'Evaluation of macroeconometric models', *Economic Modelling*, April, 125–34.

Polanyi, M. (1958), *Personal Knowledge: Towards a Post-Critical Philosophy*, Routledge, London.

Tobin, J. (1950), 'A statistical demand function for food in the USA', *Journal of the Royal Statistical Society*, Series A, **113**, Part II, 113–41 [reprinted in Chapter 2, this volume].

Turner, S. (1994), *The Social Theory of Practices. Tradition, Tacit Knowledge and Presuppositions*, Polity Press, Cambridge.

Part III

The Data

CHAPTER 21

DESCRIPTION OF THE US DATA

JAN R. MAGNUS AND MARY S. MORGAN

1. THE DATA: GENERAL INFORMATION[1]

The complete data set consists of both time series and budget survey data from the USA and the Netherlands. We use 'BS' and 'TS' to denote budget survey and time series respectively; and 'US' and 'NL' to denote data from the USA and the Netherlands respectively. The data were originally provided to experiment participants on diskette containing nine files. The full data set (including corrections made to data during the course of the experiment) is now available from the *Journal of Applied Econometrics* data archive at:

http://qed.econ.queensu.ca:80/jae/1997-v12.5/

This contains three directories: a 'readme' directory, a data directory and a documentation directory (which gives brief descriptions). Full documentation on the data is available in this chapter for the US data and in the following Chapter 22 for the Dutch data.

The US data are drawn from official reports and are in the public domain. If you use these data from the archive, please credit the relevant US Government department and cite the relevant publications (all references are given in this chapter). The Dutch data are provided courtesy of Statistics Netherlands, and some were not originally in the public domain (information about sources is given in the next chapter). If you use these data from the archive, please add a note of thanks to Statistics Netherlands.

2. THE US DATA: AN INTRODUCTION

The US data consist of four sets of cross-section observations and one time-series set.

Our aim has been to provide cross-section data on incomes and expenditures as close as possible to the type used by Tobin (1950, see Chapter 2 of this volume); and to extend the data sets where possible to provide information on certain household characteristics. The four cross-section sets are from consumer expenditure interview surveys of samples of US households undertaken in 1941 (used by Tobin), 1950, 1960–61 and 1972–73. The data provided are for groups of urban households, extended to cover all households in the last survey. The survey methods used were roughly comparable in their approach. We have not used the data available from the 1980s surveys as our investigations showed

---

[1] We are grateful to Adam Sutton and Paolo Zaffaroni at LSE for expert help with the collection of the US data. This data description is a slightly revised version of Chapters 7–8 of the *Experiment Information Pack* (see Magnus and Morgan, 1995).

Methodology and Tacit Knowledge: Two Experiments in Econometrics
Jan R. Magnus and Mary S. Morgan © 1999 John Wiley & Sons Ltd

that these were not comparable to earlier surveys in a number of important respects, and showed significant quality deterioration in some of the variables of interest.

With the time-series data, our aim has been to provide as consistent an updating as possible for Tobin's original data set. Where we have been unable to update Tobin's data, we have provided alternative series and appropriate scaling information to allow for closer comparison with household survey data. These revised and additional series cover the period 1912–1989.

The five US data files were originally provided on diskette in the form of a spread sheet (Quattro Pro version 5.00). Since a few people found difficulties in reading these data files, we sent participants ASCII versions by E-mail (as reported in our E-mail message to participants of 1 August, 1995).

The four US budget-survey data sets can now be found in the following files in the data archive (for location: see above):

> BS41US.PRN data from 1941 budget survey
> BS50US.PRN data from 1950 budget survey
> BS60US.PRN data from 1960-61 budget survey
> BS72US.PRN data from 1972-73 budget survey;

and the US time-series data in the file:

> TS1289US.PRN data from 1912–89.

The budget data are defined, described and documented in the next section, and the time-series data in Section 4.

3.   BUDGET SURVEY DATA FOR THE USA

The data are obtained from sample surveys of households carried out at four different periods (1941, 1950, 1960–61 and 1972–73) covering expenditures and incomes. The reported observations are organized into matrices, vertically by income classes within different household sizes, beginning with 1-person households and ending with all households taken together. (Different surveys use different numbers of income classes; sometimes they were reported as 1000–2000 dollars, sometimes as 1000–1999 dollars: we have stuck to the former labelling throughout.) Each observation represents a group of households in a particular income class and of a particular household size.

The budget surveys provide three different types of information, arranged horizontally in the data matrices:

1.   information on sample size/population of households;
2.   characteristics of the households in the group;
3.   income/consumption data for the households in the group.

3.1.   Variable Definitions and Data Availability

Not all surveys have all the variables listed below, and not all variables share exactly the same definition. The definitions given here are the standard shared definitions for all four surveys. Further details are given for individual surveys in following sections.

3.1.1. Sample Size/Population Shares

%INPOPH : the percent share of such (income/size) households in the population of households. It is 'population', because the sample has been grossed up using a weighting system to give

ESTPOPH : the estimated total number (the population) of such (income/size) households, measured in 000s

SAMPSIZE : the actual sample number of such households in the survey.

3.1.2. Household Group Characteristics

AHSIZE : average household size
ANCHILD : average number of children per household
ANFTEARN : average number of full-time earners per household
ANOV 65 : average number of persons over 65 years per household
AGEHH : average age of head of household in years
EDUHH : average years of education of household head
EDUHH 1 : % of heads of household with 1–9 years education
EDUHH 2 : % of heads of household with 9–12 years education
EDUHH 3 : % of heads of household with over 12 years education
NONWHITE : % of households which are non-white
HOMEOWN : % of households which are homeowners
RENTER : % of households which are renters
AUTOOWN : % of households owning one or more automobiles.

3.1.3. Income and Consumption

HINC : average household disposable income in $ (all incomes after taxes, excluding net asset changes)

TOTCON : average household total current consumption expenditure in $ (excludes personal insurance, gifts and contributions and net changes in assets)

FOODCON : food and beverages consumption expenditure in $ (including at home and away from home)

NETASSCH : average household net asset change in $

ACCBAL : account balancing item in $.[2]

---

[2] The account balancing item is calculated as: ACCBAL = Total receipts − total disbursements (including personal insurance, gifts and contributions) − net increase in assets. (Note that this is not the same as HINC − TOTCON − NETASSCH because TOTCON is not equal to total disbursements.) ACCBAL is either reported in the tables, or calculated from them. According to the 1960–61 survey report, it is a 'net reporting discrepancy' and so it is given here as one indicator of the accuracy of the reported information. When positive, it indicates that reported income exceeds reported disbursements, when negative that reported spending plus saving exceeds income.

3.1.4.   Variables Available (and In Order)

	1941	1950	1960–61	1972–73
%INPOPH	—	yes	yes	—
ESTPOPH	yes	—	yes	yes
SAMPSIZE	yes	yes	part	—
AHSIZE	part	yes	yes	yes
ANCHILD	part	—	yes	yes
ANFTEARN	—	yes	yes	—
ANOV 65	—	—	—	yes
AGEHH	—	yes	yes	yes
EDUHH	—	yes	yes	—
EDUHH 1	—	—	—	yes
EDUHH 2	—	—	—	yes
EDUHH 3	—	—	—	yes
NONWHITE	—	yes	yes	yes
HOMEOWN	part	yes	yes	yes
RENTER	part	—	—	yes
AUTOOWN	part	—	yes	yes
HINC	yes	yes	yes	yes
TOTCON	yes	yes	yes	yes
FOODCON	yes	yes	yes	yes
NETASSCH	part	yes	yes	yes
ACCBAL	—	yes	yes	yes

yes   =   data present
part   =   data partly available
—   =   data not available.

Missing data are entered as −999. Observations entered as zero indicate where a percentage was less than 0.05% or a dollar amount rounded down to zero in the accounts.

3.2.   1941 Urban US Budget Survey: Tobin's Data Set

The data used by Tobin (his Table 2) for his cross-section analysis of expenditure on food by family size came primarily from the 1942 survey designed to collect information on income, expenditure and saving over the period 1941 and the 1st quarter of 1942. This was an interview field survey, covering sixty-two urban areas (urban areas started at 2500 population). The usable number of interviews in the 1941-period sample ended up at 'about 1300' (according to a footnote, p. 32, this was 1220 full-period units and 79 part-period units). The design appears to have been rather successful with a high response rate (the main difficulty being a rather high 'refusal' rate, necessitating substitutions, of those in the highest income brackets) and remarkably complete recording. The interviewers seem to have been so effective at obtaining data that net asset change reported is equal to the net surplus/deficit on current income/disbursement flows. (Thus there is no reported ACCBAL variable.)

Not all the collected information (for example on household characteristics such as race and occupation) were reported in the published tables, and Tobin used what was reported very effectively. Wherever possible, we have added data which was available in the survey to the set of data Tobin used in his paper. Thus, we have included information on total consumption expenditures (*TOTCON*) by family size; we have included data for the category of *all* households where certain additional information is available for them; and we have included data on the highest income groups, which Tobin did not use possibly because of the poorer quality of the sample.

Although the basic sample sizes for each group are not reported for the survey, the estimated (from the sample) population of US households which fall into each group are given (*ESTPOPH*). In addition, during the experiment, we found we were able to reconstruct the sample sizes for most cells in the data matrix, and these were e-mailed to participants on 19 August 1995. This variable (*SAMPSIZE*) is now included in the archived data set.[3]

Finally, we have corrected two small and one larger error in the data reported in Tobin's Table 2 (p. 119):

> 5th income observation for 1-person households = 2149
> 3rd income observation for 3-person households = 1358
> 5th income observation for 3-person households = 2498.

3.2.1. 1941 Variables

There are nine possible income classes (ranging from 0 to over 10 000 dollars annual pre-tax money income) and six household size classes (1, 2, 3, 4, 5 and more persons, and all households). Non-reported data occur where the original sample size was too small to admit reporting.

ESTPOPH: estimated number of such families in US urban population (000s) weighted up from the sample numbers. In some cases these are grouped: e.g. income classes 2000–2500 and 2500–3000 incomes classes combined contain an estimated 341(000) 1-person households. The final figure after each household size, in a separate row, is the total for that household size (e.g. there are an estimated 4043(000) urban single-person households).

SAMPSIZE: reconstructed sample size for number of households in each household/income category.

HINC: average household disposable income in $ (money and non-money incomes after tax and minus half of gifts and contributions: see Tobin's explanation, Chapter 2, footnote to Table II; excludes net changes of assets).

---

[3] We are grateful to Professor J. S. Cramer of the University of Amsterdam who suggested the method by which we reconstructed the actual sample sizes for the individual cells in the 1941 survey (the variable *SAMPSIZE*). We have used the figures given for 'percentage reporting' in various tables to work out the implied number of households sampled for each income/family size group and for all households taken together. We are reasonably confident that these individual cell estimates are correct because they sum to 1213, very close to 1220, the total sample size given elsewhere in the text for the 1941 study. However, the larger the number of households involved, the less precise the calculations in the 'All' households column, which may vary by 1 or 2 units in the first seven categories. Our level of confidence for the individual family size cells, and for the final two categories for all households is near 100%. Note that there are some cells missing — this is where the survey had either 0, 1 or 2 households in the cell, and so reported no data.

TOTCON: average household total current consumption expenditure in $ (includes goods received in kind; excludes personal insurance, gifts and contributions and net changes in assets).

FOODCON: food and beverages consumption expenditure in $ (includes meals at home, away from home, and alcoholic beverages).

The following additional variables are available only for 'all households':

AHSIZE: average household size
ANCHILD: average number of children 16 years and under per household
HOMEOWN: % of households which are homeowners for entire year
RENTER: % of households which are renters for entire year
AUTOOWN: % of households owning one or more automobiles
NETASSCH: average household net asset change in $.

3.2.2. Data Source

The source for the data and discussion of the survey is *Family Spending and Saving in Wartime* Bulletin no 822 of the Bureau of Labor Statistics, US Department of Labor, Washington DC 1945. Tables 1 and 1A, pp. 68–9 provide estimates of the groups in the US population. Table 2, p. 70 provides average household size. Table 18, pp. 94–101 and Table 25, pp. 127–8 provide the raw material for reconstructing the sample sizes. Tables 18 and 19, pp. 96–105 provide incomes. Table 20, pp. 106–19 provides consumptions. Table 22, p. 123 provides housing information. Table 26, pp. 139, provides information on numbers of children. Table 29, p. 180, provides information on automobile ownership. Table 35, pp. 187–9 provides asset information.

3.3. 1950: Urban US Budget Survey

The 1950 survey was an interview field survey carried out in early 1951 to collect information on all major items of expenditure and income for the whole year of 1950. It resulted in complete collection from 12 489 consumer units covering 91 urban areas. It was of the same type as the survey of 1941, but broader in coverage in every respect, in particular providing data on household characteristics.

All data are based on 'complete reporters' only: those households where there was a certain consistency and completeness of all information about expenditures and lifestyles. This does not mean that all items are completely reported. The account balancing difference (*ACCBAL*) shows that the households' incomes and disbursements were not equal, and indicates the degree of incompleteness due to 'errors' (forgetfulness and reluctance) on the part of those interviewed and to errors by the interviewees. These differences are rather small, and it appears that in general income is under-reported, expenditure under-reported to a lesser extent and savings greater (or dis-savings less) than shown. Smallness of some samples also leads to under-reporting of savers.

Generally the data are more reliable on expenditure than on income, for the middle income groups than for the higher and lower groups and for the major items of expenditure than for minor ones. Some cell sizes are quite small, and sampling error is, of course, particularly likely to be a problem in these. Sample sizes for each cell are given however, and since all reporting families in the class are used for the purposes of calculating all relevant averages reported in the tables, the cells can be grouped with a relevant weighting procedure using the cell sizes.

3.3.1. 1950 Variables

There are nine income classes (ranging from 0 to over 10 000 dollars annual pre-tax money income) and seven household size classes (1, 2, 3, 4, 5, 6 and more persons, and all households).

%INPOPH :	the percent figures represent the estimated percentage share of an income/ household size class in the total of all urban US households. These figures are based on weighting the samples from different cities to get an accurate estimate of the class share in the total urban population estimated at 31 539 000 households. (One percent therefore represents approximately 315 000 families in the estimated urban population.) These figures therefore sum to 100 for all household sizes taken together.
SAMPSIZE :	the actual sample size for a class of households.
AHSIZE :	average household size. This is not a round number because it measures the average number of full-year members in the household.
ANFTEARN :	average number of full-time earners per household is the average number of household members who were gainfully employed for at least 48 weeks in 1950.
AGEHH :	average age of head of household in years.
EDUHH :	average years of education of household head. Less than or equal 8: elementary schooling. 9–12 years: high school. 13–16 years: college. More than 16: postgraduate.
NONWHITE :	% of households which are non-white; Hispanic households counted as white.
HOMEOWN :	% of households which are homeowners at the year end.
HINC :	average household disposable income in $. (All incomes after tax, excluding changes in assets. Includes some small items of goods in kind.)
TOTCON :	average household total current consumption expenditure in $ (excluding personal insurance, gifts and contributions and changes in assets).
FOODCON :	food and beverages consumption expenditure in $ (including meals at home, away from home and alcoholic beverages).
NETASSCH :	average household net asset change in $.
ACCBAL:	account balancing item in $ (reported in the published tables: see footnote 2 above).

3.3.2. Data Source

The source both for data and discussions is *Studies in Consumer Expenditure, Incomes and Savings* tabulated by the Bureau of Labor Statistics, US Department of Labor for the

Wharton School of Finance and Commerce, University of Pennsylvania, 1957. Vol. III, Table 17 for samples sizes. Vol. XVIII, Tables 1–1 and 1–2 (pp. 2–3) for all household categories; Tables 2–1 and 2–2 (pp. 14–15) for family size breakdown.

3.4. 1960–61: Urban US Budget survey

The 1960–61 survey was similar to the 1950 interview survey (and also involved a diary survey, which provided no data in this case). It was somewhat broader in geographical scope (though it covered only 66 urban areas) and time period. Two samples of households were interviewed in 1961 and 1962, covering, respectively, the years 1960 and 1961. This resulted in a total sample of 9476 usable ('complete reporting') households.

The average sampling error calculated for average total current consumption expenditures (*TOTCON*) is reported to be $45 (less than 1%). Individual expenditure subcategories (e.g. *FOODCON*) have larger sampling errors (but less than 1.5%). The largest relative error was for net changes in assets and liabilities (15%).

Particular care is needed with the extremes of the income distributions (as with all other survey data used here). Again, since all the estimated population of households (*ESTPOPH*) are used for calculating all relevant averages reported in the tables, the cells can be grouped with a relevant weighting procedure based on cell sizes.

3.4.1. 1960–61 Variables

There are ten income classes (ranging from 0 to over 15000 dollars annual *after*-tax money income) and seven household size classes (1, 2, 3, 4, 5, 6 and more persons, and all households).

%INPOPH:	the percent share of the estimated population of households for each income class within the particular household size class (i.e. summing to 100% for each household size).
ESTPOPH:	the estimated total number of such income/size households in the urban population, based on weighting up from the sample (in a manner similar to the previous surveys). The total number of urban households is estimated at 40 130 895 (given in the final line of this variable).
SAMPSIZE:	the actual sample number of households is given only for each household size category.
AHSIZE:	average household size (as for 1950).
ANCHILD:	average number of children under 18 years per household.
ANFTEARN:	average number of full-time earners per household working 48 weeks or more, and 35 hours per week or more.
AGEHH:	average age of head of household in years.
EDUHH:	average years of education of head of household.
NONWHITE:	% of households which are non-white. The categories collected were 'white' 'Negro' and 'other' ('Japanese, Chinese, etc'). Non-white categories have been combined.

HOMEOWN: % of households which are homeowners the entire year.

AUTOOWN: % of households owning one or more automobiles at year end.

HINC: average household disposable income in $ (all money incomes after tax, excluding goods in kind and changes in assets). These data exclude value of *all* goods 'received without expenses' on the income side (compared with 1941 where they were included and 1950 where there was partial inclusion).[4]

TOTCON: average household total current consumption expenditure in $ (excludes personal insurance, gifts and contributions and net changes in assets).

FOODCON: food and beverages consumption expenditure in $ (including meals at home and away from home, but excludes alcoholic beverages).

NETASSCH: average household net asset change in $.

ACCBAL: account balancing item in $ (as 1950).

3.4.2. Data Sources

Consumer Expenditures and Income, Urban United States, 1960–61. Survey of Consumer Expenditures, 1960–61, Bureau of Labor Statistics Report No. 237–38, April 1964, US Department of Labor, Table 1A, p. 10, for all households; Supplement 2 — Part A, July 1964, *Cross-Classification of Family Characteristics* Tables 11a and 11c–g (pp. 3, 5–9) for households by size.

3.5. 1972–73 Urban and Rural US Budget Survey

The 1972–73 consumer expenditure survey covered all areas, not just urban ones. Like the 1960–61 survey, there were interview and diary elements, and as before we rely on the interview results. Unlike the previous surveys, this survey used a panel visited every quarter for five quarters from January 1972 to March 1973 and from January 1973 to March 1974. The data are averages of the two samples, involving 9914 units in the first period and 10 158 in the second. Expenditure information was collected in all periods, income information in periods 2 and 5, asset information in period 5.

Unfortunately, we do not have sample sizes for this set of data. For broad categories of expenditure and total expenditures, the results are thought to be rather accurate. But the survey interviewers were less concerned than in the 1960–61 and earlier surveys to balance the household accounts. Thus there are larger gaps between total incomes and disbursements due to under-reporting of income, involving both forgetfulness and error.

---

[4] On 29 August, 1995, we e-mailed participants the following response to a query:

'One of the participants commented on the 1960 US survey data. The household income (*HINC*) variable is negative (-964) for the lowest income section of the 5-person family group. This number is 'correct' in the sense that it is as reported in the published tables. However, you may note that

(a)   the sample size is small. There are 4 families in the cell (0.4% of 984);
(b)   the cell seems to be dominated by some households with very large negative asset changes (see the *NETASSCH* variable); and
(c)   the *ACCBAL* item also suggests considerable inaccuracy in recording.'

This is reflected in the relatively greater magnitude and variance of *ACCBAL* compared to earlier surveys (despite the omission of incomplete reporting units from the tables) suggesting a greater unreliability in the overall totals in this survey (see footnote 2 above). In addition, in the 1972–73 survey, large items of expenditure were placed fully in the year even if they were paid for over several years, whereas the 1960–61 survey managed to cope with lumpy expenditures rather more satisfactorily. Further information about accuracy is discussed below under *ESTPOPH*.

3.5.1. 1972–73 Variables

There are twelve income classes (ranging from 0 to over 25 000 dollars annual pre-tax money income) for the six individual household size classes (1, 2, 3, 4, 5, 6 and more persons) and sixteen income classes (ranging to over 50 000 dollars income) for all households taken together.

ESTPOPH: the estimated total number of such income/size households in the population of all 67 447 000 US households. This is based, as before, on weighting up from the sample data. Unfortunately, sample sizes are not provided. But there is a warning accompanying these figures that 'data in columns [our rows] which represent less than 218 000 consumer units or in cells which represent less than 18 500 consumer units are likely to have large sampling errors'. Since the reported numbers here are in 000s, this means any household/income group with less than 218 (000) is suspect.

AHSIZE: average household size.

ANCHILD: average number of children under 18 years per household.

ANOV 65: average number of persons over 65 years per household.

AGEHH: average age of head of household in years.

EDUHH 1: % of heads of household with 1 to 9 years' education.

EDUHH 2: % of heads of household with 9 and not more than 12 years' education.

EDUHH 3: % of heads of household with more than 12 years' education.

NONWHITE: % of household heads who are non-white. The categories reported were 'white', 'black' and 'other'. The 'other' group were usually 1% or 2% of the total, rarely 3% and have been combined with 'black' to give comparability with previous survey results.

HOMEOWN: % of households which are homeowners for the entire year.

RENTER: % of household which are renters for the entire year.

AUTOOWN: % of households owning at least one automobile at some stage during the year.

HINC: average household disposable income in $ (all money incomes after tax, excluding goods in kind and changes in assets).

TOTCON: average household total current consumption expenditure in $ (excluding personal insurance, gifts and contributions and changes in assets).

FOODCON: food and beverages consumption expenditure in $ (including meals at home, away from home and meals as pay; excluding alcoholic beverages).

NETASSCH: average household net asset change in $.

ACCBAL: account balancing item in $, calculated from the data available (see the
                discussion at the beginning of this section).

3.5.2. Data Sources

Consumer Expenditure Survey Series: Interview Survey 1972–73, Bureau of Labor Statis-
tics Bulletin No. 1985 (August 1978), US Department of Labor. Data are contained in
Tables 1 and 6–11. Further information comes from the December 1974 *US Monthly
Labor Review* volume 97:2, pp. 16–23.

4. THE US TIME-SERIES DATA

Our aim with the time-series data has been to provide not only Tobin's original data
set, but also as consistent an updating as possible for that data set. Where we have been
unable to update Tobin's data, we provided alternative series and appropriate scaling
information to allow for closer comparison with household survey data. These 'revised'
and 'additional' data series cover the period 1912–1989.

4.1. Variable Definitions and Data Availability

The US time series consist of three sets of data series:

Tobin's original data series: (1912–1948, with 1942–1944 missing; index numbers:
1935–1939 = 100)

TOBPCFC: Tobin's per capita food consumption (his *S*)
TOBPCY: Tobin's per capita disposable income in $ (his *Y'*)
TOBFP: Tobin's food price index (his *P*)
TOBNFP: Tobin's non-food price index (his *Q*).

Revised series: Best estimates of Tobin's series, revised, updated, re-referenced (to
1967 = 100 where appropriate) and as complete as possible (1912–1989)

PCFC: revised *TOBPCFC* for 1912–1976
PCY: revised *TOBPCY* for 1912–1989
FP: revised *TOBFP* for 1913–1989
NFP: revised *TOBNFP* for 1913–1989.

Additional data series: Provides alternative data for income and expenditures (1929–1989),
and data on population and numbers of households for scaling purposes (1912–1989)

AGGEXP: aggregate personal expenditure in billion $
AGGEXPF: aggregate personal expenditure on food in billion $
AGGY: aggregate personal disposable income in billion $
POP: population in thousands
NOH: number of households in thousands.

4.2. Data Description

4.2.1. Food Consumption and Expenditures

TOBPCFC: Tobin's series of food consumption, an index from the Bureau of
                         Agricultural Economics (US Department of Agriculture), was a price-
                         weighted quantity index which measured the per capita 'disappear-
                         ance' of the physical quantity of food to the civilian population. His
                         index was 1935–39 = 100, with price weights for the same year, and
                         years 1942–44 missing. Of all the data series, Tobin's data for food
                         consumption are the most difficult to bring up to date.

PCFC: The Bureau provided a similar food consumption index for the years
                         1913–1976 involving price base weights from 1947–49 for the years
                         up to 1954 and weights from 1957–59 for years after that. This index
                         has a reference year 1967 = 100. Because the price base weights have
                         changed, this index does not replicate exactly the movements shown
                         in Tobin's index. (It is very close up to 1941, but decidedly different
                         from 1945.) We have provided this index.

AGGEXPF   Since Tobin pointed out that his quantity series was not strictly compa-
and AGGEXP: rable to those used in budget studies, we have included two alternative
                         series, namely time series of total personal consumption expenditures
                         and of the sub-category for personal expenditure on food (including
                         alcoholic beverages but excluding tobacco). The data are in billions of
                         dollars, at current dollar prices.

These two data sets cover the period 1929 to 1989. They are consistent with each other
and with the series for disposable personal income (AGGY and PCY), since they all form
part of the national income and product accounts produced by the Bureau of Economic
Analysis at the US Department of Commerce. (These appear to be of the same type as
used by Stone in his reworking of the data to provide the Tobin-Stone estimates in his
discussion of Tobin (1950); see Chapter 2, p. 56.) The income and expenditure totals were
recently revised, but only for part of the period, and apparently not fully for the food data
series. We therefore decided to end the data series at 1989, in order to provide a consistent
set of series going back to 1929. Data for the period before 1929 were more than 5%
different on the 1929 figure, were only partially available, and have been omitted.

4.2.2. Disposable Incomes

TOBPCY: Tobin's per capita disposable income figures were computed from the then
           currently available national income data divided by population figures. As
           elsewhere, 1942–44 were missing.

PCY: There have been many revisions to the national income accounts and some
           also to the population figures. We have provided an updated and revised series
           for 'disposable personal income', per capita, in current dollars, using Tobin's
           data until 1918 and thereafter data drawn from the national income accounts
           data provided by the US Department of Commerce, Bureau of Economic
           Analysis, and divided by the population series included in this data set. This
           series runs from 1912–1989.

AGGY: In addition, we have provided the aggregate series used to calculate the above per capita series for the period 1919–1989. This is total 'disposable personal income', in billions of current dollars, drawn from the national income accounts provided by the Bureau of Economic Analysis at the Department of Commerce. Disposable personal income includes all incomes (wages, rental incomes, benefits, etc.) of the personal (non-government, non-corporate) sector minus tax payments by the sector.

4.2.3. Population and Households

Figures for resident population and for numbers of households are given to provide a choice of unit for scaling both total and food expenditures and disposable income. These figures come from the US Department of Commerce, Bureau of the Census.

POP: The population figures are for total resident population in thousands including armed forces abroad. They are derived from the decennial census as bench marks using other data (such as on births, deaths and immigration) to estimate between census dates for July 1st each year. From 1959, the data are averages of quarterly estimates, and from 1960, the figures include Alaska and Hawaii. This adds an additional 0.43% increase to the 1959 figure (i.e. 1959 excluding them is 177 073 000; including them gives 177 830 000) over and above the 1.6–1.7% annual increase in population at that time. For the period before 1928, the resident population figures excluded armed forces overseas. These amounted to around 110 000 or 0.09% of the population in the period 1929–1935. The only years for which an adjustment has been made are 1918–19, when the known numbers for armed forces overseas have been added in.

NOH: The number of households, also in thousands, is based in part on census data and for later years in part on the Current Population Survey (CPS: a monthly sample survey used to estimate population characteristics). The data from these sources matched consistently with two historical series for earlier years to provide a continuous series. The only problem arises with the data for 1980, where household numbers based on 1970 census estimates proved to be 2.1% different from the numbers based on the 1980 CPS which creates a hiccup in the series. For information, the two numbers are as follows: the 1970 census based count of 1980 households was 79 108 000; the 1980 CPS based count for 1980 households (given in our data series) was 80 776 000.

4.2.4. Prices

TOBFP and *TOBNFP*: Tobin's price series were obtained from the Bureau of Labor Statistics data series of Consumer Prices Indices for middle income families in large cities. The series were for food, and for all items less food. They had reference years 1935–39 = 100 and years 1942–44 were missing.

FP and *NFP*: These series have seen many weighting revisions and widening in coverage over the years since 1950 (and incidentally rely on the consumer expenditure surveys data to provide quantity weights). Despite all these changes it is possible to provide a continuous series from individual series which overlap in a satisfactory way using Tobin's series for 1913–1941, the 1967 = 100 weighted series for 1942–74, and the 1984 = 100 weighted series for 1975–1989. The first and last of these have been re-referenced so that food prices and non-food prices are each represented by an index with 1967 = 100.

4.3. Sources

Food disappearance (*TOBPCFC* and *PCFC*): For 1912–1970, Series B 444, food consumption per capita comes from the *Historical Statistics of the United States, Colonial Times to 1970* (US Bureau of the Census, Washington DC, 1975). For 1970–1976, observations came from the *Statistical Abstract of the United States 1975* (US Department of Commerce, Bureau of the Census, Washington D.C.) (Table 147) and *1978* (Table 196).

Personal Consumption Expenditures: Total (*AGGEXP*): *The National Income and Product Accounts of the United States 1929–1976* (Washington DC, 1981), Table 2.4 line 1, provided data for 1929–1942. The *Economic Report of the President* for 1991 (US Government Printing Office, Washington DC), Table B-14, provided figures for 1940–1989. The 1978 *Economic Report of the President*, Table C-27, contained overlapping and agreeing data for 1929, 1933, and 1939–1986.

Personal Consumption Expenditures: Food (*AGGEXPF*): The *Historical Statistics* (see above) series G 419, gave figures for 1929–1950 which overlapped with those obtained for 1940–1989 from the *Economic Report of the President* for 1991 (see above), Table B-14. These food data are consistent with the figures for total consumption expenditures discussed above.

Disposable Personal Income (*TOBPCY*, *PCY*, *AGGY*): The *Historical Statistics* (see above) series F-9 provided data on aggregate disposable personal income for 1919–1932. *The National Income and Product Accounts* (see above), Table 2.1, line 25, provided data for 1933–1944. The *Economic Report of the President* for 1991 (see above), Table B-26 provided data for 1945–1989. These were divided by the population series (discussed below) to provide *per capita* figures. Tobin's original *per capita* data were used for 1912–1918.

Population (*POP*): The resident population including the armed forces overseas was taken from the annual estimates made for July 1st each year given in the *Historical Statistics* (see above). Series A-7 provided data for 1912–1929 (adding in armed forces given in footnote for the Great War). Series A-6 has been used for 1930–1959, which overlaps with data for 1929 and 1959–1970 in *Economic Report of the President* for 1990 (see above) Table C-27. The equivalent *Report* for 1994, provides data for 1970–1989 in Table B-6.

Households (*NOH*): The number of households were taken from series A-350 and A-288 from the *Historical Statistics* (see above). A-350 provided data from 1912–1960. A-288 provided matching data from 1955–1970. (Years 1955–60 matched exactly. Earlier decennial census year data were less than 1% different from A-350.) For years from 1970, data were provided by successive volumes of the *Statistical Abstract of the United States* (see above), from the Population Section tables and from reports in the P-20 series of *Current Population Reports*.

Prices (*TOBFP*, *TOBNFP*, *FP* and *NFP*): Tobin's article provided the data series *TOBFP* and *TOBNFP* for the period 1913 to 1941. The data for 1942–1974 came from the *Economic Report of the President* for 1984 (see above), Table B-54. Data for 1975–1989 came from the *Economic Report of the President* for 1994 (see above), Table B-61. These reports provided overlapping data years, and further supporting evidence on food prices was provided by a longer series for 1967 = 100 available as series E-137 in *Historical Statistics* (see above).

REFERENCES

Magnus, J. R. and M. S. Morgan (1995), *The Experiment in Applied Econometrics: Information Pack*, CentER for Economic Research, Tilburg University.
Tobin, J. (1950), 'A statistical demand function for food in the USA', *Journal of the Royal Statistical Society*, Series A, **113**, Part II, 113–49 [reprinted in Chapter 2, this volume].

CHAPTER 22

DESCRIPTION OF THE DUTCH DATA

JAN R. MAGNUS AND MARY S. MORGAN

1. THE DATA: GENERAL INFORMATION[1]

The complete data set consists of both time series and budget survey data from the US and the Netherlands. We use 'BS' and 'TS' to denote budget survey and time series respectively; and 'US' and 'NL' to denote data from the USA and the Netherlands respectively. The data were originally provided to experiment participants on diskette containing nine files. The full data set (including corrections made to data during the course of the experiment) is now available from the *Journal of Applied Econometrics* data archive at:

> http://qed.econ.queensu.ca:80/jae/1997-v12.5/

This contains three directories: a 'readme' directory, a data directory and a documentation directory (which gives brief descriptions). Full documentation of the data is available in this chapter for the Dutch data and in the previous Chapter 21 for the US data.

The Dutch data are provided courtesy of Statistics Netherlands, and some (the budget data) were not originally in the public domain (information about sources is given later in this chapter). If you use these data from the archive, please add a note of thanks to Statistics Netherlands. The US data are drawn from official reports and are in the public domain. If you use these data from the archive, please credit the relevant US Government department and cite the relevant publications (all references are given in the previous chapter).

2. THE DUTCH DATA: AN INTRODUCTION

The Dutch data consist of three sets of household level data and one time-series data set. The three budget surveys are for the years 1965, 1980 and 1988. The 1965 survey gives data on 26 groups of households. The 1980 and 1988 surveys are at household level and contain 2859 (in 1980) and 1950 (in 1988) households, respectively. The time series runs from 1948–1988 (41 years).

The data sets were originally sent to experiment participants on diskette, in ASCII format. They are now available in the data archive (see above) under the following names:

---

[1] We are grateful to Adriaan Kalwij at Tilburg University for expert help with the collection of the Dutch data. This data description is a slightly revised version of Chapters 9–10 of the *Experiment Information Pack* (see Magnus and Morgan, 1995).

Methodology and Tacit Knowledge: Two Experiments in Econometrics
Jan R. Magnus and Mary S. Morgan © 1999 John Wiley & Sons Ltd

BS65NL.TXT data for the 1965 household survey
BS80NL.TXT data for the 1980 household survey
BS88NL.TXT data for the 1988 household survey
TS4888NL.TXT time-series data for 1948–1988.

The household data are defined, described and documented in the next section and the
time-series data in Section 4.

3.   BUDGET SURVEYS FOR THE NETHERLANDS

3.1. Introduction

Since 1978, Statistics Netherlands (Centraal Bureau voor de Statistiek (CBS))
has conducted Budget Surveys (BSs) annually. Before 1978, Statistics Netherlands
conducted BSs only occasionally. The aim of the BSs is to gather information on the
expenditure behaviour of Dutch households in relation to household characteristics
such as household composition, income and education level of all members of the
household.

We have expenditure data for three years: 1965, 1980 and 1988. The 1965 survey gives
data on 26 *groups* of households. The 1980 and 1988 surveys are at household level and
are therefore much larger. They contain 2859 (in 1980) and 1950 (in 1988) households,
respectively. We thank Statistics Netherlands for providing these data and allowing their
usage in the experiment. We also thank Statistics Netherlands for permission to reprint
their appendix of technical notes applicable to the 1980 and 1988 surveys as part of this
section.

For all three surveys total household consumption ($V1$) is divided into six groups (the
sum $V11 + \cdots + V66$ is not exactly equal to $V1$ due to measurement error):

$V11$ Food
$V22$ Housing[2]
$V33$ Clothing and footwear
$V44$ Hygiene and medical care
$V55$ Education, recreation and transport
$V66$ Other consumption.[3]

More detailed expenditure data are available for seven subgroups of food (again, the sum
of $V110$ to $V119$ is not exactly equal to $V11$ due to measurement error):

$V110$ Bread, pastry and flour products
$V111$ Potatoes, vegetables and fruit
$V113$ Products containing sugar and beverages
$V115$ Oils and fats
$V116$ Meat, meat products and fish

---

[2] Includes rental value for owner occupied homes.
[3] Includes banking and insurance services.

V118   Dairy products
V119   Other food products.

Further information available for each survey is discussed below.

3.2. The 1965 Survey

The 1965 BS was conducted between June 1963 and May 1965. The information provided is scarce, mainly because the original micro data have been lost and all information has thus been gathered from the official Statistics Netherlands publication (CBS, 1966).

The survey provides data on groups of households, not on individual households. These groups are based on household income (*HINC*: two classes), number of persons in the household (*HSIZE*: five classes) and degree of urbanization (*URB*: three classes). All together we have 26 groups of households (rather than 30, since four groups are empty).

The 1965 survey is not as rich as the 1980/88 surveys. The degree of urbanization, however, is only available for this cross-section. Only households with more than two persons, where the head of household is a blue or white collar worker or an agricultural worker or a farmer are selected.[4] To make the data set representative for the Dutch population, weight variables were created based on profession (blue or white collar worker, agricultural worker or farmer) and number of persons in the household. The weights themselves are not available.

Thus, apart from *NUMH* (the number of households within the group), the data set also includes *WNUMH*. At the household level, each household and its consumption expenditures[5] were weighted before aggregating over households within the 26 groups of households. The resulting variables are the weighted number of households (*WNUMH*) and the average weighted consumption expenditures (*V1* to *V66*). Thus *WNUMH* is simply the sum of the weights within one group.

Statistics Netherlands also provides information about the 'food equivalent' household sizes. A child eats less than a grown man and this is reflected in *ADULTEQ*, the weighted number of adult equivalents in the household.[6]

3.2.1. The file BS65NL.TXT

The ASCII file contains 26 rows (groups of households) and 21 columns (variables). Each variable occupies eight positions. Thus each row contains $8 \times 21 = 168$ positions as follows:

---

[4] The main reason for this selection is, as far as we know, that the resulting tables should be comparable with earlier studies. These studies only investigated consumption behaviour of households with two adults and two children where the head of the household was a blue or white collar worker, an agricultural worker or a farmer.

[5] Consumption is the use of goods and services for non-productive purposes of which the creation is considered as production in the National Accounts. The consumption of a good or service is not necessarily equal to expenditure on it. For instance, for owner occupied homes the rental value is noted as consumption, not the actual mortgage payments and interest. Purchase and sale of durable goods are included. This may result in negative expenditures, especially in transport (car sales).

[6] The contribution of each member of the household is based on the following scheme: a child, age $< 2 = 0.2$, age $2-3 = 0.3$, age $4-5 = 0.4$, age $6-7 = 0.5$, age $8-9 = 0.6$, age $10-11 = 0.7$, age $12-13 = 0.8$, a man, age $14-59 = 1$, woman, age $14-59 = 0.8$, a man or woman, age $> 60 = 0.8$. It is important to note that these equivalence scales only apply to food consumption.

Position	Name	Description/Code
1–8	*YEAR*	Year of the survey
9–16	*HSIZE*	Household size, the number of persons within the household *Code*: 2 = 2 persons 3 = 3 persons 4 = 4 persons 5 = 5 persons 6 = more than 4 persons if URB = 2 more than 5 persons if URB = 3
17–24	*NUMH*	Number of households within the group
25–32	*WNUMH*	Weighted number of households
33–40	*ADULTEQ*	Number of adult equivalents in the household
41–48	*URB*	Degree of urbanization *Code*: 1 = three largest cities: Amsterdam, Rotterdam and The Hague 2 = other cities/urban areas 3 = villages/rural areas
49–56	*HINC*	Gross (!) household income in 1965 Dutch guilders *Code*: 1 = f6000–f9000 2 = f9000–f12 000

Consumption Expenditure variables (average weighted expenditures per household group)

57–64	*V1*	Total household consumption
65–72	*V11*	Food
73–80	*V110*	Bread, pastry and flour products
81–88	*V111*	Potatoes, vegetables and fruit
89–96	*V113*	Products containing sugar and beverages
97–104	*V115*	Oils and fats
105–112	*V116*	Meat, meat products and fish
113–120	*V118*	Dairy products
121–128	*V119*	Other food products
129–136	*V22*	Housing
137–144	*V33*	Clothing and footwear
145–152	*V44*	Hygiene and medical care
153–160	*V55*	Education, recreation and transport
161–168	*V66*	Other consumption

3.3. The 1980 and 1988 Surveys

Information at the household level is available in the 1980 and 1988 BSs. The survey design, the data collection procedures and definitions are described in the 'Technical notes to the Dutch budget surveys' provided by Statistics Netherlands (see CBS, 1992) and which we reprint with their permission as Section 3.4 below.

   The survey data are provided by a combination of household record keeping on standard expenditures and consumptions for a given period (either a month in 1980, or a half-month in 1988, which is grossed up into an annual record) and additional year long records on larger expenditures and holidays. Further data are collected by interview.

The sample drawn takes account not only of geographical distribution but also of socio-economic characteristics to obtain representativeness. Not all households were willing to participate in a survey and in 1980 the population of employees was intentionally oversampled. Therefore, a weighting variable is constructed (*WEIGHT*) which can be used to make the sample representative for the Dutch population.[7]

Although most information is contained in the 'Technical notes' (Section 3.4 below), several further points are worth noting:

1. The head of the household is defined to be the person (man or woman) who owns or rents the house where the household resides.
2. Some consumer expenditures are negative in the data set (seven observations in 1980; ten in 1988). This is not a measurement error (see footnote 5 above).
3. Both income and consumption data for the top classes are censored and replaced by averages for the class. The relevant averages for income are given below (and see footnote 9); see the paper by the Maastricht team (Chapter 8, Section 2.3) for a discussion of the consumption data.

3.3.1.   The Files BS80NL.TXT and BS88NL.TXT

The two ASCII files each contain 24 variables organized in four rows per household. Each variable occupies 11 positions, except the first variable in each row which occupies 9 positions. Missing observations are always denoted by −999. The 1980 budget survey contains 2859 households and the 1988 survey contains 1950 households. The corresponding ASCII files thus contain $4 \times 2859 = 11\,436$ and $4 \times 1950 = 7800$ rows, respectively. The positions are defined as follows:

Row	Position	Name	Description/Code
1	1–9	*YEAR*	Year of the survey
1	10–20	*WEIGHT*	Weight variable per household
1	21–31	*HSIZE*	Household size, the number of persons within the household *Code*: 1 = 1 person 2 = 2 persons 3 = 3 persons 4 = 4 persons 5 = 5–12 persons
1	32–42	*HTYPE*	Type of household *Code*: 0 = other types 1 = single person 2 = one-family household

---

[7] The weight variable is based on the following characteristics: socio-economic category (self-employed, employee, non labour force participant) combined with household income, household size, home owner or renter, gender and single person or not.

Row	Position	Name	Description/Code
1	43–53	AGEHH	Age of head of household *Code:* 1 = 12–34 years of age 2 = 35–44 years of age 3 = 45–54 years of age 4 = 55–64 years of age 5 = 65 years of age and older
1	54–64	EDUHH	Education level head of household *Code*: 2 = primary school 3 = secondary school 4 = intermediate vocational education 5 = higher vocational education 6 = university education (and higher)
1	65–75	LFPHH	Labour force participation status of head of household *Code*: 1 = full-time job 2 = part-time job 3 = otherwise
2	1–9	LFPHP	Labour force participation status of partner *Code*: 1 = labour market status partner equals that of head of household 2 = labour market status partner is not equal to labour market status of head of household[8]
2	10–20	SOCGHH	Socio-economic group head of household *Code*: 1 = employee 2 = self-employed 3 = unemployed/non-participation
2	21–31	HINC	Household Income,[9] net of taxes and social security premiums (Dutch guilders). If net household income is smaller than f 80 000, then $HINC$ = net household income. If net household income is larger than f 80 000, then $HINC = f$ 97 300 (1980 only) and $HINC = f$ 100 800 (1988 only) respectively

3.3.2. Consumption Expenditure Variables

2	32–42	V1	Total household consumption
2	43–53	V11	Food

---

[8] It is important to note that in case the head of the household is working full-time, it is not possible to know whether the partner is working part-time or is not employed.

[9] Net household income is fully defined in the 'Technical notes'. It is important to note that net household incomes above f 80 000 are not recorded in this data set. The average household income for the group of households with net household income above f 80 000 is recorded instead. For this group of households f 97,300 is the average net household income in 1980; in 1988 the average equals f 100 800.

2	54–64	*V110*	Bread, pastry and flour products
2	65–75	*V111*	Potatoes, vegetables and fruit
3	1–9	*V113*	Products containing sugar and beverages
3	10–20	*V115*	Oils and fats
3	21–31	*V116*	Meat, meat products and fish
3	32–42	*V118*	Dairy products
3	43–53	*V119*	Other food products
3	54–64	V22	Housing
3	65–75	V33	Clothing and footwear
4	1–9	V44	Hygiene and medical care
4	10–20	V55	Education, recreation and transport
4	21–31	V66	Other consumption

3.4. Technical Notes to the Dutch Budget Surveys 1978–1991

Source: Statistics Netherlands (reprinted with their permission)

3.4.1. Introduction and Purpose of the Survey

3.4.1.1 Introduction

Statistics Netherlands (hereafter CBS) has been conducting an annual Budget Survey since 1978 representative for all households in the Netherlands. In a number of years certain socio-economic categories of the population were intentionally oversampled: in 1980 employees, in 1981 the non-economically active population, in 1982 the self-employed and managing directors of limited liability and private companies and in 1985 and 1990 the so-called price index (employee) households. In 1978, 1979, 1983, 1984, 1986, 1987, 1988, 1989 and 1991 there was no oversampling.

These technical notes will examine:

— the purpose of the survey (Section 3.4.1.2);
— the survey design (Section 3.4.2);
— the most important concepts and definitions (Section 3.4.3).

For more detailed information about the justification of the survey, see Budget Survey 1978, part 1 methodology; survey documents (1982, Staatsuitgeverij, The Hague).

3.4.1.2 Purpose of the Survey

The most important objective of the present annual Budget Survey is to give as complete as possible a picture of consumer and non-consumer expenditure by households, in relation to household characteristics such as income, socio-economic category and household size and composition. The typical information supplied by the survey is the household budget or spending patterns. This is a systematical overview in sums of money, proportions or amounts of expenditure or consumption by groups of households. In its present form the Budget Survey serves various purposes.

In addition to the above mentioned main objective, the information is used for:

— the weighting scheme for the price index for household consumption;
— studies in aid of socio-economic policy;
— improvement of consumption estimates in the National Accounts;
— studies of nutritional values and the cost of food;
— information on household expenditure and household budgets;
— distribution-planning studies;
— market research;
— special studies on indirect tax burdens, the cost of children, energy use, etc.;
— the estimation of parameters in consumption models.

3.4.2. Survey Design

3.4.2.1   Sampling, Recruiting and Non-Response

As in many other CBS household surveys, the sample is drawn in two steps. First the municipalities, then the addresses — i.e. households — in these municipalities. A number of large municipalities is always included in the sample. From the others, a sample is drawn in which the chance of being selected is proportional with the number of addresses in the municipality (note 1).

To ensure a certain number and composition of participating households, about six times this number have to be included in the recruiting process, in order to compensate for the non-response during the recruiting stage and drop outs during the survey period. The recruiting takes place in the autumn preceding the survey year.

The following table shows the number of households that took part in the various Budget Surveys:

year	Net response (number of households)	year	Net response (number of households)
1978	1987	1985	2852
1979	2032	1986	3003
1980	2859	1987	2570
1981	2897	1988	1950
1982	2809	1989	1946
1983	3151	1990	2767
1984	3185	1991	1067

3.4.2.2   Data Collection

Up to the 1984 survey, the following method was used. For one month — the so-called reporting month — participating households noted in a housekeeping book:

— all expenditure; for every purchase (i.e. good or service): the date, amount, description, quantity and place of purchase;
— consumption of home grown or self-manufactured products;
— all sales.

For the remaining months the household is requested to:

— note less frequent purchases of 20 guilders and more for durables (purchases, main-
   tenance, repairs) for house and garden, fuels and moving costs (the so-called annual
   report);
— keep a holiday housekeeping book during the holidays in aid of a later interview
   on holiday expenditure;
— fill in a questionnaire about car ownership/use;
— fill in a form on medical expenses;
— fill in a form on the level and composition of the household income.

The survey further comprises interviews during which the interviewer completes ques-
tionnaires about:

— a number of household characteristics in aid of the selection of households before
   the survey;
— a number of household and personal characteristics and the possession of durables;
— periodic expenditure (subscriptions, rent, etc.);
— holiday expenditure.

In 1985, 1986 and 1987 the method of data collection was changed. The lower limit for
the annual report was raised to 50 guilders for 1985 and 1986 and to 100 guilders for
1987 and, unlike previous years, all expenditure of over 50 guilders and 100 guilders
respectively per purchase is noted throughout the year (i.e. including periodic payments
and medical expenses, etc.). With respect to expenditure covered by insurance, households
were requested to note not the difference between the cost and insurance compensation,
but to record the items separately.

As from 1988 the so-called 'reporting month' has been changed to a reporting 'half-
month' period. To reduce the loss of quality for the smaller expenditures, the amount of
the lower limit to be noted throughout the year has been lowered from 100 guilders to
25 guilders per purchase.

3.4.2.3   Calculation of Annual Expenditure

Part of the total expenditure is noted — as described above — for only one month or half
a month, while another part is noted during the whole year. As these data must form the
best possible basis for the annual consumption of each household, the information must
be converted to an annual basis. In this respect, four categories can be distinguished.

— monthly expenditure;
— annual expenditure (excl. periodic expenditure);
— holiday expenditure;
— periodic expenditure.

The monthly expenditure is raised by a certain factor to get an annual figure while account
is taken of the number of days holiday of the household. To this expenditure is then added
the annual expenditure above a certain amount (in 1978: 40 guilders; in 1979: 45 guilders;
1980–1984: 50 guilders), the periodic expenditure converted to an annual basis and other
expenditure. In this way the annual consumption per household is calculated.

In the calculation of annual expenditure for 1985 and 1986 all expenditure of less than 70 guilders and all expenditure on food was raised to an annual basis in the same way as in preceding years, while all other expenditure was already observed on a yearly basis.

3.4.3. Definitions

This section gives a brief explanation of the main concepts and definitions.

A *household* is defined as a single person or group of persons who live together domestically and run a household together. People living in homes (including homes for the elderly) are not included in the survey.

Income is defined as net household income. This includes income from employment, profit from enterprise, income from capital (up to 1987 *excluding* the own home, as from 1988 and further *including* own home), social security benefits and other income such as rent subsidies, state contributions for house owners, employers' contribution to the state medical insurance scheme, minus pension premiums, social security contributions and wage/income tax.

The item wage/income tax is the difference between tax paid and tax received. The limits of the 10% income groups are determined on the basis of the total number of households observed, regardless of the subgroup to which they are applied.

Consumption is the use of goods and services for non-productive purposes, of which the creation is considered as production in the National Accounts. The consumption of a good or service is not necessarily equal to expenditure on it (note 2). For instance, for owner occupied homes the rental value (estimated by an estate agent) is noted as consumption, not the actual mortgage payments and interest. The concept of consumption corresponds in principle with that used in the National Accounts.

However, for a number of reasons it is not possible to simply compare the raised Budget Survey results with household consumer expenditure in the National Accounts, as there are differences in, among other things, consumer expenditure by non-profit institutions and expenditure on health care.

Notes

(1) When the municipalities and addresses are drawn, the desired representativity with respect to the geographical distribution (province, degree of urbanization) and household characteristics (socio-economic category, income level) is taken into account.

(2) Furthermore, experience shows that certain expenditure categories (e.g. hotels, restaurants, cafes, entertainment, recreation, alcohol and tobacco) are systematically underestimated in a Budget Survey, and therefore total consumption also turns out too low. In addition to consumer expenditure there is also non-consumer expenditure and alternative expenditure. Non-consumer expenditure includes, among other things, transfers between households, club membership fees etc., donations, and a number of transfers to the state, among other things for permits, passports, driving licences, school fees and refuse collection rates. Alternative expenditure comprises specific expenditure, costs or values which, added to consumption would lead to double counts. The most important example

of this is mortgage payments on owner-occupied dwellings of which the rateable value is already included in consumption.

4. TIME SERIES FOR THE NETHERLANDS

We have annual observations from 1948–1988 (41 years). The data set contains first of all the number of inhabitants in the Netherlands (*POP* in thousands), the number of households (*NOH* in thousands), and the aggregate disposable income (*AGGY* in millions of guilders).

The data for *POP* are only available from 1960 onwards. In providing the data for *POP* and *NOH*, we made a serious error which was brought to our attention by a participant in May 1996. The details are given in the footnote below.[10] The data in the archive are corrected.

Disposable income (*AGGY*) consists of consumption and household savings. These savings *include* contractual savings, e.g. savings through pension funds or life insurance companies. Savings through pension funds are mandatory in the Netherlands for most employees. It is important to note that in the budget surveys these contractual savings are not part of 'savings'. (In the budgets surveys, savings are 'private' savings only.)

The data set also contained consumption expenditure variables (in millions of guilders) for total household consumption (*V*), which is divided into six groups (*V11*, *V22*, ..., *V66*). The first group is food, which is further divided into seven subgroups. (The other groups are not subdivided.) Price indices are given for each commodity group

---

[10] Our e-mail message to experiment participants regarding errors in our time-series data, dated 1 May 1996, entitled 'correction on file TS4888. NL' reads as follows: 'In the Dutch data set (file TS4888. NL, printed on page 54 of the Information Pack) a mysterious mistake has occurred in the first two variables *POP* and *NOH*. We apologize for the mistake and provide the correct numbers below.

YEAR	POP	NOH	YEAR	POP	NOH
1948	9716	−999	1969	12798	3890
1949	9884	−999	1970	12958	3986
1950	10027	−999	1971	13119	4094
1951	10200	−999	1972	13270	4211
1952	10328	−999	1973	13388	4337
1953	10436	−999	1974	13491	4454
1954	10551	−999	1975	13599	4561
1955	10680	−999	1976	13734	4660
1956	10822	−999	1977	13814	4752
1957	10957	−999	1978	13898	4839
1958	11096	−999	1979	13986	4911
1959	11278	−999	1980	14091	5006
1960	11417	3171	1981	14209	5103
1961	11556	3231	1982	14286	5239
1962	11721	3286	1983	14340	5367
1963	11890	3342	1984	14395	5494
1964	12042	3419	1985	14454	5613
1965	12212	3508	1986	14529	5711
1966	12377	3602	1987	14615	5814
1967	12535	3698	1988	14715	5888
1968	12661	3790			

In view of this error and various requests, we have decided to postpone the deadline for submissions for one month. The new deadline is therefore August 1st.'

(*P1* to *P66*). The price indices are Laspeyres index numbers. The base years are 1951, 1959, 1964, 1969, 1975, 1980 and 1985; the indices are referenced to 1951 = 100). The categories of expenditure (and corresponding prices) are those listed in Section 3 above.

4.1. The Data File TS4888NL.TXT

The data are contained in as ASCII file with 41 rows (years) and 32 columns (variables). Each variable occupies eight positions. Thus each row contains $8 \times 32 = 256$ positions as follows:

Position	Name	Description/Code
1–8	*YEAR*	Year of observation
9–16	*POP*	Number of inhabitants (thousands of persons)
17–24	*NOH*	Number of households (thousands of households) (−999 indicates a missing value)
24–32	*AGGY*	Disposable income (millions of guilders)

Consumption Expenditure variables (millions of guilders)

Position	Name	Description
33–40	*V1*	Total household consumption
41–48	*V11*	Food
49–56	*V110*	Bread, pastry and flour products
57–64	*V111*	Potatoes, vegetables and fruit
65–72	*V113*	Products containing sugar and beverages
73–80	*V115*	Oils and fats
81–88	*V116*	Meat, meat products and fish
89–96	*V118*	Dairy products
97–104	*V119*	Other food products
105–112	*V22*	Housing
113–120	*V33*	Clothing and footwear
121–128	*V44*	Hygiene and medical care
129–136	*V55*	Education, recreation and transport
137–144	*V66*	Other consumption

Price indices for each commodity group (1951 = 100)

Position	Name	Description
145–152	*P1*	Total household consumption
153–160	*P11*	Food
161–168	*P110*	Bread, pastry and flour products
169–176	*P111*	Potatoes, vegetables and fruit
177–184	*P113*	Products containing sugar and beverages
185–192	*P115*	Oils and fats
193–200	*P116*	Meat, meat products and fish
201–208	*P118*	Dairy products
209–216	*P119*	Other food products
215–224	*P22*	Housing
225–232	*P33*	Clothing and footwear

233–240	*P44*	Hygiene and medical care
241–248	*P55*	Education, recreation and transport
249–256	*P66*	Other consumption

4.2. Data Sources

POP (the number of inhabitants) and *NOH* (the number of households) are obtained from a publication of Statistics Netherlands (CBS, 1989).

The data on *AGGY* (aggregate disposable income) are given in various publications of the National Accounts (*Nationale Rekeningen*). Consumption expenditures are also taken from the National Accounts.

In 1977 a revision of the National Accounts took place. This was not so much a change of definitions, but rather an improvement on the precision. The revised data are available from 1969 onwards. Before 1969, only consumption based on the old classification is available. For disposable income, the revised definition is available only from 1977 onwards.

REFERENCES

Centraal Bureau voor de Statistiek (1966), *Nationaal budgetonderzoek 1963/'65: verbruiksrekeningen van hand-, land- en hoofdarbeiders en boeren, onderscheiden naar inkomensgroepen, grootte van de huishouding en woonplaatsen*, Staatsuitgeverij, 's-Gravenhage.
Centraal Bureau voor de Statistiek (1989), *1899–1989, Negentig Jaren Statistiek in Tijdreeksen*, Voorburg/Heerlen.
Centraal Bureau voor de Statistiek (1991), *Private Consumption Expenditure and Price Index Numbers for the Netherlands, 1921–1939 and 1948–1988*, Voorburg/Heerlen.
Centraal Bureau voor de Statistiek (1992), *Gebruikershandboek budgetonderzoek 1988–1989*, Voorburg/Heerlen.
Centraal Bureau voor de Statistiek, published annually, *Nationale Rekeningen*, Voorburg/Heerlen.
Magnus, J. R. and M. S. Morgan (1995), *The Experiment in Applied Econometrics: Information Pack*, CentER for Economic Research, Tilburg University.